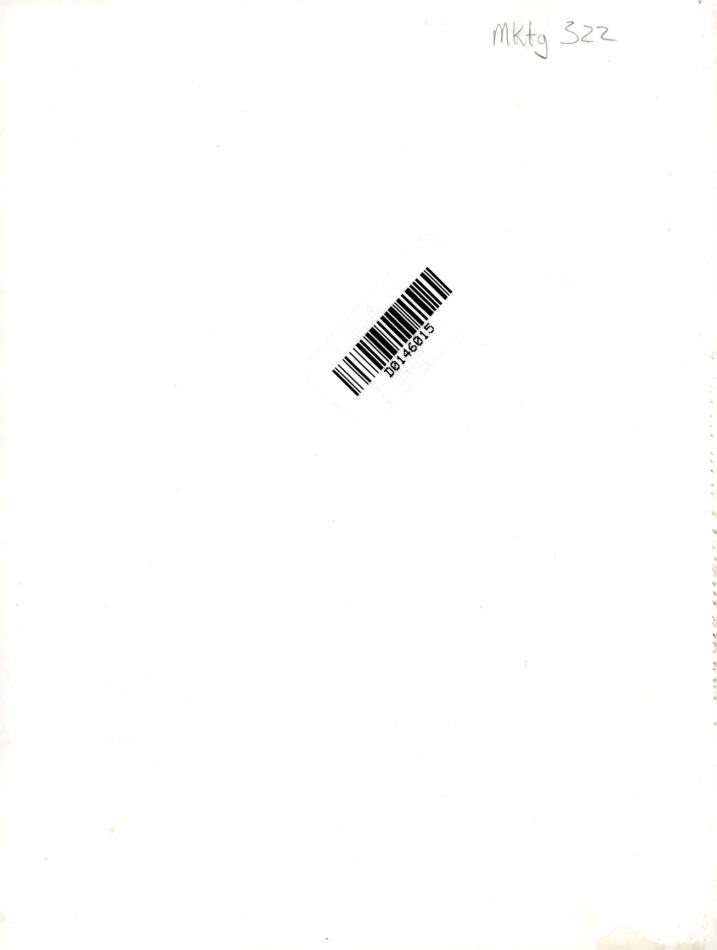

Customer Behavior
CONSUMER BEHAVIOR AND BEYOND

Customer Behavior
CONSUMER BEHAVIOR AND BEYOND

Jagdish N. Sheth

Emory University

Banwari Mittal

Northern Kentucky University

Bruce I. Newman

DePaul University

Ⓓ
The Dryden Press
Harcourt Brace College Publishers
Fort Worth   Philadelphia   San Diego   New York   Orlando   Austin   San Antonio
Toronto   Montreal   London   Sydney   Tokyo

The Dryden Press Series in Marketing

Parente, Vanden Bergh, Barban, and Marra
Advertising Campaign Strategy: A Guide to Marketing Communication Plans

Rosenbloom
Marketing Channels: A Management View
Sixth Edition

Sandburg
Discovering Your Marketing Career CD-ROM

Schaffer
Applying Marketing Principles Software

Schaffer
The Marketing Game

Schellinck and Maddox
Marketing Research: A Computer-Assisted Approach

Schnaars
MICROSIM

Schuster and Copeland
Global Business: Planning for Sales and Negotiations

Sheth, Mittal, and Newman
Customer Behavior: Consumer Behavior and Beyond

Shimp
Advertising, Promotion, and Supplemental Aspects of Integrated Marketing Communications
Fourth Edition

Talarzyk
Cases and Exercises in Marketing

Terpstra and Sarathy
International Marketing
Seventh Edition

Weitz and Wensley
Readings in Strategic Marketing Analysis, Planning, and Implementation

Zikmund
Exploring Marketing Research
Sixth Edition

Zikmund
Essentials of Marketing Research

Harcourt Brace College Outline Series

Peterson
Principles of Marketing

Publisher: George Provol
Acquisitions Editor: Bill Schoof
Product Manager: Lisé Johnson
Developmental Editor: Tracy Morse
Project Editor: Rebecca Dodson
Art Director: Scott Baker
Production Manager: Lois West
Picture & Rights Editor: Adele Krause
Cover image: SuperStock

ISBN: 0-03-098016-X
Library of Congress Catalog Card Number: 98-72504

Address for editorial correspondence:
Harcourt Brace College Publishers
301 Commerce Street, Suite 3700
Fort Worth, TX 76102

Address for orders:
Harcourt Brace & Company
6277 Sea Harbor Drive
Orlando, FL 32887-6777
1-800-782-4479

Website address:
http://www.hbcollege.com

THE DRYDEN PRESS, DRYDEN, and the DP Logo are registered trademarks of Harcourt Brace & Company.

Printed in the United States of America
   9 0 1 2 3 4 5 6 7   048   9 8 7 6 5 4 3 2

The Dryden Press
Harcourt Brace College Publishers

To my older brothers:
Himatlal N. Sheth and Gulabchand N. Sheth—JS

To Meena, Pratik, and Mayank whose constant exploration of the
marketplace mirrors my own—BM

To my wife Judy, son Todd, and daughter Erica—BN

About the Authors

Jagdish N. Sheth

Jagdish N. Sheth is the Charles H. Kellstadt Professor of Marketing in the Goizueta Business School and the founder of the Center for Relationship Marketing (CRM) at Emory University. Prior to his present position, he was the Robert E. Brooker Professor of Marketing at the University of Southern California and the founder of the Center for Telecommunications Management; the Walter H. Stellner Distinguished Professor of Marketing at the University of Illinois, and on the faculty of Columbia University, as well as the Massachusetts Institute of Technology. Dr. Sheth is nationally and internationally known for his scholarly contribution in Consumer Behavior, Marketing, Global Competition, and Strategic Thinking.

Jag has published more than 200 books and research papers in different areas of marketing. His book, *The Theory of Buyer Behavior* (1969) with John A. Howard is a classic in the field. He is also a co-author of *Marketing Theory: Evolution and Evaluation* (1988) and *Consumption Values and Market Choices* (1991).

Jag is an American Psychological Association Fellow and past President of APA's Consumer Psychology Division and Association for Consumer Research (ACR). He was the recipient of the Viktor Mataja Medal from the Austrian Research Society in Vienna (1977) and the 1989 Outstanding Marketing Educator Award from the Academy of Marketing Science. Jag was also awarded the P.D. Converse Award for his outstanding contributions to theory in marketing in 1992 by the American Marketing Association. In 1996, Dr. Sheth was selected as the Distinguished Fellow of the Academy of Marketing Science. In November of 1997, Dr. Sheth was awarded the Distinguished Fellow award from the International Engineering Consortium.

Professor Sheth has worked for numerous industries and companies in the United States, Europe and Asia, both as an Advisor and as a Seminar Leader. His clients include AT&T, BellSouth, Comstream, Cox Communications, Ford, Motorola, Nortel, 3M, Whirlpool and many more. He has offered more than 6,000 presentations in at least 20 countries.

Banwari Mittal

Banwari ('Ban') Mittal holds a Ph.D. in marketing from the University of Pittsburgh, with specialization in consumer choice process. Currently, he is a member of the marketing faculty at Northern Kentucky University where he teaches consumer behavior, advertising and promotion, services marketing, and marketing management. He has previously taught at University of Pittsburgh, State University of New York at Buffalo, and University of Miami. His research topics deal with consumer attitudes and response to marketing communications and promotions, and to services marketing programs. His papers have been published in the *Journal of Marketing*, *Journal of Marketing Research*, *Journal of Economic Psychology*, *Psychology and Marketing*, *Journal of Retailing*, *Journal of Market-focused Management*, *Journal of Applied Social Psychology*, *Journal of Services Marketing*, *Health Care Marketing*, and *Journal of Consumer Marketing*, among others. He also serves on the editorial board of *Psychology and Marketing*.

Ban's current passion is understanding what constitutes a market value for the customer.

Bruce I. Newman

Bruce I. Newman earned a B.S., M.B.A., and Ph.D. in marketing from the University of Illinois at Urbana—Champaign, and is currently Associate Professor of Marketing at the Kellstadt Graduate School of Business, DePaul University. He has published several books and articles on the subjects of political marketing, voting behavior, and consumer behavior, including *The Marketing of the President* and *Consumption Values and Market Choices* (with Jagdish N. Sheth and Barbara L. Gross). In 1993, Professor Newman received the Ehrenring (Ring of Honor) from the Austrian Advertising Research Association in Vienna for his widespread research in political marketing, the first American recipient of this honor in the 30 years it has been awarded. Professor Newman is an Editorial Board Member of *Psychology & Marketing*, and is also a frequent contributor to mass media, with Op-Ed pieces appearing in *The Christian Science Monitor* and *The Chicago Tribune*.

From the Authors

Dear Reader:

The best thing about learning and teaching customer behavior is that we can relate to the subject matter at a personal level. As we reflect on our own behavior as a customer and those of others we know, one thing becomes amply clear: we are not always the user of a product or service we buy and/or pay for, nor are we always the payer for what we buy or use. Moreover, as payers, buyers, and users, we seek different values from market transactions, whether they be in our capacity as individuals or on behalf of an organization. This fundamental insight led us to design our framework of three customer roles (user, payer, buyer) and the market values they seek.

Four beliefs have guided our journey through this book:

1. The much heralded clarion call to marketers to become customer oriented is only half the story; the other half is the need to recognize all three roles of the customer and pay attention to the specific and unique market values each role seeks.

2. A lion's share of the marketplace transactions occur between businesses—i.e., where the customer is a business firm. The chances are more than even that students of marketing, as they assume professional roles, will be marketing not to a household but to a business customer. A modern-day study of customer behavior must therefore dwell equally on both the individual and business customers. Moreover, the context of customer behavior should not be limited to the items of everyday consumption; rather it should include a range of significant products and services such as homes, financial investments, education, health services, etc.

3. Customers are becoming globe trotters, whether in person or via telecommunications, and as marketers and as learners of customer behavior, our perspectives should reflect a global orientation.

4. Customer behavior is not merely a theoretical field of study. Rather its subject matter can and does immensely benefit the world of practice. Indeed, informed business response to customer behavior is imperative for businesses to be sustained as viable and useful social institutions. A study of customer

behavior should be made relevant, therefore, to managerial strategy, and to societal and public policy concerns.

Accordingly, in this book, we: (a) constantly speak to and of both the household and business customers; (b) illustrate concepts with both products and services; (c) cull together examples from around the world; (d) seek to make an intimate connection between theory and practice; and (e) weave all concepts and applications around the three customer roles and the associated market values. This is what takes us beyond *Consumer* Behavior.

Our key motivation for writing this book was this. Customer behavior is an extremely dynamic field, increasingly exercising visible influence on corporations, small and large, domestic and global. There is a huge body of knowledge, both on theory and practice, not published before. We have sought to bring together and give form to this knowledge, accumulated through some 30 years of research, consulting, and teaching experience, and conversations with CEOs and senior executives, business and household customers, researchers, teachers, colleagues, and students on many continents.

We are often asked, why should a college professor change over to this book, or any new book for that matter. Our answer, to ourselves and to our colleagues, is always a simple one: because teaching is about learning and the best way to learn is to teach. There is no greater reward for a teacher, in our opinion, than to learn the latest on a subject, and to invite the student to partake in the excitement that learning can be.

Indeed, in writing this book, we have tried to be as playful as informative. We have sought a marriage between profound subject matter and conversational writing style. Three years in the making, and encouraged and supported by the advice and help of a large number of friends, associates, and representative readers (whom we acknowledge separately), we have endeavored to make this book worthy of your time and effort—every page, every chapter. Our aim has been to learn, to describe, and to explore customer behavior. We ourselves learned a lot in writing this book, and it is a pleasure to invite you on this stimulating journey.

Jagdish N. Sheth

Banwari Mittal

Bruce I. Newman

Customer Behavior: Consumer Behavior & Beyond

This is a book about the behavior of customers around the world. It is comprehensive in its coverage, managerial in its focus, global in its orientation, and innovative in its organization and presentation. It dwells on the traditional issues in the field, and then extends them to emerging topics both in theory and practice. The book goes beyond the conventional subject matter of "consumer behavior" textbooks in four ways:

- It covers the behaviors of customers both in the household market and the business market. The term *customer* is used to apply to both the individual household members as well as business units who buy products and services in the market.

- As examined in Chapter 2, the person who pays for the product or service is not always the user, nor is the user always the buyer. This book reaches beyond the usual scope of this field by focusing not only on the buyer but also on the role of the user and the payer. The authors recognize that a person may play one or more of the three customer roles: user, payer, and buyer. Each role makes the person a customer.

- The book adopts a managerial, action-oriented approach to the study of customer behavior. It makes a connection between customer behavior principles and the elements of marketing strategy, allowing students to see how an understanding of customer behavior is crucial to successful marketing programs.

- The book also casts its view beyond packaged consumer goods which dominate mass media advertising. In illustrations and applications, we constantly draw upon both products *and* services, consumers and business customers, and the domestic and international marketplaces.

A New Orientation: Customer Values

Customer Behavior: Consumer Behavior and Beyond has adopted a new perspective and framework: customer values. In this perspective, all customer behavior is deemed to be driven by the market values customers seek. Six values are proposed, two for each role. For each role, there is a "universal" value category, sought by all customers, and a "personal" value category, sought by customers as individuals. Specifically, for the user, the universal value is performance; personal value is a social/emotional value. For the buyer, the universal value is service value; personal value is convenience and personalization; and for the payer, the universal value is price value, and personal value is credit and financing. This framework is used throughout to explain the significance of all concepts to diverse customers. The practice of marketing is shifting from a transaction focus to a relationship marketing orientation, and the kingpin of this orientation is the long-term customer retention. We believe that the six-values framework offers marketers an avenue to the practice of relationship orientation and, as a result, to achieving customer satisfaction and retention.

CONTENT AND ORGANIZATION

While striving for uniqueness in content and the three-customer-roles framework, the book is organized for easy understanding.

Following Chapter 1, which sets the tone and motivation for customer behavior as a field of study, Chapters 2 and 3 present *the three customer roles and six values* framework for easy grasp. The rest of the chapters cover conventional as well as new topics in a fashion familiar to most teachers of consumer behavior.

Part Two focuses on *the determinants of customer behavior* including trends in these determinants: this section examines the "external influences" on the customer—e.g., climate, economy, public policy, technology, culture, reference groups, age, gender, and race.

Part Three, *the mind-set of the customer*, examines the "internal influences" on customer behavior—e.g., perceptions, learning, motivation, personality, and attitudes.

Part Four, *customer decision making*, examines the choice process of customers, including the growing body of literature on consumer information processing. A separate chapter is devoted to the decision making of individuals, households, business and government organizations, and, uniquely to this book, retailers and buying clubs as customers.

The final section, Part Five, is focused on *customer behavior topics with direct relevance to managerial action*: here brand and store loyalty are discussed both from customer motivations and potential managerial response standpoints; the new and still emerging field of relationship marketing is reviewed from the customer's point of view—the discussion examines how and why household and business customers engage in relationship-based buying, and how marketers may respond to this emergent customer behavior. The final chapter identifies a set of action strategies for management to deliver each of the specific values sought by the three customer roles.

Each topic, whether traditional or new, is presented with the most current body of knowledge. Where knowledge is still emerging or gaps exist in the current literature, we develop new frameworks and concepts, extending the frontiers of knowledge of the field. The textbook is enriched with topics new to the field, and unprecedented in their comprehensive treatment. In this aspect, the book is unique: it educates the student mind with well established knowledge, and then it piques student curiosity to question and explore the still-brewing pot of emergent knowledge.

SPECIAL FEATURES

Customer Behavior: Consumer Behavior and Beyond also goes beyond the conventional subject matter by examining such issues as:

- The notable influence of our physical environment: climate, topography, and ecology
- Government buying behavior
- Researching customer behavior
- Intermediary customer decisions such as resellers, buying clubs, and membership groups
- Relationship-based buying, reverse marketing, and supplier partnering
- Strategies for creating customer values
- Trends in customer behavior, such as anticipated developments in economic, technological, and public policy environment worldwide

In addition, the book provides expanded and innovative treatment of such topics as models of customer loyalty; intergenerational influence in household buying behavior; simulation, virtual reality, and the Internet as research tools; emotional basis of customer motivation; personality in business buying; the role of culture in business buying; major international cultures and subcultures; customer resistance to innovations; a model of customer store choice; and brand equity from the customer's point of view.

ILLUSTRATIONS AND APPLICATIONS

The subject matter is made relevant and practical by describing applications and narrating stories. Each chapter features illustrious boxes called Window on Research and Window on Practice. In the former, we showcase current research on a significant topic covered in the chapter. Examples include:

- The Zaltman Metaphor technique for customer research
- Reasons for delay in customer decisions
- Determinants of customer proneness for store brands
- Components of customer orientation
- Perceived risk and the business buying behavior: 25 years of research findings
- Group influences on Chinese shoppers
- A virtual shopping study

Windows on Practice is a unique collection of current practice stories from the business press. For example:

- How Willow Creek Community Church in the Chicago suburb of South Barrington makes religion relevant to churchgoers.
- How E-Bank of South Africa is helping the innovation adoption of ATM among its rural customers.
- How, based on customer research, NEC created the hot-selling UltraLite Versa.
- The new face of Purchasing at Eli Lilly & Co.

Additionally, each chapter opens with a vignette, narrated to engage the student from the very beginning, by such captivating titles as:

- Tom Hanks, toy transformers, and customer insight
- Brides, brides-to-be, and brides wannabe
- Let's go shopping in China

Last but not least, the subject matter is illustrated by advertisements and photos, assembled from around the world.

CASES

To help students apply the concepts, 14 short cases have been included in the book. These cases cover all major topics, and the settings range from consumer products to industrial goods, from professional services to corporate image, and from North America to Europe and Japan.

A LEARNING EXPERIENCE

Writing a textbook is as much about learning the subject ourselves as it is about teaching the student. Although our learning of customer behavior has spanned three decades, the last three years have been most intense. In gathering material for the book and in formalizing what we thought we knew, we were impressed to discover the vast amount of knowledge both in the academic writings and among the practitioners. It is our eclectic sourcing of materials, combined with our own endeavor to fill gaps in the current body of knowledge, that made us at once feel both humble and energized. Truly, we have learned a lot. But our learning has just begun. We expect to continue our journey by benefiting from the feedback from readers and adopters like yourselves. We hope you would write, call, question, and advise us as you use this book.

JS
BM
BN

A Complete and Innovative Support Package

Instructor's Manual

The IM includes Conversion notes for changing texts, sample syllabi, notes on using the PowerPoint CD-ROM, notes on using the Video Package, description and instructions for using Discovering Your Marketing Career CD-ROM, notes on using the Web in your classroom, and information on marketing careers that will be of use to your students. Also, the following helpful sections are included for each chapter:

- Learning goals & teaching suggestions
- Lecture outline
- Key terms defined
- Lecture illustration file
- Answers to critical thinking questions
- Answers to review questions
- Answers to application questions
- Answers to practical experiences section
- Experiential exercises
- Guest speaker suggestions
- Term paper suggestions
- Questions/Answers/Suggestions for Video Case Usage

Electronic Instructor's Manual

This instructor resource system includes an electronic version of the Instructor's Manual available to professors upon request.

Test Bank

Double- and triple-checked for accuracy, the revised and updated Test Bank includes 2,500-plus questions. Questions include multiple choice, true/false, and short essays to emphasize the importance of the concepts presented in each chapter.

Computerized Test Bank

Available in IBM-, Windows-, and Macintosh-compatible formats, the computerized version of the printed Test Bank enables instructors to preview and edit test questions, as well as add their own. The tests and answer keys can also be printed in "scrambled" formats.

RequesTest and Online Testing Service

The Dryden Press makes test planning quicker and easier than ever with this program. Instructors can order test masters by question number and criteria over a toll-free telephone number. Test masters will be mailed or faxed within 48 hours. Dryden can provide instructors with software to install their own online testing program, allowing tests to be administered over a network or on individual terminals. This program offers instructors greater flexibility and convenience in grading and storing test results.

PowerPoint/CD-ROM Media Active Presentation Software

Classroom lectures and discussions come to life with this innovative presentation tool. Extremely professor friendly and organized by chapter, this program enables instructors to custom design their own multimedia classroom presentations, using overhead transparencies, figures, tables, and graphs from the text, as well as completely new material from outside sources.

Videos

In the tradition of the main text, this exciting and innovative video package adopts the user, buyer, payer approach to customer behavior through its video segments which are tied to chapter concepts and material from the text. Companies such as Kmart, J.C. Penney, Pier 1 Imports, and Fossil Watches are highlighted.

Discovering Your Marketing Career CD-ROM

This interactive, student-friendly software helps students learn about and assess their compatibility with marketing careers. In one comprehensive, multimedia CD-ROM, students receive broad guidance and practical advice on everything from clarifying the depth of their interest in a particular marketing career to preparing and implementing an effective job search strategy. Comprehensive career profiles present a detailed, up-to-date picture of actual job responsibilities, career paths, and skills needed, along with information on current compensation levels, useful directories, and other relevant information for finding out more on the chosen career of interest. Also, the CD-ROM includes a free copy of the student version of *Career Design*, the landmark career planning software program based on the work of John Crystal, the major contributor to the most widely read career text, *What Color Is Your Parachute?* by Richard N. Bolles.

Please contact your local Dryden representative for *Discovering Your Marketing Career* and *Internet Guide* packaging options.

Internet Marketing Connection

Students owning a copy of *Discovering Your Marketing Career* CD-ROM included with this text can download the Internet Marketing Connection, an online guide to a wide variety of marketing links. This resource is run from the student's favorite Web browser, enabling the user to read the link's description and click on an icon if interested.

This resource is updated regularly to ensure links are current. Visit **www.dryden.com/mktng/careercd/** for the latest version.

Internet Guide

An Internet Guide can be packaged with each copy of *Customer Behavior: Consumer Behavior and Beyond*. All students can be Internet-savvy with this invaluable guide to the Internet. The handbook's Internet terms and popular Web site addresses—over 160 ranging from the American Stock Exchange to the White House—get students where they want to go on the Internet.

ACKNOWLEDGMENTS

A project of this magnitude cannot be completed without the support of many individuals. An important group among them is the colleagues and teachers of consumer behavior, who reviewed the book at the draft stage. As reviewers, they worked hard to (a) ensure the accuracy of facts, (b) improve readability, (c) suggest leads and research references, and (d) in general serve as a "second opinion." Their valuable contribution is reflected in the significant improvement of the book.

Avery Abernethy, Auburn University

Ronald Adams, University of North Florida

Eric Arnould, University of South Florida

Russell W. Belk, University of Utah

Dennis Clayson, University of Northern Iowa

Dena Cox, Indiana University

Andrew M. Forman, Hofstra University

Ronald Goldsmith, Florida State University

Cathy L. Hartman, Utah State University

David E. Hartman, University of Virginia

Ronald Paul Hill, Villanova University

Jerome Kernan, George Mason University

Shanker Krishnan, Indiana University

Steven Lysonski, Marquette University

Shelley Rinehart, University of Oklahoma

Maria Sannella, Boston College

Linda Showers, Illinois State University

Patricia Sorce, Rochester Institute of Technology

Eric Spangenberg, Washington State University

Bruce Stern, Portland State University

Gerald Stiles, Mankato State University

Gail Tom, California State University–Sacramento

Stuart Van Auken, California State University–Chico

Meera Venkatraman, Suffolk University

Rhonda Walker Mack, College of Charleston

Other individuals contributed more directly to the contents of the book and accompanying support materials. Foremost among these is the help of Reshma Shah of Emory University who contributed a majority of advertisements and end-of-chapter review questions. She also contributed immensely to the Instructor's Manual. Rajiv Vaidyanathan, University of Minnesota–Duluth was instrumental in developing the PowerPoint Presentation Software that accompanies the textbook. Also, Eric Spangenberg, Washington State University, contributed his time and talent in authoring the Test Bank.

The book would have never seen the light of day but for the unflinching hard work of our good friends at The Dryden Press. Acquisitions editor Bill Schoof was instrumental in keeping us energized as well as focused. He brought to the project invaluable experience and organizational and leadership skills. Karen Hill's contribution as developmental editor is unparalleled: her many thoughtful additions brought clarity and balance to the material, and her copyediting made the book much more readable for students. Tracy Morse, also our developmental editor, took day-to-day responsibility for seeing the book through production. Her energy and enthusiasm sustained the fast pace of the project. Equally helpful were the other members of the book team: editorial assistant, Bobbie Bochenko; project editor, Becky Dodson; designer, Scott Baker; production manager, Lois West; and product manager, Lisé Johnson. To all these fine individuals, we express our sincere thanks.

BRIEF CONTENTS

CONTENTS

Customer Behavior

CONSUMER BEHAVIOR AND BEYOND

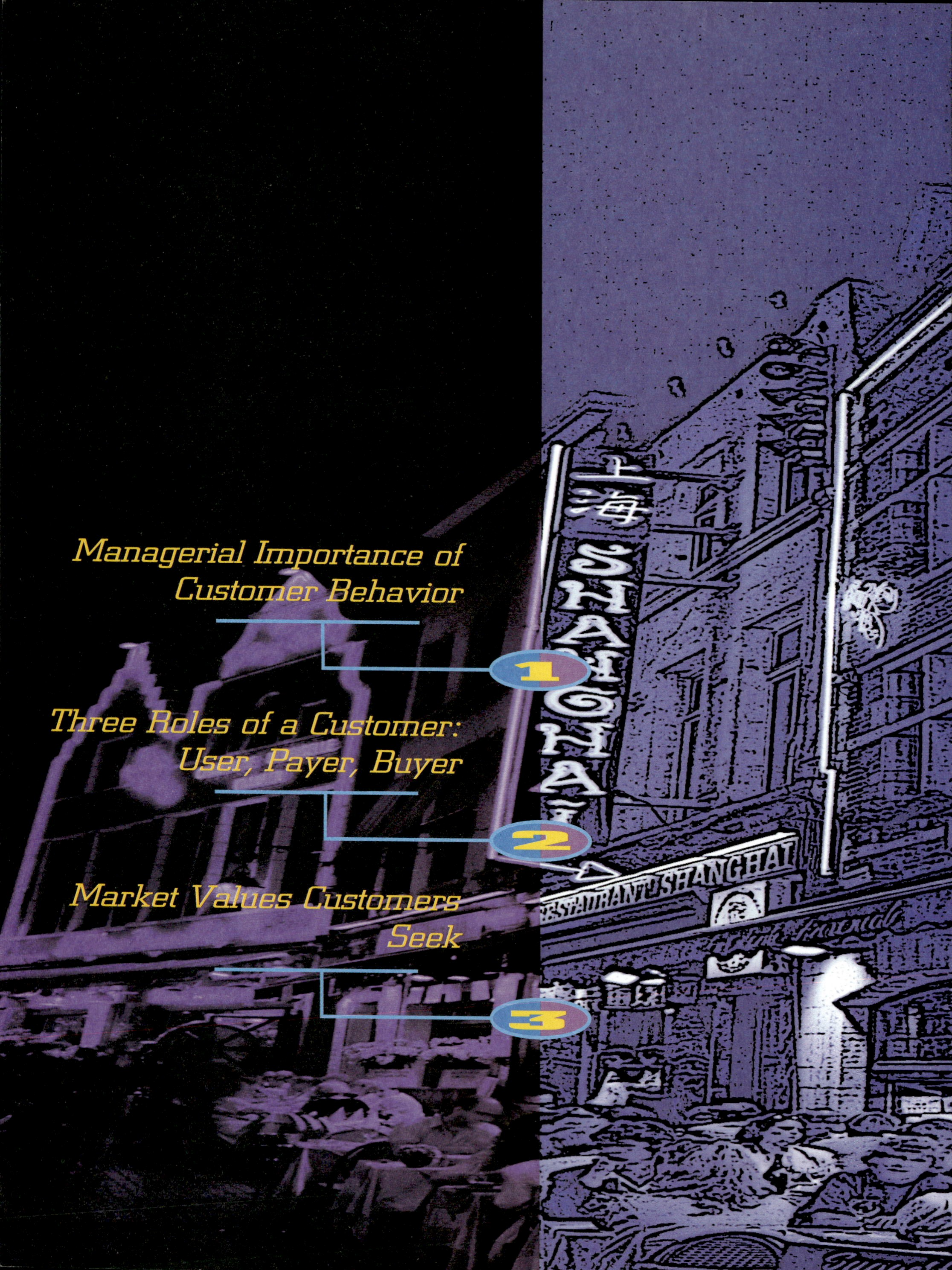

Managerial Importance of
Customer Behavior

1

Three Roles of a Customer:
User, Payer, Buyer

2

Market Values Customers
Seek

3

part one

The Customer: Key to Market Success

CHAPTER 1

After reading this chapter you should be able to:

- Describe the scope of this book, and explain how it goes beyond what is generally studied in consumer behavior textbooks.

- Introduce the concept of customer and its three roles.

- Describe the importance of studying customer behavior.

- Discuss both products and services that customers in household and business markets buy.

- Discuss the benefits of adopting a customer-oriented approach.

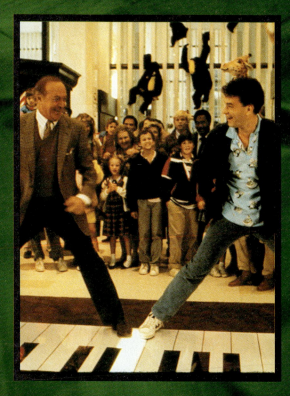

Managerial Importance of Customer Behavior

Tom Hanks, Toy Transformers, and Customer Insight

In the U.S. film *Big*, American actor Tom Hanks plays Josh, a 13-year-old kid who accidentally acquires an adult body but retains the mind of a child. This juvenile trapped inside the body of an adult continues to behave like a child—innocent, curious, and playful. To sustain himself, he gets a computer job in a toy company. One day, he was in a toy store, and the president of the company he worked for spotted him. Intrigued by this "young man's" fascination with the toys, the president asked his views on some of the toys on display. Impressed by the insights Josh offered, the president promoted him to the position of the Vice President for New Product Development.

His presence on the new-product review committee was quite a trip. One day, the company's marketing research executive was presenting the test data for a new transformer which looked like a skyscraper but could turn into a robot. Tom Hanks continued to play with the prototype toy throughout the presentation, just as a 13-year-old would.

"These tests were conducted over a six-month period using a double-blind format with eight overlapping demographic groups. The focus tests showed a solid base in the 9- to 11-year-old bracket. . . . robots and transformers, . . . and that is one-fifth of the total revenue of the last year," the research executive was saying. Everyone applauded as he finished the presentation.

Everyone, that is, except Josh. Raising his hand timidly, he said, "I don't get it!"

Here is how the conversation went after this:

Research Executive: What don't you get?

Tom Hanks: It turns from a building into a robot, right? Well, what is fun about that?

Research Executive: Well, if you had read your industry breakdown, you would see that our success in the action figure area has climbed from 27 percent to 45 percent in the last two years. Here, this might help [*hands him a sheet of paper with a graph on it*].

Tom Hanks: [*looks at the sheet briefly, looks puzzled, and raises his hand again with the same timidness*] I still don't get it!

Research Executive: [*losing his cool*] What? What? What don't you get?

Tom Hanks: [*silence*]

Company President:	[*in the nurturing voice he always exhibited for Hanks*] What exactly don't you get, Josh?
Tom Hanks:	There are a million robots that turn into something. This is a building that turns into a robot. What's fun about playing with a building?
Research Executive:	This is a skyscraper!
Tom Hanks:	Well couldn't it be, like, a robot, like, that turns into something, like a bug or something. . . . Like a prehistoric giant insect that . . . can crush cars. . . .
Executive 2:	So the robot turns into a bug.
Executive 3:	A robot transformer, eh?
Executive 4:	The robot turns into a bug. A very good idea, here! [*Everyone nods approvingly.*]
President:	The robot! The bug! Robot into a bug! This is a great idea, Josh [*addressing Tom Hanks*]. Great work, Josh!

As the committee adjourns and members leave the room, let us ponder briefly why Josh makes such a good VP of New-Product Development. The reason is simple. No other executive, including the executive who had directed the marketing research project, could so totally identify him- or herself with the customer—the child who would ultimately play with the toy.

No one else could so directly bring to the marketing decision process so intimate an understanding of customer behavior! That is why.

Introduction

Unlike Josh in *Big,* real-world marketers are rarely able to experience their customers' perspective directly. However, they can—and should—educate themselves about their customers. Successful marketers need to know what their customers need and want, as well as how their customers make decisions about buying and using products. For this purpose, marketers study customer behavior.

This book is about customer behavior and about the role it plays in deciding the fate and fortunes of corporations around the globe. As we head toward the turn of the century, understanding the customer behavior will become even more important for the success of businesses everywhere. In this chapter, we define customer behavior, identify different customer types and customer roles, and specify their domain. We then discuss the significance of customer behavior for the very purpose of business, and identify the competitive advantages a firm gains as it adopts a customer orientation.

In this and the subsequent chapters, we link customer behavior with managerial actions. Customer behavior is not merely an academic field of study. Rather, it is the basis for sound managerial response to customers. Our discussion of managerial response includes how the conventional marketing mix is adopted to customer behavior. But it also covers the emerging topics of buyer-seller relationships, business-to-business marketing, delivering customer value, and relationship marketing—topics we discuss in subsequent chapters. We thus seek to connect customer behavior principles with the elements of marketing strategy.

What Is Customer Behavior?

We define **customer behavior** as the **mental** and **physical activities** undertaken by household and business customers that result in decisions and actions to pay for, purchase, and use products and services. Our definition of *customer behavior* includes a variety of activities and a number of roles that people can hold. Figure 1.1 illustrates the dimensions of customer behavior. As we will explain, these dimensions go beyond marketers' more traditional focus on *consumer* behavior.

Types of Customers

In general, a **customer** is a person or an organizational unit that plays a role in the consummation of a transaction with the marketer or an entity. A business's customers may be acting as household members or as representatives of a company. Thus, our definition covers the behaviors of customers in both the **household** and the **business** markets. Conventionally, the term **consumer** has referred to household markets only. The corresponding term for the business market has been "customer." We use the term "customer" to refer to both markets.

Actually, even the usage of the term "consumer" to refer to the household market has been seen more in textbooks than in practice. For example, retail stores generally refer to their patrons as "customers" (rather than as consumers); so do utility companies (e.g., gas, electricity, and telephone service providers), financial companies (e.g., banks, credit card issuing firms, etc.), service companies (e.g., lawn maintenance, seamstress, dry cleaners, etc.), or even personal service providers (e.g., palm readers and fortune tellers, massage therapists, and boutiques that do the piercing and tattooing of body parts). Professional service providers refer to individuals in household markets as clients (e.g., lawyers, real estate agents, tax advisors) or by their more context-specific roles (e.g., doctors call them

Figure 1.1

CUSTOMERS: TYPES, ROLES, AND BEHAVIORS

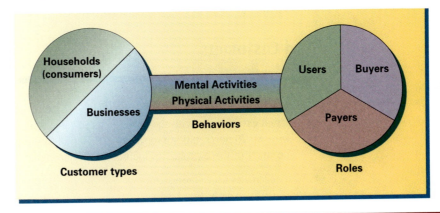

"patients," educators call them "students," fund-raisers call them "donors," etc.). Only manufacturers who do not routinely deal with the end users of a product refer to these household end users as "consumers" (e.g., Procter & Gamble, Johnson & Johnson, Kraft, and General Foods would generally refer to the end users of their products as consumers). To overcome this divergence of terms in current usage, we use the term "customer" all inclusively.

Customer Roles

A marketplace transaction requires at least three customer roles: (1) buying (i.e., selecting) a product, (2) paying for it, and (3) using or consuming it. Thus, a customer can be (1) a buyer, (2) a payer, or (3) a user/consumer. The **user** is the person who actually consumes or uses the product or receives the benefits of the service. The **payer** is the person who finances the purchase. Finally, the **buyer** is the person who participates in the procurement of the product from the marketplace. Each of these roles may be carried out by the same person or an organizational unit (e.g., a department) or by different persons or departments.

For example, many teenagers buy groceries and household items for the entire family because both parents work. Parents pay for the purchases but do not always specify what specific food items to buy, and/or which brands to purchase. Or they specify broadly, leaving the final decision to the teenager. Similarly, if you have a job that involves using a computer system, you are the user but may not be the person who actually made the purchase or paid for the system. Your firm's purchasing department may have selected the supplier, and your department head may have paid for the purchase out of the department budget.

This book thus goes beyond the conventional subject matter of consumer behavior—the behavior of "end users" (whether they be in household or business markets)—to include the behavior of payers and buyers. As we explain in detail in Chapter 2, the person who pays for the product or service is not always the one who is going to use it. Nor is the person who uses it always the person who purchases it. Any of the three customer roles (user, payer, and buyer) makes a person a customer.

In both household and business settings, conflicts develop among the user, payer, and buyer. For example, the decision to attend a particular university could be a source of conflict within a family. If your parents are paying for your education, for example, they may have determined that it is financially wise to choose a university in your hometown, whereas you, the student (the user), may prefer to attend school away from home. Or if your employer is paying for your education, cost considerations might lead your employer (the payer) to restrict your options as a user. Understanding customer behavior entails addressing the separate goals of and tensions among the three customer roles. (We elaborate on this point in Chapters 2 and 3.)

Behaviors of Customers

Our definition of *customer behavior* includes both mental and physical activities. Examples of mental activities are assessing the suitability of a product or service brand, making inferences about a product or service's qualities from advertising information, and evaluating actual experiences with the product. Physical activities include visiting stores, reading *Consumer Reports,* talking to salespeople, and issuing a purchase order.

The study of these processes includes such questions as:

- Who undertakes which processes?
- Who plays each of the three customer roles?
- Why do certain processes occur in the manner they do?

■ Which characteristics of customers themselves determine their behavior?

■ What environmental factors influence customer behavior processes?

The Domain of Customer Behavior

A customer's mental and physical activities involve some type of product or service. Throughout this book, we discuss products *and* services that households buy and use regularly, such as: automobiles, appliances, shirts, banking, dry cleaning, and insurance. But the discussion also goes beyond these typical household products and services and includes products and services that businesses use, such as office supplies, equipment, and bookkeeping services. Figure 1.2 presents the four types of products and services that constitute the domain of customer behavior discussed in this textbook. Within the business domain, we include both profit and nonprofit companies.

In the upper left-hand quadrant of Figure 1.2 are household products targeted exclusively to the household market. One example of a household consumer product is food, like bread or milk, items that are used daily that need to be replenished often. Another household product is clothing, like a blouse or a shirt, items that will last for some period, but will still need to be replaced over time because they get worn out, outgrown, or go out of fashion. A third type of household product is the one that lasts quite a long time, like an electric razor or an iron—items that are built to withstand the wear and tear of daily use.

In the upper right-hand quadrant are business products that are sold exclusively to business firms or to individuals who use them for conducting their business. Examples include machine tools, corporate jets, internal power generators, raw materials, lubricants, employee uniforms, and so on.

Of course, some products, like automobiles, are targeted to both household and business markets. Automobiles may be used in households to run daily errands or by salespeople to conduct business. Other examples of products used by both household and business customers include cellular phones, fax machines, desktop computers, bottled drinking water, and wall fixtures. In many instances, although the product categories are common, the design specifications might differ for the household and business markets. Illustrative instances are plush carpets for household use versus commercial grade carpets, office furniture versus home furniture, and heavy-duty versus light-duty smoke detectors and other security systems.

In the lower left-hand quadrant are consumer services targeted exclusively to the household market. Examples include hair styling, dental cleaning, baby-sitting, home-cleaning service, home-appliance repairs, drapery-cleaning services, and so on. This sector is witnessing exciting innovations, fueled by technology and the business strategy of using customer service as a competitive tool. Major banks like Citicorp are altering the

Figure 1.2

CUSTOMER BEHAVIOR DOMAIN

	HOUSEHOLD	BUSINESS
PRODUCTS	Consumer products	Business products
SERVICES	Consumer services	Business services

delivery of their products and services by offering customers the option of banking by phone and, most recently, banking at home through the use of the Internet. Some in the industry foresee the installation of video-conferencing kiosks installed in the mall so that a customer could just walk into it and talk to a bank official without visiting the bank.

In the lower right-hand quadrant is the business services sector, targeted exclusively to businesses. Examples include management training and consulting services, employee benefits services, janitorial services, and document delivery services. There is currently a trend toward "outsourcing," where more and more companies are farming out services that typically were performed in-house, such as data processing, payroll, security, travel and others. One recently introduced service is online data-storage servers that enable users to back up their systems over the Internet, for a monthly fee. One such company is Surefind Information Inc., which offers a $100,000 guarantee against lost data. Their service is the equivalent of a safe deposit box, offering its customers security and confidentiality.[1] The case of marketing services to business customers is perhaps the most challenging but also most intriguing task. No matter what the service, the ultimate benefit the business customer is seeking is help in doing its business better.

Marketing Services to Business Customers: Helping Them Meet New Challenges in Global Markets. The Italian caption in the ad says, "Are all your talents working in concert?"

As with products, some services are used both by household and business customers. Examples include banking, security of physical premises, telecommunications, insurance, and so on. While the same service company might target both markets, specific features are often tailored to businesses much more than for household customers.

It is important to note that the line between household consumer services and business services is thin. It is not uncommon to see a company engaged in a household service expand its market by offering it to the business market, and vice versa. For example, American Express jumped into the business service market by introducing its Corporate Purchasing Card for office supplies and services at big companies. This is a sizable market for American Express, expected to bring in as much as $300 billion in annual billings. Another example is Service Master of America, traditionally known for offering office and industrial janitorial services, which recently moved into the house cleaning market.[2]

Why Understanding Customer Behavior Is Important

Businesses everywhere are recognizing the importance of understanding the customer behavior as a key to their success. As we head toward the turn of the century, understanding the customer will be the key to business success. It is the first step toward meeting the challenges of the exciting world of business. The study of customer behavior provides the basic knowledge necessary for successful business decisions. To see for yourself, try answering the following questions about actual companies:

1. The Gap stores in Hong Kong were turning up losses. Then, a new president arrived and instituted some changes. One of these changes pertained to getting salespeople to behave differently. The strategy worked, and the company has successfully increased its revenues and profits since then. What do you think was the change in salesperson behavior?

   a. Becoming more friendly and personally showing the customer all the merchandise.

   b. Following the customer closely to be available to answer questions as the customer looked at the merchandise.

   c. Leaving the customer pretty much alone to find and examine the merchandise.

2. As a retailer of kitchen appliances, you have been carrying two brands of home breadmakers—Toastmaster at a regular price of $139 and Panasonic at a regular price of $179. Then, one day, you add to your product line a slightly larger Panasonic unit priced at $209. How will this affect sales of the $179 Panasonic model?

   a. Decrease sales, since customers who were inclined to buy Panasonic would now be split between the two Panasonic models.

   b. Decrease sales, since some of the customers who would have bought it would now buy the $139 Toastmaster unit.

   c. Increase sales, since some of the customers who would have bought the $139 Toastmaster unit, would now prefer this model.

3. Recently, Delta Airlines announced that it will buy all of its jets from Boeing. Understandably, Airbus, the other big supplier of jets, was infuriated. It thought that Delta's action was anticompetitive and offered an unfair advantage to Boeing. Why did Delta give such a large chunk of its business to Boeing?

   a. Delta Airlines' purchasing executives were swayed by personal friendship they felt toward the marketing executives of Boeing.

   b. Boeing offered Delta a low-price deal that Delta just couldn't refuse.

   c. Delta wanted a long-term relationship—one that would focus on creating long-term value for Delta—and Boeing offered it.

The correct answer is "c," in each case. By learning about customer behavior, businesspeople can understand why customers buy what they buy or, more generally, why they respond to marketing stimuli as they do. Without this understanding, their behavior, their response, remains a mystery. The Window on Practice box discusses the U.S. car industry's need for understanding customers.

WINDOW ON PRACTICE

When Detroit Misread Customers, Again!

During the oil crisis of the 1970s, American carmakers were caught by surprise when Americans bought small Toyotas and Hondas in droves, shunning their past favorites—the gas guzzling U.S.-made cars. At first reluctantly, and then in a nervous hurry, U.S. carmakers climbed on the "small car" wave, although late by a full decade.

You would think that Detroit (the city where the big three car manufacturers are located) would have learned a lesson. To some measure it did—designing small cars, and then acquiring a new religion of quality and cost efficiency. The share of foreign-made cars was 40 percent in 1997, up 3 percent from the previous years. Even though Detroit attempted to regain some of the lost share, some in Detroit thought that the foreign-car buyers were different, that they were not true Americans. But the big three (Ford, General Motors, and Chrysler) had 85 percent of the truck market. Why would Americans prefer U.S. makes for trucks and vans, but buy imports when it comes to cars? Part of the reason is that the truck buyers are a different set of consumers than the car buyers. But it may also be that U.S. trucks fill their needs (both in utility and quality) as well as do import trucks.

If import car buyers buy import cars, it is for a good reason. In some categories, the U.S. carmakers simply do not offer the car these consumers need. Take the luxury car segment. The flagship U.S. brands in that segment are Cadillac and Lincoln. Many consumers love Cadillacs and Lincolns. But just as many hate them. And it has nothing to do with the fact that they are domestic makes. Look at how big these cars are; each can carry up to six passengers. How many consumers, especially the affluent kind who can afford these pricey luxury models, really ever need to carry six passengers? But instead of making smaller luxury cars, when many of the luxury car seekers went in for the much smaller Lexuses, BMWs, and Mercedes, Detroit just blamed it on the differentness of these consumers—they were import lovers, period!

Only now are the U.S. carmakers waking up. GM is offering the Cadillac Catera, a smaller and sportier car now made in Germany. Lincoln is working on a smaller model but will take at least 18 months before it can roll one out. Why is Detroit so late in catching up? Because it misread the import buyers as import lovers, when in fact these consumers were just looking for small but prestigious, luxury models.

Based on Jerry Flint, "Hey, Just Give Me a Great Car," *Forbes*, June 2, 1997, p. 65.

How does customer behavior explain how the salespeople in The Gap stores in Hong Kong should behave? Becoming friendly with customers or at least following the customer closely to answer questions is not wrong; many customers in the United States and other countries would, in fact, desire such behavior. It is just that these behaviors are not preferred by Chinese customers. Chinese customers like to browse on their own, and they feel very uncomfortable with a salesperson looking over their shoulders. Without this knowledge, The Gap management might try to improve customer service by following U.S. notions of good customer service, which likely would alienate these customers. We will discuss this and other cross-cultural influences on customer behavior in Chapter 6.

Figure 1.3   REASONS FOR UNDERSTANDING CUSTOMER BEHAVIOR

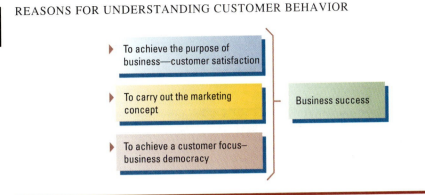

Knowledge about customer behavior also explains why the introduction of a second Panasonic model improves sales of the existing Panasonic model. This occurs because of how customers frame the decision problem. The original Panasonic model now has a new reference point: the $209 model. Compared with this new point of reference, $179 for a Panasonic bread maker looks like a much better deal. In comparison, the Toastmaster model ($139) has no point of comparison, so customers are unable to infer the "deal" it might represent.[3] In Chapter 14, we will explore further how sets of alternatives influence customers' choices.

With regard to Delta's purchase of its fleet from Boeing, for years the selling wisdom has been that if you can offer the best price to the customer, you will make the sale. That, or else you have to wine and dine the customer. Or so the thinking went. The real key to gaining a business customer's patronage, however, is to offer customers long-term *value* and develop a *relationship* based on meeting their needs. Boeing adopted this perspective and structured a relationship that would offer Delta the most long-term value. Delta's old fleet was from McDonnell Douglas (DC-9s and DC-10s) and from Boeing (Boeing 737s and 747s), and it was planning to replace these old planes with newer aircraft. Since Boeing was in the process of acquiring McDonnell Douglas, it was able to offer Delta the opportunity to upgrade *all* of its diverse fleet by using a single-source supplier. Delta Airlines valued the convenience of such "one-stop shopping," and Boeing was able to offer that and other benefits of relationship marketing. These topics are the subject matter of Chapters 18 and 19. It is the first step toward meeting the challenges of the exciting world of business.

Indeed relationship marketing and delivering long-term customer value are new approaches to doing business, and we illustrate these approaches throughout the book. These examples illustrate three broad reasons why it is important for firms to understand customer behavior. It helps them satisfy customers, adopt the marketing concept, and become customer focused (see Figure 1.3).

Customer Satisfaction: The Purpose of Business

Peter F. Drucker, considered to be one of the leading management gurus in the world, believes that the purpose of business is to create and then retain a satisfied customer.[4] Although firms have to make money, Drucker argues that making money is a necessity, not a purpose. It is, in fact, the end result, a desirable outcome, of creating a satisfied customer. Similar sentiment is expressed by Theodore Levitt, a Harvard Business School professor, who explains this by an analogy with human beings—all humans have to eat to survive, but eating is not their purpose. Furthermore, making money does not provide a legitimate reason for society to support the money-making enterprise. A society supports businesses because they serve its members by catering to their needs to leave them satisfied. Dissatisfy enough customers, and not only will these specific customers stop buying from the firm, but the society at large will condemn the firm and may even penalize it—to the point of its extinction.

Understanding Customer Behavior Makes Religion Relevant to Churchgoers

This is the story of Willow Creek Community Church in the Chicago suburb of South Barrington, Illinois.

William Hybels is the founder and senior pastor. Hybels' audience is different—an odd mix of true believers, along with atheists, agnostics, and those who once believed in Christianity but are now unsure. In their yearning for spiritual fulfillment, they have been failed by conventional churches. Many have developed the attitude that the Bible and Christianity are not relevant to them.

Enter marketing. Hybels believes that the basic products—the Bible and Christianity—are good. What is needed is presenting it in ways that make it relevant to these alienated folks' lives. So Hybels has revamped the typical ways the church sermons are offered. No more conventional religious props at Willow Creek—no more crucifixes, incense, or confessions; no more rituals. And he has devised new delivery platforms, the ones based on an intimate understanding of his target customers.

One such group of target customers is 20-year-olds—typically absent from the Sunday prayers. So Hybels has started a Saturday night service with rock music. The audience consists of young men and women—guys with faded jeans and goatees, girls in black boots and purple-streaked hair. To be sure, there is rock music. And then there is the sermon—delivered in ways that echo its young audiences' ethos. Dieter Zander, director of this service, stands up before the group and proclaims: "The leadership style of your generation is different from previous generations." Then he talks about the problems of drugs, divorce among parents, sex, and racial conflicts.

How does his young congregation take it? Very religiously, really. "God doesn't feel distant here," said one attendee. "They talk here about real life; it is dirty and it is grungy, and that is what I have been looking to hear about."

Willow Creek has 145 acres of lushly landscaped grounds, with a man-made pond. The church complex has a food court and a bookstore. Also available are day care services. The service is held in a stadium-like round with seating capacity of 4,540.

Hybels got his marketing ideas from management guru Peter F. Drucker. After attending one of Drucker's seminars, Hybels started asking some hard questions: "What is our business? Who is our customer? What does the customer consider value?" His answers: People find church boring and sermons irrelevant to their lives. He discovered that most people believed in God but not in church. So he created a service using rock music, and used skits to bring sermons to life. He invited people of all beliefs. No dress code, either. And he started ministries to deal with divorce, single-parenting, finding a potential spouse, and, with help from members, even offering car repair services to single parents. Thus, repairing psyches, marriages, and cars became part of the church's offerings.

Today, Willow Creek's success is being copied, with help from Hybels, by other churches. It has as affiliates some 2,300 churches in 15 countries. The average audience there is 400 worshippers, compared to 100 as a national average. At the heart of this success lies one fundamental lesson: understanding the customer's motivations, or needs and wants, and designing services so that they respond to these customer needs and wants.

Hybels is a pastor. But he is also a student of customer behavior par excellence. Nowhere else can one find a better showcase for the value of understanding customer behavior than in Hybels' church services. To students of customer behavior, Willow Creek is poignant proof that understanding customer behavior matters!

Source: Katrina Burger, "Jesus Christ.com," *Forbes*, May 7, 1997, pp. 76–83.

In response to such messages, companies and their employees have dramatically changed the way they treat customers, striving to continually satisfy them. Customer satisfaction has been identified as the key to business success. Although some companies use this concept more in words than in deeds, there is a definite movement in diverse enterprises—foreign and domestic, for-profit and nonprofit, and in household and business markets—on a global basis towards a "customer culture"—a culture that incorporates customer satisfaction as an integral part of the corporate mission, and utilizes an understanding of customer behavior as input to all of its marketing plans and decisions.

North Pacific Paper, a Weyerhaeuser subsidiary in Washington, sells newsprint rolls to printing presses. The paper maker has its employees work for a customer for a week, forcing them to see their business from the customer's side of the fence. According to Trig Pedersen, an hourly employee, "Just because you manufacture a roll of newsprint doesn't mean you understand what the demands are going to be on it in a high-speed press." In fact, a Weyerhaeuser employee found that a small bar code put onto the newsprint rolls was sticking to the presses. Relocating the bar code resolved the problem. Trig Pedersen recently returned from his third trip to Japan, where he videotaped, for two nights, newspaper presses working between the hours of 10 P.M. and 2 A.M. After returning to the plant, Trig gave his co-workers presentations for two to three weeks.[5]

A customer culture can be readily seen today in such diverse business firms as U.S. economy retail chain Wal-Mart and upscale Harrod's of London, premium hotel chain Marriott and budget-minded Motel "6," long-distance phone giants AT&T and France Telecom and smaller local phone companies, luxury business airline British Airways and U.S. economy king Southwest Airlines. It is just as likely to be seen also, and increasingly, in all sorts of nonprofit enterprises that are constantly surveying their members, students, patients, citizens, and public benefit recipients, to ensure the satisfaction of all these "customers." The Window on Practice box discusses one church's customer focus. And how can businesses learn what will satisfy their customers? First, they must know the basics of customer behavior.

Applying its customer culture, British Airways (BA) found out that first-class passengers want good service on the ground as well as in the air. Responding to a desire on the part of these first-class travelers to simply sleep once they get into the jet, the airline now offers flyers the option of having dinner on the ground in the first-class lounge. Once they get on board, the passengers then slip into BA pajamas and sleep through an uninterrupted flight to their destination. After arriving, BA serves breakfast, offers the use of comfortable dressing rooms and showers, and will even press their clothes before they go off to a business meeting.[6]

The Marketing Concept

According to Philip Kotler, a world-renowned marketing professor at Northwestern University and consultant to several major corporations, the marketing concept is an improvement over the selling concept.[7] In the selling concept, a firm's principal focus is on finding a buyer for the product it makes, and somehow "selling" that customer into parting with his or her cash in exchange for the product the firm has to offer. In contrast, under the marketing concept (which reflects a more contemporary view of the field), the firm's obsession is to make what the customer wants. For this reason, the market-oriented firm focuses on understanding its customers' dynamic needs and wants.

Every year, Ford surveys 2.5 million customers and invites car owners to meet engineers and dealers to discuss quality problems. The company has also designed a software system that makes it easier for executives and engineers to implement customer feedback. For example, in the mid-1980s even though the chairman himself wanted to eliminate the boxy Lincoln Town Car, the company kept the sedan after surveys showed that the older drivers still loved it. The revamped Town Car won *Motor Trend* magazine's Car of the Year award shortly thereafter. Other automobile manufacturers follow the marketing concept as well. To ensure that their customers are satisfied, carmakers such as Nissan, Acura, Toyota, and Chrysler have hired outside research firms to call every customer after he or she has purchased a car or obtained service at one of the dealerships. The survey asks customers how they were treated during their purchase or service visit.[8]

Ford is serious about following the marketing concept. This advertisement outlines the steps that Ford takes to ensure that it meets the needs of its customers.

Customer Focus Is Business Democracy

Focusing on the customer leads to serving society's needs better. In government, democracy refers to, as Abraham Lincoln put it, "government of the people, by the people, and for the people." Likewise, in the marketplace, business democracy means that companies are governed by and for the customers. This indeed is the foundation for Adam Smith's seminal work, *The Wealth of Nations*. Paying attention to customer behavior and fashioning a business to respond to customer needs, desires, and preferences amounts to business democracy for a nation's citizens and serves both the public interest and private interest.[9]

Your travel lines to India match mine

There's a lot in common between us.
We speak the same language.
We share similar tastes.
We enjoy similar comforts and luxuries.

DAILY NON-STOPS TO INDIA
For the same price, fly to any Indian destination where
AIR INDIA operate

एअर-इंडिया
AIR·INDIA

FLY WITH YOUR VERY OWN
RESERVATIONS LONDON 071.491 7979   BIRMINGHAM 021.643 7421   MANCHESTER 061.236 3958
CARDIFF 0222 224930 GLASGOW 0475 530536   G.S.A. 071.439 3627

Air India appeals to cultural familiarity of its customers.

Citizens cast their economic votes by patronizing the marketer they believe responds to their needs best. This is antithetical to state-owned enterprises, such as those that existed in the former Soviet Union, where it became obvious that centrally run businesses do not serve their customers well. The most efficient system to serve the public interest is business democracy. In other words, we stand to create a more efficient system for both household and business customers if companies pursue the goals of business democracy, giving customers freedom of choice, and depending for their own well-being on the economic patronage of their customers. The changes taking place in Eastern Europe demonstrate how economic democracy is taking a foothold in countries around the world, benefiting both businesses and the newly liberated (in both political and economic terms) citizens (i.e., "customers").[10]

Customer Behavior and Customer Orientation

The principles of customer behavior serve a company best when they are applied to developing and maintaining a customer orientation. Customer orientation (also referred to as **market orientation**) means a thorough understanding of customers' needs and wants, the competitive environment, and the nature of the market, used to formulate all of the firm's plans and actions to create satisfied customers.[11] General Electric Company's vision of itself as a customer-oriented firm (or a "boundaryless firm" as GE management envisions) is articulated in its 1990 GE Annual Report as follows:

> [In a boundaryless company] customers are seen for what they are—the lifeblood of a company. Customers' vision of their needs and the company's view become identical, and every effort of every man and woman in the company is focused on satisfying those needs.

Marketing scholar and Dartmouth College marketing professor Frederick E. Webster, Jr., has articulated the role of the marketing function and organization in the corporation as follows: "At the corporate level, marketing managers have a critical role to play as *advocates for the customer and for a set of values and beliefs that put the customer first* in the firm's decision making."[12] At this point we invite you to take the quiz in the Customer Insight box.

Kookmin Bank of Korea adopts a new logo depicting a "big man," symbolizing the bank's renewed commitment to the idea that, as the headline proclaims, "Nobody is bigger than the customer."

When firms and organizations become customer oriented, they reap impressive gains, in both of the two broad areas of business success. First, they gain a remarkable competitive advantage in the external marketplace. And second, internally (that is, within the organization), they are able to cultivate satisfied employees who feel pride in their jobs. Employees are "internal customers" for an organization. Through customer orientation, then, the firm is able to offer value to both the internal and external customers. We discuss each in turn.

CUSTOMER INSIGHT

How Customer-Oriented Is Your Firm?

If you are employed by a business firm, take the following survey, from your business's perspective. If you are a customer, answer this survey for a company you do business with, based on whatever impressions you may have formed about the firm.

Scale:

Not true	Partially true	True
−1	0	+1

1. In this business unit, we meet with customers at least once a year to find out what products or services they will need in the future.

2. Individuals from our manufacturing department interact directly with customers.

3. We periodically review the likely effect of changes in our business environment on customers.

4. Marketing personnel in our firm spend time discussing customers' future needs with other departments.

5. Data on customer satisfaction are collected regularly and disseminated at all levels in this business unit on a regular basis.

6. Our business plans are driven more by customer research than by technological advances.

7. Customer complaints never fall on deaf ears in this business unit.

8. When we find out that customers are unhappy with the quality of our services, we take corrective action immediately.

9. According to top management, serving customers is the most important thing our business unit does.

10. Top managers keep telling all employees that they must gear up now to meet customers' future needs.

11. All managers' salaries and bonuses are partly linked to the levels of customer satisfaction.

12. At this firm, everything that is done is always done with the customer uppermost in mind.

13. The firm welcomes customer comments and complaints and tries to do whatever it takes to win over a customer.

14. The employees of this firm with direct customer contact treat their customers as if their pay depends directly on customer feedback.

15. Over time, the firm has offered its customers better value than the competitors.

Scoring: The score could range from −15 to +15. If your score is negative, the firm is *not* customer oriented. The firm is unlikely to retain its customers for long. For a score in the positive range, the closer to +15 the firm is, the more customer oriented it is. Customers of this firm are probably very satisfied with its products and services. If you are a stockholder, you have reason to be happy, for the firm is likely to be profitable in the long term.

Source: Ajay K. Kohli, and Bernard J. Jaworski, "Market Orientation: The Construct, Research Propositions, and Managerial Implications," *Journal of Marketing* 54 (April 1990), p.3. The first 10 questions are adapted from Professor Jaworski and Kohli's research. The last five questions, the scoring method, and suggested score range interpretations are based on authors' intuition and are offered here to advance student understanding of the "customer orientation" concept.

Competitive Advantages through Customer Orientation

Following a customer orientation will provide a company with competitive advantages that lead to higher corporate performance in the form of increased profitability and revenue growth. There are six advantages, three of which increase profitability and three that generate revenue growth (see Figure 1.4). The three advantages that increase profitability are (1) cost efficiencies from repeat customers, (2) price premiums from established customers, and (3) customer loyalty in corporate crisis. The three advantages that generate growth are (1) increased word of mouth; (2) one-stop shopping; and (3) new-product innovations.[13]

COMPETITIVE ADVANTAGES ARISING FROM A CUSTOMER ORIENTATION

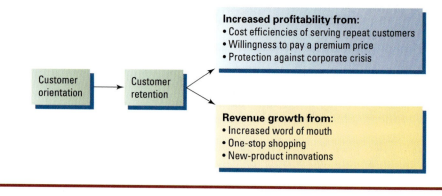

COST EFFICIENCIES FROM REPEAT CUSTOMERS

In a mature market, perhaps the best way a company can maintain a competitive advantage is through retaining its customers. Competitive strategies for retaining existing customers tend to be less costly than those for gaining new customers. According to some estimates, it costs five times more to attract a new customer than to retain one. Customer retention is the overarching advantage of a customer orientation. Customer orientation enables businesses to become more responsive to customers' needs and wants. Consequently, a firm that has adopted a customer orientation is able to keep its customers satisfied and therefore retain them over the long run. The firm's current customers become its repeat customers, year after year.

Repeat customers mean cost efficiencies. The costs of serving the established customers are considerably less than the cost of serving new customers. This occurs due to several reasons.

First, there are economies of scale in manufacturing. To produce the same item for the same customer would cost less due to accumulated learning and resulting increased productivity. This is especially true for firms offering customized products. But the marketing costs go down as well. Consider the effort a firm has to go through to replace a customer. First, it has to spend time and money in advertising and personal selling to persuade a customer to try its products. Second, for many products and services, it has to spend time and energy in offering pre-sale and post-sale service, which new customers need to a much greater extent than do continuing customers (because the former are less familiar with the firm's product or service). For example, new users of a computer system or software would need much more user support. Salespeople servicing new accounts need more time to familiarize themselves with the customers' operations (e.g., a pharmaceutical company's sales representative needs to learn a pharmacy's or a doctor's purchasing procedure). The new customer and salesperson also take time to understand each other's preferences and personalities and develop relationships where they would feel comfortable dealing with each other.

These costs of replacing a lost customer are not directly visible and have therefore been ignored by many firms in the past. We all know that with repeat customers, the cost of doing business with satisfied customers goes down. However, what we often do not realize is that it goes down exponentially with a very sharp decline in costs in the early stages of repeat buying as shown in Figure 1.5.

ECONOMIES OF SCALE FROM REPEAT BUYING

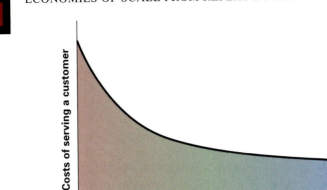

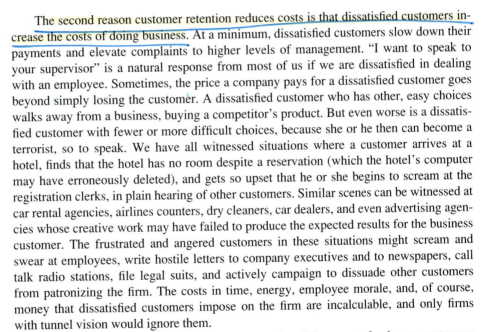

The second reason customer retention reduces costs is that dissatisfied customers increase the costs of doing business. At a minimum, dissatisfied customers slow down their payments and elevate complaints to higher levels of management. "I want to speak to your supervisor" is a natural response from most of us if we are dissatisfied in dealing with an employee. Sometimes, the price a company pays for a dissatisfied customer goes beyond simply losing the customer. A dissatisfied customer who has other, easy choices walks away from a business, buying a competitor's product. But even worse is a dissatisfied customer with fewer or more difficult choices, because she or he then can become a terrorist, so to speak. We have all witnessed situations where a customer arrives at a hotel, finds that the hotel has no room despite a reservation (which the hotel's computer may have erroneously deleted), and gets so upset that he or she begins to scream at the registration clerks, in plain hearing of other customers. Similar scenes can be witnessed at car rental agencies, airlines counters, dry cleaners, car dealers, and even advertising agencies whose creative work may have failed to produce the expected results for the business customer. The frustrated and angered customers in these situations might scream and swear at employees, write hostile letters to company executives and to newspapers, call talk radio stations, file legal suits, and actively campaign to dissuade other customers from patronizing the firm. The costs in time, energy, employee morale, and, of course, money that dissatisfied customers impose on the firm are incalculable, and only firms with tunnel vision would ignore them.

The costs of dissatisfied customers are staggering: 96 percent of unhappy customers don't complain about rude service people, but 90 percent who are dissatisfied will not buy again or will tell their story to at least nine other people,[14] and 13 percent of those unhappy former customers will tell of their experience to more than 20 people.[15] Dissatisfaction, in short, gets broadcast widely.

PREMIUM PRICES FROM ESTABLISHED CUSTOMERS

Established customers are already satisfied with the firm. Unless there is a strong reason to do so, established customers are unlikely to switch their current suppliers. After all, these customers have invested a significant amount of their time and effort in searching and selecting the right vendor or business firm in the first place. There are always some costs in switching, and sometimes these costs can be prohibitive. For example, if you have invested money in a computerized ordering system linked directly to the supplier, switching to a new supplier would mean retooling your computer network or installing a new one. Therefore, if a competitor wants to capture your satisfied customers, it must offer significantly better value either in the form of lower price or higher performance. This was the experience of Airborne Express and Emery Worldwide delivery services against Federal Express, which had accumulated a large base of satisfied customers. Similarly, this has been the experience of most of the long-distance telephone companies such as MCI and U.S. Sprint as they try to capture AT&T's customer base. And, of course, very few mainframe computer companies can compete with IBM, which still has the largest market share for mainframes.

Thus, while competitors are trying to lure away your satisfied customers with a lower price, you can continue to charge a premium price compared with the new competitors. It is estimated that a minimum of 5 percent price advantage is generated through customer satisfaction. This minimum advantage is a conservative estimate for such commodity businesses as industrial chemicals, farm products, electronic components, and basic raw materials. In niche markets and for specialty products, the price premium that a company may charge without losing its satisfied customers to lower price competitors is much higher, as much as 30 percent!

This price advantage occurs not only because established customers are unwilling to go through the hassle of switching for a lower price but also because a customer-oriented firm is able to offer its customers value from four other avenues: (a) product excellence, (b) service excellence, (c) brand reputation, and (d) a customer-oriented culture in general (see Figure 1.6). Customer-oriented firms are constantly innovating and

Figure 1.6   SOURCES OF VALUE OTHER THAN LOW PRICE

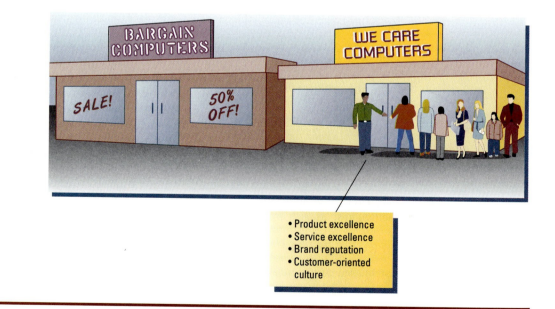

• Product excellence
• Service excellence
• Brand reputation
• Customer-oriented culture

improving their product performance to match their customer's needs better. Likewise, they are constantly upgrading their service levels to bring them in line with customer expectations. Their brand reputation, maintained through adherence to high standards of quality, is also a great value to customers. Brand reputation is important when customers cannot judge the quality for themselves or when they are unable to control its consistency. Thus, brand reputation has been important in such businesses as McDonald's in fast food, Marriott in the hospitality business, and Boeing in the aircraft industry. Brand reputation is also critical in professional services such as health care (Mayo Clinic), consulting (e.g., McKinsey) and financial services (American Express). Finally, the customer-oriented culture directly influences the customer experience in dealing with the company. Customers come away with the feeling that this company "cares for me." In return, they feel a sense of loyalty and would not switch to a lower-priced competitor.

Examples of companies that convey the "we care" culture are Nordstrom department stores, Singapore Airlines, and American Express, to name a few. Likewise, Kennametal, a tool manufacturer, has been busing employees to customers' plants to sensitize them to the kind of pressure their tools are subjected to. The company once drove 300 employees who worked at a factory in Tennessee to the plant of Dana, an automobile parts manufacturer located in Virginia. Employees were able to get a firsthand look at what happens when their tools break down. Additionally, executives at Kennametal believe that such visits create stronger bonds with their customers.[16]

PROTECTION AGAINST CORPORATE CRISIS

The third way a customer orientation enhances profits is by providing insulation against a corporate crisis. When a company uses a customer orientation to cultivate more committed customers, they will be willing to assist the company to ensure its survival.

For example, a company crisis may come from product tampering. When the Tylenol brand of analgesics was tampered with, company loyalty built up over the years prevented an erosion of the company's customer base. Note that Tylenol's customer base extended beyond the household, and included doctors and hospitals, both of which were instrumental in helping to rebuild Tylenol's market share. Tampering with products is not limited to the drug or food industries; it can also take place in the software industry, where "viruses" are becoming more prevalent.

Loyal customers also will resist unfair and unethical business practices of competitors against a company they really like. These loyal customers happily share the information they have about competitors and expose any illegal or unethical activities they might come to know. Similarly, large and highly visible companies like McDonald's, Coca-Cola, and Procter & Gamble are sometimes targets of rumors and social protests. For example, not too long ago it was rumored that McDonald's products contained spider webs or that Coca-Cola is a narcotic. Loyal customers tend to ignore rumors and calls to boycott products and continue to patronize the firm.

Another source of corporate crisis is internal operational problems that are created by breakdowns, strikes, shortages, or sabotage. Again, loyal customers would, to the extent possible, patiently wait or postpone their purchases. UPS's recovery from its recent labor strike suggests that its customers are loyal. Instead of switching carriers permanently, they returned to UPS in large numbers.

In recent years, a common source of corporate crisis has been industry restructuring, the result of either consolidation within the industry or a government mandate.

Industry restructuring has hit the oil industry and infrastructure industries such as telecommunications and airlines. Companies that have maintained a strong customer orientation and, consequently, a loyal customer base have survived these changes, whereas companies with high levels of customer dissatisfaction have not. For example, in the airline industry, Delta and United survived, but Eastern Airlines did not. Also noteworthy is the fact that the breakup of the Bell System by the government to induce more competition has not dampened the strong performance of the Bell operating companies and AT&T, largely because these companies have had a strong base of loyal customers.

INCREASED WORD-OF-MOUTH

The best way to grow a business is to gain new customers without significant investment of product, marketing, or sales resources. This is possible through word-of-mouth communication. For many years, the legal and medical professions relied on a referral system to acquire new customers. These and other professional services only recently started advertising, and to this day, they still rely on referrals for generating new customers.

A customer orientation produces satisfied customers, who will then be willing to invest their own time to tell others about your company. Research indicates that satisfied customers talk to three other customers. (Dissatisfied customers are even more communicative; they talk to nine other customers.) Word-of-mouth communication is especially important when the product or service is risky. Customers will want reassurance from others if there is a performance risk (e.g., What if the machine breaks down?), safety risk (e.g., What if the chemical is unsafe to handle?), economic risk (e.g., Is this a good economic investment?), or social risk (e.g., Is the style of this suit appropriate for the business interview?). For such risky products or services, new customers almost always look to word-of-mouth (W-O-M) advice from the company's current, satisfied customers. Hospitals, doctors, law firms, business consultants, local service firms such as car mechanics, plumbers, construction crew suppliers, recruitment firms, and so on, gain new customers largely by W-O-M.

ONE-STOP SHOPPING

The second source of business growth is the increase in the number of products a satisfied customer buys from the same company. Satisfied and loyal customers give additional business to the company. Both household and business customers prefer to do one-stop shopping for several reasons. First, it is more economical for a customer to do business with the same firm because of volume discounts, favorable terms, better support service, and savings on procurement paperwork. Second, it is more convenient, since the procedures for ordering, payments, and delivery are standardized. Finally, it eliminates the uncertainty that comes with doing business with a new company. As was mentioned earlier, there are risks associated with purchase decisions, and this is one way to avoid those risks.

A competitive advantage that comes with one-stop shopping is the ability of a company to expand its product line and generate more growth without significant risk. For example, McDonald's has expanded its product line from hamburgers to include a breakfast menu, chicken, salads, and other new products. The same is true for companies like IBM, which has recently expanded its marketing efforts to include consulting for its customers.[17]

To measure this advantage, businesses use the concept of **lifetime revenues**—the cumulative business the customer would give a firm over his or her lifetime.[18] Consider a typical supermarket customer. During any particular visit, the customer may spend as little as $1 to pick up a half-gallon of milk; on a weekly shopping trip, he/she may spend as much as $100. Yet this amount is but a minuscule portion in a stream of revenues. According to some studies, a typical family spends about $7,200 annually in supermarkets in the United States (average annual family income is $36,000, and grocery expenses are about 20 percent of household income). This adds up to $216,000 over a 30-year period! Likewise, studies indicate that an American family will spend, on average, approximately $300,000 for automotive accessories and repairs over their lifetime.[19] And these lifetime revenues are going to increase as people live longer. The potential for gaining lifetime revenues from customers, provided you satisfy them, are even greater in other societies and countries, including developing economies, because customers there tend to patronize neighborhood and small stores, do business with the same companies, or stay with their childhood brands or family brands much more. Will firms reap these lifetime revenues? Only if they realize the value of adopting a customer orientation and make it their mission to understand and respond to their customers' needs and preferences.

NEW-PRODUCT INNOVATIONS

A third way that a customer orientation generates revenue growth is by facilitating the introduction of new products. Satisfied and loyal customers are more open to sharing their experiences with a firm. Industrial customers not only allow, but encourage suppliers to visit their facilities to learn all they can about the use of their products. This open communication is very important for product innovations. Customer input in the early stages of new-product development is one of the major reasons for success of an innovation because it allows the Research and Development departments to incorporate customers' wishes as they develop new technologies.

Often, new-product disasters occur due to the failure of management to take into account the necessary market assessments. This means a customer orientation must exist throughout the new-product development process. That is, from idea generation to com-

---

WINDOW ON PRACTICE

Reinventing Sears

What do women want? That is a question that Sears CEO Arthur Martinez seems to have finally answered. Before coming to Sears in 1992, Martinez was vice chairman at Saks Fifth Avenue, a good training ground for researching women's tastes and desires in clothing. Soon after taking over the helm at Sears, Martinez commented, "We had a company run by guys who thought they were in the 'dirty fingernails' business of autos and hardware." Today, Sears has been successfully repositioned to meet the needs of its core customers.

One of the first things Martinez did was to take a hard look at who Sears' customers were. After carrying out extensive consumer research studies, Martinez found out that the core customers at Sears were not men, but, in fact, women between the ages of 25 and 54 with an average household income of $38,000 a year. More importantly, Martinez found out that this core customer was not only the purchaser of clothing for herself but also the de facto purchaser for other members in the household. In that role, the women purchased appliances, electronics, tools, and auto parts. This was, in Martinez's words, a very big "ah-hah" discovery to the top brass at Sears.

The goal at Sears became very clear: to make the store and merchandise attractive to women. In line with this thinking, Sears rid itself of its catalog, the nonretailing side of the company (including Allstate Insurance, Dean Witter brokerage, and the Coldwell Banker real estate chain), and over 50,000 workers and 100 stores. In the stores that remained, shelves were restocked with popular national brands such as B.U.M., Arrow and Champion, and new casual lines of clothing designed by Sears, like Canyon River Blues and Crossroads.

When Tammy Ray walked into a new 139,000-square-foot store, she wondered if she had wandered into the wrong place. Instead of seeing intimate apparel from the same rack fixtures used to sell paints, she saw well-designed racks of sequined evening gowns, fashionable suits, and clothes that were "cool" enough for her teenage children to wear. With a new customer culture in place at Sears, the company is using its vast databases of detailed service records to keep their customers satisfied. With his sights sharply focused on the new core customer, and no intentions of changing tactics now, Martinez said, "We have no desire to become an upscale retailer."

The customer culture is clearly working at Sears. Sales were up in 1996 about 9 percent to $38 billion. In 1995, Sears was generating $353 per square foot, compared with Kmart's $195 and J.C. Penney's $156 per square foot. Wall Street also seems to be quite happy with the change. The stock has tripled in price since Martinez arrived at Sears.

John Greenwald, "Reinventing Sears," *Time* (December 23, 1996), pp. 53–55.

mercial testing, the firm must be guided by customer preferences and reactions. Companies must devote adequate resources to market-oriented idea generation, such as marketing research through surveys and focus groups. A strong customer orientation should also guide concept testing, actual product design, and test marketing phases of new product development. The key point is that a customer orientation must be an input into the design decision, not an afterthought following the product development.[20] Product design teams that are unable to fully immerse themselves into the role Tom Hanks plays in the movie *Big* are unlikely to innovate products of any real lasting value to customers. Such immersion presupposes a customer-oriented culture in the organization. The Window on Practice box discusses Sears' rediscovery of its customer base.

WINDOW ON RESEARCH

Customer Orientation Makes a Business More Profitable

Two recent studies both found a link between a customer orientation and profitability. Marketing professors Bernard J. Jaworski and Ajay K. Kohli define a firm's market orientation as comprising three sets of activities: (1) organizationwide generation of market intelligence pertaining to current and future customer needs, (2) dissemination of the market intelligence across all departments, and (3) organizationwide response to it. Professors Jaworski and Kohli surveyed 222 business units in some 100 firms sampled from the Dun and Bradstreet *Million Dollar Directory.* Among some of their findings:

- The greater top management's emphasis on market orientation, the greater was the generation and dissemination of customer information widely in the organization, and the greater the firm's response to customer needs.

- The greater the market orientation of the firm, the higher was:

  (a) the firm's business performance in profit terms;

  (b) the commitment of employees to their organization;

  (c) the morale among the employees.

In a second study, marketing professors John C. Narver and Stanley F. Slater surveyed 113 strategic business units (SBUs) of the forest products division of major western corporations, including SBUs that offered commodities, specialty products, and exports. They measured each SBU's customer orientation by asking its managers about the degree to which their units engaged in six practices: (1) commitment to customers, (2) creating customer value, (3) understanding customer needs, (4) having customer satisfaction as an objective, (5) measuring customer satisfaction, and (6) providing after-sales service. They measured each SBU's profitability in terms of return on assets (ROA). Across the SBUs, they found that ROA was positively correlated with the degree of customer orientation.

What was remarkable about this research was that Narver and Slater also assessed the degree to which the SBU engaged in "low-cost-based competitive advantage strategy" (i.e., a strategy in which a firm tries to outdo its competitors by cost control and the resulting cost efficiencies), and likewise the degree to which it employed a "product-differentiation" strategy (e.g., offering new products, differentiated products, or a broad product line). They found no link between profits and the low-cost strategy, and only a modest correlation to the differentiation strategy. Thus, product differentiation was beneficial, but not as beneficial as the customer orientation.

Sources: Bernard J. Jaworski and Ajay K. Kohli, "Market Orientation: Antecedents and Consequences," *Journal of Marketing* 57, no. 3 (July 1993), 53–70.

John C. Narver and Stanley F. Slater, "The Effect of Market Orientation on Business Profitability," *Journal of Marketing* 54, no. 4 (October 1990), 20–37.

Customer Orientation Creates Pride in Employees

Employees brag about a company that gives them a sense of pride. This is especially true for front-line employees if they experience job satisfaction. Front-line employee satisfaction depends greatly on the extent to which they are able to satisfy their customers. By doing well by the customer, employees feel a strong pride in their company. Hal Rosenbluth, co-author of *The Customer Comes Second,* says that companies should put their employees first if they want to offer stellar service. The reason is that satisfied employees create satisfied customers. But the influence flows in the reverse direction as well. Happy customers lead to employee happiness. Grudging, complaining, dissatisfied customers actually take a toll on employee morale. Bad employees drive out good customers, and bad customers drive out good employees. How often have we as consumers found ourselves switching hairdressers or dry cleaners because we were mistreated by an employee? Likewise, it is not uncommon for employees working in retail settings to leave their jobs as a result of harassment by dissatisfied customers.[21]

The effect of satisfied customers on employee morale goes beyond front-line employees. To satisfy customers, a company has to produce a quality product and service. A company has to invest in quality, providing training and tools to its workers, enabling them to produce high quality work that utilizes their skills well, and of which they can be proud. Motorola is legendary in producing quality products, and its quality thrust has engendered a workforce proud of its "craftsmanship." Likewise, Ford Motor Company's "Quality Is Job 1" program was a "shot in the arm" for employee pride. To take an example from the service industry, Disney spends a great deal of effort on training employees on how to deal with customers who are viewed as "guests" of the Disney village. Len Berry and A. Parasuraman, two marketing professors who have written extensively on the services industry, stress the importance of socializing employees into the corporate culture of good customer service.[22] Thus, both the interaction with satisfied customers and the feedback received from them in formal customer surveys, as well as the ownership of quality work or service that a customer-satisfying organization necessarily produces, generate pride and happiness among employees. The Window on Research box discusses the link between customer orientation and business profitability.

Customers as Competitors

Make-versus-Buy Decisions

Customers are likely to make rather than buy products if they have the expertise (like do-it-yourself consumers), and if it is convenient, cheaper, or yields a better product than what exists in the marketplace. Therefore, one of the potentially biggest competitors to a company is the customer himself or herself, particularly in the case of business customers. In considering their competition, therefore, companies must always recognize the possibility that dissatisfied customers may decide to produce the product or service themselves. Even a monopolistic company has reason to be concerned about this potential competitive threat.

A few examples will clarify this. In the telecommunications industry, many business customers found that the existing suppliers were not responding well to their needs; consequently, some of them began building their own private networks and even getting government policy changed to do it. One of these companies was Southern Pacific Railways;

it designed better telecommunications services for its own use, and later supplied its service to others. The company was then called Southern Pacific Railways Information Technologies, which today goes by the more familiar name Sprint. As another example, some companies believe that universities are not addressing the need for employee education. So they have started their own executive education centers or schools. For example, AT&T has its own AT&T Business School focused solely on its own employees; Motorola has Motorola University. Today, there are at least 30 corporate universities in the United States.

For household customers, developing such self-reliance is not as easy. Yet we should not dismiss the extent to which they can threaten a business, either by boycotting its product or service, finding a substitute product or service, or somehow developing the capacity to self-produce those products or services. For example, during the energy crisis of 1974 and 1975, customers in Vermont, Maine, Washington, and Oregon (U.S.A.) responded to skyrocketing electricity prices by shutting off their electricity. Close to 40 percent of the residential customers shut off their electricity and relied on wood-burning stoves as a heating alternative, something that came as a big surprise to the electric companies.

Some families like to prepare their own foods rather than buying them packaged, like salad dressings or pizzas. The reason is not just because these customers have the skills, but also because of a failure of the marketplace to meet the customer's unique needs or wants effectively. An even clearer example is families who have religious or philosophical preferences or restrictions against certain processing methods or certain ingredients. Either the marketers do not offer such products (e.g., until recently there were no vegetarian burgers available in the marketplace), or the customer just does not trust the marketer to follow the regimen required to produce the product in the "pure" form.

Furthermore, the highly personal nature of many household services can make some households reluctant to hire outsiders for them. Besides cooking, such services might include baby-sitting, house cleaning, lawn maintenance, and care for elderly parents. Until recently, most homemakers performed these household services themselves, and in most of the traditional societies and emerging markets such as China, Malaysia, Haiti, Sudan, and Ethiopia, they still do. The use of marketplace transactions for these services is due to increasing pressures on a homemaker's time. But if a market does not supply the quality that matches, in all respects, the quality of the home-produced service, then the customer is likely to abandon the market-supplied services in favor of producing them himself. In child care services, for example, parents seek not just a place where children can pass time under adult supervision, but also an environment that conveys the values they have themselves. If they would perceive a shortcoming, many parents would resort to caring for their children themselves, even if it meant sacrificing their careers.

Thus, in a number of industries, and in both the household and business markets, there are products or services that offer opportunities for the customer to make rather than buy. Whether customers will buy a product/service from the marketplace, or instead make it themselves, depends on how well marketers understand customers' needs and wants, and how affordable and acceptable they make their products.

Summary

In this chapter, you learned that a customer is a person or organizational unit that plays a role in the consummation of a transaction with the marketer or an entity. The three roles a customer plays are those of a user (the person who actually consumes or uses the product or receives the benefits of the service), the payer (the person who finances the purchase), and the buyer (the person who participates in the physical exchange of the product with the marketer). Customer behavior consists of the processes undertaken by customers (both household and business) leading to their decisions and actions to pay for, buy, and use products and services.

You learned why companies need to be customer driven, and what the managerial implications are to taking a customer orientation. First of all, creating and maintaining satisfied customers is the purpose of business. Second, according to the marketing concept, business should focus its efforts on the customer. Third, it leads to economic democracy by serving the society's needs better.

Next, you learned what is meant by customer orientation, and the specific benefits that accrue to businesses when they follow a customer orientation: These benefits consist both in a competitive advantage in the external market and success internally in producing a workforce that feels pride in its job. The competitive advantages in the external market are due to increased profits and revenue growth from satisfied customers. Increased profits come from the reduced costs of doing business with repeat customers, ability to maintain price premiums, and customer loyalty in corporate crisis. Revenue growth comes from increased favorable word-of-mouth, one-stop shopping, and new-product innovations.

The next chapter will explore in detail the three roles of the customer and the forces in the marketplace that sometimes make it necessary for the role of the payer and buyer to be fulfilled by someone other than the user.

Key Terms

Customer Behavior 5	Consumer 5	Marketing Concept 13
Mental Activities 5	User 6	Customer Orientation 15
Physical Activities 5	Buyer 6	Market Orientation 15
Customer 5	Payer 6	Lifetime Revenues 23
Household Customers 5	Customer Culture 13	
Business Customers 5	Selling Concept 13	

Review Questions

1. Why is it important to study customer behavior in marketing? In providing your response, describe the interrelationship between customer behavior and the marketing concept.

2. Smart marketing companies are increasingly realizing the enormous value of becoming "customer oriented." What does it mean to be customer oriented? What are the specific benefits of being market oriented?

3. Car companies like General Motors, with several different divisions, offer a wide range of choices to keep customers loyal over their lifetime. What does life cycle revenue mean and why should marketers be concerned about this?

4. What does "make-versus-buy decision" mean and why should marketing companies be concerned with this?

5. In what way can a customer become a competitor? Provide one example each of this phenomenon that may occur in both household and business markets.

6. Explain the title of this book. Specifically, enumerate the three ways in which this textbook goes beyond the coverage of a conventional textbook in "consumer behavior."

Applications

1. Like the examples of American Express and Service Master of America described in this chapter, give two examples of companies that have expanded their markets by starting out in either consumer or business services and then taking their offering to the other.

2. The story of the film *Big* shows the advantage of being able to walk in your customer's shoes. Describe two examples of how companies have tried to better understand their customers by getting close to them or by taking the customers' perspective in designing their products and services.

3. A fellow MBA student in your accounting class did not register for this course with you. Her argument: "My company is in industrial products, not in consumer products. Therefore, this course would not be useful to me in my job." Is she right? Write her a note explaining why her presupposition about this course is misplaced.

4. Review the questionnaire on page 17 for measuring a firm's customer orientation. Select any two firms you do business with as a customer, and based on your impressions, use this questionnaire to rate these firms. Compute their score. Do these scores match your own impression of how customer oriented these companies are? Comment on your findings.

5. Visit three or four ethnic stores (e.g., Vietnamese, Indian, Greek, etc.). Write a summary of your visits. Describe your total experience in terms of various elements of culture (language, products, customer service, social conversations between customers and the store owner, etc.).

Practical Experiences

1. Using a 1-800 telephone number or the Internet, call up or access three international airlines that fly from the United States to Europe, Asia, and Latin America, and get a list of the different types of special meals that can be ordered. Use that information to discuss the importance of taking a customer orientation, and how this might influence the prosperity of these airlines.

2. Interview the marketing managers of two companies, one who is operating in a very competitive environment, and the other in a relatively monopolistic industry. Ask them to answer the customer orientation survey. Which company's scores are higher? Is your finding consistent with your expectations? Please comment.

Notes

1. James Karney, "Online Storage Services Provide a Virtual Vault for Your Data," *PC Magazine* 15, no. 17 (October 8, 1996), p. 50.

2. *Chicago Tribune,* January 13, 1994, Section 3, p. 3.

3. The questions and related discussion are inspired by the research of marketing professor Itamar Simonson. See Itamar Simonson, "Get Closer to Your Customers by Understanding How They Make Choices," *California Management Review* 35, no. 4 (Summer 1993), pp. 68–84.

4. Peter F. Drucker, *Management: Tasks, Responsibilities, Practices* (New York: Harper & Row, 1973).

5. *Fortune* 130, no. 6 (September 19, 1994), pp. 215–20.

6. Ibid.

7. *Chicago Tribune,* January 13, 1994, Section 3, p. 3.

8. Stephen Phillips, "King Customer," *Business Week,* March 12, 1990, pp. 88–94.

9. This was echoed by Adam Smith in his work, *The Wealth of Nations.* For a more recent discussion of Smith's thinking, see Athol Fistzgibbons, *Adam Smith's System of Liberty, Wealth, and Virtue: The Moral and Political Foundations of The Wealth of Nations* (New York: Oxford University Press, 1995).

10. For a very provocative essay on the role of consumers in business democracy, see Roger A. Dickinson, "Consumer Citizenship: The United States," *Business and the Contemporary World* (in press), and also Roger A. Dickinson and Stanley C. Hollander Dickinson, "Consumer Votes," *Journal of Business Research* 23 (1991), pp. 9–20.

11. Ajay K. Kohli, and Bernard J. Jaworski, "Market Orientation: The Construct, Research Propositions, and Managerial Implications," *Journal of Marketing* 54 (April 1990), p 3.

12. Frederick E. Webster, Jr., "The Changing Role of Marketing in the Corporation," *Journal of Marketing* 56, no. 4 (October 1992), pp. 1–17.

13. Jagdish Sheth, "Competitive Advantages through Customer Satisfaction," *BMA Review* 2, no. 1 (January–February 1991), pp. 13–25.

14. Robert G. Cooper, "New Products: What Distinguishes the Winners?" *Research-Technology Management* 33 (November/December 1990).

15. Roger L. Desatnick, *Keep the Customer* (Boston: Houghton-Mifflin Co., 1990), p. 4.

16. Ibid., *Fortune,* September 19, 1994.

17. For further discussion on this topic, see: Roger L. Desatnick, *Keep the Customer* (Boston: Houghton-Miffin Co., 1990), p. 4; Brent Gloy, and Jay Adridge, "Measuring Customer Profitability: A Look at Lifetime Value," *Feedstuffs* 68, no. 23 (June 3, 1996), pp. 20–21.; Lisa S. Howard, "Rebuilding Customer Loyalty: A Global Phenomenon," *National Underwriter Life & Health-Financial Services Edition* no. 33 (August 12, 1996), p. 6; Mark Lacek, "Loyalty Marketing No Ad Budget Threat; Major Target Is Bigger Share of Customer," *Advertising Age* 66, no. 43 (October 23, 1995), p. 20; Richard C. Whitley, *The Customer-Driven Company* (Reading: Addison-Wesley, 1991); Stambaugh-Cannon, "What Type of Business Partnerships Will You Build in 1994?" *Aftermarket Business* 103, no. 12, (December 1993), p. 4.

18. For further discussion on this topic, see: Brent Gloy, and Jay Adridge, "Measuring Customer Profitability: A Look at Lifetime Value," *Feedstuffs* 68, no. 23 (June 3, 1996), pp. 20–21; Lisa S. Howard, "Rebuilding Customer Loyalty: A Global Phenomenon," *National Underwriter Life & Health-Financial Services Edition* no. 33 (August 12, 1996), p. 6; Mark Lacek, "Loyalty Marketing No Ad Budget Threat; Major Target Is Bigger Share of Customer," *Advertising Age* 66, no. 43 (October 23, 1995), p. 20; Richard C. Whitley, *The Customer-Driven Company* (Reading: Addison-Wesley, 1991).

19. Stambaugh-Cannon, "What Type of Business Partnerships Will You Build in

1994?" *Aftermarket Business* 103, no. 12 (December 1993), p. 4.

[20] Robert G. Cooper, "New Products: What Distinguishes the Winners?" *Research-Technology Management* 33 (November/December 1990).

[21] Hal Rosenbluth with Diane McFerrin Peters, *The Customer Comes Second* (New York: Morrow Publishing Co., 1992).

[22] Leonard L. Berry, and A. Parasuraman, *Marketing Services: Competing through Quality* (New York: The Free Press, 1991) p. 111.

CHAPTER 2

After reading this chapter you should be able to:

Describe the three roles that a customer plays— user, payer, and buyer.

Summarize the conditions that cause the user to delegate the other roles of the customer to a different person.

Distinguish the needs and wants of the user from the needs and wants of the payer and the buyer.

Discuss the marketing implications of the three roles.

Identify how the marketing strategy differs according to the role of the customer being targeted.

Three Roles of a Customer: User, Payer, Buyer

Chelsea, Hillary, Bill; Shauntae, Ahmed, Mirjana— Will the Real Customer Please Stand Up?

Chelsea Clinton. The First Daughter. In May 1997, she accepted an invitation to enroll at Stanford University for her undergraduate degree. Asked how he felt about his only child leaving Washington, D.C. on the East Coast of the United States for Stanford on the West Coast, her father, U.S. President Bill Clinton, commented, "Well, the planes run out there, and the phones work out there. And the e-mail works out there. So we'll be all right." But who made the decision? Who is going to be footing the bill (tuition at Stanford averages $28,857)?

First Lady Hillary Rodham-Clinton, Chelsea's mother, is reported to have accompanied her daughter on various campus visits. Did she play a role in Chelsea's choice? And who should Stanford look to satisfy? Just Chelsea, the student? Or her mom Hillary, who would very likely keep an eye on the quality of education her daughter is getting? Or her dad Bill, who, along with Hillary, would be concerned, for example, if the tuition fee were to go up considerably? Who is the real customer here? Chelsea? Hillary? Bill? All three? Perhaps we will never know.[1]

We know more about the Abdul-Jabbars, an African American family in Chicago, who were facing a similar decision about college. Shauntae Abdul-Jabbar (no relation to U.S. basketball star Kareem Abdul-Jabbar) is a top student in her senior high school in Buffalo Grove, Illinois. Her father, Ahmed Abdul-Jabbar, is an advertising executive in the prestigious Leo Burnett agency. Her mother, Mirjana Abdul-Jabbar, a second generation immigrant from Poland, is a curator in the Chicago Museum of Art. Shauntae, who wants to pursue a double major in art and business administration, received admission invitations from the University of Illinois, Urbana-Champaign, the University of Chicago, Stanford University, the University of California at Berkeley, the Wharton Business School, Penn State, and Columbia University.

Both Urbana-Champaign and State College, Pennsylvania (home of Penn State), are college campus towns, and Shauntae is torn between the charm of campus town living versus the throbbing lifestyle of a major metropolis like Philadelphia (the home of the Wharton School) or New York (the home of Columbia University). Chicago, too, is a big metropolis, but this would bind her to living at home; she wants to experience independent living. Columbia and Stanford, both private schools, present another contest: would she prefer the lifestyle of the East Coast or the West Coast?

Shauntae knows that her parents will play a big role in the decision. Mirjana, her mother, is probably going to be more influential. She is the one who visited campuses with Shauntae, partly because she was able to get days off from work more easily than Ahmed would have. Besides, she has a very intense emotional involvement with her daughter. Nothing would please her more than to have her daughter stay home. But she would just as happily accept Urbana-Champaign, so her daughter could come home at least on weekends. "You could just bring your laundry home, and I would take care of it for you," she tries to bribe her daughter.

Shauntae's father wants her to go to the best school, regardless of the location, but both parents are concerned about the expenses. Living at home would save some money, and tuition at a public university such as Urbana-Champaign, Berkeley, or Penn State would be much less than at a private school like Stanford. At Urbana-Champaign, the tuition would be at the low rate charged to residents of Illinois, and the school's standards are as high as those of most private schools. But Shauntae is leaning toward a private school, because she believes that, among other things, she is more likely to get a job at one of the prestigious firms that tend to recruit more heavily at leading private schools such as Stanford or Columbia.

Where should Shauntae spend these four crucial years of her life? Who should have the right to decide? Who, in other words, is playing the customer role? Will the real customer please stand up?

Introduction

Is it right for Shauntae Abdul-Jabbar's or Chelsea Clinton's parents to attempt to influence their daughters' college choices? The choice will have an enormous impact on both girls. But the Clintons and Abdul-Jabbars also have stakes in the outcome.

This question of who is and is not a customer touches all markets and all customer groups. In both business markets and household markets, product or service users are not always the only people affected by a purchase decision. Thus, for any transaction, more than one person may be a customer.

This chapter elaborates on the distinction among the customer roles of user, payer, and buyer. It answers questions such as "What are the wants and needs of users, payers, and buyers?" and, "How do they coordinate their actions and desires?" The chapter begins by identifying the ways in which customer roles may be divided among individuals and groups. We then summarize basic reasons why customers adopt these specialized roles. The chapter then turns to a discussion of customer needs and wants—what they are and how they are determined. Finally, we explore the importance of the three roles and their implications for managerial decisions.

Types of Role Specialization

As we explained in Chapter 1, the person who uses a product is not always the same as the person who selects or pays for it. Rather, different individuals or groups may carry

| Figure 2.1 | THE THREE ROLES OF THE CUSTOMER |

out one or more of the three customer roles. Anyone who carries out at least one of these roles meets our definition of a customer (see Figure 2.1). Thus, in the opening story for this chapter, Chelsea Clinton and Shauntae Abdul-Jabbar are users of the service of a college education. However, their parents are also customers to the extent they helped the girls choose and pay for that service. Dividing up the customer roles—user, payer, and buyer—among individuals or groups is called **role specialization.**[2]

The broader concept of the customer brings into focus three different roles, which may or may not be played by the same individual. Regardless of whether the same person is the user, payer, and buyer, each role dictates a different set of values that are sought out by the customer. For example, an office worker who is using a personal computer is concerned with the performance of the machine, whereas the purchasing agent for the company who buys the PC is more concerned with the price. Likewise, a student who picks a college, like Shauntae Abdul-Jabbar in our opening story, may be more concerned with whether the college has a "fun campus," desired courses, or good athletic teams, whereas the parents will be more concerned with the tuition. Or the small-business owner looking to purchase health care services for his employees will be concerned with the costs of the health plan, whereas employees will be more concerned with the quality of healthcare. The three roles, whether played by a single individual or by different individuals, seek to fulfill different goals, or values.

Successful marketers are aware of the possible ways in which customers divide their roles among themselves. They adapt their marketing effort to the type of role specialization.

User Is Neither Payer nor Buyer

In some cases, the user is distinct from both the payer and the buyer roles of the customer. For example, parents typically pay for and actually buy most of the products their children use. Pet foods are certainly one product category, and veterinary care one service category where the user is definitely different from a buyer and a payer. But other products and services can sometimes fall into this category (e.g., a car bought and paid for by parents for their son or daughter or a health insurance policy bought by the working head of the household and paid for by the employer, but used by the nonworking members of the household). Likewise, in a business setting, an employee is the user of office furniture, like a desk and chair, but the payment and purchase of these products are made by someone else, such as the purchasing and the accounts payable departments of the business.

The user is neither a payer nor a buyer.

User Is Payer but Not Buyer

In other cases, the user is also a payer, but not a buyer. For example, in the financial markets, stockbrokers act as agents for clients who enlist them to buy stocks of various companies. A disabled person (whose mobility has been confined) may ask a living aide to buy a product he or she (i.e., the disabled person) would use and pay for. In business markets, an office secretary may purchase office supplies for someone else's use and paid for by the departmental budget. Similarly, an external agent may be retained to purchase some equipment, supplies, or raw materials for a company, but it is the company who pays for and then uses them.

User Is Buyer but Not Payer

The user may be a buyer but not a payer for the products or services. A household example of this situation is a customer picking and using a car towing service whose invoice is then reimbursed by an insurance company. Bridal registry is another clear example, in which the bride chooses the items to buy and will be using the items, but prospective gift-

givers are the payers. In the business market, this pattern of enabling the product usage is known as sponsorship: the sponsor pays for something that someone else uses and purchases. A business corporation might sponsor, for example, the building of a new AIDS care facility as an annex to an existing hospital. The hospital does the buying (of a construction contractor's services, for example) and will then be the user both of the contractor's service and the end product of the contractor's work. Likewise, in many companies, a large variety of health-care plans are offered from which employees choose. Although the employee will be the user and buyer, in companies where the plan is fully reimbursed, the user is not the payer.

User Is Buyer and Payer

Finally, the user may also be both the buyer and the payer for a product or service, combining all three roles into a single person or department. Most consumers purchase and pay for products for their personal use, such as clothing, watches, airline tickets, haircuts, and colognes and perfumes. In the business markets, small-business owners often combine all three roles when they acquire office equipment, furniture, and the services of an accountant or a bookkeeper.

Reasons for Role Specialization

When a single customer carries out all of the roles, marketers will likely use a different strategy than when different people act as user, payer, and buyer. Thus, it is helpful to be able to

Often what the user wants, the payer can't afford. Here, the marketer responds to the wants of both the roles.

identify the conditions under which the various kinds of role specialization occur. In general, users are unlikely to play other customer roles when they lack expertise, time, buying power, or access to the product, or when the product is either unaffordable, subsidized, or free.

Lack of Expertise

In many situations the user just doesn't have the adequate knowledge to make an informed choice. Whenever the user does not have the relevant knowledge and expertise, she or he is

REASONS FOR ROLE SPECIALIZATION

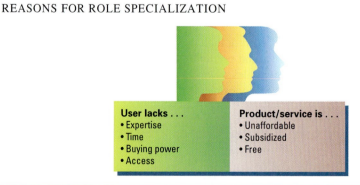

User lacks . . .
- Expertise
- Time
- Buying power
- Access

Product/service is . . .
- Unaffordable
- Subsidized
- Free

likely to delegate the buying task to someone else, who then becomes the buyer. For example, patients lack expertise and depend on their doctors for medication choice. Elderly persons who need a nursing home may not physically or mentally be able to evaluate, choose, and arrange for the nursing home; consequently, they may depend on their family to act as the buyer. As another example, it is not unusual for parents to rely on their teenage children to provide the expertise and knowledge when it comes to the purchase of electronic equipment. In business markets, a firm may hire a consultant to give advice on and execute the buying task for a complex piece of machinery because the firm does not have in-house expertise relating to evaluating alternative suppliers. Executing the buying task may entail identifying alternative suppliers, evaluating their products, and negotiating the deal.

Based on her specialized position at her company, this business customer plays the buyer role for relocation services for other employees, the users.

Lack of Time

Another reason a user may delegate the purchasing task to someone else is lack of time. For example, executives delegate purchase decisions to their assistants or secretaries, such as making airline and hotel reservations, or choosing a mail carrier service. Likewise, more and more homemakers these days are delegating many household buying chores to their spouses, teenage children, or paid shopping consultants because they are too busy themselves.

Lack of Buying Power

Often users have to delegate the buying task to someone else because they lack the buying power. Corporations often adopt the "centralized procurement" practice to take advantage of economies of scale. For example, an internal corporate travel department may handle airline travel for all its employees to get better rates and use executive time wisely. Another example is "multiple listings" of real estate properties for sale, in which real estate information is shared among many real estate brokers to, again, achieve economies of scale. Similarly, membership clubs, such as Sam's Club, are examples of consumers delegating the buying responsibility to a professionally managed organization. Of course, many neighbors form their own informal buying clubs in order to profit from the economies of scale. (We will discuss buying groups in a later chapter.) Lack of buying power can also bring about partnering between customers, but in this case, not only to purchase a product or service, but also to help pay for it.

Lack of Access

Many times, the consumer is prohibited either by law, by physical barriers, or simply by industry practice from buying a product directly from the marketer. An example of prohibition by law is that of prescription drugs. Even though patients may know, based on past experience, what medicine works best for them, they cannot make the purchase decision; rather, they need a doctor's prescription. A global supplier often presents a physical barrier. Because of language, distance, and other access barriers, the user has to go through a middleman, a trading or import/export agent, or a bank if it is a financial transaction. In such cases, customers must partner with other firms that have better access to markets in order to purchase a product or service.

Lack of Affordability

When a product is not affordable to the user, the role separation is between the user and the payer. The user may be the primary decider of what to buy, but the payer (who also becomes the customer by virtue of playing the payer role) may also influence the decision, by restricting the choices that would qualify for the payer's funds. College tuition is an obvious example: Parents are often the payers and influence which college their son or daughter chooses. Disadvantaged households that buy food with government food stamps are restricted to buying from stores that accept food stamps. In this case, the food stamp recipient is the user, and the government is the payer. This distinction also holds true in the business sector when corporations offer their employees child care services at reduced rates. Within managed health-care programs the payer—such as a health maintenance organization (HMO) in the United States or the government in Germany and Canada—restricts a patient's (user's) choice of care providers. For many treatments, the users may also have to accept substantial waiting periods before they may obtain service.

When the Product or Service Is Subsidized by Payers

In other situations, payers provide partial subsidies. An example is benefit programs offered by a company to its employees for health-care services. Another example is corporate cafeterias, where the employees' cost is only a percentage of the actual cost because of the subsidy paid by the company. Universities often subsidize education by giving fellowships and grants to selected students. When the customer is a business, like a company that will subsidize a service offered to its employees, the marketer must offer something of value to both the user (e.g., the employee) and the payer (e.g., the company).

When the Product or Service Is Free

Finally, the user and the other roles of customer are separated when the product or service is given free to the user. The user accepts these products and services, not due to lack of affordability, but simply because of their free availability. Public parks, free music concerts, taking a book out of the public library, and free coffee on some interstate highways represent instances of such free products and services. In these situations, the user of the service is not the same as the purchaser. As a publisher of books, supplier of coffee, or a construction company engaged in building public parks, the marketer has to deal with city governments in their role as the purchaser and the payer, separated from the role of the user. To the city government building the park, the important concerns are costs and ease of dealing with the contractor (including the dependability of the contractor). In contrast, the residents who will use the park will be more concerned with the performance and safety of the swing sets and jungle gyms their children will be playing on.

Customer Needs and Wants

It is important to understand what the needs and wants of users, payers, and buyers are. It is the needs and wants of customers that marketers have to satisfy. Consumer behavior theorists John A. Howard and Jagdish N. Sheth have suggested that need arousal is a critical component of the motivation process, and that the arousal of a need moves the customer toward action.[3] The specific action that is taken will depend on the three roles of the customer. As stated earlier, users, payers, and buyers seek different values in products and services. They do so because they have different needs and wants. The Window on Practice box discusses one hypothetical Dutch firm's considerations of different needs and wants in selecting a corporate travel agency.

The Distinction between Needs and Wants

A **need** is an unsatisfactory condition of the customer that leads him or her to an action that will make that condition better. A **want** is a desire to obtain more satisfaction than is absolutely necessary to improve an unsatisfactory condition. In other words, the difference between a need and a want is that need arousal is driven by discomfort in a person's physical and psychological conditions.

Wants occur when and because humans desire to take their physical and psychological conditions beyond the state of minimal comfort. A hungry stomach, an unprotected body exposed to extreme temperatures, a headache, or dandruff constitute a need. So also do social isolation, boredom, disrespect from peers or others, lack of emotional support

Corporate Travel at Nico Duin: Who Plays the Customer Part?

Nico Duin BV, a small Dutch firm that makes milling machines, is deciding on a travel agency. The company plans to expand its business internationally, particularly in Western Europe and the United States, so it wants to choose its corporate travel agency carefully.

Four agencies offer excellent corporate travel services, particularly for travel to and from the United States: American Express, Thomas Cook, Carlson-Wagonlit, and Rosenbluth. The question the Nico Duin executives are considering is, Which would satisfy everyone's desires the best. Ric De Bont, the executive vice president for human relations, knows that employees have complained vehemently in the past that their current agency did not offer a full array of choices in airline and hotel bookings. He was concerned that the agency they now choose should be able to serve the diverse needs of individual travelers relating to convenient itineraries and handling emergency travel situations. Jan-Benedict Pieters, the vice president of purchasing was concerned about the hassle in dealing with an outside travel agency. As purchasing agent, she is responsible for ensuring that, in whatever she purchases for the corporation, the user departments are satisfied with the performance of the vendor. Accordingly, she wanted to ensure that the chosen agency serves the needs of employees well.

At the same time, she is also responsible for administering the purchase contract and monitoring it, so she wanted an agency that would be easy to do business with. Finally, there was Liisa Veen, the corporate comptroller, whose main concern was keeping the expenses under control. She wanted an agency that would offer bulk corporate discounts, present choices to employees that are somewhat biased in favor of cost-efficient itineraries, and manage expense statements categorized and itemized for easy review and long-term analysis. Handling the travel business in-house versus contracting it out (i.e., "make versus buy") was certainly an important option to consider.

Everyone knew that business travel can be a lot of hassle or a lot of fun, depending on the choice of the right travel agency. Once again, being a business traveler is not as simple as "pick up the overnighters and go." Not when some nontravelers make it their business to decide how the traveler should travel.

This illustrative story by the authors is based on personal observations—all names are fictitious.

from loved ones, and unreciprocated love. But beyond these states of discomfort, desires for more or better products and services indicate wants.[4]

Thus, food satisfies a need, and gourmet food additionally satisfies a want. Just any car satisfies a need for transportation from point A to point B, whereas a Miata, Porsche, Lexus, or Mercedes, in addition, satisfy a want to get the excitement of performance, or gain prestige among one's peers, or project the right self-image to significant others.[5] Only when needs are satisfied do wants surface.

Needs and wants are distinguished by the fact that the minimal satisfaction of needs must be done to sustain people as healthy organisms. On the other hand, wants have an element of customer discretion; that is, their satisfaction is desired but not essential.

Needs and wants also differ in terms of the factors that cause them. Customer needs are determined by the characteristics of the individual and the characteristics of the environment. In contrast, customer wants are determined by the individual context and the environmental context. See Figure 2.3.

Determinants of Needs

A person's needs are determined by two factors: the individual himself or herself and the person's environment. These determinants have to do with the physical characteris-

DETERMINANTS OF CUSTOMER NEEDS AND WANTS

Figure 2.3

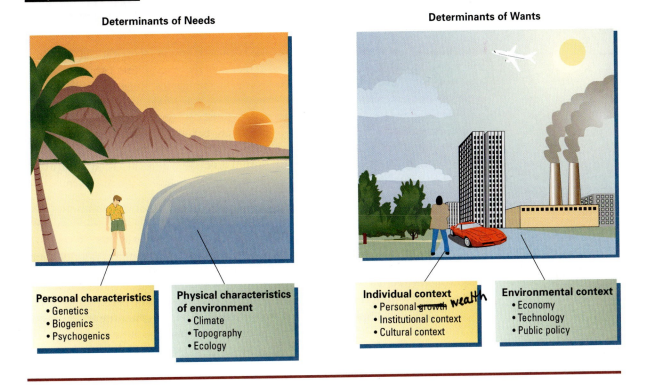

Determinants of Needs

Determinants of Wants

Personal characteristics
- Genetics
- Biogenics
- Psychogenics

Physical characteristics of environment
- Climate
- Topography
- Ecology

Individual context
- Personal growth *wealth*
- Institutional context
- Cultural context

Environmental context
- Economy
- Technology
- Public policy

tics of individuals and the environment, rather than with the social and institutional context.

PERSONAL CHARACTERISTICS OF THE INDIVIDUAL

Three personal characteristics of the person determine needs: genetics, biogenics, and psychogenics.

GENETICS.   **Genetics** is a branch of science that deals with the heredity and chemical/biological characteristics of organisms. Genetic researchers have identified deoxyribonucleic acid (DNA) as the thread of life, a molecule found in the nucleus of cells. Since 1952, researchers have known that DNA is the link to our understanding of heredity. The Human Genome Project at the National Institutes of Health is a 15-year effort aimed at drawing the first detailed map of every gene in the human DNA. Headed by Professors Anderson and Collins, the project has armed a vast body of scientists with the ability to unravel the molecular secrets of life. Labeled as a biomedical revolution, this research has created the possibility of manipulating genes in animals, plants, and even humans, and opening up the door to changing what we eat and wear as users, and even how we live and die.[6]

From a customer behavior perspective, knowledge about the role of DNA can shed light on the behavior patterns of users who have similar genetic makeup. For example, allergy to certain foods and to certain materials is due to a person's genetic make-up. Moreover, customers from different parts of the world have different clusters of gene types, and their food habits and needs differ accordingly. In general, people's food needs depend on their genetic makeup, cultural practices, and plant and animals available in the area. Thus, genetics is one factor that influences customers' food needs.

BIOGENICS. Another determinant of needs consists of the biological characteristics that people possess at birth, such as gender, race, and the year of birth (which translates into age). The study of these characteristics is called **biogenics.** Biogenic characteristics create obvious differences in the needs of men and women, young and old, and so on.

Many consumption decisions are attempts to satisfy biogenic needs, such as drives of hunger, thirst, and sleep. For example, as people age beyond 50 years, they begin having difficulty falling asleep. This occurs because an aging brain slows down the production of melatonin, a substance needed to produce sleep. This may give rise to a need for an external drug to stimulate melatonin production in the brain—such as those currently sold under the brand name Melatonex.

PSYCHOGENICS. The third individual characteristic of the individual is **psychogenics**—which refers to individual states and traits induced by a person's brain functioning. These states are such entities as moods, emotions, perceptions, cognitions, and experiences stored in memory. Thus, mood swings and emotional states necessitate the consumption of certain products. For example, the need for social conversation and interaction, need for affection, need to succeed, need to feel in control, need for recreation, and need to express oneself are all psychogenic needs. Although these are not traditionally considered needs or physical needs, their deprivation causes near traumatic effect on the person both physically and mentally. Thus, it is reasonable to classify these psychogenic effects as needs to the extent that their minimal satisfaction is imperative rather than discretionary.

Consumers often buy products or services to satisfy a need based in their mood or emotions, such as buying a greeting card, jewelry, perfume, and so on, or buying domestically produced products or services only. The Pepsi-Cola Co. understands very well the importance of creating an emotional link with consumers. On September 16 every year, Mexican-Americans celebrate Mexican Independence Day. In downtown San Antonio, close to 650,000 people typically show up for the annual parade. The grand marshal in the past has been Paul Rodriguez, better known as "Pepsi Man" to millions of Hispanic consumers. He has become Pepsi's cola-war hero and is used by Pepsi to very carefully craft an image of Pepsi as a "young, fun-loving brand," an image that plays particularly well in the Latino market. Driven by the Rodriguez campaign, sales of Pepsi in the Texas market grew by 22 percent in the first year after Rodriguez became the spokesperson in the South.[7] This particular program by Pepsi recognizes the needs of Hispanics—individuals who differ from other customer groups both in biogenics as well as in specific emotions or psychogenics.

PHYSICAL CHARACTERISTICS OF THE ENVIRONMENT

Three physical characteristics of the environment affect customer needs: climate, topography, and ecology.

CLIMATE. The **climate** of the customer's environment includes conditions such as temperature, altitude, and rainfall. Climatic conditions affect consumers' needs for food, clothing, and shelter. For example, needs for clothing are different in cold climates versus those in warmer climates. As an example of service, flood insurance on homes is needed in climates marked by heavy rains and not in drier climates.

TOPOGRAPHY.   The **topography** of a geographic area refers to the physical condition of the location on earth, the spatial profile of the territory (e.g., mountains or plains), and the presence of bodies of water (e.g., river, ocean, etc.). Topography generates customer needs relevant to managing life in the specific terrain. For example, customers living in the mountains will need hiking boots, four-wheel-drive vehicles, and a whole range of other products. On the other hand, individuals living near water will be more likely to own boats and water skis. In the business markets too, topography produces particular needs, such as the ability of products to withstand temperature and humidity conditions.

ECOLOGY.   The third physical characteristic of the environment that has a significant influence on customer needs is **ecology,** which includes the quality of air, the ozone layer, and the food chain. For example, the ozone layer is essential for screening out harmful rays of the sun. But ozone pollution at ground level due to smog affects the quality of the air we breathe, resulting in ozone alerts that keep individuals with heart or breathing conditions indoors on those days. Similarly, pollen in the atmosphere at the onset of spring or fall affects a large portion of people who suffer from cough and cold allergies. Both of these ecology concerns can affect individuals' activity levels and need for medications.

Determinants of Wants

Like the determinants of needs, the determinants of wants operate on both an individual and an environmental level. They consist of individual and environmental context factors.

THE INDIVIDUAL CONTEXT

The **individual context** consists of three dimensions: an individual's personal financial worth, institutions, and culture.

PERSONAL WORTH.   The context of **personal worth** refers to the financial resources available to a customer. These comprise a person's income, assets, inheritance, and borrowing power. Similarly for businesses, personal worth includes earnings, equity, and borrowing power. These resources influence wants by giving the customer the purchasing power to buy products that would satisfy more than the basic, physical needs.[8] Thus, rather than merely buying a car, a person with economic resources is able to buy a luxury car with higher driving thrill and greater social prestige. Likewise, a business with ample borrowing power will *want* to purchase a PC with more bells and whistles than they may actually need. And it is because of the prospect of future income that college students obtain, as soon as they graduate, immediate borrowing power from credit card institutions.

INSTITUTIONAL CONTEXT.   The **institutional context** is the second dimension, and it refers to the groups and organizations a person belongs to. The institutional context includes the workplace, religious and educational institutions, and family and friends and peer groups. All of these serve as settings that can shape our wants as users and customers. The workplace requires a particular style of clothing, for example.

CULTURAL CONTEXT.   The third dimension affecting wants comes from an individual's or businesses' **cultural context.** Culture's influence on customers is pervasive, for culture shapes everything we do, desire, or become. Customers' culture and cultural values influence their goals, and, consequently, wants for products. For example, in some cultures, a person is valued for what he or she is, rather than for what he or she possesses. Customers in these cultures are less likely to seek conspicuous consumption goods. As another example, some cultures value age (for age is supposed to give wisdom) while others value youth. Accordingly, customers from the former culture are less likely to want anti-aging products and services (such as plastic surgery) compared with customers from the latter culture. Also, business customers from the former cultures are likely to be much less receptive to a young sales executive or, say, a young business consultant compared to the customers in the latter cultures.

THE ENVIRONMENTAL CONTEXT

The environmental context also consists of three dimensions: economy, technology, and public policy.[9]

ECONOMY.   **Economy** refers to the economic development and cycles in a nation's economy. The economic level of a nation, the level of inflation, unemployment rate, and wage and income growth all have an impact on customers both in the household and business markets. For example, high inflation can impact a consumer's decision not to purchase a house because interest rates may be too high, or it may influence a business company to postpone capital budget spending if the money is to be borrowed at a high interest rate.

TECHNOLOGY.   The environmental influence of technology on customers' wants is manifested in many ways. **Technology** is the man-made inventions and devices used to sustain, facilitate, and enhance human life and activities. With respect to infrastructure, some countries have better technology deployment, such as in highways, transportation, energy, telecommunications, or educational systems. For instance, the merging of the telephone and cable technologies in the United States in the near future will give cable companies the capability of two-way communications, with the result that customers will be able to watch their favorite movies "on demand" (i.e., they can have the movie start at whatever time they wish, pause it in the middle, and resume later). This will change the video rental business (e.g., Blockbuster) in profound ways.

The proposed national information superhighway will similarly influence business customers' wants for new communications services. For example, Internet video-conferencing now offers businesses new and inexpensive alternatives to flying employees around the world to speak to business partners. The participants of a video-conference can use a whiteboard connected over the Internet, with participants' written comments appearing on all conferees' whiteboard screens instantaneously. Some of the more advanced features of this technology include the ability to copy files from one system to another; the ability to print and save the file; the use of a remote pointer that can be used to highlight without actually marking the screen; and image compression, which speeds data transfer between participants.[10]

PUBLIC POLICY.   The final influence within the environmental context is public policy, especially as it relates to market behavior. **Public policy** is governmental or societal, laws and regulations that control human behavior, and, thus, business activities. For example, in Saudi Arabia and Kuwait, public policies have been enacted to create a dress code for women. Likewise, in Singapore and Malaysia, very strong policy initiatives have been instituted to make drug usage a crime punishable by death in some cases.

Figure 2.4

MATRIX OF PERSON AND ENVIRONMENT CHARACTERISTICS

	ENVIRONMENT CHARACTERISTICS	
	PHYSICAL	CONTEXTUAL
PERSON CHARACTERISTICS — PHYSICAL	1. Needs-driven markets (e.g., allergy medicine)	3. Personal needs & environmental wants (e.g., microwavable food)
PERSON CHARACTERISTICS — CONTEXTUAL	2. Personal wants & environmental needs driven markets (e.g., fur coat)	4. Wants-driven markets (e.g., theatre attendance)

In the United States, political action committees, interest groups, and lobbyists for corporations attempt to influence the policy-making decisions of government officials through persuasive appeals in the mass media. The current health-care debate in this country evidences this type of influence.[11] The U.S. government is constantly monitoring the types of drugs that are prescribed by doctors versus those that can be bought by individuals over-the-counter. Several customer groups are impacted by these decisions, including physicians, drug companies, and individual users. The health-care reform currently underway will also have a dramatic impact on these same groups of customers. Other laws affect suppliers and intermediaries in a channel of distribution, such as interstate commerce laws, which affect the banking industry in setting up branches around the country, or the laws against deceptive advertising and unsafe products and packaging, which influence demands for certain packaging materials.

Impact of the Determinants

Figure 2.4 summarizes how each of the determinants shapes the needs and wants of customers in the marketplace. Their impact falls into four broad categories:

1. **Needs-driven markets.** When both personal and environmental characteristics are physical, pure needs drive customer behavior. Examples include climate-relevant clothing, allergy medicine during the allergy season, flood insurance for personal or business property in flood zones, and so on.

2. **Personal wants and environmental needs.** When the relevant environmental characteristics are physical, but personal characteristics are contextual, the driver of customer behavior is a personal want but an environmental need. Examples include product categories that are driven by climate, topography, or ecology, but where brand usage reflects one's wealth, social standing, self-concept, and so on (e.g., name brand warm clothing, fur coat, a contemporary off-road vehicle, etc.).

3. **Personal needs and environmental wants.** When the relevant personal characteristics are physical but environmental characteristics are contextual (economy, technology, public policy), customers seek something that will satisfy a personal need but an environmental want. Examples would include microwavable food, home-shopping network, technological gadgets, and so on.

4. **Wants-driven markets.** Finally, when both personal and environmental contexts are salient, customer behavior is driven by pure wants. Examples include consumption of arts and theater, participating in political rallies, voting, buying designer clothing, sporting the grunge look, and so on.

As a rule, needs are driven more by physiology and are less likely to change over time. Wants, on the other hand, are more context driven and are therefore more likely than needs to change over time. Personal wants are basically driven by the personal context, whereas environmental/societal wants are driven more by the environmental context.

Importance of the Three Roles

In identifying and satisfying customer needs and wants, it is important to recognize the value of each customer role. Ignore one of them, and you lose the customer. First and foremost, the user role is important in the very design of the product or service. The features of the product or service have to be the ones that the user is seeking and that will meet the user's need or want the best.

But the other two roles are important as well. Consider the critical role the payer plays. If price or other features do not satisfy the payer, the user and buyer simply cannot buy the product. Without the payer, no sale will ever occur. This role has largely been ignored in the marketing literature, but it is being acknowledged increasingly in marketing practice. The mushrooming of consumer credit card companies is testimony to this acknowledgment. Today, financing and leasing for both business and household customers is a booming business. Increasingly, more and more cars are sold through lease agreements today, and businesses are increasingly resorting to buying equipment through leasing with options to buy, such as the recent agreement by Continental Airlines to "lease-buy" its fleet from Boeing.

Educating the user about what is prudent from the payer's perspective.

Shoppers in the Store Maze

"I'll bet you the bouillon is down here with soups. Ha! Ha! I was wrong. I'm looking for a little square package. The bouillon cubes, I'm assuming, come in a square package or an envelope type of thing."

—A shopper in the supermarket talking [Actually, the shopper was wrong about the packaging, not the location. The bouillon cubes were in the soup aisle, but were packaged in plastic bottles.]

"Bouillon cubes were very hard to find. They're in such small packages and they're in jars. I wouldn't think of them as being in jars. I was looking for boxes."

—Another shopper in the supermarket

"We forgot bouillon cubes. They're in a stupid spot, right by the spices, I think . . . No, they're not here. If they're not here, they're with [pause] try gravies in aisle nine. . . . OK, they're not here either."

—A third shopper in the same supermarket

Marketing professors Philip A. Titus and Peter B. Everett studied how supermarket shoppers find their way around the store aisles. For this purpose, they gave a random sample of supermarket shoppers a shopping list, instructing them to find these items and to speak their thoughts into a cassette recorder. The monologues you just read are from a sample of these shoppers' thoughts.

What do these thoughts reveal about the customers playing the purchaser role? By analyzing these monologues for patterns and classification, Professors Titus and Everett found that shoppers attempt to locate their product by first inferring the product category that might contain the product (e.g., is powdered milk going to be with baby foods or with coffee, tea, and other beverages?). In addition, shoppers make various navigational errors in finding the merchandise in the store. These errors include:

- Shopper orientation errors. Not knowing where one is. Misidentifying the section one is in.

- Destination selection errors. Make a mistake as to where one should look (e.g., look for powdered milk in the baby food section instead of the powdered beverages section).

- Destination identification errors. Misidentifying a section (e.g., being in the refrigerated section and mistaking it for the freezer section).

- Environmental assessment errors. Being in a section and dismissing it as a likely location for the product that it does contain (e.g., being in the pasta section and ignoring it as a potential location for a limited selection of wines).

- Product analysis errors. Not knowing what a product is, or what it should look like (perhaps because the shopper is buying it for someone else, or buying it for the first time and is going to be using it for the first time; e.g., household dyes—I wonder what they look like, and what kind of a package they come in?).

- Product recognition errors. Shoppers may mistake one product for another (e.g., picking up a can of "furniture polish" only to find, upon closer inspection, that it is really air freshener).

Shopper confusion in finding merchandise can frustrate shoppers, causing them to become angry, buy fewer items, leave the store, or even decide never to shop at that store again. Marketers should therefore make it convenient for shoppers to locate merchandise. Possible actions include: (a) making the signage and shelf displays more visible; (b) clearly marking aisles with identifiers, making the list of merchandise on aisle signs more inclusive; (c) offering in-store clerical assistance; (d) including in the advertisement the aisle location or category identification (e.g., find it on the coffee and tea shelf); and (e) offering an electronic kiosk that displays merchandise location along with the aisle map. Yet another solution would be to place an item in more than one location, particularly if the item is one that shoppers may differ in associating with one or the other product category. Better product package designs with clearer product and brand name logos can also help the shopper. In other words, both manufacturers and retail stores should be concerned with not only attracting the product users, but also appealing to customers in their purchaser roles.

Source: Philip A. Titus and Peter B. Everett, "Consumer Wayfinding Tasks, Strategies, and Errors: An Exploratory Field Study," *Psychology & Marketing* 13, no. 3 (May 1996), pp. 265–90.

To understand the role of the payer, just ask college students today which car they drive and which car, if they had their way, they would actually like to drive. Affordability to the payer constrains marketplace transactions like no other factor does.

Finally, the buyer role is also critical. The buyer's task is to find the merchandise and find a way to order or acquire it. If the buyer's access to the product or service is constrained, the buyer will simply not buy the product, and thus, the user would not have the product available for use. For example, suppose a 13-year-old girl wants to buy a specific bicycle, based on her seeing the bike in a TV commercial and also in a catalog. But her mother does not have the time or the means to go to a distant store where that particular brand of bike is sold. The girl would eventually end up having to use a bike that the neighborhood store has. Indeed, playing the buyer role—finding and acquiring the product or service—can be very frustrating sometimes, as the excerpts from some shopper reactions in Window on Research box show. Marketers must facilitate the buyer's task by making it convenient to buy and acquire the product/service.

Managerial Implications: Pull and Push Strategies

The importance of differentiating among the user, the payer, and the buyer centers on how marketers can most effectively target their products and services to their chosen markets, with an eye towards creating a loyal following. When the buyer, the user, and the payer are different, marketers must tailor their product and service strategies. A product can be promoted to either the end user or the payer and buyer. For these, the marketer needs to use, respectively, a pull or a push strategy. A **pull marketing** strategy is executed when the marketer directly appeals to end users, inducing them to ask the buyer to buy the marketer's product. In a **push marketing** strategy, the marketer appeals to the buyers to induce them to buy the product and then promote it to the end users.[12]

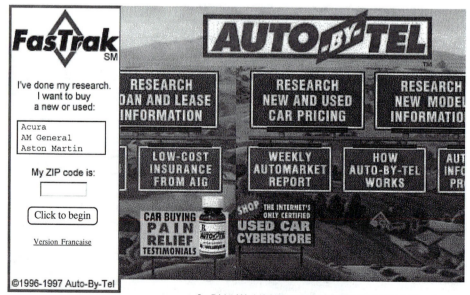

For example, when a company like Johnson & Johnson (makers of Tylenol) advertises its products directly to the end user, it is relying on a pull strategy to create a preference for its products among consumers who will then seek it out from the pharmacy. Or the same company can use a push strategy to target drugstore owners (who will purchase and pay for the product), who will then recommend the product to the consumer. Likewise, the same company uses a push marketing strategy by targeting the payer (government, corporations, or insurance companies) and the buyer (doctors, hospitals) for its prescription drugs in situations where the patient has no choice.

Another example is the marketing of children's cereals. This is a product category in which the user and the buyer are usually different, since parents typically do the actual purchasing. Cereal marketers can direct their persuasive communication, therefore, either to children or to parents, or both. If the marketer decides to persuade children directly, as most children's cereal companies do, then the marketer is using a pull strategy. On the other hand, if the cereal marketer were to use coupons and special price promotion, then it is appealing to the payer and the buyer, namely, the parents who do the shopping. This is push marketing.

An interesting strategy recently employed by Starbucks Coffee Company also illustrates this concept. Starbucks is a U.S. company marketing gourmet coffee via its own franchised coffee shops. Recently, it ran an advertisement that sought to attract their satisfied customers (who consume, buy, and pay for their coffee in retail locations) to join their mail order service. This is an example of a pull strategy.

In some industrial buying situations, the engineers and production managers (who are the users of the production materials) will specify the product they want, when they want it, and even request a supplier by name. Here, the two user departments are assuming the responsibility for supplier selection, instructing the procurement department on what to order. In this situation, the marketer targets the users in the manufacturing or engineering departments and thus employs a "pull" strategy. If, in contrast, the procurement department had the authority to decide on the supplier, then the marketer would target the procurement department (rather than the end users), thus employing a "push" strategy. In some cases, the purchasing department in a business is relegated to becoming an order taker when users specify a brand name and supplier to buy from.

In a classic pull marketing example, IBM implemented a pull marketing strategy two decades ago when it introduced their Selectric typewriters. IBM did this by placing their typewriters in classrooms to condition young women in high school to use their product. Once these young women got out of high school and went on to become secretaries, they didn't feel comfortable with a Remington or an Olivetti (the other two major brands of typewriters), so they requested or, in some cases, even demanded that the company buy a Selectric for them to use.

The decision whether to use a push strategy, a pull strategy, or both depends on who the decision maker is (see Figure 2.5). If the user is the decision maker, then a pull strategy is needed. If a buyer (who is not the end user) is the decision maker, then a push strategy is called for. If both are decision makers, with the buyer as well as the user exercising influence on the decision, then both pull and push strategies are desired.

For some products, the decision-making roles shift. A prime example is the health-care industry, where decision making has shifted from the doctor to the patient over the years. In the past, when a patient needed a hospital, she or he relied entirely on his or her physician to choose the hospital. Today, although doctors still influence patients' choice of hospitals, patients are playing a more active role in consultation with their doctors. In today's health-care marketplace, more and more hospitals advertise their facilities and

Figure 2.5	CUSTOMER ROLES AND PUSH-PULL STRATEGIES

		USER CHOOSES THE SUPPLIER?	
		NO	YES
PURCHASER CHOOSES THE SUPPLIER	YES	Push marketing (e.g., office supplies)	Push & pull marketing (e.g., cereals, office furniture)
	NO	No market	Pull marketing (e.g., personal care products, cigarettes)

services directly to consumers (i.e., potential patients). The push strategy of supporting and motivating the physicians continues at the same time.

Summary

In this chapter, you learned how customers differ from consumers, and why the customer is a broader and more inclusive concept than the consumer. It was pointed out that the "consumer," a term most commonly used in marketing interchangeably with the term "customer," is actually only one of the three roles of the customer, namely, the user. The chapter then built on this role distinction to identify the conditions under which the three roles of the customer are likely to be separated. The conditions include a lack of expertise, lack of time, lack of buying power, lack of access, lack of affordability, and situations where the product or service is free. In each of these conditions, the buyer and/or payer will be a different person than the user.

The next section in the chapter covered the needs and wants of customers—whether as users, payers, or buyers. A need was defined as an unsatisfactory physical condition of the customer that leads him or her to an action that will satisfy or fulfill that condition. A want was defined as an unsatisfactory psychological/social condition of the customer that will lead him or her to an action that will satisfy or fulfill that condition.

Needs are determined by the personal characteristics of the customer and by the physical characteristics of the environment. The personal characteristics of a customer are genetics, biogenics, and psychogenics. The physical characteristics of the environment are climate, topography, and ecology. Wants are determined by the individual context and by the environmental context of the customer. The individual context can be broken down into three areas: culture, institutions and groups, and net worth. The environmental context is shaped by the economy, technology, and public policy.

Finally, the last section of the chapter covered the managerial implications of the three roles of a customer. The distinction was made between using a push and a pull marketing strategy when targeting the user, payer, and buyer. A pull marketing strategy is executed when the marketer directly appeals to end users, inducing them to ask the buyer to buy the marketer's product. In a push marketing strategy, the marketer appeals to the buyer to induce that person to buy the product and then promote it to the end user.

Now that you understand the forces in the marketplace that sometimes make it necessary for the role of the buyer and payer to be filled by someone other than the user, the next chapter puts forward a framework that classifies market values corresponding to each of the three roles a customer plays.

Key Terms

Role specialization 35
Needs 41
Wants 41
Genetics 43
Biogenics 44
Psychogenics 44

Climate 44
Topography 45
Ecology 45
Individual context 45
Personal worth 45
Institutional context 45

Cultural context 46
Economy 46
Technology 46
Public policy 46
Pull marketing 50
Push marketing 50

Review Questions

1. How do consumers differ from customers? Why is making this distinction important to marketers?

2. Give one example each of the following from product and service categories:

   a. When the user is neither a buyer nor a payer.

   b. When the user is a payer but not a buyer.

   c. When the user is a buyer but not a payer.

   d. When the user is also the buyer and payer.

3. When users (consumers) lack the buying power to make a purchase, they often look to others to buy and pay for the products and services they need. Give one example each of a household user and a business user who depend on others to play the payer and buyer roles.

4. Refer to the Matrix of Person and Environment Characteristics on page 47. Fill in that matrix with fresh examples of your own, drawing examples from both the household and business markets.

5. How do needs differ from wants? How are needs and wants determined?

Applications

1. Some consumer groups and consumer rights advocates have accused marketers of unfairly creating needs and wants by offering customers unnecessary and often high priced items. How would you defend the marketer's point of view that needs and wants cannot be artificially created?

2. Marketplace behavior is often influenced by a customer's cultural context, one of three personal contexts described in this chapter. How does cultural context impact customer behavior? Illustrate with examples of some consumers from different cultural contexts that you may know.

3. In marketing, two options that companies use to attract and retain customers are a pull strategy and a push strategy. How do these strategies differ, and when should a company use one or the other? Illustrate your answers, citing push and pull strategies being employed by various companies that serve household and business markets.

Practical Experiences

1. The "Do-It-Yourself" market is growing bigger and bigger around the world, and entrepreneurs who are seeking new niches in the marketplace are rapidly turning to this growing group of customers. Go to the library and identify the fastest-growing or the most unique companies that cater to the "Do-It-Yourself" customer in each of the following four areas: consumer product, consumer service, business product, and business service.

2. You are the new marketing assistant to the vice president of admissions at a premier liberal arts college. Historically, the marketing program of this college has consisted of a college team visiting the various high schools around the country. In these visits, the college team meets with students during their class periods. This arrangement does not make it feasible for parents to be present, nor has the team considered it necessary. Write your boss a memo about why she should consider others (rather than merely high school students) as prospective customers and what appeals would make sense to these other customers.

Notes

1 Based on or adapted from "Chelsea Clinton to Attend Stanford," *Washington Times,* May 1, 1997, p. A4.

2 Berkman and Gilson (1986) recognize the terms "consumer" and "buyer" but align this distinction with the household versus institutional settings, respectively; we view the terms to be separate in both settings. Runyon and Stewart (1987) also recognize that sometimes the buyer may be different from the user, but they elect to use the single term "consumer" to include both the roles. Likewise, Solomon (1992), while recognizing the separation of the "buyer" and "user" roles in some situations, uses the term "consumer" inclusively to encompass the processes of "buying, having, and being." See Harold W. Berkman and Christopher Gilson, *Consumer Behavior: Concepts and Strategies* (Boston: Kent Publishing Company, 1986), p. 7; Kenneth E. Runyon and David W. Stewart, *Consumer Behavior—And the Practice of Marketing* (Columbus: Merrill Publishing Company, 1987), p. 5; Michael R. Solomon, *Consumer Behavior: Buying, Having, and Being* (Boston: Allyn and Bacon, 1992), pp. 4–5.

3 John A. Howard and Jagdish N. Sheth, *The Theory of Buyer Behavior* (New York: John Wiley and Sons, 1969).

4 This treatment differs from that in Philip Kotler, *Marketing Management: Analysis, Planning, Implementation, and Control* (New York: Prentice Hall, 1992), p. 7. Kotler defines needs as "felt deprivation of some basic satisfaction," and includes esteem, belongingness. Wants are, to Kotler, "desires for specific satisfiers of the needs." By these definitions, food is a need satisfier, whereas for want satisfaction, one needs to choose a pizza, or a sandwich. Although Kotler's examples of want satisfiers (e.g., buying a Mercedes rather than just any car) are congruent with the definitions presented here, they do not follow strictly from his definitions.

5 Some consumer researchers highlight this distinction by using the dichotomy of primary and secondary (or innate and acquired) needs. See Leon G. Schiffman and Leslie Lazar Kanuk, *Consumer Behavior,* 4th edition (Englewood Cliffs: Prentice Hall, 1991), p. 70.

6 *Time,* January 17, 1994, pp. 46–57.

7 Karen Benezra, "Tactics May Not Translate but Strategies Often Do; Mainstream Players Learn Fluency at Tapping into Non-whites," *Brandweek* 35, no. 29 (July 1994), pp. 28–29.

8 See George C. Katona, *Psychological Economics* (New York: Elsevier Scientific Publishing Co., 1975).

9 For a comprehensive essay on this topic, see Rudolf H. Moos, *The Human Context: Environmental Determinants of Behavior* (New York: John Wiley & Sons, 1976).

10 Jon Hill, Jan Ozer, and Thomas Mace, "Real-time Communication: Connecting on the Net," *PC Magazine* 15, no. 17 (October 8, 1996), pp. 102–14.

[11] For a discussion of the use of marketing in politics, see Bruce I. Newman, *The Marketing of the President: Political Marketing as Campaign Strategy* (Thousand Oaks: Sage Publications, 1994); and Bruce I. Newman and Jagdish N. Sheth, *Political Marketing: Readings and Annotated Bibliography* (Chicago: American Marketing Association, 1985).

[12] Adapted from Kotler, *Marketing Management,* pp. 619–20.

CHAPTER 3

After reading this chapter you should be able to:

Identify the various market values that customers seek.

Describe how these values differ for the roles of the customer—user, payer, and buyer.

Summarize the characteristics of these values.

Explain how these values can be measured.

Discuss how the marketer can assess its value-satisfying score vis-à-vis competitors.

Market Values Customers Seek

Brides, Brides-to-Be, and Brides-Wannabe

It is 4 o'clock on a cold winter morning. Customers from all corners of Boston leave on their pilgrimage a few miles away. Also joining them are several out-of-towners, who came into town the previous evening and stayed with friends, relatives, or in hotels. They came just to join this consumer pilgrimage. The destination: Filene's Basement—an off-price clothing store. A store so famous that it attracts 15,000 to 20,000 shoppers per day. A Boston landmark, which is also a tourist attraction. On this particular day, the store is holding a special event—the Bridal Gown Sale, an event held four times a year, to clear unsold inventory. Filene's carries gowns that are regularly priced from $1,000 to $8,000. Today, they are marked down to $249—one and all.

The store will open at 8 A.M., but customers start lining up at 5 A.M. to get a good place in line. As soon as the doors open, the crowd instantly turns into a frenzied mob, rushing in, running down the stairs to the basement store. There on racks are wedding gowns, thousands of them. Shoppers grab them by the dozen, without regard to size or style. A thousand gowns disappear in less than one minute. The shopping teams hold on to them, hoarding their inventory while someone—bride-to-be—tries them on one by one. Rather than wait for the fitting rooms to become available, the hopefuls don't mind undressing in the aisles, "public stripping" in plain view of bystanders. They try one and then another. The gowns they discard are quickly grabbed by others waiting and hovering around the shopping teams. Media have described this event as "a magical event, a mystery tour, a lovable, thrilling hole in the ground, as transforming and madcap as Alice's entry into Wonderland."

By the end of the day, many lucky "Alices" will have walked away with the gown of their dreams. Many of them are soon-to-be-brides. But the lure of the merchandise is such that others—with no wedding plans in the immediate future—also come seeking and purchasing the dress of their dreams—just in case! Filene's Basement—an extraordinary oasis of market value customers seek; customers—brides-to-be and brides-wannabe alike.[1]

Introduction

Whether in Filene's Basement or in a United jet high above the Pacific, all customer behavior is driven by customer needs and wants, whose satisfaction customers seek and value. Thus, all customer behavior is driven by the value received through the acquisition and use of a product or service. Customers do not buy a product or service for its own sake; rather they buy it for what it does—what benefits or value it offers to the customer. Thus, when customers buy toothpaste, they are actually buying oral hygiene. When they buy a Range Rover vehicle, they are not buying 3,600 pounds of sheet metal fabricated in a particular shape; rather, they are buying a solution to their problem of transportation and the problem of how to project a certain image to others.

This chapter explores the role of market values. It begins by formally defining market value, then identifies the kinds of market value sought by customers carrying out each role. Next, we give example of how various kinds of products can deliver a bundle of values. We then summarize basic characteristics of customer values. Finally, we explain how market values can be measured so that companies can evaluate how well they create value for their customers.

What Is a Market Value?

The recognition of customers as seekers of problem solutions and the resulting value is fundamental to long-term business viability. Indeed it goes to the very core of how a business firm defines and views itself. Marketing scholar Theodore Levitt has argued that many companies do not know what business they are in! They view themselves too narrowly and thus suffer from what Levitt calls "marketing myopia."[2] Marketing myopia refers to the narrow vision wherein firms view themselves in limited, product- or service-centered ways—as makers and sellers of products and services they produce and sell. Thus, firms that thought they were in the buggy business rather than in the business of providing their customers transportation solutions suffered from marketing myopia and were replaced by the automobile industry. Businesses that thought they were in the slide-rule business are also extinct today, replaced by electronic calculating devices. As Levitt puts it, when customers buy three-quarter-inch drills, basically they are buying three-quarter-inch holes. Some day firms that make drills will be ousted by firms making laser guns that cut three-quarter-inch holes with greater precision. Such a myopic view continues among some business firms even today. Some hospitals think of themselves, for example, as collections of doctors, nurses, and medical equipment, and as purveyors of medicine and ambulatory and surgical care. Patients, on the other hand, look to hospitals as *providers of value* in terms of good health and physical well-being. Likewise, in obtaining a life insurance or a health insurance policy, customers are not seeking merely a paper document; rather they are seeking "peace of mind"—freedom from anxieties about the unknown future. Thus, in every product and service that customers buy, their basic goal is the same: to solve some problem. The problem-solving abilities of products and services are what constitute value to the customer.

In sum, a market value is the potential of a product or service to satisfy customers' needs and wants. The concept of potential is central to the discussion of values. Value is created only if the product or service has the capability to satisfy a customer's needs and wants. Since not all customers' needs and wants are identical, a product or service may

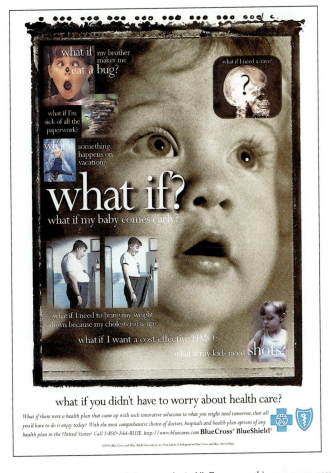

In obtaining health insurance, customers seek "peace of mind." For users, this may mean assurance that their health care needs will be met; for payers, it may mean predictably low costs.

be more valuable to one and less valuable to another because it satisfies one customer's needs and wants better than another customer's needs and wants. Furthermore, the customer's context or situation may make a product or service more or less valuable. For example, a product/service may be very valuable in one climatic zone but totally valueless in another climate, or the value may vary within the same climatic zone from one situation to another (e.g., an umbrella is valuable when it rains).[3] Thus, value is created by the convergence of a product's capability with the context of the customer (see Figure 3.1).

It must be clarified that there is another sense (different from ours) in which the term "value" is used in consumer behavior literature. In this other interpretation, "values" are thought of as desirable life goals for a society, culture, or person. These are exemplified by such terminal end-state values (the end states we strive for) as world peace, self-respect, wisdom, happiness, and so on, as well as by such instrumental values (means for reaching the end states) as acting honestly, hard work, and so on.[4] This interpretation of values is discussed in this book later in the discussion of consumer personality. Usually, however, we use the term *values* to refer instead to the problem-solving benefits (tangible or intangible) a person receives from a product or service.

MARKET VALUE: THE CONVERGENCE OF CAPABILITIES
WITH WANTS OR NEEDS

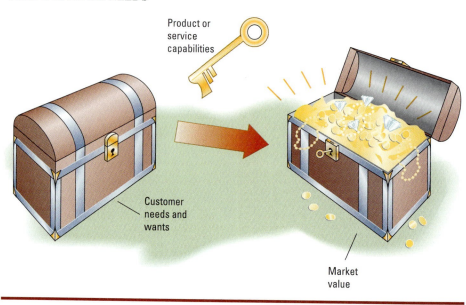

Classification of Market Values

In general, a product or service's market values may be universal, personal, or both. **Universal values** are values that satisfy the *needs* of the customer. These pertain to the basic purpose of buying a product or service or for doing business with a firm. They are termed "universal" because invariably all customers seek them in a product or service, and they are sought alike by customers across nations and cultures. As such, they are the bare minimum that a marketer should offer.

Personal values are those which satisfy the *wants* of the customer. They are called "personal" because wants are more diverse than needs and differ from person to person. Personal values pertain to something beyond the basic or universal reason for buying a product or service, or for doing business with a firm. Some personal values, called group-specific, are desired by and offered alike to a segment or group of customers. Other personal values, called individual-specific, are more individualized, more internal, more related to one's personal enjoyment or comfort. Products offering such value are more personalized or customized for the customer one-on-one, and the customer is able to relate to them as if they were being offered to him or her specifically.

Each class of values corresponds to a marketing strategy. Universal values are the basis of product differentiation strategies (those that seek to distinguish a product from the competition). Group-specific personal values are the basis of segmentation strategies (those that focus on subsets of the total market). Finally, individual-specific personal values are the basis of one-to-one marketing as well as relationship marketing (strategies that emphasize meeting unique customer needs). These topics are discussed in later chapters.

As shown in Figure 3.2, each of the three customer roles seeks a particular category of universal values. The universal value that the user seeks is different from the universal value sought by the payer, which is in turn different from the universal value sought by the buyer. Likewise, each of the three roles seeks a particular pair of personal values.

Figure 3.2

MATRIX OF VALUES AND CUSTOMER ROLES

| | CUSTOMER ROLES | | |
	USER	PAYER	BUYER
UNIVERSAL VALUES	Performance value	Price value	Service value
PERSONAL VALUES Group–specific	Social value	Credit value	Convenience value
Individual–specific	Emotional value	Financing value	Personalization value

For the user, the universal value is performance value; the personal value is social at the group level and emotional at the individual level. For the payer, the universal value is the price; the personal value is credit at the group level and financing at the individual level.[5] Finally, for the buyer, the universal value is service value, the group-related personal value is convenience, and the individualized personal value is personalization value.

Market Values Sought by Users

UNIVERSAL VALUE: PERFORMANCE

A product or service's **performance value** is the quality of physical outcome of using the product or service, (i.e., it refers to how well a product or service serves its principal physical function consistently). The physical function of clothing is to protect a body against the elements; for food it is to give body nutrition and energy. For a fan, it is to circulate air. For a cleanser, it is to clean. The performance value resides in and stems from the physical composition of the product or from the design of the service. It depends therefore on design features and manufacturing quality. Many market choices depend on the degree of performance value associated with different alternatives. This is the position advanced by utility theory in economics, where performance value is generally called functional or utilitarian value. According to the utility theory, a person acts rationally in making his or her choice. Accordingly, as a "rational economic man," a customer buys products that will offer maximum performance value.[6]

When customers buy detergents, for example, they seek such performance values as dirt and stain removal from clothing and protection against color fading. The performance value of a telephone consists in enabling a person to communicate with sound clarity with another person not within a hearing distance; of shampoo, to remove oil as well as the dust and dirt collected from the atmosphere. Of course, this is a broad performance value, but different users may need different kinds of performance value even from the same product. Consumers with dandruff desire a strong shampoo that eliminates

The performance value is nearly universal. Here Tide speaks to users in the Arab countries in a universal language—the language of performance.

dandruff; on the other hand, consumers with flat and limp hair want a shampoo that gives them the performance value of "body."

For business products, performance consists in how accurately and reliably the products perform: for example, that blood testing equipment in a hospital gives correct measurements; that the machine tool cuts metallic surfaces within certain tolerance limits; that the copier gives good color reproduction and does not jam the paper; that the downtime on the computer network is minimal; that the chemical ingredients for producing chemical compounds are pure; or the seafood delivered to a supermarket or restaurant be fresh.

In services, the performance value of a hair salon is simply cutting hair in patterns. The performance value of a travel agent is to find the traveler the most cost-effective travel plan. In business-to-business services, performance value is generally of paramount importance for the user. In the delivery of time sensitive documents, for example, the performance value consists in the speedy delivery of documents at the promised time. In pest control services, likewise, the performance value consists in the extent to which cockroaches, rats, and so on, do not breed on the business premises. When custodial services are outsourced by business, their performance value consists in keeping the premises clean and ensuring 100 percent security against break-in or unauthorized personnel entry into the building or office premises.

Performance is a very important value for those business services whose interruption or failure would cause the business processes to stop.

PERSONAL VALUES: SOCIAL AND EMOTIONAL VALUES

Products are bought and consumed not just for their physical function, but also for social benefits. For the user, these benefits are termed *social* and *emotional* values. These include sensory enjoyment, attainment of desired mood states, achievement of social goals (e.g., social status or acceptance by one's reference groups), and self-concept fulfillment. Take clothing, for example. In addition to their obvious performance value (protecting the body from the elements), customers often seek self-expressive value from the clothes they buy. At the very minimum, customers in their user role would ask, "Will it look good on me?" Some see deep meaning in their clothing, asking, "What kind of a person will I be, donning that outfit?" Similarly, some products are sought for emotional satisfactions (sometimes exclusively, and at other times in addition to their performance value), such as a high school class ring or visiting your homeland or buying a cedar chest similar to your mother's or not buying mink or fur coats due to your concern for cruelty to animals.

SOCIAL VALUE. Some market choices may be determined primarily by social value. Users driven by social value choose products that convey an image congruent with the norms of their friends and associates or that convey the social image they wish to project. Social value exists when products come to be associated with positively perceived social groups. Of course, a product associated with a negatively perceived social group has negative social value. Users both in household and business settings are often concerned with the social meaning of the product or service they use. Certain types of clothing, for example, are associated with certain groups and are either embraced or avoided, depending on whether that group is desirable or undesirable. As a business person, or as a corporate employee, the kind of clothes you wear, the kind of car you drive, the kind of house you live in, and even the kind of hair salon you patronize can signal to others whether you fit in. In the office, even the furniture and decor you choose have to be appropriate to your status. The choice of a hotel during a business trip and even the credit card you flash as you pay your bills may signal to the client your status within the organization.

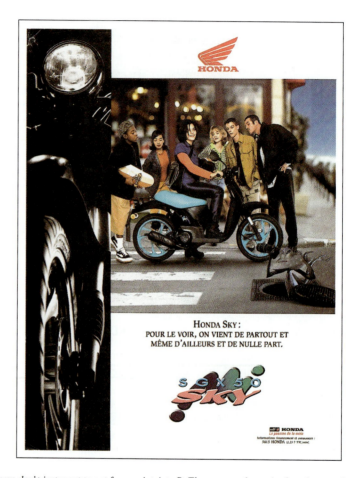

Some customers don't just want to get from point A to B. They want to be noticed as they get there. That is the "social value" this proud user of Sky Motor Scooter receives.

Highly visible products lend themselves to acquiring positive or negative social value.[7] A New York restaurant called Daniel is fashionable, exclusive, and small. And it is expensive. But for the well heeled, the main obstacle to getting a table at the restaurant is not the cost, but a lack of the right connections. You have to know the maitre d' Mr. Bruno Jamias by name, or at least know someone else who does. In late November 1996, a staffer for Bob Dole (then a U.S. presidential candidate) reportedly could not get a table at Daniel for her boss—until she called again, asked for Mr. Jamias by name, and identified the guest by name. The same exclusivity reigns at

New York's Mesa Grill or Coco Pazzo, Chicago's Frontera Grill, San Francisco's Bix, and New Orleans' Emeril. What do customers seek from restaurants such as these so that they put up with this unwelcoming attitude? Superb performance value from the exotic cuisine for one; social value from being among the select celebrity circuit for another.[8]

Utilitarian versus Expressive Product Appeals

WINDOW ON RESEARCH

If you would like to read some research literature on customer values—or at least user values—you will find it in the writings of several consumer researchers. In searching through the literature, you will meet such well-known consumer researchers as Russ Belk, Bill Bearden, Joel B. Cohen, Kenneth DeBono, Michael Etzel, Beth Hirschman, Morris Holbrook, Bernard Jaworsky, J.S. Johar, Jean Kepferer, Gilles Laurant, Debra MacInnis, Paul Miniard, Banwari Mittal, Jim Munson, Bruce Newman, C.W. Park, Paul Prabhakar, Brian Ratchford, Sharon Shavitt, Jagdish N. Sheth, Joseph Sirgy, Mark Snyder, and Michael Solomon, among others.

Several consumer researchers have argued that two major appeals of products and services for consumers are utilitarian benefits and value-expressive benefits. (In using the word "consumer," they refer to what we call the user role of the customer.) These two values are analogous to our performance and socio-emotional user values, respectively. Consumer researchers have defined utilitarian appeals as those that stem from the functional features of the product or service (i.e., what physical job the product or service does). The value-expressive appeals are designed to create an image of the typical user of the product (i.e., what social or self-image the product's use will give its user). It draws on the concept of self-concept, personality, and lifestyle research.

Various consumer researchers have argued that customers seek products whose functional benefits match their functional needs. Likewise, customers seek those products whose social image fits with consumers' self-concept.

In one research study, a sample of consumers were given the names of several products and asked to write down the associations they made with these products. Their thoughts were coded by independent judges who did not know what products elicited particular responses. For such utilitarian products as air conditioners and aspirin, the associations were mostly related to the product's attributes and objective benefits; in contrast, for such expressive products as wedding rings and the American flag, the associations were image and emotion related. In a follow-up experiment, consumers were shown advertising appeals that centered on functional benefits or, alternatively, on image appeals, each for both types of products. As expected, consumers found image appeals more persuasive for image products and functional appeals for functional products. Furthermore, for such twin user-value products as watches and sunglasses, one type of appeal was more persuasive for one set of consumers and the other type for another set of consumers. Further analysis revealed that consumers who were high in self-monitoring (i.e., those who are conscious of the impressions they generate on others) found image appeals more persuasive, whereas those low in self-monitoring found functional appeals more persuasive. This shows that consumers who seek performance value in a product find performance benefits more appealing; in contrast, those who seek socio-emotional values look for products that promise these values.

Source: P.W. Miniard and J.B. Cohen, "Modeling Personal and Normative Influences on Behavior," *Journal of Advertising Research* 21 (1983), pp. 37–46; Banwari Mittal, Brian Ratchford, and Paul Prabhakar, "Functional and Expressive Attributes as Determinants of Brand Attitudes," *Research in Marketing* (JAI Press, 1989); J.S. Johar and Joseph M. Sirgy, "Value Expressive Versus Utilitarian Advertising Appeals: When and Why to Use Which Appeal" *Journal of Advertising* 20, no. 3 (September 1991), pp. 23–34; Morris Holbrook and Elizabeth Hirschman, "The Experiential Aspects of Consumption: Consumer Fantasies, Feelings, and Fun," *Journal of Consumer Research* 9 (September 1982), pp. 132–40; and Shavitt, 1990 (Ibid), and Sharon Shavitt and Tina M. Lawrey, . . . 1992, ACR.

However, virtually any product can be associated with social value. In the early stages of a product's introduction into the marketplace, mere possession of the product might designate social status. For example, when the television was first introduced, being among the first in a neighborhood to have a TV showed the prestige of that household. Later, the same social meaning was attributed to the possession of the color TV in its introductory phase.[9] As the product class (e.g., televisions) and the product form (e.g., color televisions) move along on the product life cycle, social value shifts form mere possession of the product to the possession of *specific* brands. Thus, today, in advanced, industrialized nations, the mere possession of an automobile has long ceased to offer any social value (since almost everyone possesses a car); what gives the user a social value is whether he or she is driving a Jaguar or a Range Rover or a Cadillac or a Plymouth Voyager, for example. In contrast, in low income, emerging economies such as Eastern Europe or Asia, the mere possession of a car is still a status symbol.

EMOTIONAL VALUE. Still other market choices are made primarily because of their potential to arouse and satisfy emotions (see the Window on Research box). **Emotional value** refers to the enjoyment and emotional satisfaction products and services offer their users. Many products and activities offer desired emotions. While such emotions are often positive and therefore enjoyable (e.g., feelings of attractiveness aroused by a special perfume or enhanced confidence from wearing attractive clothing), others are enjoyable even though they may generally be described as negative (e.g., fear aroused by viewing a horror movie or anger at reading about a villainous historical figure).

Most experiential consumption offers emotional value. **Experiential consumption** refers to the use of a product or service where the use itself offers value. The satisfaction and enjoyment accrues in the customer participation per se as the consumption process unfolds. It is the immediacy of the consumption event that offers value, not its delayed outcome. Examples of experiential consumption abound: watching a movie, eating a favorite dessert, savoring a glass of wine, a bubble bath, playing a sport, gardening, camping, fishing, or traveling to Disneyland or an exotic place like Paris, Amsterdam, China, or Singapore. In business-to-business settings, attending a convention can be, for some, an experiential consumption.[10]

IMPORTANCE OF USER VALUES

Users seek products that are want driven (such as jewelry, music, paintings, or antique collections) primarily for their social and/or emotional values, whereas they seek products that are need or physiology driven (such as medicine) primarily for their performance value. Of course, some products may acquire different values depending on the brand (or model) that a user chooses. For example, the value of a Chevrolet car may be limited to the universal value of providing transportation for a user, whereas a Porsche may provide both a universal value (transportation) and personal value by the status associated with driving such a car.

Clients of the Kripalu Center for Yoga and Health in Lenox, Massachusetts, visit the center to learn yoga and meditation and how to live healthy life-styles. They stay in dormlike rooms with bunk beds, or single or twin-size wooden platforms covered with simple linen and blankets and absolutely no wall furnishings. This spartan living does not come cheap—during the holiday season, a single bunk bed costs $90, or $250 for a room for the whole family. What customers seek and get are user values—peace of mind while at the center and some tools for living a peaceful life upon return to the everyday world. Some would call it performance value. Others could call it emotional/experiential value. In either case, it has an immense user value to those who find solace in such experience.[11]

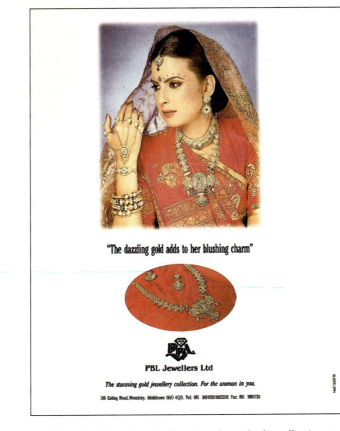

"The dazzling gold adds to her blushing charm"

PBL Jewellers Ltd

The stunning gold jewellery collection. For the woman in you.

186 Ealing Road, Wembley, Middlesex HA0 4QD. Tel: 081 9024282/9023218 Fax: 081 9001726

For Indian women, gold jewelry with intricate handiwork—and pounds of it—offers important social and emotional values. Not all can afford as much, but for those who can, this is a product where the payer role takes a back seat to the user role.

Market Values Sought by Payers

UNIVERSAL VALUE PRICE

For a payer, the universal value is **price value**—the fair prices and other financial costs incurred in acquiring the product (e.g., shipping, maintenance, etc.). When payers consider prices and costs, they of course also consider the payoffs they will receive. Thus, judgments about the *reasonableness* of price and costs are always made within the context of product benefits.[12] Nonetheless, affordability is a dominant criterion in judgments of reasonableness of prices charged. Marketers have to constantly work toward increasing the price value of their offering. This they do by improving the product benefits, reducing costs through productivity, or both. For example, J.C. Penney stores have begun offering better price value in the form of better clothing at lower prices. Stein Mart (a value-priced store in many U.S. cities) sells name brand merchandise at considerably lower prices than department stores and has as its advertising theme the tagline, "You could pay more, but you'll have to go somewhere else!" Similarly, Wal-Mart focuses on offering customers good economic value, with its "Always the Low Price" strategy. In supermarkets and drug stores, many private labels owe their customers' patronage to the excellent price value they offer.

Note that the cost of obtaining the benefits that a product gives is more than the purchase price; it includes the operational and maintenance costs. Interestingly, for example, the major cost of an air conditioning unit is not the purchase price, but rather the operating cost (i.e., the charges for electricity). So the marketer of an air conditioner or a refrigerator must use as his or her selling points the higher operating efficiency of the unit, and installation and maintenance cost advantages his or her unit may have. True price value consists in computing the life-cycle costs of owning and using a product.[13] Figure 3.3 shows the life-cycle costs of owning a car, for example.

PERSONAL VALUES: CREDIT AND FINANCING

Both credit and financing values consist in making it easy for the customer to pay for the good or service. Credit is an arrangement that allows the customer to delay the payment for the good or service. Financing is a credit arrangement with a greater degree of personalization, as explained below.

CREDIT VALUE. In their payer role, customers desire the freedom from having to exchange cash at the time of purchase or from becoming liable for immediate payment. They receive this value, called credit value, when the seller accepts a credit card issued by a third-party financial institution. Some sellers also issue their own credit cards (e.g., Sears credit card, Firestone credit card, or even a gas station credit card), and thus they offer credit value to customers who may not have been able to obtain bank-issued credit cards. In

Figure 3.3

LIFE-CYCLE COSTS OF OWNING A HONDA CIVIC EX FOUR-DOOR SEDAN

Purchase Price		
Car Item	Dealer Cost	List
Base Price	$14,535	$16,200

Ownership Costs	
Cost Area	5 Year Cost
Depreciation	$7,627
Financing ($342/month)	$2,867
Insurance	$7,973
State Fees	$669
Fuel (Hwy 35 City 29)	$2,838
Maintenance	$3,710
Repairs	$385

Warranty/Maintenance Info	
Major Tune-Up	$180
Minor Tune-Up	$78
Brake Service	$239
Overall Warranty	3 yr/36k
Drivetrain Warranty	3 yr/36k
Rust Warranty	5 yr/unlim. mi
Maintenance Warranty	N/A
Roadside Assistance	N/A

Cumulative Costs					
	1995	1996	1997	1998	1999
Annual	$6,760	$4,448	$4,394	$4,619	$5,848
Total	$6,760	$11,208	$15,602	$20,221	$26,069

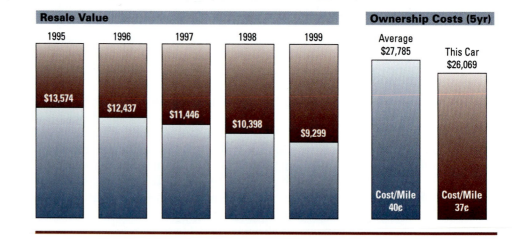

Resale Value

1995	1996	1997	1998	1999
$13,574	$12,437	$11,446	$10,398	$9,299

Ownership Costs (5yr)

Average $27,785 — Cost/Mile 40¢

This Car $26,069 — Cost/Mile 37¢

less-developed economies, or in developing countries where credit cards are available but not widely in use, merchants open credit accounts for their regular customers, maintaining the credit ledger themselves. In a rural town in Bangladesh, for example, a grocery store owned by a small businessman may have regular customers who are all known to the store-keeper personally, and who may be illiterate; consequently, there may be no paper receipts documenting the credit transactions. These customers depend on the store owner to tell them what their credit balance is. Thus, whether it is through the plastic credit cards so ubiquitous in the modernized countries, or through a handwritten ledger kept by a small grocer in a tiny village in Bangladesh, any freedom from immediate, on-the-spot delivery of money in exchange for the product or service granted by the seller to the customer consti-tutes credit value to the customer in his or her payer role. The purpose of credit value (as different from the financing value, discussed below) is not so much to offer long-term de-ferment of payment liability as to offer "convenience" to the payer in making the payment. Consider the American Express card offered both to individuals and to corporations (i.e., Corporate Purchase Card). The company requires payment of the entire outstanding amount upon receipt of the bill. Thus, the card offers (merely but importantly) the convenience of making payment only once for all of the purchases made during the preceding billing cycle.

To business customers, their supplier's credit policy is crucial. The usual credit terms are 30 days, net 2 percent (i.e., 30 days' deferred payment, 2 percent discount if paid in cash). Most businesses will forgo a 2 percent price value advantage to avail them-selves of the credit value. In some industries, customers are allowed a "float"—always carrying the credit equivalent to a given number of months' inventory. For example, in the diamond trade, the usual float is six months—if a customer's annual sale is $10 mil-lion, that customer is allowed to carry $5 million of outstanding dues.

FINANCING VALUE. Payers value affordability as well as convenience. Financing value consists of offering the terms of purchase that make the payment more affordable by distributing the liability over an extended period of time. It consists in offering an affordable graduated payment schedule (e.g., installment payment plan). Financing allows and often en-tails more "customized" payment schedules, designed with customer-specific requirements.

Marketers can add value to the economic/price dimension of a purchase by offering the customer financing options that are attractive (see the Window on Practice box). The

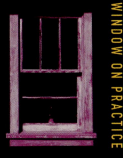

U.S. Air Force Seeks Payer Values

In late 1996, the U.S. Air Force made arrangements to buy four new Boeing 757s, to upgrade Air Force Two, the fleet that flies the U.S. Vice President, Cabinet Secretaries, and other Washington VIPs. Air Force One, the fleet that flies the U.S. President had been updated earlier, replacing the older Boeing 707s with Boeing 747s. The acquisition of the four 757s was to replace the aging 707s of Air Force Two. The purchase cost of these four 757s was $335 million. Guess what? The Air Force didn't think it could afford a straight out cash purchase. So it paid a cumulative total of $365 million—$30 million more than the cash purchase price; the deal was structured as a seven year lease with purchase op-tion. With defense budgets under close scrutiny from U.S. Congress, governmental defense agencies are increasingly seeking financing value in their buyer role, and leasing options such as the one for Air Force Two fleet upgrade offer the buyer that value.

Source: Stan Crock, "Your Rental Jet Is Ready, Mr. Gore," *Business Week*, December 23, 1996, p. 8.

WINDOW ON PRACTICE

financing value becomes more salient in those choice settings where the price of a product or cost of a service is relatively high. Chrysler Credit Corporation and GM Financing Corporations are now separate profit centers of these automakers, which are good sources of profit in their own right but which are also helping the car sales divisions sell more cars by offering the financing value. In recent years, leasing has become a very attractive option in automobiles, office equipment, and machinery. It lowers the entry price barriers, often requiring zero or a small amount in down payment. G.E. Capital, as the largest leasing company, provides this value to airline industries. Likewise, Lucent Technologies, a 1996 spin-off from AT&T, has won many business contracts on the basis of offering better financing value to its customers.

IMPORTANCE OF PAYER VALUES

Just as the performance values for the user are universal (every user seeks them at least in some minimum measure), so too, for the payer, the price value is more universal; if the product or service is not worth the price, then you would not even consider the purchase. If the price value seems reasonable, then you assess the feasibility of cash purchase. Those who can spare the cash need not seek credit and financing values. Credit is a personal value offered to a qualifying *group* of customers. Financing is a personal value more individualized in that it makes it easier for the payer to afford. Moreover, just as the individualized value for the user is emotional satisfactions, so too financing gives some payer customers the joy of being able to buy something otherwise beyond their immediate means.

Market Values Sought by Buyers

UNIVERSAL VALUE: SERVICE

For buyers, the universal value is **service value**, the assistance customers seek in purchasing a product or service. It has three elements:

1. Prepurchase advice and assistance.

2. Post-purchase advice and assistance in maintaining the product's use-worthiness.

3. Freedom from risk of a mispurchase by being able to refund or exchange the merchandise.

Pre- and post-purchase services and purchase assurance are benefits or values almost all customers in their buyer role would seek to some degree. Hence, the service value is a universal value for the buyer (see the Window on Practice box).

Buyers value prepurchase assistance because they seek product or service information. For example, they want to know the technical feature and performance information about various models of cellular phones, the purpose of caller ID service from the local phone company, the itinerary and activity schedule of a cruise trip, the availability of a vegetarian menu in a restaurant, or about the comparative features of various types of investment accounts. In business-to-business buying, they want clearly explained bids, or a well-documented request for proposals (RFPs), or technical data on two models of machine tools, or an executive proposal for a consultancy contract, or help in defining the specifications of equipment the purchaser firm needs. Product demonstration and service explanations, key aspects of a salesperson's job, are also included in prepurchase service.

Second, customers seek post-purchase advice and assistance in keeping the product use-worthy. Thus, when they receive delivery of a car, appliance, or (for business-to-business customers) a production machine, they look to the salesperson or customer service

Customers' Service Value Expectations Vary around the Globe

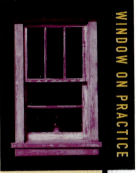

If you visit a large department store in Tokyo, you will be delighted at the behavior of store personnel. They are polite and courteous. As soon as they are face-to-face with you, they will bow. And then they will bow again when you leave the store. Perhaps more than one. And why not. This is not only their custom, but as a customer to Japanese salesmen, you are a king or a queen!

Now visit a store in Russia. At some of the stores that have not altered their ways from the days of the former Soviet Union, you will be surprised to notice that store personnel behave as if *they* are the king! And they were: in the days of the former Soviet Union, products were usually scarce, so merchants decided who got served!

Let us visit a fine dining restaurant at the Izmailova Hotel. There, the waiters are busy playing chess. Try attracting their attention for service, and one of them is likely to yell at you: "Can't you see we are one move away from checkmate?" You may have to wait as long as an hour to get a waiter to come to your table.

It is easy to see how residents of these divergent countries would differ vastly in the service value they would seek. A Russian customer is likely to seek primarily user values; not only is he or she unlikely to seek buyer values, but would in fact be oddly surprised to see the ser-vice levels he or she would encounter in the Western world. On the other hand, a Japanese customer would seek not only user values but buyer values as well. Indeed, the standards of service value that Japanese customers seek are known to be so high that many of them find even the service value offered by such countries as the United Kingdom wanting. A Japanese customer was visiting a department store in the U.K. when he saw two store sales assistants conversing in a distant corner while he waited a few minutes. He left without buying anything!

In fairness to Russian business, more and more Russian stores are now becoming market oriented. They have to, if they want to satisfy the desire for service value from an increasingly global customer.

Source: Adapted from: Valarie A. Zeithaml and Mary Jo Bitner, *Services Marketing* (New York: McGraw Hill, 1996), p. 414. Sources cited: "Japanese Put Tourism on a Higher Plane," *International Herald Tribune,* February 3, 1992, p. 8; Jack Kelley, "Service without a Smile, Russians Find a Friendly Face Works Better," *USA Today,* January 22, 1992, p. 1.

engineer to explain the maintenance procedures. Furthermore, customers seek prompt and reliable repairs and maintenance service so that the product is always use-worthy: for example, the car is always in working condition and a substitute car is available during repairs; the office copying machines are kept on an effective preventive maintenance schedule; if the cable service for households or a communication network for business customers breaks down, the cable company would send the repair person promptly upon notification, or better still, act proactively based upon electronic monitoring of the network.

Third, customers seek freedom from risk of a mispurchase. They seek this value in the form of being able to easily return the purchased merchandise for refund or exchange if they later come to realize that they made a wrong decision, or if the merchandise turns out to be defective after some use.

It may be noted that service needed specifically by the user during a product's use is a *user* value (e.g., technical advice on how to run software on a computer, or how to take the medication). Here, we are concerned instead with buyer values—that is, services that a person needs to keep a product use-worthy. When the two roles are played by the same person, it might appear that the user needs to keep the product use-worthy. More correctly, the user only wants the product to be usable; how to keep it available to the user is a buyer's concern.

PERSONAL VALUES: CONVENIENCE AND PERSONALIZATION

CONVENIENCE VALUE.   Acquiring a product or service requires time and effort. The effort includes the distance the customer has to travel to acquire the product, the hours of operation during which the customer may conduct the exchange transaction, the ease with which the customer can locate the merchandise, and the ease with which the customer can acquire title to (i.e., ownership of) the product or service and consummate the exchange. **Convenience value** refers to savings in the time and effort needed to acquire the product.

Certain retailers specialize in offering convenience value. Convenience stores feature easy-to-reach locations, parking spaces near the door, and limited selection to make shopping fast and easy. Home shopping networks, banking by computer, shopping on the Internet, or home delivery of products such as a pizza are examples of easy physical access. Stores that are open 24 hours, or catalog companies that take orders around the clock offer better convenience value than do those with limited operating hours. Customers also receive convenience value from stores with clear directions about merchandise location or in-aisle signs. These benefits appeal especially to "convenience shoppers." In a classic study of "shopper types," shoppers identified as convenience shoppers shop at stores that are conveniently located and are open for extended hours, especially for low ticket daily use staples.[14]

Besides convenient location and hours, customers seek other sources of convenience value. That is, once they have accessed the seller, customers want to conclude the transaction efficiently. They seek convenience value during the exchange transaction itself in

One-stop shopping is a great convenience value to many industrial customers.

that they want the acquisition of title on goods and consummation of exchange made easy. For example, they want short checkout lines, bar-coding of the merchandise so that it can be scanned quickly, ability of the seller (say, a car repair mechanic) to retrieve the customer's record quickly, and quick credit check procedures. If the transaction requires the purchaser to fill out forms, the task should be easy.

Note that convenience in buying is different from convenience in use. Many products have built-in convenience features, such as a redial button on a telephone. This is a value for the user and is properly included within the performance value. Here the reference is to convenience in product acquisition, a value relevant only to the buyer role.

For services, customers seek convenience value in the way the service is provided. For example, in the installation of a phone or cable service, there was a time when the local cable company could not tell customers when the repair person would show up for service installation, forcing them to stay home and wait the whole day. Now many cable and other utility companies have improved their operations so that they can give you a two-hour time window during which their repair person will show up. This has improved the convenience value for the buyer considerably. See the Window on Practice box for service and convenience values of one segment of the population—seniors.

Seniors Seek Service and Convenience Value

Imagine grandparents buying a toy as a surprise gift for their grandchild. They are at a store named Toys "R" Us, a warehouse store with the strategy of offering aggressive pricing with limited in-store service. In their role as payers, they love a bargain (i.e., price value), as all of us do. But buying a toy (at Toys "R" Us or anywhere else) can be a nightmare for grandparents. First, the physical access can be a big problem, with all those 10-foot-high shelf displays of Barbie dolls or monster trucks, and with in-store help hard to come by. Even when they eventually get someone to pull down the merchandise for inspection, there is no one to advise them (especially advise them without bias) about the suitability of a toy for a youngster. "For ages 8 and up" is too broad, and they want to know what colors and what toys are popular this year. Mortal Kombat II may be the most popular toy among kids (the users), but Grandma or Grandpa is unlikely to be aware of the toy's appeal, unless the in-store advisors take the time to educate these two-generations removed buyers about the value to the user the modern electronic and action figure toys offer. They want to know, too, if parental supervision is merely recommended, preferable, or absolutely necessary for a particular toy. This is the prepurchase assistance service value that grandparents seek in their customer role as buyers.

Banks face a similar challenge to serve this generation. Because of the aging population in advanced industrialized nations, there will be an unprecedented demand among older customers to transfer wealth to their baby-boomer sons and daughters. This represents a great opportunity for banks, but the kind of productivity-raising automation that banks are adopting does not sit well with senior citizens. They don't like to do business with faceless corporations. The reason is that in marketplace exchanges they seek positive interaction value along with other values. They look forward to interacting with salespersons, tellers, bankers, restaurant servers, and retail store clerks. Retired and isolated in suburban living, older customers look to errands as an opportunity for socializing. They even expect to run into other acquaintances in the store, at the post office, and at bank branches. Recognizing this need, Home Savings Bank trained tellers to be friendly. Furthermore, it offered coffee and doughnuts in its branches so older customers could hang out at the branch and use it as a meeting place.

Source: Paco Underhill, "Seniors in Stores," *American Demographics,* April 1996, pp. 44–48.

For business-to-business customers as well, convenience value plays a significant role. Business customers are increasingly seeking marketers who make it easy for them to do business with. Small businesses operating out-of-home seek and appreciate (as indeed do employees in corporations) office deliveries of such wide-ranging products as packed lunches, office supplies (Office Depot, a supplier of office supplies in the United States, offers this service), mail pick-up, delivery of car parts to repair mechanics, windshield replacement at customers' premises (both homes and offices), and so on.

Consider the convenience value you might seek in your role as a buyer. Suppose you want to buy a music CD by Nine Inch Nails, the Spice Girls, or any of your favorite artists. You will have to drag yourself to a music store, sift through a warehouse of CD collections to find the artist you want, wait in line for the cashier, bring it home, play it, and hope it is the one you like. And of course you must visit the store only during normal business hours. But what if you want to visit the store at midnight, when you have the sudden urge to acquire this new CD? What if you don't want to wait in line, and you want to listen to the CD before buying it? In that case, you want the convenience value of an Internet or telephone service. For example, with MCI Telecommunications, you dial in a toll-free number, make your selection, listen to it, order it, pay for it with your credit card, and have it delivered to your home the next day.

PERSONALIZATION VALUE.   Buyers also may want to be able to consummate the transaction in a personalized or individualized manner. This **personalization value** has two aspects: customization and interpersonal relation. **Customization** refers to receiving the product or service in a manner tailored to an individual customer's circumstance. Note that we speak here not of the *content* of the product or service being customized (for that would be a *user* value), but rather the manner in which it is transacted. If you want your pizza delivered between 7:00 and 7:30 P.M. on Mondays, and between 6:00 and 6:15 P.M. on Wednesdays, both days at your home address, and at 4:30 P.M. on Fridays at the office, and you want to place a one-time order for the entire month, you are seeking a customization of the delivery schedule. Such customization, while uncommon for household markets (largely because marketers have not offered it), is quite valued in business markets. A business customer who needs materials and parts for the production line may desire to receive them as close to the production schedule and as close to the production site as possible. Many customers now receive from suppliers the ordered parts directly (i.e., directly from the supplier to the individual production section or even an individual production worker without it first going to the customer's warehouse).

This aspect of personalization is quite distinct from the interpersonal aspect (discussed next). Many automated or technology based services could be delivered in a customized way without any interpersonal interaction. For example, your voice-mail messages could be delivered to you in any manner you like—on your E-mail, by fax, on the personal pager, and so on, without your ever talking to a live person.

The second aspect of personalization is the desire for the transaction to occur in an environment of pleasant interpersonal interaction. Customers seek this value in the form of positive experience in interacting with the sales or customer service employees. Two purchase transactions could be equally hassle-free in physical terms, yet one could be quite impersonal or, worse, negative, while another, very personal and socially rewarding. Basically, the attitudes and behaviors of employees interacting with the customer determine this value. Employees who are personable and friendly, who exhibit understanding and empathy, and who enjoy interacting with customers offer this value to the buyer.

Customers in their role as buyers do not always seek this market value. In many transactions, they come to expect fairly impersonal employee behavior. For example, we

"Welcome, Mr. Jonathan Lee." Such personalization appeals to many customers. The hotel shown here also provides the convenience of one-stop shopping—taking care of all your needs.

generally don't expect any rewarding social interactions from the cashier at the gas pump or the cable service installation person or the dry cleaner, although even in these transactions of limited interaction, a rude employee would become bothersome and constitute negative interaction value, discouraging the buyer from future patronage. But in many other purchase situations, we expect some positive interaction (e.g., if we are buying jewelry, if we are dining in a restaurant, or if we are banking at our regular bank). In department and specialty stores, we expect the salespersons to be friendly and empathetic. Detached salespersons, high-pressure selling tactics, a condescending manner, or even intimidation (e.g., a waiter reeling off exotic menu items rapidly) offer negative interaction value. Of course, these expectations would vary from culture to culture.

Some shoppers purposely seek positive interpersonal experience during shopping. In the classic study of shopper types referred to earlier, one category of shoppers was identified as the "personalizing shoppers." Thus, some shoppers sought mom and pop stores because they could socialize with the store owners. In many stores today, the salespersons are chosen to match the demographics of typical clientele. Thus, The Gap store (a U.S. store for clothing for young adolescents) has teenagers as sales employees, The Limited stores have young adults dressed in Limited clothing, Merry-Go-Round has offbeat dressers, while Gentry men's suit department has middle-aged persons in business suits. The hope is that by being similar to prospective target customers, the salespeople will be able to exhibit empathy and offer the positive interaction element of service value.

Personalization enables personal attention to the customer. Not only does this personal attention make the interaction more pleasant, but it also gives the salesperson an opportunity to customize the offering to some extent. For example, beyond the usual in-

Many busy customers seek high service value in the form of a personal shopper service for their wardrobe needs.

store sales assistance, some department stores offer what they call a *personal shopper*. A personal shopper acts as your wardrobe consultant, who over time comes to learn your preferences and tastes and advises you on your wardrobe needs for various business and social occasions. He or she also offers you convenience by allowing you to shop by phone. Likewise, a personal banker offers the customer personalization value. For business customers, or for a high-asset-value household customer, the personal banker would, for example, come to pick up your checks or do other transactions, and would also prepare account activity statements personalized to meet your specific needs.

Several service companies are offering more customized (i.e., personalized) customer services. For example, if you have an investment account with Merrill Lynch investment company, you can open a Cash Management Account (CMA). With this account, your account manager will automatically manage the portfolio—transferring funds as needed from cash/checking to investment accounts, or the reverse—to maximize your total returns from the assets. One customer we know was able to get his financial account manager to do all that is needed to transfer the specified funds to specified charities before the end of tax year 1996 (i.e., at a couple of weeks' notice). The account service manager took care of the entire business without further effort from the client—she got the forms from the specified charities, including their tax exemption number, filled them in, faxed the forms back, transferred the funds, and sent the tax-free donation certificates to the client, all well before the deadline! Thus, personalization is both a one-to-one relationship with the customer and an extreme form of service and convenience.

Both convenience and personalization go beyond the basic minimal pre- and post-purchase assistance that is universally required. Convenience is an additional value sought by customers, and the value of this benefit differs across customers according to the time pressure and desire to avoid effort and hassle. Goals of minimizing time and effort are personal (rather than universal) but not idiosyncratic. That is, segments of customers with certain time pressure and certain resources to enable reduced effort would value this goal. In comparison, personalization is totally idiosyncratic. It is aimed at pleasing a buyer's unique sense of the kind of seller attention he or she desires.

Products and Services as Value Bundles

A particular product or service usually offers customers more than one of the values we have identified. In other words, products and services deliver bundles of values to the various customer roles. This is true for each basic category of products and services, from consumer durables to business services.

Consumer Durable Goods

The automobile is a good example of values from consumer durable goods because all six values play a role. To begin with, two very common performance values people look for in an automobile are safety and reliability. Performance value also includes repair and maintenance service; and to satisfy a user's need in this area, the dealership needs to offer high-quality repair service (so that repeat visits for the same problem are not needed). Furthermore, because a car is a highly visible product, some consumers seek a car that has social value—that is, it makes a social statement about its owner, such as the socioeconomic and reference group associated with a particular model. For example, *Fortune* magazine has identified the Range Rover as the status symbol of the 1990s. This is a far cry from the status symbol that was identified in the 1980s, the Mercedes Benz.

The emotional value of a car is derived from a personality dimension, where one could say, "I feel as if the car fits me." Some even develop deep attachments with their cars, referring to their cars as "my Porsche," "my Miata," and so on.[15] For some, emotional satisfaction might accrue from buying a domestic car, if one has strong patriotic values. Indeed, some domestic car manufacturers and dealers are promoting their cars on the "buy American" sentiment. In Anchorage, Alaska, for example, one Chrysler–Plymouth dealer showed scenes of the Japanese attack on Pearl Harbor in newspaper advertisements. In Detroit, one Ford dealer used radio spots to offer American flags free to anyone who agrees with his feeling that buying imports puts Americans out of work.

The two values for the payer are (1) price and (2) credit and financing. The universal value of price incorporates both whether the car is worth its price, and whether the price is affordable. Parents as payers for a car might decline to buy their son or daughter a specific make or model of car, either because they can't afford it, or, even if they could afford it, because they might feel that the car is a luxury or is overpriced. Finally, the financing value would be defined in terms of availability of credit, lease arrangements, and so on. Leasing has become a popular option these days, largely because of the scarcity of both money and time (required to maintain a car one owns).

The universal value for a buyer is the service value. When the salesperson does not use high pressure tactics, it constitutes a service value for the buyer. Recognizing the importance of a hassle-free shopping experience, Saturn Corporation has adopted the policy *not* to negotiate the price of the car.

The convenience value for the car buyer accrues from the time and place flexibility, namely, the ease with which you can either buy the car or obtain the required service on it. You can, if you like, buy your car over the Internet. And some car dealerships will deliver the car to your home for a test drive. This action combines both convenience and personalization. In the case of Saturn, the hassle-free shopping experience has also made the interpersonal interaction very pleasant. To further augment the personalization element of the personal value, the Saturn dealership organizes a brief celebration just before the customer drives off with a new car.

Jewelry is another durable good in which customers seek most of the values. The principal reason for buying it is no doubt social and emotional—the satisfaction of receiving social acclaim and feeling good about oneself. Even so, performance value is important as well—that the item should not be fragile and should not show wear.

For payers, price value is important due to substantial financial investment and to be sure that the piece's quality is worth its price. Special deals (such as holiday sales) are therefore especially attractive for customers. Finally, also because the jewelry purchase entails substantial financial outlay, the availability of easy financing credit is a plus.

Customer service is an important value—buyers need credible advice about the quality and craftsmanship of the jewelry, patience (on the part of the seller) with their long deliberation process and desire to try many items before choosing one, and need for sizing or slight design adjustments. Customers also need to be able to return the merchandise for a refund or exchange if they change their mind. Moreover, although for the store the item may be only one of hundreds of exchanges on any given day, for the customer, it is often a once-in-a-blue-moon big purchase. Salespeople who are not only personable and friendly but who help a customer feel good about the purchase will help meet a buyer's needs.

Nondurable Goods

In the category of nondurable goods, food products offer many of the six values. Their performance value comes, of course, from the energy and nutrition they offer. The social value comes from social class associations some foods have acquired in a society. In America, for example, upper socio-economic status customers view meat and potatoes as a lower-class food, and asparagus and other uncommon vegetables, and imported cheese, and so on, as upper-class food items.[16] The emotional value stems from childhood associations of certain foods, and with the contingency of certain food usage occasions, such as the enjoyment of certain foods at holidays and other festivities. Children enjoy looking at the package while they eat their cereal, and in fact are likely to influence their parents' decision to buy it based on their recognition of a well known character on the box, like Tony the Tiger for Frosted Flakes. There are often negative social and/or emotional values associated with certain foods and beverages; for many years, prunes (even though they offered a performance value) were rejected by consumers because of their association with old age.

For the payer, price value is important for most families who must manage household food (and other) expenses on a fixed budget. Marketers of food products attempt to enhance the price value by offering coupons or private brands, whose use is growing. Credit and financing values are likely to be least relevant for food buyers except for those who are getting public assistance through government food stamps.

For the buyer, the convenience value is seen in home delivery of cooked food such as Domino's Pizza. As regards the service value, while it is less relevant in home-delivered pizza, clearly, in a restaurant it acquires significant importance in terms of advising on the ingredients and varieties offered. Moreover, in the dine-in restaurant, even the interpersonal behavior of the person taking the reservation and of the server could add to customer satisfaction or dissatisfaction.

Consumer Services

The six values are equally applicable to services (see the Window on Research box). Take an airline for example, where the performance value revolves around safety, reliability, physical accommodations, and on-time flight schedule. The social value comes from the class one flies in (namely, economy, first, or business class) and also from the interpersonal behavior of in-flight crew members. The emotional value of flying triggers feelings of fear or excitement for some. The price value is the cost of the ticket, and the credit and financing value is depicted in the use of credit to buy an airline ticket. Finally, the service and convenience values are the provisioning aspect, such as the ease of making reservations and buying tickets, say, with a credit card. The personalization value consists in whether the airline could customize such aspects of your travel as food and dietary restrictions. And the interpersonal element of personalization consists in whether or not the airline's ticket agents or travel agents at the travel agency are appropriately personable and friendly.

BUSINESS PRODUCTS

Customers of business products also seek various market values. Consider an office copying machine, for example. The performance value for the user consists in fast and good-quality copying and in various features such as two-sided copying or automatic collating. The social and emotional values are not very relevant to this particular product, although having the most advanced copying machine could be a source of some emotional satisfaction. But such business products as corporate jets are clearly as much a source of social and emotional value for the user as performance value. Both for jets and copying machines, the buyer seeks service value in the shape of pre- and post-purchase advice, and post-purchase maintenance and repair work. Convenience in doing business with the supplier is very relevant. And, at least for a corporate jet, the personalization value is

Values Customers Seek in Various Service Purchases

What market values do customers seek in various services they buy? Are these values equally important for different services? These questions were recently studied by two customer researchers, Banwari Mittal and Walfried Lassar. These researchers measured the extent to which various services offered three service attributes: reliability, responsiveness, and personalization (they also measured a fourth attribute, the appearance of equipment, physical facilities, etc., which is not relevant to our present purposes.) Of these, reliability was measured by such questions as "The firm performs the service right the first time"; as such it may be deemed to be equivalent of performance value in our framework. Responsiveness was measured by such questions as "Employees of this firm are always willing to help you"; as such responsiveness can be deemed to be equivalent to the prepurchase and during-purchase assistance component of the service value in our framework. Finally, personalization was measured by such questions as "Employees are friendly and pleasant," and "They take the time to know you personally." These can be deemed to represent the personalization element of the service value in our framework.

The researchers studied customer satisfaction for two services: health care and car repair. They argued that since how well the car was repaired could always be credited to or blamed on the car mechanic, whereas recovery from illness did not always depend on the quality of the doctor, reliability (i.e., performance value) should be specially influential in customer satisfaction for car repair compared to health-care services. In sharp contrast, personalization should have the opposite influence. Since there was not much opportunity for interpersonal interaction in car repair services, personalization should not play much role in customer satisfaction for car repair services. On the other hand, since there were opportunities for extended interaction with health-care personnel, how well customers received the personalization value (i.e., service value in our framework), should have as strong an influence in their satisfaction with the health-care service providers.

Their results supported the researchers' expectations. Personalization had a strong influence in satisfying health-care customers, whereas it played no role in car repair services. For car repair services, the performance value (reliability) was most influential in satisfying the customers.

Source: Banwari Mittal and Walfried Lassar, "The Role of Personalization in Service Encounters," *Journal of Retailing* 72, no. 1, (1996), pp. 95–109.

---

important. Since businesses always try to save costs, price value is very important. Finally, due to high costs of business products, customers always seek finance and credit values.

BUSINESS SERVICES

An example of a business service is executive MBA (EMBA) programs. Many *Fortune 500* companies are now actively involved in keeping their employees updated on the latest technologies and management concepts in their industry. Here, the performance value translates into knowledgeable professors who possess relevant expertise in the topic area. The social value may come from the image of the professor and the status of the degree-granting institution. The emotional value would consist in the employee's career tracking, how one feels about his or her self-respect and self-image. The cost of getting this education bears on its price value, with financing an equally critical issue, since the price of an executive MBA degree may cost as much as $40,000 at some universities. Lastly, the service and convenience values come from the ease with which you can register for courses.

Characteristics of Customer Values

There are several characteristics of customer values. As summarized in Figure 3.4, values are instrumental, dynamic, and hierarchical. As we move up the hierarchy of values, they become increasingly diverse. In addition, customer values are synergistic and role specific, and they vary among customers.

Values Are Instrumental

Instrumentality of market values refers to products and services being instrumental to fulfilling needs or wants of customers. Being *instrumental* means they are a means to an end. Thus, it is important for marketers not only to create values in their offerings but also to *link* or associate these offerings to specific customer needs and wants.

A person will perceive a product, object, or idea to be useful only if the person can establish its instrumentality in achieving his or her goals. No matter how good the product or idea, if its value instrumentality is not apparent, customers will not accept it. If recreation is not a particular customer's goal, then watching sports has no value for this customer. If you are thirsty, then water or other drinks have value instrumentality, not a music CD.

If you open any business magazine such as *Business Week* or *Fortune,* or even a consumer magazine like *Newsweek* or *Time,* you can find an advertisement for one month's free trial of Prodigy, Compuserve, or America Online—interactive information services on your computer. Yet only some people take advantage of the free offer. Others do not respond to such free offers simply because they do not see how the free service meets any of their needs or wants; that is, they do not see any instrumentality in the free offer.

Accordingly, marketers are in the business of managing people's perceptions of the benefits of their product and service offerings; these offerings, via their benefits, must be linked with customers' perception of their needs and wants. To be successful, a marketer must both create value and connect it to customers by proper communication and positioning.

CHARACTERISTICS OF CUSTOMER VALUES

Customer values are:

Instrumental

Dynamic

Hierarchical

Increasingly diverse at higher levels

Synergistic

Role specific

Variable across customers

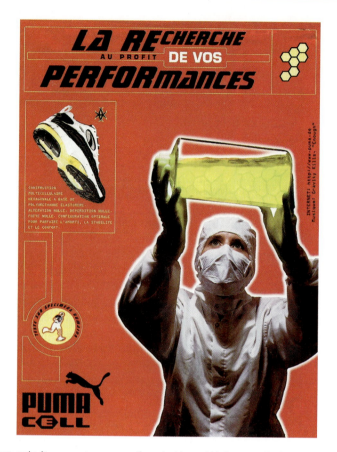

An athletic shoe must assist its wearer to move easily and withstand high-energy, high-impact foot movement. This ad tells users that such performance value is delivered by Puma's scientifically formulated cell design.

Values Are Dynamic

Market values that customers seek change over time. First, they change because individual customers' needs and wants change due to alteration in their life stage and resources. Second, they change because of rising expectations of the entire market. As marketers meet or exceed market expectations, those expectations become the new baseline against which the marketers will be judged. If no one in the market offers a first-class service, then customers will be contented with a merely adequate service, for instance. But if a few marketers offer higher levels of service, then the customer comes to expect that level from all marketers. The more the marketer satisfies customer values, the higher the customer's value expectations become.

Consider an example from a third world country. In India, on some days the electricity fails every four to five hours, but because people expect it, there is no negative response. However, if a similar power outage occurred in the United States, where expectations are different, there would be great dissatisfaction and anger. Likewise, when you lift the handset of your telephone, you expect to hear a dial tone. The expectation in the United States is that telephone service will be uninterrupted, unlike the expectations of customers in lesser-developed nations, where it is not unusual not to have a dial tone at times.

In business, as well, network reliability of services is expected to be nearly 100 percent since many market suppliers have indeed met this level. American businesspeople expect punctuality from the salespeople who call on them; in contrast, punctuality is an exception in the third world countries such as India. Accordingly, Asian Indian businesspeople (and even more so, public officials in these countries) seldom seek punctuality/performance value from their suppliers.

Values Are Hierarchical

Values are arranged in a hierarchy, with the universal values at the foundation (see Figure 3.5). These are the market values a product or service must offer first and foremost. If the universal values are absent, the customer would not even care if the product or service provided personal values. However, once universal values are met, personal values become relevant. Customers look for personal values—first group-specific, then individual-specific.

This hierarchy of values is similar to classifications of needs, such as Maslow's needs hierarchy (which ranks needs from physiological to safety, social status, self-esteem, and self-actualization) and Katona's classification of needs (survival → comfort → convenience → spiritual). Need hierarchies will be described in more detail in Chapter 8.

Diversity of Customer Values Increases with the Hierarchy

A market for any product or service category will be more homogenous if it is dictated primarily by universal values and more diverse if it is dictated by the personal values. Since most commodities (such as grain, steel, coal, electricity, computer timesharing, etc.) serve only universal values, there is homogeneity among various suppliers' products and services. Likewise most necessities (e.g., medicines, vitamins, salt and pepper, shoe polish, detergents, appliances, etc.) have limited potential for diversity among market offerings. Of course, even for products and services sought primarily for performance value, feature variations do exist because of customers' differentiation of needs (e.g., shampoo varieties for dry, oily, thin, thick, damaged, or sensitive hair). Yet this variety is much greater for products and services sought for personal (e.g., socio-emotional) values. For example, washing machines have fewer varieties than television sets or cars.

The same holds in business markets. In buying raw materials and components, customers mainly seek universal values; in contrast, from personal office furnishings, customers seek socio-emotional values as well. That is why customers want to simplify the number of alternatives for raw materials and components while they want a great number of alternatives for office decoration.

THE HIERARCHICAL ORDER OF VALUES

Figure 3.5

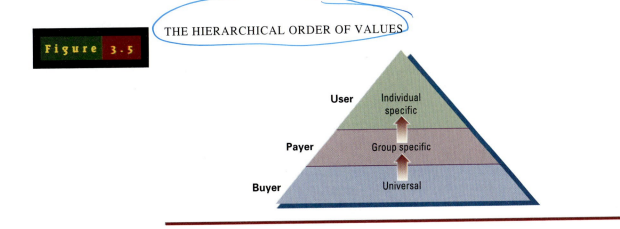

When marketers make too many brands or alternatives available for universal-value products, product proliferation and consumer confusion result. While product variety may offer better performance value to the user role of the customer, it detracts from the convenience and service values for the buyer role. Realizing such buyer confusion, some marketers have recently acted to cut down on the number of alternatives they offer. For example, Procter & Gamble cut the Head and Shoulders shampoo line in half; likewise, Max Factor in Japan reduced its cosmetics from over 1,300 in mid-1995 to about 800 by March 1996.[17] In your own experience, if you stood in a supermarket aisle, you would be facing a confusing array of brands—far more than you would prefer to see. In contrast, consider the diversity of market offerings for products driven by personal (socio-emotional) values—whoever has complained about the variety of clothing stores proliferating the urban malls or Beverly Hills Rodeo drive?

Values Are Synergistic

Value synergy means that one value enhances the utility of another value. That is, performance value, price value, and service values (the three universal values) are highest when there is no trade-off among them. Likewise, the social or emotional value, convenience or personalization value, and credit and financing values work best without a trade-off among them:

* Best Universal Value = (Performance) × (price) × (service value); and
* Best Personal Value = (Social and emotional) × (convenience and personalization) × (credit and financing).

In other words, the relationship among universal values (and likewise among personal values) is multiplicative instead of additive. Similarly, when the relationship between the personal values is multiplicative instead of additive, the marketer is able to create the best personal value. The idea is to create a synergistic relationship among the values. For example, performance should not be traded off at the expense of cost. The best strategy for the marketer is to keep costs low and to increase the performance. Therefore, a marketer must utilize resources in a way that creates synergy.

Even though economic value is most vividly embodied in the Filene's Basement Sale event described at the beginning of this chapter, the event offers performance value as well. The gowns are not only bargain priced, but they also have high quality in materials and styling. If they did not offer any value to users, there would be no reason to buy them, no matter how appealing they were to the payer. After all, nobody spends $249 just because it is less than $1,000 or $500 or $349 or even $250. They spend $249 because that expenditure buys them some user value. Also, taking advantage of the sale is very inconvenient; but with user and payer values like these, the buyer value takes a back seat. Or, more accurately, only those customers show up for the sale for whom the buyer value of service and convenience take a backseat to the user and payer values.

Values Are Role-Specific

The role-specific nature of values means they differ among the user, payer, and buyer, as Figure 3.2 shows. Because of role specificity, customers may change priorities among diverse values when they change their roles. For example, employees who are paying out of their own pockets may choose differently than when the company pays for travel and restaurants. Similarly, when children have to pay for the purchase of a product themselves, they choose differently than when someone else pays for them. In fact, children become as cautious and rational as are adults when they have to pay for a product with their own money. For example, at the age of 11 or 12, children become very suspicious of advertisers. This change in their attitude toward advertising takes place at a time when they start to pay for products themselves. Similarly, as users, young adults may be embarrassed to let their friends know that they use or wear products purchased at Kmart or Sears. However, when they become parents and have a household to run, they start to shop at these same stores in an effort to maximize their household savings.

Values Vary Across Customers

As we have already stated, what is valuable in a product or service to one customer may not be valuable to another. Consequently, a product or service is more versatile if it is capable of generating multiple values to satisfy different customers. For example, personal computers have a high degree of versatility because they must satisfy different needs: word processing, storage of information, communication with the outside world via E-mail, and bringing information from the outside world via the Internet, and so on. However, because a computer is so versatile, it is important for the marketer to understand how to target different benefits (or values) it offers to different customer segments.

Polaroid's instant-camera technology offers instant gratification through immediate development of pictures. This value was adapted to the business market by providing industrial users the ability to monitor many aspects of the production process. Applications of this technology include observation of the fatigue in metals for engineers; the ability to take pictures of homes in the appraisal business; and, for architects doing remodeling work on homes, the ability to take pictures to use in developing blueprints.

Nylon has multiple uses in both the consumer and business markets. During World War II, when there was a shortage of silk, nylon served as a substitute for silk stockings, as it had the feel of silk. The government took over the production of nylon during the war and used it to make military parachute chords. After the war was over, nylon was used to make draperies and curtains, wall-to-wall carpeting, astroturf in stadiums, and even replacement valves for human organs. In fact, nylon has even been used for artificial ski slopes. This product has a degree of versatility that allows it to be of value in various applications.

Measurement of Market Values

Some products provide a bigger bundle of values than others, and customers will prefer the products whose values best satisfy their wants and needs. For a firm to assess how well it satisfies customer needs and wants, it needs to measure customer perceptions of the values its products and services offer. One way to measure these customer perceptions is to ask a representative sample of customers whether specific choices possess any of the specified values. Here, customer choice refers to three levels of customer decisions:

1. Whether to buy a product or service category (e.g., whether to buy a computer).

2. Which brand or make to buy (e.g., should one buy IBM, Apple, Compaq, Dell, or some other make?)

3. From which supplier to buy it (e.g., from Computerland, Circuit City, mail order, or any other).

The values can be assessed at any of the three levels.

The first step in generating a measurement scale is to specify the "content" of various values. This is best done by questioning a sample of customers (buyers, users, and payers), such as in a focus group setting. The questioning would pertain to each of the values customers take into account while evaluating a set of choice alternatives. Some examples of the questions to be asked in the focus groups would be:

1. When people decide whether or not to buy a ――― (product name), what needs and wants are they expecting to satisfy?

2. When customers such as yourselves are deciding which brand of ――― to buy, what social associations (which brands of ――― would have) would they generally consider?

3. Sometimes people expect certain emotional satisfactions from their use of ――― (product name); what might be the various emotions people might look to experiencing in their selection and use of this product?

Note that these are merely examples, and such questions need to be framed for each of the values discussed in this chapter.

The next stage would be to elicit from customers a rating of a given brand or supplier (i.e., an alternative) on the "value items" generated in the focus groups. Suppose focus groups generate five social associations from the ownership of a car; then we would list these five associations and ask customers (users, in this case) to check which associations apply for a given brand. For example, people who buy a *Saab* are: (1) successful, (2) financially prudent, (3) mature, (4) youthful, and (5) outdoorsy. Similarly, one could list various emotions (the list generated from the focus groups) and ask which emotions are likely to be experienced by the user of a particular brand. For example, when you own and drive a *Saab,* you are likely to feel: (1) overjoyed, (2) confident, (3) embarrassed, and so on. In the same manner, we could measure performance value by asking the user to score *Saab* on (1) gas mileage efficiency, (2) "will not break down," (3) road handling, and so on (the list of performance features based on focus groups).

Likewise, for the payer, the economic/price value can be measured by such items as: (1) this brand or store offers good value for the money; (2) this brand at this price is a good bargain; (3) this brand is priced too high (reverse scored); and so on. The credit/financing value can be measured by having payers rate the accuracy of statements such as (1) the company or store offers good credit terms; (2) the installment payment system for this brand/store makes it possible for me to afford this item.

Finally, for the buyer, the service value can be measured by such aspects as: (1) this company (company or store name) makes it easy for me to do business with it; (2) I do not get the necessary assistance for purchasing the product at this store or from this firm (reverse scored); (3) it is a big hassle to deal with this firm (reverse scored). The convenience value can be measured as: It is convenient for me to shop at ――― (store name). The personalization value can be measured by rating statements such as (1) the employees at this store or firm are very polite and friendly; (2) I enjoy talking to sales clerks at this firm or store; (3) employees at this firm or store make shopping a pleasure for me.

These examples are only an introductory outline, but they demonstrate that the various values discussed in this chapter need to be measured, and how these measures can be obtained from customers. Table 3.1 shows illustrative measures of user values for riding mass transit as an alternative to driving.

To fully understand its markets, a firm would need to assess these values for its own brands as well as for competitors' brands. Moreover, these assessments need to be obtained from its own customers as well as from the customers of the competing brands.

Table 3.1

MEASURING USER VALUES FOR MASS TRANSIT

1. Measuring Performance Value
Which of the benefits and problems are associated with the use of mass transit?
Using mass transit . . .
a. provides reliable transportation.
b. gets me where I want to go.
c. saves energy.
d. takes too much time.
e. eliminates parking problem.
f. is unsafe
g. is safer than driving.
h. deprives me of my privacy.

2. Measuring Social Value
Which of the following groups are most and least likely to use mass transit?
a. College students
b. Senior citizens
c. Office workers
d. Poor people
e. Professionals

3. Measuring Emotional Value
Which of the following feelings would you personally experience with your decision to use or not use mass transit?
a. I feel relaxed when I use mass transit.
b. I feel bored when I use mass transit.
c. I feel socially responsible when I use mass transit.
d. I feel nervous when I drive rather than use mass transit.
e. I feel impatient when I use mass transit.
f. I feel independent when I drive rather than use mass transit .

Source: Jagdish N. Sheth, Bruce Newman, and Barbara Gross, *Consumption Value and Market Choices: Theory and Applications* (Cincinnati: South-Western Publishing Co., 1991), pp. 90–91.

Figure 3.6

Marketers need to assess customer perceived positioning of their own brands vis-á-vis competitor offerings on customer value grids.

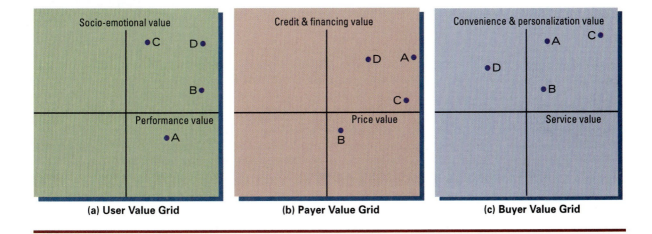

(a) User Value Grid   (b) Payer Value Grid   (c) Buyer Value Grid

These consumer data would then enable a firm to map its position on a value grid against its competitors (see Figure 3.6). Such grids help identify which customer values the firm satisfies better and which it satisfies worse than its competitors. This, in turn, suggests which values need to be improved.

Summary

In this chapter we defined values as the potential of a product or service to satisfy customers' needs and wants. Two broad clusters of value were named: universal values and personal values. Each cluster has three values, one each for the three roles of the customer. The three universal values are performance value for the user, price value for the payer, and service value for the buyer. Analogously, the three personal values are social and emotional for the user, credit and financing for the payer, and convenience and personalization for the buyer. Consumer and business products and services offer a bundle of values in some or all of these categories.

We then identified and described important characteristics of values. Values are instrumental, dynamic, and hierarchical; they work synergistically, they are role specific, they vary across customers, and their diversity increases with the hierarchy.

Finally, we introduced the methods of measuring these values from the customer's viewpoint. This measurement would enable a firm to identify which values the firm needs to make improvements on.

Key Terms

Marketing Myopia 58
Market Values 58
Universal Values 60
Personal Values 60
Performance Value 61
Social Value 63
Emotional Value 66

Experiential Consumption 66
Price Value 67
Credit Value 68
Financing Value 69
Service Value 70
Convenience Value 72

Personalization Value 74
Customization 74
Instrumentality of Market
  Values 81
Value Synergy 84

Review Questions

1. What is marketing myopia? Why is it important for companies to guard against becoming myopic in their business outlook?

2. From your personal experience, illustrate each of the six values you yourself as a customer or your business customers have sought in various marketplace transactions within the past one year.

3. Several characteristics of values were described in the chapter. Assess these characteristics by using the same examples of values as in the preceding questions. That is, to what extent do the characteristics hold true for the specific values you have described. To structure your answer, you may prepare a matrix of characteristics versus value examples, and write your assessment in the cells.

4. Why is it important to measure values? If you were to measure them for customers in three countries, say, the United States, the former Soviet Union, and an Asian country like India or Malaysia, would you find any differences? Please explain your answer.

5. In the busy times most consumers today face, two elements of doing business have become extremely important in ensuring customer satisfaction and loyalty: customer convenience and customer service. Assume you are a consultant responsible for helping department stores reorganize their sales staff to maximize convenience and service value for their customers across all the departments. Traditionally, department store salespeople assumed that to increase customer convenience, they had to reduce customer service and practice more of a "hands-off" policy on the sales floor. You know that this logic is flawed. What will you tell the department store managers and how will you show them that convenience and service are not trade-offs, but complementary attributes?

6. Think about three recent purchases you have made. What values were important in your decision making? Were you satisfied with your decisions?

Applications

1. You are a product manager responsible for developing a new line of toys for babies between the ages of 6 and 12 months. Your goals for this new line are that (a) it be radically different from what is already out there, and (b) the toys be appealing both from "play value" and learning perspectives. Of course, usual concerns for the products' safety, durability, and reliability hold. As you bring together your team of designers, salespeople, engineers, and accounting people to begin development of your new line, two important questions come to mind: (1) Who will your customer be? and (2) What customer values will you attempt to satisfy? Prepare a brief for the team on these two questions.

2. As a customer, you have no doubt encountered many instances when a particular product or service has either (1) exceeded your expectations in terms of satisfying your needs or (2) has been less that satisfactory, and may even have been completely unsatisfying. Describe one example of a product or service that has exceeded your expectations and an example of one that has delivered less value than you expected. In describing your experiences, clearly indicate the customer values that were either met or unmet.

3. Describe the process of measuring values. Design a questionnaire for measuring all customer values for the following products:

   a. Washing machine for household use.

   b. Long-distance phone service in household markets.

   c. Employees recruitment and outsourcing services for business customers.

   d. Baby-sitting services in hotels for guests from diverse foreign countries where parents' child-rearing goals differ vastly.

4. As the number of advertisements that consumers see every day continues to increase at an exponential rate, marketers are becoming more and more concerned that their messages are drowning in a sea of advertising. Therefore, it is becoming increasingly important that companies use images and messages that are eye-catching and that have the power to capture their audience's attention. At the same time, it is a well-known fact that providing information about a product or service's basic performance or functionality is one of the best ways to attract customers. As an advisor to the advertising industry, what advice would you give regarding the power of highlighting the performance value of a good through advertising versus highlighting any other universal or personal value such as its emotional or social value? Do you believe that by stressing performance value, advertisers can "cut through" the advertising clutter? Why or why not?

Practical Experiences

1. Maytag is recognized as the highest quality brand in washers and dryers by 40 percent of the consumers, yet its market share is only 10 percent (based on a 1996 survey). Visit washer and dryer appliance stores in your city, and collect whatever information you need to make sense of why its brand share remains low compared to its quality reputation. Frame your answer using the values framework discussed in this chapter.

2. This chapter discusses the concept of marketing myopia. Call four companies or access their Web pages: one that manufactures consumer products, one that manufactures business products, one that is a service (consumer or business), and one international company; obtain information (e.g., annual report or press release) or talk to someone in the company who can tell you what line of business the company is in and what the main mission of the company is. Based on this information, discuss whether these companies have a clear view of themselves. Why or why not?

3. Find three friends or classmates to interview. Ask each of them about their recent purchases of the following items:

   a. Jeans or slacks

   b. Athletic shoes

   c. Jewelry or watch

   Ask them what value(s) they were most concerned with as they chose from different brands and whether they made trade-offs between values in their decision making.

4. As the director of marketing of a major international hotel chain, you are faced with increasing competition in your home country (the U.K.) as well as in other countries in which you are currently doing business and in those that you wish to enter. Your main concern is that customers be fully satisfied with the diverse customer values they seek from your offerings. Design a hotel management manual (which will also serve as a basis for all staff training) that would enhance your value-delivery potential to diverse groups of guests.

Notes

1 Source: "Bridal Wave Sweeps Store," *Chicago Tribune,* November 8, 1994. Patrick Collins, "Charge of the White Brigade," *Sunday Standard Times,* January 15, 1995, Vol 87, no. 4, E1-E2, New Bedford, Massachusetts. Susan Davis, "No Blushing Brides in Filene's Frenzied Mob," *Westwood Suburban World,* May 25, 1995, n.p.

2 Theodore Levitt, *Marketing Imagination* (The Free Press, 1985).

3 Vast consumer research literature exists on the role of situation in consumer behavior. For example, see Russell W. Belk, "Situational Variables and Consumer Behavior," *Journal of Consumer Research* 2 (December 1975), pp. 157–64; Richard J. Lutz, "On Getting Situated: The Role of Situational Factors in Consumer Research," *Advances in Consumer Research* 7 (1980);

Joseph A. Cote and John K. Wong, "The Effect of Time and Situational Variables on Intention-Behavior Consistency," *Advances in Consumer Research* 11 (1984), pp. 374–75. U.N. Umesh and Joseph A. Cote, "Influence of Situational Variables on Brand Choice Models," *Journal of Business Research* 16 (March 1988), pp. 91–100.

4 Milton Rokeach, *Understanding Human Values: Individual and Societal* (New York: Free Press, 1979).

5 Jagdish N. Sheth, Bruce I. Newman, and Barbara L. Gross, *Consumption Values and Market Choices: Theory and Application* (Cincinnati: Southwestern Publishers, 1991), pp. 7–10.

6 For further discussion, John A. Howard, and Jagdish N. Sheth, *A Theory of Buyer Behavior,* (New York: Wiley & Sons, 1969);

Jagdish N. Sheth, David M. Gardner, and Dennis E. Garrett, *Marketing Theory: Evolution and Evaluation* (Canada: John Wiley & Sons, 1988).

7 See Roger S. Mason, *Conspicuous Consumption: A Study of Exceptional Consumer Behavior* (New York: St. Martin's Press, 1981).

8 Amy Stevens, "Does Monsieur Have a Reservation? Let Me See . . . ," *The Wall Street Journal,* December 6, 1996, pp. B1, B10.

9 See Michael R. Solomon, "The Role of Products as Social Stimuli: A Symbolic Interactionism Perspective," *Journal of Consumer Research* 10 (December 1983), pp. 319–29; and Sidney J. Levy, "Symbols for Sale," *Harvard Business Review* 37 (July–August 1959), pp. 117–124.

10 See Morris B. Holbrook and Elizabeth C. Hirschman, "The Experiential Aspects of Consumption: Consumer Fantasies, Feelings, and Fun," *Journal of Consumer Research* 9 (September 1982), pp. 132–40; Elizabeth C. Hirschman and Morris B. Holbrook, "Hedonic Consumption: Emerging Concepts, Methods, and Propositions," *Journal of Marketing* 46 (Summer 1982), pp. 92–101; Peter Weinberg and Wolfgang Gottwald, "Impulsive Consumer Buying as a Result of Emotions," *Journal of Business Research* 10 (March, 1982), pp. 43–57.

11 Lisa Miller and Daniel Reed, "Silent Nights," *The Wall Street Journal,* December 6, 1996, p. B10.

12 See Valarie A. Zeithaml, "Consumer Perceptions of Price, Quality, and Value: A Means-End Model and Synthesis of Evidence," *Journal of Marketing* 52 (July 1988), pp. 2–22.

13 See Milind M. Lele and Jagdish N. Sheth, *The Customer Is Key* (John Wiley, 1991).

14 Edward M. Tauber, "Why Do People Shop," *Journal of Marketing* 36 (October 1972) pp. 46–59; also see Lew G. Brown, "The Strategic and Tactical Implications of Convenience in Consumer Product Marketing," *The Journal of Consumer Marketing* 6 (Summer 1989) pp. 13–20.

15 Peter H. Bloch, "Involvement beyond the purchase process," in A. A. Mitchell, ed. *Advances in Consumer Research,* Vol. IX, pp. 413–417; and Russell W. Belk, "Possessions and the Extended Self," *Journal of Consumer Research,* September, 1988, pp. 139–168.

16 Sydney J. Levy, "Interpreting Consumer Mythology: A Structural Approach to Consumer Behavior," *Journal of Marketing* 45, no. 3 (Summer 1981), pp. 49–61.

17 Zachary Schiller, "Make It Simple," *Business Week,* September 9, 1996, pp. 96–104.

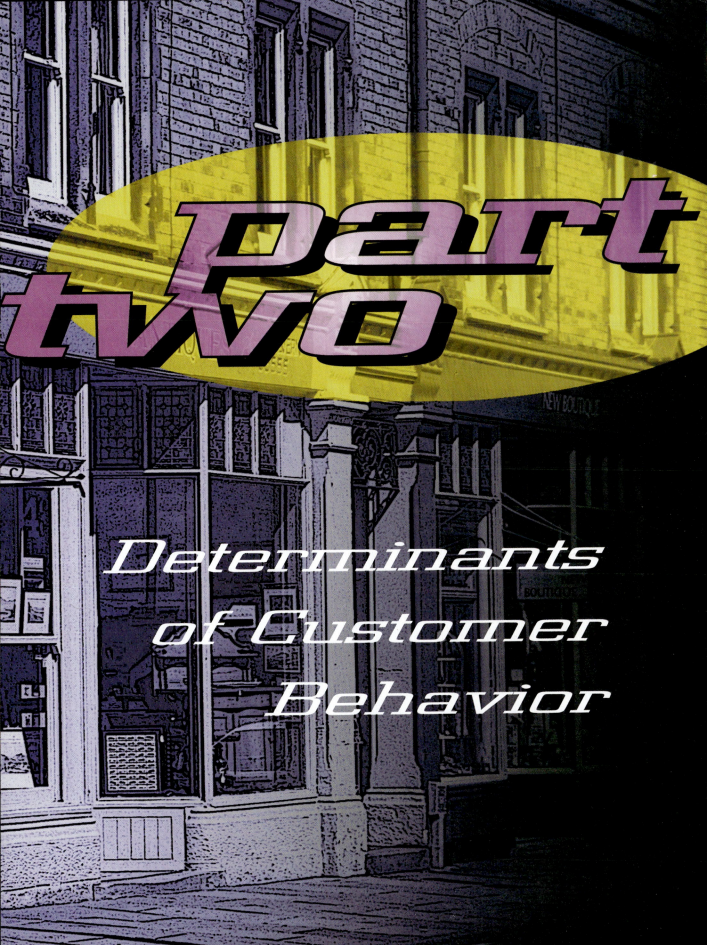

part two

Determinants of Customer Behavior

CHAPTER 4

*After reading this chapter
you should be able to:*

*List the elements of the
geophysical environment
surrounding the market*

*Describe how these elements vary
on various locations of the earth.*

*Explain how they influence customer
needs both for the household and
for business customers.*

*Discuss how marketers are
affected by annual climate changes.*

*Summarize how marketers are
adopting "regional marketing"
as a strategy based on customer
differences by geographical variations.*

*Explain how a concern for the
environment is influencing customer
choices, and how savvy businesses
are responding to customers'
environmental concerns.*

Market Characteristics: Climate, Topography, and Ecology

A Tale of Two Merchants: The Ice Cream Maker Sobs While the Coffee Brewer Sings

It was a particularly cold day in January 1997 in much of Europe. For two weeks, snow had blanketed much of France, England, Germany, Switzerland, and Belgium. Temperatures as low as 5°F had increased the demand for heating oil, but in Belgium all the canal routes had been frozen and the barges could not distribute oil. Across Europe, the lakes, rivers, and canals were all frozen and closed to traffic. The schools had also been closed. And the metro buses were running five hours late. The ice cream parlor on a busy street in Brussels that is usually buzzing with the constant chatter of customers was totally deserted. Not a soul there—save the lone parlor owner.

The real estate brokerage firm next door was doing no better. Across the street, it too was calm and quiet at the car dealership. Fortunately, not every business was down. The car towing company was doing brisk business. The phones at the plumbers were ringing off the hook. At the fast-food chains, at gas stops, and in small pubs, there were fewer customers, but those who did venture out were buying more food, more hot chocolate, and more bar drinks!

Across the border from Paris, the ski resorts in Switzerland were doing better than ever. Not only had the snow started the influx of skiers early, but a weak Swiss franc was a substantial draw for skiers from countries with stronger currencies. Here the combined magic of weather and economy was working to stimulate customer behavior for the ski towns. And the coffee shop at the ski resort was a stark contrast to the deserted ice cream shop in Brussels—its cash register had rung nonstop.

Back at the ice cream parlor, Maria van Waterschoot, who inherited the store from her father, hadn't given up hope. She knew that the summer would eventually come. And then it would be her turn to sing again![1]

Introduction

Imagine, if you will, that you are Maria van Waterschoot, the ice cream parlor owner in Brussels during that bitterly cold winter week. Right now, you appreciate all too well the impact of market characteristics such as climate on customer behavior! You understand how weather affects customer demand for a range of products, shifting it away from products incompatible with the day's weather in favor of products more suited to shelter from or enjoyment of that weather. But climate-induced shifts in customer behavior are not limited to the "see-saw" between ice cream and hot coffee. They affect customers' needs and wants in all areas of life—in food habits, in clothing tastes, in leisure choices, to name a few. And these influences are not merely weather related, but are related more broadly to customers' habitat, including the climate, topography, and ecology—that is, the *nature*-created environment of the place where people are born and live.

A marketplace, first and foremost, is a physical place. Customers live in a physical place. Products and services are produced, transported, stored, and used in physical space. In turn, these products and services also affect physical qualities of the place where they are produced and used. The physical characteristics of the marketplace—where customers live, purchase, and use products and services—are the focus of this chapter. We will consider the man-made market environment in the next chapter.

We begin by distinguishing the two facets of the market environment—natural (the market characteristics) and man-made (the market context). Then we identify the market characteristics of climate, topography, and ecology, describing examples of each. We then discuss ways that market characteristics affect the three customer roles. We conclude the chapter by exploring ways marketers interpret and respond to market characteristics by studying regional preferences and developing regional marketing strategies.

Market Environment

We divide market environment into two broad classes: market characteristics and market context (see Figure 4.1). **Market characteristics** refer to the physical characteristics of the surroundings in which customers select, use, and pay for products and services in both household and business markets. There are three physical characteristics of a place: climate, topography, and ecology.

Market context refers to the man-made market forces (as opposed to the nature-made forces) of the market as a physical place that affect customer needs and wants. It has three components: economy, government policy, and technology. Whereas the geophysical market characteristics remain largely unchanged over a person's lifetime, the market context can change rapidly and can result in discontinuity, as was witnessed recently in the former USSR. Market context is discussed in Chapter 5.

Market Characteristics

The market characteristics—climate, topography, and ecology—influence customers' needs as opposed to wants. For example, customers need air conditioning year round in

Figure 4.1

ENVIRONMENTAL DETERMINANTS OF CUSTOMER BEHAVIOR

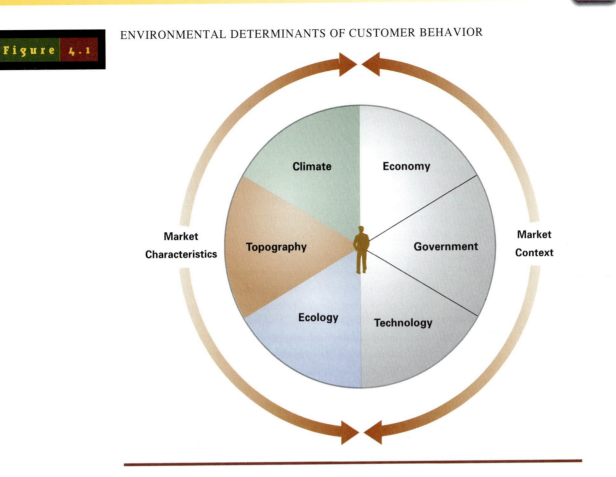

their homes, offices, or cars in Florida or other southern states, but not in northern states. In the business setting, employees are not required to wear a tie, jacket, or business suit in tropical countries such as Indonesia, India, and Mexico, in contrast to the more formal dress codes of northern European countries.

Climate

Consider why the per capita annual consumption of Coca-Cola is only 64 bottles in some countries but as many as 400 bottles per year in others. Why? The reason is not immediately obvious. Most managers assume that it is due to differences in per capita income or culture, availability of substitute beverages, and poor quality of drinking water. While these factors also contribute, the single most important factor is climate. Generally, people living in colder climate countries tend to drink a lot less Coca-Cola than those in warmer countries. For example, Swedish people drink a lot less Coca-Cola (less than two bottles per month) than do people living in Mexico (more than 30 bottles per month).

Climate is the first major component of the geophysical market environment. It consists of temperature, wind, humidity, and rainfall in an area. The patterns of these four elements vary on different locations of the earth, depending on latitude—the distance north or south from the equator.

TYPES OF CLIMATES

There are four basic types of climates (see Figure 4.2). The **equatorial** or tropical climate is found in the Amazon Valley, Central Africa, India, and Southeast Asia and consists of high humidity and high temperature. The **desert** climate is found in the Southwest United States, parts of northern Mexico; the desert belt stretching from North Africa, Arabia, Iran, and Pakistan; coastal regions in Peru and Chile; and parts of South Africa and of Australia. The **temperate zone** is located well north and, likewise, well south of the equator. Its temperature varies greatly by season, and there is significant rain or snow for the most of the year. The **polar zone** is always cold and quite dry.[2]

EFFECTS OF CLIMATE

Climate influences all forms of life (plants, insects, marine life, other animals, and humans). It plays a significant role in the development of human culture. Consider early civilization: man had to learn to make tools to cope with the climate. Since the beginning of civilization, climate has been a determinant of what crops could be grown and what types of animals could be raised in particular geographic areas. Having to cope with climate and the climate-dependent availability of food, plants, animals, and building materials has intimately influenced people's consumption of food, use of clothing, housing patterns, and the geographical distribution of population itself. In fact, even various cultural differences among people are, in some measure, climatic adaptations. Climate affects all three areas of people's basic needs: food, clothing, and shelter.

FOOD Food consumption patterns differ dramatically between the tropical and arctic countries. In the colder arctic countries, there is a lot more reliance on animals for food as

MAJOR CLIMATE ZONES

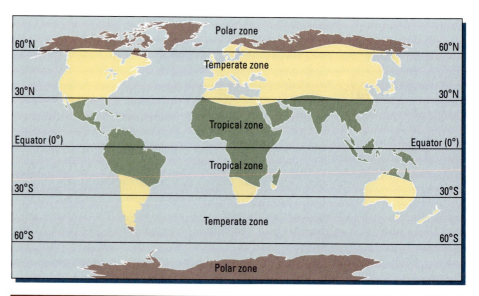

well as clothing. Northern Europeans eat more red meat and much less fruits and vegetables compared with southern Europeans. Similarly, foods in Mediterranean countries contain more spices than in arctic countries. In general, the closer to the equator, the spicier and hotter the food gets.

Differences are also found in the consumption of cheese and other dairy products. Colder countries tend to consume a lot more cheese per capita than warmer countries and the fat content of the cheese they consume is also much more. Swiss cheese contains more fat than feta or mozzarella cheese. In many tropical countries, in fact, cheese is not common as staple food. Likewise, differences occur in alcoholic beverage consumption. In colder climates, alcoholic beverages consumed are those with higher alcohol content (e.g., whisky and scotch) compared to those consumed in warmer countries (e.g., Campari and rum and liquors—generally diluted with mixers). See the Window on Practice box for one company's solution to climate and country differences.

CLOTHING There are striking differences in clothing across different climates, with respect to materials, design, and style. People living in colder climates tend to rely more on wool and leather; those living in warmer climates rely much more on cotton, silk, and other lighter fabrics. Furthermore, in the colder countries, people utilize more layers of clothing and sew their garments to fit tighter compared to those in warmer countries. In warmer countries, the clothing style tends to be loose and flowing, and color preferences also tend towards brighter colors and flower patterns; in comparison, people in colder climates tend to use darker or basic pastel colors.

SHELTER Differences can also be found in customer needs for shelter. Colder countries utilize wood and stone as materials compared to clay and brick in warmer countries.

Chiclets Gum

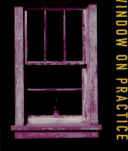

WINDOW ON PRACTICE

Warner-Lambert's Chiclets are a popular brand of chewing gum in many countries around the world. The story of its introduction in India is a lesson both in climate and economics. At first, Chiclets was a flop. And certainly not because Indian consumers didn't like its taste—they did. Rather, its packaging did not suit the Indian conditions.

In the United States, Chiclets were being packaged with 8 to 12 small pieces of gum lined up tightly in rows in a light cardboard box. Consumers would open the package, eat one or two pieces, and put the pack back in their pocket. This procedure works perfectly in the United States. In India's hot and humid climate, in contrast, the remaining pieces of gum become one messy mass, often sticking to the cardboard. Nobody in India wanted to put that in the mouth!

There was another problem—this one economic. Many people in India don't have the money to buy a whole packet of gum. Cigarettes, for example, are sold one cigarette at a time. Of course, many people do buy by the pack, but just as many buy it by the piece.

Warner-Lambert learned its lesson quickly. The company repackaged Chiclets in units of two individually wrapped pieces. That overcame both the problems—climate and customers' limited buying power. Since then Chiclets has been a popular brand in India.

Source: From Jagdish N. Sheth, *Winning Back Your Market: The Inside Stories of the Companies That Did It* (New York: John Wiley & Sons, 1984), pp. 82–83.

Also, roofs in colder climates tend to be pitched (A-frame type) to let the snow roll off, whereas they tend to be flatter in warmer climates. Indoors and outdoors are tightly segregated in colder countries, whereas they tend to be blended in warmer countries. The color and decor of homes also vary by climate.

LIFESTYLE DIFFERENCES IN THE UNITED STATES

The United States has all four climate zones, and U.S. lifestyles vary accordingly. For example, in the South, where it is warm and humid, very similar to the Equatorial climates, people move rather slowly, drink a lot of fluids, and generally engage in more outdoor activities like bicycling and gardening than do people in the North polar zone. States like Montana and Wyoming in the Northwest experience very harsh winters, so the residents there are much more likely to be skiers than bike riders.

Climate and topography affect what people do and what they consume.

The more temperate regions include Seattle, Washington, where it rains quite often, or Buffalo, New York, which experiences the most snow in the country. As a marketer, you can expect to sell a lot of rain gear in Seattle and Vancouver, but not much snow removal equipment; in contrast, in Buffalo, New York, you can expect to sell a lot of snow removal equipment and warm clothing, but not much of sunscreens.

Finally, in the desert regions like parts of Nevada and Arizona, summers are very hot, so people stay indoors most of the time during summer; but in the fall and winter the region becomes the resort capital of the world. Palm Springs, California, and Scottsdale, Arizona, are known for resort hotels and many renowned golf courses. You can expect to sell a lot of air conditioners, cold beverages, and sunscreen in these desert regions but not much warm clothing and ski equipment.

CLIMATE AND BUSINESS CUSTOMERS

Climate also affects business customers' needs and purchases. All industrial machinery and equipment must be designed to withstand the climatic conditions in which the business customer is located. For example, heat, humidity, and dust affect the performance of trucks, tractors, and farm equipment. Computers and other machinery often need climate control environments to perform. Climate also affects the storage and use of materials in warehouses, in laboratories, and during transit.

Climatic differences certainly played a significant role in the strategy the U.S. military used in Operation Desert Storm—a 1991 U.S.-led international military operation against Iraq to reverse the Iraqi occupation of Kuwait. The desert climate affected the materials and equipment the army needed and utilized in this war. The soldiers' clothing had to be light and the ground equipment designed for extreme desert conditions. In general, defense equipment manufacturers supplying to armies of various nations must take into consideration the climate where weapons will be used.

Climate also dictates the need for special packaging materials that are used for packaging and shipping various products to business firms. As the marketplace continues to expand globally, and countries ship products around the world, packaging becomes more critical if there are severe differences in the climate. For example, a warehouse in Chicago in the middle of winter will not have the same temperature as a warehouse in Bangkok, Thailand, during the same time of the year. Consequently, products must be packaged to accommodate the climatic variations that are present around the world.

Prima Fruit Packing Co. is one of many fruit packers in California that recently switched to bulk crates made of plastic. The high density polyethylene bins offer the packers better protection against harsh conditions in cold storage.[3] In York, Pennsylvania, Graham Packaging is using corrugated reshipping containers for household cleaners and laundry detergents to transfer their products to retailers and warehouse clubs. In warm weather, the inside of an enclosed truck trailer can get as hot as 140°F; the product packaging must be able to withstand such extreme temperatures.[4]

SEASONALITY AS CLIMATIC VARIATION

In addition to climatic variations from one location to another, climate in any one place also varies during the year, causing the annual cycle of seasonality. Clothing stores change merchandise with fall, winter, spring, and summer collections. Stores like Kmart

Seasonality affects the clothing that customers wear.

and Sears stock snow shovels, insecticides, lawn mowers, garden supplies, fans, and so on, according to the season. In a supermarket, fruits and vegetables and certain kinds of foods such as soups, soft drinks, heating fuel, and so on, all move slow or fast depending on the season. All seasonal merchandise in stores across the world must be delivered at the right time of the year, and to the right geographic locations.

Business sales vary from month to month in a calendar year. This seasonal variation is caused by three factors: (1) annual climate changes; (2) calendar events such as school year, football season, and so on; and (3) holidays and festivities. To a degree, the last two factors are themselves related to or influenced by the first factor. Thus, climate affects variations in customer buying behavior both directly and indirectly.

ANNUAL CLIMATE CHANGES   The effects of annual climate changes on customer purchases are most obvious. Customers need and buy warm clothing during winter and cool clothing during summer. Firewood, snow salt, snow tires, and so on, are bought during winter, and garden supplies and barbecue grills are bought during summer. And spring brings in an increase in the purchase of spring cleaning materials and supplies (e.g., window washing soaps), as well as dining out, for example. Around the world, coffee, tea, and other hot beverages are purchased more during cold months, and soft drinks and ice creams more during warm months. In the still industrializing countries like India, Thailand, and Mexico, you can see changes in sidewalk stalls that appear and disappear according to the season—every summer, even small children trying to supplement family income typically set up make-shift stalls around street corners to sell fresh lemonade, sugarcane juice, and fresh coconut water.

CALENDAR YEAR EVENTS   Calendar year events (many related to annual climate variations) impel other purchases. A typical calendar year for a North American family with children may run something like the following. January and February are flu season, necessitating purchases of cold remedies. Also, New Year resolutions after a binge of holiday indulgence raise consumer purchases of self-help books and memberships in weight-loss, quit-smoking, and other lifestyle improvement clinics. March is a month most watched for weather—people want it to be spring but Mother Nature waffles. Allergy season due to pollen, and so forth (which will last the entire summer) has just begun, once again creating the need for allergy medication. April begins the spring cleaning season, and home improvement projects mushroom. Banks promote home improvement loans heavily during this month. May begins the four-month-long summer season, and customers start outdoor activities such as bicycling, gardening, swimming, and sports. Accordingly, they buy products related to these activities and summer clothing in general during May through August. Indeed, bicycle sales peak in May and June.

June is the peak wedding season as well as a month of graduation, both inducing purchases of party goods and other celebration merchandise, among other things. July and August are peak months for family travel—both vacationing and moving. Barbecues and cookouts, swimming classes for children, amusement parks, ball games, and garage sales occupy most customers during these months. August is also the back-to-school month, and school supplies and children's clothing sales peak during August and September. In fact, all book and shoe (adults as well as children) sales increase during August and September.

October is noted for the World Series and Halloween; along with the purchase of Halloween costumes and candies, customers begin to seriously shop for winter clothing and for getting the house ready for winter. November begins the early holiday shopping season, and December peaks the purchase of all kinds of retail items, including clothing, toys, books and shoes, and gifts. Many households treat themselves to a gift of a household appliance or furniture or even a car, having postponed the purchase of these "necessities" until the Christmas season so that one member of the family could give these as gifts to another family member. Thus, seasons influence customer attitudes towards purchasing.[5]

For businesses, the calendar year has a massive impact on purchases—as the budget year comes to a close, firms rush to complete their purchases to take advantage of the available budget and tax write-offs. This is referred to as the "fourth quarter purchase rush." For car dealers, the arrival of next year's models (typically, next year's models become available in the last quarter of the current year) induces inventory clearance sales to make room for the new inventory.

Topography

Another major component of the geophysical environment is **topography,** that is, the terrain, altitude, and soil conditions of the market where customers buy and use the product or service. Food, shelter, and clothing preferences differ across topographical regions. Cities surrounded by mountains are likely to have more air pollution (e.g., Los Angeles, Salt Lake City, Denver), which is likely to influence the need for special automobile emission control systems. Gasoline in high altitude areas needs to have a different composition and octane rating. Customers around rivers and lakes on the coast have very different lifestyles, with fish as their principal food.

Would you ride the camel, or would you prefer the boat? DHL needs both to serve two markets with divergent topography.

A number of products and services are needed principally due to topographical conditions. Examples include flood insurance, erosion-resistant foundations for homes, special water treatment plants and supplies for both households and municipalities. The means of transportation depend on the terrain: four-wheel-drive jeeps for mountainous regions, boats and ferries in the intracoastal waters of Miami and Amsterdam, camels in the desertlands of the Middle East, mules on the trails of Grand Canyon in the United States and in the hills of Simla and Himalayas in India. Military clothing and all camouflage materials need to be in desert sand color in the Middle East but forest green in the jungles of Somalia.

REGIONAL PREFERENCES

Consumption varies across different regions of the world, and indeed within a single country. For example, snack food consumption varies across different parts of the United States; compared to the United States' annual per capita consumption of snack food in recent years of 20.6 pounds, it varied from 18.6 pounds in the Pacific and Southeast regions to 23.9 pounds in the West Central states. Regional preferences were even more pronounced for the specific types of snack food consumed. The Pacific region consumed only 5.1 pounds of potato chips per capita, the West Central region consumed as much as 8.6 pounds. And, in pretzel consumption, the Mid-Atlantic region stands out—4 pounds per capita compared to a U.S. average of 2 pounds.

The regional consumption differences are due to two factors: (1) geophysical conditions comprising climate, topography, and ecology and (2) cultural and/or ethnic heritage. For example, one reason that food tends to be spicier in tropical countries (e.g., Mexico and India) is that it helps the human body adapt to the hot temperatures of the tropics. Other geophysical conditions may also play a role. Within India, snacks are spicier in the western state of Rajasthan than in the southern state of Madras, because the drinking water is "harder" in composition in Rajasthan, and the chili powder helps the body digest food in hard water environments. In contrast, cultural and ethnic heritage plays a major role in the variation in pretzel consumption in the United States. A significant proportion of the population of New York and the Mid-Atlantic states is of European heritage, accounting for greater consumption of pretzels there.[6]

Although cultural and ethnic factors often influence regional preferences, we describe them as a market characteristic. From a theoretical perspective, many ethnic/cultural practices have themselves developed as an attempt to adapt to the physical environment. Furthermore, regions are the most practical way of delineating and segmenting markets even when the geographically distinct preferences might sometimes be culturally driven.

REGIONAL CONSUMPTION MAPS

To capture regional preference differences, it is illuminating to draw and study maps of regional variations in product consumption. These maps show **geographical variation—** that is, different patterns of consumption in different regions.

Consider bicycle riding. About 47 million Americans ride a bicycle at least once a year, according to the U.S. Bureau of the Census.[7] About half a million Americans commute to work on their bicycles. But bicycling as a mode of commuting to work is not evenly distributed across America (See Figure 4.3). The Pacific region has the greatest concentration, with more than 10 bike commuters per 1,000 commuters (the ratio exceeded 50 per 1,000 commuters in some communities in California); Alabama,

Figure 4.3

GEOGRAPHICAL DIFFERENCES IN CUSTOMER BEHAVIOR: BICYCLE RIDING (NUMBER OF BICYCLE RIDERS PER 1,000 COMMUTERS BY CENSUS DIVISION 1990)

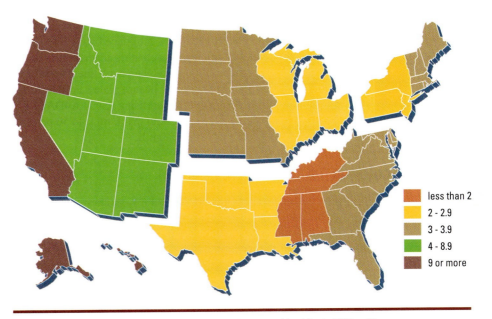

▮	less than 2
▮	2 - 2.9
▮	3 - 3.9
▮	4 - 8.9
▮	9 or more

Source: Jan Larson, "The Bicycle Market," *American Demographics,* March 1995, p. 50.

Mississippi, Tennessee, and Kentucky show the lowest rate of less than 2 bike commuters per 1,000 commuters. These differences occur due to variations in climate, topography, and facilitative infrastructure such as biker lanes in city traffic.[8]

Pizza as a fast food also shows substantial geographical variation. According to some records, pizza's first home in America was a Manhattan restaurant called Lombardi's opened in 1905. Although it is a popular food all across America, its consumption is concentrated on the East Coast. This reflects pizza's Italian influence, since its consumption is highest in areas with high Italian populations. Of the 14.7 million Americans of Italian ancestry, 5.7 million are concentrated in New York, New Jersey, or Pennsylvania; 1.5 million live in Massachusetts or Connecticut; and 1.8 million in Ohio, Michigan, or Illinois. These states show a concentration of pizza stores, with at least 3.5 quick-serve pizza stores per 10,000 people.[9]

REGIONAL MARKETING

To address such differences, marketers may use a strategy of **regional marketing,** the practice of adapting marketing programs according to segmentation based on geographic differences among customers. The marketer recognizes customer diversity from one region to another and tailors the entire marketing mix to each region. This is a recent strategy, and a sharp departure from the mass marketing practices of the companies that promote national brands. Some regional marketers focus on a particular region, and by offering a special product suited to that region, they take on national market leaders. For example, while Procter & Gamble's Crisco oil brand is the market leader on a nationwide basis, in New Orleans, Louanne's oil, designed especially for Creole cooking, has the largest market share.

conscious and avoid foods high in salt, sugar, or fat. They are consumers who look for useful information in advertising and don't like sex in commercials. If they are insulted by an advertisement, they won't buy the product. They think pollution is a serious threat to people's health and are willing to reduce their standard of living in the effort to tighten pollution standards. They do believe that the individual can make a difference in making the environment healthier. To these people, environmentalism is not a passing fad, but rather a way of life.[13] For more details about the customer behavior of green consumers, see the Window on Research box.

Of course, not all consumers are green consumers, and among those who are, not everyone shows the same commitment. People who show some commitment to the envi-

---

Knowing the Ecologically Conscious Consumers

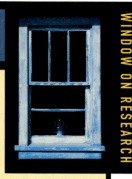

WINDOW ON RESEARCH

A number of consumer researchers have tried to identify whether ecologically conscious consumers are different in any characteristics from nonconsciousness consumers. For example, marketing professors Gregory M. Pickett, Norman Kangun, and Stephen J. Grove (all affiliated with Clemson University) surveyed consumers' environmental conservation behavior (e.g., recycling, water and electricity conservation). They found no demographic differences between the conserving and nonconserving consumers. And there is no reason to expect any.

What we would expect, instead, is that conservers would differ from nonconservers in their psychological make-up. This relationship was tested in a study of consumers in Singapore. This study is important because Singapore has taken the leadership in the greening of South east Asia with its vision of becoming a model of an "Environmental City."

The researchers were Prem Shamdasani, Gloria Ong Chon-Lin, and Daleen Richmond—all affiliated with the National University of Singapore. They too classified consumers into "green" and "nongreen" based on consumers' performance of 12 environmentally friendly behaviors (e.g., buy products in recyclable packages, return containers for recycling, etc.). They then compared these two groups on their attitudes and self-perceptions. Their findings are as follows:

- Compared with nongreen consumers, green consumers (a) possess a more favorable attitude toward the environment; (b) are more willing to sacrifice personal comfort for environmental gain; (c) are more likely to believe that environmental crisis is real and legitimate; (d) believe in the power of individual consumers in saving the environment; (e) believe that the job of saving the environment should not be left solely to government, scientists, environmentalists, etc.; (f) are more cosmopolitan, sociable, and socially integrated.

- Compared with nongreen consumers, green consumers were also (a) willing to pay more for green products, and (b) willing to make the extra effort to find green products.

- Promotional and distribution factors (i.e., the easy availability of green products, and promotional feature displays to make them conspicuous) were the most significant predictors of consumers' green buying behavior, taking precedence over the role of attitudinal and belief factors (e.g., willingness to satisfy comfort).

These findings point to the necessity of both types of managerial actions: (a) using marketing mix in such a way as to make green products convenient to purchase, and (b) providing educational communication to mold consumers' attitudinal beliefs (e.g., credibly communicating that the environment problem is real and legitimate).

Source: Gregory M. Pickett, Norman Kangun, and Stephen J. Grove, "Is There a General Conserving Consumer? A Public Policy Concern," *Journal of Public Policy & Marketing* 12 no. 2 (Fall 1993), pp. 234–43; Prem Shamdasani, Gloria Ong Chon-Lin, and Daleen Richmond, "Exploring Green Consumers in an Oriental Culture: Role of Personal and Marketing Mix Factors," in *Advances in Consumer Research* 20 (1993), pp. 488–493.

Table 4.1

ENVIRONMENTAL SEGMENTS

1. True-Blue Greens (20%)	The most deeply committed to environment, they are in the forefront of the green movement in America, and they express their concern both by advocacy as well as by pro-environmental consumption behavior, such as recycling and buying products made from recycled materials.
2. Greenback Greens (5%)	This group backs its commitment to environment by showing willingness to pay more for environmentally friendly products.
3. Sprouts (31%)	This group shows a moderate level of commitment to environmental issues with a limited amount of pro-environmental behavior.
4. Grousers (9%)	They display a lack of pro-environmental attitudes and behavior and rationalize their inaction by blaming others.
5. Basic Browns (35%)	Environment is not a concern to them and they do not want to be bothered with environmental issues. Majority of them are poor and are more preoccupied with just making their ends meet than with worrying about anything else.

Source: "The Environment: Public Attitudes and Behavior," a report by The Roper Organization and S.C. Johnson & Sons, Inc. (New York, 1992).

ronment in their marketplace choices are termed **environmentally conscious consumers—** defined as "those who actively seek out products perceived as having relatively minimal impact on the environment."[14] Consumer researchers have identified differences in consumers according to the degree of their "greenness." Two resulting schemes of segmentation are presented in Table 4.1.

BUSINESS RESPONSE TO ENVIRONMENTALISM

Businesses from a variety of industries are responding to customer demand for environmentally friendly products. To illustrate, in 1992, Archie Comic Publications Inc. started printing all its comic publications on 100 percent recycled paper. This decision was motivated, according to the publisher, by a number of its readers who are young children. Similarly, Harmony (formerly Seventh Generation) is exclusively a green product supplier and the nation's leading catalog house for green products. Its sales rose tenfold between 1988 and 1991 (from $1 million to $10 million). Many greeting card companies have followed suit in using recycled paper.

In their effort to respond to the consumer demand for a healthier environment, marketers engage in **environmental marketing,** which refers to the marketing of products and services in a manner that attempts to minimize the damage to the environment. This might entail conservation of scarce resources such as trees and energy; use of recycled, recyclable, or biodegradable materials in the production of the product as well as in its packaging; product design changes to reduce air or water pollution due to product use; and adapting manufacturing processes to minimize air and water pollution. Environmental marketing is a response to increased public and consumer concern about safeguarding our environment. Studies show this concern to be rising among American consumers.

Wal-Mart Stores, Inc. has been an early pioneer in stocking green products and encouraging suppliers to be more environmentally conscious. Its Green Aisles program flags over a thousand green products. The store now reports that its green labeling program has increased its sales by 25 percent.[15] For educating consumers at large, in

BECAUSE WE RECYCLE OVER 100 MILLION PLASTIC BOTTLES A YEAR, LANDFILLS CAN BE FILLED WITH OTHER THINGS. LIKE LAND, FOR INSTANCE.

We can't make more land. But we can do more to protect what we have. In fact, last year Phillips Petroleum's plastics recycling plant processed over 100 million containers. This effort reduced landfill waste and helped conserve natural resources. And that left another little corner of the world all alone. At Phillips, that's what it means to be The Performance Company.

PHILLIPS PETROLEUM COMPANY 66

For an annual report on Phillips' health, environmental and safety performance, write to: HES Report, 16 A1 PB, Bartlesville, OK 74004.

Phillips Petroleum—echoing customers' ecology concerns.

The Greening of the Golden Arches

By the end of the 1990s, McDonald's produced 2 million pounds of waste per day. During the 1980s, more and more consumers were choosing products based on environmental criteria, and the McDonald's foam clamshell used to package its burgers had become a symbol of ecological evil. School children vilified its beloved mascot, calling him Ronald McToxic and mailed their Mctrash back to the company—personally addressed to Shelby Yastrow, the company's chief legal officer. Consumers were banding together for a Styrofoam-packaging ban.

This consumer protest forced the company to take some pro-environmental action. Of course, the company also had an economic motive: With landfills running out of room, especially in the Northeast, the actual cost of garbage disposal was rising as fast as the company's public relations bill. In November 1990, McDonald's announced it would no longer use its signature polystyrene clamshell sandwich boxes. The step was an outcome of a joint project with Environmental Defense Fund, which was aimed at identifying sources of waste at the Big Mac. Later, in April 1991, the chain announced that it would recycle all its corrugated cardboard, use less paper in its napkins, and test a refillable coffee mug. It also asked all its suppliers to use boxes made from 35+ percent recyclables.

1991, Procter & Gamble, along with Giant Food, and local government and media agencies, formed a recycling educational program entitled *Closing the Loop*. Perhaps the best-known case of consumer protest against a business's environmentally damaging practices is the case of McDonald's; in turn, McDonald's response was a total embrace of environmentally friendly corrective actions (see the Window on Practice box).

MARKETING STRATEGY IMPLICATIONS

The three market characteristics have implications for marketing strategy. (See Figure 4.4) The climate introduces both spatial and temporal variations within the marketplace. This in turn creates variations in the products and services customers would need to satisfy their physiological needs. Marketers respond to spatial variations by adopting a regional marketing strategy. Furthermore, they respond to temporal variations with a strategy of seasonal marketing. Topography directly causes variations in consumption across regions, and the strategy of regional marketing is designed to take advantage of topographical differences across regions. Finally, ecology, the third geo-physical market characteristic, alters the suitability of products, making some products more suitable for the local ecology than others. Where ecology is at risk, this market factor causes customers to adopt the preservation of the environment as a "value." Marketers respond to this factor by offering ecologically-friendly products to environmentally conscious customers.

Figure 4.4

MARKETING STRATEGY IMPLICATIONS OF
THE GEOPHYSICAL ENVIRONMENT

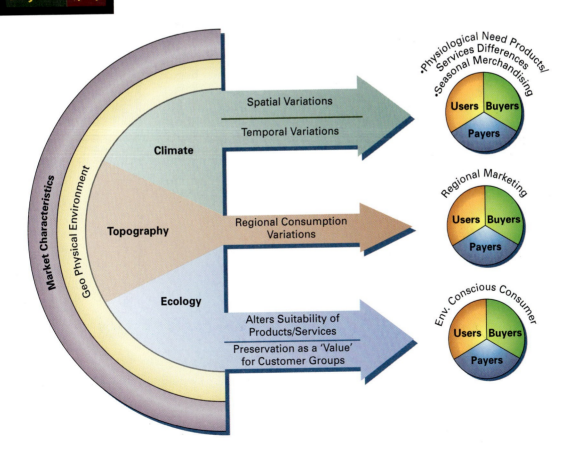

Table 4.2

RELATIONSHIP BETWEEN MARKET CHARACTERISTICS AND CUSTOMER BEHAVIOR

CHARACTERISTIC	OVERALL IMPACT	INFLUENCE ON CUSTOMER ROLES			MARKETING RESPONSE
		USER	PAYER	BUYER	
Climate	Needs vary among climates and according to seasonal changes within a climate	Certain types of food, clothing, and shelter are needed. Weather-related products are needed. Suitable packaging is required.	Out-of-place products cost more. Out-of-season products cost more.	Climate-appropriate storage facilities affect accelerated buying. Bad weather may require postponement of purchase. Pickup/delivery services may be needed in bad weather.	Regional marketing Seasonal marketing
Topography	Regional consumption variations	Products adapted to local conditions (e.g., flood insurance, bottled water) are needed. Available means of transportation may be limited.	Special-needs products must be budgeted for.	Transportation difficulties may require minimizing trips, buying in bulk, or delegating purchase to others.	Regional marketing
Ecology	Altered suitability of products/services	Pollution control products are needed. Environmentally friendly products/services are needed.	Ecologically friendly products may cost more.	Ecologically friendly products may require a special search effort.	Green marketing Targeting environmentally conscious customers

Market Characteristics and the Three Customer Roles

The three market characteristics affect all three customer roles. Not all characteristics affect all roles equally. We have already given many examples that focus on the user role. We briefly refer to these and then add the effects on the payer and buyer roles, where applicable. Table 4.2 summarizes these effects.

As stated in Chapter 2, the physical market characteristics affect the *needs* of the customer, whereas market context affects the wants. Let us consider each of the three market characteristics in turn. Climate affects the users' need for food, clothing, and shelter, as all these have to be adequate and compatible with the climate (e.g., warm clothing for colder climates). Topography affects needs for particular means of transportation (e.g., the camel in the deserts of Arabia), insurance against topography-based mishaps such as floods, hurricanes, and so on; water and soil conditions necessitating water purification treatments, and so on. Ecology makes ecology-unfriendly products nonviable and channels customer needs toward biodegradable and other environment-friendly products and services.

For the payer role, some physical environment factors imply greater expense. Suppose you lived in a tropical country such as Pakistan or Afghanistan, and you wanted to visit the Swiss Alps. You would need very warm clothing such as down-filled jackets, which are unlikely to be available in your country. If they are available at all, they would be priced exorbitantly because of the specialty nature these products acquire in such out-of-place merchandise stores. Similarly, if your dietary restrictions require you to consume certain foods throughout the year (e.g., avocado in summer and winter both), you may have to pay more for such out-of-season merchandise. You will also have to allocate in your budget for products necessitated by the topography of the area (e.g., flood insurance). Finally, of course, ecology-friendly products are more expensive (e.g., organically grown fruits are about twice as costly). The user in you may very much want to use pro-environmental products and services, but the payer in you may have to just hold the purse strings tighter.

The buyer role is also affected by the physical market characteristics. If you live in a very hot climate, either you have a good cold storage facility, or else you buy products in quantities sufficient for immediate consumption. Accelerated buying to take advantage of price and promotional deals is made infeasible if the storage facilities are inadequate for the climate of the place. Bad weather also leads purchasers to postpone the shopping trip and/or order home delivery rather than in-store acquisition. For customers who live in towns where the road to the market is uneasy to navigate, buyers would minimize shopping trips and would tend to buy bulk. They may also delegate the purchase task to others (e.g., "you are going that way; could you please buy—for me").

As these examples illustrate, each of the three market characteristics has varied and significant influences on each of the customer roles. Successful marketers identify and communicate the ways their products meet the resulting needs.

Summary

This chapter focused on market characteristics (i.e., the characteristics of the market as a physical place). You learned that there are three geophysical characteristics: climate, topography, and ecology.

Climate plays a very important role in shaping the market values customers would seek and affects the three basic necessities of life: food, shelter, and clothing. Market behaviors of the user, buyer, and payer are greatly affected by climate. At the same time, you learned that businesses are also affected by climate, including the type of packaging that must be used in warm and cold climates, and the fact that there is a seasonality with products and services.

Another market characteristic is the topography of a country, which refers to the terrain, altitude, and soil conditions where customers (both household and business) use products and services. Just as with climate, topography affects the choices households and businesses make with respect to food, clothing, and shelter. For example, you learned that the consumption of snack foods varies based on the topography of a region. Likewise, office designs in businesses will also vary depending on the natural make-up of the location where the business is conducted.

The last market characteristic is ecology. Ecology refers to the natural resources and the balance that exist among the humans, animals, and vegetation. You learned about many changes taking place ecologically around the world, including the global warming, air pollution, water pollution, and ozone layer depletion, and how each of these is affecting both household customers and businesses. One outcome is the movement by activists around the world to save the environment, and the impact it is having on marketers as they attempt to respond to demands put on them by users of various products and services.

Key Terms

Market Characteristics 96
Market Context 96
Climate 97
Equatorial 98
Desert 98
Temperate Zone 98

Polar Zone 98
Topography 103
Geographical Variation 104
Regional Marketing 105
Ecology 106
Global Warming 106

Green Consumer 107
Environmentally
  Conscious Consumer 109
Environmental Marketing
  109

Review Questions

1. You read about the ice cream maker and the coffee vendor and how climate affects their businesses. Give two other examples when climate affects customer behavior in the household markets and likewise two examples for the business customers.

2. Why should marketers be aware of global climatic differences? How does understanding this help marketers to better satisfy basic customer needs such as those for food, shelter, and clothing?

3. Describe how specific calendar year events, business cycles, and holidays impact the purchases of both household and business customers. How can marketers capitalize on these events?

CAMCORDER CONSUMERS

Figure 4.5

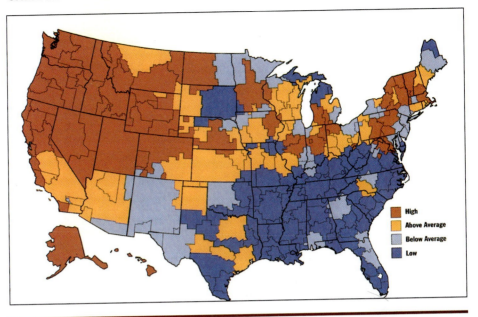

High
Above Average
Below Average
Low

Source: Michael J. Weiss, "Camcorder Consumer," *American Demographics*, September 1994, p. 60.

4. When people refer to the 1990s as the "age of the green consumer," what are they referring to? What implications does this "age" have for marketing managers?

5. What is meant by "regional marketing"? What is its significance and rationale? What customer factors are driving regional markets? Why is regional marketing growing?

6. What is ecology? What are its elements? How is customer behavior affected by it?

7. Based on the regional consumption map in Figure 4.5, in what areas of the United States do camcorder owners reside? Where is their lowest concentration? What might explain this geographic variation?

Applications

1. As the Director of Product Development for a medium-sized international producer of soap, lotion, and detergent, you are fundamentally concerned with the movement worldwide towards protecting and preserving the environment. In many countries, specific raw materials have been banned and certain packaging materials have been discontinued. In addition to consumer and government pressure to become a "green" marketer, your major competitor, The Body Shop, has exhibited its commitment to the environment in several meaningful ways. What will you do to move your company towards being more environmentally friendly and how will you communicate this to your customers?

2. Not all market characteristics have the same influence for each product or service. Different characteristics may affect different market values that customers seek, and this influence may

further differ across products and services. For each of the following products and services, assess the effect of market characteristics (climate, topography, and ecology): (a) a chain of gourmet coffee shops across the European continent; (b) an exporter of bottled water to third world countries; and (c) a worldwide supplier of exterior paint for houses.

3. Different market characteristics may also have different implications for different elements of the marketing mix (product, price, distribution, and promotion). For the same products and services as in the previous question, please assess the marketing mix implications of the three market characteristics.

Practical Experiences

1. Contact a marketing manager or access the Web site at two companies producing packaged consumer goods, say, Procter & Gamble and Campbell's Soup. Gather and analyze information on each company's efforts at regional marketing. Compare and contrast their approaches.

2. Obtain monthly sales data for at least three products for which you would expect seasonality and three for which you would not. Gather data from published sources or by contacting the business firm. Explain the seasonality that the data reveal, comparing it with your prior expectations.

3. Review the annual reports of International Paper and Georgia Pacific Company to find out about their efforts at "green marketing" or how they have or are going about becoming more environmentally friendly as they embark on global expansion efforts. Describe your findings. Which company is doing a better job in terms of environmental friendliness, and how much of a competitive advantage does it represent?

4. Interview five consumers to rate them on how "environmentally conscious" they are. Then ask them about how their environmental consciousness affects the products and service they have bought within the past one year. Verify if "environmental consciousness" relates to customers' purchasing behavior.

Notes

1 Based in part on "As Bitter Cold Keeps Europe in Its Grip, Economy Could Be in Danger of Cooling," *The Wall Street Journal,* January 7, 1997, p. A14.

2 For a more detailed 12-fold classification (including such climate zones as the Mediterranean and subpolar), see Robert Clairborne, *Climate, Man, and History* (New York: W.W. Norton & Co.), p. 41.

3 *Packaging Digest* 32, no. 8 (July 1995), pp. 56–58.

4 *Packaging Digest* 32, no. 17 (December 1995), pp. 44–46.

5 This section is adapted from Judith Waldrop, "The Seasons of Business," *American Demographics,* May 1992, pp. 40–44.

6 Adapted from Marcial Mogelonsky, "The Geography of Junk Food," *American Demographics,* July 1994, pp. 13–14.

7 U.S. Bureau of the Census, *Statistical Abstract of the United States,* 115th edition Washington, D.C., 1995.

8 *American Demographics,* March 1995, p. 50.

9 Brad Edmundson, "Pizza Parties," *American Demographics,* August 1994, p. 60.

10 Larry Carpenter, "How to Market to Regions," *American Demographics,* November 1987, pp. 44–48.

11 Roger C. Olsen, "Regional Marketing's Comeback at Ford," *Marketing Communications,* September 1984; also, Thomas W. Osborn, "Opportunity

Marketing," *Marketing Communications,* September 1987, pp. 49–54.

[12] See Jacquelyn A. Ottman, *Green Marketing* (Lincolnwood), Ill.: NTC Business Books, 1992).

[13] Joseph Winski, "Lifestyle Study," *Advertising Age,* October 5 1990, in Ottman, *Green Marketing.*

[14] Ottman, *Green Marketing.*

[15] Adapted from Eric Wieffering, "Wal-Mart Turns Green in Kansas," *American Demographics,* December 1993, p. 23.

CHAPTER 5

After reading this chapter you should be able to:

Explain how the economy affects customer demand for specific products.

Define the role of the index of "consumer sentiment" in terms of customer behavior.

Summarize how government's fiscal, monetary, and other public policy both constrains and encourages customer purchase and use of products and services.

Explain how public policy creates consumer confidence in the marketplace.

Describe how technology is revolutionizing the marketplace, giving customers more choices, shaping their expectations, and enabling them to buy "anything, anytime, anywhere."

Market Context: Economy, Government, and Technology

Let's Go Shopping in China!

China may be one of the world's oldest civilizations, but you don't immediately associate trade with that country—military strength maybe, but not trade. From 1966 to 1969, Communist Party Chairman Mao Zedong, led the Cultural Revolution, purging the country of intellectuals and bourgeois tendencies. As a result, the counter-revolution was all but suppressed, and the country became politically stable, militarily strong, and closed to the rest of the world. Capitalism and intellectualism were in disdain. Peasants were nurtured. Everything seemed to be going well. Everything, that is, except the economy. Much of the Chinese population could barely buy life's necessities.

Then, in 1978, the Communist government reversed the decade-old "closed door" policy, which had kept all international business out of China. Reaching its peak under the charismatic leadership of Deng Xiaoping (who remained China's president until his death in early 1997), the new "open door" policy welcomed foreign investment. In 1992, China allowed six Chinese cities and five special economic zones to form joint ventures with foreign retailers. And in 1996, it reduced tariffs on imported retail merchandise. Today, Chinese consumers can shop in Western-style department stores such as Giordano's, discount stores and warehouse clubs managed by U.S. retailers Wal-Mart and CP Pokphand, 7-Eleven convenience stores, and Park "N" Shop supermarkets. There is a new entrepreneurial class in China, with money to spend. And while the general public's resources remain limited for shopping at pricey department stores such as Japan's Yaohan in Shanghai, the large middle class is now fully exposed to a full display of Western-style consumerism.

And these Chinese middle-class consumers are about to join the class of global consumers—with access to world-class products and services, and with resources to afford them. The Chinese economy is on a steep growth curve. China is now the world's third largest economy, catching up with Japan. The expected annual growth rate in the remaining years of the 20th century is 9.1 percent, compared with less than 3 percent for non-Asian countries. By the year 2020, China's economy is expected to grow three-fold, dwarfing that of the United States.[1]

What a testimony to the power of government policy in stimulating the national economy and of the national economy in opening a wide array of choices for the customer. For a long time, Hong Kong has been a shopper's paradise. It is entirely possible that someday in the near future some global consumers will think of China and say, "Let's go shopping!"

Review Questions

1. What is meant by the statement "The general state of a nation's economy influences customer behavior by affecting their sense of optimism"? Elaborate your response by comparing and contrasting necessary versus discretionary expenditures.

2. Define and explain each of the following: (a) Index of Consumer Sentiment; (b) business cycles; (c) monetary and fiscal policy. Also explain how each relates to customer behavior.

3. Briefly enumerate the various ways in which government policy influences each of the three customer roles.

4. What is meant by negligent consumer behavior? Give three examples. How can society discourage these kinds of customer behaviors?

5. Technological advances have been identified as a major market context factor and have been shown to affect customer behavior in four fundamental ways. Discuss each of these, illustrating your answer with two new examples of each influence.

Applications

1. Part of the government's influence on customer behavior is through public policy setting and more specifically by protecting the consumer. One area for which the government provides protection is to safeguard against potentially deceptive advertising practices of companies. Give an example of advertising that, in your opinion, is deceptive. What medium does it appear in and why do you perceive it to be deceptive? What might the government do to protect consumers in this case?

2. The chapter talks about the differences between technophiles and technophobes. Briefly describe these differences. Next, identify two products/services for which you consider yourself to be a technophile and two others for which you consider yourself to be a technophobe. Justify your rationale for categorizing yourself with these products/services in this way.

3. Find a magazine advertisement for a product that represents a new technological innovation. First, identify any elements in the ad that might appeal to techophiles. Next, find any elements in the ad that might appeal to technophobes. Briefly describe your findings and determine which of the two groups of customers is more likely to respond favorably to the ad.

4. The personal computer industry praises Dell Computer's fantastic success, partially as a result of its use of mass customization. Access the Dell Web site, talk to employees at Dell, and interview customers who have bought Dell computers. Describe how Dell's use of mass customization has affected both the company and its customers.

Practical Experiences

1. Assume you are an entrepreneur and you are about to introduce to the market a revolutionary new product—an interactive kiosk—which enables convenient, easy, Internet access and offers a host of value-added services for business travelers. In general, your target group will be fairly computer savvy and will be familiar with most office equipment such as faxes, E-mail, and voice-mail sys-

tems. What specific customer values will this new technology product satisfy? How will you introduce your new technology given the barrage of new innovations in the marketplace? How will you show that your product has the ability to appeal to both technophiles and technophobes?

2. One of the recent debates regarding the government's role in customer protection revolves around the use of airbags and mandating their presence in all new vehicles. On one hand, the airbags, when deployed as intended, have saved countless lives during accidents. On the other hand, airbags have killed several children and small adults—those found to be too small to withstand the force of the airbag upon impact. Assume the role of an advisor to one of the government's safety boards responsible for determining the future role of airbags in all automobiles sold in the U.S. market (both domestic and foreign makes). Would you recommend that airbags continue to be mandatory? Draft a memo that considers the implications on market values customers seek.

Notes

1. Based on Charles Lip and Kanmy Chan, "Global Powers of Retailing: Hong Kong/China," *Chain Store Age,* December 1, 1996, p. 40B.

2. James C. Cooper and Kathleen Madigan, "Shy Shoppers, Crowded Shelves Spell Slower Growth," *Business Week,* August 1, 1994, pp. 21–22. Also, "The Fed May Keep the Economy On Cruise Control," *Business Week,* April 24, 1995, pp. 31–32. Also, Rob Norton, "Where Is This Economy Really Heading?" *Fortune,* August 7, 1995, pp. 54–56.

3. George Katona, "Consumer Saving Pattern," *Journal of Consumer Research* 1 (June 1974), pp. 1–12.

4. Richard T. Curtin, "Indicators of Consumer Behavior: The University of Michigan Survey of Consumers," *Public Opinion Quarterly* 46 (1982), pp. 340–52. Also see, E. James Jennings and Paul McGrath, "The Influence of Consumer Sentiment on the Sales of Durables," *Journal of Business Forecasting,* 13 (Fall 1994) pp. 17–20.

5. Joe Schwartz, "Hard Times Harden Consumers," *American Demographics,* May 1992, p. 10.

6. W. Fred van Raaij, "Economic Psychology," *Journal of Economic Psychology* 1 (1981), pp. 1–24. Alf Lindquist, "A Note on Determinants of Household Saving Behavior," *Journal of Economic Psychology* 1 (March 1981), pp. 39–57.

7. See James C. Cooper and Kathleen Madigan, "Consumers Won't Stand for Higher Prices," *Business Week,* September 26, 1994, pp. 13–14. Also, Louis S. Richman, "Managing through a Downturn," *Fortune,* August 7, 1995, pp. 59–64.

8. "India: The Fashion for Going Dry," *The Economist* 339, no. 7971 (June 22, 1996), pp. 38–39.

9. Gordon Cramb, "Lending Bubble Is Deflated," *The Financial Times,* no. 32609 (February 24, 1995), p. SII.

10. John Greenwald, "The Air-Bag-Safety Saga," *Time* 148, no. 25 (December 2, 1996), p. 40.

11. *Ward's Auto World,* "NTSB: Enforce Seatbelt Laws, Airbag Injuries Will Decline" 32, no. 10 (October 1996), p. 10.

12. Anna Mulringe, et al., "Window Blinds That Can Poison Kids," *U.S. News & World Report* 121, no. 2 (July 8, 1996), p. 76.

13. Helen Mundell, "High-Tech Fries and Computer Campouts," *American Demographics,* December 1993, p. 25.

14. *Chain Store Age Executive with Shopping Center Age,* "Going beyond EDI" 69, no. 3 (March 1993) pp. 150–51.

15. Glenn Rifkin, "Digital Blue Jeans Pour Data and Legs into Customized Fit," *New York Times,* November 8, 1994, pp. A1/D8.

16. Jeff Moad, "Let Customers Have It Their Way," *Datamation* 41, no. 6 (April 1, 1995), pp. 34–37.

17. Susan Mitchell, "Technophiles and Technophobes," *American Demographics* 16, no. 2, February 1996 pp. 36–43.

18. Adapted from Susan Mitchell, *American Demographics,* February 1994, p. 36.

19. Richard G. Pignataro, "Strategic Agility: Flexibility Is Key," *Chief Executive,* no. 114 (June 1996), pp. 40–43.

CHAPTER 6

After reading this chapter you should be able to:

Define what culture is, identify its elements, and describe how we learn it.

Discuss how corporate culture influences business customers' behavior.

Summarize ways in which cultures differ and how those differences are important for international marketers to understand.

Identify major institutions and groups to which customers belong, and how these act as reference groups for customers.

Explain how reference groups influence the different market values customers seek.

List the components that define a customer's personal worth and describe the implications for customer behavior.

Explain the concept of social class, including the way it is measured.

Summarize how social class and income groupings affect customer behavior.

Describe how marketers adapt their strategies to respond to different economic conditions of the customer.

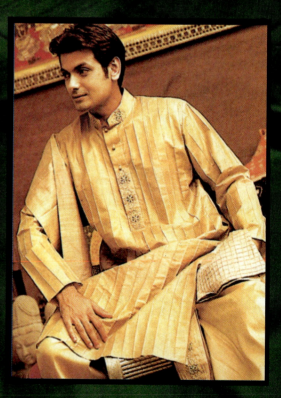

Personal Context: Culture, Reference Groups, and Personal Worth

Ram Dass Gandhi is immersed in his thoughts, reflecting on the day's events, when his wife Rita barges into the room complaining about a severe headache she has had for two days. "I want to take a Tylenol," she tells her husband, whose advice she always values. "Take an extra dose of Amritanjan," he says, referring to the Ayurvedic herbal extract from India, believed to be a cure-all for marginal ailments.

Gandhi—no relation of the Indian political leaders Mahatma Gandhi and Indira Gandhi—moved to the United States some 11 years ago, when he was only 19. Sponsored by an Indo-American scholarship program, he attended Carnegie Mellon University in Pittsburgh, and after finishing his bachelor's degree, he went on to work on a graduate program. He met Rita at a cultural festival organized by the International Student Association. Rita was born of Italian parents in the United States, and, in her views and tastes, was totally Westernized. When she met Ram Dass, she was just finishing her M.B.A. from the neighboring University of Pittsburgh. They married two years later and moved to Atlanta, where they now live.

Rita's Western tastes have certainly rubbed off on Ram Dass—for example, he now enjoys wine and pasta dishes she so much relishes, and together they go to church and to Western-style music concerts. For her part, Rita has cultivated a taste for Indian cuisine and has become a total convert to *Ayurveda*, the Indian system of medicine. To Ram Dass, of course, vegetarianism, Indian-style clothing for lounging at home, and total faith in Indian medication are lifelong values, culturally ingrained from early childhood.

But make no mistake; Ram Dass is no caveman. With a Ph.D. in computer science, he is a network engineer for a start-up company in Atlanta. His work takes him around the globe, and he speaks to diverse groups at international conferences. Outside of home, in dress, speech, and mannerism, he is as Westernized as they come. He carries medical insurance, which he plans to use for major medical catastrophes, such as when hospitalization or surgery would be needed, or for Rita's use for childbirth.

But Western-style, day-to-day medication? "We don't need chemicals in our bodies," Ram Dass's father often used to say, deriding the Western system of medication. Instead, the senior Gandhi had a cabinet full of herbs and extracts, which he would prepare himself, and information books on "how to prepare and how to use" natural medication for all occasions. Does Gandhi Junior prepare his medicines too? No, he just orders them from Dr. Vasant Ladd's Ayurvedic Supply Co. in Louisiana. He and his wife often shop at the supermarket, but the over-the-counter drug section is one aisle they have not visited. And don't hope to. Ever!

Introduction

When Ram Dass and Rita met, some of the differences between their beliefs and practices were so obvious that they could not help but be aware of their cultures. Does this story make you think about your own culture? What are the beliefs and practices of your family, religion, or ethnic group? For example, think about the kinds of foods you eat (or don't eat), the methods of health care you choose, the holidays you celebrate, and the amount of time you spend with family members. Can you think of any friends, fellow students, or co-workers whose values and practices differ from yours?

Such values and practices also define appropriate behavior in a business context. For example, businesspeople from different countries have different expectations concerning punctuality, the giving of gifts, and the contents of discussions. They also differ in terms of whom they involve in the purchasing process.

This chapter explores these and other differences that constitute the customer's **personal context**—the social, economic, and cultural environment in which the customer has lived and is living. The chapter begins by identifying each dimension of the personal context: culture, groups and institutions, personal worth, and social class. We then discuss each of these dimensions in detail. Finally, we summarize ways in which marketers address the personal context of the customer in the roles of user, payer, and buyer.

The Impact of Personal Context

Our personal context—the characteristics of the socio-econocultural environment in which we have lived and are living—has intimately influenced our resources, tastes, and preferences. It therefore affects our behavior as customers by helping to define what we can and want to use, pay for, and buy.

As shown in Figure 6.1, the personal context has four dimensions: culture, institutions and groups, personal worth, and social class. Of these, culture and reference groups influence customers' tastes and preferences, and personal worth influences resources. This

THE PERSONAL CONTEXT OF CUSTOMER BEHAVIOR

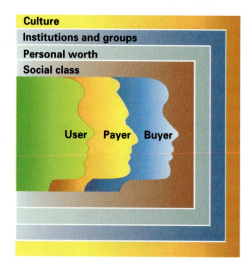

quartet of contextual factors forms the conduit through which all customer behavior is channeled. Without an understanding of these contextual factors, it is nearly impossible to understand why customers from different countries, different subcultures, different economic means, and different religions, families, and other institutions seek different values from the marketplace.

Culture

Webster's New Collegiate Dictionary defines **culture** as "the integrated pattern of human behavior that includes thought, speech, action, and artifacts and depends on man's capacity for learning and transmitting knowledge to succeeding generations." Thus, culture is everything a person learns and shares with members of a society, including ideas, norms, morals, values, knowledge, skills, technology, tools, material objects, and behavior. Culture excludes genetically inherited instincts, since these are not learned, as well as individual behaviors, norms, knowledge, and so on, not shared with other members of society. In a sense, culture represents collective mental programming. It is part of our conditioning that we share with other members of our nation, region, or group but not necessarily with members of other nations, regions, or groups.

We learn our culture by the processes of enculturation and acculturation. **Enculturation** is the process of learning one's own culture. **Acculturation** is the process of learning a new culture.

Learning a culture entails becoming knowledgeable about its various elements:

- *Values*—Values are conceptions of what is good and desirable versus what is bad and undesirable.
- *Norms*—Norms are rules of behavior. They are a do's and don'ts guide. Norms are more specific than values and dictate acceptable and unacceptable behavior.
- *Rituals*—Rituals are a set of symbolic behaviors that occur in a fixed sequence and tend to be repeated periodically. Being symbolic behavior, they have a meaning in that culture. Table 6.1 lists various rituals.
- *Myths*—Myths are stories that express some key values of society. For example, the story of Santa Claus is a myth in much of the Christian world.

Table 6.1

TYPES OF RITUALS IN A SOCIETY

TYPE	EXAMPLES
Exchange rituals	Giving gifts; the practice of dowry in India.
Possession ritual	House warming party; worship ceremony in India, China, Japan before starting a business.
Grooming rituals	Bathing; using or not using scents and perfumes.
Divestment ritual	Redecorating a house; exorcising ghosts and spirits.
Religious rituals	Going to church on Sunday (Christians); praying five times a day (Muslims).
Social interaction/ Relational rituals	Greeting, mating, and so on.
Rites of passage	Marriage, graduation, birthday, and so on.
Family rituals	Mealtime, bedtime, and so on.
Public celebrations	Cultural/civic celebrations; fireworks or parades on national holidays.

Holidays are a type of cultural ritual related to customer behavior. Purchases of a variety of items are concentrated around holidays. In much of the Western world, Christmas is the most festive holiday season, accounting for a disproportionately large share of annual purchases of discretionary goods and services. In the United States, for example, in 1996, each household spent an average of $806 during the Christmas holiday season on discretionary items, up from $655 in 1995.[1] For most retailers in the Western world, the months of November and December are critical—approximately 40 percent of total retail department store purchases are concentrated during these two months. And sales in jewelry stores nearly triple during December. No wonder—December is the month when engagements peak![2]

Other holidays induce their own sales. The fourteenth of February, celebrated as Valentine's Day in much of the Western world, generates the highest 24-hour floral sales of the year and is second only to Christmas for the number of greeting cards sent. Products such as candy, stuffed animals, wine, perfume, and all restaurants receive a big boost on this day. Overnight on one February the 13th, Federal Express delivered more than three million pounds of roses! That was enough to fill seven 747 cargo jets—flying from South American to North American florists. By the next morning, there were $331 million worth of flowers in the shops of florists and retailers around the country.[3] In the rest of the world, the influence of holidays on customer purchase behavior is just as prominent. In Israel, Passover is celebrated by nearly every household. In much of the Muslim world, Ramadan is the period of fasting and prayers (when many businesses and stores actually close down), followed by a bout of festivities and consumption. In India, Diwali and Holi are two major Hindu holidays, celebrated with much color and pomp and show (see the Window on Practice box).

Holi and Diwali Holidays Affect Customer Purchases in India

WINDOW ON PRACTICE

Holi is a festival of fire and color, literally—actually a national campfire and paint-spraying party! People come out in their old and torn clothes, ready to spray (and be sprayed on) wet paint and dry color, on friends and strangers alike. For weeks before that, guess what people buy the most? Color and color-spraying guns!

Diwali is something else—a Hindu Christmas of its own, and preparations begin months before. Houses are whitewashed and painted. Floors are freshly scrubbed (if made of stone or marble) or covered with a fresh coat of cow dung (if made of mud). Murals are painted on walls and on the floor. Everyone buys or gets tailored a new set of clothes, generally white for men and bright and colorful for women and girls. During the whole week surrounding the day of Diwali, houses and business premises are decorated with strings of pottery lamps filled with ghee (a purified form of butter), candles, and, in the modern version, electric lights. Music is everywhere. Tons and tons of candies are made—at home as well as by retailers in the market—and consumed. As a good omen, everyone buys a silver, steel, or brass utensil regardless of whether he or she needs it. The affluent order custom-made jewelry. Every home cooks a festive meal. There are fireworks everywhere, with little boys and little girls playing with hand-held sparklers.

Considered a day of worship of Lakshmi, the goddess of wealth, Diwali heralds for many new hopes for a new year of fortune and wealth. Businesses worship the goddess as well as their "account book"! Many business firms still following the Indian conventional calendar (which begins on Diwali, not on January 1) start their new accounting year on this day, replacing their old accounting ledgers with new. Therefore, accounting books are the single largest item purchased by businesses at this time of year. For businesses and households alike, Diwali in India is a time of optimism, engendering a cycle of buying and consuming.

Characteristics of Culture

The concept of culture has the six characteristics illustrated in Figure 6.2.

First, *culture is learned.* We are not born with it. Thus, instinctive behavior, which we possess since birth, is not culture. Thus, the act of crying or laughing is not culture; however, knowing when it is proper to cry or laugh in public is culture since that is something we have to learn. Cultures differ, for example, in permitting public expressions of emotions, such as crying or laughing.

Culture regulates society. It does so by offering norms and standards of behavior and by sanctioning deviations from that behavior. Everyone in a culture knows what rules to live by. Thus, in a small community everyone may drive calmly and follow common courtesy, and the traffic moves smoothly. Where this norm is not enforced, such as someone driving aggressively in parts of New York City or New Delhi, traffic is chaotic.

Culture makes living more efficient. Because culture is shared (by definition), we don't have to learn things anew as we encounter new people and new situations within the same culture. Once you have learned the Japanese culture, for example, you can use the same etiquette in interacting with all Japanese customers.

Culture is adaptive. Culture is a human response to the environment, and as environment changes, culture is likely to adapt itself to the new environmental demands. In wartime, the battle situation requires everyone to act in a coordinated way according to a central command. The military culture is therefore one of central command and control with virtually no room for individual whims. An entrepreneural organization, on the other hand, allows plenty of individual freedom since that is the task demand of innovation.

Figure 6.2

CHARACTERISTICS OF CULTURE

Survival makes adaptation imperative—a U.S. firm doing business in Latin America, for example, would have to adapt its ways of dealing with Latin American customers or else face failure.

Culture is environmental. It envelopes everyone's life alike and always. Like environment, we take culture for granted until something unexpected happens. That is, if a cultural norm is broken, only then is our attention drawn to the otherwise quiet existence of culture. There is a culture in the Western world, for example, of not sharing a table with strangers at fast food restaurants. Nobody thinks about it; the norm is followed and taken for granted until someone breaks it, such as a customer from another culture, say, someone from Amsterdam, where in many restaurants, customers are assigned a seat, not a table.

Finally, multiple *cultures are nested hierarchically.* The culture of the larger group constrains and shapes the culture of the smaller group within it. Imagine that you are a middle-income Hispanic family in the United States with two teenagers. What is the culture in your family? It is actually the culture of the middle class, nested inside the culture of the Hispanics, in turn nested inside the U.S. culture. Within the middle-class Hispanic culture of this family, you will also see youth culture, since the family has some teens. Thus, many of the activities and behaviors you would witness in this family would be different from a family of the same ethnic heritage but without teenagers living in it. For business customers, to take another example, a Japanese advertising agency in the United States would display the culture of an advertising agency within the culture of a Japanese company within the larger culture of the United States. Its culture would be different from that of a Japanese advertising agency in Japan, or from a Japanese legal services company in Japan (since a legal service company will have much more formal culture than an advertising agency), or from a Latin American advertising agency in the United States.

National Culture versus Subculture

National culture refers to the culture prevalent in a nation. It comprises the norms, rituals, and values common to everyone in that nation regardless of the subgroup affiliation. In Appendix 6A, we have summarized the national cultures of selected countries. A related concept is that of "popular culture." **Popular culture** is the culture of the masses, with norms, rituals, and values that have a mass appeal. For example, Hollywood and the movie industry has had an influence on popular culture in the United States.

In contrast to national and popular cultures is the concept of subcultures. **Subculture** is the culture of a group within the larger society. The group may be based on any common characteristics identifying that group as distinct from other groups or from the society at large. For example, group identification may be based on characteristics such as the following:

- *Nationality of origin*—Hispanic, Italian, Polish.
- *Race*—African American, Asian American.
- *Region*—New England and the Southwest in the United States, Northern and Southern Italy.
- *Age*—Youth culture; boomer culture, and so on.
- *Religion*—Moslem culture, Jewish culture, and so on.
- *Gender*—Male and female cultures.
- *Social class*—Middle-class culture; the culture of the nouveau riche.
- *Profession*—Blue collar workers' culture; the culture of the professionals, and so on.

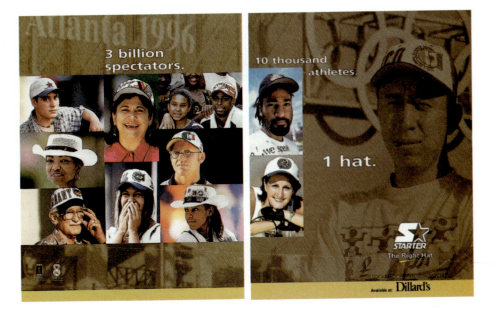

Olympics 1996, perhaps the biggest event in history, brought together customers—spectators and athletes—from all over the world. They represent different nations, diverse cultures.

Corporate Culture

Corporations have culture, too.[4] Tandem Corporation, for example, has a culture of "making things work." Ingrained in its culture was the idea of product reliability. So much did Tandem want to ensure that its products would work that it placed two computers inside the mainframe so that if one failed, the other would keep the machine running. Its slogans illustrate its philosophy:

"It takes two to Tandem."

"Tandemize it—means make it work."

"It's so nice, it's so nice, we do it twice."

Corporate culture is reflected in a company's values, rituals, and customs, and even in corporate myths and celebration of its heroes. Values such as "People are important," "Merit matters," and "Prosper through diversity" define what success means in the corporation. The Window on Practice box on page 152 tells how some companies have expressed their culture by letting managers invent job titles.

Cultural heroes in an organization are the persons who embody the corporate culture and by their example inspire others. They personify the culture's values and provide tangible role models for others. In organizations, heroes make success look attainable and human, set a standard of performance, make values look desirable, motivate everyone else, and symbolize the company to the outside world. Examples of some cultural heroes in the corporate world are Henry Ford at Ford Motor Co., Thomas Watson at IBM, Colonel Sanders at KFC, Bill Gates at Microsoft, and Robert Hass at Levi's.

Examples of rituals and customs include Friday casual dress days and other social gatherings to engender camaraderie and team spirit—morale. Companywide celebrations are staged on important holidays, or there might be annual events like a summer barbecue,

What's in a Title?

Seen any zany titles on business cards lately? Here is a sample of some actual job titles: Chief Yahoo, Chief Knowledge Officer (CKO), Visionary, Ambassador, Chief Growth Officer, Minister of Progress.

The cofounder of Chromatic Research Inc, a microprocessor maker, chose the title of Visionary. Mike Maples, who handles "special assignments" for Microsoft, carries a card that reads Ambassador. The Krispy Kreme Doughnut Corporation's head of marketing communications is titled Minister of Culture.

For even more zany titles, Silicon Valley takes the prize. You won't see executives in pinstripe suits and wingtip shoes here. And you won't meet anybody called Vice President of Corporate Development. As far back as 1984, Guy Kawasaki of Apple Computer Company had the title of Software Evangelist. He described his job as "using fervor and zeal—not money—to motivate developers to write software." Likewise, Linda Jacobson of Silicon Graphics is titled Reality Evangelist.

These titles mesh well with the "loosened tie" culture of the Silicon Valley. However, this cultural playfulness is not always shared by customers. Business customers in South America, for example, won't be happy to see someone called an Evangelist. In Asia, Linda Jacobson becomes "Manager of Virtual Reality Development." But Chief Yahoo, the title of the CEO of Yahoo!, Inc., worked well with Japanese billionaire Masayoshi Son; Mr. Son got a kick out of the title and handed Chief Yahoo over $100 million for an equity stake in the company.

If you were a creative director in an advertising agency, would you call yourself a Senior Creatologist? Or if you were an Internet provider firm's director of marketing, would you call yourself Net-net? Think twice about it. With some of your clients, a zany title can be an ice-breaker. With others, it may be suicidal. It all depends on your customer's corporate culture.

Source: Josh McHugh, "Who Did You Say Is Calling?" *Forbes*, March 10, 1997.

---

annual golf outing, and so on. Celebrations and ceremonies provide visible and potent examples of what the company stands for.

Dimensions of Cross-Cultural Values

Although culture includes a host of shared beliefs and behaviors, the bedrock of culture is values. Cultural values may apply to things, ideas, goals, and behaviors. These define and distinguish one group or society from another—for example, a capitalistic versus a socialistic society. To make generalizations, we can compare cultures across different nations in terms of their people's value orientations. One of the most useful and widely recognized classifications of value orientations is the system developed by Dutch social scientist Geert Hofstede.[5] Based on research in a number of countries, Hofstede has identified the five dimensions of culture shown in Figure 6.3: individualism/collectivism, power distance, uncertainty avoidance, masculinity/femininity, and abstract or associative thinking.

INDIVIDUALISM VERSUS COLLECTIVISM

This dimension concerns the value individuals place on their own individual advancement and benefits versus the good of the groups and institutions of which they are members. Cultures marked with individualism exhibit loose ties among individuals, self-interest over the group interest, large amount of personal freedom, and survival of the fittest. Contrarily, cultures of collectivism exhibit close ties between individu-

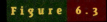

Figure 6.3

FIVE DIMENSIONS OF CULTURAL VALUE ORIENTATIONS

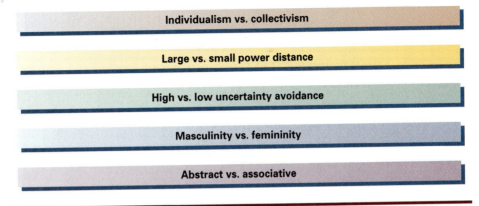

Individualism vs. collectivism

Large vs. small power distance

High vs. low uncertainty avoidance

Masculinity vs. femininity

Abstract vs. associative

als, group interest over self-interest, limited amount of personal freedom, and group protection.

The United States is an example of individualism, whereas Asian societies value collectivism. Accordingly, individualistic appeals are used extensively for American consumers, whereas collective appeals will be more effective in Asian markets or to Asian and Hispanic customer groups in America. (For more details on this difference, see the Window on Practice box below.) Some specific countries that score high on collectivism

WINDOW ON PRACTICE

Group Influences on Chinese Shoppers

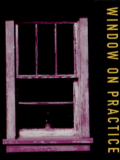

Recently, the China Europe International Business School (CEIBS) did a study of Chinese consumers. It interviewed young chinese consumers (age 25–35 years old) to learn their views about advertising and about how they make buying decisions. The study found that young consumers in China liked advertisements and used them as part of the total shopping experience—which to the Chinese means "learning about the products." Chinese spend a lot of time in stores, simply browsing and window shopping. They then use the information they gather from advertisements and store visits to buy the product, which may be from a store different from the one where initial visits were made for gathering the information.

For Chinese consumers the opinions of friends, colleagues, and family members matter more than the information obtained from the market sources. Chinese consumers want to blend in with their group rather than stand out. This motive guides their choices in favor of brands that are "middle-of-the-road," rather than unique or attention-getting. This is in sharp contrast to North American consumers whose market choices are influenced much more by their desire to stand out and be more individualistic.

Chinese consumers are influenced strongly by their peers, and they try to buy what everyone else is buying. If you knew this about Chinese consumers, which of the three options would you adopt to sell a line of personal-care items, say, cosmetics: (a) selling them through stores, (b) selling them via mail catalogs, or (c) by organizing house parties where a group of friends would gather to look at the merchandise? The correct answer is option c. The American firm Mary Kay did just that for its line of cosmetics; in the first six months, it was successful in selling more than all the department stores combined.

Source: "Japanese Retailing: A Matter of Convenience," in *The Economist,* January 25–31, 1997, p. 62.

are Chile, Egypt, Ethiopia, Indonesia, Kenya, Russia, Mexico, South Korea, Panama, Taiwan, Venezuela, and Zambia. Besides the United States, countries that score high on individualism include Australia, Canada, Denmark, France, Italy, Sweden, and the United Kingdom.

LARGE VERSUS SMALL POWER DISTANCE

Power distance refers to the extent of social inequality and the extent of submissive relationship with authority. In cultures with large power distance, there is greater authoritarianism among persons of different strata in the larger population, among members of the family, and among managerial hierarchy in organizations. In cultures of small power distance, there is greater egalitarianism among members of different strata, among family members, and among managerial hierarchy in the organization. Consequently, decision making is more participative.

Power distance also refers to the extent to which personal relationships are allowed to be formed between members holding different levels of power and authority. In societies with large power distance, subordinates are required to maintain a distance from their superiors and always act in a subservient way. In societies with small power distance, relations between members at different vertical ranks are not as formal.

Some countries with large power distance are Egypt, Guatemala, India, Iraq, Malaysia, the Philippines, Saudi Arabia, and Venezuela. Some countries with small power distance are Australia, Canada, the United States, Germany, Great Britain, Israel, Netherlands, New Zealand, and Switzerland.

Suppose you were conducting negotiations with managers of a foreign firm or were trying to sell your company's services to this firm or even a domestic firm with a corporate culture different than your own. For business customers whose organizations have large power distance, subordinates and middle managers have no say in decision making. You would have to find the right decision-making authority and have access to the upper management, and these are likely to be the customers most concerned with the payer role. In companies with smaller power distance, on the other hand, you would have to involve and engage middle managers and subordinates either because the decision making is likely to have been delegated to them or because, at any rate, the ultimate decision maker is likely to seek counsel from them. These lower-level managers are more likely to be concerned with the user value of performance.

STRONG VERSUS WEAK UNCERTAINTY AVOIDANCE

Uncertainty avoidance can be defined as the extent to which people in a society feel the need to avoid ambiguous situations. They try to manage these situations by providing explicit and formal rules and regulations, rejecting novel ideas, and accepting the existence of absolute truths and superordinate goals in the context of work organization.

Some societies socialize their members into accepting a certain degree of uncertainty and not becoming upset by it. People in such societies tend to accept each day as it comes. Other societies socialize their members into trying to beat the future. However, because the future remains essentially unpredictable, in these latter societies there will be a higher level of anxiety, which then manifests in greater nervousness, emotionality, and aggressiveness.

Uncertainty avoidance is directly related to the importance of quality assurance and service guarantees. People who cannot tolerate uncertainty would be expected to seek greater dependability, reliability, and guarantees when buying products and services. Northern Europeans generally have lower tolerance for uncertainty than Mediterranean cultures.

MASCULINITY VERSUS FEMININITY

This dimension refers to the extent to which male and female roles are segregated and the degree to which masculine roles are considered superior (masculine culture) or inferior (feminine culture). The United States is becoming a society free of this dimension, with greater equality between the genders. In contrast, Asian societies are markedly masculine.

In a masculine society, there are sharp distinctions between assertive roles that men perform and service roles that women are expected to fulfill. The role of women in society clearly generates gender differences in customer values. In a culture where male–female segregation is strong and women have more rigid norms imposed on them (for example, as in the Islamic culture), obviously, market values for products and services for one gender versus the other will be strong and stereotyped.

This dimension can also be interpreted as the extent to which dominant values in a society emphasize assertiveness, acquisition of money and status, and achievement of visible and symbolic rewards. In a masculine society, dominant values are money, success, and material things. A feminine society more strongly values quality of life, preservation of the environment, helping others, putting relationships before money and achievement, and thinking "Small is beautiful."

ABSTRACT VERSUS ASSOCIATIVE

Thinking cultures also differ in terms of the thinking associated with the creation of values in products and services, that is, whether values are engineered into them or added by associative processes such as celebrity endorsement of the products and services. In abstract cultures, cause-effect relationships and logical thinking are dominant. Abstract cultures emphasize the use of cause-effect relationships, face-to-face communication, field independence, and eagerness to change and innovate.

In associative cultures, people utilize associations among events that may not have much logical basis. In these cultures, thinking and communication are characterized by linkages without a logical base, mass media communication, the importance of context, and a resistance to change. For example, associative cultures tend to link events to the influence of gods or the supernatural or to link a personality (e.g., Michael Jordan) to a product or service.

The "How" Aspect of Cultural Differences

In his book *Silent Languages of Doing Business Overseas,* anthropologist Edward Hall describes and illustrates the "how" aspect of cultural influences—that is, how a culture's norms and values are manifested through friendship, time, distance, agreements, and other similar actions. Hall calls these behaviors "silent languages." With regard to business relationships, he identifies five of these silent languages: the basis of agreements, the role of friendship, the importance of relationship, timeliness, and personal space. More recently, consumer researcher Jagdish N. Sheth has identified five additional silent languages: status consciousness, the role of women as executives, dress code, religion, and astrology. Hall and Sheth's silent languages are summarized in Figure 6.4. If marketers fail to interpret one of these correctly, they may fall short in their effort to serve customers in cross-cultural markets.

AGREEMENTS

Cultures differ in whether people base agreements more on rules of negotiations and legal framework or on business customs and moral practices. The Middle East operates on the

Figure 6.4

EXPRESSIONS OF CULTURE IN A BUSINESS CONTEXT

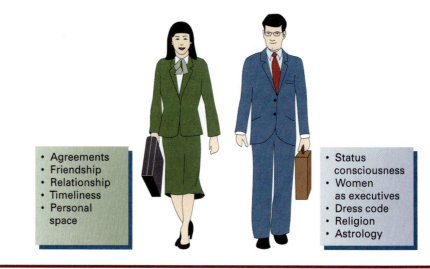

- Agreements
- Friendship
- Relationship
- Timeliness
- Personal space

- Status consciousness
- Women as executives
- Dress code
- Religion
- Astrology

basis of entrenched business customs, which are different from the legal framework used in the United States. Middle Eastern contracts are founded on personal trust rather than on legal paperwork, while the reverse is the case in the United States.

FRIENDSHIP

In some cultures, such as those of India and the Middle East, friendships and personal connections become symbols of power, respect, and status. In these cultures, people like to do business with friends, or only after business associates develop a certain level of friendship and trust. In contrast, in the United States, friends are not as important as good business allies are. Business is conducted on a more impersonal basis, according to the mutual benefit the two parties expect.

RELATIONSHIP

As with friendship, getting to know one another prior to conducting business is a practice followed in many cultures. The Japanese tea ceremony is a good example of this. In the United States, a golf foursome is not uncommon as a means of building relationships in corporate America. In many other cultures such as Latin America, Asia, and Eastern Europe, establishing a personal relationship is often a prelude and a prerequisite to doing business with anyone. For a more detailed example, see the Window on Practice box on page 157.

TIMELINESS

Businesses place different emphasis on promptness and time consciousness in business dealings. In the United States, punctuality and timeliness are very important. In contrast, in Latin America, time is thought of as events, rather than clock hour; thus, events and meetings are scheduled in relation to one another, and a subsequent event begins *whenever* the preceding event ends. Greater concern with timeliness in the United States, of course, has implications for service industries, where excessive waiting time may cause great customer dissatisfaction.

WINDOW ON PRACTICE

Getting to Know You: Building Relationships in Russia

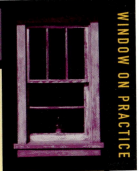

International business consultants H. Ned Seelye and Alan Seelye-James narrate this case story about the importance of relationships:

In the aftermath of *perestroika,* a British engineering firm struck a deal with the Russians to support them in a plant start-up. To staff this project, the firm appointed two Britons, Diana and Horace, who would use interpreters. In the remaining slot of a site consulting engineer's position, Nigel Johnson was appointed. Johnson was a brilliant engineer, plus he spoke Russian fluently. His only drawback was that he was dark, short, and young! This conflicted with Russians' expectations that consultants are tall, light-skinned, and have grey hair and wrinkled faces, reflecting years of experience and wisdom. A middle-aged British colleague had warned him, with the typical British politeness of course, that "there may be a problem."

When Johnson arrived at the plant, he gathered plant managers and supervisors and spent the whole morning talking to them, not at all about engineering and the plant, but rather about himself and his family, asking his audience about their family and answering their questions about life in England and other matters, related to business at hand or not. This perplexed Johnson's own supervisor, who admonished Johnson not to waste any more time in nonbusiness talk. Johnson paid no heed and continued with the relaxed pace and informal conversations during the next few days. A few days later, Johnson was asked into a meeting with the Russian managers and supervisors, and his advice was sought on a particular problem. Although the plant director did not agree with all of his advice, the director let it be known that he was happy to have Johnson to help them.

What to Johnson's supervisor was a waste of time was in fact time well invested in establishing relationships. In countries and cultures such as Russia, relationships are a prelude to doing any business at all. Business customers in such relationship-oriented cultures want to spend time with you in social and informal situations to assess your character in order to judge your trustworthiness. Without trustworthiness, they will do no business with you. In such customer cultures, a seller who gets right down to business would likely scare off more than a few customers.

Adapted from H. Ned Seelye and Alan Seelye-James, *Culture Clash: Managing in a Multicultural World* (Lincolnwood, Illinois: NTC Business Books, 1995).

PERSONAL SPACE

Personal space is the physical distance at which people must stand in face-to-face conversations. In Latin America, this distance is much less than in the United States. An American salesperson meeting a Latin American customer, for instance, could feel offended if he or she were unaware that close physical distance in business conversations is a normal practice in Latin America.

STATUS CONSCIOUSNESS

The status of the person negotiating a business deal is important in some cultures. Sending the right person with appropriate title and power to negotiate is very important in Japan. In the United States, too, business executives take into account the power and background of the person they are dealing with.

WOMEN AS EXECUTIVES

Women's roles in business dealings are perceived differently in different cultures. In the United States, women play a significant role in business dealings. In other countries, however, such as in the Middle East, women executives are less likely to be treated as equal, something that U.S. businesses need to be aware of.

DRESS CODE

Cultures also differ in dress codes. In the United States, dress code is very important. Most male business executives dress in a suit and tie and would not be taken very seriously if they negotiated a deal dressed any other way. On the other hand, in Israel, the dress code is much more informal, and one would not be expected to dress in a suit and tie. This is due in part to both the climate and to business customs.

RELIGION

The influence of religious beliefs in business dealings also varies across cultures. In the Middle East, a business deal can be won or lost on the basis of religious beliefs. In the United States, this will usually not be a problem, unless of course the religious beliefs of an executive interferes with his or her ability to carry through with a deal. For example, in the Jewish faith, the Sabbath (Saturday) is considered a holy day when business is not conducted by those who are Orthodox observers of the religion. This would be a problem to a company if none of its employees could work on Saturday, but it had business that must be conducted on that day.

ASTROLOGY

Some cultures believe in astrological blessings in closing a business deal, as is the practice in China. In the United States, during Ronald Reagan's term as president, there were

Language is not the only difference between two cultures. A sleeveless dress on a female model would be a "no-no" in the culture of the Middle East.

numerous stories circling around the use of astrologers by his wife, Nancy Reagan. No one really knows just how important those considerations were in decisions made which affected the whole world.

The Myth of Homogenized Global Culture

Today, you can be in any corner of the earth, and you will be able to find your favorite brand of clothes, toiletries, luggage, watches, soft drinks, and even fast food. Coke is everywhere, and McDonald's and Kentucky Fried Chicken (KFC) are opening stores in once forbidden central economies of China and Russia. In every sense of the word today, Gucci and Banana Republic, Timex and Rolex, Levi's, and IBM are global brands. The TV series *Dallas* and *Dynasty* were watched worldwide. The Volkswagen beetle mania is back worldwide, and the American-style rap music is being integrated with domestic music in India and other countries. In dress, cuisine, and media viewership, Western capitalism is evident everywhere.

Is cultural diversity on its way to extinction? Are we headed toward a culturally homogenized world? The answer to this question, according to Russel W. Belk, is no. Belk, a creative consumer researcher affiliated with the University of Utah, argues that obliteration of distinct cultures is not the real threat. (See his tongue-in-cheek tale in the Customer Insight box, "The Consumer Revolt against the Saints of Commerce.") The real threat, Belk suggests, is the "creation of a sterilized, sanitized, and trivialized version of consumer life as spectacle." But there are very clear possibilities for resisting such trends:

- *Local resistance to globalization*—Local resistance is offered by three elements: localism, ethnogenesis, and neonationalism. Localism consists in adopting foreign goods but with altered localized meanings, or as a point of departure from the local culture. According to one analysis cited by Belk, the Japanese kept the American facade on Tokyo Disneyland so that they could maintain the "other" separate and distinct from what is one's own. The ethnogenesis factor is that with the break-up of the communist regimes in Eastern Europe, there is a revival rather than demise of ethnic identity. The ethnic groups are eager to separate themselves from one another within the same region, a practice counterproductive to a global village mentality. Finally, neonationalism refers to a renewed pride in one's national identity and national culture. Becoming a global consumer is not the same thing as becoming a global citizen.

- *Hyperreality in globalization*—Consider Main Street U.S.A. in the Disney village. We see in it an idealized and romanticized version of small-town America at the turn of the century. As consumers, we know that it is not real; yet we believe it as if it were (i.e., we enjoy taking in the experience). This is hyperreality—a sanitized version of reality, free from strife, prejudice, dirt, and other problems of everyday living. As consumers we prefer this hyperreality, yet we can distinguish it from the reality. Thus, imported global culture is viewed as hyperreality, while the native culture is viewed as reality.

- *Individualization of the global*—Consumers adapt the globalized, homogenized products and services to their individuality. Thus, at London's council housing estate, residents redecorate the kitchen according to their taste even though they know that they will have to restore it in the standard condition at departure. As another example, motorscooters were originally targeted to women in Britain, but young men made them a trendy male vehicle. Belk states, "In each case, consumers have used standardized objects of the marketplace in a way that asserts identity, reclaims controls, and successfully counters the globalization trend." "Such resistance and quiet rebellion offer," argues Belk, "some small hope that the seemingly inexorable progress toward the age of Ronald McDonald will not go unopposed."[6]

The Consumer Revolt against the Saints of Commerce

The year is 2995 A.D.

Archaeologist Gucci Toyota Rolex, a recent graduate of Ralph Lauren University (once Karl Marx University) in Budapest, sits in his IBM sensatorium seeking clues that will help him understand the obscure origins of the major world holidays. He believes that some of these holidays, including Coke Day, Elvis Day, Saint Johnny Walker Day, the Day of the Levi's, Sony Feel-Man Day, and the Feast of the Seven-Eleven, may have originated almost a millennium ago in the 20th or 21st century. But the evidence is far from clear. No major catastrophe or war has obliterated the relevant data. In fact, the period since the likely origin of these holidays is now known as the Pax McDonald's, due to the extended period of world peace that was ushered in after McDonald's first entered what were then known as China, the Soviet Union, and Eastern Europe. This signaled the peaceful global conquest by Saint Ronald McDonald, at a time when McDonald's sold only food products and the people of the world spoke a variety of languages. No, there is a lack of data because, at some point after the development of United World Government and Entertainment Incorporated, history simply lacked any tension to make it interesting. There was also convincing evidence that history was a source of discontent and neuroses. So when people learned to stop recording the trivia of daily and yearly events, history stopped as well.

As a result, even the details of Saint Ronald's birth and life are lost in the mists of antiquity, along with the biographies of lesser deities such as Colonel Sanders, the Michelin Man, and Mickey Mouse. Although he accepts the catechism that history is bunk, Gucci hopes that if the roots of current celebrations and their patron saints can be pieced together, this proof of divine inspiration will help stop a strange sociopathology spreading among a growing number of the people of the earth: heretic asceticism! Not only does this barbaric and nihilistic cult refuse to worship Saint Ronald, but they reject all of our major holidays and refuse to consume the associated products and services to which they are constitutionally entitled. Recently they have also begun to boycott such sacred sites as Marlboro Country, Ford Country, Sesame Street, Disney Universe, and even McDonaldland. What is worse, they fail to show any enthusiasm for the games, even when such arch rivals as Nissan and Toyota contest. Obviously, such hereticism is dangerous and threatens not only the economy but our essential values. Gucci has no desire to kindle nostalgia for a long dead past, but by returning to the origins of world holidays, perhaps the nonbelievers can be made to accept the legends celebrated by these holidays and their sacrilegious apathetic behavior can be stopped before it spreads farther.

Source: Reproduced with permission from Russell W. Belk, "Hyperreality and Globalization: Culture in the Age of Ronald McDonald," *Journal of International Consumer Marketing*, 8, no. 3/4, (1995) pp. 23–37.

Institutions and Groups

Besides being part of a culture, customers are members of various institutions and groups, which together form the second factor of the customer's personal context. **Groups** can be defined as two or more persons sharing a common purpose. Groups can be transient (such as two or more strangers sharing a cab ride and sharing expenses); or they can be more permanent such as co-workers. **Institutions** are more permanent groups with pervasive and universal presence in a society, such as schools, religions, and the family.

It is important to distinguish between a collection of people and a group. A collection of people may be simply two or more persons sharing physical proximity for a short term. The people in a group have a *common purpose*. To pursue this common purpose, the group members share some values, recognize interdependency, assume specific roles, and communicate mutual expectations and evaluations. Passengers on an interstate bus are simply a collection of people. A small crisis, such as a wheel swung into a ditch, turns this collection into a group, with the common purpose of safely extracting the bus from the ditch, with passengers showing concern for one another's safety, some assuming leadership roles, others dutifully following, each asking for and offering help and co-operation.

Although a collection of people pursuing common goals during a short-term crisis can be thought of as a group, in general, groups are more enduring. The ongoing, enduring existence is in fact what may turn a collection of people into groups. Thus, regular commuters on a metro bus might form friendship groups, and people living on the same street become a group—a neighborhood group, if not a friendship group.

Consumers are social creatures. As such, they live, work, play, belong to, and consume in groups of other consumers. These groups influence customer decisions immensely, as customers try to buy and consume products and services that will please the groups they belong to. Since institutions and groups influence individual behavior by serving as points of reference, as sources of norm, value, and conduct, they are also called reference groups. **Reference groups** are persons, groups, and institutions whom one looks up to for guidance for one's own behavior and values, and whose opinion about oneself one cares for. Of course, the same person or group or institution may be a reference group for one individual but not for another. Thus, sports celebrities are reference groups for some, whereas successful businessmen are for others.

Types of Groups

Groups have been classified in many ways. The most common classifications divide groups according to frequency of contact, nature of membership, formality, and group members' ability to choose whether they belong.

PRIMARY VERSUS SECONDARY AND MEMBERSHIP VERSUS SYMBOLIC GROUPS

Primary groups are the ones that a person interacts with frequently (not necessarily face-to-face) and considers their opinion or norms important to follow. In **secondary groups,** the contact is infrequent, and the norms of the group are considered less binding or obligatory. Examples of primary groups are family, work organization, church groups, business cartels, and so on. Examples of secondary groups are distant relatives; occupational groups like doctors, lawyers, engineers, musicians, theater artists, and so on; credit unions; stockholders groups; volunteers for any political campaign; annual fund-raising committees; the external appraisers group for the Malcolm Baldrige National Quality Award, and so on.

A second dimension to differentiate groups is whether the membership is real or symbolic. **Membership groups** are the ones where an individual claiming to be a member is recognized as such by the head or leader and/or the key members of the group. In **symbolic groups,** on the other hand, there is no provision or procedure for granting membership, and the group leader or key members may even deny membership, but the individual regards him- or herself to be the member and voluntarily and unobtrusively adopts the group's norms and values, and identifies him- or herself with the group. Membership groups are family, the YMCA or other community organization, credit unions, warehouse clubs, professional associations, and so on. Symbolic group memberships are generally one-sided in that the other person does not recognize or is unaware of your self-identification with him

Table 6.2

TYPES OF GROUPS

	PRIMARY	SECONDARY
MEMBERSHIP	■ Family ■ Work organizations ■ Church groups ■ Fraternities/sororities	■ Professional associations ■ Credit unions ■ Political campaign volunteers ■ YMCA
SYMBOLIC	■ Personal role model ■ A significant other ■ The person one "secretly admires"	■ Celebrities ■ Fortune 500 companies ■ Other artists (for an artist)

or her. Examples are celebrities and heroes as sources of inspiration for many who emulate the norms, values, and behavior of their hero.

As shown in Table 6.2, these two bases for classifying groups can be combined to describe many groups.

FORMAL VERSUS INFORMAL AND ASCRIBED VERSUS CHOICE GROUPS

Two other dimensions on which groups differ are the degree of formality and whether or not the person has the freedom to choose the group. In formal groups, conduct and behavior tend to be highly codified. Informal groups, in contrast, have few explicit rules about group behavior. A choice group, as its name implies, is a group a person voluntarily decides to join. An ascribed or assigned group is one in which membership is automatic for someone who has the characteristic that defines the group. Together, these two dimensions lead to four types of groups depicted in Table 6.3.

First, there are groups that are informal in their organization and based on voluntary participation by their members. These choice-based informal groups include neighborhood community and social or volunteer groups such as a homeowners association, the YMCA, the Red Cross, and other volunteer groups. On the other hand, workplace, school, and fraternities or sororities (which even have formal rites of initiation) are more formal groups joined by choice. They are more codified and the group norms as to how a member should behave make a person's conduct subject to rewards and sanctions.

Table 6.3

CLASSIFICATION OF GROUPS FOR HOUSEHOLD CUSTOMERS

	TYPE OF INSTITUTIONS/GROUPS	
	INFORMAL	FORMAL
CHOICE	■ Volunteer groups ■ Community ■ Friendship groups ■ Cultural heroes	■ School ■ Workplace ■ Fraternities
TYPE OF MEMBERSHIP		
ASCRIBED OR ASSIGNED	■ Family ■ Relatives ■ Tribes	■ Religion ■ Prisons

Table 6.4

CLASSIFICATION OF GROUPS FOR BUSINESS CUSTOMERS

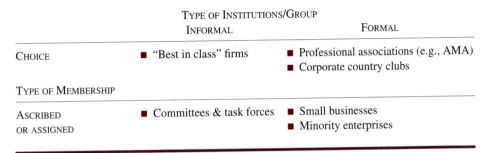

| | TYPE OF INSTITUTIONS/GROUP | |
	INFORMAL	FORMAL
CHOICE	■ "Best in class" firms	■ Professional associations (e.g., AMA) ■ Corporate country clubs
TYPE OF MEMBERSHIP		
ASCRIBED OR ASSIGNED	■ Committees & task forces	■ Small businesses ■ Minority enterprises

Membership in the assigned or ascribed groups is usually by birth (e.g., family, relatives, or a tribe) or by some formal process such as becoming a prisoner or being declared a minority for receiving government benefits. Strictly speaking, only the family you are born into is an ascribed group. All other groups have some degree of choice. Thus, the family you form by marriage, and even your religious group if you abandon your religion of birth and join another religious group—these entail some choice. However, since most people stay in their religion of birth, we will consider religious groups along with families as ascribed groups. Of these, family is an informal institution and religious group is a formal institution.

As shown in Table 6.4, this typology of groups applies just as well to business customers. Informal but choice-based groups are "best in class" companies that a business customer firm may consider itself to be in league with (e.g., "In home appliances, we are what Motorola is in technology"). Informal but ascribed or assigned groups are committees and task forces. Many of these are of course more formalized, particularly if they have the resource allocation responsibility, such as a purchasing committee; but many committees are formed for advisory purposes and on matters not centrally related to the main business of the firm, and these are often informal groups. Examples are a company picnic committee, the beautification committee, volunteers for urban renewal committee, and so on.

Examples of choice-based formal groups include professional associations such as the American Marketing Association (AMA), or corporate country clubs that have well-codified rules of admission and behavioral customs. An example of a formal but ascribed or assigned group in a business setting is a business being identified as a small business and then being accorded all the privileges but also the responsibilities of the small businesses as a group. Similarly, as a minority-owned business, you automatically become a business belonging to the minorities business. Of course, if there is a formal organization (such as a "small business association"), then you have the choice of becoming a member or not. But independent of your joining a choice-based formal organization, you are considered part of a community of small businesses or a minority business class. Of course, many businesses, particularly in diverse cultures, also consider family and religion as their reference groups. For example, as discussed in the previous section of the chapter, Mexican businesses value family more than work, and Japanese businesses consult a priest before any business enterprise.

CONDITIONS FOR REFERENCE GROUP INFLUENCE

Although we all belong to a number of groups, reference groups do not influence every decision to use, pay for, and buy a product or service. When we are buying mulch for our lawn, or hiring a carpenter to build a deck in our backyard, or deciding where to go for a quick lunch, or buying a toner for the laser printer in the office, or choosing a contractor for janitorial services in the office building, we are not thinking of any reference groups we might have. But if we are buying a tree to plant in the front yard of our house, we might worry about our neighbors' opinion on it. Or if we are going to the annual office Christmas party, we had better think twice before putting on that bell-bottomed high-fashion outfit we so proudly wore at the 10th college reunion earlier this month. If we are entertaining a business guest, we had better choose our restaurant wisely.

The important question, therefore, is When or under what conditions does reference group influence occur? Behavioral scientist Francis S. Bourne addressed this question in a pioneering work that proposes that a product's or service's conspicuousness is the principal factor that affects whether or not users of that product or service will be susceptible to reference group influence.[7] Moreover, Bourne proposed that there are two dimensions of conspicuousness: exclusivity and public visibility. If everyone owns and uses a product or service, then the ownership and use of that product or service has no exclusivity. Accordingly, there will be no basis for being concerned about others' opinions on it. The second dimension, visibility, is critical because a product or service has to be visible and identifiable in order for reference group members to approve or disapprove of it.

Based on Bourne's ideas, marketing professors and consumer researchers William O. Bearden and Michael J. Etzel have suggested that the reference group influence may occur for the ownership of the product per se, or for the choice of a specific brand, or both. This will depend on whether a product is a luxury or a necessity (capturing the "exclusivity" dimension of conspicuousness in Bourne's proposal), and whether the product is used in private or in public (capturing the "visibility" dimension of conspicuousness). Accordingly, four combinations can occur (see Table 6.5):[8]

Table 6.5 PRIVATE-PUBLIC, LUXURY-NECESSITY, PRODUCT-BRAND INFLUENCES

		PUBLIC	
PRODUCT / **BRAND**		WEAK REFERENCE GROUP INFLUENCE (−)	STRONG REFERENCE GROUP INFLUENCE (+)
NECESSITY	Strong reference group influence (+)	*Public necessities* ■Influence: Weak product and strong brand ■Examples: Wristwatch, automobile, man's suit	*Public luxuries* ■Influence: Strong product and brand ■Examples: Golf clubs, snow skis, sailboat	LUXURY
	Weak reference group influence (−)	*Private necessities* ■Influence: Weak product and brand ■Examples: Mattress, floor lamp, refrigerator	*Private luxuries* ■Influence: Strong product and weak brand ■Examples: TV game, trash compactor, icemaker	
		PRIVATE	

Source: William O. Bearden and Michael J. Etzel, "Reference Group Influence on Product and Brand Purchase Decisions," *Journal of Consumer Research* 9 (1982), pp. 183–94.

1. *Publicly consumed luxuries*—In this case, reference groups will influence both whether or not the product will be owned and which brand is purchased.

2. *Privately consumed luxuries*—Here, reference group influence will be strong for the ownership of the product (because it is a luxury) but weak for the brand choice (since it will be used in private, out of public visibility).

3. *Publicly consumed necessities*—In this case, product ownership influence will be absent or weak since everyone owns it anyway, but brand level influence will be strong due to public visibility.

4. *Privately consumed necessities*—Finally, for products that are necessities and, in addition, are consumed privately, neither product ownership nor the choice of specific brands is likely to be influenced by reference groups.

TYPES OF REFERENCE GROUP INFLUENCE

Whether the reference group influences decisions about a brand or a product category, the influence may operate through several types of power. The nature of influence power exercised by reference group members may be of three types: expertise, reward and sanction, and attractiveness. Corresponding to each type of power is a type of reference group influence: informational, normative, and identificational, respectively.[9] (See Table 6.6.)

INFORMATIONAL   Informational influence occurs when a consumer seeks and accepts advice from someone else because of the latter's expertise on the performance characteristics of the product or service being bought. Examples of informational reference groups include: (a) professional advisors such as doctors and pharmacists, stock brokers, lawyers, car mechanics, and salespeople; (b) product enthusiasts among your informal groups such as a friend who is a computer buff; and (c) other consumers having previous experience with the product or service, such as a family member or relative or friend who might have bought or tried a product or a brand. Much of the word-of-mouth communication occurs simply because of consumers' desire to seek and accept experience-based information from other consumers. Business customers seek and accept informational influence as well. For instance, they contract with legal, technical, and managerial consultants if they don't have the necessary expertise in-house.

Table 6.6

✳ TYPES OF REFERENCE GROUP INFLUENCES FOR HOUSEHOLD CUSTOMERS

Type of Influence	Basis	Exemplars	Products
Informational	Expertise	Professional advisors Product enthusiasts Experienced consumers	Medication Computers Travel destinations
Normative	Material rewards Sanctions	Work groups Family	Work clothes Alcohol
Identificational	Self-concept enactment	Cultural heroes (e.g., sports athletic celebrity)	Shoe brand

Source: Adapted and modified by the authors based on Robert E. Burnkrant and Alain Cousineau, "Informational and Normative Social Influence in Buyer Behavior," *Journal of Consumer Research* 2 (December 1975) pp. 206–15.

NORMATIVE   Normative influence occurs when a consumer lets his or her decision be influenced by his or her desire to conform with the expectations of someone else. This influence stems from the reference group's power to reward or sanction the consumption behavior of others. Thus, family members exercise influence on what others, especially children and adolescents, may or may not watch, read, eat, wear, and drive. Organizations have dress codes, and employees abide by them even when, to some of them, the required clothes are "boring." Some organizations are now allowing Friday as a day to wear casual clothing, and some have relaxed their dress codes entirely; presumably this offers employees more individuality and freedom of expression. Businesses are also subject to normative influence from government: for example, in regard to doing business with minorities.

IDENTIFICATIONAL   Identificational influence occurs when a consumer buys something because it helps him or her to be like somebody else. Everybody has some role model, someone he or she aspires to be similar to and identifies with; the consumer then emulates, to the extent possible, the lifestyle of people he or she admires, buying products associated with, used by, or endorsed by these admired people. Cultural heroes such as entertainment, sports, or political celebrities inspire and serve as reference groups for multitudes of consumers, especially in their more impressionable adolescent years. Popular brand names such as Nike (sponsored by future Hall of Fame sportsman Michael Jordan) in athletic wear, Polo or Tommy Hillfiger in clothing, and Giorgio or Calvin Klein in colognes are examples of products consumers buy principally under the identificational influence. Brand choices made under this influence help consumers enact their self-concept, living and becoming the kind of person they want to be.

In business markets, identificational influences are at work when companies look to other corporations as "best in class," or the most admired companies. They emulate these "best in class" companies to try to gain their advantages. Another example is the Malcolm Baldrige Award given by the U.S. government to companies demonstrating outstanding quality. Many companies covet this award and the prestige that goes with it. To win it, companies adopt many practices required for raising their quality. One of the recommended practices is building long-term relationships with suppliers. Thus, companies desirous of winning the award adopt better supplier management practices. This exemplifies the role of reference groups in modifying customer behavior.

TYPES OF REFERENCE GROUP INFLUENCES FOR BUSINESS CUSTOMERS

Type of Influence	Basis	Exemplars	Products
Informational	Expertise	Legal and technical consultants	Business contracts
Normative	Material rewards and sanctions	Political advisors Government	Equipment purchasing Campaign resource allocations Doing business with minorities
Identificational	Self-concept enactment	Most admired companies/best in class	Emulating "business practices"
		Malcolm Baldridge Award	Adopting recommended sourcing practices

FAMILY: THE MOST INFLUENTIAL REFERENCE GROUP

Perhaps the most influential reference group for any individual customer is that person's family. Family can be defined as a group of people related by marriage and biology. Generally, families are characterized by a sharing of a common residence, presence of ties of affection, an obligation for mutual support and caring, and possession of a common sense of identity.[10]

Family is the institution in which children, the future adults of a society, receive their precepts and guidance. The concept of what is good and right is transmitted through the family. Family members socialize with each other as citizens and as consumers participating in a common consuming unit.[11] The influence of family members on one another's buying decision process is discussed in a later chapter. It is sufficient to note here that families are primary groups where members interact continually in intense and face-to-face communications and where member preferences and desires receive constant feedback and are channeled and shaped by reinforcement or sanctions by other members. Of all reference groups, families most intensely influence the values their members seek in marketplace exchanges. Families are important and exercise influence on customer behavior across all cultures. However, family as a source of life satisfactions and as a source of values and aspirations is even more influential in Eastern cultures such as those of India, China, Japan, Indonesia, the Middle East, Latin America, and Mexico. Many individuals are proud of the family they come from, such as the Kennedy family in the United States and the Nehru family in India. Likewise, many businesses proudly carry the founding family's name as well as values, such as the Ford Motor Company, Toyota and Mitsubishi of Japan, Siemen's of Germany, and the Tata Enterprise in India.

A family is the most influential reference group.

RELIGION AS A REFERENCE GROUP

Like family, religion is a reference group that exercises substantial influence on customers—their values, customs, and habits. Religion refers to a system of beliefs about the supernatural, spiritual world, about God, and about how humans, as God's creatures, are supposed to behave on this earth. Religious institutions indoctrinate and offer tenets by which their followers ought to live. As such, these institutions influence customer values, both in respect to the importance and value of material possessions and the goals or benefits of the products. As a historical example, sociologist Max Weber attributed the industrialization and rise of capitalism in Western Europe to the Protestant ethic.[12]

Major denominations (i.e., religious affiliations) in the United States are Catholics, Protestants, and Jews. Major religions of the world include Christianity, Islam, Judaism, Hinduism, Buddhism, and Confucianism. The major ideas and tenets of each are summarized in Appendix 6B.

Religious affiliation affects customer behavior principally by influencing the customer's personality structure—that is, his or her beliefs, values, and behavioral tendencies. These personality structures, in turn, affect customers' marketplace behaviors. For example, if you contrast the personality structures of, say, Protestants and Catholics, you would find that compared with Catholics, Protestants are much more stoic, nationalistic, ascetic individualists who believe they have control of their fate and accept delayed gratification. In contrast, Catholics are more traditional and fatalisic, with belief in collec-

How Religious Beliefs Impact Consumer Preferences

To examine the customer behavior differences due to people's religious affiliations, Beth Hirschman, then a consumer research professor at New York University, surveyed a sample of consumers in New York City. Among her respondents were 96 Catholics, 114 protestants, and 120 Jews. She asked them to indicate what criteria they would use to decide what to do on a weekend evening for entertainment. She also asked them to list the kind of activities they might consider doing.

Consumers' choice criteria (i.e., the considerations they use in making their choice among a set of alternatives) differed significantly across the three religious groups. Moreover, these differences were explainable by religious affiliations and the personality structure shaped by them. Specifically, among the choice criteria, price was mentioned much more by Protestants, as was also the expected enjoyment. This may result from an emphasis (found among Protestants) on capital accumulation and on using time productively. Desire for companionship and personal feeling (how "I feel about it") were other important criteria, mentioned much more by Jews than by the other two groups. This is most likely because Jews are much more sociable and emotional.

Preferred leisure activities differed significantly as well. Dinner and/or entertaining at home was mentioned much more by Catholics than the other two groups (63 percent of Catholics mentioned it compared to 18 percent of Protestants and 45 percent of Jews). This is an outcome of the fact that Catholics place much more emphasis on family and home. In contrast, going to a nightclub or attending

a ballet was mentioned the least by Catholics but the most by Jews. The reason is that Jews are more cosmopolitan and also more hedonic (seeking sensory pleasure) in comparison to the other two groups. Visiting friends was cited the most by Jewish consumers, attesting to the gregarious, emotional, and sociable personality character their religious affiliation inculcates in them. Reading was mentioned the most by Protestants, the second most by Jews and the least by Catholics. Note that both Protestants and Jewish religions prescribe seeking knowledge of the world from nonreligious scriptures. Also, reading is a very productive use of time, a value Protestants seek. Finally, making love was mentioned considerably more by Jews (53 percent compared to 3 percent and 13 percent by the other two groups). This too is explainable by religious affiliation. Both Protestant and Catholic religions consider sex as an activity whose main purpose is reproduction. In contrast, the Jewish religion recognizes sex as a legitimate hedonic (i.e., enjoyment) value!

Although this study is based on a small sample of customers, and is dated, its principal arguments appear logical. At the very least, it is a powerful illustration of the pervasive influence of religion on one's personality, and, in turn, on consumption preferences.

Source: Elizabeth C. Hirschman, "Religious Affiliations and Consumption Processes: An Initial Paradigm," in *Research in Marketing*, J. Sheth, ed. (Greenwich, CT: JAI Press, 1983), pp. 131–70.

tivism (rather than individualism) and in external locus of control (i.e., fate tends to control them). They also emphasize family and home.

On the other hand, Jews differ from both these groups. They tend to be more innovative (rather than traditional), more achievement oriented, and more emotional, but also more anxious socially. These personality differences in turn affect consumer preferences for products or services. See the Window on Research box.

Personal Worth

Along with culture and reference groups, the customer context that influences the market values the customer seeks includes personal worth. In this context, **personal worth** means only financial worth and has nothing to do with a person's worth as a human being, or a person's worthiness in terms of his or her character.

Measurement of Personal Worth

As shown in Figure 6.5, personal worth has three components: income, wealth, and borrowing power.

INCOME

A person's **income** is the amount of monetary earnings that person receives periodically on a more or less regular basis. The general income level of a society has strong bearing on what will be produced and consumed by it.

Although no two families spend their money in exactly the same way, there is, on the average, quite a consistent pattern of how income is allocated over expense categories. Based on statistical analyses of data from families with diverse income groups, economists have discovered that a nearly constant proportion is spent on various items. Poor families, of course, spend their incomes largely on food and housing and on some basic

Figure 6.5

COMPONENTS OF PERSONAL WORTH

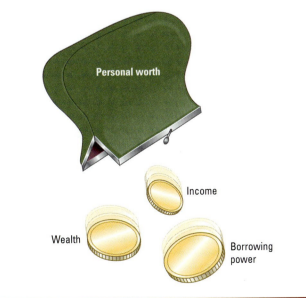

clothing. As income increases, people tend to eat more food and also more of the food that is less staple (and therefore more expensive). As income increases, the proportion spent on food declines; after all one can eat only so much!

Your proportion of income spent on housing rises with income in the very low-income range, but then it remains pretty constant. Expenditures on clothing, automobiles, and luxury goods rise sharply with income, until a very high upper limit is reached. Finally, savings rise dramatically with income, and they never decline. Because of low incomes, affordability for luxury items is severely restricted in many third world countries.

For example, in China, less than 15 percent of the households can afford to buy a refrigerator. In fact, Chinese people's incomes are so low that even affording such items as detergent or packaged food is a luxury, within reach of only about 15 to 20 percent of Chinese, whose annual incomes exceed $1,000. If you were a foreign firm hoping to market consumer goods produced in the more modernized nations such as North America, Europe, or Japan, you would be dismayed at the low market size that China offers. This is certainly what a Japanese retail company *Yaohan* discovered in operating one of the world's largest department stores in Shanghai.[13]

These spending patterns are called "Engel's laws" after the 19th century Prussian statistician Ernst Engel. See Figure 6.6. According to **Engel's law,** the lower the per capita income of a nation or people, the more they tend to spend on basic necessities such as food and clothing. As discretionary income rises, consumers spend more on discretionary items, such as vacations, art collections, or even plastic surgery.

Figure 6.6

ENGEL'S LAW

Lower-income customers spend a large proportion of their income on food, clothing, and housing.

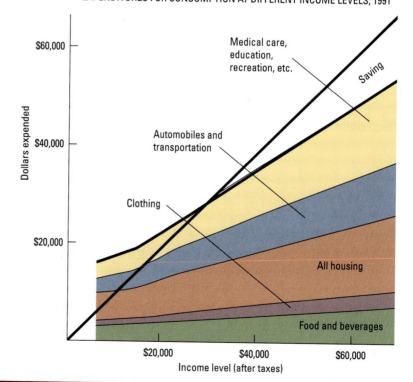

EXPENDITURES FOR CONSUMPTION AT DIFFERENT INCOME LEVELS, 1991

Source: Paul A. Samuelson and William D. Nordhaus, *Economics* 14th ed. (New York: McGraw, 1992), p. 43B.

Similarly, in business markets, cash flow influences what will or will not be bought. Many small business failures are mostly due to cash flow problems. On the other hand, rapid growth can also create cash flow problems from corporate acquisitions. For example, General Motors became the largest corporation through acquisition of smaller automobile companies such as Chevrolet, Pontiac, Buick, and Oldsmobile, which had cash flow problems during the great Depression of 1929. Similarly, General Foods was built on buying out small local or regional brands and making them national brands, including Yuban, Maxwell House, and Sanka coffees and Bird's Eye frozen vegetables.

WEALTH

The second component and measure of personal worth is wealth. In household markets, **wealth** is assessed as the net worth of an individual. Net worth of an individual is defined as current dollar value of all assets owned minus the current dollar value of all liabilities. Households with net worth exceeding $1 million are generally regarded as wealthy. There were an estimated 1.2 million millionaires in the United States in 1987.

As illustrated in Figure 6.7, wealth is created by five means: (1) inheritance, (2) high-income accumulation, including "passive income" from investment of one's wealth; (3)

COMPONENTS OF WEALTH

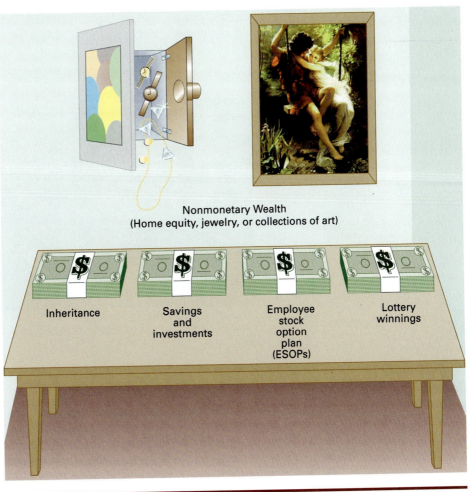

Nonmonetary Wealth
(Home equity, jewelry, or collections of art)

Inheritance   Savings and investments   Employee stock option plan (ESOPs)   Lottery winnings

by employee stock option plans (ESOPs)—for example, Microsoft has created at least 5,000 millionaires from its ordinary workers due to ESOPs; (4) accumulation of nonmonetary wealth such as equity in home ownership, jewelry, or art; (5) lottery winnings—most states have lotteries or legalized gambling and a lotto as a weekly jackpot, generally worth more than a million dollars. Additionally, illegal gambling, prostitution, and drugs have created enormous wealth for a few.

For individual households, the concept of net worth is relevant. Its counterpart for the business market is the concept of shareholder equity. The net worth of a business customer is reflected in its balance sheet. Net worth is the book value of a business. The book value may or may not be commensurate with the business's market value.

BORROWING POWER

Borrowing power is the final indicator of a customer's economic condition. In consumer markets, **borrowing power** is the anticipated level of income of the person (lifetime disposable income and asset accumulation through savings). The best examples of market offerings that are based upon an accounting of the customer's borrowing power include consumer credit cards, home mortgages, and automobile financing.

The business market equivalent is the firm's ability to repay debt in the future. It is measured by creditworthiness of the organization based on ratings by A.M. Best Company and Standard & Poor's ratings ("AAA" rating is the highest). It is also reflected in letters of credit for financing the working capital (inventory and accounts receivables). Finally, the lease of equipment (machinery, office equipment, and computers) is another good indicator of the business borrowing power.

A scooter or a bicycle? Which one would you ride? To each, according to his personal net worth.

The Poor, the Rich, and the Middle Class

To understand how customer behavior differs by personal worth, it is useful to divide all customers into three groups: poor, middle class, and affluent. How are these groups defined? How many people fall into these groups—worldwide and in selected countries? How do the needs and wants differ across these groups? How do they differ in terms of the market values they seek in each of the three customer roles? And what is the marketplace behavior and the underlying psychology of customers in each group? Finally, how are marketers responding to the needs and wants of these customer groups? These questions are addressed next.

THE POOR

A 1963 study by sociologist David Caplovitz showed that poor consumers actually pay more for goods and services than the rest of society. This occurs both because poor consumers do not have the skills and transportation to shop for bargains and because merchants exploit their weaknesses.

DEFINITION OF POVERTY   In general, **poverty** is a level of personal wealth at which a household cannot even pay for all of its basic needs, such as food, clothing, and shelter. For the U.S. population, the federal Department of Health and Human Services defines the poverty level relative to the cost of food. To do this, the department first specifies a daily market basket of foods needed to provide an adequate, nutritious diet on an "emergency" basis (i.e., when income is very low) for families of various sizes and composition. This food basket is then priced according to prevailing prices, and in turn multiplied by three because at low-income levels food represents about one-third of all expenditures. This figure defines the poverty-threshold income level. In 1995, this figure was $15,569 for a U.S. family of four. The number of people below the poverty level was 36.4 million, representing 13.8 percent of the U.S. population.

THE PSYCHOLOGY OF POVERTY   The poor see themselves as relatively deprived, powerless, cut off from the rest of society, and manipulated. Their attitudes toward life differ from well-to-do consumers as follows:

- *Insecurity*—The poor feel that their jobs are unstable, that their resources are inadequate to take care of sickness or other emergencies, and that police and courts exercise excessive and unfriendly vigilance against them.
- *Helplessness*—The poor feel they lack political muscle, and because of their low-level education and limited life experiences, they are subject to the whims of others.
- *Fatalism*—The poor feel that their own destinies are not in their hands and that chance, luck, or others control their future.
- *Present orientation*—Since they perceive a lack of personal control of future events, the poor feel they might as well enjoy life now and let the future take care of itself.

These attitudes are responsible, according to some researchers, for the poor accumulating debt, not saving, and buying unwisely (without putting in the required effort to obtain good price values).[14]

Some studies have found that the poor do not follow wise purchasing strategies. That is, the poor are less likely to read newspapers (and therefore newspaper advertisements), less likely to do comparison shopping, less likely to patronize low-price discount and warehouse stores and to buy private or generic brands, and are more likely to accept high-interest credit. Whereas some may view these as *ir*rational behaviors, the poor might actually be quite rational, given their goals and situation.

THE MIDDLE-INCOME GROUP

There is no single definition of what "middle income" is. One conventional grouping deems income levels of less than $25,000 as low income, from $25,000 to $75,000 as middle income, and greater than $75,000 as upper income. In 1994 dollars, the percentages of U.S. households in these three groups were 39.4, 47.0, and 13.6 percent respectively. Note that this approach defines the low-income group (income <$25,000) more broadly (39.4 percent) than the "poverty group" identified earlier.

INCOME DISTRIBUTION OF U.S. HOUSEHOLDS

	RANGE	PERCENTAGE
Bottom fifth	<$17,940	4.2
Second fifth	$17,941 to $31,300	10.0
Third fifth	$31,301 to $47,000	15.7
Fourth fifth	$47,001 to $69,998	23.3
Top fifth	>$69,998	46.9
All households		100.*
Top 5 percent	>$120,043	20.1

Note: Percentages do not total 100 percent due to rounding.

Source: Bureau of the Census, U.S. Department of Commerce.

Another way of reckoning income groups is to divide the population into fifths, as in Table 6.8. Considering the second, third, and fourth groups as middle-income groups, 60 percent of U.S. households were in the middle-income group, accounting for 47.3 percent of aggregate income.

In Europe, average income has gone up in most European Union (EU) nations. In Belgium, France, Italy, the Netherlands, and the United Kingdom, however, the trend is toward a two-tier income distribution, where both upper- and lower-income groups are expanding but the middle-income group is shrinking. The marketing implication of this situation is simultaneous demand for luxury products and for inexpensive products.

THE AFFLUENT

There is, of course, no universal definition of affluence. One convenient identification is to designate the top fifth of households as affluent. In the United States, this group's annual income exceeds $70,000, with their average income exceeding $100,000. Furthermore, the top 5 percent may be deemed as "superaffluent." Their annual income exceeds $120,000. In recent years, this top 5 percent of U.S. households has accounted for more than 20 percent of total aggregate U.S. household income.[15]

The top one-fifth of households account for some 35 percent of all wine consumption in the United States, more than 60 percent of all airline travel, and 54 percent of all new-car sales. Obviously, the exquisite products advertised in such magazines as *Town and Country, Smithsonian, Architectural Digest, Southern Accent,* and *Worth* are consumed almost exclusively by the affluent. In third world countries, domestic servants—chauffeurs, butlers, valets—and imported cars are the status symbols for the affluent.

Social Class

Many sociologists, consumer economists, and consumer researchers consider social class, rather than personal worth, to be a more meaningful characteristic to understand and predict customer behavior. Income is an important factor in deciding a person's social class, but it is not the only determinant. Social class also depends considerably on one's education and occupation so that, despite relatively low income, a highly educated person and/or someone in a more prestigious occupation could be accorded higher social class, and vice versa.

Social class is the relative standing of members of a society so that a higher position implies a higher status than those in the lower social class. Status results from wealth,

Table 6.9

CONSUMPTION PATTERNS AMONG U.S. SOCIAL CLASSES

PRODUCT CATEGORY	UPPER CLASS	MIDDLE CLASS	LOWER CLASS
House	Large estate plot secluded from public view; multi-room; extensively landscaped; unique; custom-made	Housing developments	Crowded urban or inner-city housing
Furnishings	Marble or parquet floors; oriental rugs; color-coordinated window treatments in pastel or earthtone colors; original works of art; selected large portraits of ancestors; certificates or diplomas and trophies in study or individual children's room	Wall-to-wall carpeting; mass-produced art prints in mass-produced frames; portraits of family members placed sparingly	Vinyl floors; portraits of family members crowding the walls; certificates, trophies, and other memorabilia in every room
Food	Dining out at full-service restaurants with exquisite cuisine; limited at-home cooking; gourmet foods (such as asparagus); wine, light liquors, martinis, premium beers; bottled water, iced tea	Dining out at national chains (e.g., Pizza Hut, Don Pablo's, Olive Garden); significant cooking at home; frozen foods, vegetables, fish; mixed drinks, beer	Eating out at fast-food restaurants; substantial cooking at home; meat and potatoes, staple foods; beer, malt liquor, liquor with higher volume alcohol; soft drinks with greater sugar content; tend to be heavy beer drinkers
Clothing	Designer brand; custom tailored; cotton, silk, wool, and blends; upscale department stores, specialty stores, boutiques	Name brands; store brands; designer brands from off-price store; polyester blends, denims	Discount department stores; thrift stores; garage sales; polyester and other synthetic fabric; T-shirts with sports heroes and baseball caps are popular
Leisure	Vacation in exotic resorts abroad or domestic; travel by air; cruise ships; memberships in country clubs	Vacation travel to popular and fun spots, e.g., Disney World, Smokey Mountains	Vacation travel mostly to relatives and friends in nearby cities
Sports	Golf, polo, cricket, skiing	Bridge, team sports like volleyball, baseball, soccer	Bowling, bingo, weight lifting, fishing, motorcycle riding
Media	Less TV, more magazines and newspaper	Average TV and more newspaper and magazines	A lot more TV; extensive interest in local news and events, sitcoms, and soap operas
Shopping	For marketplace information, rely on specialists and advisers; quality and features important and desired at any price; coupon nonusers	Use newspapers, consumer magazines, and product brochures; extensive planning and need evaluation based purchasing; heavy use of coupons	Use in-store displays and salesperson advice as a source of information much more than do other classes; price a predominant consideration; prefer to shop at small local stores with acquaintance with the owner; buy on as-needed basis without prior planning (contributes to poor paying more); not much use of coupons

Source: Adapted and modified by the authors based on Paul Fussell, *Class* (New York: Summit Books, 1983), pp. 190–192. Copyright 1983 by Paul Fussell.

political power, education, professional success, and so on. In many less-developed societies, social class is ascribed rather than achieved—that is, one's social class is defined by birth. In more industrialized nations, social class is defined by one's achievements, whether material (e.g., wealth) or otherwise (e.g., education, work success, political position).

Sociologist W. Lloyd Warner defined social class as "classes of people who were approximately equal in community esteem and were made up of men and women who regularly socialized among themselves, in both formal and informal ways and shared behavioral expectations."[16] Studies done at the University of Chicago and Social Research, Inc., documented that members of different social classes differed in their purchase goals and shopping behavior. In sociologist Richard P. Coleman's words, these classes were "motivational groups," not just status categories—i.e., they caused different purchase behaviors.[17]

Coleman introduced, along with a colleague Lee P. Rainwater, a new social class grouping.[18] This grouping is based on a study sponsored by the Joint Center for Urban Studies of MIT and Harvard. Researchers interviewed some 900 residents in Boston and Kansas City areas, questioning respondents on their perceptions of the social hierarchy and their own participation in it. They found, for instance, that the middle mass of citizens most readily talk in terms of "people like us in the middle," "people above," and "people below." In such perceptions of hierarchy, economic status plays the primary role, and education and behavioral standards the secondary (but nonetheless important) role.

Social Class Characteristics

Some characteristics of the concept of social class are as follows:

1. *Rank ordering*—Social classes are ranked in terms of social prestige.

2. *Relative permanence*—Social classes are relatively permanent characteristics of the family. A person's social class does not change from day-to-day or even year-to-year.

3. *Intergenerational class mobility*—Although it does not change year-to-year (or even less often), it is possible for a person or a family to move in and out of a social class, such as from lower to middle class or vice versa. In particular, it is possible for a person to move out of the social class of his or her birth to a higher or a lower class by acquiring the values, resources, and behaviors of the new class. Of course, some societies prohibit such social class mobility.

4. *Internal homogeneity*—Classes are homogeneous within each strata or within themselves. As such, the persons belonging to the same social class tend to be similar in terms of the types of occupations, the kinds of neighborhoods they live in, food habits, socializing, and so on.

5. *Distinct from income*—As mentioned before, although income is an important determinant of social class, there is no one-to-one correspondence between the two. Since social class depends as much on other factors—education, occupation, personal tastes, and so on, it is not uncommon for a person of relatively middle income to be in the upper social class and vice versa. For example, a university president with a salary of about $150,000 to $200,000 is in the same upper social class as a CEO of a Fortune 500 company, who can make about $500,000 to $1,200,000 annually. Likewise priests, politicians in power, and educators command the prestige and status significantly disproportionate with their income earnings.

Impact of Social Class

Social classes exist everywhere. In centrally controlled economies and polities, social classes can be divided into the ruling classes, those close to the ruling class, and the masses. In once-traditional societies such as India, social class is the caste a person is born in. Among Hindus, it is Brahmin (the priest and learned), the Kshatriya (the ruler, prince, and warrior class), the Vaishyas (or the trader class), and the Shudras, the untouchable class—although these caste barriers are weakening in modern India. In feudal systems, classes are the landlords and the peasants; in pre–Civil War America, classes consisted of the slaves and other servants and the white European gentry. In industrializing nations, the bourgeois and the proletariat form the social classes. Democratic societies boast egalitarianism, but the class system is alive and well. Everywhere, class distinctions are almost a sociological need: People need, it would seem, a class system to belong to, to aspire to, and to associate with.

People everywhere identify themselves with some class, even if it is a class higher than their current objectively defined class. You will often find a person say, "That is not a class act," "That is not what people of my class do," or the like. It seems as though without a self-identification with some class, people would sense a loss of identity.

At the same time, being identified with a class imposes a set of "normative" behaviors. People expect others of the same class to behave like they do—observe the class norms, so to speak. A broad range of behaviors is expected, as detailed below.

Persons belonging to the same class also share their values, possessions, customs, and activities. In the next section, we will describe examples of how this occurs in the United States.

Social Classes in America: A Brief Profile

The broad social groups in Coleman's scheme—namely, Upper, Middle, and Lower Americans—differ markedly in their marketplace behaviors. Social classes determine customers' marketplace behaviors, in terms of both what they buy and how they buy it. Correspondingly, their tastes, activities, preferences, and possessions differ markedly. In leisure, for example, lower classes prefer and engage in such sports as bowling, and such pastimes as boxing, fishing, watching wrestling, hunting, visiting casinos, and watching TV. Upper-class groups play golf and polo, go on cruises, patronize symphonies, operas, and plays. People of middle class play team sports (e.g., volleyball), play cards, and spend a lot of time shopping and visiting friends. Table 6.9 summarizes some important differences in consumption across the three social classes.

LOWER AMERICANS

Typically, Lower Americans are "family folks," deriving their emotional and psychological support from family members and relatives. "Locational narrowness" marks their preference in housing, travel, sports, and news—they live close to their kin, travel nearby or to meet relatives, favor local sports heroes, and take interest mainly in local rather than national news. Illustrating the loyalties and "locational narrowness" of this class for automobiles, Coleman writes:

> By the mid-1970s, ownership of an imported car had penetrated 40 percent among the upper, and 25 percent among the middle-class families but less than 10 percent among working-class families. This was three years after the gas price shock! . . . gas-guzzling pick-ups and standard- and large-size cars were still in favor. Thus was the working class remaining the xenophobic heart of resistance to the foreign-car invasion and dragging its heels in accepting the idea that America should reduce the size of its automobiles; the men of this class were not yet ready to give up this macho symbol of roadway conquest.

MIDDLE AMERICANS

This class is most concerned with wanting to "do the right thing" and buying what is popular. Middle-class persons tend to emulate the lifestyles of the Upper Americans, a tendency working classes do not exhibit. This "upward gaze" makes them patronize dinner theaters and all the other trickle-down culture. Physical activities (particularly the ones in which parents can participate with their children) are becoming popular with this group. Indeed, physical activities are becoming core to middle-class life "in which possessions-pride has yielded to activities-pleasure." Of course, the middle-class struggle to uplift themselves continues, evidenced in increased enrollment from this class into local colleges and universities. "Imaged as a mental challenge and storehouse for knowledge, the home computer will do particularly well here when it reaches mass-market pricing." This prophecy, made some 10 years ago seems to ring true today.

UPPER AMERICANS

This class as a whole remains concerned with buying quality merchandise, favoring prestige brands, and spending with good taste. Significant numbers of upper-uppers are adopting less circumscribed ways of consumption. Two points about the Upper Americans group are noteworthy. First, a subdivision of this group has been identified and referred to by sociologist Irving Kristol as "The New Class." Consisting of media influentials (TV anchor persons, talk-show hosts, newspaper editors and journalists) and nonprofit professional (educators, government officials), the members of this subgroup tend to be anticapitalists, and their basic thrust in ideology and consumption style has been to establish themselves above the Middle American classes. Marketing scholar Fred Webster calls them "socially conscious consumers."[19]

The second point Coleman makes is that more than any other group, Upper Americans are a more heterogenous group today: "Upper America is now a vibrant mix of many lifestyles, which might be labeled post preppie, sybaritic, counter-cultural, conventional, intellectual, political, etc. Such subdivisions are usually more important for targeting messages and goods than are the horizontal, status-flavored, class-named strata."[20]

Marketing Response to the Customers of Different Economic Means

In light of the customer behavior differences linked to personal worth and social class, marketers respond by targeting the means and values of the different socioeconomic groups. The following discussion identifies marketing strategies for reaching low-income and high-income consumers. Some companies, as described in the Window on Practice box, have broadened their customer base by targeting customers at two points along the economic spectrum.

MARKETING TO THE LOW-INCOME CONSUMER

The marketing response to poor customers has not always been admirable. In a recent book, *The Low-Income Consumer: Adjusting the Balance of Exchange,* consumer behavior researchers Linda F. Alwitt and Thomas D. Donley detail how low-income consumers get the short shrift at the hands of marketers.[21]

One reason may be that, when it comes to low-income consumers, marketers do not trust poor consumers to have enough resources to pay for the goods they want to buy, and to shop with honesty. As a result, retail stores in low-income areas tend to keep low qual-

Upscale, Downscale

Meet Winnie-the-Pooh twins. The older of the twins, whom we will call Pooh-D, is a plump, cartoon-like hug-gable bear clad in a red T-shirt. Its cartoon-like pictures appear on polyester bedsheets sold in Wal-Mart stores. Its goofy smile also peers at you from plastic key chains sold at five-and-dime shops. The younger twin (whom we will call Pooh-U) looks less plump and less goofy, and its soft line-drawn likeness adorns fine china sold in such depart-ment stores as Nordstrom and Bloomingdale's. If you have a baby, which twin will your son or daughter grow up with? That depends on your income and social class. If you are an upscale customer, Walt Disney Co., the parent of the twins, will make sure that Pooh-U ("U" for up-scale) meets you where you shop on merchandise you seek. If, on the other hand, you are a downscale person, the twin "D" (for downscale) is available to you at a price you can afford. A New York–based public polling com-pany, Roper Starch Worldwide, has recommended to clients that there are *Two Americas,* reflecting the great economic divide among the social classes. And Walt Disney Co. has seized the opportunity.

Similarly, The Gap Inc., a U.S.-based casual clothing chain, owns Banana Republic for upscale and Old Navy for downscale consumers without the ap-pearance of downscale (the store chain is pretty hip in its ambiance and sales persona). And it is pushing the expan-sion of both these, much more than its mass-market flag-ship Gap Stores. "To each, according to his class," is an age old refrain in marketing, but it is now being played with a never-before fervor.

Source: Adapted from David Leonhardt, "Two-Tier marketing," *Business Week,* March 17, 1997, pp. 82–90; "Is America Becom-ing More of a Class Society," *Business Week,* February 26, 1996, pp. 86–90.

---

ity merchandise and maintain extra vigilance. Sellers may also not value as much what poor consumers have to offer in exchange (e.g., food stamps, low revenue per transaction, browsing without buying), so they may offer even less variety and charge higher prices. Marketers may also act less responsibly in dealing with poor consumers, such as not car-ing about crowding at checkout registers meant for food-stamp-paying customers only, not extending the same courtesy in customer service contacts as they do with their more well-to-do customers, keeping poor patients waiting longer, and so on.

Marketers may not value poor customers as potential long-term customers. Many marketers may not realize that for some customers, poverty may be a temporary state (e.g., students living away from their parents, a skilled worker temporarily out of job, etc.). The result is that "satisfying the customer" may not even exist as a goal of marketers who cater to poor customers![22]

Although individually their incomes (and therefore buying powers) are low, as a group, lower-income customers constitute a substantial market. Some marketers recog-nize this market potential and are increasingly targeting this group with newer value-oriented strategies, or as *Business Week* states, by providing "affordable simulations of good life."[23] This is epitomized by a store called *Children's Orchard,* which sells used clothing in a nonthrift atmosphere, packaging many of the clothing items in shrink-wrap to make it look new! Sales of used clothing and other goods has doubled since 1987. Today, car dealers are selling more and making more profit per car on pre-owned vehicles than on new cars. And at the used car store, they have learned to treat the customer with the same respect they once reserved for buyers of expensive used cars.

MARKETING TO THE AFFLUENT

In contrast to the widespread ambivalence about serving the poor, most marketers are eager to target affluent customers. Everywhere, from free market to command economies, in industrialized as well as nonindustrialized nations, and in modern as well as traditional societies, there is at least a small group of affluent, for whom marketers make available the finest, bringing it from wherever it may have been originally produced. You can thus find the most exclusive designer brands of goods in Western Europe as well as in the newly liberated Eastern European countries, in Japan as well as in Africa, in China as well as in Australia, in the United States as well as in India or Bangladesh.

In America, at least, the affluent are growing in numbers and in wealth concentration. According to an estimate by the Affluent Market Institute in Atlanta, by 2005, million-aires will control 60 percent of the country's money. Some marketers are taking note and altering their strategy. Gucci is pulling out of midscale Macy's and courting more upscale stores. And Saks Fifth Avenue has decided to direct its energies to its 100,000 "best cus-tomers." Banks missed the opportunity for a while. The "new moneyed" affluent needed investment services in addition to check cashing, and commercial banks didn't provide it. So these customers moved to investment brokerage firms such as Merrill Lynch and Fi-delity, which added check services to their investment business. Now banks are fighting back. Citicorp is setting up CitiGold offices around the country and in each of its tradi-tional branches for customers who have $100,000 in investable assets.

The Influence of Personal Context on the Three Customer Roles

Now that we have described the three personal context factors, we can pull them together and show how they influence the various market values customers seek in their user, payer, and buyer roles. Table 6.10 presents an overview of this influence.

Culture

The influence of culture on the market values that users seek (performance, social, and emotional) is pervasive and immense. Cultures vary in their insistence on performance and quality. For example, sloppiness is accepted in some Asian cultures, while in others, such as the United Kingdom and Germany, standards of personal service are very high. In developing countries, product quality is expected to be merely adequate, whereas manu-facturers in many advanced countries are now demanding from their suppliers and offer-ing their customers near-zero defect quality. Thus, culture influences the rigor with which users expect and evaluate performance quality.

Social value is also differently interpreted in different cultures. Conspicuous con-sumption is frowned upon in some cultures, such as in more egalitarian societies. Like-wise, cultures differ in whether emotional expressiveness is considered proper and nat-ural. In the more expressive cultures such as Southern Europe and Latin America, advertising and product package design need to allow for emotional and aesthetic expres-sion. Corporate culture constrains what kinds of clothes we wear and what kinds of cars we drive. Large enterprises with conservative cultures require more formal clothing, while casual clothing is in vogue in entrepreneurial business firms such as in the Silicon Valley or in the art and creative departments of advertising agencies.

**EXAMPLES OF HOW THE PERSONAL CONTEXT
AFFECTS THE THREE CUSTOMER ROLES**

Table 6.10

DIMENSION OF PERSONAL CONTEXT	USER	PAYER	BUYER
Culture	Cultures differ in their insistence on flawless performance. Conspicuous consumption is frowned upon in some cultures. Different cultures permit emotional expressiveness to different degrees. Corporate culture constrains what people wear and drive.	Cultures vary significantly in sanctioning borrowing and in living in debt. Cultures allocate the payer role to specific members of the household.	Cultures assign the buyer role according to their sex-role norms. Negotiations and bargaining practices are governed by cultural norms.
Institutions and groups	Families differ on seeking materialism and in emphasis on performance versus social and emotional values. Religion prohibits consumption of certain products and services. Employers and work groups exercise norms on clothing, cars, and business travel options.	Families differ in using credit and in individual versus joint responsibility for managing financial matters. Islam prohibits borrowing. Employers affect the payer by assuming partial or full financial burden.	Families differ in blending versus separating the buyer role from the user and/or payer roles. Some religions disallow women to go shopping. Employers' purchasing policies constrain the purchaser.
Personal worth	Economic classes have distinct cultures of consumption.	By enabling or limiting the resources, economic conditions affect the payer role most directly.	Greater personal worth supports a more confident approach to vendors. Economic means may limit access to vendors. Higher economic condition leads customers to seek more convenience and personal shopping experience.

Culture influences the payer role in at least two ways. First, it is a determinant of who plays the payer role. In some cultures, it is the female head of the households, while in others it is the male head. In some cultures, where joint families are prevalent, such as in Mexico, Latin America, and Eastern countries, other members of the household remain dependent on the head of the household for allocating the budget to individual needs, and the family remains a unit in managing finances and in deciding what can be bought for whom. In Western cultures, in contrast, even teenagers become responsible for and acquire independence for allocating money for at least their personal, nonmajor purchases.

Second, cultures influence the payer role in that they differ significantly in their prescription for borrowing money. In non-Western cultures, for example, borrowing is a sign of being poor; the well-to-do don't borrow money. For the wealthy in these cultures, the house, the car, the business assets are all paid for. In Western cultures, in contrast, even millionaires may borrow money, since borrowing is a sign of managing money (e.g., in investment portfolios) rather than a sign of not having money. Cultures also differ in sanctioning the practice of living on borrowed money. Asians, for example, don't buy what they can't afford, whether or not they use credit. In the United States, on the other hand, it is not uncommon for many to accumulate a massive amount of personal debt.

Want to do business with these customers? You will have to know their customers—or know someone who does—like Telstra, the telecommunications company in the Asia-Pacific.

Finally, culture influences the buyer role both in terms of who plays the buyer role and what specific values the buyer may tend to seek. In many cultures, there is a clearer allocation of sex roles, including a norm as to what kinds of products will be shopped for mainly by the female members of the household, and what kinds by male members. For example, women may do all the food shopping, and males may buy all the furniture, appliances, and so on. In addition, expectations about personal service and convenience differ across cultures. Cultures also vary in negotiating tactics and in allowing the practice of bargaining. Fixed-price merchandising is not a universal practice, and customers always bargain in the shops and bazaars of many third world countries. Similarly, in business negotiations, the level of direct confrontation considered prudent differs across cultures. These cultural nuances make playing a buyer role an art form in many societies.

Institutions and Reference Groups

Next, let us consider institutions and groups and their influence on the three roles. Actually, institutions are embodiments of culture (i.e., it is through them that culture lives). So culture's influences on the three roles, as outlined above, are also the influences of institutions and groups. But specific institutions have their own additional influence. Illustratively, the larger culture of a society or country shapes all families in it, but each family also has its own culture, norms, and practices. Thus, different families differ in the value they place on materialism and on simplicity versus indulgence, in permitting debt (i.e., living on deficit financing, so to speak), and in the extent to which the user, payer, and buyer roles are blended versus separated. In one family, it might be the practice that either one member or the family as a unit does the shopping for household items. In others, each member might do his or her own shopping (e.g., a teenager picks up food he or she needs and orders CDs he or she likes versus Mom buying everything in the weekly shopping trip using a shopping list that includes everyone's desired items, food, toiletries, books, magazines and CDs, and the like).

Religion certainly influences what people may or may not consume, as detailed earlier in the chapter (e.g., kosher food by Jews). Religion also affects the payer role by sanctioning the practice of borrowing. Islam, for example, forbids the practice of borrowing and lending, since usury is considered a sin. Again, certain religions prohibit women from going to the market, so the buyer role becomes the exclusive prerogative of men.

Employers and work groups influence all three roles. Beyond a norm about clothes and cars, employers also influence other *user* decisions such as what kind of personal computer you can buy for your office desk, what airlines and which fare class you may fly, which hotels you may stay at, and whether or not you may take your spouse on business trips—in other words, determining whether emotional and social values are allowed in these business-related consumptions. Employers affect the payer role in letting or not letting employees manage their own budget, in terms of allowing certain business expenses (e.g., entertainment, social club membership, etc.), and in the extent to which they partially or fully assume the financial burden for the things you buy as an employee and as a consumer (e.g., health-care insurance, company car, housing rent subsidy, home phone, paid annual vacation). Finally, purchasing practice is dictated by employers—some allow individual employees to do their own purchasing while others mandate centralized purchasing (e.g., use your own travel agent, or use only corporate travel agency).

Personal Worth

Finally, consider the influence of personal worth on the three customer roles. Personal worth influences customers' behavior primarily by constraining their resources. Its influence is greatest, therefore, on the payer role. Not only is the amount of money (whether equity or credit) available for market transactions relatively abundant or scarce, but it also affects the extent to which money is tightly controlled among the user, buyer, and payer roles. Customers with more personal worth, for example, may give children a higher allowance, which the children might then be free to spend as they wish, or employees in prosperous companies might be given more financial freedom to allocate budgets for their personal need items (e.g., office furnishing, travel and entertainment, etc.). In low-income families, and in money-strapped companies, on the other hand, one person—other than the user and the payer—might tightly regulate how money is spent.

Personal worth affects the other two customer roles as well. Economic classes acquire their own consumption cultures, so there is the consumption culture of the poor, of the middle class, and of the rich, for example. These differences in consumption cultures were amply described and illustrated earlier in this chapter. Likewise, for business customers, it is fashionable to consume according to your class—*Fortune* 500 companies expect their executives to belong to certain social and professional clubs, to own and use corporate jets, and to entertain clients in certain restaurants. Small, fledgling businesses, in contrast, are supposed to live more modestly within their means. As to the buyer role,

---

The New Rich—They Are on All Continents!

CUSTOMER INSIGHT

Champagne Veuve Clicquot is one of the classiest and most expensive of champagnes. Until recently, its cap bore the face of the empire's grandmother, Nicole-Barbe Clicquot, squinting at the choosy superrich set around the globe who revel in this exquisite sparkling wine. This face has been replaced by Nicole-Barbe's younger face—27 years of age to be exact, the age at which she inherited the empire from her husband—put together by a computer reimaging program. The new bottle caps were launched not for the Armani set on New Year's Eve, but on Halloween 1997—targeted at the merrymaking Generation Xers!

Such refurbishing of image to broaden the appeal to newer (and younger) affluent segments is the hallmark of the new strategy of LVMH—Louis Vuitton Moët Hennesy—who owns the Veuve Clicquot label. LVMH is attempting—and successfully—a strategy of seeming contradiction: mass marketing of luxury goods—such labels as Givenchy (a French couture brand), Berluti (an Italian shoe company), Christian Dior (another French clothing designer), Louis Vuitton (a fashion statement in leather luggage), Celine (a designer brand of leather accessories), and Guerlain (a French perfume). Bernard Arnault, the aggressive CEO of LVMH is taking these carriage-trade brands more mainstream. And not as much by introducing more affordable products—"You get better value for your money now, but it is still a lot of money," observes one industry expert. Rather, the kingpin of Arnault's strategy is to put a new bloom on these somewhat staid labels by courting a fresh breed of hip designers, by sporting trendier graphics and store fronts, and by buying stores in new markets—not in Madrid, Lyons, or Milan, but rather in such Asian cities as Hanoi and Guangzhou. For this is where the *new money* is.

Consider the Asian share of French luxury goods, such brands as Hermès, Chanel, and, of course, all of the LVMH's products. Ten years ago, that share was 16 percent; today, Asian consumers account for 35 percent of the revenues (some $2.4 billion worth). "Luxury is crossing all age, racial, geographic, and economic brackets," says an executive of LVMH.

In broadening its market beyond the traditional wealthy segment, the company has read the new customer reality well: Customers in a large segment of the market, much beyond the wealthy segment, have fulfilled their basic needs. They want to use their money to go beyond the basics, to indulge somewhat. And it is not as much about conspicuous consumption, a motive attributed (somewhat oversimplistically) to the "old money" bourgeois; rather it is about self-expression. It is about pleasing oneself. If this assumption about the broadening segment of affluence is correct, LVMH's Arnault will have proven that it helps to found entrepreneurial zeal on a solid base of understanding the trends in customer behavior.

Source: Based on Joshua Levine, "Liberté, Fraternité—but to Hell with Égalité!" *Forbes*, June 2, 1997, pp. 80–89.

personal worth affects both the broad mind-set of customers and their specific purchase strategies. In broad terms, it influences the confidence versus timidness with which buyers can approach their suppliers and vendors. It influences their choice of vendors; for example, poor consumers may only shop at warehouse and off-price stores, at stores accessible by public transportation, and at stores that might offer them special credit terms or terms of exchange such as pawn shops or barter stores or stores where they might take food stamps. Greater financial worth also makes buyers desire more convenience and more personal shopping experience, since they have the means to pay for it. In general, then, low personal worth focuses customer attention on universal values in each of the three roles. Only when economic conditions are better does the consumer move up to seeking individual values, whether as a user, as a payer, or as a buyer.

Summary

The personal context of the customer comprises the enduring circumstances that surround the customer. It is the cultural, social, and economic milieu that a customer is a member of and in which the customer resides. We described three context factors: culture, institutions and groups, and personal worth.

In this chapter, we defined what culture is and discussed its characteristics and components. We described national and popular culture, and argued that the concept of culture applies to business customers as well. Corporate culture has a significant bearing on the behaviors of individuals or departments in it, and when these individuals and departments act as customers, we should be aware of the cultural influence on them. We identified five dimensions of cross-culture value orientations and also 10 dimensions of the "how" aspects of culture.

Institutions and groups were discussed as the second context factor. Here the principal idea was that these diverse groups act as reference groups for individuals—groups that we use as reference for our own behavior. Depending on the frequency of contact, groups can be primary or secondary, membership or symbolic, choice or ascribed. Their influence depends on conspicuousness in consumption, and as such it can occur at the product or brand choice level. This influence is of three kinds in nature, as described in the chapter.

The last context is the economic condition surrounding the customer. Its components, as discussed, are income, wealth, and borrowing power. The concept of social class was discussed. It was argued that social classes are motivational in that they motivate customer behavior toward certain activities and possessions. The three major social classes (upper, middle, and lower) were contrasted in regard to their consumption behavior. In the last section, we brought together the three context factors and spelled out the effects of each on the behavior of customers—customers as users, payers, and buyers.

Key Terms

Personal Context 146
Culture 147
Enculturation 147
Acculturation 147
National Culture 150
Popular Culture 150
Subculture 150

Groups 160
Institutions 160
Reference Groups 161
Primary Groups 161
Secondary Groups 161
Membership Groups 161
Symbolic Groups 161

Personal Worth 169
Income 169
Engel's Law 170
Wealth 171
Borrowing Power 172
Poverty 173
Social Class 174

Review Questions

1. Culture has been identified as an important personal context factor that influences customer behavior. Explain in your own words what culture is and why it is important to study for understanding customer behavior.

2. What are the five cultural dimensions proposed by Hofstede, the cultural researcher? Illustrate the relevance of each for a household product or service.

3. In understanding the "how" aspect of cultural differences, why is it important to understand the cultural differences that deal with friendship and personal space in a business context?

4. What are the components of personal net worth? How does net worth affect customer behavior? Give two examples from the household market.

5. Describe the three different income groups discussed in this chapter and how marketers treat each group differently in terms of their strategies to appeal to them. Use current company examples to explain your points.

6. How do institutions to which consumers belong vary? Why should marketers be concerned about the different types of institutions or groups that consumers belong to? Be specific.

7. Describe the fallacy of the poor in America. How does their psychology and their general attitudes affect their overall behaviors as well as their consumption behavior?

Applications

1. Give three examples from your own experience of how marketers have utilized the relationship between consumer behavior and religion. Some of the links may be in terms of symbols or rituals. Others may deal directly with customs and practices, while still others may deal with specific religious mandates or restrictions.

2. How is normative influence different from identification influence in the context of reference groups? Give two examples of each type of influence and show how marketers have capitalized on the reference group influence phenomenon.

3. Your friend missed the last lecture and was concerned about making up the material. You inform him that part of the class was devoted to culture as a part of personal context and that your favorite part of that discussion was the topic of socialization. Your friend, being a party animal, gets very excited about it and wants to hear more on it. You calm him down and explain to him that socialization is different from socializing. What exactly do you tell him about socialization in the context of consumer culture? Explain it to him by drawing from his own life.

4. The chapter discusses three different types of reference group influences. Think about your own experience in college. First, identify the three different types of reference group influences. Next, identify the person, types of people, or groups that have exerted their influence on you while you have been at college. Finally, list the products or services for which you have been influenced (for example, the classes you selected or your place of residence).

5. Identify five consumers who come from different national cultures. Interview them to identify how their customer behaviors are different in each of the three roles.

Practical Experiences

1. Select two households featured in two different TV series or sitcoms. First, classify each household into one of the social classes discussed in the chapter. Then, analyze each household's lifestyle and consumption behavior. Compare the two households if they fall into different social classes.

2. At your university or college, find one person who belongs to and represents each of the five major religious institutions presented in the chapter (you may include yourself if appropriate). First, ask them to think about the various routines in their daily life (e.g., food preparation, dressing, and grooming). Next, ask them to identify one ritual and to describe it to you. Is the ritual in any way connected to their religion? Do any of these people have any common rituals? In your view, what are the implications of this individualistic ritualistic behavior to the marketers of the products and/or services used during these religious rituals?

3. The chapter presents several examples of culturally based marketing mistakes. Most of them involve U.S. firms attempting to enter foreign markets. Go to the library and identify four companies (U.S. or otherwise) that have implemented international marketing programs. From a cultural perspective, discuss the positive and negative aspects of their international marketing decisions and actions.

4. Take any two national cultures from Appendix 6A. A team of your company's sales engineers is visiting a business customer in each of these two countries. Assuming that it is better for the team to visit a country where the culture is less dissimilar to their host country, in which sequence would you advise the team to visit the two customers. Also write the team a memo on what cultural adjustments the team members should make in their behavior when visiting the first customer and then again when visiting the second customer.

Appendix 6A: Selected Cultures from around the World

A marketer whose customers are from other countries needs to be aware of those customers' cultures, especially cultural norms and values regarding business relationships.

China

Historically, Chinese tend to be ethno-centric, considering their country to be the center of the universe, and their race to be superior. The Chinese character for the name *China* means the central nation!

Chinese welcome foreigners but are cautious about trusting them. Some knowledge of Chinese language and culture is appreciated, but show too much of it, and they are likely to become suspicious that you might be trying to get too close to them!

If you pay a Chinese customer a compliment, he is unlikely to respond with a "thank you." This shows, not arrogance, but modesty, as Chinese tend to deny or diminish the value of their accomplishment.

Family is very important and its well-being comes before anything else. Senior family members are revered and obeyed. Aging brings dignity and status (unlike in Western cultures where youth is at a premium) and elders are sought for advice as well as blessing.

An important Chinese value is faith in *feng shui,* meaning wind and water, implying the principle of harmony between man and nature. Before constructing any building or business site, Chinese will consult with a feng shui man, who will advise how to design the structure and its furnishings to embody that harmony. By extension, they also ask the feng shui practitioner for blessing before any new venture.

In initial business contacts, connections and relationships help. The term *Guanxi* means both connections and graft, as the party providing the connection expects to profit from the favor. Thus, using a connection or Guanxi helps you get the contact with the target customer, but it also obligates you to the middle man who provides the connection.

Chinese pride themselves for not showing emotions, especially in the first meeting, and accordingly tend not to smile much at first greetings. In nonbusiness settings, they greet one another with a slight bow or a nod of the head; in business settings, a handshake upon greeting as well as departure is common.

Personal courtesy in yielding at a door and in choosing seats is expected; business cards are handed with both hands; personal space is shorter so people stand closer together. Meetings begin with tea drinking and informal conversation, including introduction of oneself and a brief history of your business. Trust is necessary before substantive business talks can begin. Chinese tend to remain formal at business meetings. Informality is welcome but is misinterpreted as being much more than intended by the casual manner in which Westerners display it.

Negotiations proceed slowly and are best conducted at a low-key tone and without publicity. Chinese consider negotiations basically a win-lose proposition and thus attempt to seek as many concessions as possible, sometimes restarting the negotiations just when you thought you had concluded them; or they often delay the progress in the hope that you will make concessions at the last minute to close the deal. Furthermore, they don't like to say "no," so they will say things like "It will be inconvenient." In general, you will hear them say "yes," but this implies not agreement but only that "I am listening." It is important to them that all parties maintain "face."

France

French business organizations are highly centralized, with well-defined formal command and control lines of authority. The planning is centralized, and consequently, there is little commitment to it by those who would implement it. On the surface, at least, there is rigid formality in how managers interact with each other and in adherence to the written rules. Below the surface, however, there is an invigorating subculture of informal networking and tacit flexibility. While rules are seldom broken, they are constantly distorted or ignored. The familiar phrase in French organizations is—*le cas particulier*—"this is a special case!"

French managers are very competitive (as opposed to cooperating in teams). Indeed a manager would be dismayed if others did not compete with her or him. Group consensus takes the back seat to individual initiative. Most of the decision-making oriented communication is via written reports and proposals (rather than by oral presentations or verbal discussions). These are detailed, well structured, comprehensive, clear, and well written. Managers call meetings with a detailed agenda to inform and coordinate rather than to discuss. People come prepared to contribute, to answer objections, and to question others, but never more than mildly. To ask tough questions is considered a personal attack, and this norm for interacting in public keeps in check the otherwise fiercely competitive rivalry.

Business colleagues use last names, at least in public, and they shakes hands no matter how well they know each other. Bosses do not socialize with subordinates after work; business lunch with the boss is rare and formal. Usually, lunch is regarded as "private time," and food is deemed to deserve the main attention. Thus, the working lunch eaten alone or with colleagues or with salespersons is a recent innovation, restricted to some companies and only practiced occasionally.

French people enjoy abstract thought and consider themselves philosophers. The pragmatic matters less than the clarity of logic. They will tolerate the impractical but not the inconsistent. In business dealings, they will react negatively to your idea initially because they want to hear the arguments. Rational arguments supported by facts rather than sentimental pleadings are key to successful negotiations. French managers dislike direct confrontations and prefer to work around problems.

The French seek novelty and elegance. This shows up in French consumers' quick adoption of gadgets and other innovations, and in their valuing aesthetics in product design and also in the use of language. They prefer wit to a belly-laugh and use humor that is more intelligent and satirical. In business presentations and meetings, humor is rarely used. If you used humor in presentations to business clients in France, you would be regarded as flippant. Similarly, personal remarks should be avoided.

Business begins with establishing a personal relationship. The French want to know you and expect you to show interest in their country. Personal relationships are valued for their own sake. The French believe that there is more to life than work; accordingly, they admire hard work but not workaholism. Work and family are considered separate. Being successful at the job is not considered adequate. Colleagues are expected to be lively and interesting, and well-informed and appreciative of finer things in life.

When you meet people as well as when you take leave of them, you shake hands with everyone, including children. When you praise a French person, you are likely to hear a self-deprecating comment since French are modest in accepting compliments. French are well-informed about other countries and cultures, so it pays to be informed about French history, politics, and culture.

In public, French avoid laughing or speaking loudly, chewing gum, or walking and drinking, or walking and smoking simultaneously.

Germany

Germans are very ambitious, success oriented, and competitive. The outward signals of success are the size of a person's office and the car he or she drives. Work and home are considered separate, and few Germans ever take the work home.

German organizations are hierarchical with strict lines of authority. Planning is top down. Superiors are supposed to govern out of competence and knowledge even though subordinates always take down orders unquestioningly. The organizations are very bureaucratic: everyone's role is well defined and written down. Procedures are well documented, and everyone is supposed to work by the book. Perfectionism both in business and private life is a hallmark of Germans. Obsession with detailed planning is accompanied by low tolerance for uncertainty. Opportunism is seen as a lack of organization and planning.

Decisions are taken conservatively and cautiously, with contingency plans and fallback options. Decisions are taken by senior management rather than by consensus with those who would be affected. However, anyone with expertise is invited to offer opinion, which is seriously listened to. Subordinates are expected to offer opinion only if well informed. Meetings between managers and subordinates are largely for conveying information rather than for discussions. Compliance rather than consensus is expected. Communication is top down, largely when it is necessary to inform subordinates.

German views on the role of women in society are the most traditional. Progress toward accepting women in top positions in the organizations has been slow.

Germans are very formal and private persons. German society is very normative, and eccentricity of even the mildest form is frowned upon. A German would not hesitate to point out if you do something out of line, even something as trivial as taking off your jacket. Policing each other's behavior is deemed as a social duty.

German businessmen and managers always keep their jackets on unless alone. They address each other formally by their last names, especially in meetings. There is no place for humor in business meetings. Joking is common among close colleagues in private, but among strangers or in formal meetings, it makes people uncomfortable. Colleagues often take lunch together, but lunch hour is not to talk business. After office hours, getting together for drinks is not a regular practice, but when it does happen, it is used as an occasion for camaraderie and having a good time.

In sharp contrast to the excessive formality in public life is the informality in private life. There, friendship and warmth are highly valued. Intimacy is restricted to a few and is highly valued.

Punctuality is very important to Germans. Everyone arrives on time and leaves on time. Working late is neither expected nor rewarded. During the working hours, you work hard, but then that is the end of it.

India

As the largest democracy in the world, India embodies the value of egalitarianism alongside the deeply rooted caste and class system. Persons born in lower castes were discriminated against for centuries, but now it is common for even the lowest classes to command high positions both in politics and civil service. However, labor or menial work, historically the exclusive occupation of lower castes, continues to be considered undignified. Most middle-class and upper-class families will hire household help for dishes, laundry, and cleaning, not necessarily because the homemaker is working but simply because it is the proper thing to do. Until recently, most people who owned cars also retained a chauffeur rather than drive their car themselves (except in big cities and centers of commerce).

In businesses, rank and the respect that comes with it are zealously guarded. Accordingly, subordinates display a subservient behavior, and superiors treat their subordinates in a condescending manner. A Westerner who behaves in a more egalitarian manner toward the subordinates of his or her counterpart at the negotiating table may therefore discomfort both the subordinates and the superior alike. Since physical labor is not respected, superior managers will never do any physical work, including moving their own chair, for example; they wait for the subordinate to do it for them. Clerks and personal assistants disproportionately occupy an office roll, and it is not uncommon for an executive office to have a lower staff person simply waiting outside the closed office door for the call bell to ring. Peons will bring for you whatever you need, including carrying your briefcase. As a seller, you may not usurp this custom by insisting on carrying your own briefcase, or by otherwise treating the peon in an egalitarian fashion. However, many business firms are becoming Westernized, and such customs and rituals may be conspicuously absent in such firms.

Age is revered in India, as in most other parts of Asia (unlike in the West). Family members are respected. Even friendships formed during adult years manifest more respect than informal camaraderie. Except in childhood or adolescent friendships, where informality is common and first names are used, adults refer to each other with respect, adding the Indian equivalent of "Mr." or "Mrs." or "Dr." after the last name of acquaintances, friends, business associates, seniors as well as juniors and subordinates, and of course business customers. If you are younger than your customer, even if your rank in your own company is higher, you would be offending if you did not address the customer with respect.

Indians have a strong belief in destiny or fate and, for this reason, tend to work less hard or work fewer hours, and also tend to be contented with what they have.

Guests and visitors to homes are considered a godsend and are welcomed with a sense of duty and reverence ("A guest/visitor is a god" is a popular adage in India, followed in words as well as deeds). Even if a stranger knocks on the door, he or she will be welcome, invited into the house, and offered at least a glass of water. Friends drop by without announcement, a carryover from the days when virtually no one had phones to make the prior appointment—thus the Indian name for guests is "dateless," meaning those who came without an appointment.

This social practice spills over to business. While business introductions from mutual friends help, "cold" calling or, more generally, a cold letter is quite accepted. Requests for impromptu meetings or showing up without prior appointments is not frowned upon either. Indeed, the executive you are calling upon will make an effort to see you, if at all feasible.

Indians are famous for being late, although in business appointments, this is changing. In part, this practice is the consequence of Indians (as in Latin and Arab cultures) marking time not as much by clock as by events so that the proper beginning time for a subsequent event is whenever the preceding event concludes. If you delight at the prospect of meeting your business customer without appointment, you should understand why keeping time is generally not in the Indian character.

Indians generally greet one another with a *Namaste*—the word is audibly spoken along with a gesture in which both palms are placed together at the chest level with a slight bow of the head. However, when greeting customers, a handshake is accepted and appropriate, with these exceptions: when greeting women customers, a "namaste" is appropriate, not the handshake (though younger women executives or younger businesswomen would gladly shake hands if offered); when greeting very senior or older executives or business customers; when greeting government officers; and, definitely, when greeting political cabinet members, even a junior minister in the foreign trade department.

Business cards are given by the caller such as a salesman, rather than by the customer (but they are willingly offered if you ask for it), and they are given casually (unlike the elaborate protocol that Japanese follow). Generally, small talk begins the business exchange, but it is brief and the customer is eager for you to come to the point quickly. Touching (such as for putting your arm around the shoulder or for patting) is considered awkward among business exchange parties. During the same meeting, smiles are as common as seriousness in face expressions, reflecting the emotional reaction of the moment, as Indians do not try to hide their emotions or their opinions.

In consumer markets, haggling over price is as common in India as in Latin America and Mexico. Even though fixed price shops and one-price merchandise are becoming prevalent, especially in large cities, the practice of bargaining or seeking some concessions is quite accepted everywhere. Merchandise is being sold in bulk, and such buying options exist along with the option of buying prepackaged consumer goods. Despite the popularity of manufacturers' brands, both domestic and imported, the reputation of the retailer is crucial in store selection, and retailers influence brand choice, since their advice is often sought and accepted.

When **you** step into my house you **honour me.** It is my privilege to take **care** of you.

Welcome to the National experience.
Whatever be your need,
we try our best to fulfill it.
By serving you from our 1000 offices
and offering you the widest range of policies.
Because what inspires us is a basic belief —
Atithi Devo Bhava.
The guest is God.

National Insurance Company Limited
(A Subsidiary of General Insurance Corporation of India)

A t r a d i t i o n o f r e s p e c t .

"The Guest Is God." The customer is a guest for this company, and so it follows that as a customer you would be treated like God! Where else can you run an advertisement like this? Only where "the guest is God" culture exists.

Italy

At the middle- or upper-management levels, executives relate to one another on the basis of personal alliances and trust rather than being limited by the formal organization. For an outside supplier, therefore, finding the decision maker becomes an art. In sharp contrast to the German organizational culture, rules and formal procedures are almost always ignored, and flexibility is considered an Italian virtue. Getting things done is what counts.

Planning is generally absent. Businessmen and managers value an entrepreneurial recognition of opportunities rather than strategic plans.

Personal relationships are valued among colleagues. The delegation of responsibility is by trust in the individual rather than by position. Teams work only with a respected leader.

Meetings are small and informal. Often they appear to be social gatherings. Formal presentations are not common. People use meetings as an opportunity to exhibit their status, style, and elegance. Everyone is entitled to offer an opinion, and everyone is expected to be agreeable to the speaker. The worth of the idea depends more on status than on its intrinsic validity. The purpose of the meetings is to sense people's mood regarding a decision rather than to make decisions. Most decisions are taken in informal, behind-the-scene discussions.

Business managers consider it important to demonstrate intelligence and education. Even the most mundane conversations about business are filled with references to such notable figures as Aristotle, Adam Smith, and John K. Galbraith. Being well educated and familiar with the classics is considered a social necessity.

For business, Italians dress formally. Looking sharp is considered a sign of good taste.

In social interaction, courtesy and good manners are desired. Italians will easily tolerate inefficiency and even incompetence, but not arrogance or rudeness.

Italians are not sticklers for punctuality, but it is considered rude to keep others waiting. While it is considered desirable not to be late for the next appointment, it is also considered rude to break off the current meeting or engagement. Thus, time and being on time are considered tools to organize activities rather than as ends in themselves.

Thus, it is second nature to Italians to be constantly juggling each other's appointment schedules. If you are a salesperson calling on an Italian businessperson, for example, you may be invited into the tail-end of the previous meeting, which may then take a significant amount of time to conclude.

Japan

To Japanese, harmony is more important than honest opinion or truth. Saving face and maintaining dignity are critical in all situations. Individuality is sanctioned, and blending in and being a team player are rewarded. People with higher rank, political position, seniority, or age are respected and obeyed. Japanese corporations are very hierarchical. Japan has been a male-dominated society, and Japanese are unaccustomed to dealing with woman businesspeople, although among younger businesspersons, this is changing.

Decisions are made by consensus. The consensus building process, called *ringi seido,* is very time consuming. Written proposals, called *ringi-sho,* are circulated throughout the departments and then upward, with prolonged discussion and analyses at each level. In business, Japanese are very process oriented, following procedures and rules closely and disfavoring any bending of rules.

Japanese smile generously. They speak softly and dislike aggressive mannerism of Western businesspersons. They stand two to three feet apart, in part to allow body language such as the bow. They will escort you to the door or the elevator and expect you to do the same.

Japanese place great importance on relationships and contacts. Accordingly, cold calling is unwelcome, and a business person must obtain an introduction from third parties, and yet be careful not to ask too much of them, for this will obligate them to those whose favor they are seeking for you. A great deal of time is spent at first meetings just to get acquainted.

Socializing among business colleagues and with clients is important and considered part of a workday, so much so that many will leave the office in the early evening hours to socialize (eat and drink) and then return back to the office in the evening to conclude the workday. Many business deals are, in fact, made in social settings such as over dinner or on a golf course.

Japanese businesses are tied into a web of financial and nonfinancial relationship of cross-ownerships and mutual obligations. These network arrangements, called Keiretsu, have made it difficult for foreign businesses to penetrate, all the more reason why introduction by mutual associates is important.

Presenting business cards is an elaborate protocol. The card is presented with both hands and with words while facing the receiver, who then reads it slowly and carefully to show respect for the giver of the card. It is then placed on the table facing you so you can refer to it from time to time; it is rude to put it in the pocket right away.

To Japanese, bowing is an art form. Junior executives and younger persons bow first and at a steeper angle than do senior executives and older persons, although they do not expect it from foreigners. Handshakes, offered in deference to Western custom, are light.

Gift giving is a conspicuously noticeable part of Japanese social life, and, by extension, of business life as well. The gift selection and its presentation (i.e., packaging) is done with great deliberation and care. Aesthetic presentation is as important as the appropriateness of the gift content. First-time business gifts should be low- or moderate-priced, lest they obligate the receiver more than is in order, and because room is needed for subsequent gifts that need to be more expensive. But more than the price, the reputation and quality of the gift is of paramount importance.

Mexico

If you can learn only one thing about the Mexican culture, it is the mañana syndrome. *Manana* is Spanish for "tomorrow," but the cultural meaning of the term goes deeper than its literal meaning. It connotes priorities rather than procrastination.

To Mexicans, family and social obligations come first; business later. The *familia* (Spanish for "family") is a broad term extending to several generations, and horizontally to aunts and uncles, nephews and nieces, grandparents, cousins, and their families. Holidays are grand family reunion days, and old and young alike enjoy being at these gatherings. Teenagers do not view these as social obligations and they do not look bored. They enjoy their elders and respect them and in turn receive much valued affection. If you are invited to their home, remember, they are putting their family, their life, their pride on display for you to admire and respect. Show interest in the family, treat all family members with respect, and never, never ask or expect a Mexican to postpone a family concern to deal with the business at hand more efficiently.

Mexican businesspersons are not aggressive (and so they won't like it in you); they work at a relaxed pace but this should not be mistaken for laziness. Therefore, you must learn to work at a relaxed pace.

Mexicans like flexibility, and, from their vantage point, they perceive most U.S. and Canadian businessmen to be "set in their ways." In Mexico, deadlines are flexible, as a rule; in all contracts, therefore, you need to allow for inevitable extension of deadlines.

Lunch hours are long, lasting two to four hours, with a multicourse meal over the relaxed atmosphere and conversations about friends and family. A business lunch with a salesperson is the same, without any talk of business. But the Mexican customer is trying to assess you in this social set up as to your worthiness for his trust and dealing with you; this therefore, from the Mexican's viewpoint, is a *business lunch*!

Along with mañana and familia, a third cultural element guides the Mexican cultural life, namely fiesta. Fiesta means fun, enjoyment, pleasure. If you see men drinking and dining with friends, with free-flowing tequilas, with Mariachi bands, colorfully dressed señoritas, and colorful pinatas for children, you are witnessing a fiesta in progress. This zeal for living, for fun and celebration, is what sustains a Mexican's morale and high productivity during work hours. Whatever else you may sell to Mexicans, you can't sell them "stress-release seminars"!

Netherlands

The Dutch have a strong belief in the power of human aspirations and effort; at the same time, however, they believe that the forces of nature have to be respected. Dutch like to innovate but also wish to minimize risks.

The Dutch are predominantly egalitarian; they are frugal, using money wisely. Dutch organizations are generally egalitarian and open, and it is common for people to cut across reporting lines if needed. The hierarchical nature of organization and authority seen in other cultures is anathema to the Dutch. The authority is to be camouflaged rather than exhibited. The boss is deemed to be "one of us," as a collaborator rather than as an authority figure.

Communication in the Netherlands is open and sincere. Nobody attempts to hide things or manipulate information. There is preference for oral communication rather than written. This practice is termed *buurten,* which means "visiting" (i.e., exchanging or communicating information orally).

Dutch businesses have frequent and regular meetings based on a formal agenda. The Dutch are open to and welcoming of new ideas, but will adopt them only after thorough research and clarity. In sharp contrast to Italian practice, ideas are seen separate from the person who offers them and are therefore judged on their own merit. The Dutch therefore tend to be direct in offering comments and ideas, a trait that might be offensive to those from cultures where speech is vague, indirect, and nonconfrontational.

Decisions are made by consensus (not by majority vote), which may take a long time to reach. But since these are based on consensus, the implementation is fast.

Dutch businesses value frugality. Showing off is to be avoided. Offices, clothes, cars, even food—all are kept simple and subdued. Socializing takes place over coffee rather than over meals, so if you are invited to someone's home, it is more likely to be after dinner.

Punctuality is valued, and there is an obsession to use every minute productively. The Dutch look for solid personal relationships and consider it important to honor commitments.

United Kingdom

Meetings are considered very important in the United Kingdom. Most decisions are made in meetings. They are discussed, analyzed, ratified, and implemented in meetings. Meetings take up a good proportion of any given business day, and they are not considered an interruption of work. They are informal in style, and, although participants are not always well prepared, they do not hesitate to make comments and express opinions. Decisions are made by consensus, and all meetings have to have a resolution and a decision; otherwise they are considered a failure.

British are very group oriented. Individual initiatives are frowned on. Individuals always seek group support before implementing any idea or action plan.

The British tend to use first names among colleagues and also among all business contacts, even without a face-to-face meeting. Handshaking is limited to first meetings. The usual greeting is "How do you do?" with the expected response being the same interrogative.

Rank and status distinctions are common; British would generally feel less comfortable without them.

In social dealings, it is important to be "a nice person." One is supposed to be courteous and unassuming, rather than assertive and arrogant. Humility and self-deprecation are valued. Being polite in conversation is a British trademark. Direct confrontation and argument are avoided, and vagueness and hints mark the British conversations. These may mislead a foreign manager into thinking that British managers lack clarity and decisiveness.

Work does extend into private life. It is acceptable to take work home or to work in the office after hours, and sometimes even on the weekends.

It is considered impolite to come on time to social gatherings! Usually, you are expected to arrive 10 to 20 minutes late. This has extended to business life, where everyone is generally 10 minutes late for meetings.

In sharp contrast to German and French business etiquette, humor is expected and desired. Business discussions are filled with levity and witty remarks. British humor can be sarcastic, self-deprecating, sexist, jocular, or racist. Both men and women participate equally in humor, including sexual innuendo. Women are easily found in managerial positions in British businesses, particularly in service industries.

It is common for colleagues and business associates to lunch together. Conversations can be social or shop talk. After-hour socializing at the pub is also common.

Appendix 6B: Major Religions of the World

This appendix provides a very general overview of the world's largest religions: Hinduism, Buddhism, Islam, Christianity, Judaism, and Confucianism.[24]

Hinduism

Perhaps the oldest of all religions, Hinduism holds a strong belief in "Karma"—the idea that a person's activities determine his or her destiny in the next life and liberation of the spirit from the human body and its union with God. An important element of its belief system is the caste system, the group each person is born into; caste defines one's status. In India, the home of Hinduism, class mobility would be an inappropriate appeal for promoting products. Family is highly valued in this religion, and most Hindus live in extended families and even operate businesses as a family unit.

Buddhism

The Buddhist religion branched out of Hinduism in the sixth century B.C. and is found in such countries as China, Tibet, Sri Lanka, Japan, and Korea. Buddha, the Enlightened One, preached, "Blessed is he who overcomes sin and is free from passion . . . and the highest blessedness comes to him who conquers vanity and selfishness." The tenet of Buddhism most relevant to customer behavior is the one about asceticism—Buddhism teaches that material things cannot bring happiness.

Islam

Islam is the religion of the followers of the Prophet Mohammed. These followers, called Muslims, are concentrated in India, Pakistan, and the Arab nations of the Middle East. Muslims follow a detailed way of life and daily routine prescribed in the Koran, their sacred book. This routine includes prayer five times a day, a practice marketers visiting their Muslim customers should be aware of. Another noteworthy practice is fasting, especially during the lunar month of Ramadan, when Muslims must eat or drink nothing during the day. This religion holds rather traditional views on women, which may entail their seclusion and permits polygamy. Finally, Islam is a missionary religion—the faithful are supposed to uphold their religion and oppose the unbelievers.

The number of Moslems in America is estimated to be three to four million. About one in four Moslems in America is black. Moslems favor close-knit families, support religious education, and have conservative social values. Use of alcohol, dating, and sexual freedom are prohibited among traditional Moslems, although the younger generation growing up in America tends not to adhere to such strict norms of their religion.[25]

Christianity

Christianity comprises two main groups—Catholics and Protestants. Roman Catholicism centers around the church and its religious order. The church is supposed to mediate between God and humans. In the Catholic religion, the proper source for rules on the way to live is considered to be the Vatican. Therefore, outside knowledge not originating from the clergy is considered invalid. Consequently, Catholics are likely to be more fatalistic, traditional, and less innovative. In the United States, Catholics identify themselves with the Democratic Party.

Protestants believe that everyone has direct access to God (without the mediation of the church) and that God has intended for every person to do His work. Thus, work becomes important as a means of carrying out God's will. This work ethic, referred to as Protestant ethic, leads its followers to produce more material wealth. Protestantism does not seek to provide to its followers knowledge of the external world. It encourages them, instead, to seek scientific knowledge for that purpose. Compared to Catholics, Protestants are less authoritarian, more open to change, and have a work ethic; they consider leisure nonproductive and hence a waste of time. Politically, they may be conservative and align themselves, in the United States, with the Republican Party. Protestants believe in getting ahead by personal effort rather than by government handouts, and they strive for upward mobility.[26]

Judaism

In Judaism, God is viewed as an abstract and omniscient presence; however, God is presumed to be inclined to communicate with the individual directly (as opposed to through the clergy as in the Catholic system). Judaism believes that man can only comprehend God through self-education. It also believes, similar to Protestants, that man is responsible for his own actions and for his destiny or position in life.

The Jewish personality has been described as follows:[27] Compared to Protestants and Catholics, Jews are more liberal and democratic, more flexible and rationalistic, higher in achievement motivation, more enthusiastic, gregarious, and emotional, more impatient and hurried, more inclined to postpone gratification, and politically most liberal.

Confucianism

There are about 350 million adherents of Confucianism, mostly in China, Japan, Burma, and Thailand. Confucianism is a philosophy rather than a religion. It guides almost every aspect of Chinese life. Confucians urge people to strive for righteousness and improvement of one's character. Prominent Confucian values are harmony in the family, order in the state, and peace in the empire. Human duty is emphasized, and the ideal of the "superior man" rather than the divine is stressed. Man is supposed to cultivate the qualities of benevolence, propriety, wisdom, and sincerity.

Notes

1. June Carolyn Erlick, "IMRA High on Holiday: Sees Consumer Spending Up 20%," *HFN: The Weekly Newspaper for the Home Furnishing Network* 70, no. 46 (November 11, 1996), pp. 1–2.
2. Albert Niemi and Jeff Humphreys, "The Retailer's Calendar," *Georgia Trend* 11, no. 12 (August 1996), pp. 14–15.
3. *Maclean's* 109, no. 9 (February 26, 1996), p. 14.
4. Parts of this section are adapted from Terrence E. Deal and Allan A. Kennedy, *Corporate Cultures: The Rites and Rituals of Corporate Life* (Reading, MA: Addison-Wesley Publishing Co., 1982).
5. Geert Hofstede, *Cultural Consequences: International Differences in Work-Related Value* (Beverly Hills, CA: Sage., 1980); Geert Hofstede and Michael H. Bond, "Hofstede's Culture Dimensions: An Independent Validation Using Rokeach's Value Survey," *Journal of Cross-Cultural Psychology,* 15 (December 1984), pp. 417–33.
6. Russell W. Belk, "Hyperreality and Globalization: Culture in the Age of Ronald McDonald," *Journal of International Consumer Marketing* 8 (March/April 1995), pp. 23–37.
7. Francis S. Bourne, "Group Influence in Marketing and Public Relations," in *Some Applications of Behavioral Research*, eds. R. Likert and S.P. Hayes (Basil, Switzerland: UNESCO, 1957).
8. William O. Bearden and Michael J. Etzel, "Reference Group Influence on Product and Brand Purchase Decisions," *Journal of Consumer Research* 9, (1982), pp. 183–94.
9. See C. Whan Park and V. Parker Lessig, "Students and Housewives: Differences in Susceptibility to Reference Group Influence," *Journal of Consumer Research* 4, no. 2 (1977), pp. 102–110. and Robert E. Burnkrant and Alain Cousineau, "Informational and Normative Social Influence in Buyer Behavior," *Journal of Consumer Research* 2 (December 1975), pp. 206–215.
10. Faith Robertson Elliot, *The Family: Change or Continuity* (London: Macmillan Education, 1986).
11. Ruth Nanda Anshen, *The Family: Its Function and Destiny* (New York: Harper & Row, 1959).
12. Bronislow Malinowsky, *Magic, Science, Religion, and Other Essays* (Boston: Beacon, 1948); Robert E. Wilkes, John J. Burnett, and Roy D. Howell, "On the Meaning and Measurement of Religiosity in Consumer Research," *Journal of the Academy of Marketing Science* 14, (Spring 1986), pp. 47–56; Stewen W. McDaniel and John J. Byrnett, "Consumer Religiousity and Retail Store Evaluative Criteria," *Journal of the Academy of Marketing Science* 18, no. 2 (Spring 1990), pp. 101–12.
13. "Japanese Retailing: A Matter of Convenience," in *The Economist,* January 25–31, 1997, p. 62.
14. Alan R. Andreasen, *The Disadvantaged Consumer* (New York: Free Press, 1975); David Caplovitz, *The Poor Pay More* (New York: Free Press, 1967); and David Hamilton, *The Consumer in Our Economy* (New York: Free Press, 1962).
15. Elia Kacapyr, "Are You Middle Class," *American Demographics,* October 1996, p. 31.
16. W. Lloyd Warner, Marchia Meeker, and Kenneth Eells, *Social Class in America* (Chicago: Science Research Associates, 1949).
17. Richard P. Coleman, "The Continuing Significance of Social Class to Marketing," *Journal of Consumer Research,* 10 (December 1983), pp. 265–80.

[18] Richard P. Coleman, and Lee P. Rainwater, with Kent A. McClelland, *Social Standing in America: New Dimensions of Class* (New York: Basic Books, 1978).

[19] Frederick E. Webster, Jr., "Determining the Characteristics of the Socially Conscious Consumer," *Journal of Consumer Research* 2 (December 1975), pp. 188–96.

[20] Coleman, "The Continuing Significance of Social Class to Marketing." *Journal of Consumer Research,* 10 (December 1983), pp. 265–80.

[21] Linda F. Alwitt and Thomas D. Donley, "The Low-Income Consumer: Adjusting the Balance of Exchange," (Thousand Oaks, CA: Sage Publications, 1996).

[22] E.J. Boyer and A. Ford (1992), "Black-owned Businesses Pay a Heavy Price," *Los Angeles Times,* May 8, pp. A1, A5.

[23] "Two-Tier Marketing," *Business Week,* March 17, 1997, p. 82.

[24] Benson Y. Landis, *World Religions,* (New York: E.P. Dutton & Co, 1965).

[25] "Understanding Islam in America," *American Demographics,* January 1994, pp. 10–11.

[26] See Elizabeth C. Hirschman, "American Jewish Ethnicity: Its Relationship to Some Selected Aspects of Consumer Behavior," *Journal of Marketing,* 45 (Summer 1981), pp. 102–10; Elizabeth C. Hirschman, "Religious Affiliations and Consumption Processes: An Initial Paradigm," in *Research in Marketing,* J. Sheth, ed. (Greenwich, CT: JAI Press, 1983) pp. 131–70; Priscilla LaBarbera, "Consumer Behavior and Born-Again Christianity," *Research in Consumer Behavior* 2 (1987) pp. 193–222.

[27] See Raphael Patai, *The Jewish Mind* (New York: Charles Scribners & Sons, 1977).

CHAPTER 7

After reading this chapter you should be able to:

Describe how genetic traits influence a customer's personality.

Discuss characteristics of customers of diverse races.

Describe how marketers respond to the needs and wants of diverse race groups.

Identify men-women differences in customer behavior, changes in gender roles, and marketer responses.

Distinguish the needs and wants of customers of different age groups.

Identify the intergenerational differences in household and business customer behavior.

Define personality and tell how personality traits determine customer behavior.

Personal Characteristics: Genetics, Race, Gender, Age, and Personality

The Color of Money Is Green, Isn't It?

Meet Ricardo and Janet Bermudez—proud owners of a home in Babylon, New York, since October 1991. The Bermudezes financed their purchase with a $46,000 mortgage by the Long Island Savings Bank (LISB). Then, one month later, they applied for a home improvement loan for $10,000. But LISB turned it down. Four months later, a contractor obtained a preapproved $16,000 home improvement loan for them from the same bank. Why was their own application for a smaller amount turned down, while an application for a larger amount made by someone else on their behalf was accepted? The contractor was white. And the Bermudezes? Take a guess.

The black couple confronted the bank and got the original application approved. When it comes to money, from now on, the only color that matters is green, the Bermudezes assured themselves. And they went about their normal life—until 1993.

Then it happened all over again. Encouraged by the low 6.75 percent interest rates in 1993, the Bermudezes applied for refinancing on their old 8.75 percent, 15-year mortgage with the same bank. The bank's response: application denied! But this time they were ready. With the help of a local fair-housing organization, the couple filed a complaint with the Department of Housing and Urban Development (HUD). Three years and reams of paperwork later, they won. LISB granted them a 15-year loan at the 6.75 percent rate and paid an additional $23,000 in damages!

Source. Marjorie Whigham-Désir, "Fight back," *Black Enterprise*, July 1997, pp. 62–66.

Introduction

The treatment that customers like the Bermudezes receive in the marketplace and, in response, their customer behavior are profoundly affected by their characteristics—that is, by who they are. We refer here to the personal characteristics that they largely inherit from birth—and over which they have little control. We describe these characteristics and the role they play in determining the market values customers seek.

As we stated in Chapter 3, the market values that customers seek stem from customers' needs and wants. These needs and wants are in turn determined by the personal situation or context of the customer, as described in the last chapter. In addition, they are also determined by certain personal characteristics. In this chapter, we will describe the determinant role of three categories of personal characteristics of customers: genetics, biogenics, and personality. Included in biogenics are three personal characteristics: race, gender, and age.

Genetics, Race, Gender, Age, Personality. All Different. All Different Customers.

Personal Characteristics

By **personal characteristics,** we mean characteristics customers possess as individuals. They include those biological and physiological features a person is born with and those that develop as a person grows but whose origin derives from biological heredity. There are two types of personal characteristics: the traits of the individual himself or herself and group traits.

Group traits consist of common biogenic categories including race, gender, and age. These are considered group traits because they are not unique to an individual; rather

PERSONAL CHARACTERISTICS THAT DETERMINE CUSTOMER BEHAVIOR

Figure 7.1

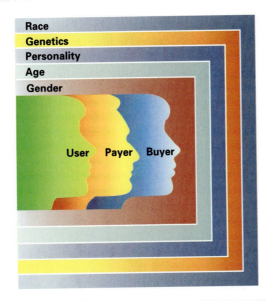

they are shared by and describe a group of persons such as "all men 25 years of age." Furthermore, a person is born with these traits and does not have the ability to alter them. These group traits allow researchers to analyze customers at a group or segment level (e.g., all men or all women) to see whether trends or significant differences exist between groups of customers with different traits. Examples include men-women differences in food, clothing, and shelter; young-old differences; and ethnic differences.

Individual traits consist of unique (not common) biogenic and psychogenic aspects of an individual customer. The biogenic individual trait is called "genetics." The psychogenic individual traits are called "personality traits." As we shall see, genetics are unique to each individual, and so are personality traits. Moreover, like race, gender, and age, genetics are ascribed (i.e., a human inherits them from birth). Personality traits, on the other hand, are produced by a combination of genetics, group traits, and a person's external environment.

Genetics: The Cards We Are Dealt at Birth

Jon Pepke is 6 feet 9 inches tall at age 28; Charles du Pont is 4 feet 5 inches at age 35. Angela Infonsino has blue eyes; Maria Ramirez has brown. Atsuko Linuma has dark hair; Ayesha Golub has red. Abu Khan weighs 350 pounds at age 32; Saleem Taher weighs 140 at 24. Meera Patel has an allergy to mink; Alex Rodriguez to milk. Josh Wijaya likes to shower with cold water and likes to stay outdoors in winter; Gilles von Raaij likes warm water showers and staying indoors by the fireplace. Chung Ka-shing wears eyeglasses at age four; Kim Ju-Yung does not at age 53. Mikhail Baryshnikov is happy-go-lucky; Jirri Anston is introspective.

Why are these customers different? The answer lies at least partly in genetics. Genetics refers to the biochemical heredity of an organism, specifically to sequences of chemical compounds in DNA. **DNA,** an acronym for deoxyribonucleic acid, refers to the chem-

Genetic Research, DNA, and Human Behavior

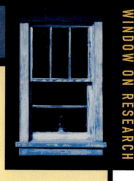

The Human Genome Project is seeking to catalog and describe all the genes in the human body—that is, the *human genome*. Often described as the biological equivalent of the Apollo moon mission, the Genome Project is expected to prepare a complete readout of our biological blueprint by the year 2005 (at a cost of around $4 billion).

In 1983, the first partial gene map was assembled around the discovery of the specific mutation for the devastating neurological disorder known as Huntington's chorea. Since then, geneticists have located genes responsible for hundreds of "monogenic" (single-gene) diseases, such as cystic fibrosis and sickle-cell anemia. One particularly interesting finding shows that DNA regulating the activity of one specific gene in humans has been found in two variations. The slightly longer version causes the gene cell to churn out more of a substance called serotonin transporter. The more transporter it produces, the more neurotic the person becomes. Serotonin is one of the most important of the 50 or so neurotransmitters identified so far. It plays a role in appetite, sleep, reproduction, cognition, and emotion, and especially in anxiety and depression.

So far, about 6,300 human genes (around 6 percent of the total) have been mapped. About half of these cause disease when present in mutated form; most have been traced to specific locations on chromosomes.

One practical application of this research is correction of genetic defects—and, with it, prevention or cure of diseases. Many commercial firms are lining up to invest in and reap the benefits of genetics research. A growing number of new commercial laboratories are rushing into the fray, marketing genetic tests for an ever-increasing number of gene-related disorders. Hundreds of these tests—including nearly 200 prenatal tests—are already available.

Sources: See "Human Genetics: Anxious Natures," *The Economist,* November 30, 1996; Christian Tyler, "Darwin Still Gets under the Skin: His Descendants Claim He Has an Answer for Everything," *Financial Times,* February 15, 1997, p. 1; "The Proper Study of Mankind," *The Economist,* September 14, 1996, p. 19.

icals in cell nuclei that form the molecular basis of heredity in organisms. Genes—segments of DNA—synthesize the proteins of which the human body is made. In so doing, the 100,000 or so genes within each human cell provide the code that determines our characteristics. Currently, research is in progress on genetics and DNA, seeking to discover secrets of the human condition and behavior (see the Window on Research box).

Biological Determinism

Advances in neurology are uncovering various chemicals that regulate human emotions and behavior. These discoveries support the idea of **biological determinism**—the belief that human behavior is determined by biological factors such as genetics and DNA. One example of biological determinism is the current debate in U.S. courts against cigarette companies. An argument is being made that cigarette companies, rather than the smoking individual, are responsible for the suffering and addiction of the individual. At issue here is the fact that nicotine in cigarettes is chemically addictive, and consequently, a person's smoking behavior is determined by the biological factor of chemical dependency caused by the cigarettes. Regardless of how this argument is conclusively settled, the issue illustrates the currency in public policy of the principle of biological determination of at least some of customer behavior.

A note of caution is needed, however. It is misleading to take biological determinism as an absolute. Certainly, other factors, nonbiological in nature, such as culture, perception, learning, and individual motivation, determine much of adult behavior. At the same time, many physiological abilities and conditions and consequent behaviors are determined by neurological and genetic factors. A more appropriate statement is therefore that *some* human behavior is determined by biological factors.

Impact of Genetics on Customers

Genetics affects customer needs and behavior in at least four ways: by establishing (1) physiological differences, (2) diseases and mental disorders, (3) circadian rhythm, and (4) emotions and behavior.

PHYSIOLOGICAL DIFFERENCES

The most direct and vivid effect of genetics is on a person's physical features and other physiological characteristics. A person's height, weight, skin color and tone, color of eyes, color and texture of hair, and bodily reactions to variations in temperature and other environmental changes (i.e., allergies) are all caused by genetics. A consequence of these gene-based physical differences is that customers need different products and services to be compatible with their individual bodies. Thus, shorter people may have difficulties with automobile airbags and people of different sizes and shapes need adjustable office chairs for comfort. The differences in products and services necessitated by genetic effects on customers are pervasive and often dramatic.

DISEASES AND MENTAL DISORDERS

Genetics and biological makeup intimately affect human susceptibility to certain diseases. Currently, geneticists are researching the genes that cause susceptibility to diseases such as cancer, diabetes, and cardiovascular diseases. While some of these diseases are caused by the interaction of genes and the physical environment (e.g., exposure to carcinogens), certain types of colon and breast cancer are thought to be primarily genetic. Breast cancer, for example, may be caused both by biology (e.g., errors in DNA, inherited mutations of

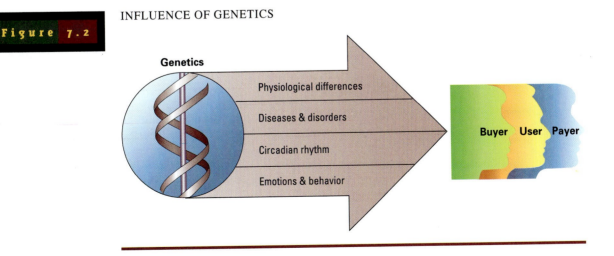

Figure 7.2

INFLUENCE OF GENETICS

Genetics

Physiological differences

Diseases & disorders

Circadian rhythm

Emotions & behavior

Buyer   User   Payer

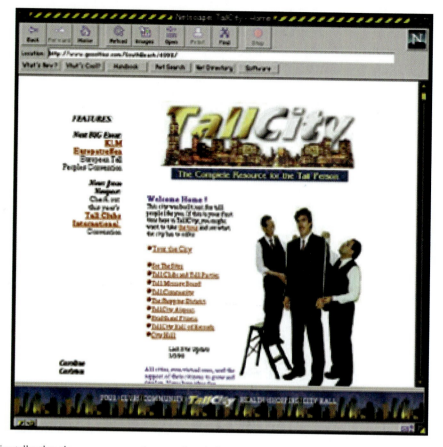

Being taller than the average person is a genetic trait that can require specialized products and services. Finding the right size bicycle or clothing is made easier at the TallCity Web site where over 1,800 suppliers of goods and services are provided for the tall consumer.

genes) and by environmental factors (e.g., exposure to carcinogens). Many other diseases are also caused by genetic deficiency: Huntington's chorea and hemophilia are caused by a single faulty gene. Similarly, Alzheimer's disease, schizophrenia, depression, diabetes, and a range of allergic reactions are caused by genetic factors. This effect of genetic makeup causes customer needs to avoid certain environments, foods, and other materials and to seek special products and services and environments; possible drugs to alleviate symptoms or reactions; and possible medical services and treatments to alleviate or cure genetics-produced diseases.

CIRCADIAN RHYTHM

All living creatures, humans included, have a daily cycle of activity, called their **circadian rhythm.** This biological "clock" governs rhythms like sleep-wake cycles. These behavioral cycles are in turn governed by the daily ebb and flow of various hormones and brain chemicals according to the time of the day, a process that depends, in part, on the amount of light perceived. The amount of light perceived regulates the onset and rate of certain neurological processes.

Why are some people night owls, while others are at their best in the morning? The answer is in the genes (or their biological clock). People's rhythms affect, among other things, when shoppers like to shop. If you have ever wondered who shops at Wal-Mart in the wee hours (since Wal-Mart is open 24 hours), the answer lies in circadian rhythm: people who are night owls. Some research is currently examining whether consumers might process advertisements differently at different times of the day, according to their circadian rhythm.

EMOTIONS AND BEHAVIOR

Finally, many emotions or emotional disorders and behaviors themselves are rooted in biological factors. Take child behavior. Twelve percent of U.S. children and teenagers suffer from brain disorders.[1] Some of the emotional and mental disorders in children have historically been blamed on the family and on parents' child rearing practices. Recent advances are now discovering that many of these problems are, in fact, based in brain chemistry, in the hard-wiring, that is.

Nature versus Nurture Argument

An interesting debate concerns whether human behavior is determined by nature (i.e., the biological factors) or nurture (the familial and social environment). Those who favor nurture argue that behavior is determined by a person's upbringing, by family life, by parental values, by peer group influences, by school, and by church groups. The nature argument, on the other hand, credits a person's genetic makeup for much of the human behavior. After all, two siblings reared in the same household will grow up to be dissimilar.

Genetics makes people different (not similar). Except for identical twins, all children inherit a unique genetic combination that never existed before and is not duplicated ever! That is why physical characteristics differ even among siblings—one baby has blue eyes; his sister has brown. Furthermore, their temperaments are different. Although no gene is yet linked to a specific personality trait, thousands of genes in combination could establish a person's personality type and behavior patterns.

Conservative. Serious. Upbeat. Introspective. Sociable and outgoing. Aloof. A follower or a leader. What are you like? Modern evolutionary psychologists now tell us that, at some basic level, our behavior can be scientifically explained by our genetic history. This history influences our behavior and predispositions in a range of areas: our emotions, our sexual preference, tribalism, love of status, notions of beauty, our sociability, creativity, and morality itself.

Adherents to the nurture-based argument insist that we learn these behaviors by observing how we and others are treated. Nevertheless, two siblings may, due to different genetic make up, react differently to the same parental behavior. When Dad insists that Tom and Jerry, two brothers, get good grades in school, for example, Tom might perceive that his father is looking out for his interests, and Jerry might see him as an overbearing authoritarian figure.[2]

One particular biological factor researchers have studied is the birth order of children. **Birth order** is the sequence among all siblings born of the same mother. Frank Sulloway, a science historian at MIT, has studied thousands of famous people of the last five centuries and has concluded that birth order matters. According to the theory of birth order, espoused by Sulloway in his book *Born to Rebel,* a person's birth order determines his or her temperament and behaviors. Specifically, older children are control freaks and are aspiring, ambitious, and driven. Having no one younger in the family during their initial childhood years, they identify with adults and learn to act responsibly and maintain and enforce law and order. They graduate with good grades and end up running corporations. The younger siblings, in contrast, take themselves much less seriously, are more sociable and less judgmental, more risk taking and more open to new things and change.

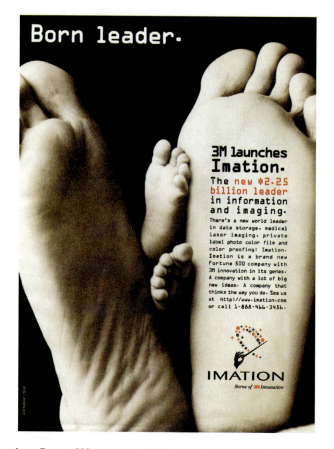

"Imation is a brand new Fortune 500 company with 3M innovation in its genes," claims this ad. Who says genetics does not influence personality—be it an individual's or an organization's!

We discuss personality and its customer behavior effects in the last section of this chapter. Presently, we turn to the three biogenic personal characteristics that influence customer behavior: namely, race, gender, and age.

Race

Not only do people have a unique collection of traits, but they share many traits with their relatives. **Race** refers to the genetic heritage group a person is born in. A related concept is **ethnic identity,** which refers to the ethnic heritage one is born in. In the United States, the Bureau of the Census specifies the following four race categories:

1. Caucasian.

2. African American.

3. American Indian and Alaskan Eskimos.

4. Asians and Pacific Islanders.

The U.S. Census asks for ethnic identity separately, and Hispanics are included as a category there. It is interesting to note that Hispanics are not identified as a separate race category. Accordingly, many Hispanics mark themselves in the "other" category. Another point to note is that not all Asians have the same genetic heritage, and therefore are not the same race. Asians tend to mark the fourth category because they interpret it as a geographic identity group rather than race. Thus, the U.S. government race identification is an "administrative" designation rather than a scientific or cultural classification.

Race in the American Marketplace

Los Angeles, California, is a quintessential multiethnic city. People here speak 80 plus languages and come from 100 plus cultural and ethnic backgrounds. Perhaps only in the United Nations buildings will you find a more diverse population. In Los Angeles, at every turn of the road, you will see people who look different from you, no matter what your own race is. You will meet Filipinos, Koreans, Mexicans, Salvadorans, as well as Chinese, Ethiopians, Indians, Indonesians, Iranians, Pacific Islanders, Druze, Tamils, and Vietnamese, and, of course, infrequently, white Americans. As Marlene S. Rossman, the author of *Multicultural Marketing* observes, you can eat every night in a different ethnic restaurant without repeating the food for a year![3]

Los Angeles: The quintessential multiethnic city.

Although the ethnic potpourri is not as dramatic elsewhere, its presence is unmistakable almost anywhere in the United States, and it is on the rise. In the 1980 census, one in five persons was of nonwhite, non-European origin; in the 1990 census this number had gone up to one in four. According to a report by the U.S. Census Bureau, in 1996 there

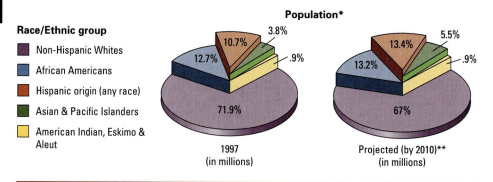

Figure 7.3

U.S. POPULATION MAKEUP BY RACE/ETHNIC GROUP

Population*

Race/Ethnic group

- Non-Hispanic Whites
- African Americans
- Hispanic origin (any race)
- Asian & Pacific Islanders
- American Indian, Eskimo & Aleut

1997
(in millions)

3.8%
10.7%
12.7%
.9%
71.9%

Projected (by 2010)**
(in millions)

5.5%
13.4%
13.2%
.9%
67%

Source: Bureau of Census, *Statistical Abstract of the United States,* U.S. 1996.

were 33.5 million blacks (13 percent of population); 27.7 million Hispanics (11 percent), 9.5 million Asians (4 percent); and 2.3 million American Indians (1 percent). By 2010, one in three American children will be minorities (see Figure 7.3).

The ever-increasing presence of immigrants and their U.S.-born offspring is altering mainstream culture and customs. Consider some popular foods in America: bagels, pizza, hamburgers, sushi, Szechuan chicken, burritos—all are ardently consumed by Americans. Today, tortilla chips are consumed in 60 percent of U.S. households, and salsa outsells ketchup! Given such diversity, marketers need to understand the ethnic makeup of U.S. customers.

The marketing literature identifies four race/ethnic groups in the United States: European Americans, African Americans, Hispanics, and Asian Americans. The culture, values, norms, and behaviors of these four race/ethnic groups differ markedly.

European Americans

Even though European Americans are the descendants of European immigrants themselves, they are the largest racial group, and it is now conventional to deem them as the mainstream population. It is also conventional to refer to this group simply as "whites" or "Caucasians," although neither term is exact. Hispanics are also white and are counted in the U.S. census as Caucasians. A more accurate label therefore would be "non-Hispanic Caucasians."

DEMOGRAPHICS

Americans of European descent number about 200 million, about 4 million of them foreign born. Immigration from Europe boomed between 1980 and 1995, a period during which about 1.2 million Europeans migrated to the United States, in large part spurred by a breakdown of communist regimes in Eastern Europe. Although these European descendants are themselves a diverse group, representing some 15 different countries of origin, they do share some common characteristics as a group.

According to a recent survey, about one in three is a member of a household with two or more persons working full-time. More than 10 percent are business owners, and one in four has a professional job. More than one-third of them have a household income that exceeds $50,000 a year, indicating the relative prosperity of this population. Of course, the prosperity of different ethnic people within this population varies: in general, the more recent the immigration, the poorer or less prosperous the group. Thus, the median household income is highest among European Americans of French origin (<$75,000 for 40 percent of them), the majority of whom have been in the U.S. for more than 10 years. The lowest income is among those of Polish origin (<$25,000 for about 40% of them), the majority of whom have had a U.S. residence of less than 10 years.[4]

VALUES AND MARKETPLACE BEHAVIOR

European Americans are very competitive, aggressive, and explicit and direct in their communications. They seek and desire change and consider time as "money." They value youth and also materialism. Although egalitarianism is the professed ideal, class consciousness is very much alive in the mainstream culture. These cultural values and norms influence their marketplace behavior. Market transactions tend to be impersonal, apparently rational, and efficiency driven. Products and services are purchased with self-centered benefits in mind. Salespeople tend to be pushy and customers demanding. These values as well as market behaviors are in sharp contrast with those of the other ethnic/race groups.

Not all European Americans think of themselves as ethnic, but many do. This latter group maintains strong ties with their homelands. These "ethnic Europeans" exhibit somewhat different marketplace behavior than non-Hispanic whites in general, and, of course, than other ethnic minorities in particular. Some of these consumption differences are as follows.[5]

These ethnic European Americans work longer hours than other non-Hispanic whites, and they spend the fruits of their labor liberally on material goods and on recreation. For example, they take cruises substantially more than does an average American: compared with a 3 percent rate among the general population, the cruise travel rate among the Americans of Swiss origin is 6 percent, and among those of Russian or Norwegian origin it is 17 percent. Another conspicuous recreational activity is casino gambling, with as many as half of Germans, Italians, and Portuguese identifying themselves as "having gambled in the past year."

Conspicuous consumption is especially conspicuous among the ethnic whites. Home electronics (VCRs, stereos, etc.) are owned by more than 90 percent of ethnic whites, compared to about 50 to 60 percent among all non-Hispanic whites. Indeed, among the recent immigrants from Eastern Europe, buying American consumer goods is a symbol of having become an American. One European immigrant explained it thus: "It takes a long time to become a citizen or to be able to vote or to perfect one's English. But as soon as a person has a steady job and an income, he or she can start buying the symbols of what it is to be an American, whether it be the TV and the VCR or the designer sneakers."

MARKETER OPPORTUNITY AND RESPONSE

To reach ethnic Europeans—that is, those Americans of European descent who still maintain ties with their homeland and its language and culture—marketers have to adapt their mainstream strategies. Cruise marketers catering to ethnic Europeans, for example, target different cruises to ethnic segments—Greeks, Italians, Eastern Europeans—and they customize food and entertainment to each group. Another strong marketing tool is the use of ethnic languages in advertisements—German, Italian, French, Russian, and so on; ethnic whites still find their mother tongue very appealing. Often, the product benefit or appeal too needs adaptation. For instance, AT&T found that its "True Voice" campaign with Whitney Houston had no appeal to recent ethnic European immigrants. The quality of the sound (true voice) was not a value to them because they were used to having to scream into the phone in their homeland. Actually, to an immigrant from Eastern European countries, true voice often meant "the voice of Pravda"! And Whitney Houston had no relevance to them either. So on Russian-language TV, AT&T instead used a Russian comic promoting its service.

Such customization is not needed for the larger group of European Americans (i.e., those other than recent immigrants). Long in residence in America, most constitute, as already mentioned, what has come to be known as the "mainstream culture." This culture, in contrast to that of African Americans, Hispanics, and Asian Americans, values individualism over the rights of the family and society. It also values a small and nuclear family, whereas the other groups value extended families.[6]

African Americans

DEMOGRAPHICS

African Americans number some 33.5 million (13 percent of the total U.S. population) and are expected to grow to some 38 million by 2010. They are concentrated in the South, mostly in major cities, with Atlanta being the major center for this subpopulation. Other major metropolitan areas with large populations of African Americans are Chicago; Los Angeles; Detroit; Washington, D.C.; and New Orleans. Their median age is 25.6 years (compared with 43 years for whites), and average household size 3.1 (compared to 3.5 for whites). Many children live in single parent families (58 percent of the children compared to 20 percent white children), and most of these are female-headed families. A large proportion is poor: the annual household income is less than $25,000 for 60 percent of African Americans compared to 40 percent of whites. At the same time, many have middle and upper incomes and are well educated.

VALUES

Family and religious values are very important to African Americans. Taking care of their loved ones comes first. Middle-class African Americans display a high degree of achievement motivation, attempting to succeed financially, and are keen to make a mark, in part to show the world what an African American can do. They are self-image conscious and like to display style. They are trendsetters and tend to define their own style. In his book, *African Americans: A Celebration of Life,* author Ronald L. Freeman writes: "Style— whether captured in an elegant hat, an eloquent phrase, a sophisticated step, or a smooth move—lies at the very heart of African American culture."

MARKETPLACE BEHAVIOR

African Americans enjoy shopping, many using it as a social occasion. Compared to the general population, African Americans spend disproportionately more on clothing, shoes, and home electronics. African American children have a greater awareness of fashion. Although all kids are fashion and brand conscious, African Americans are substantially more so. African Americans show loyalty to well-known brands, but they are also willing to try new brands. Patronage of generic and store brands is higher among middle- and upper-class African Americans than among poor African Americans. This counterintuitive behavior may be due to unawareness among the poor or lack of access to these brands (i.e., they may be unaware of private brands, or warehouse stores that carry many private brands may not be located in poor neighborhoods.)

For this African-American man, only dark and natural will do.

African Americans tend to drink regular colas (rather than diet versions) and flavored drinks such as Mountain Dew. Drinks with a lot of sugar (such as Jolt) are also popular among this group. This group also accounts for some one-third of the U.S. consumption of malt liquor.

In many product categories, African Americans tend to buy premium brands. They buy premium liquor because it is an *affordable* status symbol. Many urban youth wear gold jewelry. To them, gold is expensive but still more affordable than, say, a suburban house. While some of this conspicuous consumption is to keep up with the mainstream Joneses, it should not be assumed that all of it is to impress their white counterparts; many middle- and upper-class African Americans spend much on clothing, cars, audio equipment, and they buy other luxury products simply because doing so signifies their lifestyle, tradition, and relative affluence.

MARKETER OPPORTUNITY AND RESPONSE

Marketers have not directed much of their resources to African Americans. Until the 1980s, cosmetic companies marketed the same make-up products for whites and African Americans; then Flori Roberts introduced a new line of foundations and make-up products specially formulated for the dark skin. Likewise, for years, African American children had to make do with white dolls, white cartoons, and even white fairy tales

(Goldilocks). Today, Huggy bean dolls, and Kulture Kids, smaller dolls wearing kente cloth (a fabric motif style popular in Africa), and black hero comic books are in the offing. In another exemplary case of custom-targeting African Americans, *Essence* magazine created a designer line of eyeglasses with a broader nose bridge and longer temple stems, to suit African American faces.

Most African Americans have reported feeling that most TV and print advertisements are designed mostly for whites. In a recent study, the New York Department of Consumer Affairs studied some 2,000 plus advertisements in 10 general readership magazines (e.g., *Better Homes and Gardens*) and found that African Americans appeared in only 3.4 percent of the advertisements!

There are, of course, special media for African Americans that offer opportunity for marketers to target this group. Black Entertainment Television (BET) network reaches more than half of the African-American households, and among magazines, *Ebony, Essence, Black Enterprise, Emerge,* and *YSB* are very popular among African Americans. Now, some marketers and advertisers have begun to adapt their efforts for this segment. For example, the Allstate logo is a pair of hands along with the slogan, "You are in good hands with Allstate." In some advertisements, those hands are black.

J.C. Penney offers African Collection women's clothing in some 22 of its stores. These boutiques offer a wide range of African clothing and fabrics for the home, many based on kente cloth, a richly patterned fabric produced in West Africa. Originally worn by African royalty, woven of cotton and sometimes silk, this cloth was traditionally worn by men as togas and by women as dresses. Many African Americans say that kente clothing helps them appreciate the African in African American.

Hispanics

DEMOGRAPHICS

With over 27.7 million in number in 1996, Hispanics are an important customer group in America. Growing at the highest rate of any ethnic minority, Hispanics are estimated to become the single largest ethnic minority group by 2010, surpassing African Americans by about a million or so. Presently, they are concentrated in Miami—accounting for about half of the total local population. In Los Angeles County, they account for about 37 percent of the population, and New York is another major area. Youngest of all groups in the United States, their median age is 24 years. There are four major subgroups:

1. *Mexicans*—Sixty-four percent of Hispanics are of Mexican origin, and two-thirds of them are U.S. born. Most of them live in the West and Southwest. They are the youngest of all the Hispanic groups, and some have entered the country illegally, crossing the border and taking any job in the border states. Low-income Mexican Americans tend to stay in these border towns and states such as in Arizona, Texas, and California.

2. *Puerto Ricans*—About 12 percent of U.S. Hispanics are of Puerto Rican origin. However just as many are of Puerto Rican ancestry but born in the United States. Puerto Ricans have been entitled to U.S. citizenship since 1917, when Puerto Rico became a U.S. commonwealth. Half of all immigrants from Puerto Rico have settled in New York. Many college-educated Puerto Ricans have settled in the Sunbelt States. They can move freely between the United States and Puerto Rico; however, many feel that their home is Puerto Rico. This reduces their desire for or interest in assimilation. Puerto Ricans, like other Hispanics, are warm and sociable people.

3. *Cuban Americans*—Only 4 to 5 percent of U.S. Hispanics are of Cuban origin, and 72 percent of them were born in Cuba. A vast majority of them live in South Florida (e.g., Miami, Tampa), although a large concentration can also be found in the New Jersey area. Cuban Americans are the

most affluent Hispanics, and they are also the most educated: Of all Cubans above 25 years of age, 20 percent have completed four years of college; this compares with 6 percent for Mexican Americans and 10 percent for Puerto Rican Americans.

4. *Dominicans*—Immigrants from Dominican Republic are new in the United States and were half a million in the 1990 census. Black and brown in skin color, most tend to settle near the Puerto Rican communities in the North (although a few do live in Miami and New Jersey), and yet they don't really assimilate with Puerto Ricans. They make up 40 percent of New York's Hispanics, and own 70 percent of Hispanic small businesses (predominantly supermarkets).

Hispanic median income is $31,500 for Cubans, $23,350 for Mexicans, and $18,000 for Puerto Ricans. While these four groups share a broadly common language, cultural values, and customs, there are many important differences in tastes and activities. The style of music is different. They have different holidays and like different sports. Mexicans play soccer, whereas Cubans and Puerto Ricans play baseball. Their family size is different. Cubans tend to have smaller families than Mexicans (3.2 versus 4.4, on average). They also differ by their region of U.S. residence. In San Francisco, about half of them are churchgoers, whereas in Phoenix and Tucson, only about one in four are. Hispanics also differ by income groups, as do all customer groups. Affluent Hispanics are more assimilated than are low-income Hispanics. Finally, they differ by the length of their residence in the United States. Recent immigrants exhibit more of their native culture and customs.

VALUES

Family and children are very important to Hispanics and take precedence over work. Religion and tradition are also respected. Hispanics are more religious than whites, and a greater proportion of them are churchgoers. Play and work are interwoven—During a normal workday, they entertain social visitors or engage in extensive social conversation with business visitors; on the flip side, they tend to work late hours (especially if they have had a prolonged, fun-filled lunch hour) and make substantial business deals over food and beverage fiestas. Hispanics—both men and women—have a strong interest in appearance. Finally, Hispanics are fascinated by technology. In Miami, Florida, for instance, everywhere except in the low-income neighborhoods, you find Hispanics nearly all carrying pagers, and one out of every two carries a cellular phone.

MARKETPLACE BEHAVIOR

Good looks and appearance being important to Hispanics, they are heavy buyers and users of cosmetics and toiletries, much more than mainstream America. Hispanics love to shop—on a typical weekend, either the whole family will go to the mall, or the women would pick up their children and go shopping with a group of friends. They prefer shopping in person rather than by catalogs (see the Window on Practice box). Hispanics also have a tendency to buy from those companies that are involved in community activities. Hispanics tend to be more brand loyal—45 percent of them buy their usual brands. Many U.S. brands have made inroads in their native countries, so they continue to show loyalty to those brands. One reason is that since family is very important to them, they want to do the best for the family by buying prestige goods. Many Hispanics, of Mexican origin, in particular, don't trust putting checks in the mail, because back in their homeland of Mexico, they trust neither the bank nor the post office. So they tend to pay by cash. Nationally, only one in three Hispanics has a checking account or owns a credit card (compared to more than two-thirds of all Americans).

Why Do Hispanics Prefer Vended Water?

In Los Angeles, consumption of vended water is much more prevalent among Hispanics than among the Anglo population (26 percent versus 7 percent in 1989). The reason is their past experience with the poor quality of water in their countries and the media reports about the poor quality of water in Los Angeles; furthermore, they prefer to buy their water from the vending machine rather than from a store because at the vending machine they do not have to speak the language. When Sparkletts Water System developed an advertising campaign, they employed the Hispanic values of family orientation, respect for the elderly and for tradition, and brand-consciousness. The commercial showed a grandfather bringing his two grandchildren to the vending machine to teach them why he buys water there. In another commercial, advanced technology in the vending machines was highlighted because Hispanics are fascinated with technology and like things that work perfectly.

Source: "Quenching Hispanic Thirst," *American Demographics*, December 1989, pp. 14–15.

MARKETER OPPORTUNITY AND RESPONSE

Since Hispanics are close knit and community oriented, word-of-mouth is very effective for them; hence, event marketing (sweepstakes, music festivals, sporting events, religious holidays) is a good tool. In mass media, Spanish TV, and among magazines, *Hispanic* and *Hispanic Business* are important. Some marketers adapt their products to Hispanic tastes; an example is the introduction by Dannon yogurt of guava, papaya, mango, and pineapple flavors.

One vexing question facing marketers is whether the Hispanic customers of different origins can be treated as a single market? The most significant common factor, from marketing communications standpoint, is their common language, Spanish. But even here, regional nuances exist, and smart marketers ensure that their communications are free of such local or regional variations. A few years ago, Segmented Marketing Services of Winston-Salem, North Carolina, an ethnic marketing agency, prepared a magazine in Spanish called *Tradiciones de Familia* and distributed it free to more than 2 million Hispanics across the United States, along with free product samples from Procter and Gamble, its sole sponsor. But great care was taken to eliminate regional variations: three Hispanic editors from three different regions of origin worked on the magazine.[7]

To account for differences among Hispanic groups, Donnelley Marketing Information Services (DMIS) of Stamford, Connecticut, has identified as many as 18 segments. For example, two of those segments are "Puerto Rican high-income, younger, established homes," and "Mexican, lowest income, younger, low-mobility Hispanic neighborhoods."[8] Such microsegmentation helps local, regional, and national marketers temper national campaigns with local variations. These local adaptations can supplement a national effort, which is based on an understanding of common Hispanic cultural values—family and relationship orientation, respect for tradition and elders, religiousness, equi-importance of play and work, and desire to acquire "Americanness," without losing pride in their language and culture.

Marketers are increasingly responding to Hispanic customers. GM recently bought advertising for its cars in Latina Style *magazine. Shown is publisher Anna Maria Arias.*

Asian Americans

DEMOGRAPHICS

Between 1980 and 1990, the Asian-American population more than doubled. Asian-Americans' median age is 27 years, and they have the highest median household income, $40,600 in 1995 (compared with $37,200 for non-Hispanic whites). They also have a high rate of completing college, 39 percent, compared to the 17 percent U.S. average. Fifty-five percent of all Asians live in California, greater New York, or Honolulu. Many live in acculturated neighborhoods and pricey suburbs. Asian American is merely a convenient label, since, in fact, it comprises immigrants from several countries:

- Chinese Americans (23 percent)
- Filipinos (19 percent)
- Japanese (12 percent)
- Asian Indian (11 percent)
- Korean (11 percent)
- Vietnamese (14 percent)

CHINESE AMERICANS   Chinese Americans are about 1.6 million in number, and account for over 20 percent of all Asian Americans. They sometimes identify themselves as either American-born Chinese (ABC), who are more educated, and well-to-do, who live in upscale communities and are more assimilated into the mainstream culture; or as fresh off boats Chinese (FOB), who live in downtowns and Chinatown and tend to be patriarchical, blue-collar, and conservative. They may speak one of the two major Chinese languages: Cantonese (spoken in Hong Kong) and Mandarin (spoken in Taiwan).

JAPANESE AMERICANS   There are about 850,000 Japanese Americans in the United States, and more than 80 percent of them live on the West Coast. Close to 50,000 Japanese describe themselves as "salarymen," people who are sent by corporations to the United States on temporary assignment and have extended visas. Due to loyalty to their employers, they return to their country. Accordingly, they attempt to "stay Japanese" and believe that others have turned their backs on their homeland. However, a majority (close to 90 percent) are born in the United States, most have attended college, and this group's median family income is 32 percent above the U.S. average. Most of these U.S.-born Japanese don't even speak Japanese, and close to 50 percent of third-generation Japanese Americans have married whites. Many are well assimilated, breaking the stereotype and doing things the mainstream population does. Overjoyed at Kristi Yamaguchi's success in figure skating, one young Japanese-American fan commented, "We are not all math or science wizards or laundry operators or restaurant owners, but skaters, architects, writers. And more. And less. Without hyphens."[9]

Breaking the Stereotype: Kristi Yamaguchi, a U.S.-born Japanese and the 1992 world champion of figure skating.

ASIAN INDIANS   About one million in number, immigrants from India, Pakistan, and Bangladesh are, as a group, the most educated of the entire U.S. population. A large number are professionals, and many are owners of small businesses (e.g., motels, gas stations, and convenience stores). Among recent immigrants, most came to study in polytechnic schools and in Ivy League colleges. Indian students are the most significant presence of all foreign students on college campuses, especially in doctoral programs.

KOREAN AMERICANS   There are over one million Koreans in the United States, and 90 percent of them are foreign born. They tend to cluster in large metro areas, mostly in New York, Los Angeles, Chicago, and Honolulu. They have the highest self-employment rate and the highest business ownership rate of any group in America. Many of them own small supermarkets and convenience stores.

FILIPINO AMERICANS   In 1990, there were 2 million Filipinos in America, constituting the largest (28 percent) and probably the best assimilated of all Asian Americans. Because of the 400-year long colonization by Spain, the Philippines is a Christian nation; hence, 85 percent of Filipino Americans are Roman Catholic. They are concentrated in San Francisco and Los Angeles, and, in lesser numbers, in Chicago, New York, New Jersey, and Connecticut.

VIETNAMESE AMERICANS   Vietnamese comprise the largest number of the rest of Asian Americans. About one million in number, they make up about 14 percent of all Asian Americans. About half of them live on the West Coast (about one-third in California). Their median income is lower than that of all other Asian Americans.

VALUES

Confucianism has had a big influence on many Chinese. This system of beliefs (propagated by the Chinese philosopher Confucius) values hard work, long-term reciprocal relationships, respect for authority (especially, teachers and parents), harmony in all things, and discipline or delaying gratification. Accordingly, the cultural values of Chinese Americans emphasize familial relationships and obligations. Many Chinese Americans do not trust banks, preferring to borrow within their own community, and to put cash in a safe rather than in the bank.

Core Japanese-American values are hard work, loyalty to the group (work group, employer, family, community, or whatever other groups they may join), an obligation to return favors, and respect for age and tradition. Education is also valued highly, so much so that doing well in school is considered an honor to the family or community.

Filipinos share many cultural traits with Hispanics: family values, courtship rituals, allowing enough "play" time, and so on. They are outgoing and sociable; they love having a good time and enjoy a good laugh.

Korean Americans are very hardworking—especially in the family-owned stores where the family works about 11 hours a day, six days a week. For this reason, they also tend to be tired and insulated from other communities. Like other Asians, Koreans too value family loyalty, education, and frugality, and show respect for elders. Koreans prefer *Kye* (a system of borrowing from individuals), rather than from banks or government. Like Chinese, they distrust banks due to bad past experience with Korean banks.

More than any other minorities, Koreans prefer to maintain their culture, resisting assimilation. Many Koreans see themselves as Koreans rather than as Korean Americans and may return to Korea if economic conditions are perceived to have improved. Koreans value self-reliance, extending the self to their own communities so that when they need help they tend to reach into the community rather than reach out to the mainstream population, thus causing insulation.

Among Asian Indians, one of the most remarkable traits (but not easily visible to outsiders) is a faith in the Hindu philosophy of *Karma*. Karma, a gospel from Hindu Lord Krishna, emphasizes two seemingly contradictory dictums: (1) a person is predestined to get and achieve whatever is his or her due, based upon his or her deeds in previous life, or, otherwise, whatever the God has willed for him or her; and (2) at the same time, it is a person's duty to do his or her work diligently since that work too is willed by God. Many outsiders misunderstand Karma to imply fatalism (belief in fate) and, correspondingly, no desire to make the effort. Traditional Indians are fatalist, but this implies not that they should shirk the effort, but rather only that they must make peace with whatever is the outcome of their effort (i.e., whatever is their Karma). Likewise, Asian Moslems often use the expression, "Insha Allah," which means "whatever be Allah's—God's—wish."

Asian Indians value their families and many live in extended families, where adults and children care for the elderly. Many are deeply religious and like to maintain their tradition and customs. Many Asian Indian families, especially those with U.S.-born children, who act as acculturation agents for their parents, adopt modern lifestyles but at the same time preserve their customs in their activities at home and within the community, such as in dress, language, food habits, and religious rituals. They, like other Asians, are hard working; like Japanese, they are very ambitious. But unlike most other Asians, they are also contented with what they manage to achieve, a trait acquired by their faith in Karma.

Among Asians in general, humility and self-denial for the sake of the group are valued. And Asians (from all regions) don't show emotions in public.

MARKETPLACE BEHAVIOR

The marketplace behavior of Asian Americans differs from the mainstream population as well as from other racial/ethnic minorities. Let us consider some examples:

- Japanese Americans, both permanent immigrants and salarymen, are very sophisticated consumers, have a good deal of money to spend, and buy high-quality mainstream brands.
- Many Asian Indians are vegetarians. But even among those who are not, certain kinds of meats are prohibited; for example, Hindus will not eat beef, and Muslims will not eat pork or drink alcohol. Many Indians prefer Pizza Hut to McDonald's.
- Saving face is very important to Asians. Therefore, they do not take kindly to advertisements that disparage a competitor's product—It is considered bad to make someone (e.g., a competitor) lose face.
- Koreans prefer a soft sell and face-to-face shopping. Koreans will, however, say "no" more directly than other Asians.
- In Hawaii, Chinese tend to pay cash for a car, whereas Japanese finance it.
- Looking the customer in the eye is expected in the United States, but Asian customers would view it as undesirable. Similarly, in the United States, it is a practice to smile a lot at customers, but for many Asian-American customers, such as Koreans in America, this would be out of place, since smiling is done selectively in Asia, reserved for good acquaintances and friends only. Smiling at strangers is considered artificial or "false." (See Window on Practice box, "To Smile or Not to Smile.")

MARKETER OPPORTUNITY AND RESPONSE

Language obviously is a key factor in targeting ethnic customers. Marketing communications need to be in the language that minorities are comfortable with. Most businesses in Miami offer Spanish as a menu option on their voice mail. Chemical Bank teller machines offer a Russian language option in its Brighton Beach-Brooklyn branch to cater to the sig-

To Smile or Not to Smile?

The employee procedures manual at many fast-food restaurants such as McDonald's, Burger King, or Wendy's demands that employees "look the customer in the eye, smile, and hand over cash into customers' hands." This procedure would not be natural in a store run by Korean Americans; in fact these actions would be considered disrespectful. But not adopting this procedure may have contributed to the looting of Korean stores by African American customers in the wake of the Los Angeles riots.

The riots were a reaction of the local black community to a white policeman's beating of an African-American man who was alleged to have resisted arrest. In the midst of the riot, many African Americans resorted to looting the Korean-owned stores in their neighborhood. During interviews, the African Americans who had shopped at the stores confided that they used to resent the Koreans because they (the Koreans) were not friendly.

Proof? "Because they would never make eye contact with us, never smile at us, and will not place the change in our hands," replied these angry customers.

Ask any Korean to explain this behavior, and you will discover something amazing. In the Korean culture, it is rude to look someone in the eye, it is improper or "false" to smile at someone whom you do not know socially, and it is definitely unbecoming to touch a stranger's hand!

Now a community volunteer group is trying to bridge the gap in cultural awareness—teaching Koreans what the American mainstream norms on interacting with customers are and getting the local customers to appreciate the cultural explanation to what otherwise appears as unfriendly Korean behavior.

nificant Russian immigrants there. The New York Downtown Hospital, near Manhattan's Chinatown, serves Chinese food. And Dreyfus Corporation offers, at its San Francisco investment center, a money market prospectus in Chinese. But targeting ethnic groups goes beyond a simple language translation. Many ethnic minority customers can't identify with the American models most advertisers predominantly use. In a recent analysis, Cover Girl was found to have shown only one minority model out of 236 ads! Beyond the use of different models, the communications should reflect the particular minorities' cultural values and marketplace norms. Since Filipinos enjoy a good laugh, humor works very well for them. Also, because of their strong community orientation, sponsorship of community events is a very effective marketing tool. For example, the Moon Festival banquet is a very special festival in the Chinese culture. And Deepawali is the Christmas-like festival for Asian Indians of Hindu origin. Many local marketers take advantage of these ethnic events and sponsor contests, prizes, and so on.

Most Asian Indians can be reached via English-language media, and since most Japanese now living in the United States are third- or fourth-generation persons, mainstream media appeal to them. However, the communication appeals need to be adapted to specific cultures of specific minorities. To Japanese Americans, don't advertise "You will stand out with this car," because Japanese do not value standing out; they desire to blend in. Similarly, Chinese do not like technology much; therefore, advertising something as being "high tech" is not a good strategy for them. Asians value tradition, so the "new and improved" appeal is likely to be unattractive to them; instead, marketers should emphasize how long the company has been in business or how well established the brand is, and how long-standing its reputation is.

Gender

Gender is a group trait that divides customers into two groups—males and females. This group trait remains constant through a person's life, and it influences customer values and preferences. Concerning food, gender differences exist in health-oriented perceptions of foods and beverages. Women tend to buy fresh vegetables more because these are healthier than canned vegetables. Diet foods and diet drinks are also more popular among women than among men. In the 25–34 age group, single men spend more of their food budget (65 percent) away from home (i.e., in buying food at restaurants) compared with women, who spend 55 percent.

In clothing, men-women differences exist in respect to color, fabric, and style. Certain fabrics are exclusively (e.g., chiffon) or predominantly (e.g., silk) employed in women's clothing. Bright, full-spectrum colors are usually used for women, whereas men are mostly clothed in white, blue, black, brown, and grey. In terms of cut and style, while both men and women have a variety of clothing to choose from to suit their own personality, women's clothing entails a wider range. Men tend to use women's clothing styles as indications of the wearers' motivations and moods. Even though unjustified, this use of women's clothing as "signaling" is widespread in U.S. culture. Therefore, in office settings, there are some unwritten rules about what is correct office wear. The marketers of clothing understand these differences. Manufacturers like Anne Klein have gone to the extent of setting up hot lines for women who may need advice about their choice in clothing for the office.

Men-women differences in shelter preferences are also well known. In the purchase of a house, for example, men and women look for different features. Women are generally much more concerned with such functional features as the amount of closet space in bedrooms, the size and shape of the kitchen, and the proximity of the house to a playground. Men, on the other hand, have historically been more concerned with such functional aspects as the construction of the house; the heating, cooling, and electrical systems; and the kind of building materials utilized. Likewise, home decorating or redecorating choices are influenced by gender. According to a survey done by Home Furnishings Council, in redecorating their home, husbands focus mainly on dens (where men generally gather during parties or where men retire to relax or watch sports), whereas wives focus on the living room and kitchen, where they spend a lot of time daily. Marketers should, however, be watchful for changes in gender-based preferences since many of the traditional gender roles in the United States are changing. (For some examples of gender differences in transition, see the Customer Insight box.)

Men-women differences permeate many other consumption situations. For example, one study of U.S. brides and grooms found that brides considered the wedding ceremony itself as the most important event, whereas grooms considered the reception as the key event. Thus, brides considered the wedding dress immensely significant and even sacred, requiring great planning and extensive deliberation. Also greatly significant to the bride were the choice of the church and the minister, the flowers, decorations, and the music. In contrast, grooms saw the success of the wedding more closely associated with a judicious selection of the reception hall, hearty food, and good socialization during the reception.[10]

Successful marketers use their knowledge about male-female preferences to meet the needs of both groups of customers. Today, a large number of men are buying groceries, and women are buying cars. By the early 1990s, women had become 49 percent of all new-car buyers! And they exercise an influence on some 80 percent of all new-car sales. So carmakers are paying attention to women's needs. Chrysler Corporation has an Advisory

CUSTOMER INSIGHT

Full-time Dads, Homemakers, Shoppers: The Changing Role of Men

In April 1991, a new magazine for men appeared on the newsstand. *Full-time Dads* contains stories about the joys and frustrations of childrearing. Utterly familiar to women, these topics were largely new to men.

At least until the 1970s, a man in much of the Western world didn't spend much time at the supermarket, in the kitchen, or changing the baby's diapers. But in the 1980s, and much more so in the 1990s, men started sharing more and more in the homemaking chores, partly because women were increasingly in the labor force, and partly because of a movement toward equality of sexes. The old adage "Real men don't . . ." changed into "Enlightened men do . . ."

According to a recent survey by Maritz Marketing Research, a U.S. marketing research company, only 45 percent of men buy all of their personal items, compared to 82 percent of women who buy or control all of their personal purchases. Retailers generally believe that while women shop, men buy—meaning that men don't enjoy shopping and that they don't do comparison shopping. Moreover, the objective men and women expect their purchased product to satisfy differ: As one clothing retailer has put it, "Women shop to look beautiful; men shop not to look stupid."

Men are also less likely to be buyers of household products—cleaning supplies, for example. Only 28 percent of men buy these products, but 77 percent of women do.

Men have a greater motivation for knowing how things they buy work. Dubbed the "must-know" segment of men (some 25 percent of those with annual income $20,000), these are good at "do-it-yourself" jobs and influence others about products.

In media, men read more newspapers compared to women, who read more magazines and books. Men also read more nonfiction, whereas women read more fiction. On TV, men watch more sports, action, or scientific programs, whereas women watch more daytime dramas, feature films, game shows, and sitcoms.

Men are becoming more savvy about household products. And women are learning to buy cars, electronics, and power tools. Still, some activities remain mostly the "men thing" like watching sports or drinking beer. 85 percent of the beer drinkers are men.

Sources: Quoted in Bill Saporito, "Unsuit Yourself," *Fortune,* September 20, 1993, pp. 118–120; Diane Crispell, "The Brave New World of Men," *American Demographics,* 14, no. 1 (January 1992), pp. 38–43.

Committee on the Women's Auto Market. Cars for women are designed differently. For example, doors and other parts are made to open easily, and the rear deck in minivans is supposed to lift easier. Also, many minivans now have integrated child seats and a purse carrier. Some car dealers have built play areas for children and diaper-changing stations in restrooms. Finally, many dealers have women salespersons, and male salespersons are learning not to treat lightly women who accompany their husbands car shopping. Sales-pitches about cars' technical performance are no longer directed only to male customers.[11]

Men-Women Differences for Business-to-Business Products and Services

As in the consumer market, there are men-women differences in business products and services. The choice of decor to go into a home office or an executive corporate office, for example, will be highly influenced by nonfunctional values, which will be different for men and women. Women may prefer very different designs, colors, and types of furnishings than do men. The choice of a telephone design, cabinet, desk, bookcase, and other

Chronological Age-based Grouping of Customers in the United States

Marketers most often use chronological age, counted from the year of birth, to identify different market segments. The book *Generations* identifies four age groups in the U.S. population.[15] These are: (1) The **GI Generation**—born from 1901 to 1924; (2) **Silent Generation**—born between 1925 and 1945; (3) **baby boomers**—born between 1946 to 1964; and (4) **Generation X**—Post–1964. In addition, teenagers and children are important age segments for many marketers.

THE GI GENERATION: OVER 70 AND STILL STRONG

The G.I. generation accounted for some 29 million persons in the United States in 1991 (of the total 63 million ever born), of whom 9 percent are immigrants. Among the icons of this generation are such people as Ronald Reagan, Walt Disney, Joe DiMaggio, Ann Landers, Katharine Hepburn, John F. Kennedy, Walter Cronkite, John Wayne, and Lee Iacocca. The GI generation was raised by parents determined to have "good kids," protected from urban danger and adult vices. They became America's first Boy Scouts and Girl Scouts, thus channeling their gang instinct to useful purposes. School was important for this generation, with emphasis on vocational education. Staying in school and being a "regular guy" and a team player (rather than be individualistic and stand out) were the virtues instilled in the youth.

In the late 1920s, the Great Depression tested the fervent optimism of this generation; somehow, the youth spirit stayed high. Two decades later, World War II came, and the GI generation emerged triumphant, feeling heroic and ever more optimistic. The GI Bill aided a financially secure life that the war heroes thought they deserved. A suburban house with a friendly neighborhood and comforts of new technology defined the adult GI Sameness rather than being different was celebrated.

Vietnam triggered an angry generation gap between the GI parents and their children, who brought crime waves, urban riots, substance abuse, eroticism—contrary to the GI generation's life mission. In politics, at work, and at home, the GI men faced opposition and rebellion from their youngsters. "Something has gone sour, in teaching and in learning," lamented a GI author George Wald.

When these GI's entered their senior years, they vowed not to grow old, tired, and defeatist, as their predecessors had; accordingly, they fought the myth of "a lonely, unhappy old person." They have worked hard to be active, energetic, happy, and hopeful senior citizens. Most live today in retirement, heavily subsidized by public funds, which they believe they have richly earned, something with which lawmakers in their children's generation don't quite agree. In any case, their rising affluence enables them to live in "seniors only" retirement communities, in a lifestyle filled with cheer and vigor. A record number participate in travel, leisure, investing, and loans or gifts to youngsters in their extended families—in 1988, a record high of 25 percent of all gifts to children were bought by grandparents! To the dismay of these aging GI's, however, their adult children look to them for material help, but not for advice and wisdom. Indeed, what aging GI's resent is a lack of deference and appreciation.

According to a recent survey done by the Georgia State University's Center for Mature Consumer Studies, 32 million Americans aged 65 or over have discretionary incomes of roughly $7,000 per year, roughly twice that of debt-immersed baby boomers. Seniors are not as attracted by fantasies about a leisurely life or escapist appeals; rather, products must be shown to help them attain their values. With aging, consumers process informa-

How Mature Adults Differ from Young Adults

According to David B. Wolfe, the author of *Serving the Ageless Market,* as a person matures, his or her modes of thinking change. In early childhood, his or her cues to thinking come from within. During adulthood, the person is more oriented to cues from the external world. During mature years, the person tends to turn again toward internal cues, assimilating the external information within the internal cues from experience and values one holds.

Based on his research, David Wolfe believes that mature persons hold five key values:

- Autonomy and self-sufficiency
- Social and spiritual connectedness
- Altruism
- Personal growth
- Revitalization

Thus, to mature adults, direct benefits of products (e.g., clean hair) are less appealing than a product's role in fulfilling these values. Some examples illustrate this distinction:

1. Kimberly-Clark's promotion of Depends undergarments was hugely successful by showing an actress playing golf and going about her active life; in contrast, competitors promoted the functional features such as absorbency and were not as successful.

2. Freedom Group of Florida developed a senior housing community and recruited residents by having a mortgage-burning party signifying self-sufficiency and autonomy.

3. Mature adults tend to patronize mom-and-pop stores to a greater degree because their owners are able to offer them personalization and social connectedness.

4. Thrifty Car Rental Co. found that a donation to a social project was more appealing to seniors than a direct discount.

5. Elderhostel offers mature adults travel programs in conjunction with educational programs at universities worldwide; close to 300,000 adults participate annually in this personal growth and revitalization opportunity.

These examples show that marketers can benefit greatly by being aware of these values. Each communication and advertising campaign and each product offering should be preassessed on how well it reflects the values mature adults hold.

Sources: David B. Wolfe, *Serving the Ageless Market* (McGraw Hill, 1990); David B. Wolfe, "Targeting the Mature Adults," *American Demographics,* March 1994, pp. 32–36.

tion more slowly, but they have a richer store of information to supplement the slowly acquired new information. Therefore, older consumers don't fall for advertising hyperbole. Also they have more time to do comparison shopping and product research.[16] (For more details about the values of this age group, see the Customer Insight box.)

THE SILENT GENERATION: THE GOLDEN YEARS

Among the first wave of the silent generation are such people as Marilyn Monroe, Clint Eastwood, Neil Armstrong, and Martin Luther King, Jr., and among the last wave, such names as Barbra Streisand, Elvis Presley, Woody Allen, John F. Kennedy, and Jesse Jackson.

While the GI generation faced the Great Depression and World War II in their adulthood, the Silent Generation (some 40 million in 1991) faced these crises during its youth. They believed in the success of the system rather than in individual enterprise, seeking secure careers in big corporations. One GI historian described them as "withdrawn,

spend it all, since saving for the future is not their goal. They buy clothes (e.g., T-shirts, baseball caps to wear backwards), sneakers, athletic wear, team sport memorabilia, fast food, books, movies, long-distance phone services, and personal items, and patronize restaurants and bars.

In military base towns, you can find about 1.6 million military troops, about 40 percent of them aged 18 to 24. Although far fewer than college campus youth, their access to income and money is markedly more substantial. Each new military recruit gets about $700 a month. Businesses that thrive near the military bases are, according to one report, insurance agencies, car rental companies, domestic car dealerships, long-term storage facilities, bars, and tattoo parlors. Many Xer service members live with their families in nearby offbase sites. They are a source of business to gas stations, McDonald's, toy stores, garden suppliers, bowling alleys, and supermarkets.

Other youth, as well, live with their parents (as do, of course, most teens). According to a recent report, nearly half of the never married adults aged 18 to 24 live with their parents. Many return after a brief sojourn living out of the home. They find living at home attractive because food is generally free, and the rent is either waived or subsidized, and chores are also shared. Many who live at home are motivated to save and build their bank accounts so that they can buy a car, or when they get a job, they can afford the down payment on a house.

Youth living at home participate increasingly in household purchase decisions. Their advice is generally sought for technology products, and many times they are the sole decision makers on their parents' behalf.

All youth, whether they live at home, on college campuses, or at military bases, differ from the previous boomer generations. Their music is not rock 'n' roll or classic rock or retro. It is rap, urban rhythm and blues, and industrial dance music. They wear clothing that ranges from punk to preppie, from sloppy grunge look to environment-friendly eco shirts. They are dead serious about getting a job and about getting an education so they may get a job—unlike their parents who were sometimes in college just for the experience, or to engage in political protest and reform. Of course, youth is different from their preceding cohorts everywhere. This is even more the case with American youth. Their image of the boomers is that of Woodstock—that they, the boomers, had a big party and didn't clean up.

The baby busters are more accepting of diversity in race, ethnicity, religion, language, and lifestyles. Social issues have a big appeal for today's youth. Issues like the environment, drug abuse, AIDS, and discrimination arouse young people, and young adults reward those businesses that support such social causes. Another important characteristic of this group is its dislike of hype in advertising. They dislike overstatement, hypocrisy, and false pretense of status image for the advertised products. To them, a product must be advertised and sold on its utility, rather than hype. This is not to imply that Xers don't buy for image, but the image is the one they give a product, and the one they perceive from their social observations and from peer group, not the one the advertising hypes. And they are appalled at telemarketers—that anyone would make the assumption that it is allright to disturb people at home. They reject conspicuous consumption.

Despite their hip-hop culture and counter-fashion grunge look, American youth are a serious set of customers. The U.S. 1992 and 1996 elections are proof. In the 1992 elections, the incumbent President George Bush refused an invitation to appear on MTV (the most popular TV station for American youth), dismissing it as a "teeny-bopper network." In contrast, then-candidate Bill Clinton appeared on the network extensively, holding townhall-like question and answer sessions. He won the American youths' hearts. And votes.[21]

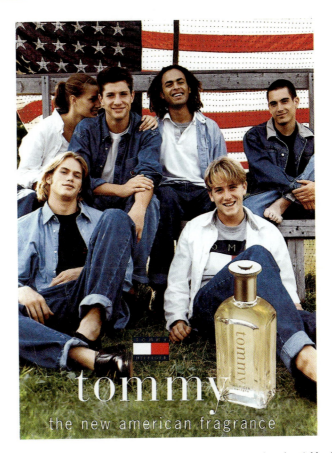

Neither race nor gender is shared here. The common tie is age. Young, casual, and sociable. And their Tommy fragrance.

TEENAGERS AND CHILDREN: MOVE OVER XERS

Beyond the four age groups described in the book *Generations,* two more age groups deserve attention: teenagers and children.

TEENAGERS Today's teenagers are the children of baby boomers, born after 1975, or more specifically during the late 1970s and early to middle 1980s. About 30 million in number, U.S. teenagers spent an estimated $103 billion of their own money in 1996. In addition, they spend about $33 billion of their parents' money.[22] Of all the people, teenagers have the most time available to spend in the checkout lines. Not surprisingly, a large number of them do family shopping. One of the important teen traits is that they like to look a couple of years older than they are (i.e., a 14-year-old likes to look 16). An older teen will never seek advice from, or be influenced by younger teens. Savvy marketers recognize the potential teens represent and have made special efforts to respond to their needs and offer them the market values they seek. (For an example, see the Window on Practice box on page 232.)

CHILDREN In the United States, children 4 to 12 years old now number 33 million. According to a national survey of this group, children spend about $9 billion annually, with an average income (including allowances, gifts, and household or outside work) of

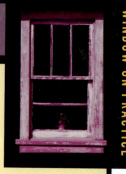

Teen Shoppers: Dressing Up Is in Fashion Again

The store is Ulta[3] Inc. in Las Vegas, and it is opening day. MTV personality Daisy Fuentes is making an appearance. Also on display is a male M Professional representative, smeared with lipstick—the M Professional brand—designed to remind us of the cosmetic company's motto: "not tested on animals . . . unless you count men." Just the kind of thing teenagers would find appealing.

Ulta[3] carries a vast array of product lines: Ultima II, Studio Gear, and Trucco at the upper end of the price spectrum, and Bonne Bell, Prestige, and M Professional at the lower end.

Many mass market retailers looked at teenagers as trouble rather than opportunity. They thought teens were in the store to pilfer and loiter. Now the likes of Wal-Mart is waking up to the market potential teens represent. For example, while only 60 percent of women over 24 wear eyeliner and shadow, 75 percent of teens wear eyeliner, shadow, or mascara, both during the day and the night. And 90 percent of them wear lipstick. As shoppers, when they visit a store, they buy more things—everything from blush to eye shadow. Adult women, in contrast, tend to pick just one or two items that they came to the store for. Of course, teens buy more than makeup. One company to capitalize on their buying potential is Delia's Inc., a start-up catalog company. The conventional wisdom about teen shopping was that teens go to the mall, buy a CD or two, hit the food court, and maybe buy a pair of platform slides and blue nail polish on their way out. The company saw it otherwise and started a now successful catalog with teen clothing. Just a few years ago, the teen stores like Merry-Go-Round and Jean-Nicole were closing in mall after mall—a direct fall-out of Generation Xs abandoning of fashion in favor of the grunge look. Now, the next generation, the children of baby boomers, are embracing fashion again. New teen fashion clothing companies like Quick Silver and Gadzook are rolling out new stores every day. Spurred by this trend, the catalog features hip fashion on fresh-faced models. And the catalog has become a favorite pass-along magazine among many high school girls. The company's catalog sales soared to $30 million in 1996.

Source: Jennifer Steinhauer, "Mail Order: Like Mother Like Daughter," *The New York Times*, July 6, 1997, Section 1, page 21; Faye Brookman, "Stores Open to Teen Scene; Ulta[3] Inc; Beauty Report 2," *WWD*, February 28, 1997, vol. 173, section 40, page 10.

$4.42 a week, or $229.84 a year. Children spent about $1 billion during a recent Christmas selling season, and about half of this came from their piggy bank savings. Annually, this group spends about $2 billion on toys, and an equal amount on candy, soft drinks, desserts, and snacks. They spend about $1.1 billion on entertainment, about $700 million on clothes (the rest of their clothing expenditures are paid for by adults), and $265 million for other items such as cosmetics, electronic equipment, or stamp/coin/card collections. By age eight, all children make some independent purchases while shopping with their parents. A 10-year-old averages about five visits a week to five different stores![23]

Even more significant than their own purchases is the amount of influence they exercise on their parents' purchase decisions. Children influence such adult decisions as where to dine out, where to vacation, which entertainment and electronic gadgets to consider, and which brands of household groceries to purchase. This influence is estimated at upward of $150 billion a year.[24]

Growing up in the age of the information superhighway and multimedia entertainment, kids of the 1990s are much more sophisticated than their predecessors, and in many aspects of life, more knowledgeable than their parents. Their influence stems both from personal preference (e.g., which brands of cereals they like and insist their parents buy) and from product expertise. Older kids can offer expert advice on such high-tech products as athletic shoes, video equipment, and even automobiles! One 10-year-old told in a Simmons Kids Study, "My little brother begged my dad to get a sports car. He got it."[25]

Intergenerational Differences in Household Markets

The intergenerational differences among the age groups affect their customer behavior with regard to basic consumer goods—food, clothing, and shelter. The market values sought by customers with respect to these three basic goods have been transformed across the four generations.

There has been a significant change over the last 80 years with respect to what customers value. In regard to the universal values customers seek, there has been a general shift from a functional and economic orientation for the prewar (GI) segment to a preoccupation with personal values by successive generations. The prewar segment went through the Great Depression as young adults, and it never forgot what it meant to have a sense of financial security. Hence, there is still a preoccupation with the price value on virtually any product this age group buys. Furthermore, the prewar segment and Silent Generation grew up in the United States at a time when manufacturing was the engine that drove the economy. Hence, there was always an appreciation among these segments for performance/functional value and good quality in any product they bought. The prewar generation was not as concerned with the nonfunctional values (i.e., the personal values of social and emotional satisfaction) as are the baby boomers and Generation X. Conspicuous consumption became a driving force in the American marketplace only after television became popular in the 1950s, and this new technology showed customers how people in different walks of life were living relative to them.

Similar intergenerational differences occur in respect to the relative importance of user versus payer and buyer values. Baby boomers and Generation X grew up in a service-oriented society, where service and convenience were valued over product quality and even price in some cases. The pervasive influence of "convenience" in life has impacted the prewar generation and Silent Generation as well as the other two segments. However, in respect to financing value, baby boomers and Generation X are more concerned with it than the other two older groups. The reason is the relative affluence of the older consumers.

How do the values of different age groups differ across food, clothing, and shelter? With respect to food, the universal value of product quality itself is the driving force for all of the segments, except that for baby boomers and Generation X, the value of convenience-in-use (time taken to prepare the food) is also very important. Baby boomer parents are usually both working, and as a result, buy foods with time-saving convenience value. The ability to use a credit card at the supermarket is a credit value sought and used by the baby-boomer and Generation X segments, in contrast to the two older segments who are just not used to paying for food with a credit card. Also, the performance value is different across age groups, as preferences for specific food types are affected by aging. Concern about nutrition grows, and some medical conditions such as diabetes introduce dietary restrictions. Foods need to be less spicy due to less tolerant gastrointestinal systems.

The intergenerational differences are even more acute for clothing. Clearly, there will be a difference between the importance placed on the universal and personal values by the four segments. The prewar segment is much more concerned with performance values like durability, quality, and the universal price/economic value, whereas the younger segments, while not ignoring universal values, tend to place greater importance on the nonfunctional, personal value of social image associated with various items and styles of clothing. Popular brands of clothing like Guess Jeans and Levi's Dockers certainly appeal to the nonfunctional or personal value that younger customers place on brand recognition in the marketplace.

The market values from shelter are similar across age segments, especially with respect to the importance customers place on the economic and financing values they must carefully consider before they buy a home. However, people typically buy a home only when they are at least 30 years old, and rarely after they reach the age of 70. That leaves two segments, the Silent Generation and the baby boomers, to buy most goods and services related to the home industry (such as major appliance dealers, mortgage companies, carpet stores, and so on).

Among services, insurance is a good example of an industry where age plays a significant role in the shaping of customer desire for diverse market values. Customers in the prewar segment have much less of a need for life insurance, as their dependents have already grown up. However, among the Silent Generation and baby-boomer segments, there is a much greater emphasis on the universal value for financial coverage as well as the personal value of the security of knowing that their loved ones will be provided for should something happen to themselves. In regard to automobile insurance, the universal value of reliability and prompt claim settlement would be equally important to all age segments. Also constant across the four segments is the personal value of security. However, customers in Generation X, and especially teenagers, will be much more sensitive to the universal economic/price value of the cost of coverage, as their premiums are much higher and their own incomes (or allowances) rather limited.

Intergenerational Differences in Business Markets

In business markets, we consider generational differences in three business services: payroll benefits, support services, and employee career path. The influence of age on payroll benefits is significant, since employees look for different benefits from a company as they grow older. For example, a Generation X customer will want to start to build a pension, and therefore seek out a company that affords him that opportunity. In contrast, a younger employee would be more concerned with life insurance and disability insurance than a person in the prewar segment. Health-care benefits would be of concern to all age segments, but more critical to an older worker. Baby boomers building a family will be more concerned with health-care coverage for pregnancy and maternity leave (for women).

Even though the needs of each of the segments may vary, the specific universal and personal values they seek out will be similar. In employment benefits, everyone is concerned with the universal values of service and reliability, and the personal values of security, convenience, and financing.

Support services vary to a certain degree, especially for workers who have special needs. For example, office employees today must be computer literate. For younger workers who grew up with the computer, the functional universal value that comes with having an in-house computer expert is not that vital, so computer-related technical assistance can be outsourced. However, to an older worker from the prewar generation, these same services would be more crucial to their success in a company, especially if they were not computer literate. Other support services such as travel, employee cafeterias, and parking would all have both universal and personal value to workers, but would not vary as significantly as computer services.

Customer Personality

An individual's **personality** refers to a person's consistent ways of responding to the environment in which he or she lives. Everyday descriptions of people as innovative or tradition-bound, dogmatic or open-minded, sociable or aloof, aggressive or meek, penny-pinchers or splurgers are all references to these persons' personalities. Note that if we observe a customer adopting a new idea or product or service on a single occasion, we still do not know whether or not he or she is an innovator; only if we find the person to be one of the first to buy new products repeatedly can we say that the person has the personality characteristic of being innovative. Thus, a *consistent* repeated pattern of behavior is what constitutes personality.

Humans develop personality because it is efficient to build a standard repertoire of responses to one's environment, as opposed to thinking up a new response every time a situation arises. Some of these standard responses will apply to a person's behavior as a customer.

How Is Personality Developed?

Customer personality is a function of two factors: genetic makeup and environmental conditioning.

Personality = Genetics $\times$ Environment

In everyday language, you can bear references to both these themes. When someone says, "He's got his father's temper," he or she alludes to the genetic determination of personality. On the other hand, when someone says, "He was born with a silver spoon in his mouth" or "She has expensive tastes," that person is alluding to the environmental determination of personality. (For an example of the research behind these views, see the Window on Research box on page 236.)

These two factors have emerged from separate streams of research: The leading proponent of environmental determination was American psychologist B.F. Skinner, and that of genetic determination, the British psychologist Hans Eysenck. Skinner's theory, known as **behaviorism theory,** is that a person develops a pattern of behavioral responses because of the rewards and punishments offered by his or her environment. Therefore, personality (a consistent pattern of behavioral responses) is formed and can be molded by a society by means of environmental shaping.

Eysenck, on the other hand, considered biogenetic factors as important causes of individual differences. Eysenck has been a pioneer in studies of the relationship between genetically produced biological variations and personality. In studies of twins, for example, Eysenck and those who followed his work found that the personality trait of sociability was markedly determined by genetic effects. Such physiological measures as electroencephalographic (EEG) recording of the brain's alpha wave activity and the subject's heart rate differed between twins from two separate eggs (as opposed to twins from the same egg) and thus are genetically produced; since nervous arousal (which is measured by EEG and heart rate) is in turn related to personality differences, both physiological and psychological differences are shown to be genetically produced.

As an illustration of the genetic origins of personality, consider the trait of introversion/extraversion. Eysenck demonstrated that a person's relative extraversion/introversion

Genetics and Personality Traits

Why are some people thrill seekers, while others lead a more subdued life? The answer lies in chromosome 11. Thrill-seeking behavior is affected, according to a recent discovery, by how brain cells process a neural messenger chemical called dopamine. The transmission of that chemical message is determined by a gene called D4DR. Individuals who have a certain kind of extra-long DNA sequence on part of chromosome 11 also score much higher on psychological tests measuring a personality trait called "novelty seeking."

This is the finding of two independent researchers. The one is by Richard P. Ebstein and colleagues, at Herzog Memorial Hospital in Jerusalem, who examined 124 unrelated Israeli subjects, giving them a test that measures four personality dimensions: novelty seeking, harm avoidance, reward dependence, and persistence. The researchers took blood samples from each subject for genetic analysis. They found that subjects who scored highest on novelty seeking—characterized as impulsive, exploratory, fickle, excitable, quick-tempered, and extravagant—were much more likely to have the long seven-segment component of D4DR. In contrast, subjects with the shorter version scored significantly lower, and tended to be reflective, rigid, loyal, stoic, slow-tempered, and frugal. The same findings were obtained in another study, conducted by Jonathan Benjamin of the Laboratory of Clinical Science

at the National Institute of Mental Health and colleagues, who tested 315 American subjects.

The studies do not indicate that novelty seeking is controlled by a single gene or a number of genes. Upbringing, life experience, and numerous environmental factors clearly play a major role in complex human behaviors. Indeed, the researchers note that the genetic factor had a relatively minor impact, accounting for some 10 percent of the variance in the novelty-seeking behavior.

In another study of nearly 2,300 twins, psychologists at the University of Minnesota found that on a rating scale for happiness, genetically identical twins scored more similar than even fraternal twins. A person's proclivity for being happy is explained, according to psychologists, only 3 percent by such factors as level of education, family income, marital status, and religious belief; in comparison, it is explained as much as 50 percent by our genetics.

Sources: "Genetic Studies Suggest Connection between Heredity and Behavior," *The Buffalo News,* January 2, 1996, Tuesday, City Edition, p. 3A; Curt Suplee, "Researchers Find Personality Gene: Chromosome Pattern Markes People Seek Thrills," *International Herald Tribune,* January 3, 1996; Kathleen McAuliffe, "Born to Be Happy," *Self,* December 1996, p. 33.

is greatly dependent upon arousal of the brain, as mediated by their body systems. Introverts exhibit a more intense state of arousal than extraverts. With intrinsically lower levels of stimulation, extraverts tend to seek it in their external environment, "whereas introverts tend to avoid additional stimulation because their internal mechanisms are chronically switched to a 'high-gain' position."[26]

In a stirring book published in 1975, *Sociobiology: The New Synthesis,* psychologist Edward Wilson argued that much of human personality, society, and culture are the outcome of evolutionary and genetic processes. Even altruistic acts such as self-sacrifice could be caused by unconscious biogenetic processes aimed at ensuring the survival of a large number of related individuals. In *Imperial Animal,* anthropologists Robin Fox and Lionel Toger argue that every species has its own *biogrammer*—a behavioral language and a repertoire of actions. They argue that "agricultural and industrial civilizations have put nothing into the basic wiring of the human animal. We are wired for hunting" (p. 39).[27]

In the psychology literature, two of the dominant theories for explaining the concept of personality are the Freudian theory of personality and personality trait theory.

FREUDIAN THEORY

Sigmund Freud, the founder of psychoanalysis, was the first to suggest the concept of the unconscious. He argued that human personality is driven by both conscious and unconscious motives (i.e., desires). He proposed three divisions of the human psyche: **id, ego, and superego.** The *id* is the basic source of inner energy directed at avoiding pain and obtaining pleasure and represents the unconscious drives and urges. The *superego* is the moral side of the psyche, and it reflects societal ideals. The *ego* is the conscious mediator between the id and the superego: that is, between the unconscious and impulsive desires of the id and the societal ideals internalized by the superego. The ego helps the person respond to the world in societally acceptable ways.

Because many of the id's urges are societally unacceptable, they are suppressed and find their expression in alternative ways that are more acceptable. Behaviors that express themselves in this manner are called "defense mechanisms."

Defense mechanisms are psychological processes that stem from a person's need to protect his or her ego. Since the ego mediates between the urges of the id and the moral imperatives of the superego, it is often involved in conflicts and anxiety. For example, the id may want to own an expensive car, but the superego would remind the ego that, given the person's financial means, it would be unwise to buy an expensive car. The ego has to resolve this anxiety—caused by the person wanting to really buy the expensive car, but being frustrated in this desire by limited financial means. The person saves his or her ego (sense of self) by arguing, for example, that an expensive car is a show off, used by people with not enough confidence in their inherent ability or talent. This argument, made to others or to oneself, is an example of a defense mechanism.

These defense mechanisms make a behavior acceptable to a person's own sense of right or overcome guilt and frustration. They entail mentally redefining the stimulus or redefining the motive for that response (i.e., by explaining it away). Thus, to prevent anxiety, by keeping the unacceptable id impulses or other threatening material from reaching consciousness, the ego employs a variety of unconscious tactics:

■ *Aggression*—To become aggressive is to display or inflict pain on someone out of frustration and without justification. Examples: A customer who suspects the retailer of taking advantage of a market shortage spoils merchandise in the store. A poor person deprived of basic transport smashes a luxury car.

■ *Rationalization*—To explain some action by a motive that is more acceptable than the actual motive, which is suppressed from consciousness. If you bought a model of a car to impress others, but do not want to admit this motive, you might rationalize the decision by citing a superior performance feature even though that feature played no role in the decision. Corporate jets and country club memberships are rationalized as needed for business efficacy, although the real motive and reason in many cases is prestige and personal sense of vanity.

■ *Projection*—To blame others for a person's own shortcomings or to attribute personal feelings to others. For example, a customer breaks an appliance by wrongful use, then blames the manufacturer or the workmanship. A person who enjoys buying name brand clothes from off-price stores assumes that others are there for the joy of unearthing bargains.

■ *Repression*—To devote a great deal of energy to keeping a particular thought or feeling at the unconscious level. Repression is one of the most primitive mechanisms. Examples of repression include situations in which consumers avoid products that are associated with unattractive situations and at the same time deny that association to be the reason for their choice. For example, products associated with a person's ex-spouse (or consumed by the consumer in previous marriage) may be avoided. Children of immigrants, eager to fit in with the new environment, may avoid their own parental preferences, but may deny a conscious motive to distance themselves from their ethnic origins. In business-buying situations, many subordinates repress their inner conflicts stemming from cultural differences across departments or functions. Likewise, participants in business-buying situations may repress their desires to choose or avoid particular supplies due to personal prejudices.

- *Withdrawal*—When not successful in a situation, to simply withdraw from the situation. Thus, both household and business customers literally withdraw from associations, conferences, PTA meetings, book clubs, and so on, if they believe they are not respected in those gatherings.

- *Regression*—To "revert" to childhood behaviors. At special sale events in stores where item supply is limited, many adults resort to fighting like children to get to the merchandise.

TRAIT THEORY

In the **trait theory of personality,** a person is viewed as a composite of several personality traits. *A personality trait is a consistent, characteristic way of behaving.*[28] Thus, compulsive people consistently and characteristically act compulsively; persons with the personality trait of dogmatism consistently hold on to their beliefs; and variety-seeking persons are constantly changing their preferences. Although it is possible to build a list of a large number of personality traits (e.g., compulsiveness, innovativeness), Cattell, a leading trait theorist, identified 16 fundamental traits that account for a person's behavior (see Table 7.1).[29]

Table 7.1

SIXTEEN FACTORS OR PERSONALITY SOURCE TRAITS
IDENTIFIED BY CATTELL

Reserved, detached, critical, aloof, stiff	vs.	*Outgoing,* warmhearted, easy-going, participating
Dull, low intelligence	vs.	*Bright,* high intelligence
Affected by feeling, emotionally less stable, easily upset, changeable	vs.	*Emotionally stable,* mature, faces reality, calm
Humble, mild, easily led, docile, accommodating	vs.	*Assertive,* aggressive, competitive, stubborn
Sober, taciturn, serious	vs.	*Happy-go-lucky,* gay, enthusiastic
Expedient, disregards rules	vs.	*Conscientious,* persistent, moralistic, staid
Shy, timid, threat-sensitive	vs.	*Venturesome,* uninhibited, socially bold
Tough-minded, self-reliant, realistic	vs.	*Tender-minded,* sensitive, clinging, over-protected
Trusting, accepting conditions	vs.	*Suspicious,* hard to fool
Practical, "down-to-earth" concerns	vs.	*Imaginative,* bohemian, absentminded
Forthright, unpretentious, genuine, but socially clumsy	vs.	*Astute,* polished, socially aware
Self-assured, placid, secure, complacent, serene	vs.	*Apprehensive,* self-reproaching, insecure, worrying, troubled
Conservative, respecting traditional ideas, conservatism of temperament	vs.	*Experimenting,* liberal, free-thinking, radicalism
Group dependent, a "joiner" and sound follower	vs.	*Self-sufficient,* resourceful, prefers own decisions
Undisciplined self-conflict, lax, follows own urges, careless of social rules	vs.	*Controlled,* exacting will-power, socially precise, compulsive, following self-image
Relaxed, tranquil, torpid, unfrustrated, composed	vs.	*Tense,* frustrated, driven, overwrought

Source: Adapted from R.B. Cattell, H.W. Eber, and M.M. Tatsuoka, *Handbook for the Sixteen Personality Factor Questionnaire* (Champaign, Ill.: Institute for Personality and Ability Testing, 1970), pp. 16–17. Reprinted by permission of the copyright owner.

He termed these "source traits," since, in his view, these were the source of other "surface traits" or overt behavior.

Another set of personality traits is the Edwards Personality Preference Schedule (EPPS), which consists of the 15 traits also shown in Table 7.2. In fact, early personality research in consumer behavior used the EPPS to identify brand preferences of different consumer segments. Yet another classification is by psychologist Karen Horney. Horney grouped people into three categories: compliant, aggressive, and detached. The **compliant** type seeks others' friendship, acceptance, appreciation, and/or love, and tries to be likable and agreeable. The **aggressive,** on the other hand, values personal accomplishment over friendship and seeks power and admiration from others. Finally, the **detached** person is independent minded, entertains no obligations, and admits little social influence on personal choices.

The first reported studies of personality traits in marketing is by Franklin B. Evans, who, in a survey in 1959, examined whether Ford owners and Chevy owners differed in their personality traits. He used the EPPS measures of personality; however, he failed to

Table 7.2

A SUMMARY OF PERSONALITY TRAITS MEASURED BY THE EDWARDS PERSONAL PREFERENCE SCHEDULE

1. *Achievement:* To do one's best, accomplish tasks of great significance, do things better than others, be successful, be a recognized authority.
2. *Deference:* To get suggestions, follow instructions, do what is expected, accept leadership of others, conform to custom, let others make decisions.
3. *Order:* To have work neat and organized, make plans before starting, keep files, have things arranged to run smoothly, have things organized.
4. *Exhibition:* To say clever things, tell amusing jokes and stories, talk about personal achievements, have others notice and comment on one's appearance, be the center of attention.
5. *Autonomy:* To be able to come and go as one pleases, say what one thinks, be independent in making decisions, feel free to do what one wants, avoid conformity, avoid responsibilities and obligations.
6. *Affiliation:* To be loyal to friends, do things for friends, form new friendships, make many friends, form strong attachments, participate in friendly groups.
7. *Intraception:* To analyze one's motives and feelings, observe and understand others, analyze the motives of others, predict their acts, put one's self in another's place.
8. *Succorance:* To be helped by others, seek encouragement, have others feel sorry when sick, have others be sympathetic about personal problems.
9. *Dominance:* To be a leader, argue for one's point of view, make group decisions, settle arguments, persuade and influence others, supervise others.
10. *Abasement:* To feel guilty when wrong, accept blame, feel need for punishment, feel timid in presence of superiors, feel inferior, feel depressed about inability to handle situations.
11. *Nurturance:* To help friends in trouble, treat others with a kindness, forgive others, do small favors, be generous, show affection, receive confidence.
12. *Change:* To do new and different things, travel, meet new people, try new things, eat in new places, live in different places, try new fads and fashions.
13. *Endurance:* To keep at a job until finished, work hard at a task, keep at a problem until solved, finish one job before starting others, stay up late working to get a job done.
14. *Heterosexuality:* To go out with opposite sex, be in love, kiss, discuss sex, become sexually excited, read books about sex.
15. *Aggression:* To tell others what one thinks of them, criticize others publicly, make fun of others, tell others off, get revenge, blame others.

find any personality differences. Three years later, another researcher, Westfall, conducted a similar study (using a different personality measure) and found no difference between the owners of Ford and Chevrolet brands. However, he did find personality differences between the owners of convertible and standard/compact models: for example, owners of convertibles were more active, sociable, and impulsive, exactly as we would intuitively expect. Another noteworthy study of personality traits was by consumer researcher Joel B. Cohen. Cohen used Horney's compliant, aggressive, and detached (CAD) typology of personality. Cohen's study attempted to find product purchase and consumption differences across these three personality types. Although the differences were not found for 8 of the 15 product categories included in the study, some interesting findings were these: mouthwash and Dial soap were used substantially more by compliants than by the detached group; among deodorants, "Old Spice" was the favorite of the aggressive personality types, whereas the leading brand, Right Guard, was the choice of the other two types. Aggressives used colognes more and preferred Coors beer, whereas the detached types drank tea more than the other groups.

Other recent studies also support the role of personality in explaining selected consumer behaviors. In a study of cosmetics buyers, for example, marketing researcher Shirley Young identified a number of personality traits related to consumption of cosmetics. In another study, psychologist and consumer researcher Raymond L. Horton examined the effect of selected personality traits on the decision-making process of consumers and found that consumers with high levels of anxiety and low task orientations, as well as consumers of low intelligence showed a higher preference for well-known brands.

Some consumer researchers have studied the personality trait of **tolerance for ambiguity,** which, as the name implies, refers to how comfortable a person feels with uncertainty and lack of complete information. In a study on this trait, consumer researchers Michael B. Mazis and Timothy W. Sweeney found that consumers with low tolerance for ambiguity tended to delay trial of low-cost convenience goods. Similarly, consumer researchers Charles M. Schaninger and Donald Sciglimpaglia found that consumers with low tolerance for ambiguity and higher self-esteem tended to use more product information in their brand choice decision.[30]

There have been two problems with personality research in consumer behavior, especially in the early years. First, no personality scales have been developed especially for consumer behavior. Second, researchers have not considered which personality traits should matter for which consumer choices before conducting their studies.[31] For example, there is no reason to expect any personality differences between the owners of Fords and Chevrolets, but you would expect such difference between the owners of convertibles and compact cars. This explains why the Evans study was not successful, whereas Westfall's study was. Today, trait-oriented personality research has fallen out of favor with consumer researchers, who now increasingly use a lifestyles view of personality, discussed in Chapter 9.

Personality of the Business Customer

In business organizations, people are not simply employees, co-workers, managers, or subordinates. They are not simply engineers, accountants, financial controllers, or purchasing managers. Rather, in addition to being whatever their job title and job responsibility indicate, they are also people. That is, they have a personality that they bring to the work they do and, for our purposes, to how they play their customer role. They could be aggressive or subdued; fast or slow in their speech and movement; emotional or unemotional; demanding or easygoing; social or aloof; task oriented or relationship oriented. These personality differences have implications for you if you are trying to sell something to a business customer, or if you are negotiating a business deal with your business associate.

One apt personality typology for business customers is the "social styles" classification, proposed by Dr. David W. Merrill of the research group at Tracom Corporation, Denver, Colorado.[32] This classification uses two personality traits:

1. *Assertiveness*—the aspect of behavior that measures whether the person tends to tell or ask and the degree to which others see us as trying to influence their decisions. Assertive persons take a stand and make their position clear to others. They are demanding, aggressive, and forceful. In social situations, they are likely to initiate the conversation and display a take-charge attitude. In contrast, unassertive people are unassuming, contented, quiet, and easygoing. They tend not to express their ideas and beliefs, but instead tend to listen to others and be supportive of others' ideas. The "telling" kind of individuals, when placed in an uneasy social situation, tend to "fight" or confront the situation. The "asking" kind prefer "flight" or to avoid the situation.

2. *Responsiveness*—a person's tendency to emote rather than control feelings, and the extent to which others see that person as an individual who displays feelings or emotions openly in social situations. A more responsive individual readily expresses anger, joy, or hurt feelings and tends to be warm, emotional, or lighthearted. The unresponsive, or the controlling types tend to be reserved, cautious, and serious; to be independent of or indifferent to others' feelings; and to use reason or logic more in making decisions. Such people tend to avoid personal involvement with others and be more formal and stiff in social relationships. Thus, an unresponsive or controlling person is task oriented rather than relationship oriented, while the opposite is the case with responsive or emotive persons.

By combining these two traits, we can identify the four social styles shown in Table 7.3: driving, expressive, amiable, and analytical. The driving types want to dominate in interpersonal situations, want their opinion to prevail, demand compliance with their wish, and they do so in a "cold" manner, without any regard for the others' feelings. The expressive types

CLASSIFICATION OF PERSONALITY INTO SOCIAL STYLES

Table 7.3

LOW
RESPONSIVENESS

Analytical Slow reaction Maximum effort to organize Minimum concern for relationships Historical time frame Cautious action Tends to reject involvement	**Driving** Swift reaction Maximum effort to control Minimum concern for caution in relationships Present time frame Direct action Tends to reject inaction
Amiable Unhurried reaction Maximum effort to relate Minimum concern for effecting change Present time frame Supportive action Tends to reject conflict	**Expressive** Rapid reaction Maximum effort to involve Minimum concern for routine Future time frame Impulsive action Tends to reject isolation

LOW
ASSERTIVENESS

HIGH
ASSERTIVENESS

HIGH
RESPONSIVENESS

Source: Adapted from David W. Merrill and Roger H. Reid, *Personal Styles and Effective Performance: Make Your Style Work for You* (Radnor, PA: Chilton Book Company, 1981).

Table 7.4

IDENTIFYING SOCIAL STYLES: VERBAL AND NONVERBAL CUES

	ASSERTIVENESS	
	LOW	HIGH
VERBAL BEHAVIORAL CUES	Slower	Faster
Pace of speech	Fewer statements	More statements
Quantity of speech	Softer	Louder
Volume of speech		
NONVERBAL BEHAVIORAL CUES		
Use of hands	Relaxed or cupped	Pointing at others
Body posture	Leans back while talking	Leans forward to make a point
Eye contact	Indirect contact while speaking	Direct contact while speaking

	RESPONSIVENESS	
	LOW	HIGH
VERBAL BEHAVIORAL CUES	Monotone	Inflections
Emotion in voice	Tasks	People
Subjects of speech	Facts/data	Opinions/stories
Descriptives		
NONVERBAL BEHAVIORAL CUES		
Use of hands	Closed	Open palms
Body posture	Rigid	Casual
Facial expression	Controlled	Animated

Source: Adapted from David W. Merrill and Roger H. Reid, *Personal Styles and Effective Performance: Make Your Style Work for You* (Radnor, PA: Chilton Book Company, 1981).

are also opinionated and demanding of compliance with their requests, but they do so with emotions, using persuasion rather than authority. The amiable types are unassertive, undemanding, easygoing, but also warm, openly showing their feelings, and desirous of establishing personal relationships with those they deal with. Finally, the analytical types are neither demanding and assertive nor emotional. They tend to ask questions, collect information, and study the data carefully before forming an opinion. When asked, they will state their considered opinion objectively, without getting emotional about it.

How can marketers use this model? While the social style classification has been used in employee selection and in employee training to increase effectiveness in working with co-workers, subordinates, and superiors, it can be equally useful for salespersons or in business negotiations. It is fairly easy to classify a customer or a client just by observing his or her behavior. The four social style types display distinct behavior—both verbal and nonverbal—as shown in Table 7.4. By observing these behavioral cues, the salesperson or a business negotiator can identify the social style of the customer and attempt to adjust his or her own style for interacting with that customer.

The Influence of Personal Characteristics on the Three Customer Roles: An Overview

Throughout the chapter, we have described how the five personal characteristics (genetics, race, gender, age, and personality) influence customer behavior. In the present section, we reiterate some of these influences, organizing them along the three customer

Table 7.5   PERSONAL CHARACTERISTICS AND THE THREE CUSTOMER ROLES

| | CUSTOMER ROLE | | |
CHARACTERISTIC	USER	PAYER	BUYER
Genetics	Customers' genetic makeup determines biological needs and the specific performance features sought. Genetics determines personality and emotional makeup to influence specific social and emotional values sought.		Certain genetic disorders might incapacitate customers from making shopping trips, so value is more desirable.
Race	For personal care items, customers seek products that are compatible with their skin and hair needs. Ethnic tastes in food, clothing, and homes differ. Some minority groups seek social values as compensation.	Economic means are unevenly distributed across races and ethnic groups. Race-based discrimination in credit limits affordability for some customers.	Many customers prefer ethnic stores and suppliers. Race and ethnic group influence the preferred modes of interaction with vendors.
Gender	Many products and services are gender specific, due to either physiology or culture. In some cultures, women might use emotional products more.	Sex roles may be the basis for allocating the payer role.	Sex roles may be the basis for allocating the buyer role. Where sex roles include women in the workforce, they might seek convenience and time saving in shopping. In some cultures, men are still learning shopping skills.
Age	Product/service usage in many categories is contingent on age. Social and emotional values are more important for youth. Product/service needs are influenced by the physical limitations related to aging (such as inability to lift heavy weights or read fine print).	Age influences the amount of financial resources. The payer's role is more separate from the user's among youth (dependent on parents) and the elderly (dependent on government for income).	Elderly buyers need more service and convenience. Word-of-mouth communication about shopping is highest among youth. Older buyers (in both businesses and households) prefer to buy based on relationship with the seller.
Personality	At onset of need, some personality types may either delay or rush use of the product or service. Some personalities will be more open to cross-gender product use. Some personalities will have more need for mood and emotional products.	Some personalities will be frugal; others spendthrift. Some personalities (of business and household payers) will focus on long-term investment; others on immediate price.	Personality types will differ in their loyalty to brands and stores. Some personalities enjoy browsing; others focus on obtaining target merchandise. Some personalities focus more on seeking relationships with sellers.

roles—user, payer, and buyer. The five personal characteristics influence the three roles in distinct ways. See Table 7.5.

Influence of Genetics

A person's genetic makeup determines a person's biological needs as well as physical constitution, and hence the need for products necessitated by those biological needs or by special physiological constitution. Examples include allergy medications, sun protective skin lotions, clothing for very short or very tall persons, certain dietary restrictive foods, weight management programs, special products for the physically challenged, and so on. These genetic effects shape expectations for specific performance features in products and services. But beyond performance, genetics also affect a person's emotional state and personality, and this in turn affects a person's desire for emotion-producing experiential or hedonic products (e.g., thrill-seeking products or services such as going to an amusement park).

The payer role is not much affected by genetics directly, although it is conceivable that some of the effect is indirect: for example, via altering a customer's earning capacity and consequently his or her economic condition. But the buyer role is affected in that certain genetic disorders might incapacitate customers from going to the market, making convenience a more dominant value.

Influence of Race

Some of the effects of race and genetics are similar, while others differ. Race affects, due to related genetic differences, skin color and texture and hair type. Therefore, customers from different races need personal care items with specific performance characteristics. Beyond physiology, a customer's race also implies differences in values, lifestyle, and tastes. Customs and tastes differ, for example, for different ethnic groups in food, clothing, home decoration, and leisure preferences. Finally, some minority ethnic groups tend to seek socially prestigious consumption to compensate for their sometimes low public image.

Then, race influences the payer role for two reasons. First, economic conditions are distributed differently across races—This in turn is due to historical differences in access to opportunities and due to race-based cultural differences in individual achievement motivation and belief in upward mobility. Second, there has been a systematic bias against certain ethnic minorities in credit approval. Both of these limit the buying power of some ethnic minorities. Other ethnic minorities, such as Japanese Asians or Asian Indians are affluent (which has a positive influence on their demand for products and services), but at the same time shun credit, thus limiting their purchases to what they can afford.

Finally, the buyer role is affected by race at least in two ways. First, many ethnic groups prefer to patronize vendors, store owners, and service agents (e.g., insurance agency representatives, real estate agents) of the same race and ethnic background. Second, as buyers, ethnic groups differ in the kind of interaction they seek from suppliers and from store operators. In some races and ethnic cultures, friendship is limited to personal friends, and consequently, in commercial transactions, there is politeness but not personal warmth, so none is offered and none is expected. However, expectations may be different between the customer and the salesperson, if they come from different ethnic backgrounds, or the overt expressions for communicating good feeling may be different—a case we saw with the Korean storeowners in New York and their African-American customers.

Influence of Gender

Gender, too, has pervasive effect on customer roles. (See the Window on Research box for an example.) For the user, gender implies the purchase of some gender-specific products and services, based either in some biological or physiological needs (e.g., vitamins with iron for women and without iron for men), or in culture-generated gender-specific customs and tastes (e.g., skirts for women only, except in Scotland). Many performance-related values differ between men and women, such as the ergonomics in the design of the driver seat in cars, or the extra-security needs in hotel rooms for women business travelers. But men-women differences spill over to social and emotional values. While the fashion and public image consciousness may be present to the same degree among men and women (although this too varies across cultures), the range of fashion accessories and accoutrements suitable to reflect shades of moods and person-types is many times broader for women than for men in almost all cultures. Consequently, the drive to obtain a good "fit" (from an emotional and social value standpoint) is generally much more intense among women than among men. Also, except in the very liberated cultures, women, more than men, are also concerned lest they inadvertently send, by their clothing, a wrong message to men around them. Finally, women are also likely to consume more of the mood and emotional products such as perfumes, flowers, incense, or bubble baths. Men, on the other hand, are likely to seek emotional value more in outdoor adventures and sports.

The payer role is affected only insofar as there exists, in a given society or in a given family unit, sex-role based bias in the allocation of the payer role. Specifically, in some societies and families, the male head of the household might be the one who controls the family budget; in others, the female head of the household might be the one shouldering this responsibility (as likely happens in matriarchical cultures).

The buyer role is affected by gender both in allocation of the responsibility and in gender differences in the specific values the customer seeks as a buyer. Regarding role allocation, again, there are norms about who should be the buyer, which differ across families and cultures. Often and mostly in traditional societies, women do the shopping for routine household items, while men do the shopping for major purchases (appliances, cars, and so on) or for certain technical items (e.g., chain saw). In modernized societies and families, the sex roles are more egalitarian, so both sexes assume an equal share of purchasing, often shopping jointly. Where women do assume the purchasing role, their time is becoming scarcer due to their taking up a job; consequently, they are increasingly seeking more convenience and time-saving means of shopping. Also, men are being forced to assume more of the purchasing role, and many are still novices, learning the necessary skills.

Influence of Age

As users, the needs and wants for product and service categories obviously differ across different age groups (e.g., youth will rarely use dentures, and the elderly as a group are unlikely to use in-line skates). Medical services needed for different age groups differ greatly. As users in business markets, older workers can't use heavy equipment or parts, and therefore they seek different performance value from raw material, parts, and equipment, and so on, from those that younger workers seek. Moreover, social and emotional values are likely to be more important to youth than to the elderly, and more important to the latter than to the middle-age customers.

Why Women Go on Binge Eating: Or Gender Differences in Emotional Eating

Everyone occasionally eats without actually being hungry—that is, when there is no physiological need for food. We eat because we are feeling bored, alone, overwhelmed, anxious, and so on. These instances of food consumption are called *emotional eating*. It has generally been observed that women indulge in emotional eating much more than do men. This hypothesis has been tested in some research studies. Three studies done in Germany and Denmark found that both men and women indulge in emotional eating, but this behavior is more prevalent among women.

Why these gender differences? Suzanne C. Grunert, a marketing professor at Odense University, Denmark, has reviewed available sociological and psychological theories on the topic and has proposed the following explanation for the emotional eating behavior more prevalent among women. Grunert's model attributes this behavior to four factors:

1. *Gender differences in personal values*—Women more than men have hedonistic values (concepts about what is worth having) such as pleasure, fun, and enjoyment. These values lead women toward emotional eating.

2. *Gender differences in personality traits*—Women tend to score higher than men on such personality traits as empathy, guilt, fear, altruism, and social anxiety. Women who are experiencing negative emotions tend to resort to eating as a compensation. By giving, worrying, and so on, they feel a lack of something (e.g., self-esteem, security, and so forth), so they compensate for it by some other behavior such as eating. Compensatory eating is thus a kind of emotional eating.

3. *Gender-specific roles*—In most societies, women are loaded with a greater number and diversity of roles (as mothers, wives, and workers) than men. Moreover, women consider these diverse roles as more central to their self-identity (whereas men may consider only one or two of all of their roles as defining of their self-concept). Failure to fulfill all roles well causes them anxiety, which in turn causes compensatory eating.

Also, situations in which new role expectations emerge while the old ones still remain may also call for some compensations through relatively easily available pleasures such as eating.

4. *Body image*—Society's concepts about appearance and attractiveness, applied differently across genders, also influence women's feeling of well-being and satisfaction. More preoccupied with their body weight and appearance, women go on diets more often than do men. Then, to compensate for the sacrifice they made in dieting, they indulge in periodic temporary eating binges.

This model is a rich illustration of how a multitude of factors covered in this textbook such as cultural values and norms, gender roles, and gender-specific personality traits explain a customer behavior phenomenon we frequently observe in Western societies.

This phenomenon does not occur uniformly across nations and across cultures. In developing countries, for example, we are unlikely to observe the greater prevalence of emotional eating among women than men. One reason is that a slim body is not necessarily considered more attractive in these cultures. Furthermore, eating is more of an organized activity—undertaken at specified times of the day, and as a family unit as a whole. The individual snacking, or "grazing" as it is often called, is just not the custom or habit. But even in the Western context for which the above model is proposed, Professor Grunert is careful to note that these are hypotheses, based on whatever research findings exist and that they still need verification for women consumers in a specific country.

Source: Suzanne C. Grunert, "On Gender Differences in Eating Behavior," in Janeen Arnold Costa, ed., *Gender Issues and Consumer Behavior* (Thousand Oaks: Sage, 1994), pp. 63–83.

As payers, customers are affected by age, because age influences their station in their career, and, accordingly, their financial resources. Today, older consumers who have retired and have accumulated their lifetime savings are the most financially resourced customers. Age also affects the separation of the payer and the user role. Generally, these two roles are separated for youth, and again for many elderly who now depend on the government for medicare and retirement benefits.

Finally, age influences the buyer role. Elderly purchasers need and seek more service and more convenience. Also, older customers, in both business and household markets, prefer to buy based on a relationship with the seller. Finally, word-of-mouth communication about shopping is the highest among youth. The youth talks, more than do other groups, about what is new in the market and where.

Influence of Personality

The role of personality is overarching, affecting all domains of customer behavior. In a sense, personality is the conduit through which the influence of other characteristics passes. Thus, a person genetically prone to headaches or allergies could bear the

Personality is the conduit through which all customer behavior flows. Here, Bijan appeals to customers who possess spontaneity.

discomfort stoically, shunning early medication, or he or she could show hypochondriac tendencies and seek intense medication at the earliest onset of symptoms. An overweight person could be concerned or unconcerned about his or her physical condition and may or may not seek weight reduction programs. A young person could be staid and be content with "consuming" TV all the time, while a 70-year-old could be hiking and skiing. A woman could wear unisex clothes and smoke cigarettes with a macho image, and a man could be a heavier user of cosmetics (men's fragrances, of course) than an average woman. Many ethnics break all stereotypes and are sometimes more cosmopolitan than the mainstream population. Even role models cross ethnic lines, so, in effect, a customer could be from one race and ethnic group by birth, but of another in lifestyle and consumption aspirations. For example, during the 1990s, rap music and the accompanying rebellious clothing style of the inner-city black youth were widely sought and adopted by suburban white teenagers. Thus, personality is a filter that screens and shapes the consumption effects of other personal characteristics.

But personality influences the three customer roles in its own right. Outgoing persons would participate in outdoor and social activities more and therefore consume products and services relevant to these recreational activities. Similarly, pleasure-seeking individuals would like experiential products more. People with artistic tastes would be users, payers, and buyers of performing art events. Achievement-oriented adults would seek to improve their skills and aptitudes and register for college courses and buy the products and services needed to complete their training. As payers, some customers would be spendthrift, and others very frugal and conservative. Some would like to live on credit; others well within current cash resources. Customers as payers could differ in adopting a long-term versus short-term perspective (which is a function of personality), and this could in turn affect their perception of the relative value of two options such as two models of cars or appliances or even the choice of a school to send their son or daughter to.

Customer personality also affects the buyer role. Brand loyalty and, likewise, store loyalty vary from person to person, a topic we cover in later chapters. These individual differences in brand and store loyalty are basically personality differences. Some individuals like to stick with the tried and tested; others like to explore new options. Another manifestation of personality is in the shopping style, again a topic we cover in a later chapter. Suffice to say, however, that some customers are browsers, scanning the store environment for opportunities; others are, in contrast, focused shoppers, using a shopping list and getting out of the store as quickly as they can. Impulse buying (discussed in a later chapter) is also primarily a personality trait.

The personality of the business customer is influential, likewise, across the three roles. The choice of the office decor, the choice of airline and hotel during business trips, and even the choice of performance features such as speed versus memory in a computer (impatient users want faster speed), the safety factor in design specifications (e.g., the torque specification of industrial motors—risk avoiders build in a higher safety factor) are dependent on the personality of the user. As payers, the long- versus short-term perspective definitely affects the business customer's choice between options or allocation of funds to a business activity or service. For example, managers with short-term perspective might spend less in image-building advertising and more in sales promotion. Finally, as buyers, the four social styles—driving, expressive, amiable, and analytical—directly bear on the kind of interactions they would seek with sellers and business negotiators.

Summary

In this chapter, we discussed customers' personal characteristics and showed how these affect customer behavior. These characteristics are genetics; the three biogenic features of race, gender, and age; and personality, which is a function of genetics, biogenics, and environment. All these characteristics affect customer behavior, and they affect each of the three customer roles—user, payer, and buyer.

The influence of genetics is through their determining role in the physiology of the individual, the diseases to which a person is made susceptible, circadian rhythms, and moods and emotions. Each of these affects what the customer will need and or want, such as specific food products, medications, mood-enhancers, and so on. Race and ethnic background influence customers' needs for skin-specific personal care items, taste differences in food and clothing, and in preferred interaction styles with store owners. We discussed the origins of the human race, and the profile of major races and ethnic groups in the United States (e.g., the Hispanics, African Americans, Asian Americans, and Ethnic European Americans). Next we discussed the customer behavior differences between the two genders. These differences relate to the consumption of clothing, personal items, and emotional or mood-enhancing products in the household market, and the need for greater security for women in business travel for the business customer, for example. Payer and buyer roles are allocated differently across the genders in various cultures so that marketers must be cognizant of whom to target—the man or the woman in the household.

Next, we discussed the diverse categories of age: GI generation, boomers, baby busters, Generation X, teenagers, and children. These customers need and want different products and services, both because their physical characteristics are different and because their tastes differ according to the age of their subculture.

Finally, we explained what personality is and how it is formed. The Freudian theory illuminates the nature of personality as a set of conscious and subconsciousness motives and urges. Trait theory views personality as a pattern of behavior. Defense mechanisms were described as the ego's attempt to manage anxiety and to protect the self from being slighted. Many defense mechanisms account for significant occurrences of product and service uses. For a business customer, we introduced a specific personality typology—social styles—and we showed the relevance of this typology on customer behavior in business interactions.

All five personal characteristics influence, and, along with the environment, shape a person's psychological makeup—her or his motives, emotions, and lifestyles. These are the topics of the next chapter.

Key Terms

Personal Characteristics 202
Group Traits 202
Individual Traits 203
DNA 203
Biological Determinism 204

Circadian Rhythm 206
Birth Order 207
Race 208
Ethnic Identity 208
GI Generation 226
Silent Generation 226
Baby Boomers 226

Generation X 226
Baby Busters 229
Personality 235
Behaviorism Theory 235
Id 237
Ego 237
Superego 237

Review Questions

1. What are the four ways in which genetics influences customer behavior? Illustrate each influence by a new example. Identify whether the influence is on needs or wants or both.

2. One important reason for studying age in consumer behavior is to help determine the lifetime revenue from a given customer. Link the family life cycle approach of classifying customers by age to the determination of lifetime revenue.

3. List some of the men-women differences in their behavior as customers, separately in their user and buyer roles.

4. List all the major races in U.S. markets and identify at least two characteristics typical of each race; illustrate their influence on their customer behavior.

5. Explain the concept of personality traits in your own words. Select any four personality traits and explain how each trait might affect customer behavior. Illustrate each influence by one example each from household and business markets.

Applications

1. Cosmetic companies have product lines targeted specifically to African American women. In contrast, under public pressure, R. J. Reynolds canceled its plan to introduce Uptown, a cigarette targeting African Americans. Do companies have the right to use a subculture's unique characteristics to increase the sales of products? Was R. J. Reynolds simply following the marketing concept, which states that companies should design products to meet the needs of specific market segments? What are the ethical issues involved in subcultural market segmentation?

2. Select two ads from a magazine that are deliberately targeting customers by age. First, describe the ads. Next, show which aspect of age is being highlighted. Finally, give your opinion of the ads in terms of their ability to attract the customers they are targeting.

3. Describe some of the general gender differences that affect consumers in both household and business markets. What have marketers done to handle these differences? Recently, companies like Calvin Klein have tried to minimize gender differences. Do you think this strategy is a good idea?

4. How can marketers use the information in this chapter to develop promotional campaigns designed to increase market share among Asian-American, Hispanic, and African American consumers for the following products:
   - Cameras.
   - Ready-to-eat cereals.
   - Fragrances (perfume or cologne).

5. David B. Wolfe, author of *Serving the Ageless Market,* describes how a person's mode of thinking changes as he or she matures. He describes five key values that are generally held by mature

individuals: (1) autonomy and self-sufficiency; (2) social and spiritual connectedness; (3) altruism; (4) personal growth; and (5) revitalization. Provide one example each of a consumer product and a consumer service that caters to mature individuals and describe how these companies have tapped into consumers' generally held values.

6. Assume you are in charge of a new line of clothing that will directly compete with the Tommy Hilfiger brand targeted to the Generation X market. What do you need to know about this age segment to make your clothes more appealing? How can you distinguish yourself from your major competitor in terms of tapping into the market values (universal and personal) that your target customers seek?

7. In general, how should marketers promote products and services to working women? What appeals should they use? Now assume that you are the owner of a luxury automobile dealership. What kind of marketing strategies will you use to target working women?

Practical Experiences

1. Interview two baby boomers and then separately interview two Generation Xers. Based on your conversations, describe how the universal and personal values for the following two services—medical checkups and vacations—may be different for baby boomers and Generation Xers.

2. Next time you are watching television, pay attention to the advertising instead of channel "surfing" through it. Find an ad that is deliberately meant for small children. How have the needs of children been addressed in this ad? For which customer roles has this marketer targeted children—user, payer, and buyer? Describe in detail why this strategy may or may not work.

3. Using one of the personal characteristic categories described in this chapter (age, gender or race), identify a group that belongs to that category within your college or university. First, describe the norms, values, and behaviors of this particular group. Interview five members of that group regarding their attitudes toward the use of credit cards. What are the implications of your findings for marketing credit cards to the group you selected?

4. Select one business services company and one consumer products company. By reviewing their annual reports and their Web sites, describe how they specifically appeal to different consumer personal characteristics in their market segmentation efforts.

Notes

1 Harold Koplewicz, *It's Nobody's Fault: New Hope and Help for Difficult Children and Their Parents* (Arlington, VA: National Alliance for the Mentally Ill, 1996).

2 Gloria Hochman, "That Age-Old Question: They Have the Same Parents, the Same Upbringing, So Why Do Brothers and Sisters Turn Out So Differently?" *The Orlando Sentinel,* February 16, 1997, p. 6.

3 This section is informed by a number of prior works of other authors. Important among these are: Marlene L. Rossman, *Multicultural Marketing: Selling to a Diverse America* (New York: AMACOM, 1994).

4 This 1994–1995 survey was done by Paul Sladkus International, Inc. (PSI), a New York–based multicultural advertising and marketing firm. The survey results are reported in *American Demographics,* March 1997 issue.

5 This section is based on a report published in *American Demographics,* March 1997. See Shelly Reese, "When Whites Aren't a Mass Market," *American Demographics,* March 1997, pp. 51–54.

6 "How to Sell across Cultures," *American Demographics,* March 1994, p. 56–57.

[7] Patricia Braus, "What Does Hispanic Mean," *American Demographics* 15, no. 6 (June 1993), pp. 46–51.

[8] Ibid.

[9] Quoted in Marlene Rossman, *Multicultural Marketing: Selling to a Diverse America.*

[10] Tina M. Lowrey and Cele Otnes, "Construction of a Meaningful Wedding: Differences in the Priorities of Brides and Grooms," in *Gender Issues and Consumer Behavior,* Janeen Arnold Costa, ed., (Thousand Oaks: CA: Sage, 1994), pp. 164–83.

[11] Adapted from Frieda Curtindale, "Car Dealers Give the Lady Some Respect," *American Demographics* 14 no. 9 (September 1992), p. 25.

[12] For further reading, see Bernd H. Schmitt, France Leclerc, and Laurette Dubé-Rioux, "Sex Typing and Consumer Behavior: A Test of Gender Schema Theory," *Journal of Consumer Research* 15 (June 1988), pp. 122–28; Barbara B. Stern, "Sex Role, Self-Concept Measures and Marketing: A Research Note," *Psychology and Marketing* 5 (Spring 1988), p. 85 ff; Janeen Arnold Costa, ed., *Gender Issues and Consumer Behavior* (Thousand Oaks: Sage, 1994).

[13] Vincent J. Cristofalo. "An Overview of the Theories of Biological Aging," in *Emergent Theories of Aging,* James E. Birren and Vern L. Bengston, eds. (New York: Springer, 1988) pp. 118–27.

[14] Marion Perlmutter. "Cognitive Potential throughout Life," in *Emergent Theories of Aging,* James E. Birren and Vern L. Bengtson, eds. (New York: Springer, 1988), pp. 247–68.

[15] William Strauss and Neil Howe, *Generations: The History of America's Future, 1584–2069* (New York: William Morrow & Company, 1991).

[16] "Older Consumers Follow Different Rules, *American Demographics,* February 1993, pp. 21–22.

[17] "Raging against Aging," *American Demographics,* March 1990, pp. 42–45.

[18] Susan Mitchell, "How Boomers Save," *American Demographics* 16, no. 9 (September 1994), pp. 22–29.

[19] Cherryl Russell, "On the Baby-Boom Bandwagon," *American Demographics* 13, no. 5 (May 1991), pp. 24–31.

[20] Ibid.

[21] Susan Mitchell, "How to Talk to Young Adults," *American Demographics* 15, no. 4 (April 1993), pp. 50–54.

[22] Estimate by Teenage Research Unlimited (TRU), reported in Shelley Reese, "The Quality of Cool," *Marketing Tools,* July 1997.

[23] "Children as Customers," *American Demographics,* September 1990, pp. 36–39.

[24] S. Selina Guber and John Berry, *Marketing to and through Kids* (New York: McGraw Hill, 1993).

[25] Ibid., p. 10.

[26] Hans J. Eysenck, *The Biological Basis of Personality,* C. C. Thomas (Springfield, IL, 1967); and *The Structure of Human Personality* (London: Metheun, 1970); also, Hans J. Eysenck, *Personality, Genetics, and Behavior: Selected Papers,* (New York: Praeger Publishers, 1982).

[27] L. Tiger, and R. Fox, *The Imperial Animal* (Paladin: St. Albans, 1974); A.L. Caplan, ed., *The Sociobiological Debate* (New York: Harper & Row, 1978); S. Freud, *Instincts and their Vicissitudes,* in standard edition, Vol. 14 (London: Hogarth, 1957); E.O. Wilson, *Sociobiology: The New Synthesis* (Cambridge, MA: Harvard University Press, 1978).

[28] For a more formal definition and treatment of personality and trait theory, see Ernest Hilgard, Richard Atkinson, and Rita Atkinson, *Introduction to Psychology,* 6th ed. (New York: Harcourt Brace Jovanovich, Inc., 1975); and Walter Mischel, "On the Future of Personality Measurement," *American Psychologist,* 32 (April 1977), p. 2.

[29] R.B. Cattell, H.W. Eber, and M.M. Tatsuoka, *Handbook for the Sixteen Personality Factor Questionnaire* (Champaign, IL: Institute for Personality and Ability Testing, 1970).

[30] Raymond L. Horton, "Some Relationships between Personality and Decision Making," *Journal of Marketing Research* 16 (May 1979), pp. 233–46; Michael B. Mazis and Timothy W. Sweeney, "Novelty and Personality with Risk as a Moderating Variable," in B.B. Berkers and H. Becker, eds., *1972 Combined Proceedings* (Chicago: American Marketing Association, 1973), pp.

401–11; Charles M. Schaninger and Donald Sciglimpaglia, "The Influence of Cognitive Personality Traits and Demographics on Consumer Information Acquisition," *Journal of Consumer Research* 8 (September 1981), pp. 208–16. For a review of personality studies, see Girish N. Punj and David W. Stewart, "An Interaction Framework of Consumer Decision Making," *Journal of Consumer Research* 10 (September 1983), pp. 181–96.

[31] Harold H. Kassarjian, "Personality and Consumer Behavior: A Review," *Journal of Marketing Research* 8 (November 1971), pp. 409–19.

[32] David W. Merrill and Roger H. Reid, *Personal Styles and Effective Performance: Make Your Style Work for You* (Radnor, PA: Chilton Book Company, 1981).

CHAPTER 8

After reading this chapter you should be able to:

Describe the benefits of anticipating trends in customer behavior.

Identify expected changes in customer demographics.

Describe how technological trends are likely to affect products, services, and customer behavior.

List ways in which trends in public policy are expected to influence customer behavior.

Summarize the impact of these trends on the three customer roles.

Discuss how marketers are responding to these trends.

Trends in Determinants of Customer Behavior

Business Trip at Warp Speed

"Sophia, please get me a drug store in China, a car mechanic in Paris, and a fairy tale on the Internet multimedia to share with Cuckoo in Thailand."

Anne-Marie de Randamie is traveling in China, attempting to clinch a deal she is negotiating with Sung-Tai Lee, the head of the leading silk export house. From her hotel room in Beijing she has just finished showing the silk fabrics to her fashion designer and manufacturing director on the videoconferencing network, and together they have finalized the fabrics they want to buy for the upcoming season.

She will be returning to Paris tomorrow, driving back from the airport in her Saab 900. There is only one snag. She has just received a message on her electronic notebook computer from Sophia, her personal assistant, announcing that her car has sent a signal that the battery-charging mechanism is failing. Anne-Marie instructs Sophia to find a car mechanic who can go to the airport and fix the car. Sophia searches for mechanics, and after unsuccessful negotiations with the computers of four mechanics, she finally finds one who has agreed to perform the service in the wee hours in Paris.

She then inquires of Sophia whether the pharmacist has delivered the medications she had requested. Sophia apologizes and informs that there was some delay in getting the prescription from her regular pharmacist's databank in Paris, having it translated into Chinese, and in obtaining permission from a Chinese governmental agency, since the drug was restricted in China. Fortunately, the pharmacy retail trade has long been privatized by the Chinese government, and consequently the drugstore was set up to offer top-class customer service and offer delivery on demand at the customer's doorstep. "The medication should be here any minute now Ms. de Randamie," Sophia informs her.

Relieved, Anne-Marie plunks down in the large sofa in front of the six-foot high-definition TV screen in the room. She plans to order a Jane Austen movie, using her electronic money, and choosing from the 5,000 or so movies available on her video-on-demand menu. But before she does that, there is just one more thing she wants to do. Boot up the Internet and share with Cuckoo, her great grandson in Thailand, a multimedia bedtime fairy tale. Yes, her great grandson—Oh, we forgot to tell you that next week, on July 10, 2010, Anne-Marie will turn 105!

Part three

The Customer's Mind-set

CHAPTER 9

After reading this chapter you should be able to:

Describe the process of perception, including the factors that influence how customers perceive various marketplace stimuli.

Explain how perceptual distortion occurs and how customers interpret price information.

Summarize how customers learn through the four modes of learning.

Explain how learning helps customers with decision making.

Discuss the customer psychology of simplification (streamlining decisions) and complication (repeating a previous decision-making process).

Outline the process by which customers learn about and respond to product and service innovations.

Identify the characteristics of innovations that customers consider desirable.

Define innovators and opinion leaders in the process of customer response to innovations.

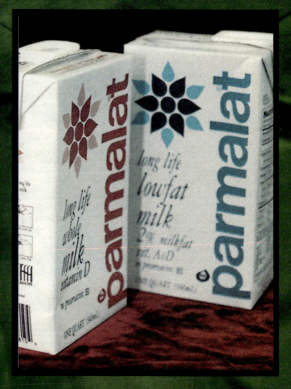

The Customer as a Perceiver and a Learner

This Is Fresh Milk?

Milk. You find it in the refrigerated section of the supermarket, and you store it in your refrigerator, not in your pantry. Right? Not necessarily. Parmalat, the world's largest milk producer, markets a type of milk called *Long Life*, which is specially processed without any preservatives. The processing technology is "ultra-high temperature," which neutralizes bacteria and thus prevents spoilage. The milk is then packaged in aseptic cartons. It does require refrigeration after opening. But until then, it can be stored on dry-goods shelves for six months.

The advantages to customers are substantial. It saves refrigerator space, which in most households is scarce. Customers can stock extra in their pantry so they don't have to run to the store at midnight because they just discovered they are out of milk.

When Parmalat introduced Long Life in the United States, it expected that customer acceptance of this revolutionary new product would be immediate and high. The product concept sounded great in theory. However, the actual product sales have been extremely slow. Somehow, U.S. customers just can't fathom fresh milk in a dry-goods can or box. This is one innovation where customers' preexisting perceptions and learning are at odds with the new product concept.

the classical conditioning principle works in advertising. In this experiment, Professor Gorn selected two musical tunes, one from the movie *Grease* (which customers in his experiment liked) and the other from classical Indian music (which the same customers disliked). Then he showed slides of two pens that were identical except for their colors—the colors were pretested to ensure that the chosen colors were preferred equally. The slide for one pen advertisement was paired with the music from Grease, while the other was paired with the Indian music. The pen paired with the liked music was preferred by more customers than the other pen. Thus, pairing liked and disliked music stimuli with two virtually identical pens conditioned customers to prefer the pen that was shown in conjunction with the liked music![15]

In another experiment at a supermarket, the music pace was varied on different days from slow to fast. On the slow-music days, shoppers spent more time in the store and bought more than on faster-music days.[16] Finally, in a third experiment with students, the mere presence of credit-card replicas induced greater spending. In this same study, experimenters made observations of restaurant patrons and data were recorded on the amount of the tip left by patrons who paid by credit cards versus those who paid by cash. Credit-card-paying patrons left higher tips than the cash-paying patrons.[17] (For yet another example, see the Window on Research box).

Marketers put this principle to use when they pair their brand with a likable celebrity. The celebrity's personality, by classical conditioning, rubs onto the product itself. Thus, CK perfume is more "youthful" because of the teenage models used in the brand's advertising, and Giorgio is more "mature" and "richer" because of its Beverly Hills heritage. Coca-Cola uses "Mean" Joe Green to convey its "real-thing" image, while Pepsi has used Michael Jackson and Michael J. Fox to promote its "New Generation" image. In the United States, milk is becoming trendy as supermodel Christie Brinkley, country music singer Garth Brooks, and well-known film director Spike Lee sport their milk mustaches. Now even *Garlique*, a brand of pharmaceutical formulation with garlic extract as its principal ingredient, is "chic" because Robin Leech promotes it!

Marketing applications of classical conditioning extend beyond advertising. Products are packaged to look expensive or more basic, natural or fancy, healthier or indulgent, special or everyday, environmentally friendly or not, and aesthetically appealing. The shopping bag given to customers is designed to convey a certain image about a company; compare, for example, Bloomingdale versus J.C. Penney shopping bags. In a restaurant, the dress norm of the waiters, the typeface on the menu, and even the appearance of paper napkins are designed to classically condition the perceived quality of the restaurant and its food. Finally, price is used to communicate quality and exclusiveness (more discussion on price later).

Such pairings expand beyond product or service characteristics. Manufacturing firms exploit the prestige of the distributors and retailers who agree to carry their products. Companies try to associate themselves with other programs with certain public appeal. In the 1960s, General Foods associated its Tang brand of breakfast drink with the National Aeronautics and Space Administration program. In 1996, major global corporations such as Coca-Cola, Visa, and Nike became the official sponsors of the Olympics held in Atlanta, Georgia. A firm that forms a joint venture with a larger, more reputable firm uses the collaboration to promote its own image, as the 1996 alliance between MCI (a small U.S. telecommunications company) and British Telecom (a British giant) shows.

Some firms even boast about their major clients, hoping that such name-dropping will boost their own public image. At least that is how one young American entrepreneur succeeded in London. Lee Nordlund, a college student and a resident of Newport Beach, California, befriended a young lady from Britain and moved to London in the 1990s. To

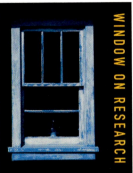

Seeking Evidence That Classical Conditioning Really Works!

Terence A. Shimp, a well-known consumer researcher and marketing professor at the University of South Carolina, joined with Randall W. Engle, a professor of psychology at the same university, and Elnora W. Stuart, a marketing professor at Winthrop College, to perform a series of 21 experiments demonstrating, in by far the most rigorous way, the classical conditioning effect in the context of the marketplace.

These researchers used four unknown brands of colas (Cragmont, Elf, My-te-Fine, and Tiger) that were not sold in the region where the experiment was conducted, two moderately known brands (Royal Crown [RC] and Shasta), and two well-known brands (Pepsi and Coke). Each of these served as the conditioned stimulus (CS). For the unconditioned stimulus (UCS), the researchers employed four attractive water scenes: a mountain waterfall, a sunset over water, a boat mast against the sky, and a lavender-hued island. An important consideration in classical conditioning experiments is that the UCS have at least some degree of relevance to the CS. Here, water scenes do have relevance to colas because both have a refreshing mood effect.

Subjects were randomly assigned to either an experimental or control group. The experimental group was shown slides of the cola product and of the water scenes in tandem. Specifically, one cola slide was shown for 7.5 seconds, followed immediately by a scene slide for 7.5 seconds, and then a two-second blank screen. This 17-second showing was termed a "trial." Each subject was shown a total of 80 such trials. Of these, 20 were conditioning trials, in which a cola slide featuring a specific cola brand was followed by a specific water scene slide; the other 60 were nonconditioning trials that paired a cola slide (other than the cola brand that had been paired with the water scene slide) with the slide of a neutral stimulus (e.g., license plate, landscape, and so on). The control group was shown all the cola slides and all the scene slides at random—none were paired.

Afterward, subjects answered questions pertaining to the evaluation of the brand under study (i.e., the brand paired with the water scene). When the colas were paired *consistently* with the water scenes, the rating of colas was more favorable than when the colas were accompanied by water or neutral scenes in random fashion. This effect occurred the most for completely unknown brands and the least for previ-

ously well-known brands. For moderately known brands, the effect was in between.

Since, in the real world, brands are exposed along with other competing brands, the experiment also used a design in which the 20 slides of the same focal brand (paired with a water scene) were interspersed with 60 slides of the other cola brands (which were paired with neutral scenes); these other colas served as the surrounding context for the focal brand. The favorable rating of the focal brand was always higher when the surrounding context was made up of unknown colas rather than known colas.

This research (comprising 21 separate experiments) was significant both from theory and practice standpoints. In terms of theory, although classical conditioning effects have been demonstrated before, none of the previous research had used a surrounding context (which in this case consisted of competing brands). Thus, it captured the real marketplace conditions better. Moreover, the experiments compared the conditioning effect for well-known, moderately known, and previously unknown brands.

In terms of practice, the research implications are that (1) pairing an unknown brand with a likable audio or visual scene or person can indeed help develop consumer liking for the brand; (2) once the brand is already well known, the brand stands on its own, and pairing it with new likable scenes or persons does not do much for its already favorable rating, and (3) for a relatively unknown brand, it is easier to take advantage of the classical conditioning effect when competitive brands are not being advertised heavily than when intense competitive advertising is occurring.

The classical conditioning effects obtained here are with relatively pallid unconditioned stimuli (UCS) of water scenes. In the real world, much more powerful UCS are typically employed; brands are paired with intense, emotionally arousing, alluring audiovisuals and with highly attractive models with a fan-like following.

Source: Terence A. Shimp, Elnora W. Stuart, and Randall W. Engle, "A Program of Classical Conditioning Experiments Testing Variations in the Conditioned Stimulus and Context," *Journal of Consumer Research* 18, no. 1, (June 1991), pp. 1–12. Additional information available at **http://www.usc.edu**

STAGES IN THE MENTAL PROCESSING OF THE INNOVATION

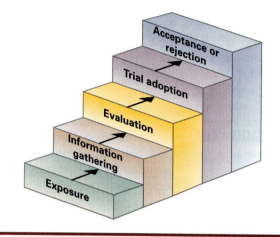

Thus, a true nonadopter is one who, following exposure, resists further evaluative processing of the innovation.

Desirable Characteristics of Innovations

Customers adopt certain innovations quickly; for others, they take a long time. Why is this so? Innovations vary along certain characteristics that render them easy or difficult for customers to adopt. The characteristics that customers desire in innovations are as follows:

- Relative advantage—What customers consider first and foremost is the relative advantage of an innovation. The **relative advantage** refers to how much better the innovation is compared to the current product for which it will substitute. For example, customers would adopt digital answering machines only if they perceive them to satisfy the value they seek better than the machines with conventional tapes do.

- Perceived risk—**Perceived risk** of innovations refers to uncertainty about whether their relative advantage will accrue and whether unanticipated harm will occur. For example, some customers might perceive risk in laser surgery or in irradiation of foods. Customers are less likely to adopt innovations with high perceived risk.

- Complexity—Customers prefer an innovation that is easy to comprehend. The easier it is to comprehend, the less **complexity** it has. For example, many customers may find the Internet too complex to understand, so they may decide to not adopt it. The more complex the customers perceive the innovation to be, the less readily they will adopt it.

- Communicability—**Communicability** refers to the extent to which an innovation is socially visible or is otherwise easy to communicate about in social groups. For example, taboo topics (such as personal hygiene products) have low communicability. Hairstyles are more visible and are therefore naturally more communicable. The greater the ease with which customers can communicate about an innovation, the more rapidly they are likely to adopt it. In some developing countries, discussing contraceptives even with one's doctor is considered a taboo. However, this taboo is felt less by the educated people, who therefore tend to seek advice regarding contraceptives less hesitantly; consequently, educated customers tend to adopt such innovations more rapidly.

- Compatibility—Customers want products that are compatible with their behavior and values. **Behavioral compatibility** consists of qualities that do not require customers to alter their behavioral routine. **Value compatibility** is consistency with customers' deeply held values.

Examples of behavioral incompatibility are vans that do not fit in the garage, electric cars that may require frequent battery charging, or a medication that contraindicates a person's favorite beverage such as coffee (as do most homeopathic medicines). Examples of value incompatibility are contraceptives for customers whose religion may prohibit contraception, or new food products that use animal derivatives for vegetarian customers.

- Trialability—**Trialability** refers to the extent to which it is possible to try out the innovation on a smaller scale. For example, among the birth control methods, oral pills have trialability, whereas a vasectomy does not. Therefore, customers are likely to adopt vasectomy less rapidly.

WINDOW ON PRACTICE

Making Modern Technology Customer-Friendly for South African Rural Customers

One Saturday morning in mid-1996, Ntombiazanele King of South Africa opened a bank account—the first bank account in her life. She is more than 50 years old, is a day-care worker, and had saved her money in a jar hidden somewhere in her shack, living in fear that someday a robber might take the jar. But now she is free from that fear. The story of her acceptance of this innovation—and the acceptance by several of her neighbors in a small underdeveloped village in South Africa—is also the story of a well-conceived marketing strategy that responds to customer motivations for or against adopting a new idea or practice.

The bank is an affiliate of The Standard Bank of South Africa, named E Bank—E is for *eyethu,* a native word meaning "okay" or E for easy for English-speaking South Africans. The bank teller who helped King open the account speaks her own native language. The teller took the application orally and keyed it directly into the computer. The computer instantly delivered a banking card that King now uses to do business on the automated teller machine (ATM). The clerk showed her how to use the machine, and with the clerk's help, King made her first deposit. The ATM is extremely user-friendly—with the monitor displaying color graphics and animation. The screen shows a keyboard identical to the one on the ATM itself, and a picture of a hand shows what keys to press.

To this South African village, opening a bank account is more than an act of ensuring money safety. To many, it is a newfound prestige to finally own an account and have an address at the bank. These "never-before—banked" customers don't want to tie up their cash in long-term deposits and are not literate enough to operate a checking account. What they need basically is a system for safe-keeping their money that is convenient and allows instant access to cash. The bank branch where King opened her account has a non-intimidating storefront setting with a glass door accessible from the street. It has no closed-off offices and no bars to separate tellers from customers. Tellers sit at desks, each equipped with a PC, where customers open their first accounts. By an adjacent wall (covered with vibrant, colorful art) are five ATMs. These customers don't mind the waiting because they use the waiting period for socializing. The bank facilitates that social atmosphere by playing MTV music, for example.

One concern these customers have is the safety of the ATM card itself against theft. To alleviate this fear and to minimize risks to the bank, the bank also issues a "Stop" card. The owners of lost cards simply need to insert their Stop card in the ATM, and their account is frozen automatically.

Ntombiazanele King is pleased to have opened the account. She is also happy that the bank clerk helped her operate the ATM. But she found the ATM so user-friendly that she could not wait to do it on her own the next time.

Source: Adapted from Ken Wells, "Its New ATMs in Place, a Bank Reaches Out to South Africa's Poor," *The Wall Street Journal,* June 13, 1996, pp. A1, A10. Additional information available at **http://www.standardbank.co.za**

Origin in the Era of Global Brands," *International Marketing Review* 9 (1992), pp. 57–76. W. K. Li, K. B. Monroe, and D. Chan, "The Effects of Country of Origin, Brand, and Price Information: A Cognitive-Affective Model of Buying Intentions," *Advances in Consumer Research* 21 (1994), pp. 449–57. J. K. Johansson, "Determinants and Effects of the Use of "Made in Labels," *International Marketing Review* 6 (1989), pp. 47–58. Murray A. Young, Paul L. Sauer, and H. Rap Unnava, "Country-of-Origin Issues," in Salah H. Hassan and Roger D. Blackwell, *Global Marketing: Perspectives and Cases* (Fort Worth, TX: Dryden Press, 1994), pp. 196–210; Sevgin A. Eroglu and Karen A. Machleit, "Effects of Individual and Product-Specific Variables on Utilizing Country-of-Origin as a Product Quality Cue," *International Marketing Review,* 6 (November), 1998, pp. 27–41; G. Erickson, J. K. Johansson, and P. Chao, "Image Variables in Multiattribute Product Evaluations: Country-of-Origin Effects," *Journal of Consumer Research* 11 (September 1984), pp. 694–99. C. M. Han, "Country Image: Halo or Summary Construct," *Journal of Marketing Research* 16 (May 1989), pp. 222–29.

12 S. Lohr, "Made in Japan or Not: That Is the Question," *New York Times* 3, no. 1 (April, 1988), cited in L. D. Dahringer and H. Muhlbacher, *International Marketing: A Global Perspective* (Reading, MA: Addison-Wesley, 1991), p. 354.

13 Jay S. Niefeld, "Corporate Advertising," *Industrial Marketing* (July 1980), pp. 64–74; "Two Different Animals: Brand Awareness and Corporate Image," *Forbes* 6 (March 1989), p. 20.

14 For a fuller description of the Pavlov experiments, see Leland C. Swenson, *Theories of Learning: Traditional Perspectives/Contemporary Developments* (Belmont, CA: Wadsworth Publishing Company, 1980), pp. 13–30.

15 See Gerald J. Gorn, "The Effects of Music in Advertising on Choice Behavior: A Classical Conditioning Approach," *Journal of Marketing* (Winter 1982), pp. 94–101.

16 Ronald E. Milliman, "Using Background Music to Affect Behavior of Supermarket Shoppers," *Journal of Marketing* (Summer 1982), pp. 86–91.

17 Richard A. Feinberg, "Credit Cards as Spending Facilitating Stimuli: A Conditioning Interpretation," *Journal of Consumer Research* (December 1986), pp. 348–56.

18 See Timothy Harper, *Cracking the New European Markets* (New York: John Wiley & Sons, 1992), pp. 41–58.

19 Neal E. Miller and John Dollard, *Social Learning and Imitation* (New Haven, CT: Yale University Press, 1941).

20 See John A. Howard and Jagdish N. Sheth, *The Theory of Buyer Behavior* (New York: John Wiley and Sons, 1961).

21 Jagdish N. Sheth and Atul Parvatiyar (1996), "Relationship Marketing in Consumer Markets: Antecendents & Consequences." *Journal of the Academy of Marketing Science* 23, no. 4 (Fall 1995), pp. 255–71.

22 Raju P. S. Raju, "Optimum Stimulation Level: Its Relationship to Personality, Demographics, and Exploratory Behavior," *Journal of Consumer Research* 7 (December 1980), pp. 272–82.

23 Alan R. Andreasen, "Life-Status Changes and Changes in Consumer Preferences and Satisfaction," *Journal of Consumer Research* 11, no. 3 (December 1984), pp. 784–94.

24 For further reading see E. Hirschman and M. Wallendorf, "Some Implications of Variety Seeking for Advertising and Advertisers," *Journal of Advertising* 9, (1980), pp. 17–25; W. D. Hoyer and N .M. Ridgway, "Variety Seeking as an Explanation for Exploratory Purchase Behavior: A Theoretical Model," *Advances in Consumer Research* 11 (1984), pp. 114–99; L. McAlister and E. A. Pessemier, "Variety-Seeking Behavior: An Interdisciplinary Review, *Journal of Consumer Research* 9 (December 1982), pp. 311–22.

25 Pamala L. Alreck and Robert B. Settle, "The Importance of Word-of-Mouth Communications to Service Buyers," in David W. Stewart and Naufel J. Vilcassim, eds., *1995 AMA Winter Educators' Proceedings* (Chicago: American Marketing Association, 1995), pp. 188–193. Lawrence F. Feick, Linda L. Price, and Robin A. Higie, "People Who Use People: The Other Side of Opinion Leadership," in Richard J. Lutz, ed., *Advances in Consumer Research*

13 (Provo, UT: Association for Consumer Research, 1986), pp. 301–5, Ronald E. Goldsmith, Melvin T. Stith, and J. Dennis White, "Race and Sex Differences in Self-Identified Innovativeness and Opinion Leadership," *Journal of Retailing* 63, Winter 1987, pp. 411–25. Pamela Kiecker and Cathy L. Hartman, "Predicting Buyers' Selection of Interpersonal Sources: The Role of Strong Ties and Weak Ties," in Chris T. Allen and Deborah Roedder John, eds., *Advances in Consumer Research* 21 (Provo, UT: Association for Consumer Research, 1994), pp. 464–69.

26 Eric Von Hippel, *Novel Product Concepts from Lead Users: Segmenting Users by Experience* (Cambridge, MA: Marketing Science Institute, 1984), Report No. 84–109.

27 Adapted from Tara Parker-Pope, "Will the British Warm Up to Iced Tea? Some Big Marketers Are Counting on It," *The Wall Street Journal,* (August, 22, 1994), p. B-1.

28 For further reading, see Frank M. Bass, "A New Product Growth Model for Consumer Durables," *Management Science,* 15 (January 1969), 215–27.

29 This section is adapted from Jagdish N. Sheth, "Psychology of Innovation Resistance: The Less Developed Concept (LDC) in Diffusion Research," *Research in Marketing* 4 (Greenwich, CT: Jai Press Inc., 1981), pp. 273–82.

30 Everett M. Rogers, "New Product Adoption and Diffusion," in R. Ferber, ed., *Selected Aspects of Consumer Behavior,* Washington, D.C.: NSF Government Printing Office, 1977, pp. 223–38, Everett M. Rogers, "Diffusion of Innovations," 3rd ed. (New York: Free Press, 1983), p. 281–84.

31 Also see S. Ram and Jagdish N. Sheth, "Hurdling the Barriers to Technological Innovation," *R&D Strategist* (Fall 1990), pp. 4–14; Pam Scholder Ellen, William O. Bearden, and Subhash Sharma, "Resistance to Technological Innovations: An Examination of the Role of Self-Efficacy and performance Satisfaction," *Journal of the Academy of Marketing Science* 19, no. 4, (Fall 1991), pp. 297–307.

32 Susan Kitchell, "Corporate Culture, Environmental Adaptation, and Innovation Adoption: A Qualitative/Quantitative Approach," *Journal of the Academy of Marketing Science* 23 no. 3 (Summer 1995), pp. 195–205.

CHAPTER 10

After reading this chapter you should be able to:

Illustrate the motivational process and summarize how it guides customer approach or avoidance behavior.

List types of needs that motivate customer behavior.

Summarize how emotions motivate behavior of both household and business customers.

Classify basic human emotions that influence customer behavior.

Distinguish customer moods and tell what role they play in influencing customer behavior.

Define psychographics and explain how they motivate customer behavior.

Describe how marketers use psychographics to identify and profile diverse customer groups.

Customer Attitudes: Cognitive and Affective

Santa Claus Arrested in Midtown Manhattan—For Showing an Attitude

During a recent Christmas shopping season, a small crowd of labor unionists and workers had assembled in front of Lord & Taylor department store in midtown Manhattan. They were protesting the sweatshop conditions prevalent in many of the garment manufacturing shops whose products Lord and Taylor was selling. Among these protesters was a Santa Claus, who, instead of working as Santa Claus, had decided to voice his antibusiness attitude.

For nearly six months, the press in North America had been abuzz with the exposé of sweatshop conditions in the garment industry. The catalyst event was a U.S. Department of Labor (DOL) discovery the preceding April that Wal-Mart's "Kathie Lee" line of clothing was manufactured by underpaid, underage workers in Honduras as well as in New York. The Honduras factory employed young children, who worked up to 13 hours a day for "starvation wages." Similarly, the manufacturer subcontractor in New York was found to employ immigrant workers off the books, to pay them less than minimum wages, and to pay them no overtime for work up to 60 hours a week.

Although stories of child-labor exploitation were not new, this particular story had become the talk of the media due to Kathie Lee Gifford's sweet TV talk show persona of an emotional, caring, and empathizing celebrity. Overnight, a vocal and indignant outrage had ensued. Gifford pleaded ignorance—she had started endorsing for Kraft Foods at the age of 17, and she didn't think, she said, that "I had to go check out the cows"!—but the hate mail continued. Ultimately, she decided to mandate independent monitoring for her line of clothing, and this obliged Wal-Mart to sever ties with the Honduran and New York factories, and to announce a new code of conduct for all its subcontractors.

Indeed, Gifford herself turned into an antisweatshop crusader. At the 1996 fashion industry summit conference in Washington, D.C., she joined then Labor Secretary Robert Reich's renewed call to fashion retailers to shun sweatshops. And in July 1996, she appeared before U.S. Congress to testify in support of Representative Christopher Smith's bill designed to clamp down on imports made in sweatshops. In these acts of child protection, Kathie Lee was echoing customer attitudes: In a study completed just before the Wal-Mart story broke, 74 percent of the women surveyed had reported believing in banning products made from child

And exploitation of child labor is the last thing Santa Claus would like. More than anyone else, Santa is the symbol of "love the children" attitudes customers hold around the world. These and other customer attitudes are at the heart of the very survival for businesses.

Source: Adapted from "Provide Women with Apparel Manufacturer Ethical Labor Standards Labels," *About Women and Marketing*, 10, no. 2, (February 1997), p. 8; Andrew Ross, "An Unfashionable Cause," www.feedmag.com/97.01ross/97.01ross.html

Introduction

Do you prefer Coke or Pepsi? Are you in favor of banning cigarette advertising? Do you think a "flat income tax" is a good idea or a bad idea? Should funding for space research be curtailed? On a test, would you rather answer true/false questions or essay questions? Who is your favorite teacher? And do you agree or disagree with the statement "there is a grade inflation in American colleges and universities today"? All these questions are designed to elicit your *attitudes*. Your answers are a window on understanding and knowing you as a person, as well as a tool for predicting some of your behavior. Because marketers are interested in predicting customer behavior, they are extremely interested in knowing customer attitudes about their product and service and other elements of the marketing mix.

This chapter introduces the current state of marketing knowledge about attitudes. First, we define and discuss *attitude* as a global concept. Next, we present a three-component view of attitude and discuss three hierarchies in which the three components are organized. Following this, we discuss various strategies of influencing customer attitudes, utilizing our knowledge of how the three components are interrelated. This description of attitude influence strategies is then followed by an explanation of the underlying psychological processes and the various theories that capture these processes. Next, we discuss a class of models (called multiattribute models) that account for how customers might combine several beliefs about something into a global attitude. In one of these models, we also discuss how global attitude combines with social pressures to produce customer action. Next, we discuss the functional theory of attitude. Knowing what functions an attitude serves will help us understand the deeper motivation of customer attitudes. Finally, we discuss a special application of attitudes to marketing—namely, how to utilize knowledge of customer attitudes in order to plan social change. In the concluding section, we outline the relevance of various topics covered in this chapter to each of the three customer roles.

Attitude: Definition and Characteristics

To fully understand the significance of attitudes, let us first review a classic definition of attitudes, offered by psychologist Gordon Allport:

> **Attitudes** are learned predispositions to respond to an object or class of objects in a consistently favorable or unfavorable way.[1]

This definition has several implications:

- Attitudes are learned. That is, they get formed on the basis of some experience with or information about the object.
- Attitudes are predispositions. As such they reside in the mind.
- Attitudes cause consistent response. They precede and produce behavior.

Therefore, attitudes can be used to predict behavior. Thus, for example, if we know that your attitude toward a candidate in some election is positive, then we could predict that you are likely to vote for that candidate. Or if you have a positive attitude toward saving the environment, then we could predict that you are likely to engage in recycling and buying environmentally friendly products. Marketers therefore use attitude measures before launching new products. For example, if you show a favorable attitude toward a new product concept, then marketers predict that when the new product is made available, you are likely to buy it.

Alternatively, behavior can be used to infer the underlying attitudes. In everyday life, we observe somebody's behavior toward us and use that observation to infer whether that person likes us; we then use that inferred attitude to predict how the person will behave toward us in the future. Marketers, too, often use this logic. When customers buy a product, this purchase behavior is used to infer a favorable attitude toward the related product class, which is in turn deemed to be an indicator of the potential purchase of an item in the related product class. For example, if you buy a ticket for a fine arts show, marketers infer that you have a favorable attitude toward fine arts; a fund-raising letter is then sent to you in the hope that your attitude (inferred to be favorable) toward the fine arts implies support for the arts in general.

Attitudes as Evaluations

Attitudes, then, are our evaluations of objects—people, places, brands, products, organizations, and so on. People evaluate in terms of their goodness, likability, or desirability. As such, it is easy to measure attitudes by getting customers to rate statements such as the following:

Please check how you feel about Olestra, [a fat substitute used as a cooking medium by Procter & Gamble for its line of snack products]:

I dislike Olestra very much   ☐ ☐ ☐ ☐ ☐ I like it very much.

Toward Olestra, I feel unfavorably   ☐ ☐ ☐ ☐ ☐ I feel favorably.

My opinion about Olestra is: Negative ☐ ☐ ☐ ☐ ☐ Positive

Attitudes are held by customers both in household and business markets. In household markets, many customers hold an attitude toward salespersons in general (for example, "Salespeople are basically all hucksters"), about specific companies (such as "Company X is a company that makes good electronic appliances but not computers"). In business markets, business customers hold attitudes about their suppliers—both toward a class of vendors and toward specific vendors. For example, a business customer might hold an unfavorable attitude toward off-shore companies or toward vendors as a group (e.g., "Vendors are, in general, opportunistic").

Three-Component Model of Attitude

The previous view of attitude as an overall evaluation of objects treats attitude as a single dimensional "global" concept. This view informs us how a person feels in overall terms about an object, but not why he or she feels that way, or what underlies that specific attitude. Psychologists have identified three underlying dimensions to global attitude: knowledge, feeling, and action. That is, when we hold an attitude about an object, typically it is based on some knowledge and beliefs about the object. We feel some positive or negative emotion toward it, and we want to act in a certain way toward it—either embracing it or

Figure 11.1 A THREE-COMPONENT MODEL OF ATTITUDES

Conation
(Action)

Affect
(Feelings)

Cognition
(Thoughts)

spurning it, for example. In this view, the three components of attitude are called cognitive, affective, and conative. See Figure 11.1

Cognitions or thoughts about brands or objects are also called beliefs. More specifically, **beliefs** are expectations as to what something is or is not or what something will or will not do. Statements of belief connect an object (person, brand, store, etc.) to an attribute or benefit. Accordingly, a **brand belief** is a thought about a specific property or quality of the brand.

There are three types of beliefs: descriptive, evaluative, and normative. **Descriptive beliefs** connect an object or person to a quality or outcome. The following sentences are examples:

- This computer has a large memory.
- This computer system will handle all our network needs.
- This airline is often late.
- This store never has any stockouts.

Evaluative beliefs connect an object to personal likes or dislikes, preferences, and perceptions. The following statements express evaluative beliefs:

- This computer is very user-friendly.
- This airline makes it easy to do business with.
- The service at this store is outrageous.

Normative beliefs invoke moral and ethical judgments in relation to someone's acts, as in the following examples:

- Cigarette companies should not advertise in a way that would appeal to youth.
- It is unfair for businesses to take advantage of innocent customers.
- People should not buy foreign-made goods.

Table 11.1	ILLUSTRATIVE MEASURES OF THE THREE-COMPONENT MODEL OF ATTITUDE

ATTITUDE OBJECT

ATTITUDE COMPONENT	DHL, FOR SHIPPING A BUSINESS'S SMALL PACKAGES	SHOPPING FOR AIRLINE TICKETS ON THE INTERNET
Cognitions or Beliefs	■ DHL is very reliable in its service ■ DHL is more economical than other package carrier services. ■ DHL is able to customize its service to my shipping needs.	■ For my airline tickets, shopping on the Internet is very convenient. ■ You can find the cheapest fares by shopping on the Internet. ■ Internet-based travel agents do not offer you a comprehensive set of airline and flight options.
Affect or Feelings	■ When I ship by DHL, I feel secure. ■ I am very happy to be using DHL for my shipping needs. ■ I don't care if DHL goes out of business.	■ Shopping on the Internet is: (please circle as many as apply) Totally cool Boring Confusing A pain in the neck I like it I hate it.
Conations or Actions	■ I use DHL for my shipping more than I use other carriers. ■ I am often recommending DHL to other business associates. ■ I am looking for alternative carriers.	■ I have used the Internet for my travel airline tickets recently. ■ I often search the Internet for planning my travel itinerary.

Affect is the feelings a person has toward an object or the emotions that object evokes for the person.

Finally, **conation** is the action a person wants to take toward the object.

Table 11.1 presents examples of each attitude component for attitudes about two services. Researchers can measure attitudes by asking respondents to rate how well each statement describes them or their beliefs.

HIERARCHIES IN ATTITUDE

If attitudes have three components, we need to know how, if at all, they are related. Do you think first and then act, or do you act first and think afterwards? Or, when you see a person, product, brand, store, or any other object, do you just feel a sudden burst of emotion immediately, and then you might think about it or act on it?

Marketers have addressed these questions by looking for an attitude hierarchy. **Attitude hierarchy** refers to the sequence in which the three components occur.

LEARNING HIERARCHY   The most commonly discussed hierarchy is the learning hierarchy. In the **learning hierarchy,** cognitions come first, affect next, and action last. (See Figure 11.2.) That is, you think first, feel next, and act last. The learning hierarchy assumes that brand beliefs underlie our feelings toward the brand. Brand beliefs lead to brand feelings, which then cause brand purchase and use (or avoidance).

Consider an example. Let us say that you need to decide where to go for spring break: Panama City; Florida; Los Angeles; Cancun; or Steamboat Springs, Colorado. You find out how far these places are in terms of the travel time, the cost of travel, and what a hotel room will cost. What activities does each site offer? Can you do snorkeling there, or white

Figure 11.2

LEARNING HIERARCHY OF ATTITUDE

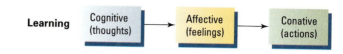

water rafting? Or would you have opportunities to ski? Is there a casino? Or whatever other information you want to consider. Then after thinking over all this information, you reach a judgment about which destination will be good for you, whether you like Los Angeles better or Panama City, whether the idea of going to Cancun excites you or not, or whether it is Steamboat Springs that you really feel the urge to go to. Based on these feelings, you then choose one of these four destinations. If you use the learning hierarchy, that is how you develop your attitude and behavior toward things that you encounter in life. Or that is how you are supposed to. We call this learning hierarchy a "rational" hierarchy.

EMOTIONAL HIERARCHY "But wait a minute," you might say. "The last time I decided on my spring break plan—well, what happened was that we were with a bunch of friends watching this show on cable TV, called *MTV Spring Break*; it was basically a live scene from Panama City Beach, where lots and lots of college students were having one big party on the beach. And we said, 'That is it. That is where we are going.'"

This description of your attitude feelings, action, and thoughts toward the Panama City Beach illustrates a different process, the **emotional hierarchy** of attitude. Here you *feel* first, then act, and think last. Based on your emotions—attraction or repulsion toward certain brands or persons or things—you embrace or avoid them, buy them, use them. Finally, through experience, you learn more about them. Thus, in this hierarchy, affect comes first, conation next, and cognition last. (See Figure 11.3.)

Of course, these hierarchies are not limited to your decisions as an individual consumer; they happen just as much for business customers. The same scenarios could be observed, for example, for a business manager choosing a site for the next national sales meeting. The manager could follow the rational route, choosing the site primarily on cost considerations, for example. Alternatively, she could follow an emotional route, choosing the site primarily based on the lure of the place.

LOW-INVOLVEMENT HIERARCHY The learning and emotional hierarchies are *high-involvement hierarchies* because the attitude object generates high involvement. As we defined *involvement* in Chapter 10, it can be viewed as the degree of importance of an object to you. It is the stakes you have in the object. It is how much owning the object matters to you. The spring break site is a high-involvement object for you if it is very important to you that you not waste the time in some substandard, less desirable place. The spring break site is not something you want to acquire an attitude toward *casually or cursorily*. Rather, you want to have the attitude that you can feel confident about, you can

Figure 11.3

EMOTIONAL HIERARCHY OF ATTITUDE

تناول عصير
الطماطم (البندورة)
مخلوطا بعصير
البرتقال او تناول
حبوب فيتامين ـ سي ،
هو افضل طريقة
لحماية المدخنين من
الاصابة بمرض
السرطان. هذا ما
يقوله البروفيسور
جورج تراسكوت
العالم الانكليزي
واختصاصي الكيمياء
في جامعة كيل
البريطانية

للمدخنين فقط

Would you still like to smoke? An emotional appeal to attitude change.

feel committed to. When you say you like Cancun and that is where you want to go, you want to be sure that is how you really feel and that is what you really want to do—no matter whether you reached this attitude state via the rational or the emotional hierarchy.

In contrast is the *low-involvement* mode. Here, not much is at stake, and it would not matter much if your attitude happened to be wrong. These are matters of relatively low importance in your life that you could take or leave. With these, you don't want to take the time to think, nor do you particularly feel strongly positive or negative about them. For these matters, then, the hierarchy is called a "low-involvement attitude hierarchy." **Low-involvement attitude hierarchy** refers to the sequence in which the three attitude components occur in a person's acquisition of attitude toward objects that are of low salience or importance to the consumer in his or her life. This model has the sequence of conation, affect, cognition, as shown in Figure 11.4.

Suppose that you are in the neighborhood bakery and you notice a new kind of bread—it has multigrains and some seeds in it, and the appearance looks inviting. The bread is new, so you don't have an attitude toward it. Now what do you do before you buy

• more typical →

LOW-INVOLVEMENT HIERARCHY OF ATTITUDE

Figure 11.4

| Low involvement | Conation (actions) | → | Affect (feelings) | → | Cognition (thoughts) |

it? Do you have to know a whole lot about it? Not really. Do you have to say, "Now, let me see; do I really, really feel attracted to it?" Not likely. Thus, neither the rational nor the emotional hierarchy is likely to apply. Instead, what you are likely to do is just put it in your shopping basket and bring it home. And you take the first bite and you say that it is good and that you like it. Then you pause to feel what grains it has and what flavor it has, and then maybe you even read the ingredients label and the nutrition information. Thus, in this case of a low-involvement product, action comes first. Basically, the customer tries the product first and then feels good or bad about it, and takes note of its features or qualities (i.e., forms brand beliefs). Thus, action comes first, feelings next, and cognitions or thoughts last.

Two clarifications are in order. One, involvement is not a property of the product or service; rather it is the view or importance of it to a customer. Thus, the same product could be low involving for some and high involving for others. In our example, bread could indeed be a high-involvement product for some consumers. These consumers will then first read the label and try to learn as much as possible about the bread. Based on this information, they will like it or not like it, and then, based on this feeling, they will choose to buy it or not. That, of course, is the high-involvement attitude acquisition process described earlier.

The second clarification is that involvement is not dichotomous (a strict choice between very high and very low). Rather it is a matter of degree. The low-involvement hierarchy occurs at the very low-involvement end when something is utterly of no consequence to the consumer. In the middle range, the high-involvement hierarchies occur, but with less intensity of processing. The emotional hierarchy still begins with affect, but at the middle range it is likely to begin with a mood rather than deep emotion. And the rational hierarchy is still relevant, except that instead of the extensive cognitions of the high-involvement condition, fewer cognitions will drive the affects. This is why relatively lower-involvement products are advertised by citing only one or two features. (See Figure 11.5.)

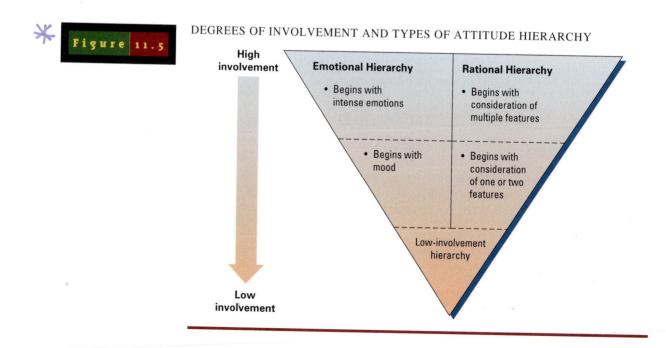

Figure 11.5

DEGREES OF INVOLVEMENT AND TYPES OF ATTITUDE HIERARCHY

High involvement

Emotional Hierarchy

- Begins with intense emotions

- Begins with mood

Rational Hierarchy

- Begins with consideration of multiple features

- Begins with consideration of one or two features

Low-involvement hierarchy

Low involvement

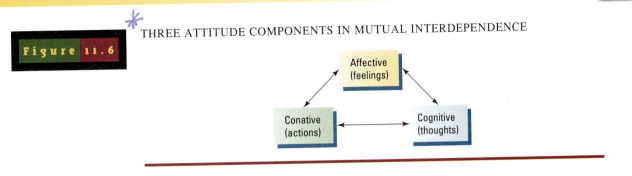

Figure 11.6   ✻ THREE ATTITUDE COMPONENTS IN MUTUAL INTERDEPENDENCE

✱CONSISTENCY AMONG THE THREE COMPONENTS

Although the three components develop in terms of hierarchies, they imply one another. A person tries to make the three components consistent and to maintain consistency among them. Certain cognitions inevitably give rise to certain affect and certain action tendencies, and vice versa.

The consistency can be related to two factors: valence and intensity. **Attitude valence** refers to favorable and unfavorable thoughts, feelings, and actions. Thus, favorable cogitions will be associated with positive affect, and unfavorable cogitions with negative affect, regardless of the sequence in which they might have arisen initially. Likewise, favorable action tendencies will be associated with positive affect and positive cognitions. If one of them needs to be modified, then the other components will need to be modified as well. For example, suppose that you have recently tried a new kind of multigrain bread, and after several uses, you don't like its taste anymore; then you will have to modify some cogitions (e.g., "The grains don't really taste as good as they first did"), and conation too (e.g., "I won't buy it in the future").

The second dimension on which the three components have to be consistent is intensity: the *strength* with which they occur. Some beliefs are strong; others weak. Likewise, some feelings are deep; others mild. Finally, there is strong action commitment toward some things and "take it or leave it" stance toward others. **Attitude strength** refers to the degree of commitment one feels toward a cognition or feeling or action. Just as on valence, so too on strength: the three components have to be balanced. Strong beliefs produce strong feelings and very committed action tendencies, and vice versa.

Since these three components must be mutually consistent, regardless of their initial sequence or hierarchy, they continue to mold one another. Accordingly, it is informative to depict them as mutually interdependent and mutually influential. Thus, in contrast to the previous hierarchy models, Figure 11.6 shows the arrows going in both directions among all three of the components.

Molding Customer Attitudes

The two dimensions of consistency have implications for how marketers may help mold customer attitudes. Since the three components are mutually consistent, it is possible to mold an attitude (all three components) by first molding or changing any component. By **attitudes molding,** we mean both helping to form an attitude where none existed before and changing a pre-existing attitude. Accordingly, there are three avenues of attitude molding: (1) via cognitive change, (2) via affective change, and (3) via behavior change.

Cognitive Route to Attitude Molding

To follow the cognitive route, the marketer provides an association (i.e., Brand A has property X) about the product or service; if the consumer accepts that association, then a brand belief is formed. Brand belief is a unit of thought that associates a brand with a property: for example, that Head and Shoulders brand of shampoo is really effective in eliminating dandruff, or that Amul brand of butter is the best tasting butter available in India, or that Makino brand of hydraulic controls are very reliable. When a brand belief is formed, the cognitive component of attitude is formed. This component then produces compatible affective and conative components. The same process works in altering a cognition if the customer already had one—that is, if you give the customer new facts on something, he or she would likely change his or her old beliefs.

A couple of examples will clarify. Suppose you knew nothing about soya, a Chinese food crop. If we were to tell you that soya is a good source of protein, then you acquired a new belief about soya (cognitive attitude *formation*). Or suppose you thought that a potato is fattening and has no good qualities. Now, suppose we were to tell you that it is fattening only when fried (as in potato chips or french fries) and not by itself and that, further, it has much-needed carbohydrates. This is likely to change your prior beliefs about potatoes (cognitive attitude *change*). Or suppose that as a buying agent in a German firm, you thought that electronic machinery from, say, South Korea or Malaysia would be of poor quality, though cheap. If you then read a report that an independent test had ranked the South Korean or Malaysia-made electronic machinery among the highest-quality products, these cognitive attitude changes will then induce affective and conative attitude changes. You would begin to have a favorable opinion about soya and potatoes and about electronic equipment from South Korea or Malaysia. And you would tend to include soya and potatoes in your diet and be inclined to buy electronic equipment from South Korea or Malaysia.

Affective Route to Attitude Molding

The marketer may also mold attitudes by attempting to create an emotional connection with the consumer in the context of the product or service being promoted. (See the Window on Research box for an example.) Domestic marketers of both household and industrial products could appeal to a sense of patriotism. Products such as soft drinks, colognes, and food are often presented with mood-inducing upbeat music. Luxury models of cars are paraded as rewards for hard work and symbols of accomplishment to the user, and cost-efficient cars as testimony to wisdom and financial prudence of the payer, even in corporate settings, by showing the choice of the financially prudent executives. Some car models appeal to the customer's sense of exploration and fun, shown by the Saab campaign titled "find your own road." For business customers, IBM had long played upon what came to be known as "the FUD factor"—fear, uncertainty, and doubt, promoting its computers as the safest bet. Recently, a package carrier company utilized the scene of a harassed business executive being the target of scorn by other executives who were shown shocked by their colleague's foolishness in *not* sending the package by the advertiser's firm ("You didn't send it by—?" was the dismayed reaction). These all exemplify strategies of attitude change by first changing the affective or emotional component.

What Makes Kids Think Smokers Are Cool?

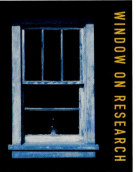

"Please look at this ad, and then tell us if you still think smokers are cool."

Is it possible to change customers' attitudes toward something—a product, service, or category of persons—by giving them information on the undesirable aspects of it? Is it possible, for example, to modify adolescents' attitudes toward smoking and smokers by exposing them to antismoking messages in advertising? This question was researched in a pair of studies by attitude researchers Cornelia Pechman and S. Ratneshwar of University of California at Irvine and University of Florida, respectively.

In study 1, Pechman and Ratneshwar showed seventh graders either antismoking advertisements, smoking advertisements, or advertisements not related to smoking. Each seventh grader saw only one type of advertisements, and research participants were randomly assigned to see one of these ads. The ads were embedded in a mock up magazine, and the research was presented as an evaluation of the magazine.

After rating the magazines, respondents participated in a second study. A computer presented information about an unnamed person. This student (Student A) was described to all the respondents as having three habits: watches TV, rides a bike, and goes to the mall. The interesting twist on this research design was that half of the seventh graders in each of the three groups from study 1 were told of only these three habits, while the other half were additionally informed that Student A was a smoker. All the participants were told certain traits of Student A; the traits were a mix of positive and negative traits, and every seventh grader was told the same traits.

Did the viewing of the antismoking ads in study 1 affect participants' perceptions of Student A when Student A was described as a smoker versus a nonsmoker? Pechman and Ratneshwar measured this by asking participants to rate Student A on such characteristics as smart, intelligent, healthy, grown-up, mature, good-looking, attractive, exciting, adventuresome, popular, has friends, and cool. They were also asked whether they (the seventh graders) might personally like the target. The results? Seventh graders who had seen the antismoking ads rated Student A much lower when Student A was described as a smoker than when he or she was described as a nonsmoker. This deterioration in the rating of Student A was much greater for the participants who had seen the antismoking ads than for those who had seen either the pro-smoking ads or the smoking unrelated ads.

It is worth noting that each student saw only one type of ad and was asked to rate only one "instance" of Student A. Thus, each seventh grader was totally unaware of the experimental manipulation (that Student 'A' is being presented in two different ways). Second, seventh graders were also unaware that the two studies were related (they were conducted by different research staff). Finally, rather than seek reactions to the ads or to the idea of smoking, researchers measured consumer reactions to a person who happened to be a smoker or a nonsmoker.

This clever research procedure went to the heart of the issue in antismoking advertising: Can antismoking advertising shape adolescents' long-term attitude toward smokers so that they don't view smokers in attractive terms as the cigarette advertising purports to show? The answer, based on this research, is a reassuring "yes."

Source: See Cornelia Pechman and S. Ratneshwar, "Advertising versus Prior Beliefs: Does Cigarette and Antismoking Advertising Alter Young Adolescents' Perceptions of Smokers?" *Report No.* 93–125, December 1993 (Cambridge, MA: Marketing Science Institute). Additional information available at **http://www.tobaccofreekids.org**

Saab creatively uses both emotional and rational appeal to mold attitudes toward its cars.

Conative Route to Attitude Molding

Finally, in this third approach, behavior is influenced directly, for example, by free product sampling or by giving incentives such as rebates, coupons, and discounted price. Once the behavior is influenced (e.g., the consumer buys a brand due to coupons), the cognitions and feelings will fall in place. Methods of influencing the customer's behavior directly are incentives, structuring the physical environment, business procedures, government mandates, and information structuring. Part of the appeal of this approach is that it can be easier to get someone to try a sample (or mandate that they do something) than to convince them to think or feel in a new way. "Just try it," we urge, confident that the experience will win the person over.

INCENTIVES

As already mentioned, special price promotions, coupons, rebates, and so on, are a frequently used means of inducing the desired behavior. Many people donate clothing and furniture to charity simply because of the financial rewards in getting tax write-offs. In the supermarket, customers tilt their purchase actions toward the brands on sale. Cars sell more when the cash rebates are announced. Three cases of behavioral change due to incentives can be distinguished:

1. In low-involvement choices, such as for many supermarket items, where the customer has no preference for one brand or the other and hasn't thought much, he or she buys the brand on sale.

2. If a product is not necessarily low in involvement per se, but two or more brands are comparable and the customer is equally likely to buy either of them, the price incentive would channel the behavior for many. For example, some people buy either Coca-Cola or Pepsi Cola, depending on which brand is on sale during a particular week.

3. If the attitude is already favorable but not yet strong enough to impel action, the financial incentive gives that extra push; it tilts the customer preference toward the brand with the incentive. Cash rebates on cars are an example. A consumer doesn't buy just any car because of a rebate; rather, only the car he or she was already considering buying.

• STRUCTURING THE PHYSICAL ENVIRONMENT

The physical facility surrounding the customer may be designed to induce behavior directly, either as an impulse purchase or as subconscious behavior.[2] Examples of the former are the display of candies, magazines, or novelties in the checkout lines in the supermarket, or need-arousing sensory display of food and beverage items (such as in-store displays of ice-cold bottles of the beverage brand Fruitopia in open containers filled with ice on a hot summer afternoon). Examples of physical environments designed to induce subconscious behaviors are store designs that are inviting, with pleasing colors, spaciousness of aisles, and lighting conditions. Other examples include the plastic seating in fast-food restaurants purported to discourage lingering, but bright, sprightly colors in Taco Bell restaurants, encouraging "hanging out" by youthful customers.

In an experiment by consumer researcher Ronald E. Milliman, a supermarket played fast-paced music on certain days and slow-paced music on certain other days.[3] The days of fast and slow music were "rotated" so that each type of music was played on each of the weekdays (i.e., say, on Wednesday of one week fast music was played and on Wednesday of the next week slow music was played, and the same with other weekdays or weekend days). Guess what happened to customer behavior? Compared to fast-paced music days, on slow-paced music days, customers themselves moved with a slower pace, spent more time in the store and had a larger average bill! And all of this occurred without awareness that they were doing so. This strategy of molding behavior is called **ecological design.**

• GOVERNMENT MANDATES

An important means of eliciting some desired behaviors is *government mandates*.[4] Making consumption or disconsumption mandatory might be the only means available when (1) consumers lack the knowledge/competence to judge their own interests (e.g., automobile insurance policies and seatbelts are examples of mandated consumption, and a smoking ban is an example of mandated disconsumption); and, (2) individual benefits are remote and are outweighed by collective public benefits, such as with recycling, observing speed limits, using unleaded gasoline.[5]

For compliance with government mandates to occur, behavioral prescriptions should be specified, and there should be enforcement mechanisms to ensure conformance. Note that the enforcement mechanisms seldom need to be invoked—the possibility of their use usually brings people into compliance.

Examples include vehicle registration renewal, the wearing of helmets by motorcycle riders, and in-store behavioral prescriptions backed by surveillance equipment. Among business "customers," many workplace environment and hiring practices are followed because of the presence of possible legal enforcement. Other examples are state regulation of building codes to include installation of smoke detectors and fire equipment, prohibition of the sale of liquor to minors, the law against highway littering, speeding, and so on.

• BUSINESS PROCEDURES

Customer behaviors can also be modified by business procedures.[6] Marketers mold customer behavior by instituting business procedures that prescribe certain behaviors and by prominently bringing them to customers' attention. These behavioral prescriptions include store hours of operations, which "force" customers to shop during certain hours; by "take a number" queue-management procedure, visibility of in-store surveillance devices, merchandise layaway procedures for unclaimed items, tow-away signs, and eligibility conditions for compensation by airlines for denied boarding (e.g., the required lead-time for check-in). Another example is the group health-insurance plans sold to employers, which then "force" all employees to participate in their health maintenance according to the prescribed schedule and options (such as "You cannot visit an out-of-network physician without approval").

INFORMATION STRUCTURING

In contrast to environmental structuring, where the physical environment is "structured," information can be structured in such a way as to "channel" the customer behavior toward the desired target. This method also differs from business procedures and government mandates, where the desired behavior is simply prescribed, without explanation. In contrast, information structuring emphasizes presenting the information that would make the person see the benefits of the desired behavior. Some salesmen or retailers adopt the practice of selectively presenting information—such as declaring the item as being the last one in stock, or display the store brand in conjunction only with those brands that would make the store brand seem a better choice.

We must note that some of these procedures may tend to be unethical (especially the one where a salesperson misinforms the customer). Moreover, it may also be self-defeating. If a customer later finds out that the information was misrepresented, the customer may not come back.

FOOT-IN-THE-DOOR VERSUS DOOR-IN-THE-FACE A particularly interesting variant of this "information structuring" method is what has been called the twin procedures of "foot-in-the-door" and "door-in-the-face" methods (see Figure 11.7). In the **foot-in-the-door strategy,** the customer is first asked for a small favor. Since the favor is really small, the customer typically complies, even if unenthusiastically. Later, he or she is asked for a somewhat bigger favor. Research has found that when a favor is presented after a small request, the bigger request is generally granted more often (or by more customers) than if the bigger request had been made at the outset. An example of this is charity organizations' seeking help from volunteers and donors. Typically, they begin by asking for small help, too small to be refused, and then follow it up by a subsequent appeal for larger assistance.

The opposite to the foot-in-the-door is the **door-in-the-face strategy.** Here the first request is large, almost certainly to be refused (hence called "door-in-the-face"). This is then followed by a much smaller request. The assumption is that the customer would have denied the smaller request, except that he or she feels bad, maybe even a little guilty, about the first refusal. That feeling increases the chances of the second request being granted.

Researchers have used both of these techniques in getting customers to respond to their surveys. In the foot-in-the-door approach, the researcher would typically request customers to answer a very short survey on the phone. Later, a longer survey is mailed. Research has found that customers who had the opportunity to participate in the smaller survey first were much more likely to answer the second, longer survey.

To implement the opposite approach, survey researchers would first ask if the customer would participate in a research study requiring a significant amount of time and effort. When refused, he or she then makes a "counter offer"—would the customer please at

TWO VARIATIONS OF INFORMATION STRUCTURING

Figure 11.7

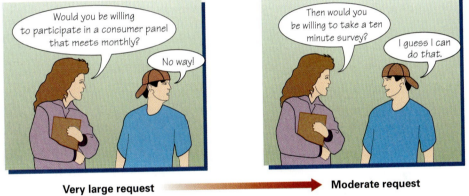

Foot-in-the-Door Strategy

Small request ⟶ Larger request

Door-in-the-Face Strategy

Very large request ⟶ Moderate request

least fill out a short survey? Again, according to the research studies done on this topic, the short survey (which, incidentally, is all that the researcher wanted the customer to fill out in the first place) is answered by many more customers if they have first been asked to participate in a much larger study that they refused.[7]

While these studies are interesting and make sense, not much research has been done to identify the conditions under which one rather than the other approach would be much better. Consider a political campaign, for example. Let us suppose that you want a lot of potential voters who are undecided to come to a rally. You could either first ask them to become active campaign workers and participate in door-to-door canvassing. Upon being refused, you could then ask them at least to come to the rally. Alternatively, you could first ask them to just display a small sign in their front yard or ask them if they would please at least come out to greet the candidate when the candidate visits their neighborhood. That having been done, you could then ask them to come to the rally. Which approach would you follow? That depends on which theory you think is more effective in that particular case!

The Psychological Processes Underlying Attitude Change

The approaches to attitude molding or change are descriptions of what an external agent (such as the marketer) does to elicit the desired attitude changes. For example, the marketer provides information, presents emotion-arousing stimuli, structures the environment, imposes procedures or government mandates, and manages information. In response to such actions, certain *internal* (i.e., psychological) processes occur to produce these attitude changes. The effort to explain these processes has generated four major groups of theories:

1. Learning theories.

2. Attribution theory.

3. Cognitive consistency theories.

4. High- and low-involvement information processing.

• Learning Theories

The four learning theories described in Chapter 10 explain how attitudes are *formed*. In addition, learning is a pathway to attitude *change*. These four learning theories are classical conditioning, instrumental conditioning, modeling, and cognitive learning.

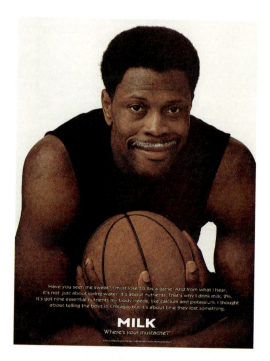

Got a negative attitude toward milk—that, somehow, it is not for the adult that you are? Look again. In this campaign by the National Fluid Milk Processor Promotion Board, the milk mustache has appeared on the lips of such celebrities as Danny Devito, Conan O'Brian, Bob Costas, Martha Stewart, Pete Sampras, Jennifer Aniston, Larry King, Dennis Rodman, and even Bill Clinton and Bob Dole. Shown here is U.S. basketball star Patrick Ewing, sporting the now famous milk mustache.

Classical conditioning methods can be used to "reposition" a brand by associating it with new celebrities and situations. Thus, milk was repositioned recently from an image of being a children's drink to being an adult drink by advertising that paired it with adult celebrities. This learning method is the explanation for (a) creating new associations (i.e., beliefs) by presenting the brand in constant conjunction with desired celebrities, situations, or user groups, (b) influencing the affective component directly by presenting emotional stimuli, such as the Saab campaign mentioned earlier; and, (c) environmental structuring method to influence behavior directly, which was described earlier.

Instrumental conditioning can also be used to change attitudes. For example, the marketer might offer frequent-use rewards on a previously disliked product or service. Also, giving a free sample induces initial behavior; the outcome of this behavior, if positive, is then instrumental in sustaining that behavior.

Similarly, modeling can change attitudes. For example, fashions come and go, and then they reappear. Their fast diffusion upon reappearance is a prime example of attitude change by modeling. This method creates desired association (e.g., "Clothing with the grunge look is cool"), and/or emotional arousal, such as the urge to wear clothes like rap musicians whose song lyrics feature themes of rebellion.

Finally, the cognitive learning method is a very potent method to alter attitudes because of its capacity to engage the attitude holder in a conscious re-examination of his or

Airwalk: Harnessing the model's coolness to get you to like its shoes.

One frequently observed customer behavior is that customers become more attentive to product or brand information after they have already bought the product. This is explained by the dissonance theory. Customers are looking for positive information to resolve their dissonance.

HEIDER'S BALANCE THEORY

According to **Heider's balance theory,** based on the principle of *cognitive consistency*, when a respected opinion leader endorses an issue not initially favored by a person, the person would either lower the opinion leader in his or her esteem or become more favorable toward the endorsed issue. If the issues are value laden and if the initial opinions are deeply negative, the endorser must be held in strong esteem to overcome the negative opinion.

An example of this strategy is presented in Figure 11.8. Suppose a consumer such as a college student (say, Mike) befriends his classmate (say, Jerry) and they become best friends. Mike is given to gambling. One day he learns that Jerry hates gambling. (In the figure, solid arrows show preexisting likes/dislikes; broken arrows are new likes/dislikes that just came to light). Now what is Mike to do? To reconcile the conflict of opinion with his best friend, Mike might give up gambling and form a new opinion of dislike toward gambling, as shown in the figure to the right. This, of course, is only one of the options. Alternatively, Mike might drop Jerry as his best friend.

Similarly, in business markets, consider a small company that buys machine tools from a Japanese supplier, believing that domestic machines are of poor quality. One day it

HEIDER'S BALANCE THEORY

Figure 11.8

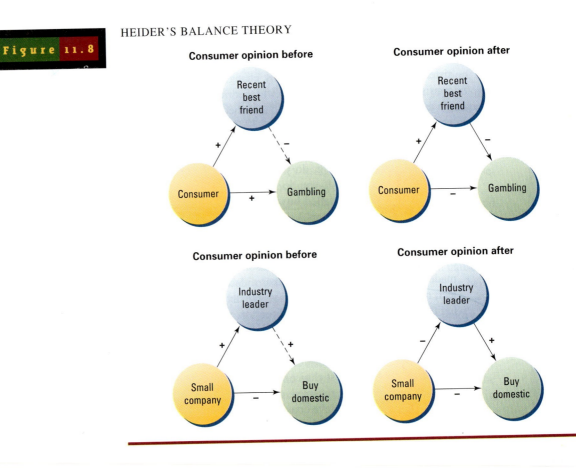

learns that the industry leader whom it respects actually patronizes a domestic supplier. As a result, then, it stops respecting the industry leader, at least as far as the latter's opinion about the quality of domestic supplier goes. Alternatively, of course, the firm could modify its opinion in favor of the domestic supplier.

High- and Low-Involvement Information-Processing Modes

Within the cognitive explanation of attitude formation and change, the second mode is the information-processing mode. When customers are exposed to an ad or other marketing communications, they process the information in either of the two modes: central or peripheral routes. In the **central processing route,** the customer attends to and scrutinizes message *content* actively and thoughtfully. This has been termed *Elaboration Likelihood model* (ELM). The consumer elaborates upon the message to examine and interpret it. Therefore, the quality of evidence presented to support the product claims plays a key role.

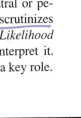

WINDOW ON RESEARCH

Central and Peripheral Routes to Attitude Formation

To test the occurrence of central and peripheral routes to attitude formation, psychologists Richard E. Petty, John T. Cacioppo, and David Schumann did an experimental research. They prepared an ad booklet containing 10 ads: some familiar, others new. The sixth ad was for a fictitious brand (brand name "Edge") of shaving razor blades. This sixth ad was different in two versions of the booklet: In one booklet, the ad featured a famous endorser (e.g. "Professional athletes agree . . .") and five strong and product relevant message arguments (e.g., "New advanced honing method creates unsurpassed sharpness). Special chemically formulated coating eliminates nicks and cuts; handle is tapered to prevent slipping; in tests, Edge blade gave twice as many close shaves; and unique angle placement of blade provides a smooth shave. The other version featured ordinary citizens and weak message arguments: floats in water without rusting; comes in various colors, sizes, and shapes; designed with bathroom in mind; in direct comparison tests, Edge gave no more than competition; and can only be used once but will be memorable. Half the respondents were given one version of the booklet, and the other half, the second version.

Subjects were placed in either the high-involvement or low-involvement mind-set (without the subjects realizing this) by telling them a cover story. Half of the respondents were told that the product would be available in their part of the country soon, while the other half were in-

formed the opposite. Furthermore, the first group was offered a free gift of a disposable razor, while the other group was offered a free gift of an unrelated product. The first group was called a high-involvement group and the second a low-involvement group.

After they had looked through the booklet, respondents answered a questionnaire pertaining to their evaluation of the advertised brands. Logically, the strong-arguments ad produced a more favorable brand attitude, but the absolute power of the argument's strength and quality was not under research here. What was of interest was how the low- and high-involvement groups differed in their attitude. The findings here were most fascinating: Strong arguments produced a positive attitude both among the low- and high-involvement groups; however, the weak arguments produced a more favorable attitude among the low-involvement group compared to the high-involvement group! The reason, argue Petty and Cacioppo, is that the weakness of the weak arguments was transparent only to high-involvement respondents, since only they processed the ad in the central route.

Source: Richard E. Petty, John T. Cacioppo, and David Schumann, "Central and Peripheral Routes to Advertising Effectiveness: The Moderating Role of Involvement," *Journal of Consumer Research*, Vol. 10 (September 1993), pp. 135–146.

In contrast, in the **peripheral processing route**, the consumer attends to the message only cursorily, and tends to make quick inferences by simply looking at the elements in the ad (such as the quality of music, the setting, spokesperson, and so on). The *form* of the message determines consumer attitude more than does the message substance.

When would you process a stimulus (e.g., an ad) in the central route versus in the peripheral route? This is easy to figure out. Suppose we were to tell you that there would be a quiz on this topic and an attractive prize for a good score. You would be likely to read this very carefully and process the information in the central route, deliberating and trying to understand it correctly. On the other hand, if you were just reading it with the knowledge that you will never have to use this information, then you would be attending to it in the peripheral processing route, forming whatever fleeting impressions the information might leave on you. Thus, the central route is followed in a high-involvement mode, and the peripheral route in a low-involvement mode. See the Window on Research box on page 407.

Multiattribute Models of Attitude

In the cognitive route to attitude change, how do various cognitions or beliefs about a product or brand combine to produce a global attitude? This question is answered by multiattribute models. The **multiattribute models of attitude** suggest that overall attitude is based on the component beliefs about the object, weighted by the evaluation of those beliefs. There are three such models: the Rosenberg model, the Fishbein model, and the extended Fishbein model.

The Rosenberg Model

The well-known psychologist Milton Rosenberg developed a model based on cognitive consistency theory. According to the **Rosenberg model,** an object may be instrumental in helping us achieve certain values (things that we value). Our attitude toward that object is a function of the extent to which the object is instrumental in obtaining various values, weighted by the relative importance to us of those values:

$$A_o = \sum_{j=1}^{n} I_j \times V_j$$

where A_o is the overall attitude toward the object, I is the importance of value j, V is the instrumentality of the object in obtaining value j, and n is the number of values.

Consider a business customer's attitude toward buying from a minority or domestic supplier. To find the customer's attitude, add together each of the values this behavior satisfies (e.g., patriotism, encouraging the disadvantaged, rewarding the spirit of enterprise, nurturance, and so on), weighted by the importance of the value to him or her.

The Fishbein Model

Martin Fishbein, a well-known scholar and a professor of psychology at the University of Illinois at Champaign-Urbana, tried to explain the formation of overall attitude by seeing the object as having a set of consequences, which could be desirable or undesirable. In the **Fishbein model,** attitude is the sum of these weighted consequences, where each conse-

Table 11.2

EXAMPLE OF CUSTOMER ATTITUDES: TWO INTERNET SERVICE PROVIDERS

EVALUATION OF ATTRIBUTE
(UNLIKELY 1 2 3 4 5 LIKELY)

ATTRIBUTE	AMERICA ONLINE	AT&T	EVALUATION OF CONSEQUENCES
1. Connection will be established successfully every time.	3	5	+3
2. The connection will be established speedily.	4	3	+2
3. The connection will be dropped in the middle of the session.	3	3	−3
4. The price (monthly fee) will be high.	2	5	−1

(Very bad −3 −2 −1 0 +1 +2 +3 Very good)

quence is weighted by the evaluation of that consequence (i.e., how good or bad that consequence is):

$$A_o = \sum_{i=1}^{n} B_i \times E_i$$

where A_o is the overall attitude toward the object,

B_i is the belief that object i has a certain consequence,

E_i is the evaluation of that consequence, and n is the number of consequences.

As an example, assume a customer rates two Internet service providers, America Online and AT&T, as shown in Table 11.2. Using the data from the table, we can compute the customer's attitude toward each service provider by using Fishbein's formula:

$$A_{AOL} = 3(3) + 2(4) + -3(3) + -1(2) = 6$$
$$A_{AT\&T} = 3(5) + 2(3) + -3(3) + -1(5) = 7$$

In this example, the customer's attitude toward both services is positive, but it is more positive toward AT&T. Other customers would have different perceptions about the four attributes, as well as different values for the attributes so that they would have different attitudes.

Fishbein's Extended Model of Behavioral Intention

Psychologist Martin Fishbein has also proposed an augmented model of attitude, which emphasizes behavior. **Fishbein's extended model** measures attitudes toward behaviors and defines the role of these attitudes in determining behaviors. Figure 11.9 is a schematic of this model. In general, a person's attitudes and subjective norms about a behavior lead to a behavioral intention, and that behavioral intention is the impetus for a behavior.

To examine this model in more detail, begin at the upper left of Figure 11.9. A person's beliefs about the consequences of a behavior, multiplied by his or her evaluation of the consequences, generate an attitude.

Figure 11.9

SCHEMATIC OF FISHBEIN'S EXTENDED MODEL

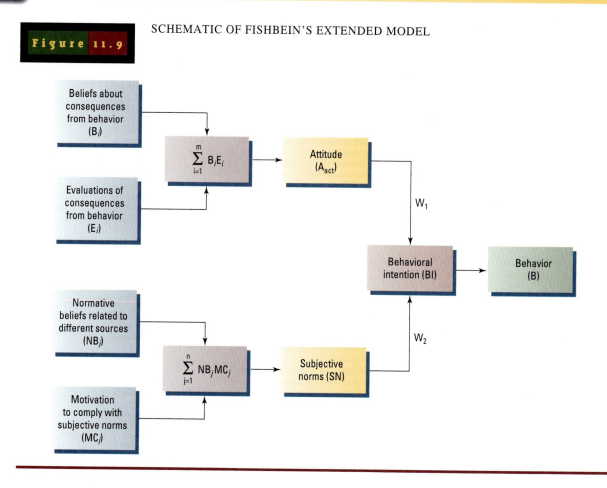

This is similar to the previous multiattribute model, except that the model is not concerned with attitude toward the object per se, but with attitude toward a specific *behavior*. This distinction is important in Fishbein's view because we may hold multiple attitudes toward different behaviors toward the *same* object. For example, suppose a city wants to build a new stadium for its football team and is holding a referendum on it. Now a person (1) may dislike the idea of a stadium, or (2) may approve of the stadium but does not like the idea of campaigning for it, (3) does not like to contribute to it, or (4) may not mind contributing but does not want a mandatory tax levy. Thus, rather than measuring customer attitude toward the stadium (or the idea of having it in the city), Fishbein's model measures attitude separately toward each of these behaviors in relation to the stadium.

Along with attitude, a person's behavior depends on social norms, called **subjective norms,** or others' desires or expectations from us. Thus, someone may *personally* have an unfavorable attitude toward giving donations to an abortion clinic, but may end up doing so due to the expectations of his or her co-workers or neighbors. Subjective norms are the product of beliefs about others' norms or expectations multiplied by one's motivation to comply with these norms (see the bottom left of Figure 11.9). In a business context, a purchasing agent might disregard the plant engineer's wishes concerning the vendor choice because there may be no motivation to comply with the plant engineer's wish.

To find the person's behavioral intention, the person's attitude and subjective norms are each weighted; then the two are added together. (For a particular situation, the weight would be obtained through empirical research.) Finally, the model uses behavioral intention as an approximation of behavior. The reason is that attitude and subjective norms can only predict an intention; actual behavior also depends on the specifics of the situation. Table 11.3 summarizes the equations used in this model.

The distinctive advantage of Fishbein's extended model is that it accounts for social normative pressures as well as one's own internal beliefs about the consequences of the behavior. Explain to a teenager all you want about how utterly injurious to health smoking is, or how wearing a seat belt can save his or her life in an automobile accident; yet if the teenager's peers consider smoking cool, or wearing a seat belt "uncool," your fact-laden pleadings are probably going to fall on deaf ears.

In many situations, the customer's own assessments and personal attitudes are in favor of one alternative, but subjective norms temper them in favor of another. At many a public university, a faculty member's personal desire to own a sporty car like a Mazda Miata, a chic European car like BMW, or a super-luxury car like a Cadillac or a Mercedes is sacrificed to conform to the campus norm in favor of conservative cars like Toyotas, a

Table 11.3

FISHBEIN'S EXTENDED MODEL OF BEHAVIOR

B	=	$f[(BI) = f(A_{act})w_1 + (SN)w_2]$
where		
B	=	overt behvaior (i.e., brand purchase)
BI	=	behavioral intention or purchase intention
A_{act}	=	attitude toward purchase of brand
SN	=	subjective norm
w_1 and w_2	=	empirically determined evaluation weights

A_{act}	=	$\sum\limits_{i=1}^{m} B_i E_i$
where		
B_i	=	belief that performance of a certain behavior—brand purchase—will lead to an anticipated outcome
E_i	=	evaluation of an anticipated outcome, either a positive benefit or the avoidance of a negative consequence
i	=	anticipated outcome 1, 2, ... m

SN	=	$\sum\limits_{j=1}^{n} NB_j MC_j$
where		
SN	=	subjective norm—the motivation toward an act as determined by the influence of significant others
NB_j	=	normative beliefs—belief that significant others (j) expect the consumer to engage in an action
MC_j	=	motivation to comply—the extent to which the consumer is motivated to realize the expectations of significant others (j)
j	=	significant other 1, 2, ... n

Ford Taurus, or, in the luxury models, a Lexus or an Acura Legend. Even on campuses (especially those of private universities) where indulgence in personal tastes is entirely accepted, the pressure of social norm is unmistakable. You could drive a sporty or a luxury or a chic European model (even a Lamborghini or a Lotus if you can afford it), but try driving a run-down 1982 Pontiac LeMans or a dirty or banged-up vehicle, or an odd-colored, graffiti-tattooed car and you will pretty much find yourself talking to yourself even when you are not alone!

Social norms influence business behavior as well. A firm buying legal and auditing services, for example, may be expected to sign a contract with the most prestigious firms in town, even if, on objective performance, other firms are better. You also may have to give in to the normative expectations of your city's mayor and shun out-of-town suppliers in favor of local firms. Your major customers' expectations may tilt your patronization of minority suppliers for your own purchases. For example, Procter & Gamble buys its raw ingredients for detergents from chemical companies; it can demand that these chemical suppliers favor minority and small business firms for its own purchase needs. Thus, normative expectations mold, in important ways, customers' own internal desires for specific products and services. It is important for marketers, therefore, to understand social sanctions and rewards surrounding their products and services.

✦ Use of Multiattribute Models

Whether or not they are extended to include social norms, the multiattribute models of attitude have advantages over the models of global attitude, which could have been measured by a couple of simple scales such as dislike/like, favorable/unfavorable, and so forth. In the global attitude measure, we know only that the customer attitude is favorable or unfavorable, but we do not know why. In the multiattribute models, we know what beliefs underlie customer attitudes and how those beliefs are weighted to yield overall attitudes. Thus, multiattribute models *explain* attitudes, rather than simply index them. They add **diagnosticity**—the ability to diagnose why certain attitudes are the way they are.

Since the multiattribute models specify what underlies attitudes, they offer us a handle on how, in the cognitive mode, we can change or influence customer attitudes. According to the multiattribute model, we can change customer attitudes in three ways:

1. By changing a specific component belief, which can be done by changing the perception of the corresponding attribute level or associated consequence.

2. By changing the importance customers assign to an attribute or the evaluation of that consequence.

3. By introducing a new attribute (i.e., evaluation criteria) into customers' evaluation process.

These three strategies can be applied to the preceding example of America Online. Suppose AOL wants to influence a particular customer's attitude toward itself relative to AT&T. It can improve its connection success rate and communicate this improvement to the customer. (If its connection success rate is already comparable to that of AT&T, then it can communicate this to correct the current misperception.) Since, in the example, AOL has a superior rating on speed, it can try to emphasize the desirability of high speed, thus raising the speed's evaluation from the current rating of +2 to, say, +3. Finally, if AOL offers very good customer support, it could communicate that customer support should be an important consideration in choosing an Internet service provider.

The Functional Theory of Attitude

The process of forming attitudes does not fully explain differences in attitudes and in people's willingness to change them. Some of this variation is related to the reasons behind people's attitudes.

Why do people hold attitudes toward things, including products, services, and brands? The most obvious answer is that attitudes help them decide how to act toward these objects—to approach them or to avoid them. But approaching or avoiding the objects, or engaging in or avoiding the corresponding behaviors must be rewarding; the behavior must serve some purposes for the person. These purposes then become the reason why people hold attitudes.

Psychologist Daniel Katz called this perspective the functional theory of attitude. According to Katz's theory, people hold certain attitudes (or come to acquire those attitudes) because the attitudes serve certain functions. Katz proposed four such functions: utilitarian, ego defense, value expressive, and knowledge (see Table 11.4).

Four Functions of Attitude: Examples

To understand these, consider four teachers and their attitudes toward student evaluations.

Teacher A has a favorable attitude toward Student Evaluations of Course and Teaching (called here, SECTs). Her evaluations are among the best in school and help her get a good annual performance review in the department. Some of her colleagues in her department get poor evaluations, and this hurts them in their annual evaluations. It is no wonder that these colleagues have an unfavorable attitude toward SECTs, whereas Teacher A has a favorable attitude. This basis of having an attitude (whether favorable or unfavorable) is termed a **utilitarian motive.** That is, the SECTs serve some utility (or offer disutility) to the person.

Teacher B is at a school where SECTs are not used in performance evaluation, so he has no reason to worry about what they will do for him. Accordingly, he has no utilitarian

Table 11.4

FUNCTIONS OF ATTITUDES

FUNCTION	DEFINITION	EXAMPLE
Utilitarian	Related to whether the object serves some utility	I prefer no-crease jeans because they are easy to care for.
Ego-defensive	Held to protect a person's ego	My income may not be high, but I can buy this luxury car.
Knowledge	Related to whether the object adds to a person's knowledge	I like to work with this salesperson, because he spends a lot of time learning my needs and explaining how his company's products will help our company.
Value-expressive	Manifesting one's existing values	Every year I donate to the art institute and a local dance theater because the arts are a vital part of this community.

motive or reason to dislike the SECTs. However, he is aware that his evaluations are consistently poor compared with his colleagues. How does he look at them? He dismisses them as being invalid as indicators of teacher competence. "SECTs are nothing more than popularity polls," he muses. In this way, he is able to defend his own ego. This negative attitude toward SECTs is based on the **ego-defense motive.**

Teacher C is at the same school. Her scores are average, so she finds them neither very elating nor ego-threatening and doesn't feel the need to defend her ego. At one time, the administrators stopped administering the SECTs, and she was among those who lobbied for their re-installation. And, until they were re-installed, she gave her own evaluations! The reason was that she felt uncomfortable *not knowing* how students perceived her. For her, SECTs had value because they gave her knowledge of student perceptions. This is the **knowledge motive** for attitudes.

Teacher D has had varied experience with her evaluations. Sometimes, they were exceptionally positive; at other times they were heart-breaking. She is self-confident and knows she is a good teacher. She doesn't need SECTs to tell her how good she is, nor does she feel personally threatened by poor scores. No matter what the scores, she values them, however. As a marketing professor, she takes customer orientation to heart. "All organizations must listen to the customer's voice and strive for customer satisfaction," she believes deeply. Students are customers for a university, so all teachers must seek and value student feedback. This is her personal belief, so SECTs are more than mere tools of knowledge or ego satisfaction for her. Her motive is a **value-expressive motive.** Her attitude is a manifestation of her own value that customer voice matters.

Finally, Teacher J believes that students don't know what they ought to learn and how what they are learning is going to be useful to them. In other words, they are not capable of knowing what is in their interest, nor are they qualified to make judgments on teachers' competence, knowledge, and skills. Her evaluations are great, so she has no utilitarian or ego-defensive motives to oppose them. But because SECTs are contrary to her beliefs about students as competent evaluators, she doesn't favor them. Thus, her motive for disfavoring SECTs is value-expressive. Each of the motives can be a cause for favorable attitudes as well as unfavorable attitudes.

Now consider some customer attitudes. You may like a brand of clothing, say Polo, because of its durability and nonfading color quality; your friend may dislike it for being very expensive. Both are displaying attitudes based on the utilitarian function. You may like Polo shirts because of the brand's prestige and how it represents the successful person you consider yourself to be. Your co-worker may dislike it because he thinks it is too conservative and that he himself is somewhat of a rebel at heart. Both of you have the value-expressive function for liking (in your case) and disliking (your co-worker's case) the brand of shirt.

Applications of the Functional Theory

An understanding of these functions of attitudes helps explain why certain attitudes are resistant to change, as well as why attitudes about the same object, person, or brand vary from one customer to another. Someone may have a prejudiced attitude about immigrants, for example. This person might view immigrants as taking jobs away from native-born people (utilitarian function). Someone else may hold a favorable attitude toward immigrants because they provide a cheap source of labor, particularly for menial household chores, such as for baby-sitting or cooking and cleaning (again, a utilitarian function). Yet another person may hold a favorable attitude toward immigrants because they offer a window on another culture (the knowledge function).

Stereotypes themselves are attitudes toward a *category* of objects or persons. We hold them toward a category of people (e.g., Asian Americans) and toward a group of products, such as those made in Hong Kong. Why do stereotypes occur? To enable customers to efficiently "order" the world around them— that is, to give some structure to the world, to understand it in terms of what is what. Stereotypes serve the "knowledge" function of attitudes. In the movie *Mars Attack,* when Martians land on earth, humans everywhere try to make sense of them—who they are, what they want, how to relate to them. These are questions that would leave anyone uneasy—we would not rest until we knew answers to them. We would like and value anyone who tells us the answer. Or we will value what that answer implies for the unknown object. Such is the power of the knowledge function.

In most of the industrialized countries, one is likely to be exposed to persons of all nationalities (such exposure in the less developed countries is limited to a few major cities). What are these people like? What do they mean for me? How am I supposed to behave toward them? By exposure to one or two individuals from a particular ethnic background, people form an impression, an attitude, toward the entire ethnic class. For example, you might hold the stereotype that, depending on your vantage point, immigrants from Russia are hard to understand, unsophisticated, and spendthrift people; or that they are hard working, very intelligent, and successful career professionals. Once formed, this stereotype then helps you deal with newer instances. In other words, stereotypes as attitudes help you deal with the world efficiently (but not always accurately).

Let us consider some other knowledge-serving attitudes. In Greek mythology as well as in the Hindu scriptures, forces of nature are identified as gods—thus, there is a sun god, a god for wind, and a god for rain, for instance. So weather-related calamities are explained as caused by the wrath of the relevant god. Even in modern societies, there are a sizable number of people who are unfamiliar or unaccepting of explanations provided by modern science; in traditional societies, their numbers are large. To these people, Greek mythology or the Hindu scriptures are valuable sources of knowledge about the workings of the universe. This knowledge function of the scriptures accounts for a very favorable attitude these people hold toward the scriptures and toward the myths.

These examples illustrate why it is often difficult to alter people's attitudes—these are often rooted in some critical function they serve for the individual. Only by understanding what function it is can we hope to mold that attitude in the desired direction.

Applying the Theory of Attitudes:
Planned Social Change

In every society, some individual behaviors are not in the long-term interests of the society as a whole. Examples include individuals not practicing contraception in high-population countries, producing excessive garbage, littering, driving beyond speed limits, and polluting the environment. Sometimes individual behaviors are not even in the long-term interest of individuals themselves, even though these individuals may enjoy them at the moment. Examples include unhealthy eating, smoking, drinking and driving, and not taking preventive health measures such as vaccinations or breast examinations for cancer.

Governments and other agencies that want to protect the societal and individual interests engage in programs designed to alter these individual behaviors. These programs are called planned social change programs. **Planned social change** refers to active intervention by some agency with a conscious policy objective to bring about a change in some social or consumption behavior among the members of a population. The agency implementing such programs is called a **change agent,** and people whose behavior is sought to be altered are called **change targets.** Marketing scholars Gerald Zaltman and Philip Kotler have argued that principles and tools of marketing can be applied to planned social change. This application is termed **social marketing.**

Planned social change programs utilize a number of strategies, and we review them here to understand how they relate to the attitude change models we have discussed in the preceding section. The social marketing literature has identified eight strategies of planned social change:

Conservative consumption is a desired social message, in any language.
In this ad by Public Association of Advertising Agencies in Korea the headline reads: Money saved is money made. The copy then makes these suggestions: (1) Make a list; (2) Don't buy just because others buy; (3) Compare for value; (4) Take a deep breath before opening your purse. Tagline: New Consumption Culture: You Can Create It.

1. *Informing and educating*—This strategy consists of dissemination of objective information without drawing conclusions. Examples would be information about daily nutrition requirements or how to perform a breast self-examination.

2. *Persuasion and propaganda*—This entails a dramatic, and sometimes biased, presentation of information while stressing the recommended behavior.

3. *Social controls*—This entails using group and peer pressure to adopt the group's values, norms, and behaviors. Examples include a blood drive by a work group in which co-workers would communicate their expectation of each co-worker, or a neighborhood campaign for fund raising or recycling, and so forth.

4. *Delivery systems*—This entails making it easy for individuals to engage in prosocial behavior. Examples include convenient placement of trash cans to prevent littering, mobile blood collection or vaccination units, more flexible public health clinic hours, and so forth.

5. *Economic incentives*—This entails giving monetary incentives for prosocial behavior, such as giving tax credit for home insulation or use of a solar heating system, or even a cash incentive for undergoing a surgical procedure for birth control.

6. *Economic disincentives*—This strategy entails adding to the financial costs of continuing with the undesirable behavior. Examples include increased tax on cigarettes and liquor, increased fines for speeding and littering, and so forth.

7. *Clinical counseling and behavior modification*—This entails psychiatric and psychoanalytic programs for individuals one-on-one, or programs of small-group therapy that bring about the unlearning of socially undesirable behavior or learning of socially desirable behaviors. Examples include "quit smoking" clinics, or Alcoholics Anonymous—a group in which persons with severe drinking habits discuss their problems and seek social support in their effort to overcome their addiction.

8. *Mandatory rules and regulations*—The government may enact laws to restrict the undesirable behavior, specifying punitive measures for noncompliance. Examples include mandatory reproduction restriction, smoking prohibition in public buildings, fire safety code in building construction, and so forth.[10]

Choice of Strategy

How does a manager know what strategy is appropriate for a specific social change program in a specific population? This question is answered by considering a person's attitudes about the change program. Basically, a person's attitude may be positive or negative; for each case, moreover, the person may or may not be engaged in the desired behavior. Using these attitude and behavior statuses, customers can be classified into four groups, as shown in Table 11.5. A different strategy is appropriate for each of these groups.

When attitude is positive and behavior is present (cell 1), what is needed is a reinforcement strategy, a strategy that will reward the person for his or her behavior and encourage him or her to maintain the positive attitude. The reinforcement may be either behavioral (for example, economic incentives for participation in the prosocial program) or psychological (e.g., praise).

Table 11.5

A TYPOLOGY OF STRATEGY MIX FOR PLANNED SOCIAL CHANGE

		ATTITUDE	
		POSITIVE	NEGATIVE
RELEVANT BEHAVIOR	ENGAGED	**Cell 1** Reinforcement Strategy (Behavioral or Psychological)	**Cell 3** Rationalization Strategy Attitude Change (Psychological)
	NONENGAGED	**Cell 2** Inducement Strategy (Behavioral)	**Cell 4** Confrontation Process Strategy (Behavioral or Psychological)

Source: Jagdish N. Sheth and Gary L. Frazier, "A Model of Strategy Mix for Planned Social Change," *Journal of Marketing*, winter 1982, 46(1), 15–26.

If attitude is positive but behavior is absent (cell 2), then an inducement strategy is needed. Basically, the behavior needs to be facilitated (since the attitude is already positive). Therefore, the social change programs should try to remove whatever is holding back the behavior—such as some organizational, socioeconomic, time, or place constraints. Delivery systems become important, making it as convenient for the customer to engage in the proattitude behavior.

When attitude is negative and yet the person is engaging in the desired behavior (cell 3), a rationalization strategy is called for. This situation may occur due to lack of choice (e.g., wearing a helmet while riding a motorcycle because that is the law) or due to a temporary situation (e.g., carpooling due to a temporary shortage of fuel). Social change agents need to aid and stimulate the rationalization of the behavior—that is, the person tries to justify the behavior as desirable rather than merely necessary under the circumstances.

Finally, in cell 4 is the situation where attitude is negative and the behavior is absent. Here, a confrontation process is needed. Two types of confrontations are behavioral and psychological. In the behavioral confrontation, the change agency utilizes its power to block the current behavior, thus leaving the desired behavior the only viable option. In the psychological confrontation, the change agency directly attacks the person's existing attitudes toward the desired behavior. Although the ultimate goal is to move change targets from cell 4 to cell 1, this may be too radical to attempt in one step. If so, the change targets may be moved first to cell 2 or cell 3 and then, in the next phase, to cell 1.

How do the eight strategies of planned social change relate to the four approaches recommended for the four cells in Table 11.5? Table 11.6 provides this match. As shown in the table, for behavioral reinforcement, economic incentives and mandatory rules will be appropriate, although delivery systems (that facilitate the behavior) may also be effective. For psychological reinforcement, the best strategy is information and education, although persuasion and propaganda and social control strategies may also be appropriate. For behavioral inducement, informing and educating and persuasion and propaganda are not useful, since these strategies basically mold attitudes, which are already positive. Instead, the strategies of social control, delivery systems, economic incentives, and economic disincentives will be more effective. For rationalization, which is a psychological

---

Table 11.6   APPROPRIATENESS OF THE STRATEGIES IN FACILITATING THE PROCESS OF PLANNED SOCIAL CHANGE

STRATEGIES	REINFORCEMENT BEHAVIORAL	REINFORCEMENT PSYCHOLOGICAL	INDUCEMENT BEHAVIORAL	RATIONALIZATION PSYCHOLOGICAL	CONFRONTATION BEHAVIORAL	CONFRONTATION PSYCHOLOGICAL
Informing and Educating	No	**Yes**	No	Maybe	No	No
Persuasion and Propaganda	No	Maybe	No	**Yes**	No	**Yes**
Social Controls	No	Maybe	**Yes**	**Yes**	Maybe	**Yes**
Delivery Systems	Maybe	No	**Yes**	No	No	No
Economic Incentives	**Yes**	No	**Yes**	No	No	No
Economic Disincentives	No	No	**Yes**	No	**Yes**	No
Clinical Counseling and Behavior Modification	No	No	No	No	**Yes**	No
Mandatory Rules	**Yes**	No	Maybe	No	**Yes**	No

Source: Jagdish N. Sheth and Gary L. Frazier, "A Model of Strategy Mix Planned Social Change," *Journal of Marketing* 46, no. 1 (Winter 1982), pp. 15–26.

rather than a behavioral process, persuasion and propaganda and social controls are appropriate, since these strategies give reason to justify the behavior and thus mold the underlying attitude. Finally, for the confrontation approach, economic disincentives, clinic counseling and behavioral therapy, and mandatory rules target the blocking of the existing behaviors. And for psychological confrontation, the strategies of persuasion and propaganda and also social controls are likely to be most effective.

The general lesson of the foregoing discussion is that it is important to understand the attitudes underlying a particular behavior and also to recognize the nature of the attitude-behavior gap. (For an example of an organization that has learned and applied this lesson, see the Window on Practice box.) Depending on the direction of any discrepancy, the task may be to mold the attitude first, or behavior first. In either case, certain strategies may be more appropriate than others.

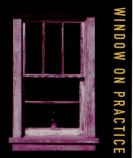

WINDOW ON PRACTICE

Would You Commit Fraud?

Attitude, they say, is everything.

Suppose Liisa Olanderkamp, your co-worker, lost a suitcase on a U.S. domestic flight, and she filed an insurance claim on her home insurance policy for $3,000; suppose, however, that her suitcase contained items worth only $500. Trusting her, the insurance agency sent her a check for $3,000. As Liisa tells you of this small "triumph," how would you feel? Can you condone Liisa's "soft" fraud?

The Washington-based Coalition against Insurance Fraud decided to find out. In a study published in September 1997, the coalition surveyed a national sample of 600 households on their attitudes toward insurance fraud committed by applicants and claimants, such as medical providers, lawyers, insurance agents, auto-repair specialists, and adjusters.

The study found that most of the respondents are concerned about the rising incidence of fraud and deem the practice to be morally wrong. At the same time, the study also found that the respondents understand why people do it and in some cases even sympathize with people who defraud, either because they are economically disadvantaged or because they believe the insurance companies deserve it.

Respondents were asked to describe their attitudes toward the insurance industry in general. Only 53 percent rated their feeling toward the industry as either very positive or fairly positive. And almost two-thirds agreed with the statement that fraud is justified because insurance premiums increase regardless of claims history and that insurers make undue profits.

On the positive side, consumers overwhelmingly believed that insurers should take a number of actions to curtail insurance fraud. Over half the respondents said insurance companies should prosecute customers for falsifying information and should deny the unjustified portion of claims. Nearly as many said insurance companies should deny insurance to a customer who has submitted false claims, deny all claims in cases of fraud on the application for insurance, and require customers to pay the investigative costs of a claim that turns out to be unjustified. Respondents were less receptive, however, to requiring more documentation to make it more difficult to falsify records or offering rewards to people who provide information about fraud.

The coalition is using these findings in formulating recommendations to curb fraud, including lobbying for new legislation. Beyond the specific measures against defrauders, however, the industry must act to improve its image among customers at large. It is only in a climate of positive customer attitudes that any antifraud measures will become acceptable or effective.

Source: Adapted from Dennis Jay, "Public Attitude Has Big Impact on Fight against Insurance Fraud," *National Underwriter,* Property & Casualty/Risk & Benefits Management Edition, Section: Special Report: Insurance Fraud Review; (September 15, 1997), pp. 23–29. Additional information available at **http://www.insurancefraud.org**

Customer Attitudes and the Three Customer Roles

The concepts of attitudes discussed in this chapter apply to all three customer roles. Customers hold attitudes relevant to each of their roles (see Table 11.7). As users, for example, we like certain products and services (e.g., vegetables if we are health conscious and power tools if we are do-it-yourselfers) and dislike others (e.g., cigarettes if we are nonsmokers). As payers, we have attitudes toward credit—some of us like it while others don't like it. Finally, as buyers, we like certain stores, vendors, and purchase methods while we dislike others (e.g., mail catalog buying).

In each of these foregoing instances, our attitudes exist in their three components. As users, our attitudes comprise beliefs we hold about products and services (e.g., "Toyota cars are reliable," or "Sun Microsystems have versatile connectivity"), have feeling toward them (e.g., "I love my Toyota," or "I like doing business with Sun Microsystems"), and manifest corresponding approach or avoidance behavior (e.g., "I will always buy a Toyota," or "My current preferred network services provider is Sun Microsystems"). Then, as payers, we have beliefs about specific credit cards, have favorable predispositions toward them, and we use certain cards and reject others. Finally, as buyers, we have beliefs about certain vendors, like some and dislike others, and patronize those we like and avoid those we dislike. For example, some of us may like to shop at warehouse club stores, believing that they offer good selection and price, while others among us may avoid them because of the belief that they offer a low level of service.

Fishbein's extended model points to the role of subjective norms—the expectations of significant others—and these norms also influence each of the three roles. As users, we are concerned about whether significant others will like what we use. We buy the cars our neighbors will not frown upon, wear clothing our friends and co-workers will admire, eat our vegetables to appease our parents, and (as business customers) fly economy class to comply with the company's new cost-saving measures. As payers, our debt behavior is shaped by parents' expectations during our teenage years when we first acquire our own

ATTITUDES AND THE THREE CUSTOMER ROLES

Table 11.7

	USER	PAYER	BUYER
Customer attitudes	Users like products/services they use, and dislike products they avoid.	Payers have attitude towards credit.	Buyers like some vendors more than others.
Three-component-model	Users hold beliefs about products and services, have feelings toward them, and manifest approach or avoidance behavior.	Payers have beliefs, feelings, and behaviors toward specific credit cards, and other forms of payment methods.	Buyers have beliefs about the attributes of vendors, have feelings of like or dislike toward them, and patronize or ignore them, accordingly.
Fishbein's extended model	Subjective norms dictate customer use or nonuse of many products/services.	Subjective norms influence a person's debt behavior, and also spending norms for specific purchases. Tipping behavior.	Subjective norms influence one's choice of vendors. Government has list of approved vendors.
High and low involvement	Users are very involved with some products, exhibiting fanatic consumption.	Payers differ in their concern with what happens to the money they pay.	Some buyers are highly involved, others not.

credit cards. Furthermore, we are expected to spend money within a normative range for specific products—for example, our spouse would expect us not to spend too much on clothing, and gift recipients would expect us to spend a certain amount on the gift. The amount of tipping is influenced by our desire to impress our dinner guest. "Cheapskate" and "extravagant" are essentially normative labels, used by others to refer to counter-normative spending behavior. Finally, subjective norms also influence our choice of vendors as well as our shopping strategy. For example, we shop at stores our friends and people of our social class shop at. We don't shop around too much if we have a friend along. Parents force teenagers to buy family groceries at the regular store rather than the one more convenient to the teenager himself or herself. And government-funded projects specify a list of approved vendors.

Involvement, an attitudinal state of the customer, also is manifested in all three roles. As users, we are highly involved in some products and services, exhibiting fanatic consumption of these—for example, a collection of art works. As payers, we differ in our concern with what happens to the money we give. Some parents, for example, might give their children an allowance and not worry about how they spend it, while other parents may want to keep a close eye on how that money is being spent. As donors to charity organizations, we might be uninterested in the exact uses of that money, or we might want to be on the board of directors so we may influence the distribution of funds. Finally, as buyers, we might shop disinterestedly, or alternately, we might enjoy shopping or take keen interest in making the most judicious purchase. As business customers, we might routinely reorder from the existing vendor or we might diligently search for new vendors.

These examples cover only the main concepts of attitude. Other concepts discussed in this chapter—the multicomponent model, attribution processes, cognitive dissonance and consistency, and the functional theory of attitude—also are relevant to the three roles. For example, as a payer, we might like and use a particular credit card simply because that card has offered us a higher credit limit, even though we would never even come close to exhausting the much lower limit of a competing card; we may do so because it serves our ego-defense function. Or we might prefer a credit card because of its higher prestige (value-expressive function). We leave it to you to reflect on and tease out the relevance of these and other attitude concepts to the three customer roles.

Summary

This chapter dealt with the concept of attitude and how it applies to customer behavior. Attitudes were described as customers' likes and dislikes toward various products and services and their predispositions to respond to them (approach or avoid them). These attitudes have three components—cognition (thoughts), affect (feelings), and conation (actions). Customers acquire these three components in a specific sequence, and three such sequences were identified: rational, emotional, and low-involvement. Because the three components usually exist in harmony (i.e., consistency), changing any one of them would usually drive a change in others. Accordingly, we have identified three routes to attitude change: the cognitive, affective, and conative routes. In the conative route, behavior is shaped or encouraged by such means as incentives, information structuring, and regulation. Corresponding thoughts and feelings then follow to become consistent with the shaped behavior.

Various psychological processes underlie attitude change. First, attitudes are changed when we learn something; accordingly, all four methods of learning (classical conditioning, instrumental conditioning, modeling, and cognitive learning) also become methods of attitude change. Attitudes change because humans have an innate need for attribution of causes (i.e., to understand causality) and seek cognitive consistency (e.g., Heider's balance theory; Festinger's dissonance theory). Furthermore, low- and high-involvement learning processes lead to attitude change in very different manners.

Computational models of attitudes seek to capture the arithmetic of how object beliefs (i.e., cognitions) combine to form an overall attitude or evaluation of the object. Two major models have been developed by Rosenberg and Fishbein. Fishbein's model also has an extended form, which adds to the basic model's cognitive component a normative component. Together, these predict a customer's behavioral intention.

Next, we discussed a functional theory of attitude. Advanced by psychologist Daniel Katz, this theory expounds on the motivational reasons why customers hold an attitude at all. They hold it, according to Katz, because these attitudes serve one or more of the four functions: utilitarian, value-expressive, ego-defense, and knowledge. Applications of these functions for customer behavior were discussed.

These attitude concepts have been applied to the task of planned social change. Concerned with changing people's behaviors so that the acquired behaviors are in the interests of the customers themselves or society at large, planned social change can use diverse strategies of "social marketing." The appropriateness of these strategies depends on the nature of attitude-behavior gaps.

In the last section, we highlighted the applicability of various attitude concepts covered in the chapter to each of the three customer roles and the market values they seek.

Key Terms

Attitudes 388
Beliefs 390
Brand Beliefs 390
Descriptive Beliefs 390
Evaluative Beliefs 390
Normative Beliefs 390
Affect 391
Conation 391
Attitude Hierarchy 391
Learning Hierarchy 391
Emotional Hierarchy 392
Low-involvement Attitude
  Hierarchy 393
Attitude Valence 395
Attitude Strength 395
Attitude Molding 395
Ecological Design 399

Foot-in-the-Door Strategy
  400
Door-in-the-Face Strategy
  400
Inference Making 404
Self-Perception Theory 404
Norm of Reciprocity 405
Buyers' Remorse 405
Cognitive Dissonance 405
Festinger's Dissonance
  Theory 405
Heider's Balance Theory
  406
Central Processing Route
  407
Peripheral Processing
  Route 408

Multiattribute Models of
  Attitude 408
Rosenberg Model 408
Fishbein Model 408
Fishbein's Extended Model
  409
Subjective Norms 410
Diagnosticity 412
Utilitarian Motive 413
Ego-Defense Motive 414
Knowledge Motive 414
Value-Expressive Motive
  414
Planned Social Change 415
Change Agent 416
Change Targets 416
Social Marketing 416

Review Questions

1. What are consumer attitudes? What are the two primary uses of the concept of consumer attitudes in marketing? How can marketers do a better job of satisfying customer needs by understanding customer attitudes? Since attitudes are learned predispositions to respond (i.e., engage or not engage in a specific behavior), why don't marketers and market researchers simply measure purchase response (i.e., behavior) and forget about attitudes?

2. Compare and contrast the learning hierarchy of attitude and the emotional hierarchy of attitude. How do these two models differ? Moreover, how do these models differ from the low-involvement hierarchy of attitudes? Give an example of each model in use in marketing.

3. In the "Conative Route to Attitude Molding," five approaches are identified in the chapter. What are these and how do they help to shape attitudes by directly influencing behaviors? Explain each approach and provide two examples of each.

4. How does the central mode of attitude processing differ from the peripheral mode? What differences in attitude might accrue as a result of processing in one way or the other? Provide one example of central processing being stressed by a company in its communications and another example of a company where peripheral processing is stressed. Under what conditions should a marketer select one route versus another in attempting to change consumer attitudes?

5. What is planned social change? What approaches should the social marketer use in different conditions of attitude-behavior discrepancy?

Applications

1. Select one ad—either from television or from magazines—for each of the three alternative models of attitude formation (learning hierarchy, emotional hierarchy, and low-involvement hierarchy). Provide some rationale about why the company has chosen one path of attitude formation over the other two. For each of the ads chosen, find another ad for that company's competitor and analyze the competitor's promotional approach. Are the paths similar or different for the competitor?

2. Put the three-component model of attitude to work by providing three measurement statements for each component of the model for the following three objects: (a) Nike running shoes, (b) Surfing the World Wide Web, (c) McDonald's fast-food restaurants.

3. One of your classmates was out partying late last night and missed a key lecture in your customer behavior class this morning. You let her know that it was pretty important since the topic dealt with molding attitude. Your friend is not that concerned and tells you that she has a pretty good attitude. You then tell her that the professor covered two techniques called "foot in the door" and "door in the face." Again, your friend is relaxed and tells you that she has had experience in sales and knows how to "get in the door." At this point you sigh and proceed to set your friend straight about the topic of attitude molding. What do you tell her? How do you explain the "foot-in-the-door" and "door-in-the-face" approaches to behavior molding to her?

4. Describe an attitude you recently developed toward a product or service in terms of classical conditioning, instrumental conditioning, modeling, and cognitive learning theory. Give one example of your acquiring an attitude in each of these four learning modes.

5. In your daily life, think about two products and two services that you use on a regular basis and the brand that you prefer. First, summarize Katz's functional theory of attitude. Next describe which of the four functions the brands of those products and services best serves (please select your product and services so that each of the four functions is covered).

6. Assume the role of strategic marketing manager for a new line of South Korean automobiles. You are very familiar with the problems that your predecessors such as Hyundai and KIA have had in creating a high-quality automobile image among U.S. customers. In South Asia and Europe your new line has tested very well and you are confident that your cars will succeed in the United States

given that you can properly shape U.S. attitudes towards Korean auto imports. Given your knowledge about the attitudes of American consumers towards their cars, which of the three alternative routes to attitude molding will you take in your promotional campaign? Why have you chosen this route? Briefly describe the types of attitudes you hope to invoke in your target customers.

7. You are in charge of market research at a company that manufactures computer components. You are concerned about a recent drop in what was a rapidly rising market share and want to gain a better understanding of your business customers' attitudes. Using Fishbein's model of attitude and your customers' beliefs as to the consequences of buying from you, assess your customers' attitudes toward your brand versus your major competitor's brand.

   a. Buying from this supplier would mean the highest quality parts.

   b. Doing business with this company will be difficult since it is a foreign firm.

   c. We would get a 15 percent price break if we work exclusively with this company.

   d. We would have to alter some of our business processes to accommodate this suppliers' parts.

   Using the above four belief dimensions, construct a questionnaire that will measure all the concepts involved in the Fishbein model; then answer it for two brands of computer components familiar to you. Then,

   a. Calculate the overall scores for each brand.

   b. Discuss your customers' perceptions of the strengths and weaknesses of your brand versus your major competitor's brand. Discuss the implications of these results for marketing your brand.

8. Despite the raging war against the tobacco industry and the general negative sentiments towards cigarette smokers, a lot of people continue to smoke. Based on the model of planned social change presented in this chapter, evaluate various strategies and identify the ones you would recommend for an antismoking marketing program of action.

Practical Experiences

1. Find someone in your class or college or university that is exhibiting a behavior that is inconsistent with his or her attitudes (e.g., attitudes towards smoking, studying, acquiring brand name products, and so on). Ask the person to elaborate on why he or she continues to elicit the behavior that is inconsistent with his or her attitudes. Now do the same exercise for a business. Find a business that publicly holds a particular attitude (e.g., being environmentally friendly is good for business), but then exhibits behaviors that are inconsistent with that particular attitude. (Hint: you may refer to annual reports, Web sites, or business magazines for company information.) Summarize your findings.

2. Find two print ads, one illustrating the use of the affective component of attitude formation, and the other illustrating the use of the cognitive component. Discuss each ad in the context of the tricomponent model. In your opinion, why has each marketer taken the approach it did in each of these ads?

3. Develop a multiattribute model for a local health food store. Recently, some health food stores have come under attack for their practice of selling products that are not FDA approved or that have no real health benefits. Based on your analysis, suggest how the health food store can improve its image via the strategies described in this chapter.

4. Part of the Kathie Lee Gifford story (see opening vignette) was drawn from the Internet. Along the same lines, using the Internet, find a story on other consumer protests. Briefly describe the nature of the protest, and identify which of the four functions of attitudes underlie this particular consumer protest.

Notes

1. Gordon W. Allport, "Attitudes," in C.A. Murchinson, ed., *A Handbook of Social Psychology* (Worcester, MA: Clark University Press, 1935), pp. 798–844.

2. See Philip Kotler, "Atmospherics as a Marketing Tool," *Journal of Retailing* 49 (Winter 1973–74), pp. 48–64; Robert Donovan and John Rossiter, "Store Atmosphere: An Environmental Psychology Approach," *Journal of Retailing* 58 (Spring 1982), pp. 34–57.

3. Ronald E. Milliman, "Using Background Music to Affect the Behavior of Supermarket Shoppers,"*Journal of Marketing* 46 (Summer 1982), pp. 86–91; "The Influence of Background Music on the Behavior of Restaurant Patrons," *Journal of Consumer Research* 13 (September 1986), pp. 286–89. Also see, Charles S. Areni and David Kim, "The Influence of Background Music on Shopping Behavior: Classical versus Top Forty," in *Advances in Consumer Research,* Leigh McAlister and Michael L. Rothschild, eds., 20 (Provo, UT: Association for Consumer Research, 1993), pp. 336–40; James J. Kellaris and Robert J. Kent, "The Influence of Music on Consumers' Temporal Perceptions: Does Time Fly When You Are Having Fun,"*Journal of Consumer Psychology* 1, no. 4 (1992), pp. 365–76.

4. Jagdish N. Sheth and Banwari Mittal, "A Framework for Managing Customer Expectations," *Journal of Market-Focused Management* 2 (1996), pp. 137–58.

5. See Robert E. Krapfel, "Marketing by Mandate," *Journal of Marketing* 46 (Summer 1982), pp. 79–85; Jagdish N. Sheth *Winning Back Your Market: The Inside Stories of the Companies that Did It* (New York: John Wiley, 1985), pp. 59–72.

6. Sheth and Mittal, "A Framework for Managing Customer Expectations."

7. See Peter H. Reingen and J.B. Kernan, "Compliance with an Interview Request: A Foot-in-the-Door Self-Perception Interpretation," *Journal of Marketing Research,* 14 (August 1977), pp. 365–69. Also, John C. Mowen and Robert B. Cialdini, "On Implementing the Door-in-the-Face Compliance Technique in a Business Context," *Journal of Marketing Research*, Vol. 17 (May 1980), pp. 253–258.

8. John C. Mowen and Robert Cialdini, "On Implementing the Door-in-the-Face Compliance Strategy in a Marketing Context," *Journal of Marketing Research* 17 (May 1980), pp. 253–58.

9. Leon A. Festinger, *A Theory of Cognitive Dissonance* (Evanston, IL: Row, Peterson, 1957).

10. Jagdish N. Sheth and Gary L. Frazier, "A Model of Strategy Mix for Planned Social Change," *Journal of Marketing,* winter 1982, 46(1), 15–26.

CHAPTER 12

After reading this chapter you should be able to:

Describe how marketers do things differently to differentiate themselves from their competition.

Define generic, targeted, and segmented differentiations and how these differentiation strategies respond to customer differences in needs and resources.

Identify various bases of segmenting the market.

Summarize how marketers use usage as a basis of segmentation.

Discuss how customers can be segmented on the basis of demographics, geography, and geodemographics.

Describe how customers' personality, lifestyles, and psychographics can be utilized to identify distinct customer groups.

Explain how marketers can use product benefits to segment the market and position the product.

Summarize how business markets can be segmented, including the application of demographics and psychographics to business markets.

List criteria for good segmentation, and tell how these can be used to assess the utility of a segmentation scheme.

Market Differentiation and Segmentation: Responding to Customer Differences

All Latinos Are Not Created the Same

Latin Americans. They live in a specific region of the world; and they speak a common language. But if you think they are a single market, think again.

San Diego-based Market Development Inc., a marketing research firm specializing in the Latin American region, recently did a psychographic segmentation analysis based on 2,000 in-depth, person-to-person interviews with adults in the four major markets of Latin America—Saõ Paulo, Brazil; Mexico City; Buenos Aires, Argentina; and Santiago, Chile. The study identifies key attitude dimensions that influence not only what products these consumers buy, but why they buy them.

The study found five major segments:

1. "Cosmopolitan Climbers" (24.1 percent) are trendy, cosmopolitan, young, and upscale, with their outlook on life being "Go for it!" They are open to new and imported products and willing to spend on those that they believe are high quality and will enhance their life style.

2. "Hopeful Homebodies" (23.1 percent) hold almost the opposite views. They like "the old ways" and are generally dissatisfied with both their financial status and accomplishments. This group is among the least likely to spend on imported products if they consider them to be foreign or alien to their experience, as well as more expensive.

3. "Relaxed Realists" (17.4 percent) are primarily the region's emerging middle class. They hold an unhurried, unplanned vision of life, more relaxed than the "Hopeful Homebodies" and less driven than the "Cosmopolitan Climbers." Work to them is simply a means of earning money, nothing more. They are willing to spend their money on imported goods, but insist on good value.

4. "Hurried Handlers" (6.6 percent) mostly women, lead jam-packed lives that leave little room for rest and relaxation and "no sympathy for whiners." This group is made up of goal-oriented planners who shop for convenience and value.

5. "Careful Copers" tend to be cautious and somewhat pessimistic. They are not adventurous in spirit or in spending. Price-conscious, they tend to buy products that they know and trust

"These are the first psychographic segments that cut across national boundaries and demographic divisions in Latin America," said Loretta H. Adams, president of MDI. **"With the MDI COMPASS study, U.S. marketers can finally segment the Latin American market with the same sophistication they are using for the U.S. general market."**

Source: "New Study Segments Latin American Consumers by Attitudes: Psychographics Reveal How Latin Americans Think," *Business Wire*, April 10, 1996.

Introduction

For Latin Americans as well as other customer groups, mass marketing is a thing of the past. In the hotly contested automobile market, for example, customers differ greatly in how they view automobiles in general and what they want from the car they would buy in particular. In such a marketplace, attempting to appeal to everyone with the same offering is both inefficient and ineffective. We live in a global marketplace where companies from around the world have figured out how to differentiate themselves from the competition by building a better product for a very small part of the market and then targeting their promotional appeals only to those customers. In other words, by using market differentiation and segmentation strategies, companies position themselves to compete in the marketplace more effectively.

This chapter explores how marketers respond to customer differences with differentiation and segmentation strategies. It begins by defining *differentiation* and identifying three broad differentiation options. Next, the chapter discusses bases for segmenting customer markets for households and businesses. Finally, we explore the ways in which marketers can use their understanding of customer behavior to select segmentation criteria.

A Typology of Market Differentiation and Segmentation

Differentiation is the way in which marketers present their offerings differently from their competition in order to become the customer's choice. Presenting offerings differently entails creating and implementing the marketing mix (product, price, place, and promotion). To differentiate themselves from their competition, marketers use three types of differentiation: generic, targeted, and segmented differentiation (see Figure 12.1).

Generic Differentiation

Generic differentiation is a global (or overall) differentiation on a nontargeted basis, which means the differentiation is not for any specific segment of customers. Rather, a firm presents an improved offering to the entire market. This type of differentiation is appropriate for companies who are able to present their products and services as superior to competitive products in the entire marketplace.

This is, in effect, what Henry Ford did. Henry Ford realized that cars available in his day were built poorly and were, at the same time, priced high. Following a generic differ-

TYPES OF DIFFERENTIATION

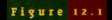

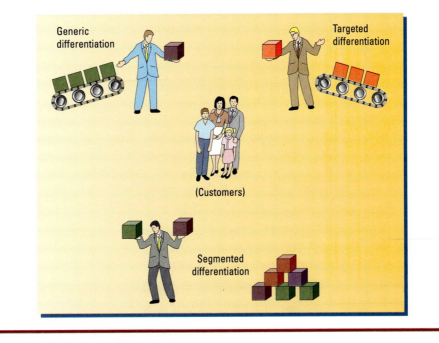

entiation strategy, Ford designed an assembly-line system that produced a more reliable car with improved productivity. Consequently, he was able to offer a better product at a lower price ($600 when it was introduced) than competitors. This approach gave Ford a lead in the marketplace.

Similar generic differentiation approach is commonly practiced by Japanese companies, especially with respect to product quality improvements. The Honda and Toyota car companies are apt examples of companies that offer more reliable cars to American consumers at comparable prices. Similarly, several years ago, when television sets were made with vacuum tubes, Japanese manufacturers moved to solid state technology, which eliminated the need for frequent repairs. This differentiated Japanese TV makers in the global market. In industrial markets too, the Japanese have practiced this type of differentiation in several markets, including flat screen technology (in the television market), memory chips (in the computer industry), and in the machine tools industry.

The generic differentiation benchmarks competitive offerings with respect to product, price, promotion, distribution, and customer service and attempts to differentiate offerings by improving over competition.

Companies can use any one of the 4 Ps—the elements of the marketing mix—to achieve generic differentiation.

PRODUCT-BASED DIFFERENTIATION

Companies use product-based differentiation by offering better products than their competitors. The product's superiority may be based on superior quality and performance reliability, or innovations in the product's performance, design features, or on brand image, and manufacturer reputation. For example, NEC differentiated its laptop computer by making it versatile (the screen could be flipped 180 degrees or detached from the keyboard); many car rental companies started differentiating themselves in late 1996 onwards by offering a navigator in the car. In the service industries, hotels started differentiating by offering such new features as upgraded business class with rooms equipped with fax, computer ports, and so on, or express check-in (e.g., Hyatt), or 5 P.M. check-out (e.g., Sheraton Hotels).

In the business services sector, several years ago, Federal Express realized that the assurance of next-day guaranteed delivery was critical to business customers. Using the U.S. Postal Service (USPS) as a benchmark, Federal Express implemented an operations system that guaranteed next-day delivery. This was accomplished in part by establishing the hub of the system in Memphis. Memphis is centrally located, permitting short flight time for all incoming and outgoing airplanes. It also had the fewest weather-related problems of U.S. airports, which minimized delays. True to its slogan, "When it absolutely, positively has to be there," FedEx continues to have a generic differentiation advantage over USPS in the time-sensitive document delivery service business. A more recent innovation FedEx has made is giving its customers the ability to track their packages online, which gives FedEx yet another generic differentiation.

NONPRODUCT DIFFERENTIATION

Nonproduct differentiation is based on distribution, pricing, and/or advertising and promotions. A good example of generic differentiation by innovation in distribution is the home delivery of Domino's Pizza guaranteed in one-half hour. Today, many supermarkets offer customers the opportunity of ordering via E-mail and have the groceries delivered at home.

Warehouse clubs (such as Sam's Club), excess-inventory buying-based stores (such as Big Lots), or brand-name discount stores (e.g., Syms, or TJ Maxx) represent generic differentiation based on the *price* advantage. In the services industry, UPS fought hard to wrench market share away from FedEx, and it did so by offering a better price than FedEx.

Finally, many companies attempt to differentiate themselves by memorable and unique *advertising*. Energizer's pink bunny, Coca-Cola's polar bears, and Infinity's introductory TV spots in which the car itself was conspicuously absent are examples of generic differentiation by advertising that departs from the expected and the ordinary. Current Infinity advertising distinguishes the brand to U.S. customers by having a spokesperson with a European accent.

Although one of the 4Ps may be utilized as the dominant basis of differentiation, some companies may have opportunity to base their differentiation on more than one or all four marketing mix elements. L'eggs pantyhose represents the case where all four elements were utilized. The product itself was improved so it would not "run", the egg-shaped introductory packaging and the apt brand name were unique; the product was priced attractively; and, most importantly, the product was distributed in supermarkets and discount stores, which made it very convenient for women to buy the product. The company has further differentiated itself by offering the product through direct marketing.

USE OF SIX VALUES FOR GENERIC DIFFERENTIATION

Each of the examples cited above can easily be linked to the six values described in the previous chapters. For example, Honda and Toyota car companies differentiate themselves from domestic carmakers on the universal value by focusing on reliability and performance. Likewise, Sony differentiates itself on the functional value of superior quality. So do Intel and Microsoft, offering technologically superior products. Infinity differenti-

it's aluminium it's recyclable it's for men it's for women it's for me it's for you it's for everyone on the planet and it smells good.*

paco
paco rabanne

Dillard's
* of course it does it's a fragrance.

The Paco promotes itself to all audiences—"everyone on the planet"—with the generic differentiation based on its appeal of a prestigious brand name and in the simplicity of its packaging in a market otherwise dominated by brands with fancy packaging.

ates by universal value (via its high-performance design) but even more by the personal value of social status. Domino's pizza represents both the service and the convenience value, as does Federal Express, which uses both convenience and service (i.e., guaranteed delivery) as its differentiating advantage. Honda also offers price value in that the car is value priced and will need fewer repairs. Price value is, of course, the mainstay of discount stores and warehouse clubs. Thus, each of the six values lends itself to building generic differentiation into one's market offerings.

Targeted Differentiation

A second form of differentiation is **targeted differentiation**, an approach in which a company identifies a specific market segment and then designs a marketing program to target and appeal to this particular segment. This is in contrast to the generic differentiation, where a single undifferentiated marketing program is offered to everyone. Companies normally act as "niche" players in this type of differentiation. As with generic differentiation, this approach uses specific elements of the marketing mix to differentiate a company's offerings.

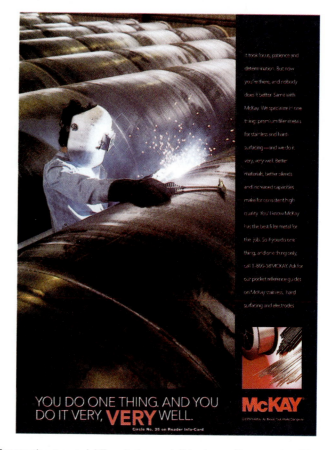

McKay practices targeted differentiation specializing in one thing: premium filler metals.

Some companies are formulating special products specifically for ethnic markets. Both Revlon and Max Factor have a line of beauty aid products specifically for the African-American population. The chemical base is different for these cosmetics, reflecting differences in the genetic and physical needs of African Americans. This differentiation strategy has now been expanded to the Hispanic and Asian populations, with each market representing a set of unique physical characteristics that require corresponding product formulations.

In consumer services, the life insurance industry has begun to realize that some ethnic groups are a lucrative segment because of their relative affluence. According to the 1990 census, the Asian-American population has 22 percent higher income than the white population, due to the fact that a majority of the former are dual-income white-collar professionals. Now, although the basic product—insurance—remains the same, the ways in which two key benefits of security and investing for the future are communicated to various ethnic groups differ. The differentiation comes in the reorganization of the sales force. In this industry, trust is a key issue because consumers are putting their life-long savings into the hands of another individual. So people are trained as agents to sell the life insurance policies to customers of similar heritage.

Small businesses represent a good opportunity as a targeted market for a number of products and services. In the long-distance telephone market, resellers (small companies that buy large blocks of long-distance time from a large carrier like Sprint or MCI) sell cheaper long-distance rates to small businesses by representing 70–80 small businesses at once. Companies like Office Depot or Staples are set up to target small businesses for their office-supply needs.

SEGMENT OF ONE

A special form of targeted differentiation is **segment-of-one marketing**. This refers to ex. Dell customizing the market offering to each individual customer. Recent advances in technology enable a firm to respond to very small segments, even single customers, without losing the economies of scale. This development is called "mass customization," and is accomplished by flexible manufacturing. In the typical flexible manufacturing arrangement, a network of computers instantly translates an individual customer's order into specifications for materials and components needed. The computer also transmits a job order to several computer-controlled work stations, which seamlessly custom-produce that particular item.[1] Motorola has the capability of offering 27 million types of pagers, all efficiently and speedily assembled *after* a customer order is received. Dell Computer Co. custom assembles a PC within eight hours after the order is received on its toll-free 800 number. Of those eight hours, five hours are taken up just in dry-burn test; in effect, then, the computer is assembled in just under three hours! Technological developments such as flexible manufacturing and cable TV capability with as many as 500 channels (which will allow communicating with increasingly narrow audiences) will enable companies to target smaller and more precisely defined segments.[2]

Segmented Differentiation

The third type of differentiation, **segmented differentiation**, involves breaking up the total market into segments that are homogeneous by some characteristics of its customers (such as demographics, psychographics, or usage patterns), and then treating each segment as a distinct market for which all elements of the marketing mix are differentiated. This method is described more formally and in detail later in the chapter. Presently, we give brief examples to illustrate how this method differs from the preceding two.

The automobile industry serves as an excellent early example of this type of differentiation. The story is classic and legendary and a pace setter in its marketing lesson, so we report it in some detail in the Window on Practice box on page 435.

A more current example is Gap, Inc. It began business in 1969 as Gap Stores, selling Levi's jeans, carrying many more styles and sizes than a typical department store did. It also displayed the merchandise in a more organized way than did other department stores. Thus, it was in itself an example of generic differentiation from other jeans stores. Later, in 1983, the company acquired Banana Republic, selling casual clothing to upscale customers. More recently, in 1994, it opened yet another chain of stores, Old Navy, this time targeting low-income customers. In 1986, it also started a new division, GapKids, targeting kids as a segment.[3]

Segmented differentiation can be practiced by business-to-business marketers as well. For example, utility companies have recognized four separate segments: residential, institutional, industrial, and commercial. These differ in their product and service needs. For example, power surge is a critical problem for industrial but not residential customers. Accordingly, more backup systems are put in place for the industrial user. A sales force is utilized for the large industrial segment (but not for the residential segment). For the industrial, business, and institutional users, the supply is metered by various categories of use, and the invoice is detailed by business unit.

Likewise, in the automotive components industry, tire companies serve at least four different markets: (1) Original Equipment Manufacturers (OEMs), namely, the

By publishing different versions of the Bible for different customer segments, Zondervan Bibles practices segmented differentiation.

automobile manufacturer; (2) tire dealers and distributors; (3) their own distribution chain, such as Goodyear dealers who sell Goodyear tires; and (4) the repair and maintenance market—referred to as the tire, batteries, and accessories market, or known as the retread market. For each of these four markets, the tire companies will use very different marketing strategies, differentiating by one or more elements of the marketing mix within each segment.

Segmented Differentiation by General Motors

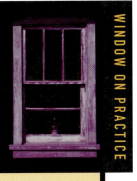

Henry Ford had the idea that customers could have any color car as long as it was black. However, General Motors (GM) knew better. GM believed very strongly that customers have different needs and wants and also different resources.

GM recognized that when it comes to the kind of automobile people want, there were four segments based upon socioeconomic class: the working class, the middle class, the upper-middle class (the affluent), and the upper class (the very wealthy). The company then came out with five automobile models. For the working class, GM manufactured the Chevrolet, targeted to the person living in a rural area. For this segment, the company also manufactured the station wagon, meant for the family that could not afford to fly, but instead could "See the U.S.A. in [their] Chevrolet" (a familiar jingle from commercials targeted to this segment at that time). Pontiac was directed to the middle class. Buick and Oldsmobile were targeted to the affluent. Within this segment, two subsegments were identified: one was the more traditional affluent customer, an honorable and family-oriented citizen, living in the metropolitan area, looking for a four-door sedan. The Buick was targeted towards this subsegment. The Oldsmobile, on the other hand, was targeted to the affluent customer who bought a car for personal enjoyment. Accordingly, the Oldsmobile had a rocket engine and an innovative (at the time) body with only two doors. Finally, Cadillac was manufactured for the wealthy.

Once the four segments were identified by GM, a unique marketing mix was developed for each. To accommodate this strategy, the company was split into divisions, with each responsible for the marketing of one of the five models. The then GM chairman Alfred P. Sloan made each division autonomous, giving each the freedom to manage its model and its segment. Divisions used their own brand names, their own advertising agency, and their own distribution channels (a Chevrolet dealer sold only Chevrolets). For each segment, the product designs and components were different (with Cadillac always leading with state-of-the-art technology); prices were different (with a Chevrolet priced initially at $3,000 and Cadillac at $15,000). Finally, promotional and positioning campaigns and media vehicles were different. For example, the Cadillac car was advertised only in the print media, never on TV, because of the belief that only working-class people watched television. Wealthy people in those days read *The New Yorker, Time, Life*, and *Look* magazines. The magazine advertisements for Cadillac showed a full-page picture of the Cadillac, with very little copy or information about the car itself; instead it showed men dressed in tuxedos and women dressed in formal gowns on their way to the opera or the theater.

This early history of GM's segmented differentiation is a perfect example of segmentation where *all* elements of the marketing mix are different for different segments. Henry Ford, who had initially exploited generic differentiation, did not later recognize the opportunity the developing market offered for segmented differentiation, so Ford Motor Company lost its lead to General Motors.

Additional information is located at
http://www.ford.com
http://www.generalmotors.com
http://www.cadillac.com
http://www.buick.com
http://www.chevrolet.com
http://www.oldsmobile.com

Customer Diversity as a Basis for Differentiation

A basic reason for differentiation is that customers' needs and wants may vary on the basis of personal and environmental characteristics, and their resources may vary with respect to time, money, and expertise. In a given marketplace, then, the most useful differentiation strategy may depend on whether needs/wants and resources are homogeneous or diverse. Table 12.1 shows the possibilities.

Table 12.1 TYPOLOGY OF DIFFERENTIATION AND SEGMENTATION

<table>
<tr><td rowspan="2"></td><td colspan="2" align="center">RESOURCES</td></tr>
<tr><td>HOMOGENEOUS</td><td>DIVERSE</td></tr>
<tr><td>Needs/Wants — DIVERSE</td><td>Targeted Differentiation (Product & Promotion)</td><td>Segmented Differentiation (Product, Service, Promotion, Price, Distribution)</td></tr>
<tr><td>HOMOGENEOUS</td><td>Generic Differentiation (Product, Price, Service, Distribution, Promotion)</td><td>Targeted Differentiation (Price and Distribution)</td></tr>
</table>

When market needs/wants are relatively homogeneous and resources (time, money, and expertise) are also relatively homogeneous, the market is a nondifferentiated mass market. In this market, generic differentiation would be a useful strategy for the marketer to become the customer's choice. Differentiating on any one element of the marketing mix is common here. One may strive to offer better quality, lower price, more convenient distribution, or better customer service.

At the other extreme, when both needs/wants and resources are diverse, it is best to segment the market into more homogeneous subgroups and practice segmented differentiation (based on demographics, psychographics, and usage characteristics, as described later in this chapter). All elements of the marketing mix (product, price, promotion, distribution, and customer service) are differentiated by creating a unique marketing mix for each segment.

In between the two extremes is targeted differentiation. This would be appropriate in situations where either needs/wants or resources are different, but not both. In that case, if needs/wants differences are the drivers for differentiation, it is better to use product and/or promotion as the primary method of differentiation. Examples include different skin-care products for ethnic customers whose skin tones indicate different needs. Car companies offer the minivan, four-door sedan, or the subcompact to accommodate the different needs of households with different family sizes. Marketing communications are used to position a brand for a very specific target segment, such as the positioning of Marlboro cigarettes for the individualistic, adventurous, masculine person.

When the resource differences (money, time, and expertise) are the primary drivers, then price, distribution, and customer service are the key differentiators. One crucial resource these days is time, and there are segments of the population that have very little time to spare, such as dual-income, white-collar, professional families. This segment therefore seeks companies that can service them at times when they are available, such as early in the morning, late at night, or on the weekends. It is in response to this that many banks, for example, are now open in some markets on Saturdays, and even on Sundays, in some cases. Some grocery stores stay open 24 hours a day. Service technicians, like telephone companies repair service, car dealerships and their service shops, and even public libraries, are also now more willing to work on the weekend. Many no-wait oil change services (e.g., Jiffy Lube, Quick Lube) represent marketer response to just such a time-pressured segment.

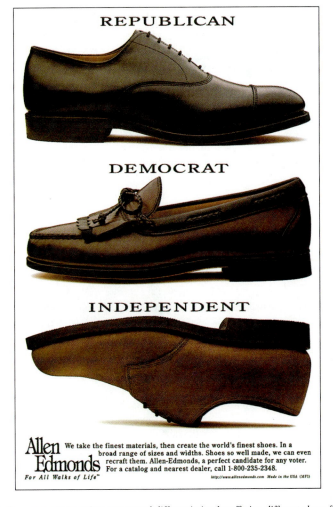

Allen-Edmonds shoe company practices segmented differentiation by offering different shoes for different customer segments.

Another resource precious to many customers is money. For example, there are people who can't afford certain products or services because they are single-wage earners with little education. This presents an opportunity for companies to market goods of acceptable quality at lower prices, such as the Hyundai car and stores that buy surplus merchandise and sell it at low prices. The growth of private labels in supermarkets is also a response to this money-constrained segment.

The final resource is expertise. Some consumers don't have the money to get household projects done by professionals and want to (or like to) do it themselves. They can find the time, but don't have quite the expertise needed to do the job. This segment of "do-it-yourself" customers requires expert advice on materials selection and some guidance in doing the work. Companies like Home Depot have responded very effectively to customers of this type by offering in-depth advice on materials and techniques.

In the business market, companies have always struggled for time. Time-sensitive document delivery has now become a big business, and Kinko's promotes itself not only as doing large quantity copying but also a quick turn-around time. Restaurants serving the lunch crowd in business districts differentiate themselves by promising a 15- (or even 10-)

Shouldice Hospital: Not All Patients Are Welcome Here!

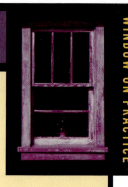

Most sick people couldn't be admitted to this hospital. And that is not because it is busy (which it is), but because the hospital *chooses* to exclude all patients save one kind. It doesn't have a maternity or obstetrician department; urology or neurology; ear, nose, or eye; pediatrician or geriatrics; heart surgery or cancer treatment; no long-term inpatient care facilities, no services for quit-smoking, antidrug, insomniac, or the like. In fact, it does not even have an emergency department. This is Shouldice Hospital in Toronto.

The only kind of patients it admits are those needing hernia surgery. And even here, if the hernia victim has a history of heart trouble or has undergone surgery in the last 12 months or is overweight, he must apply elsewhere. Only simple, uncomplicated hernia victims are welcome here. The surgeons have performed hundred of thousands of hernia repairs, more than those at any other hospital (obviously), thus boasting the most experience, and consequently, for the hospital, the highest productivity. The hospital uses only local anesthesia (which is safer and cheaper), which allows patients to recover sooner (since they are up and about sooner). That is why it does not admit complicated hernia cases.

The patients receive a warm welcome upon arrival. Nurses are attentive and personal, and doctors very com-

petent. Patients' medical needs are well attended to, but the staff acts as though their clientele is well and healthy. (One way to do this is to interact with clients with pleasure and camaraderie instead of the usual "sympathy" and "control.")

Its nurse-to-patient ratio is the lowest in the industry. It doesn't have too many wheelchairs and gurneys, beds or private rooms, or even wide elevators. Instead it has low-rise staircases, plush carpeted hallways, and centralized TV and restroom lounges. A typical afternoon sight is one of groups of patients walking in the hallways and strolling on acres of landscaped grounds outdoors, still hooked to the glucose feeder bottle on a mobile stand.

Are patients happy with this kind of "self-service" hospital care? Judge for yourself: Ex-patients hold an annual reunion to commemorate their Shouldice experience!

Source: Excerpt adapted from Case Shouldice Hospital Limited, Christopher H. Love Lock, *Services Marketing*, 3rd edition (Prentice Hall, 1996), Englewood Cliffs, NJ pp. 614–27.

Additional information located at

http://www.shouldice.com

minute-lunch service but with a limited menu. An exemplar of targeted differentiation (i.e., niche marketing) is Shouldice Hospital in Toronto, which focuses on a single surgical procedure, namely, hernia, and that too only in otherwise healthy patients. See the Window on Practice box.

Thus, both in the household and business markets, and for physical goods and services alike, new opportunities exist for identifying a segment that differs from the rest of the customer base (based on differences in either needs/wants or their resources), and to differentiate the offerings targeted to this segment.

Identification of Markets for Differentiation and Segmentation

How should companies go about identifying market subgroups to target? The various bases of identifying these groups involve some form of market segmentation. **Market segmentation** is a process of identifying subgroups of customers within a market whose needs, wants, and/or resources are different in a way that makes them respond differently to a given marketing mix.

It is a truism that a given product does not appeal equally to all. Some desire their clothes to be more comfortable than stylish, while others desire the reverse. Some need their shampoos to be strong dandruff removers, while others want gentler shampoos that would make their limp hair look fuller. Some have no use for cowboy boots and want dress shoes instead; others want good loafers rather than dress shoes. Some are attracted to natural foods for their health benefits even if they like fried foods better; to others, fried foods are more appealing even if they are not as healthy.

Such differential response occurs for other elements of the marketing mix as well. Some want the lowest-priced hotel room; others would pay more for a more conveniently located or a better-appointed hotel. Some don't mind shopping in warehouse food stores and bagging their own groceries; others would pay for a full-service store. In distribution, some consumers looking to buy, say, furniture feel comfortable ordering from a mail-order house; others want to see the merchandise before deciding to buy and therefore prefer to order it from a retail store. Some athletic shoe buyers desire a specialty store with knowledgeable salespersons who can offer them product guidance; others feel more self-sufficient in product expertise and prefer to buy them from a general merchandise store. In advertising, some seek an advertisement with detailed product information; others respond better to a celebrity sponsoring a product.

In sum, the differing responses of customers to one or more elements of the marketing mix form the rationale for segmentation. Once a marketer has identified subgroups of customers with different response tendencies the marketer attempts to target them by different marketing mixes. These different marketing mixes might differ only in their product element, or in pricing, or distribution, or promotion, or in customer service, or all of these. When all elements of the marketing mix are differentiated for each market segment, a perfect segmentation strategy is realized.

Approaches to identify different subgroups of customers who would respond differently to different marketing mixes are discussed later in the chapter. Note that once a marketer has identified various segments, the marketer has the option of following either a targeted differentiation or a segmentation differentiation strategy.

There are three board bases of identifying segments in any market—the "what," the "who," and the "why" bases of segmentation. The "what" pertains to product *usage* and results in what is commonly referred to as **usage segmentation**. The "who" basis identifies subgroups of customers based on their descriptive characteristics (e.g., age, sex, social class); this is commonly referred to as the **demographic segmentation**. And, finally, the "why" pertains to the *reasons* that customers behave the way they do; these reasons lie in different benefits customers seek from a product, and different lifestyles they want the product to fit. This basis of segmentation is commonly referred to as **psychographic segmentation** (see Figure 12.2). (The following discussion emphasizes segmentation of households; in a later section, we apply these principles to business markets.)

Usage Segmentation

The common approach to usage segmentation (based on the *what* aspect of market behavior) is to divide customers on their level of usage. Thus, segments are ranked high, medium, and low, according to the quantity consumed. For instance, for the movie theater business, you might say that those who go to a movie theater once a month or less often are light users, more than once a month but less than four times a month are medium users, and those who go to a movie theater more than once a week are heavy users.

Another popular way of segmenting by usage is called the "heavy half" theory. As a rule of thumb, one-half of the consumers consume about 80 percent of the product, whereas the other half consume only 20 percent. This 80/20 split is, of course, a general description; in specific product categories it could vary from a 35/65 split at one extreme to a 10/90 split at the other. Consider some examples in selected industries. For colas, 50 percent of the consumers—the heavy half—account for 83 percent of all cola consumption; for dog food, used by 30 percent of U.S. households, the heavy half account for 81 percent of purchase. For greeting cards, women account for 80 percent of the total cards bought in the United States. In the paper towels market, 34 percent are nonusers, 33 percent use 17 percent, and 33 percent use 83 percent of the paper towels produced. Finally, in the shampoo market, 18 percent are nonusers, 41 percent consume 19 percent of the shampoo, and 41 percent use 81 percent of the shampoo produced.

Assuming a 20/80 split in a given market, one heavy user's consumption is equal to the consumption of four light users; in other words, it has four times the value of a light user's consumption. In an industrial setting, where the split is sometimes even 10/90, companies need to manage the "key" accounts in the heavy half. Losing one of the customers who falls into the 10 percent range could result in a significant loss in revenue.

Heavy-half segments can be further split into super heavy and heavy. To do this, the marketer finds the median level of usage or consumption within the heavy half.

Once a company has decided on the three or four segments, it needs to profile each according to its demographic and psychographic makeup. Generally, one would find heavy users to share the same demographics and perhaps also the same psychographics. Illustratively, heavy beer drinkers are 25 to 50 years of age, working-class males; they are also heavy watchers of TV, and are more interested in sports than is the general public.[4] Profiling heavy users in terms of such demographics and psychographics would assist a marketer in targeting product promotions.

Demographic Segmentation

To classify customers according to the "who" aspect of market behavior marketers use demographic segmentation (see Figure 12.2). Table 12.2 summarizes the various demographic characteristics. It also details two other measures of the "who" bases: geography

THREE BASES OF IDENTIFYING MARKET SEGMENTS

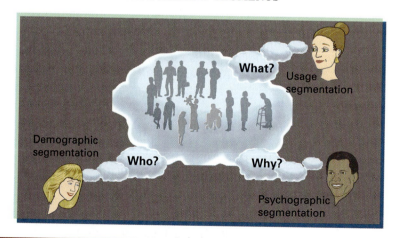

Table 12.2	THE "WHO" BASES OF SEGMENTATION

DEMOGRAPHICS

Gender:	males, females
Age:	youth, baby boomers, senior citizens, Generation X
Family life cycle:	young, single, older married couples, and so on
	religious and/or ethnic background
	income, education, occupation, and social class

GEOGRAPHY

Regions:	Northern Region, Southern Belt, West Coast, East Coast and so on
Metro size:	mega-metro (e.g., New York), mid-size towns (300–600k), small cities (100–300)
Urbanization:	urban, innercity, suburban, rural
Climate:	cold (northern), warm (southern)

GEODEMOGRAPHICS

Examples:	nine nations; PRIZM, Claritas' Cluster Plus, CCAI's ACORN.

and geodemographics. We have discussed these demographic bases in detail in Chapters 6 and 7, and geographic characteristics in Chapter 4. Accordingly, our discussion will focus on examples that apply these characteristics for segmentation.

Recently, marketers have identified a new segment, termed the "older, affluent market."[5] This segment combines both age and income, with age reflecting a needs orientation and income reflecting a wants/resources orientation. The cosmetic industry also segments its market by age, race, and ethnic groups.

DEMOGRAPHIC BASES

Perhaps the most prevalent demographic characteristic used to segment household markets is gender. Clothing, cosmetics, hair-care products, toiletries, cigarettes, and so on, are all marketed differently to men and women. Two points are noteworthy here. First, in some product categories, the product itself needs to be different for the two genders (e.g., clothing, shoes, cosmetics), so the segmentation by gender is inevitable. In other product categories, segmentation is not inevitable, but it is pursued in the hope of increasing the product's perceived attractiveness for one or the other gender. Thus, cigarettes are differentiated in their size (i.e., slimness), package, brand name, and user imagery communicated via advertising; the brand Eve is targeted toward women and Camel and Marlboro toward men. The second point about gender-based segmentation is that for product categories used by both genders, there would always be a segment that would defy gender-based differentiation, although the size of this segment would vary with sociocultural trends. Unisex clothing and adoption of Marlboro by some women smokers exemplify this cross-gender product uniformity.

Another obvious demographic characteristic by which household markets are segmented is age. For example, U.S. retailer Limited, targets adult working women with its Limited stores and teenage youth with the Limited Express stores. An important segment in the United States is the 55 plus age group, with over 60 million people and growing three times faster than the overall U.S. population. It is interesting to note that the magazine with the largest circulation in America is not *Newsweek, Time, People,* or even *TV Guide* or *Reader's Digest;* rather it is *Modern Maturity* (with 22 million subscribers in 1997). In between the youth and the 55 plus age group is the 40-something group, once targeted for example, by the magazine *Lears* with the slogan, "for the woman *not* born yesterday." Many hospitals are organizing elder-care centers specializing in care of the elderly. Barnett's Bank of Florida was a pioneer in organizing a Senior's Club to cater to its 55 plus customers. Baby boomers are recognized as another important segment, currently the prime prospect for financial planning products. Finally, there is Generation X, recently becoming more eclectic in its values, and being targeted by The Gap clothing companies.

Other demographic characteristics identified in Table 12.2 are family life cycle, income, education, occupation, and social class. Each of these has been discussed in preceding chapters, so we shall not repeat them here. Suffice it to say that each forms a useful basis of segmenting the market depending on the product category. For example, family life cycle can be used to segment the market for housing and home furnishings—for example, start-up families would need smaller houses compared to those needed by, say, full-nest families. A good example of income/social class-based segmentation is the previously cited strategy used by Gap, Inc., which owns and operates three store chains— Gap stores for middle-income, Banana Republic for affluent, and Old Navy for the lower-income customers.

GEODEMOGRAPHICS

Geodemographics is the study of relationships between demographics on the one hand and geographic location on the other. The underlying premise is that people of similar demographic characteristics (age, income, occupation) tend to live in similar geographic locations. Moreover, since the natural and economic resources of a geographic location enable and constrain people's activities, geographic location helps shape people's lifestyles and activities (which are also in part shaped by demographics). For example, people in wet and cold areas will have a different lifestyle than, say, those in desert areas. Likewise, people in farmlands will differ in lifestyle from those in industrial towns. Consequently, geodemographics can be a useful basis of segmenting customers. Two geodemographics segmentation schemes are described below.

Segmentation tools

NINE NATIONS   A good illustration of geodemographic segmentation is based on sociologist Joel Garreau's work on identifying nine regions (or "nations") in North America.[6] See Figure 12.3. Garreau traveled widely across North America, observing people and codifying their behavior and moorings. Garreau's logic was, "Each nation has,"—and here he refers to the nine subnations, actually, "its own list of desires . . . and a distinct prism through which it views the world." Thus, Garreau's nine nations differ from one another because of topography, climate, and sociocultural factors. See the summary profile in Table 12.3.

The undercurrent and the premise of this delineation are the value differences among different nations, so that two cities within the same geographic region could be classified in two different "nations." Thus, San Francisco and Los Angeles, both in the pacific region, are assigned respectively to Ecotopia and MexAmerica. Ecotopians believe that "small is beautiful," contrary to the beliefs of the MexAmerica and Empty Quarters. Ecotopians share their antidevelopment view with New England, where "voluntary poverty has become rather chic." The most distinguishing feature of the Breadbasket is that people value "honest gains from hard labor" as opposed to leisure. The Islands in contrast value "fun and enjoyment" the most.

Consumer researcher Lynn R. Kahle has studied the predominant values held by people in these "nations." He used a list of nine values and asked a representative sample of 2,235 Americans to choose the value most important to them. Later, he divided the sam-

Figure 12.3

THE EIGHT NATIONS OF THE UNITED STATES

NINTH NATION

ECOTOPIA   EMPTY QUARTER   NEW ENGLAND   DIXIE (or NEW SOUTH)

MEXAMERICA   BREADBASKET   FOUNDRY (or RUSTBELT)   ISLANDS

Source: Adapted from Joel Garreau, *The Ogilvy & Mather Listening Post* (New York: Ogilvy & Mather, 1983), p. 3.

Table 12.3

SUMMARY PROFILE OF THE NINE NATIONS

NAME	EXAMPLE CITY	DESCRIPTION
Breadbasket	Kansas City	Agricultural economy; conservative, conformist people; stable and most contented people.
The Foundry	Detroit	Urban and industrialized; work oriented.
Dixie	Atlanta	Small-town way of life; rapidly transforming economically.
The Empty Quarter	Denver	Largest area, smallest population; rich in energy and mineral resources; blue-collar concentration; hardworking and conservative.
MexAmerica	Los Angeles	Growth oriented, most entrepreneurial; large Hispanic population.
The Islands	Miami	The most diverse population with Caribbean, Latin American, and Hispanic majority; large retired communities, heavy illegal drug traffic.
New England	Boston	Poorest "nation" making economic progress; politically diverse; recent high-tech influx; "quality of life more important than material goods."
Ecotopia	San Francisco	Home of the "Silicon Valley"; high-tech economy; largest concentration of the young, educated, affluent; "small is beautiful" mind-set; most fun-living.
Quebec	Quebec City	Very homogeneous French-speaking culture; diversified economy.

Adapted from Joel Garreau, *The Nine Nations of North America* (Boston, MA: Houghton Mifflin, 1981).

ple into Garreau's nine nations and also according to the nine U.S. Census regions. His results were twofold: (1) the nine nations do differ in the values its people hold dear, and (2) similar distinctions exist across the nine Census Bureau regions. Garreau's nine nations are not any better (but not any worse) in segmenting people by values than the Census Bureau's regions. Because the suppliers of syndicated marketing research organize information according to the Census Bureau's classification of regions and not along Garreau's nine-nation scheme, marketers can more easily use the former. The most important contribution from Garreau is that he created "literary" labels with connotative meaning for thinking about the geographical differences among consumer markets.

PRIZM The most widely known geodemographic segmentation scheme is PRIZM. Its foundational premise is the maxim "Birds of a feather flock together." Devised by Claritas Corporation of Alexandria, Virginia, the scheme is based on clustering 250,000 neighborhoods into 40 groups based on their zip codes (which number about 36,000).

ZQ 11: BOHEMIAN MIX

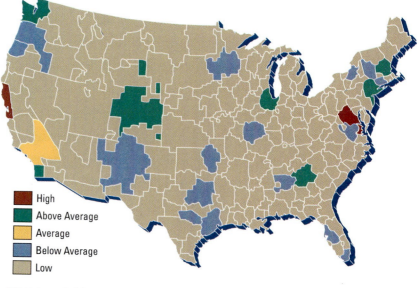

High
Above Average
Average
Below Average
Low

1.1% of U.S. households

Primary age range:	18–34
Median household income:	$21,916
Median home value:	$110,668

Thumbnail Demographics

Bohemian innercity neighborhoods
multiunit housing
racially mixed singles
college graduates
white-collar jobs

Sample Neighborhoods

Greenwich Village, New York, New York (10014)
Dupont Circle, Washington, D.C. (20036)
Cambridge, Boston, Massachusetts (02139)
Lincoln Park, Chicago, Illinois (60614)
Shadyside, Pittsburgh, Pennsylvania (15232)
Haight-Ashbury, San Francisco, California (94117)

The unit of measurement is a zip code—that is, all the households in a zip code are placed in a cluster as a group. But the basis of clustering is lifestyles, so that zip codes with residents manifesting a particular lifestyle are grouped together. People's lifestyles directly influence what they will buy and thus the market potential for specific products and services in those clusters of zip codes; hence the name Prizm (Potential Rating Index by Zip Codes). Claritas also links the zip code information with behavioral purchase data, credit card information, magazine subscriptions, and radio and TV listening/viewing data.

The 40 PRIZM groups are listed in Table 12.4, ranked by relative affluence scale called a Zip Quality (ZQ) scale. ZQ is computed from a number of indicators such as median income, education, median home value, and so on. Note, for example, that the groups Bohemian mix and Grain Belt have about equal median income but are far apart on the ZQ scale, number 11 and 33 respectively. Of course, they differ vastly on median home value and on education. They also differ on lifestyle and purchase of products and

Figure 12.4

ZQ 11: BOHEMIAN MIX *continued*

LIFESTYLE

HIGH USAGE	INDEX	LOW USAGE	INDEX
Environmentalist organizations	573	Gardening	57
Downhill skiing	306	Tupperware	45
Common Stock	248	Country records/tapes	39
1960s rock/records/tapes	235	Standard-size cars	13
Imported beer	221	CB radios	7
Health food	163		

MAGAZINES/NEWSPAPERS

HIGH USAGE	INDEX	LOW USAGE	INDEX
Atlantic Monthly	727	Family Handyman	26
Harper's	645	Seventeen	19
The New Yorker	489		

CARS

HIGH USAGE	INDEX	LOW USAGE	INDEX
Alfa Romeos	516	Buick LeSabres	16
Saabs	261	Ford Crown Victorias	16
Peugeots	222	Mercury Grand Marquises	15
BMW 3 Series	219	Dodge Diplomats	13

FOOD

HIGH USAGE	INDEX	LOW USAGE	INDEX
Whole-wheat bread	144	White bread	65
Frozen waffles	120	Pretzels	56
Fruit juices and drinks	116	Frozen pizzas	54
TV dinners	115	Meat tenderizers	49

ZQ 33: GRAIN BELT

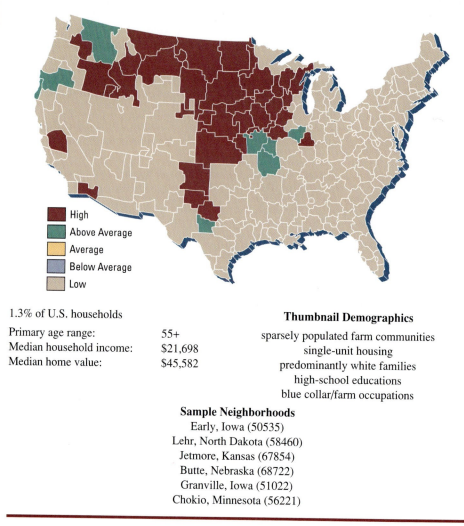

High

Above Average

Average

Below Average

Low

1.3% of U.S. households

Primary age range: 55+
Median household income: $21,698
Median home value: $45,582

Thumbnail Demographics

sparsely populated farm communities
single-unit housing
predominantly white families
high-school educations
blue collar/farm occupations

Sample Neighborhoods
Early, Iowa (50535)
Lehr, North Dakota (58460)
Jetmore, Kansas (67854)
Butte, Nebraska (68722)
Granville, Iowa (51022)
Chokio, Minnesota (56221)

services. Figures 12.4 and 12.5 depict their geographical concentration and some key facts. Let us examine these groups briefly.

Bohemian Mixers (ZQ 11) are young residents of urban hodge-podge neighborhoods; the majority never married or are divorced singles, and predominantly students, artists, writers, actors, and the like, with a U-shaped income distribution concentrated on the high- and low-income groups. They live somewhat adventuresome, funky lives, exercising both their bodies and minds hanging out at sidewalk cafes, public libraries, bookstores, discussion groups, health food stores, social and voluntary organizations, benefit programs, and public demonstrations and protest campaigns on social issues. They shun domestic cars, subscribe to literary magazines (e.g., *Atlantic Monthly*), and buy healthy foods.

In sharp contrast are Grain Belters (ZQ 33), who live in America's most sparsely populated rural communities and small farm towns now in economic decline. Barely sol-

Figure 12.5

ZQ 33: GRAIN BELT *continued*

LIFESTYLE

HIGH USAGE	INDEX	LOW USAGE	INDEX
Gas chain saws	210	Health clubs	38
Cats	172	Jazz records/tapes	24
Watch rodeo	171	Common stock	6
Tupperware	150	Burglar alarm systems	0
Horseback riding	139		

MAGAZINES/NEWSPAPERS

HIGH USAGE	INDEX	LOW USAGE	INDEX
Grit	398	Harper's	6
Lakeland Boating	222	Scientific American	2
Hunting	168	Food & Wine	0

CARS

HIGH USAGE	INDEX	LOW USAGE	INDEX
Chrysler E-Classes	191	Peugeots	19
Oldsmobile Delta 88s	189	Toyota Corollas	16
Chevrolet Impalas	168	Fiat Spiders	13
Ford Crown Victorias	167	Volvos	13

FOOD

HIGH USAGE	INDEX	LOW USAGE	INDEX
Canned stews	148	Frozen dessert pies	69
Powdered fruit drinks	130	Frozen waffles	54
Cookie-baking chips	128	TV dinners	54
Frozen pizzas	118		

vent on farm income, they are conservative, have faith in God, and are believers in Providence (the purchase rate for burglar alarms is zero). They patronize domestic brands of cars, read such magazine as *Hunting*, and spend leisure hours in such activities as watching rodeo and horseback riding. See Figure 12.5.

Since Claritas links purchase behaviors with zip code information, PRIZM is very useful for identifying the zip location and lifestyle of customers, product by product or by store category. For example, the top cluster for U.S. retailer Sears is Levittown (ZQ 12), while for U.S. retailer Kmart it is Shotguns & Pickups (ZQ 24). See Figure 12.6. For McDonald's, the top cluster is Rank & File (ZQ 20) and the bottom cluster is Tobacco Roads (ZQ 38). See Figure 12.7).

Table 12.4 provides basic data about these groups.

All the households in a zip code are placed in a cluster as a group, but the basis of clustering is lifestyles.In other words, zip codes with residents manifesting a particular lifestyle are grouped together. Two of the 40 PRIZM groups are profiled in Figure 12.5.

Figure 12.6

AMERICA'S SHOPPERS: SEARS VS. KMART

Numbers indicate percentages of people who shop at Sears or Kmart, indexed against the national average. An index of 100 equals the U.S. average: 33.2% for Sears, 43.2% for Kmart. An index of 130 means a cluster has 1.3 times the national average, or 56.2% in the case of Sears.

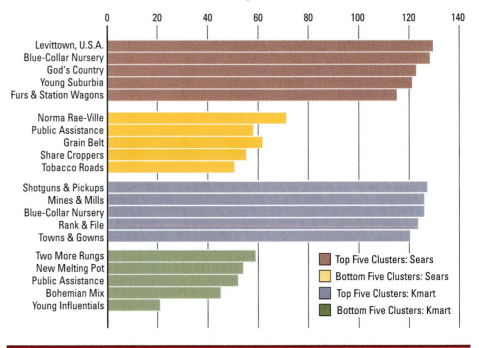

Source: SMRB 1985/86, Claritas Corp., 1987.

Figure 12.7

MCCLUSTERS: WHO EATS AT MCDONALD'S?

Numbers indicate percentages of people who frequent McDonald's, indexed against the national average. An index of 100 equals the U.S. average: 36.2%. An index of 132 means a cluster has 1.32 times the national average, or 47.8%.

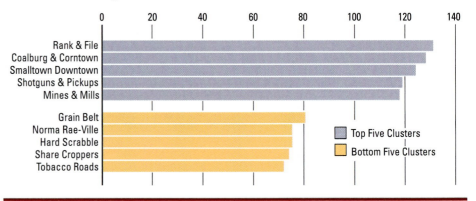

Source: MRI Doublebase 1986, Claritas Corp., 1987.

Table 12.4

40 PRIZM CLUSTERS OF NEIGHBORHOODS IN AMERICA

CLUSTER ZQ#	CLUSTER NAME	PERCENT U.S. HOUSEHOLDS	MEDIAN INCOME	PERCENT COLLEGE GRADUATES	THUMBNAIL DESCRIPTION
1	Blue Blood Estates	1.1	$70,307	50.7%	America's wealthiest neighborhoods includes suburban homes and one in ten millionaires
2	Money & Brains	0.9	45,798	45.5	Posh big-city enclaves of townhouses, condos and apartments
3	Furs & Station Wagons	3.2	50,086	38.1	New money in metropolitan bedroom suburbs
4	Urban Gold Coast	0.5	36,838	50.5	Upscale urban high-rise districts
5	Pools & Patios	3.4	35,895	28.2	Older, upper-middle-class, suburban communities
6	Two More Rungs	0.7	31,263	28.3	Comfortable multi-ethnic suburbs
7	Young Influentials	2.9	30,398	36.0	Yuppie, fringe-city condo and apartment developments
8	Young Suburbia	5.3	38,582	23.8	Child-rearing, outlying suburbs
9	God's Country	2.7	36,728	25.8	Upscale frontier boomtowns
10	Blue-Chip Blues	6.0	32,218	13.1	The wealthiest blue-collar suburbs
11	Bohemian Mix	1.1	21,916	38.8	Innercity bohemian enclaves à la Greenwich Village
12	Levittown, U.S.A.	3.1	28,742	15.7	Aging, post–World War II tract subdivisions
13	Gray Power	2.9	25,259	18.3	Upper-middle-class retirement communities
14	Black Enterprise	0.8	33,149	16.0	Predominantly black, middle-and upper-middle-class neighborhoods
15	New Beginnings	4.3	24,847	19.3	Fringe-city areas of singles complexes, garden apartments and trim bungalows
16	Blue-Collar Nursery	2.2	30,077	10.2	Middle-class, child-rearing towns
17	New Homesteaders	4.2	25,900	15.9	Exurban boom towns of young, midscale families
18	New Melting Pot	0.9	22,142	19.1	New immigrant neighborhoods, primarily in the nation's port cities
19	Towns & Gowns	1.2	17,862	27.5	America's college towns
20	Rank & File	1.4	26,283	9.2	Older, blue-collar, industrial suburbs
21	Middle America	3.2	24,431	10.7	Midscale, midsize towns
22	Old Yankee Rows	1.6	24,808	11.0	Working-class rowhouse districts
23	Coalburg & Corntown	2.0	23,994	10.4	Small towns based on light industry and farming
24	Shotguns & Pickups	1.9	24,291	9.1	Crossroads villages serving the nation's lumber and breadbasket needs
25	Golden Ponds	5.2	20,140	12.8	Rustic cottage communities located near the coasts, in the mountains or alongside lakes
26	Agri-Business	2.1	21,363	11.5	Small towns surrounded by large-scale farms and ranches
27	Emergent Minorities	1.7	22,029	10.7	Predominantly black, working-class, city neighborhoods
28	Single City Blues	3.3	17,926	18.6	Downscale, urban, singles districts
29	Mines & Mills	2.8	21,537	8.7	Struggling steeltowns and mining villages
30	Back-Country Folks	3.4	19,843	8.1	Remote, downscale, farm towns

(continued on page 450)

Table 12.4 40 PRIZM CLUSTERS OF NEIGHBORHOODS IN AMERICA *continued*

CLUSTER ZQ#	CLUSTER NAME	PERCENT U.S. HOUSEHOLDS	MEDIAN INCOME	PERCENT COLLEGE GRADUATES	THUMBNAIL DESCRIPTION
31	Norma Rae-Ville	2.3	18,559	9.6	Lower-middle-class milltowns and industrial suburbs, primarily in the South
32	Smalltown Downtown	2.5	17,206	10.0	Inner-city districts of small industrial cities
33	Grain Belt	1.3	21,698	8.4	The nation's most sparsely populated rural communities
34	Heavy Industry	2.8	18,325	6.5	Lower-working-class districts in the nation's older industrial cities
35	Share Croppers	4.0	16,854	7.1	Primarily southern hamlets devoted to farming and light industry
36	Downtown Dixie Style	3.4	15,204	10.7	Aging, predominantly black neighborhoods, typically in southern cities
37	Hispanic Mix	1.9	16,270	6.8	America's Hispanic barrios
38	Tobacco Roads	1.2	13,227	7.3	Predominantly black farm communities throughout the South
39	Hard Scrabble	1.5	12,874	6.5	The nation's poorest rural settlements
40	Public Assistance	3.1	10,804	6.3	America's inner city ghettos

Adapted from Michael J. Weiss, *Clustering of America* (New York: Harper & Row, 1988) pp. 5, 13.

The "Why" Basis of Market Segmentation

Marketers also may segment markets according to customers' underlying motives, or the reasons why they respond differently than other segments. Marketers have offered three categories of explanations for different customer responses: (1) differences in benefits sought, (2) product involvement attitude, and (3) differences in lifestyles and psychographics. The explanation based on benefits sought is that consumers differ in the specific benefits they seek in the same product or service, so they respond differently to various market offerings. Second, consumers differ in their involvement in and attitude toward the product category, and consequently differ in their response. The third explanation is that consumers differ in their personality, lifestyle, and psychographics—concepts we discussed in Chapters 7 (personality) and 10 (lifestyle and psychographics). As explained in these chapters, consumers buy products and services to satisfy the personality needs they have and to implement the lifestyle they desire to live. Accordingly, they respond differently to different marketplace stimuli.

BENEFIT SEGMENTATION

Why do some consumers prefer Head & Shoulders brand of shampoo while others prefer Pert, both made by Procter & Gamble? The reason is that for over a decade, Head & Shoulders has been advertised as a dandruff shampoo, so people who want the benefit of dandruff elimination buy Head & Shoulders. In contrast, Pert has been advertised as a shampoo that will give hair a lot of body, so people with limp hair would prefer this brand. Across a wide variety of products, the reason consumers seek one brand rather than another is that they are seeking particular benefits that brand offers better than the competitor. Products and services are bundles of benefits, and different brands contain different benefits; thus different brands appeal to different consumers according to what benefits consumers are seeking.

Benefit Segmentation refers to grouping individual customers according to the benefits they seek from a product or service. That is, consumers are grouped into a segment based on the similarity of benefits sought; different benefit segments seek different benefits.

The classic research on benefit segmentation was done by Russell Haley.[7] Back in the 60s, he identified four benefit segments among toothpaste consumers. These segments are presented in Table 12.5. In this table, although demographic and lifestyle profiles of the segments are also furnished, what makes this a benefit segmentation is that the four groups were identified by the differences in the benefits consumers sought. The resulting four groups were *subsequently* profiled in terms of their demographics and lifestyles. And although in this case the segments happen to also differ on their demographic and psychographic profiles, this may not always be the case.

An example of business-to-business services is provided by yet another classic study, done by Wharton Business School (U.S.A.) professor Thomas Robertson for air freight service (The Flying Tigers). He found several different segments, including a time-sensitive segment, a price-sensitive segment, a "no-worry" segment, and a pick-up segment. Further, in the time-sensitive segment, several subsegments emerge, including ability to handle emergencies, minimum door-to-door time, and prime night-time departures. In the price-sensitive segment, the subsegments included those who cared most about best price, lowest total cost, and daylight rates. The "no-worry" segment had the following subsegments: keep the shipper informed; honest and straightforward; and able to trace the shipment (one of the benefits that Federal Express now offers based on its state-of-the-art computer tracking system). Finally, the pick-up segment included good pickup service; minimum time between calls and pickups; and good truck driver attitude.

Although most examples cited above give the impression that consumers in different segments seek altogether different benefits (e.g., dandruff elimination versus body to limp hair), in reality such is not the case. Products are bundles of multiple attributes—for example, toothpastes clean the teeth as well as freshen the breath; or cars come with a gas consumption rating, are varyingly reliable, have some style, and cost money. Benefit segments are identified by *relative* importance of one benefit over others (as opposed to dedicated preference for one benefit to the exclusion of other benefits). Table 12.6 shows one

TOOTHPASTE MARKET BENEFIT SEGMENTS

Table 12.5	SENSORY SEGMENT	SOCIABLE SEGMENT	WORRIER SEGMENT	INDEPENDENT SEGMENT
Principal benefit sought	Flavor, product appearance	Brightness of teeth	Decay preventing	Price
Demographic strengths	Children	Teens, young people	Large families	Men
Special behavioral characteristics	Users of spearmint-flavored toothpaste	Smokers	Heavy users	Heavy users
Brands disproportionately favored	Colgate	Ultra Brite	Crest	Cheapest brand
Lifestyle characteristics	Hedonistic	Active	Conservative	Value oriented

Source: Adapted from Russell I. Haley, "Benefit Segmentation: A Decision-Oriented Research Tool," *Journal of Marketing* 32 (July 1968), pp. 30–35. Published by the American Marketing Association.

Table 12.6

A BENEFIT SEGMENTATION OF PHOTO DEVELOPING SERVICES MARKET

CLUSTER ANALYSIS

SEGMENT	QUALITY	PRICE	CONVENIENCE	SPEED	RETURN	DIVERSE
1	6.80	5.83	5.83	5.50	5.66	3.96
2	6.71	4.76	3.38	4.00	4.66	3.80
3	4.60	6.60	6.20	5.80	3.40	2.60
4	6.47	6.28	5.42	3.66	2.80	2.57
5	6.90	3.45	5.63	4.45	3.54	3.36

Scores are mean values on a 7-point scale where 1 meant "not important at all," and 7 meant "extremely important."

DEFINITION OF SEGMENTS

	SEGMENT NAME	DESCRIPTION
Segment 1	"Want It all"	All six attributes important.
2	"Will Sacrifice"	Quality very important; will sacrifice convenience and even pay more.
3	"Cheap and Easy"	Most price sensitive; most convenience oriented; quality: anything goes.
4	"Basics"	Speed, returns and diversity least important. Desire the basics of quality, convenience, and value.
5	"Price no object"	Least price sensitive; want quality and convenience.

such benefit segmentation for a photo developing service. This segmentation resulted from the following research steps:

1. Develop a list of relevant benefits of a product category. This can be developed on the basis of focus groups with customers and conversations with product design engineers or product managers.

2. Obtain consumer evaluation of these benefits in terms of their importance to consumers. These "importance" ratings can be obtained either on a rating scale such as a seven-point scale anchored by "not at all important" (a score of 1) to "extremely important" (5 points) or by a weighing scale by asking respondents to distribute 100 points over the attributes. Using either scale, the respondents rate each of the following possible benefits for the photo developing service:

   ■ Quality of developed photos
   ■ Low price
   ■ Convenience
   ■ Speed
   ■ Variety of work

3. Enter the data in the computer and perform a cluster analysis by using any suitable statistical analysis package such as SPSS or SAS. Cluster analysis is a technique that groups together (i.e., clusters) persons who share the same pattern of ratings on a set of questions. The computer can place consumers in any number of groups (2, 3, 4, and so on) as specified by the analyst, always ensuring that persons within a group (i.e., cluster) are similar among themselves but are different from members of the other groups. Obtain two, three, four, five, and even six clusters, and for each of these obtain a "cluster profile" in terms of the cluster mean values (i.e., average rating of that specific cluster) for each of the benefits evaluated. The cluster profile in the bottom panel of Table 12.6 is obtained from one such analysis.

Table 12.7 A COMPARATIVE EVALUATION OF VARIOUS BASES OF SEGMENTATION

			EVALUATION CRITERIA		
BASIS	MEASURABILITY	SCOPE	DIAGNOSTIC VALUE	ACTIONABILITY	MARKETING MIX IMPLICATIONS
Usage	Easiest	Household + Institutional	Low	Least self-sufficient	Resource allocation
Demographics	Very easy	Household + Institutional	Low	Good	Media mix, distribution and pricing decisions
Psychographics	Difficult	Household (for nonfunctional products)	Moderate	Good	Advertisement creative execution
Benefits	Moderately easy	Household + Institutional (for functional products)	High	Good	Product design and message decisions

4. Choose the correct number of clusters based on a statistical fit criterion (the SAS and SPSS print these statistical criteria automatically) as well as based on cluster interpretability. The successive breakdown of customers from two to three, three to four, and so on groups also gives useful information and guidance as to the proper number of clusters to be deemed final. For example, if going from five to six clusters did not make the new clusters significantly different in terms of their desired benefits, then it is better to stop at five clusters.

In step 2, consumer response was obtained only on one question (to rate the benefits of one service). This was done to emphasize that *one question* is all you need in order to identify benefit segments in a market. In practice however, researchers would generally ask a few related questions such as consumer ratings of various brands on the same benefit lists—that is, consumers' brand beliefs or perceptions, and brand preference and current brand use history. Also, we would definitely ask a few demographic questions. These questions will enable a further analysis, for example, to understand relative brand perceptions of different benefit segments. More importantly, we would use the demographic questions to cross-profile the benefit segments by demographics. This enables us to describe the resulting segments not only in terms of the benefits they seek, but also how they differ, if at all, on demographics—that is, do consumers with different demographic characteristics differ in the benefits they seek?

PRODUCT ATTITUDE AND INVOLVEMENT

Customers differ in their attitude toward and involvement in product categories. Some consumers are not much involved in the product and use it only to the extent necessary or take it for granted; others are so passionately involved that they are consumed by it. Thus, while everybody wear shoes, some people may not care much about their appearance, prestige, upkeep, or match with the outfit. Others may be obsessed with the style of shoes in their collection. Similarly, some people may listen to jazz once in a while, while others may be fanatic about it. Or some might consider grocery shopping a chore, while others might consider it a joy. Obviously these people who differ in their involvement in or attitude toward a product would respond differently to market stimuli; accordingly, it pays for marketers to recognize these segments.

Consider the segments of car owners found in a recent study, based on their attitudes toward cars. In fact, it may be useful for you, as you read their descriptions, to identify which segment you might belong to.

- Gearhead—These are true car enthusiasts who enjoy driving their cars. They love to maintain and care or their cars, keeping them in tip-top condition. More than any other group, this segment is most likely to believe that the kind of car you drive shows who you are.

- Epicures—These car owners drive elegant, comfortable, well-equipped, luxury cars. They want to enjoy the car without having to do any work on it; accordingly, they depend on someone else taking care of their cars.

- Functionalists—This group likes functional, fuel efficient cars without concern for style or sportiness. They tend to buy small and mid-sized cars.

- Road Haters—This group is the least involved in their car or in driving. Concerned most with safety, they don't enjoy driving and have no interest in knowledge about cars.[8]

PERSONALITY, LIFESTYLES, AND PSYCHOGRAPHICS

The clearest example of lifestyles segmentation was the VALS (values and lifestyle) groups described in Chapter 10. That example shows how the entire population of consumers in the United States, and likewise in Japan, has been classified according to their motivations (e.g., principle or status orientations), activities, interests, and opinions (psychographic question items utilized to assess lifestyle). Notably, VALS is the most well-known psychographic segmentation scheme, widely in use, especially by advertising agencies for targeting specific audiences. It is not, however, the only scheme. A few others have been published in the marketing literature, especially for specific subgroups of populations (e.g., elderly, or women) or for specific sectors of business (e.g., insurance or healthcare industry). Moreover, marketers utilize other psychographic customer profiles custom-developed for their own customer groups.

To illustrate the use of psychographic segmentation, consider one recent application. In 1995, Atlanta-based U.S. Centers for Disease Control and Prevention (CDC&P) started a social marketing effort it called the "Nutrition and Physical Activity Initiative." To target their educational campaign, CDC approached the marketing research firm of Porter/Novelli, which had just started its annual survey of U.S. consumers on health-specific issues as part of an omnibus survey of consumer lifestyles. CDC got Porter/Novelli to design a specific "health-styles" questionnaire. Based on responses to more than a hundred psychographic questions from a national sample of 3,000 adult U.S. consumers, Porter/Novelli identified the following seven health lifestyle segments (along with the percent of U.S. adult population):

- Physical fantastics (24 percent)—Low-fat nutritious diets and regular exercise, frequent conversations on health topics, and compliance with the doctor's health advice mark this group of healthiest lifestyle Americans.

- Decent doolittles (24 percent)—Although living unhealthy lifestyles (smoking, drinking, poor eating and exercise habits), consumers in this group *are* aware of the health risks they face, but do nothing about it. They see themselves as "religious and conservative."

- Passively healthy (15 percent)—Although the members of this group are in excellent health currently, and also engage in exercising, their eating habits are unhealthy and, moreover, they are rather indifferent to their health.

- Active attractives (13 percent)—This group exercises regularly and also controls fat intake. Its members are socially very active and they describe themselves as "romantic," "youthful," and "vain."

- Tense but trying (10 percent)—Although they are diet and exercise conscious, they tend to be smokers and also more anxiety prone than other groups.

- Non-interested nihilists (7 percent)—The least health-oriented group, consumers in this group reject any personal responsibility for their health. They smoke and they dislike exercise. They are less satisfied with life than most other groups, and they describe themselves as homebodies.

- Hard living hedonists (6 percent)—This group comprises heavy smokers, drinkers, and illicit drug users. Psychologically, they are the least satisfied with life and describe themselves as "moody" and "independent."

These customer segments, based on lifestyle and psychographics, are unlikely to respond to a common, generic education and communication strategy from CDC&P. Instead, messages would need to be tailored to each segment. Rather than document the strategies CDC&P used for different segments, we leave it for you to brain storm appropriate strategies for targeting these groups.

Lifestyle- and psychographics-based segmentation can also be done within a population subgroup delineated by some demographic characteristic such as age, gender, or income. In discussing the age-based segmentation earlier, we identified such groups as teens, boomers, and senior citizens. However, these groups themselves are not very homogeneous. Large in numbers, they are internally quite diverse in marketplace behaviors, because they are quite diverse in their lifestyles. Accordingly, marketers can target their demographically defined customer segments better by further delineating subsegments based on lifestyles. An example of such an application of psychographics and lifestyle segmentation is in the Window on Research box, which describes a recent segmentation study of aging consumers.

Segmentation of Business Markets

The general approach to segmenting business markets parallels consumer segmentation. However, the specific categories differ somewhat.

DEMOGRAPHICS

For the institutional/business market, demographic characteristics include size of the customer (small, medium, and large businesses), geographic location, type of business (i.e., what business the customer company is in), and the life-cycle stage. Marketing consultants John Berrigan & Carl Finkbeiner call such characteristics "firmographics." **Firmographics**, like demographics in the household markets, are easily verified, objective characteristics of a business firm.[9]

The size of the business can help in two ways. First, it translates into usage segmentation, as size is generally related to the quantity of product needed. Also, large and small businesses differ in the degree of formalization in their buying procedure, which in turn requires different selling approaches.

Geographic location can be a very useful basis to segment the business market because that has a direct implication for where to locate distribution and sales infrastructure. For example, 80 percent of the U.S. export market (for bolts, nuts, rivets, washers, and so on) is located in five countries: Canada (53 percent), Mexico (13.6 percent), United Kingdom (6.8 percent), France (3.1 percent), and Japan (3 percent). A U.S. fasteners firm can

Gerontographics: Lifestyle Segments among the Elderly

Georgia State professor George Moschis, a leading marketing researcher with focus on aging customers, uses gerontographics to identify segments within the mature consumer population. He defines **gerontographics** as a "segmentation approach based on the premise that the factors that make older consumers more or less receptive to marketing offerings are directly related to their needs and lifestyles, which are in turn influenced by changing life conditions." When people experience major life events, Moschis explains, "they often change their outlook on life as they reevaluate their wants, goals, and roles on both personal and consumer levels . . . Older people who experience similar life events and circumstances in later life are likely to exhibit similar patterns of consumer behavior."

Moschis's study uses a gerontographics lifestyle model to classify older adults into four groups:

1. Healthy indulgers (18 percent)—These 55 plus consumers have experienced the fewest life events (e.g., divorce, widowhood, retirement or chronic health conditions); consequently, their behavior is least distinguished from those of younger consumers. This group is also financially well-off and well settled in life. Their major focus is on enjoying life.

2. Healthy hermits (36 percent)—Healthy hermits are likely to have experienced a negative life event (such as the death of spouse), and consequently they are psychologically and socially withdrawn. Many are unhappy with the resulting isolation; they also resent the fact that they are supposed to behave like old people.

3. Ailing outgoers (29 percent)—Like healthy hermits, the ailing outgoers have also experienced a negative life event, but they have not allowed it to affect their self-concept and self-esteem. They also accept the fact of their old age, but they still try to get as much out of life as possible.

4. Frail reclusers (17 percent)—Like ailing outgoers, this group also accepts their old-age status and has adjusted life activities accordingly. However, unlike outgoers, members of this group have chosen to cope with detrimental changes in later life by becoming spiritually strong.

Although everyone eats, ailing outgoers like to eat out more (as part of enjoying life) but also are concerned about diet. They also have to watch their pennies. There-

use this information to treat each of these five countries as a segment with targeted distribution facilities and sales effort.[10]

The type of business is an important segmenting criterion because the product may have to be customized for different applications. Dupont sells its fibers, for example, to textile, tire, carpet, and rope-making industries, among others. The fiber is customized for each and the sales force is organized around these applications. As another example, a great deal of customization is needed in the computer hardware and software industry, where the supplier would need to target different services and products depending on the industry the company is in. Indeed, IBM has differentiated its products in the market by using a vertical breakdown of the market, and targeting different products to manufacturing, retailing, financial services, and so on. Business-to-business marketers can easily categorize their business customers, through the use of SIC (Standard Industrial Classification) codes.

SIC is a numbering system for classifying all establishments in the United States that are engaged in any economic activity whatsoever. There are 11 primary groups of these establishments, A through K, each given two digit codes: for example, 01 to 09 for group A (which represents agriculture, forestry, and fishing establishments), and 60 to 89 to

continued

fore, food stores and restaurants that cater to special dietary foods and that provide healthy meal menus at a good price value will appeal to this group. Early-bird dinner specials offered by many restaurants attract many consumers of this group. Healthy indulgers, on the other hand, require no special attention and like to eat out just like their younger counterparts do.

In terms of clothing, ailing outgoers like to be socially acceptable, but they also want clothing that suits their body needs and is easy to get in and out of. J.C. Penney's catalog offers a line of clothing called easy dressing—a line of fashionable apparel that utilizes velcro fasteners (instead of zippers or buttons), roomier armholes, partially elasticized waistbands, and so on. Healthy hermits, on the other hand, don't want to stand out and, therefore, unlike the fashionable clothing desired by ailing outgoers, hermits desire conservative clothing that will conform to the majority of seniors' own tastes.

In housing, ailing outgoers' social orientation will make them seek retirement communities with social-networking opportunities, but also nearby shopping areas and other activity centers so they can exercise their independence. Healthy indulgers, on the other hand, are looking for truly independent living. They sell their large houses of the full-nest stage and move into apartments and condos. Being upscale, they invest in home furnishings, modern appliances, and home cleaning services. Healthy hermits and frail reclusers prefer to stay put in single-family homes of their full-nest years, remodeling and doing home improvement projects. Hermits are in fact do-it-yourselfers, and accordingly, Home Depot (a U.S. home-repair and remodelling hardware products store chain) caters to this group by hiring elderly sales associates who might be better able to relate to this group of consumers. Frail reclusers, being in poor health, depend much more than hermits on outsourcing of home-maintenance services.

The segments also differ in their response to marketing communications. Since ailing outgoers don't mind acting their age, they are very accepting of promotions that portray old people as old people. Healthy indulgers and hermits, on the other hand, resent the stereotypical portrayals of older people and are turned off by promotions that identify them as old (e.g., hotel, motel, and restaurant chains offering senior citizen discounts).

Additional information is located at **http://www. demographics.com, http://www.aarp.org**

Source: George P. Moschis, "Life Stages of the Mature Market," *American Demographics*, 18, no. 9 (September 1996), pp. 44–50.

group H (which represents finance, insurance, and real estate). The specific two digits within the same basic group represent a specific industry group within that basic category (e.g., 53 for general merchandise and 54 for food stores). The subsequent digits in the seven-digit SIC codes are added to identify increasingly more specific types within nesting, broader groups of establishments. Thus, SIC 3441121 is for manufacturers of fabricated structural metal for buildings—namely, iron and steel. All U.S. government data available on industry and economic activity are tabulated and summarized by these SIC codes. Thus, business customers in industries with one SIC code may be treated as a different segment than those in another SIC code.

Finally, life-cycle stage identifies a business as either a start-up organization, a growing company, a mature organization, or an aging company. These stages reflect very different needs and wants, as well as different buying policies and procedures. Companies at the four stages also have different corporate objectives and cash-flow requirements. As a result of these differences, the buying behavior of companies tends to differ from one stage of development to another. In fact, Mack Hannan, a management consultant, has argued that an approach to becoming what he calls "recompetitive" in a mature industry is to look for customer companies that have a growth potential and then to grow with them.[11]

PSYCHOGRAPHICS

The concept of psychographics would translate in the business context as the behavioral dynamics of the customer. The formal policies and organizational structure set up for procurement serve as the broad parameters of this behavior which a marketer needs to be aware of. Some companies use centralized buying, whereas others spread this function over many employees or facilities. Some favor single-source supplier, others cultivate multiple sources. Some want to patronize local and/or minority businesses. Some seek reciprocal buying arrangements. The constellation of these variables can serve to segment markets.

THE BUYING CENTER

An important concept in industrial buying is that of "the Buying Center." This concept is discussed in more detail in Chapter 16; here, we briefly describe its use for segmentation. The **buying center** consists of all the members of a customer firm who play some role in the purchase decision. It includes five different roles: user, influencer, buyer, gatekeeper, and decider. For the purchase of industrial raw materials, for example, the production manager would be the user, the product design engineers could be the influencers who specify the technical quality standards, an assistant in the purchasing department may be the gatekeeper with discretion to allow or disallow various salespersons to see particular managers in the company, the executive vice president may be the decider, and the purchasing director might be the one who places a formal order. The information needs of these role players are different and need to be addressed.

This MasterCard ad is as adept at verbally presenting its product's core benefits as at visually capturing the psychographics of the small business organizations.

Business customers can be segmented on the basis of who plays a major role in the purchase of specific products. For example, in some business firms, the technical persons (i.e., engineers, information system specialists) or users (e.g., plant supervisors) might select the vendor; in others, purchasing managers or financial controllers might play a more dominant role. In this example, the marketer might segment business buyers into technical influence and executive influence customer groups.

Beyond the formal structure, informal organizational dynamics and political processes are important, as is the corporate culture. Members of the buying center may be purely task-oriented, or they might be caught in power games of turf-guarding. Culturally, the buyer organization may have an open and candid dialogue with the potential supplier, keeping the latter fully informed about its emerging needs and supplier selection deliberations, or it may operate in secrecy and intrigue. Furthermore, it may seek a one-time supplier, reopening the selection process anew for each purchase occasion, or it may be seeking a long-term relationship. Segmenting business customers on these psychographic variables can greatly help a business supplier plan its marketing strategy and target marketing.

Market Value-Based Segmentation

To conclude our discussion of bases of segmentation, we describe a market-value-based segmentation scheme. By market value, we refer here to the same values described in Chapter 3. Not discussed in published studies, the scheme is conceptual and broad in scope—it can be applied to almost any product or service and in both household and business markets. It is similar to benefit segmentation except that instead of specific benefits (e.g., gas mileage or style), it uses a category of market value (e.g., performance or social value). Recall from Chapter 3 that two types of market values were universal and personal. For the user, these were, respectively, performance and social-emotional.

Using the basic distinction between universal and personal values we can obtain a value-based broad division of the total market. Depending on whether universal values are important or not, and likewise whether personal values are important or not, we obtain a matrix of broad market segmentation. See Table 12.8. When universal values are of high importance but personal values are of low importance, the market is seeking "best value." The "basic product/economy market" is found in the lower-left hand cell, where both the universal and personal values are of low importance. The "premium market" is the one for which both the universal and personal values are of high importance. Finally, if the universal values are of low importance but personal values are of high importance, this segment can be called the "convenience/personalization" segment. These segments can be found in almost any industry.

VALUE SEGMENTATION MATRIX

		PERSONAL VALUES	
		Low	High
Universal Values	High	Best value segment	Premium segment
	Low	Basic Product/ Economy segment	Convenience/ personalization segment

For example, in the hotel/motel industry, basic product/economy segment customers would seek very basic accommodations without any frills, with no consideration of any social prestige or sensory or emotional outcomes—for example, in one-star or unrated motels. The best-value segment would seek high-quality, clean, and comfortable properties without frills, such as, say, Embassy Suites or Courtyard by Marriott or Le Meridian. The premium segment would desire both high quality and prestigious properties with enjoyment avenues, such as Four Seasons or resort hotels; finally, the convenience/personalization segment would seek small guest houses such as a bed and breakfast or popular tourist destination hotels.

Selection of Bases for Segmentation

An effective segmentation strategy begins with selection of an appropriate basis for segmentation. Several principles can help with this decision.

Criteria for Successful Segmentation

For a segmentation scheme to succeed, it must meet three basic criteria:[12]

1. **Substantiality**—Every segment targeted must be big enough to be profitable to the company. It would not make sense for a company in the computer industry to spend $10 million to research and develop a product priced at $2 million, if only two companies are likely to buy it.

2. **Identifiability**—Every segment must be identifiable so that the marketer can know who the customer is and what his or her needs, wants, and resources are.

3. **Reachability**—Finally, these segments must be reachable without wasting resources. That is, it should be possible to discriminate the segments by their members' media habits and demographics so that you know where to advertise and distribute the product to reach the targeted segments.

To illustrate these three criteria further, consider some off-the-wall examples. Short people would be easy to identify and measure (once the height categories were defined), but they would neither be substantial for most marketers to profitably target, nor is there any way to reach them specifically, since people do not live in any particular geographic or neighborhood pattern based on height, and they do not favor any particular communication media.

One could segment customers by, say, the color of the eyes. This will offer segments of substantive size, and it is easy to measure either by direct observation or by asking the survey respondent a simple question. However, this segment neither lends itself to any product differences (except perhaps for marketing eye makeup or tinted contact lenses) nor provides any way to reach them specifically.

A Comparative Look at the Three Bases of Segmentation

The three bases of segmentation have different strengths and weaknesses. Some are easier to measure, but less useful for customizing the marketing mix. Some contain explanation of why customers' marketplace behaviors differ across segments, while others are purely mechanistic divisions of the market. Table 12.7 on page 453 displays these comparisons across segment bases.

MEASURABILITY

The easiest type of segmentation to measure is usage segmentation, since the marketer can simply ask customers how much of a product they consume in a given time. Of course, like all measurements, even this simple measure is subject to respondent error because customers may not exactly recall or may feel embarrassed to admit how much of a particular product they consumed. For metered services (e.g., telephone, electricity), and for institutional purchases, it is easier to measure this variable by inspecting customer account information. Demographics, too, are relatively easy to measure, except that some customers may have motivation to lie about their age and income.

In contrast, the measurement of psychographics becomes quite involving, as it requires asking a long battery of wide-ranging questions. Benefits are moderately easy to assess—one merely needs to prepare a list of all possible benefits and ask respondents to rate their relative importance. The only snag is that it works for products whose benefits are relatively physical and easy to articulate. Certain intangibles, such as aesthetics or beauty, are difficult to translate into objective quantities.

SCOPE OF RELEVANCE

The scope of relevance for the usage basis extends to both the household and institutional markets. Demographics too are relevant to both the markets, except that in institutional markets, demographics are interpreted differently (e.g., by SIC codes, by industry type, by size of business, and so on). Among the "why" bases, benefit segmentation applies to both the markets, whereas psychographics apply to household markets only. Another important difference between these two "why" bases is that benefit or value segmentation is most suitable for products customers seek primarily for their functional value, whereas psychographic segmentation is most befitting for products sought for nonfunctional values.

DIAGNOSTIC VALUE

The issue of diagnostic value addresses two questions: Does a particular subgrouping make intuitive sense, and does it offer any insights about the market behavior? On these questions, the "what" and "who" bases rate poorly, whereas the "why" basis rates high. This is not surprising, since it follows from the very name of this last basis, but still its diagnostic value needs to be kept in mind. The usage basis is, of course, a purely mechanical division of the market and offers no explanation of why the resulting segments are different. At the other extreme is benefit segmentation, which tells us exactly why the segments differ in what they buy.

The demographics and psychographics are in between, with the latter being more explanatory than the former. In demographics, the reasons for differential response to marketing mix are implicit; we make sense of demographic differences, because, and only after, we interject our common-sense understanding of motivational differences among people of different demographics. Age-based segmentation makes sense, for example, because we understand different age groups have different needs and different stylistic preferences. When these common-sense assumptions prove erroneous, demographics-based segmentation becomes misleading. Thus, targeting seniors by their chronological age has been found to be defective because most seniors view themselves as about 10 to 15 years younger psychologically. That is why psychographics are more explanatory—consumers buy products as aids to their lifestyles. Sometimes, psychological variables can give deep understanding of otherwise elusive preferences, as happened in the Mason Haire study.

ACTIONABILITY

In terms of actionability, usage segmentation is the least self-sufficient; we need to cross-profile it by demographics to take any action whatsoever. Thus, it is not very useful to know that half of the consumers account for, say, 20 percent of a product's consumption; managers need to know who these people are, where they live, and so on. Of course, this problem vanishes if the customer enumeration itself is by some demographic characteristic, which is often the case for institutional markets, as, for example, rank-ordering sales territories (which are named by their geographic address) by usage or brand penetration. Finally, psychographics and benefits bases lend themselves to some actionability, particularly if they are found to be correlated with demographics. Even when they are not, they offer important guidance to how the marketing mix needs to be customized.

MARKETING MIX IMPLICATIONS

Different bases influence different elements of market planning. Usage segmentation is most useful for allocation of the total marketing resources. One allocates most resources to heavy users—unless, of course, one discerns untapped potential in the low-use segment. Either way, use segmentation helps managers decide at which markets the company's resources should be directed.

Demographics help most in media-mix decisions, as people of different demographics differ in their media habits. They also influence distribution decisions; in particular, geographic location and geodemographics tell us directly where to physically locate our major distribution or sales outlets. Income-based segmentation also has an influence on pricing decisions.

The most direct influence of psychographics is on the creative aspect of marketing communications. In advertising and mass communications, we need to depict customers similar in lifestyle to our target segment and use psychographic positioning that would appeal to our target customers. In particular, if a marketer is marketing a conspicuous product, he or she would be totally handicapped if he or she did not delineate various market segments on the basis of psychographics. Psychographics also help fine-tune a marketer's broad media choices, in particular because several print media vehicles specialize by consumer interest groups (e.g., there are magazines that appeal to golf players, to skiers, or to outdoor adventure types).

Finally, benefit and value segmentation helps most in product design and in determining what unique selling proposition one must use in communicating the product's appeal.

In sum, because different bases of segmentation offer different utility to marketers, in practice one should always attempt to cross-profile segments derived from one particular basis by other bases. Identifying what basis of segmentation would be most useful for a given product market takes creativity and marketing savvy. In a sense, success in becoming a customer's choice comes to those who segment their market in a meaningful way.[13]

Summary

The three basic strategies of differentiation and segmentation are generic differentiation, targeted differentiation, and segmented differentiation. The appropriateness of these three strategies is contingent on customers' resources and need diversity.

The chapter described different methods of segmenting the market, including demographics, psychographics, usage behavior, benefit, and value segmentation, both for the household and institutional market segmentation. These various bases of segmentation were appraised on the desirable characteristics of measurability, identifiability, reachability, relevance, diagnostic value, and actionability.

To properly differentiate and segment a market, companies must go beyond the traditional demographic, psychographic, and usage segmentation strategies to incorporate a procedure that provides "actionable" information on which to develop a marketing-mix strategy. The six consumption values model presented in this book can serve that purpose because it offers insights that go beyond the mere profiling of the segment. Profiling who your customers are is very critical to the development of differentiation and segmentation strategy, but knowing how to appeal to them, how to impact their attitudes and behavior, is even more important when it comes to making sure that a given company is the customer's choice.

Key Terms

Differentiation 428
Generic Differentiation 428
Targeted Differentiation 431
Segment-of-One Marketing 433
Segmented Differentiation 433

Market Segmentation 438
Usage Segmentation 439
Demographic Segmentation 439
Psychographic Segmentation 439
Geodemographics 442

Benefit Segmentation 451
Firmographics 455
Gerontographics 456
SIC 456
Buying Center 458
Substantiality 460
Identifiability 460
Reachability 460

Review Questions

1. The chapter identified three different types of differentiation strategies. Identify all three and then compare and contrast any two of them.

2. How does the needs/wants and resources diversity among customers impact the type of differentiation strategy that a company would choose to undertake? First, describe the diversity and then give an example for each of your responses.

3. Marketers have realized that in many product categories, a relatively small group of customers— heavy users—represents a disproportionately large percentage of the sales of that product. In some cases, 20 percent of these users can be responsible for 80 percent of the sales. What are the advantages and disadvantages of targeting this market segment?

4. What is benefit segmentation? And, what is value segmentation? How are the two related? How can the value segmentation matrix be used to identify different market segments? Give examples to illustrate your points.

5. What are firmographics? What do demographics mean for business customers? Give two examples of each demographic characteristic that can be used to segment business markets.

Applications

1. For each of the following products, identify the base of segmentation that is the most appropriate for targeting customers: (1) telephone services (2) ice cream (3) tennis shoes (4) hair salons (5) frozen pizza.

2. Geodemographics assumes that people who live in the same neighborhood have many things in common. Do you believe this to be a good assumption? Why or why not? In your opinion how useful are geodemographics in targeting the right customers for a particular product or brand?

3. Your friend has missed class lecture again. You tell him that the topic dealt with segmentation for accurate targeting. Your friend gets excited and tells you he just got back from Target and knows everything about the store and what it sells. You shake your head in frustration and begin to explain "targeting" to him. What do you say? How do you relate it to differentiation so that he understands?

4. Assume you are the director of marketing for a new soft-drink company that has to face intense competition from a large brand such as Coca-Cola and Pepsi. You know that your product definitely has what it takes to attract customers away from the market leaders. How will you use usage segmentation to determine who might become a loyal customer to your brand in the future?

5. Disney is a well-known company in the vacation and entertainment industry. Describe how the company can use demographics and psychographics to identify TV shows and magazines in which to place its advertisements.

Practical Experiences

1. Survey five friends in terms of their usage patterns of the following product/services: (1) coffee (2) television viewing (3) telephone usage. Use the steps outlined in the chapter to conduct a "heavy-half" analysis. Based on their responses, do you consider them to be heavy, medium, or light users of each product?

2. Call up three companies that offer products and services to other business customers (or look them up on the Internet). For each company, indicate the most important demographic factor and the most important psychographic used to segment their customer bases.

3. Find two companies—one in consumer products and the other in consumer services. For each company, evaluate their segmentation approaches based on the criteria for effective segmentation outlined in the chapter. Score each company on each criterion from 1 = very poor to 10 = very good. Compare the overall scores of each company and assess which does a better job at segmentation.

Notes

[1] B. Joseph Pine, *Mass Customization: The New Frontier in Business Competition* (Cambridge, MA: Harvard Business Press, 1993).

[2] For further reading on one-to-one marketing, see Don Peppers and Martha Rogers, *The One-to-One Future: Building Relationships One Customer at a Time* (New York: Currency and Doubleday, 1993).

[3] Michael R. Czinkota, Masaaki Kotabe, and David Mercer, *Marketing Management: Text and Cases* (Cambridge, MA: Blackwell Business, 1997), Case, "Gap. Inc.", pp. 631–650.

[4] Frank M. Bass, Douglas J. Tigert, and Ronald T. Lonsdale, "Market Segmentation: Group Versus Individual Behavior," *Journal of Marketing Research*, August 1968, vol. 5, pp. 264–70.

[5] Thomas J. Stanley, *Marketing to the Affluent* (New York: McGraw-Hill, 1997).

[6] Joel Garreau, *Nine Nations of North America* (Houghton Mifflin Co., 1981); Lynn R. Kahle, "The Nine Nations of North America and the Value Basis of Geographic Segmentation," *Journal of Marketing* 50 (April 1986), pp. 37–47; Sharon E. Beatty, Lynn R. Kahle, Pamela Homer, and Shekhar Misra, "Alternative Measurement Approaches to Consumer Values: The List of Values and the Rokeach Value Survey," *Psychology and Marketing* (Fall 1985) 2, no. 3, pp. 181–200.

[7] Russell I. Haley, "Benefit Segmentation: A Decision-Oriented Research Tool," *Journal of Marketing* 32 (July 1968). Also, Russell I. Haley, "Beyond Benefit Segmentation," *Journal of Advertising Research*, August

1971, pp. 3–8; Russell I. Haley, "Benefit Segmentation: 20 Years Later," *Journal of Consumer Marketing* 2 (1983), pp 5–13.

[8] Marc B. Rubner, "The Hearts of New-Car Buyers," *American Demographic*, August 1991, pp 14–15.

[9] John Berrigan and Carl Finkbeiner, *Segmentation Marketing: New Methods for Capturing Business Markets* (New York: Harper Collins, 1992), pp. 9–10.

[10] Quoted in Robert W. Haas, *Business Marketing* (Cincinnati, OH: South-Western College Publishing, 1995), p. 270.

[11] Mack Hanan, *Growth Partnering: How to Build Your Company's Profits by Building Customer Profits* New York: AMACOM, 1992 (American Management Association).

[12] See Leon G. Schiffman and Leslie Lazar Kanuk, *Consumer Behavior* pp. 45–46. (Engelwood Cliffs, NJ: Prentice Hall, 1991).

[13] For further insight, see Y. Datta, "Market Segmentation: An Integrated Framework," *Long Range Planning* 29, no. 6 (1996) pp. 797–811; Peter R. Dickson, "Person-Situation: Segmentation's Missing Link," *Journal of Marketing*, Fall 1982, pp. 56–64.

After reading this chapter you should be able to:

Identify various methods of researching customer behavior, both quantitative and qualitative.

Explain the uses of survey versus experimental research methods.

Summarize the meaning and utility of interpretive research.

Describe the methods used to measure attitudes, perceptions, and preferences.

Discuss information-processing research and various alternative concepts related to information-processing.

Explain the newer research tools such as virtual shopping and virtual test marketing.

part four

Customer Decision Making

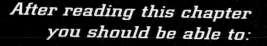

CHAPTER 14

After reading this chapter you should be able to:

Identify the steps in the individual customer's decision-making process.

Summarize the types of problems that lead a customer to begin this decision process.

Describe how customers seek information about products and services, including the sources they utilize and what determines how much information they will seek.

Discuss how customers utilize information to form evaluations of various brands, product and services.

Explain typical decision rules by which customers make their choice decisions.

Summarize customer experience after the purchase of a product or service, including the way that experience affects their future response to the marketer.

Discuss how marketers can utilize their understanding of the customer's decision-making process.

Individual Customer Decision Making

Ready, Set, Go! Buy Yourself a CD Player

So you have been dreaming of buying a CD player. Almost every one of your friends has one. Ideally you want a surround sound rack system model. But for now, a personal CD player would do. Actually, that would be better. So you could play it in your college dorm and also carry it home during vacations. Besides, your parents have made it clear that you have to pay for it with your own money. And about a hundred dollars is all you can spare for now.

The Service Merchandise store (a catalog-based discount retailer of jewelry and appliances in the United States) is far from where you live. But you have their catalog, and you think it is a good idea to study the catalog first. Personal CD players are on p. 468. The page shows seven makes and models, in pictures. Below these is a table that compares these seven brands feature by feature. You study this table.

There are two Sony models. Both have 22 tracks programmability, megabass, and rechargeable battery, and both come with headphones, AC adaptor, and a patch cord. One costs $129.99 and the other $79.99. The only difference you can see from the table is that one is shock resistant while the other is not. Shock resistance is good, but is it worth $50 more, you wonder. Surely, there must be other differences. There is a Panasonic model but it is not shock resistant; moreover, the bass boost is only XBS. You don't want it, even though it has 24 tracks programmability compared to Sony's 22 and a price of only $79.00.

In the table, there are two AIWAs and two RCAs. You don't know anything about the AIWA's reputation. So you will stay away from it. Only one of the two RCA models is shock resistant. And it is not too expensive—only $99.99. So your choice is really between the Sony model (the one with shock resistance and a $129.99 price tag) and this RCA model. Deciding between these two won't be easy. Well, you will worry about it when you visit the store. For now, you are glad you at least found something that will meet your need and is within the price range you have budgeted for it!

Introduction

If you think back to a recent *major* purchase you may have made, such as the preceding example of a CD player, you may recall that it was a complex, involved, extended, and perhaps even an agonizing process. It probably began with your realizing one day that you needed to purchase this product. You started studying some catalogs, visiting various stores, talking to friends, weighing alternative makes, models, and features in your mind. Finally, perhaps when you got tired of being indecisive, you chose one, paid for it, and brought it home. Now you are eager to find out how it works out. If it works fine, you will have solved one more problem in your life. Of course, other purchases are not as agonizing or effortful. Indeed, many customer decision processes are enjoyable experiences.

This chapter will give you an opportunity to reflect on both types of decision processes. Understanding your own decision processes as a customer might improve your future decisions. For marketers, it is of paramount importance to understand the decision process the customer goes through. Understanding the process helps marketers organize marketing efforts in a fashion that is responsive to the customer's decision-making imperatives.

To lay the foundation for such an understanding, this chapter begins by describing the role of the individual decision maker. It identifies the steps in the decision process, including the types of decisions relevant to customer behavior and the ways in which customers gather information. We present several models for the process of evaluating alternatives, and we identify conditions under which a customer is likely to use each model. Next, the chapter analyzes purchase and post-purchase behavior as part of the decision process. Finally, we gather the concepts together in a comprehensive model of buyer behavior.

The Individual Decision Maker

Purchase decisions are sometimes made by individuals in households; at other times they are made by groups of people such as spouses or by committees in business organizations. The other chapters in this part explore group decisions; this chapter focuses on *individual* decision makers. This focus includes situations when the individual decision maker is making a decision about any product or service in any context, as long as he or she is making the decision about a product or service for his or her own use. Thus, it includes purchase decisions customers make in their personal capacity, but also in their capacity as an employee in a firm. Thus, employment-related travel purchases, when made by individual employees (rather than by a corporate travel officer) are considered individual purchase decisions even though they occur in an organizational context, and even though someone else pays for them. Of course individual decisions use somewhat different criteria when someone else is the payer (as in business travel) compared with when the decision maker himself or herself is the payer. In the former case, the decision maker may be less concerned with the economic and financing values compared with the other values. But the decision process remains the same.

Roles of the Decision Maker

In individual decision making (as opposed to organizational decisions), the three customer roles (payer, user, and buyer) could all be played by a single individual, or each could be played by a different individual. Often, at least two of the roles of a customer—those of buyer and user—come together within a single person. In these cases, the individual decision maker has to be concerned with at least four of the *six* market values of our framework (i.e., the market values relevant to the user and the buyer roles). In addition, the payer role is often played by the same individual so that all six market values—performance, social/psychological, convenience, service, economic, and financing—come into play in individual decision making. But even when the same individual plays all three roles, the concerns may differ for each role, creating internal role conflict. This chapter covers the decision processes of all individual customers, whether they are playing one, two, or all three roles.

When we think of an individual making a choice, we tend to limit our attention to the benefits of a product or service (i.e., values it will satisfy), whether these be performance related or social/emotional outcomes. This is a limited view, confining the decision maker to the user role. In reality, to the individual decision maker, the buyer and payer roles are pertinent too so that the service, convenience, economic, and financing values (i.e., market values relevant to the buyer and payer roles) become equally important. In some situations, some of these values might determine the choice.

Location and Cost of an Individual's Decision

Individual consumption can occur in three places: (1) at home, (2) in business organizations (at work, at school, and so on), and (3) in public places (e.g., restaurant, airplane, on the road, in the park, on the beach, and so on). For products or services consumed at

Customers face choices all the time

home, purchase decisions tend to be made in advance, substantially ahead of time. Consumption in organizational settings and in public places is much less separated in time from the purchase decisions. When purchase decisions are made close to the time of consumption (or for immediate consumption), convenience value of the buyer role acquires much more prominence. That is why individual customers readily buy a soda can from a vending machine at one dollar a piece when they are on the road; the same customers would choose their "supermarket of the week" based on a measly 20-cent deal on a case of Coke or Pepsi for consumption at home.

Likewise, consumption in public places tends to bring into prominence the social values of the user relative to the values of the payer. Price sensitivity is lessened in favor of how good the product will look in public.

When products and services are given away free, whether by government or by organizations, the decision criteria change. A trade association organizing a business luncheon can expect a significantly greater number of guests to eat dessert they would typically skip. Or a restaurant serving an "all you can eat" buffet lunch can expect to serve many more desserts than one serving an *à la carte* lunch. Free public roads become quickly congested, whereas toll roads encourage car pooling. Customers will willingly accept any type of freebies such as a free hat or a free coffee mug as a promotional giveaway by a radio station or a business organization, disregarding its low quality; the same customers are less likely to accept that low quality if they have to pay for it. At the other extreme, if they are not the payers (for example when buying something for self-use but as employees), they would want the best quality, making user values most salient.

The more you combine the user, the payer, and the buyer roles, the more conflicting the decision process becomes. It is in individual buying decisions, then, that the values of the three roles interplay, and trade-offs become integral to the decision process, making it an intriguing process to study.

Customer Decision Process

In each of the roles, customers constantly face choices—how much to spend, what alternative to acquire, and where to purchase it from. These choices call for customers to make decisions. **Customer decisions** are decisions customers make in the marketplace as buyers, payers, and users. Typically, these decisions include *whether* to purchase, *what* to purchase, *when* to purchase, from *whom* to purchase, and *how* to pay for it. *Whether* to purchase something is the first level of decision that entails weighing alternative uses of money and time resources. Customers have finite money and time, and they must allocate them judiciously. Alternative demands on time may constrain a customer to postpone or dismiss a purchase altogether. Thus, a vacation plan may be scrapped because we have to finish this book by a deadline, or because you have to study for a test instead. Allocating *money* resources entails weighing alternative needs at the level of the product or service category. For example, a family may have to choose between taking a cruise versus investing in remodeling the house. This product/service level choice is both a *whether* to purchase and *what* to purchase decision.

An important customer behavior at this category level decision is **mental budgeting**—how the budget customers set for a product category guides their subsequent behavior as a customer. This concept of mental budgeting is explained in the Window on Research box. The concept of mental budgeting highlights the importance of the payer role. The user is ultimately at the mercy of the payer, not only when someone else is the payer but also when the customer himself or herself is in both the payer role and the user

Mental Budgeting and Customer Behavior

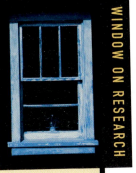

Do people set a budget for different categories of consumption, such as entertainment, clothing, food, and investment? And what happens if the money budgeted turns out to be too much or too little? Do these budgets become limiting? Do they result in underconsumption of one product category and overconsumption of another? Interestingly, the answer to all these questions from recent research is yes.

Consider two consumers, A and B. Consumer A has put aside some money for clothing to purchase a pair of slacks. After finding no acceptable slacks, he can easily put that money into another product category; instead, he just goes ahead and purchases a sweater that he had no prior intention to buy. Consumer B has allocated some money for entertainment. She receives an invitation to join a dinner group but discovers that the money she has allocated to the entertainment category is not adequate to cover the cost of dinner with the group. So she declines, even though she could have easily moved some money out of allocation to another consumption category. For consumer A to buy a sweater just to utilize the budget for clothing is an example of overconsumption. For consumer B to decline the dinner invitation even though she knew she would have enjoyed the event is an example of underconsumption.

Consumer researchers Chip Heath and Jack B. Soll studied this topic recently. They asked a group of consumers a set of questions about how much they had set aside to spend and how much they would spend if certain hypothetical incidents had occurred. Their questions and respondent answers are best illustrated by this example. Suppose a respondent said at the outset that she had set aside $100 for entertainment this week; now suppose she had already spent $30 on a dinner, how much did she expect to spend on entertainment for the rest of the week? The answer, as expected, was about $70. Now, what if the dinner was paid for by a friend; the respondent still wanted to spend about $100 rather than about $70. What if the respondent had to unexpectedly buy a birthday gift for someone costing $30? She still expected to spend $100 for entertainment. This pattern of response demonstrates the mental budgeting effects. Heath and Soll obtained this pattern of responses from a majority of their research respondents.

Additional information available at **http://www. journals.uchicago.edu/JCR**

Source: Chip Heath and Jack B. Soll, "Mental Budgeting and Consumer Decisions," *Journal of Consumer Research* 23, 1 (June 1996), pp. 40–52.

role. The payer role imposes relatively inflexible budget limits, and in this way imposes some self-discipline on the user, whose needs and wants can sometimes be infinitely expandable. Unfortunately the amount of research on mental budgeting is limited, and it is based solely on Western consumers. It is entirely possible that consumers in other cultures, and/or consumers who live from hand to mouth, might not practice the concept of mental budgeting, or if they do, they might implement it in a flexible way, adjusting the budget at the time of the purchase. This is an issue that needs cross-cultural research.

Nevertheless, the concept of mental budgeting can guide marketers' positioning efforts; a product or service may be positioned in one category rather than the other to take advantage of the budget earmarked for each category. Illustratively, a carpet may be positioned to the user as a "consumption" item with superior performance; at the same time, it might be positioned for the payer as a long-term investment. As another example, a frozen dinner of lobster may be viewed by the customer as an expensive food item; the marketer might, in contrast, present it as a relatively economical entertainment (compared to going out to eat at a restaurant).

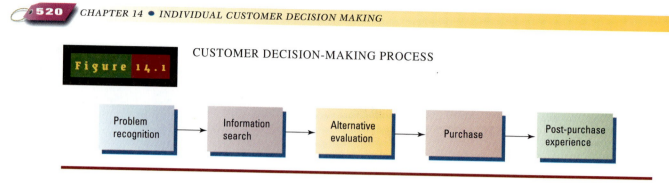

Figure 14.1   CUSTOMER DECISION-MAKING PROCESS

Following the choice at the product/service level, the customer makes another "what to purchase" decision—a choice among brands. Thus, illustratively, if a "product category level" decision is made—namely, "take the cruise"—the next decision is which brand to purchase (e.g., which travel destination to select and which cruise line to purchase tickets on).

These decisions at various levels of hierarchy can all be framed in a general way: these are all *alternatives*, and the customer task is to decide among alternatives. Thus, this section uses the term "alternatives" generically, to refer to product and service categories, brands, stores, suppliers, and so on, and deals with customer choice decisions among alternatives.

The process of customer decision making consists of the steps shown in Figure 14.1.

Step 1: Problem Recognition

The decision process begins with a customer recognizing a problem to be solved or a need to be satisfied. The customer notices, for example, that he or she is hungry and needs to get some food, that the light bulb has blown out and needs replacement, that the roof has begun to leak and needs repairing, or that Sally has not called in a while, so he, Harry, better send her a simple friendship card. The office copier has run out of paper, or the report an executive has prepared for an important meeting the next morning has an error and needs redoing, complete with all 100 copies individually addressed.

As these examples illustrate, a customer "problem" is not necessarily a physical problem such as a hungry stomach or dirty laundry. Rather a **customer problem** is any state of deprivation, discomfort, or wanting (whether physical or psychological) felt by a person. **Problem recognition** is a realization by the customer that he or she needs to buy something to get back to the normal state of comfort—physically and psychologically.

STIMULI FOR PROBLEM RECOGNITION

Problem recognition can occur in two ways: due to an internal stimulus or an external stimulus. **Internal stimuli** are perceived states of discomfort—again, physical or psychological (e.g., hunger or boredom, respectively). **External stimuli** are marketplace information items that lead the customer to realize the problem. Thus, an advertisement about multivitamins or the sight of a Pizza Hut or the smell of coffee coming from a coffee shop in a mall can all serve as external stimuli to arouse the recognition of a need. The Window on Practice box provides examples of how banks have attempted to use such stimuli.

The terms *external* and *internal* are commonly used in psychology; however, more apt terms would be "problem-stimuli" and "solution-stimuli." A problem-stimulus is one in which the problem itself is the source of information. This source could lie *within* the cus-

Problem Recognition: A Key to Selling Bank Loans

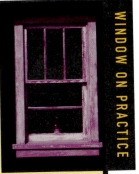

Often the trickiest part of generating a demand for a firm and satisfying customer needs is helping customers make the connection between a firm's product or service offering and the customers' needs. This connection is not always obvious to the customer, and marketers sometimes miss this opportunity. Take, for example, bank loans. Most banks market them predominantly by advertising the interest rate and other terms of financing. That works if consumers are already looking for a loan. But looking for a loan and having the need for a loan are not the same thing. Customers may want to do things for which they need money, but if those things have not been associated in the customer's mind as legitimate purposes for a bank loan, then the idea of getting a bank loan for that purpose would not occur to them. So there may be a customer need (i.e., a problem), and there may be a solution available. But the customer problem and the marketplace solution remain disconnected in the customer mind. To establish that connection is to facilitate "problem recognition." And recently, some banks have done just that.

One category of bank loans is the home equity loan—money banks loan with the borrower's house as the collateral. It is a desirable type of loan for the bank because the collateral makes the loan less risky. And it appeals to the customer because the rate is generally lower than other types of loans, and the interest is tax-deductible. Yet most customers inadvertently think that a home equity loan is for financing the purchase of a home, or at most for financing a home improvement project, and for no other purpose. That is, home equity loans are perceived the same as mortgage loans.

A number of leading banks realized this quirk in the customer assumption recently. They realized why rate ad-

vertising was not creating new demand for loans. People's Heritage Bank of Portland, Maine, is a case in point. The bank ran an advertising campaign that educated the customer about the various uses for which a home equity loan could be obtained. The bank developed three advertisements that featured people who achieved their dreams with the help of a home equity loan. In one advertisement, a veterinarian opened her practice with the home equity loan. In another advertisement, a customer bought the guitar he had always wanted. In a third advertisement, a teenager and her dad were featured with the computer they bought with the home equity loan so they could explore Europe on the Internet. By the end of the advertising campaign, which involved print and radio as well as more targeted direct mail, the bank had tripled the average number of equity loan sales each month.

Reflecting on the situation, a senior product manager commented: "There was a lot of rate advertising in the market when we introduced this product. We were offering a good competitive rate, yet we wanted to offer customers something more. We wanted to show them that our product had value." In other words, the bank needed to make a connection between the things customers valued and the product the firm offered.

Additional information available at http://www.bmanet.org.

Source: Katherine Morrall, "Marketing Loans That Make Consumers' Dreams Come True," *Bank Marketing*, April 1996, pp. 19–24.

tomer (as in hunger pangs) or outside (dirty laundry). The solution-stimulus is the information emanating from a solution itself; exposure to a potential solution arouses the recognition of the need or the problem. For example, the smell of fresh-baked cinnamon rolls from a bakery might arouse your desire for cinnamon rolls. Exposure to a new style of dress in a store might make you realize that the dress will come in handy for an upcoming party. Or listening to a pitch about Rejuvex on TV might make you recognize the need for some energy supplement. Marketing communications, product or service samples, window shopping, and so on, have their utility precisely because they serve as problem-recognition stimuli.

As customers, you can expect to encounter solution-stimuli in three states of mind:

1. When you have already recognized the problem and are looking for a solution—for example, suppose you have dandruff and are looking for a more effective shampoo than what you are using currently; or you find your current food service contractor for the company cafeteria unsatisfactory and are planning to find a new contractor.

2. When the problem had been recognized in the past, but it was just not salient (i.e., not in the top-of-the-mind awareness) at the moment of the exposure to the solution—An example would be that you had thought of needing to buy some exercise equipment, but you never pursued the thought actively; an infomercial or a product display or the fact that a friend bought it rekindles the need you had previously recognized.

3. You never recognized the need in the past, but exposure to the solution-product makes you realize that the product or service would solve a condition now perceived as a problem. Thus, a display of a "caller ID" device in a store and the salesperson's explanation of its use might make you realize that "not knowing who is calling" had been a frustrating experience all along, even though until now you never viewed it as a problem.

Life situations that cause inconvenience but have no solutions are generally not viewed as problems; they are simply viewed as life conditions, taken for granted. Only when a solution appears on the horizon does the life condition become a problem. For example, before the invention of the microwave ovens, the slow process of conventional ovens was not perceived as a problem. Or before the home delivery of pizza, going to the pizzeria was not perceived to be a problem.

This distinction is important for two reasons. First, it underscores the role of what is known as educational or pioneering communications and marketing. Pioneering marketing and communications promote a new product or a new service by educating the customer about what the product or service will do, and how it can solve a hitherto unsolved or indeed hitherto unrecognized problem. Some of these marketing efforts are intended to create "primary" demand rather than "secondary" demand. **Primary demand** is demand for the product or service category itself, seeking to convert nonbuyers of the product/service category into buyers. **Secondary demand** (also known as **selective demand**), in contrast, is simply to deflect demand from one brand to the other. There is a noteworthy controversy on this issue in cigarette advertising today. The government and antitobacco groups claim that cigarette advertising is targeted at the youth, promoting the primary demand for smoking among new customers. If this is true, then cigarette advertising is a "solution-stimulus" arousing a problem recognition among youth by presenting the product as a solution to their enduring need to be perceived by their peers as "being cool." The tobacco industry, on the other hand, argues that it is merely creating secondary demand for specific brands, rather than enticing and recruiting new smokers.

The second implication of solution- versus problem-stimulus goes to the heart of a basic controversy in marketing. An often asked and hotly debated question is, Does marketing create a need or merely satisfy one? In arguing that it indeed *creates* needs, critics cite such examples as "No one needed a VCR or a video camera or a cellular phone or a $150 pair of Nike shoes or an overnight document delivery service, until advertising came along, parading these products and services in an enticing way." Our view is that a need ought to be defined in terms of the "function" the product or service serves, rather than in terms of the product or service itself (as in "No one needed a VCR"). When needs are properly defined in terms of the function, it is easy to see that the only products or services that would be successful in the marketplace are those that serve some function. Thus, a VCR serves the function of enabling "time-shifted viewing," and the need to be able to watch a program at your convenience was always a need, albeit unrecognized as a problem and as such relegated from consciousness simply as a life condition. The invention of the VCR, like all other inventions, helped surface that latent need. Likewise, in the world of business, there is a product to which every executive and every staff member is addicted—"Post-it" notes. Yet before their invention, no one even sensed the problem now addressed by this innovative product.

PROBLEM RECOGNITION BY EACH CUSTOMER ROLE

Problem recognition can occur for each customer role and for each of the six values customers seek. The VCR and Post-it examples illustrate the latent needs of the user role. For the buyer role, the example of problem recognition is the home delivery of pizza, which offers convenience value. Before the availability of home delivery, customers apparently did not see as a problem their inability to eat a pizzeria-baked pizza at home. For the payer, the availability of leasing automobiles to individual customers or for a corporate fleet has improved affordability. Also, availability of credit makes many customers realize the need to buy a *new* car or furniture or even (as one recent bank ad targeted at students suggested) for a college student to move out of the parents' home and live on his or her own.

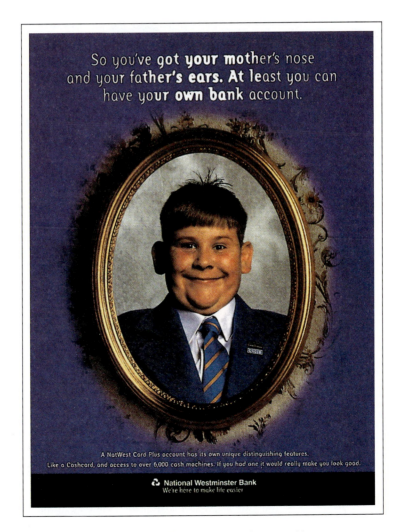

How marketers help customers' problem recognition

FOUR SITUATIONS FOR PROBLEM RECOGNITION

	VIVID	LATENT
FAMILIAR	Stock depletion	Educational marketing
NOVEL	Life stage change	New product technology

A TYPOLOGY OF PROBLEMS

To see the variety of problems customers recognize, we can classify them along two dimensions: familiar versus novel and vivid versus latent (see Table 14.1). Familiar problems generally occur due to what is commonly called "stock depletion"—for example, a hungry stomach, or a worn-out tire. Novel problems arise generally with life events that mark passage from one stage to another, as discussed in Chapter 9. Examples include a new job, a marriage, or even a child going to the next school grade. For business customers, the life-stage changes occur when firms go public, change ownership, form alliances, or undergo restructuring such as in downsizing and re-engineering.

Vivid problem situations are immediately obvious and recognized, as in a just-emptied cereal box or the arrival of the "back-to-school" month. A latent problem is not immediately obvious and needs shaping either by self-reflection or more likely by an external agent such as a salesperson. Examples of a latent problem are getting your car regularly tuned or a regular self-examination of breasts (both familiar latent problems) or to have the ability to know who is calling you on the phone (a novel-latent problem). Availability of the caller ID service from the local phone company makes the novel-latent need salient (i.e., recognized). Thus, recognition of novel-latent problems is stimulated by solution-stimuli, generally in the form of new technologies and new products/services. In addition, however, the recognition of latent problems (whether familiar or novel) generally requires educational marketing effort (e.g., counseling by a salesperson about the need for a life-insurance policy).[1]

Step 2: Information Search

Once the need has been recognized, customers search for information about various alternative ways of solving the problem. That search rarely includes every brand in existence. Rather, as shown in Figure 14.2, customers consider only a select subset of brands, organized as follows:

- The **awareness set** consists of brands a customer is aware of.
- An **evoked set** consists of the brands in a product or service category that the customer remembers at the time of decision making.
- Of the brands in the evoked set, not all are deemed to fit your needs. Those considered unfit are eliminated right away. The remaining brands are termed the **consideration set**—the brands a customer will consider buying.

Initially, customers seek information about the consideration set of brands—which is a subset of evoked sets. New information can bring in additional brands into the aware-

AWARENESS, EVOKED, AND CONSIDERATION SETS

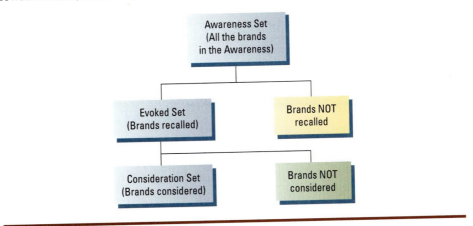

Figure 14.2

ness, evoked, and consideration set. It should be the minimum objective of all marketing communications to place the brand in the consideration set (rather than merely in the "awareness or evoked set") of its target customers.

Three elements characterize the Information search phase of the decision process: (1) sources of information, (2) search strategies, and (3) amount of search.

SOURCES OF INFORMATION

Sources of information may be categorized into marketer or nonmarketer. See Table 14.2. **Marketer sources** are those that come from the marketer of the product or service itself. These consist of advertising, salespersons, product/service literature and brochures, and in-store displays. One of the latest marketer sources is the Internet—more and more companies have opened a home page on the Internet, a site customers can visit at their conve-

Table 14.2

SOURCES OF INFORMATION FOR CUSTOMERS

MARKETER SOURCES	NONMARKETER SOURCES
■ Advertising	PERSONAL
■ Salespersons	■ Friends and other acquaintances
■ Product/service brochures	■ Past experience
■ Store displays	
■ Company Web sites	
	INDEPENDENT SOURCES
	■ Public information (e.g., *Consumer Reports*, Better Business Bureau, news reports in media, government publications such as The Census of Manufacturers)
	■ Product or service experts: (e.g., Auto Critic, home appraiser, pharmacist, and so on)
	■ Internet (bulletin boards)

nience. Since these sources have a vested interest in providing favorable information, these are also referred to as **advocate sources** (i.e., sources that have a vested point-of-view advocate or promote). As such, these sources have lower credibility compared with nonmarketer sources.

Nonmarketer sources are those that are independent of the marketer's control. Of the various marketing sources, from the customer's point of view, advertising would be considered the least credible, and inspection of in-store product displays the most credible. Product/service brochures generally contain more technical and performance data and are particularly useful for high-ticket and technical products and services. As regards salespersons as a source, customers tend to view them generally with suspicion, but do consider them a useful source of information. Salespersons aware of this customer perception can improve their effectiveness by (a) becoming knowledgeable about the product or service, and (b) avoiding serving self-interest at the expense of customer interest; that is, given the starting disadvantage of lacking in credibility, salespersons should go out of their way to provide information in a way that appears unbiased and non-self-serving.

Nonmarketer sources include personal sources and independent sources. Since these have no personal interest in biasing the information, they are viewed as nonadvocate sources and are deemed more credible. Friends and other acquaintances with past experience and/or greater knowledge of the product category are sought and valued for their advice. Customers' own past experience with the product or service is also a credible source of information, except that its relevance depends on how much the marketplace has changed (in terms of product or service advances) since the last purchase.

Independent sources are usually publications and organizations with relevant expertise. For example, *Consumer Reports*, published in the United States, provides performance data based on product trials by independent judges and based on systematically collected reports of other past users' experiences. Other independent product and service experts that can be valuable sources of information include pharmacists and financial advisors. Professional appraisers/advisors are sometimes used for very large purchases. Thus, home appraisers are used by home buyers, and car mechanics are used to appraise used cars. American Automobile Association (AAA) has a program, called Auto Critic, to thoroughly inspect a used car before you purchase it and advise the prospective buyer of the car's mechanical condition. In business-to-business buying, such as for plant and equipment, engineering consultants are utilized as sources of information.

SEARCH STRATEGIES

The choice of information sources depends partly on the customer's search strategy. A **search strategy** is the pattern of information acquisition customers utilize to solve their decision problems. Since information acquisition has costs in terms of time, physical effort, and mental effort, customers weigh the costs against the likely gains from information acquisition. That comparison helps them decide how much information they will acquire and from what sources.

ROUTINE, EXTENDED, AND LIMITED PROBLEM SOLVING Based on the amount of search deemed necessary, customer decision strategies may be routine, limited, or extended problem-solving strategies. **Routine problem solving** is a strategy in which no new information is considered. This strategy is utilized for purchase problems that have occurred and have been solved previously. Consequently, when these problems recur, these are solved simply by repeating the past choice, as in purchasing the brand bought in the past. Information search is minimal. **Extended problem solving** occurs when the search is extensive and deliberation prolonged. This strategy becomes necessary for purchases never made before, or made long ago, or where risks of wrong choice are high. Finally, **limited problem solving** is a strategy wherein the customer invests some limited amount of time and energy in searching and evaluating alternative solutions. Customers adopt this strategy when purchases are nontrivial, the risk is limited, and the product or service is not complex or technical in terms of its features. There is some familiarity with the product/service class, but a desire for variety (e.g., buying a new dress) or unavailability of previous solutions (e.g., stockout of your usual brand) necessitates some amount of search.

These three strategies are related to the problem typology discussed earlier. Generally, familiar-vivid problems are likely to be solved with routine problem solving. Novel-latent problems would tend to be solved with extended problem solving. Familiar-latent problems (e.g., starting to get your car regularly tuned) may entail routine (go to your regular mechanic) or limited problem solving (comparison shopping with coupons). Finally, novel-vivid problems may entail limited or extended problem solving, depending on the risk involved and/or prior familiarity. Note that the familiar-novel/vivid-latent typology has to do with the genesis of problem *recognition*, whereas the routine/extended/limited continuum has to do with search efforts.

SYSTEMATIC VERSUS HEURISTIC SEARCH So far, the description of search strategies may seem to suggest that customers prefer systematic strategies. **Systematic search** consists of a comprehensive search and evaluation of alternatives. Systematic searchers have been found to search information extensively, consult with a variety of sources, tend to shop with others, take a long time, deliberate a lot, and are especially price-comparison shoppers. However, customers also use a contrasting search strategy, termed heuristics. **Heuristics** are quick rules of thumb and shortcuts used to make decisions.[2]

Heuristics can be implemented in a variety of ways:

- Broad inferences are quickly drawn from partial information (e.g., price may be used to judge quality). Technical sounding terms may be used to infer overall brand superiority (e.g., many customers may not know what "Dolby sound" in stereos or even "pH balanced" in shampoos means, but they would conveniently infer that these imply "advanced" products).

- Past experiences are considered adequate.

- Others' judgments are sought and summarily adopted as final choice.

- Brand names are heavily relied on to the exclusion of seeking further attribute information.

Although these strategies are not systematic, they are also not irrational. They are rational to their users in terms of the cost versus benefit trade-offs they perceive.

Consider inferences, for example. Customers often have to make their decisions on partial information about various product or service alternatives. In purchasing a VCR, customers may use several evaluation criteria: number of heads, automatic tape rewind, on-screen programmability, slow mode operation, hi-fi, repair record, and so on. A particular model of VCR may not have information on whether or not it has an automatic tape rewind feature, or repair record information may be unavailable for another brand. In these situations, customers make product or service assessments by supplying the missing information in the form of inferences. Scholars have identified various strategies customers use for handling missing information:

Interattribute inference—The value of one attribute is inferred based on another attribute. For example, thickness of the fabric in an item of clothing might be used to infer crease-resistance (whether correctly or incorrectly).

This tongue-in-check suggestion of a heuristic is for the payer.

- **Evaluative consistency**—The missing attribute is assumed to conform to the overall evaluation of the brand. Thus, if a brand is positively evaluated in overall terms, the brand is assumed to be good on the missing attribute as well. For example, suppose you are looking at a Sony VCR, and after looking at all the features and its brand reputation, you are inclined to judge it very favorably except that you don't have information on its repair record. You might fill this gap by assuming that since the model is good on all its features, its repair record must be good as well.

- **Other-brand averaging**—The missing attribute value may be assumed to be an average of its values across all other brands. This is likely to occur, however, only if the variance in the values of this attribute for other brands is low.

- **Negative Cue**—The customer may simply treat the missing information as a negative cue and then use one of the two substrategies: avoid altogether the option with the missing information, or assume a low or poor value on this attribute.

The "Window on Research" box discusses the application of intuitive theories to these strategies.

The extent and type of inference making will depend on several factors. One is the need for inference: That is, how critical is the attribute considered for product or service assessment? For example, in assessing a fitness facility, whether or not valet parking is available may be information not considered critical, whereas whether or not it is open in the evening hours would be critical.

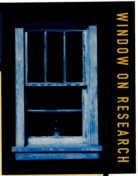

WINDOW ON RESEARCH

Intuitive Theories in Customer Inference Making

An important research issue concerning inferences is the extent to which customers' intuitive theories play a role in inference making. For example, people generally expect the length of warranties to be positively related to a product's reliability (i.e., the longer and better the warranty), the more reliable the product or service is likely to be. But what if we did not find this to be true in a specific case? For example, suppose you were shopping for a camera and you found that, across different brands of cameras there was no correspondence between reliability and warranty. Brands that had poor warranties had just as good or poor a reliability record as brands with exceptional warranties. However, another attribute, say, shutter speed, was perfectly correlated with reliability record: that is, the model that had a high shutter speed also had more reliability. Note that there is no logical connection between shutter speed and reliability. It just so happens that for all the models you examined, the reliability record happens to be uncorrelated with warranties but related to shutter speed. Now, suppose you encounter another brand and find reliability information missing. How are you going to infer its value? Is your inference going to be based more on data (i.e., in the models examined, reliability was related with shutter speed—a mere coincidence) or is it going to be based more on your general intuitive theory, which tells you that, logically, reliability should be related to warranty?

This important question was examined by customer researchers Susan M. Broniarczyk and Joseph W. Alba. These researchers presented customers information about alternative brands of cameras to choose from. After they made the choice, customers were presented with information about a new set of brands, except that the information on their reliability record was missing. In choosing from these new, incompletely described brands, customers could rely for inference about the missing attribute either on their knowledge of the value of the missing attribute on an otherwise identical brand in the previous set (which would be in conflict with intuitive theory), or they could base such an inference on intuitive theory. The experimental subjects' choices revealed that in inferring the missing information, customers drew on their intuitive theory, even when the previously exposed data were in conflict with the logical theory.

Of course, further research is needed on this topic; but this important finding of research done thus far implies that marketers should understand their customers' intuitive theories about the relationships among diverse brand attributes in particular, and about various marketplace phenomena in general.

Additional information available at **http:/s/www.ConsumerReports.org**

Source: Susan M. Broniarczyk and Josrph W. Alba, "The Role of Consumers' Intuitions in Inference Making," *Journal of Consumer Research* 21 (December), 1994, pp. 393–407.

Another factor is customer involvement in the purchase: That is, how critical is it to make the right choice? Finally, the use of inferences will depend on the customer's product or service category knowledge. More knowledgeable customers are more likely to infer the missing information.

DETERMINANTS OF THE AMOUNT OF SEARCH

Imagine that you are in the market for a CD player, or a pair of shoes, or a greeting card, or a catering service for an office party, or whatever. How much information will you seek? How much effort will you put in processing this information? Actually, this depends on several factors. These factors include perceived risk, involvement, familiarity and expertise; time pressure; functional versus expressive nature of the product or service; and information overload.

PERCEIVED RISK   The **perceived risk** is the degree of loss (i.e., amount at stake) in the event that a wrong choice is made.

There are five types of risks:

1. Performance risk—The product or service may not perform well or not as well as some other alternatives.

2. Social risk—Reference group members and significant others may not like it.

3. Psychological risk—The product or service may not reflect oneself.

4. Financial risk—The alternative may be overpriced; there may exist a better purchase.

5. Obsolescence risk—The alternative may be replaced by newer substitutes.

The financial risk is of most concern to the payer, whereas other risks are of concern to the user.

The greater the perceived risk, the greater the likelihood that the purchase will be postponed or in any case, the search and deliberation will be extensive. Marketers therefore attempt to overcome these risks by various strategies. Performance warranties are an attempt to overcome performance risks, both for physical products and in the service industries. Stores are increasingly offering price guarantees; Circuit City, for example, not only will match a competitor's price, but will refund 110 percent of the price difference. This has taken price risk completely out of the decision equation. Obsolescence risk is overcome by allowing the trade-in of the older model for the new one (as in automobiles), or by offering product upgrades (as in computers). Social and psychological risks are addressed by liberal returns, exchange, or refund policies. If you judge the product not to fit your style or if significant others dislike your purchase, you may return it to the store without any liability.

Similarly, for business customers, marketers attempt to free customers from various perceived risks by assuming the risks themselves. For office machines, for example, performance risk is minimized by offering a life-time repair maintenance contract. Financial and obsolescence risks are minimized by offering the product on lease. Many consulting firms and advertising agencies guarantee certain results for the client, and some even make their fees contingent on the degree to which intended results are achieved.

INVOLVEMENT   On the positive side of the equation, involvement is defined as the perceived importance of the product or service. We purchase and consume hundreds of products and services in our lives, but we are not equally involved in all of them. We take some for granted, not even noticing unless something wrong happens. And we purchase them routinely, just repeating the last purchase, or just buying whatever is convenient, cheapest, or available. Then there are other products and services that we consider very important in our lives (e.g., golfing equipment for ardent golfers), which we consume with full consciousness and which we purchase with great care.

Consumer researchers have further distinguished between two types of involvement: purchase decision involvement and enduring involvement. **Purchase-decision involvement** is the degree of concern and caring that customers bring to bear on the purchase decision. Purchase decision involvement is high for most of the high-ticket items, but price and involvement do not have one-to-one correspondence. Notice for example, that some customers would spend 30 minutes or more for the purchase of a greeting card costing only $2. What brings in purchase involvement is the degree of risk, whether performance, financial, or social (in the case of the greeting card, the risk that the card may miscommunicate one's true feelings).

For most products and services, customers' involvement ends when the purchase is made. After buying an appliance, for example, most customers just use it without deliberation. For some products/services, however, the involvement continues well beyond the purchase, into the product or service use. This is termed **enduring involvement,** *on-going interest* in the product or service. Many customers love using that product or service (such as Netscape an Internet access service), or are even nuts about it. Customer researchers refer to this state of enduring involvement as "deep involvement." Consider this quote from Morris Holbrook, a leading consumer researcher at Columbia University; here he speaks as a consumer himself, specifically as a fanatic consumer of jazz music:

> I just want to hear the music. What I do need is music in every location where I might spend any appreciable amount of time (say five minutes). This includes the living room, my study, Christopher's room, Sally's office, Sally's desk, the Oldsmobile, and [my other] house in Pennsylvania. For other locations and for traveling, I also keep a backup collection of portable radios and tape players.[3]

Table 14.3 illustrates measures of these two forms of involvement.

The relationship between purchase involvement and enduring product involvement is that product involvement will create high purchase involvement but is not necessary for it. That is, if there is product involvement, then high purchase involvement is likely to follow. But purchase involvement can also occur for products a consumer does not find involving in themselves. Many purchases could be highly involving without the product or service itself eliciting any long-term enduring involvement. For example, the purchase of

Table 14.3

ILLUSTRATIVE MEASURES OF CONSUMER INVOLVEMENT

PRODUCT INVOLVEMENT OR IMPORTANCE:
This product is

Unimportant	_____	Important
Means a lot to me	_____	Means nothing to me*
Unappealing	_____	Appealing
Valuable	_____	Worthless*
Unexciting	_____	Exciting

ENDURING PRODUCT INVOLVEMENT:
(Example: consumer involvement with cars)

- Cars offer me relaxation and fun when life's pressures build up.
- I prefer to drive a car with a strong personality of its own.
- To me, a car is nothing more than an appliance.*
- I enjoy conversations about cars.

PURCHASE INVOLVEMENT:
- In choosing this product, I would not care at all/would care a lot about which brand, make, or model I buy.
- How important would it be for you to make a right choice of this product?
  Not at all/Extremely Important
- It is not/it is a big deal if I make a mistake in choosing————(the product name).*

*Reverse scored.

Compiled from: Peter H. Bloch (1981), "An Exploration into the Scaling of Consumers' Involvement in Product Class," in K. Monroe (ed.), *Advances in Consumer Research*, Vol. VIII, pp. 61–65; Judith Lynne Zaichkowsky (1985), "Measuring the Involvement Construct," *Journal of Consumer Research*, 12 (December), pp. 341–352; Banwari Mittal, "Measuring Purchase Decision Involvement," *Psychology and Marketing*, 6, 1988, pp. 147–62.

a washer and dryer entails high-involvement purchase deliberation processes. But having bought these appliances, the customer does not find their usage to be of enduring interest. In contrast, a music lover wants to buy a stereo sound system. His enduring interest in music raises his purchase involvement, and his involvement in the product continues beyond the purchase occasion.

Purchase decision involvement directly affects the extent of information search and processing. Enduring involvement, on the other hand, leads customers to develop expertise on the product or service category, to search information on an ongoing basis, to take interest in product care, and to augment and upgrade it. Marketers expect these people to become opinion leaders and advocates for the brand, to purchase add-on options, to build a bonding relationship with the company, and to participate in new-product or service idea generation. Nintendo and Kool Aid companies coordinate membership clubs to channel product fans' enthusiasm.

FAMILIARITY AND EXPERTISE   Customers have familiarity and expertise as a result of prior information acquisition and prior personal experience. The relationship between prior experience and external information search is generally inverse; with increasing prior experience, less external search occurs (see Figure 14.3).

Prior experience also implies that the purchase problem is solved in the routine problem solving mode, as happens with most of the day-to-day purchases of staple items. However, even with high prior experience, routine problem solving may not be considered a desirable strategy under these conditions:

- If the experience with the prior purchase was *not* positive (e.g., last year's lawn maintenance service was unsatisfactory).

- If the technology has changed substantially since the last purchase, thus rendering prior experience obsolete (e.g., newer generation of computers).

- If the goal is to build an assortment rather than replace the older or prior purchase—for example, the purchase of clothes, music CD collection, and so on.

- If the purchase is infrequent and long after the last purchase so that there is natural desire to explore "what is new out there" (e.g., an automobile).

- If the product or service is a high-risk purchase so there is a need to optimize the purchase anew—last time's optimal choice may not be the optimal choice now (e.g., investment portfolios).

- If the product or service is one of high-interest/high-enduring involvement, so it is inherently enjoyable to search information about the alternatives in the product or service class (e.g., antiques). In these instances, information search is likely to occur, despite prior experience.

Figure 14.3

THE INFLUENCE OF PRIOR EXPERIENCE ON INFORMATION SEARCH

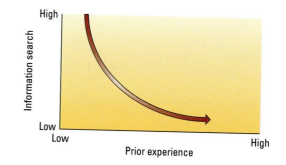

It is useful to distinguish between prior experience and expertise. Prior experience refers simply to the history of purchase and consumption and information obtained with respect to that product or service. Thus, the number of times you have bought a product or service, say, a car or a car insurance policy, the length of experience with the car, and the number of items of information about the car acquired previously all constitute prior experience. In contrast, expertise refers to the *understanding* of the attributes in a product or service class, and knowledge about how various alternatives stack up on these attributes.

Once a customer judges prior experience to be inadequate for the impending purchase and decides that new information search will be useful, expertise comes into play in determining how much search will be undertaken. Interestingly, the role of prior expertise is counterintuitive. At first marketers thought customers with low prior expertise would seek more information to overcome their knowledge deficit ("the deficit hypothesis"). However, it turns out that customers with prior expertise seek even more information about the impending purchase than do those less knowledgeable.[4] For example, in one recent study of 1,400 car buyers, it was found that the amount of prior experience was negatively correlated with the amount of search effort customers undertook prior to making their choice. However, customers' general

You have 12 minutes to make changes on a thousand copies. Is now a good time to talk copying systems?

New needs often make current products inadequate: Here Canon helps business customers' problem recognition by catching them at the precise moment they need high-speed document processing, a need Canon wants to fulfill.

interest in cars was positively correlated with their product knowledge (i.e., expertise), and both interest and expertise were *positively* correlated with the amount of search effort.[5] We term this tendency of less knowledgeable customers to seek less information rather than more, as the **"ignorance paradox"**!

The ignorance paradox occurs in that those who do not know also do not know that they do not know. Thus, naive customers do not know what questions to ask. This explains why sports enthusiasts visit and buy from a sports specialty store, whereas nonenthusiasts buy their sports needs from mass merchandisers. This is also why specialty stores have to keep more knowledgeable salespersons compared to mass merchandisers.

TIME PRESSURE   One of the most conspicuous characteristics of the customer in the 1990s is time pressure. Time has become and is becoming more and more scarce, due to (a) both spouses working, (b) many customers employed in more than one job, (c) many customers re-enrolling in school to acquire new skills necessary for a more complex employment market, and (d) new leisure activities enabled by technology. Some have called the "always on the go" customer the "harassed decision maker." Time pressure is making customers look for more convenient outlets of shopping (e.g., home-shopping networks, catalog shopping, and the Internet). In addition, time-pressed customers are likely to cut short their information search, comparison shopping, and decision-making time.[6]

FUNCTIONAL VERSUS EXPRESSIVE NATURE OF PRODUCTS AND SERVICES

In Chapter 3, we distinguished between performance value and social and psychological value. This distinction highlights the fact that people buy some products and services primarily for their physical performance, whereas others are bought primarily or significantly for their social image or for their hedonic (sensory enjoyment) utilities. These two end-goals in product/service purchases have implications for evaluation criteria.

Specifically, only performance value products and services lend themselves to choice by information processing. In the **information processing mode (IPM)**, "the customer is thought to acquire information about brand attributes, form evaluative criteria, judge the levels of these attributes in various brands, and combine these attribute-levels for overall brand evaluation."[7] Products and services sought for social and psychological values are chosen in contrast by an "affective choice mode." In the **affective choice mode (ACM)**, affect or liking for the brand ensues based not on attribute information, but based on judgments that are holistic, self-implicative, and difficult to articulate. That is, the overall style and appearance matters (holistic); the product or service is judged in relation to oneself, as in "How will I look in this dress?" (self-implicative); and the decision cannot be verbalized since it is the nonverbal cues and emotional experience (vicarious at the time of choosing) that lead to choice.

Examples of these two modes abound. For household customers, the search and evaluation of such products as detergents, appliances, and financial investments uses IPM. In contrast, the assessment of such products as clothing, perfumes, jewelry, greeting cards, and so on, occurs in the ACM. For business customers, the purchase of raw materials, components, and equipment utilizes IPM. On the other hand, for many customers, the purchase of a corporate jet, office furniture and even an office location, say, with a prestigious street address, are driven to a large extent by ACM.

The implication of this distinction is two-fold. First, for social/psychological value-fulfilling products and services, customers would not seek much feature information, but this would not mean that they don't care, and that they are executing a routine problem solving strategy. Actually, the deliberation time may still be just as much. Second, marketers should not burden the customer with a lot of attribute information; instead they

Customers face information overload all the time.

should emphasize showing the product or service in its entirety (i.e., holistically), and create social/psychological symbolism via nonverbal communication and via association with positive role models.

INFORMATION OVERLOAD Imagine that you are at a computer store, browsing at some models. The salesperson walks over to you and you ask her some questions. The salesperson is very knowledgeable and wants to tell you all she knows. Enthusiastically and with a very helpful attitude, she walks you to one model, explains it, then walks to a second model, describes its features, then to a third model, and so on. While she is explaining the third model, you remember to ask something about the first model. Back to the first model, you now inquire if a feature on the first model (but not in the second and third) is also available in another brand. She then shows you two more brands, dutifully describing all of their features. And at this point, your mind is saying, "There is too much information here. I can't handle it. I give up." You ask for brochures and tell yourself that you will study them leisurely at home and take your time to make the decision.

Your head-spinning experience in the computer store is a case of information overload. **Information overload** is the condition of being exposed to too much information—so much so that you are unable to process it to make a decision. To illustrate this phenomenon, let us review how researchers study it. Typically, some customers are asked to participate in a research study. They are provided information about a number of attributes of various brands, and asked to make a brand selection. Some customers are provided more information; others not as much. Researchers then analyze these customer decisions in terms of their accuracy. Although results of various studies are not conclusive, the findings tend to show that as the number of attributes or alternatives were increased, customers experienced the information overload and made suboptimal decisions.

These are laboratory experiments, where information is force-fed to customers. The intent of these studies is to examine if customers experience discomfort and whether decision error occurs. In the real world, of course, customers have the freedom *not* to be overloaded. The laboratory experiments imply, nonetheless, that in the real world, customers will avoid information when they are exposed to too much information.

A general principle of the customer information search, therefore, is that customers are *selective* in their acquisition of information, and because of this selectivity, they may not always make the best decisions. An important lesson from this to marketers is that they should carefully consider what information they should provide. Marketers should not overload the customer with information, should organize the information so that it is easy to process, and should ensure that the subset of information presented is still adequate for the customer to make an informed choice.[8]

Step 3: Alternative Evaluation

Now that the customer has all the information, how does he or she use that information to arrive at the choice? In this section, we discuss the specific manner in which customers select one of the several alternatives (brands, dealers, and so on) available to them. These specific processes and steps are referred to by researchers as "choice *models.*" There are two broad categories of choice models: compensatory and noncompensatory.[9]

THE COMPENSATORY MODEL

In the **compensatory model**, the customer arrives at a choice by considering *all* of the attributes for a product or service (or benefits for a service) and mentally trading off the alternative's perceived weakness on one or more attributes for its perceived strength on other attributes. A customer may go about making this calculation in two ways. One method of arriving at a choice is simply to add the number of positive attributes and subtract the number of negative attributes each alternative has, and then choose the one that has the most positive and fewest negative attributes.

Consider Monica Opalo, a student at the Emory Law School in Atlanta, planning a trip to visit her parents in Cincinnati, Ohio, during a recent Thanksgiving break. She was considering driving versus taking an interstate bus. Driving from Atlanta to Cincinnati takes about eight hours, and she doesn't really enjoy driving on interstate highways; taking the bus would avoid the tedious driving chore. However, the bus service is at odd hours, takes longer (about 12 hours), and the bus depot is located in an unsafe part of the town. Besides it would still cost $140 for a two-way ticket (compared with an out-of-pocket expense of about $50 by her car. Air travel was another option, but it will cost $200, and she will have to fly into Dayton, 40 miles north of Cincinnati, where her mom would have to pick her up. But at least air travel will be less tedious and less time consuming. But one advantage of traveling by her own car would be that she would have a car of her own in Cincinnati, which would give her more freedom of movement. Monica is at first pretty confused and undecided; after some thought, however, she decides to count the pluses and minuses for each option and choose the option with the most number of pluses and (correspondingly the least number of minuses). Shown in Table 14.4, these pluses and minuses lead Monica to happily decide to drive her own car.

This, of course, is a very simplified example. Whereas sometimes customers do make decisions based on a simple numerical count of pluses and minuses, often, the individual does not consider each plus or a minus equally significant. Some considerations are clearly

Table 14.4

COMPARING ALTERNATIVES BY SIMPLE COMPENSATORY RULES

	By Own Car	By Bus	By Air
Time consumed	−	−	+
Tedium	−	−	+
Cost	+	+	−
Inconvenience to Mother	+	−	−
Car available in Cincinnati	+	−	−

more important than others, and every minus may or may not cancel a plus on some other feature. Therefore, the simple method shown above may lead to arbitrary decisions.

A second and more systematic approach is to weigh every attribute for each alternative in terms of its relative importance (Table 14.5). To implement this approach, the decision maker also estimates the degree to which the alternative possesses each positive or negative attribute. This can be done either on a numerical scale of, say 0 to 10 where 10 means a perfect performance on that attribute, or in verbal rating categories such as "poor," "average," "excellent," and so forth. The latter ratings are then multiplied by the relative weight of the attribute. The sum of these products for each alternative provides a total score for that alternative. The alternative with the highest score is then chosen.

Let us see what happens if Monica were to follow this approach. To her, time is the most important consideration, especially since even during the break she wants to study for an upcoming test. She therefore assigns this attribute a weight of 4 out of 10. Cost is the second most important consideration, since she is strapped for money like students usually are; so she assigns cost a weight of 3. Inconvenience to the mother doesn't really matter since she knows that her mother wouldn't really mind it, so she gives it a weight of zero. Of the remaining 3 points (out of total 10), she assigns 2 to tedium, and 1 to having a car in Cincinnati, as she can easily borrow a car from her parents and friends in Cincinnati. As Table 14.5 shows, for Monica, then, the use of the compensatory choice model will lead to the decision to travel by air.

Likewise, business customers could use the compensatory model for vendor selection. Table 14.6 provides an example. In this example, Vendor 2 has the greatest total score, so the business customer would choose Vendor 2.

Table 14.5

USE OF COMPENSATORY CHOICE MODEL

Weights		By Own Car	By Bus	By Air
4	Time consumed	Average	Poor (most)	Good (least)
2	Tedium	Poor (high)	Poor (high)	Excellent (low)
3	Cost	Good (low)	Average	Poor (high)
0	Inconvenience to Mother	Good (none)	Average	Poor (great)
1	Car available in Cincinnati	Excellent	Poor	Poor

[where Poor = 1, Average = 2, Good = 3, and Excellent = 4]

Total Score for "by own car": $(4 \times 2) + (2 \times 1) + (3 \times 3) + (0 \times 3) + (1 \times 4) = 23$
"by bus": $(4 \times 1) + (2 \times 1) + (3 \times 2) + (0 \times 2) + (1 \times 1) = 13$
"by air": $(4 \times 3) + (2 \times 4) + (3 \times 1) + (0 \times 1) + (1 \times 1) = 24$

Therefore, the travel method this customer would choose is air.

Table 14.6		USE OF THE COMPENSATORY CHOICE MODEL BY A BUSINESS CUSTOMER		
		VENDOR RATINGS		
ATTRIBUTE	WEIGHT	VENDOR 1	VENDOR 2	VENDOR 3
Quality	4	Average (2)	Excellent (4)	Poor (1)
Fit with desired performance standards	3	Good (3)	Poor (1)	Good (3)
Customer support	1	Poor (1)	Good (3)	Excellent (4)
Price	2	Good (3)	Average (2)	Poor (1)
Total		$4(2) + 3(3) + 1(1) + 2(3)$ $= 24$	$4(4) + 3(1) + 1(3) + 2(2)$ $= 26$	$4(1) + 3(3) + 1(4) + 2(1)$ $= 19$

This model is called compensatory because a shortfall on one attribute may be compensated by a good rating on another attribute. Illustratively, a vacation spot that has less learning opportunity but more activities for fun for the whole family might receive the same overall rating as another destination with few family fun activities but more learning opportunities.

NONCOMPENSATORY MODELS

While there are several noncompensatory models identified in the literature, four are most common and useful. These are called conjunctive, disjunctive, lexicographic, and elimination by aspects.[10]

THE CONJUNCTIVE MODEL   In the **conjunctive model,** the customer begins by *setting the minimum cutoffs on all salient attributes*. Each alternative is then examined on each attribute, and any alternative that meets the minimum cut-offs on all attributes can potentially be chosen. If an alternative fails the cut-off, even on one attribute, it is dropped from further consideration. If all alternative fail to meet the cut-off levels, then the customer may revise his or her minimum cut-off levels or use another decision model. On the other hand, if more than one alternative meets all the minimum cut-off levels, the customer might resort to another decision model, to further eliminate alternatives until only one survives the process.

Consider a customer buying a car. He or she might want a car that is priced below $20,000, gets at least 30 miles per gallon, has at least an average reliability and repair record, and has at least a "good" safety rating (these latter two ratings can be read from *Consumer Reports*, for example). The customer eliminates cars that fall below these cut-off levels. If more than one car satisfies all these cut-offs, the customer may next decide on the basis of style, or simply raise the desired cut-offs on one or more attributes.

Since a majority of the choices household customers make in the marketplace on a day-to-day basis are for small ticket items, an illustration of conjunctive model for a supermarket product would be appropriate. Assume that a customer, Rosa is considering the four brands of potato chips shown in Table 14.7. Rosa has five important criteria, which are not listed in any order of importance, since she considers all five attributes important. Assume further that Rosa has cut-off levels of $1.25 (she won't spend more than $1.25), unflavored only, in a resealable package, fat not exceeding 2 grams, and branded only. Rosa first evaluates Brand 1 and rejects it because it fails to meet price, unflavored, and resealable package as cut-off criteria. Next, Rosa examines Brand 2 and accepts it because it meets all five cut-offs. Next, she examines and rejects Brand 3 and Brand 4, due to failure

Table 14.7

BRAND COMPARISONS CONSIDERED IN NONCOMPENSATORY MODELS

ATTRIBUTES	BRANDS OF POTATO CHIPS			
	BRAND #1	BRAND #2	BRAND #3	BRAND #4
Price	$1.50	$1.05	$1.25	$.99
Flavored	Yes	No	No	No
Resealable package	No	Yes	Yes	Yes
Fat (per serving)	1 gram	2 grams	3 grams	1 gram
Branded/generic	Branded	Branded	Branded	Generic

on different cut-offs. Brand 2 is left as the only choice. Had Brand 4 been a branded alternative (rather than generic), it too would have been included. Rosa would then have to further consider Brands 2 and 4, perhaps evaluating them on additional criteria, revising the cut-offs on the same criteria, or using some other model discussed later in this section.

The conjunctive model can be used by both household and business customers. Since businesses often buy components and raw materials that have to fit into finished products and production processes, meeting the minimum specifications becomes a necessity. For example, in the chemical industry, required chemicals have to meet certain minimums on such attributes as purity, side-effects, and disposability. Such indispensable minimums serve as cut-offs in the conjunctive model. The conjunctive model is therefore especially important in business-to-business markets.

THE DISJUNCTIVE MODEL   The **disjunctive model** entails *trade-offs between aspects of choice alternatives*. Sometimes the customer is willing to trade off one feature for another. For example, a home buyer might say that the house he or she would be willing to consider buying should have either five bedrooms or, if it has only four bedrooms, a finished basement. A business customer buying a copy machine might be willing to trade off copying speed if the machine has dual-side copying capability, because in a sense, automatic dual copying saves time and inconvenience. Of course, these trade-offs vary across customers. A business customer whose copying needs are always for one-sided documents may not value dual-copying capability in lieu of copying speed.

Although these trade-offs are made also in the compensatory model, there are important differences. First, the disjunctive model considers the sheer presence or absence of attributes, rather than the degree or amount in which these attributes are present. Thus, the attributes tend to be those that do not vary on a graduated scale. For example, gas mileage rating tends to be used in a compensatory fashion, whereas the presence or absence of a finished basement tends to be traded off in a disjunctive model. This categorical ("Is it present or not?") rather than graduated ("How much of it is there?") appraisal of an attribute makes the disjunctive model simpler to execute than the other models.

Second, in the compensatory model, the attributes traded off need not serve the same purpose, while in the disjunctive model they tend to. Thus, In the compensatory model, lower gas mileage of a car can be compensated by superior rating on a totally unrelated attribute such as safety. In the disjunctive model, on the other hand, gas mileage could be traded off only with other cost saving features such as low-maintenance costs. Or for copiers, their high speed versus the dual-copying capability address the same time and convenience utility.

THE LEXICOGRAPHIC MODEL   Another model customers use to make a choice is termed the **lexicographic model**. In this model, *attributes of alternatives are rank-ordered in terms of importance*. Customers examine all alternatives on the most important criterion and identify the one with the highest level on that criterion. If more than one alternative remains in the choice set, then they consider the second most important criterion and examine the remaining alternatives with respect to that criterion. The process continues until only one alternative remains.

This process can be illustrated for the potato chips customer in Table 14.7. This time however, we need to assume that not only does the customer consider those five salient attributes, but he or she also has an importance ranking for these. Let us say that fat content is most important, flavored/unflavored next most important (with unflavored "fat" being preferred), resealable package next most important (with preference for a "resealable"), branded/generic next in importance ('branded' preferred), and price last in importance. The customer looks at all four brands on fat content, and retains Brand 1 and Brand 4 since they have the lowest amount of fat. Then, he or she looks at the second most important criterion, flavored/unflavored. Of the remaining Brands (1 and 4), Brand 4 is "unflavored" and is therefore preferred. The choice is made. Had Brand 1 also been "unflavored", then the customer would look at the short-listed brands with respect to the third most important criterion, namely, resealable package—again Brand 4 would have been the choice since it is the only one available in a resealable package.

For an example of business-to-business service, consider a business traveler (a salesperson, say) deciding on a hotel for an out-of-town trip. His most important criterion might be the hotel location within the downtown business district (rather than in the outlying areas of the city); therefore, he does not even bother looking at the listing of the outlying area hotels (in the AAA guide books, hotels are listed in separate sections for downtown and outlying areas). Since there are several hotels in the business district listing, he next considers the second most important criterion, availability of office and business services (FAX, copying, a VCR- equipped TV Monitor in the room, and so on). Suppose only four hotels in the AAA listing meet this criterion. He next considers the third most important criterion, say, price. He then chooses the one with the lowest price, and the decision is made. But if two hotels (or more) had the same low price, the customer would have to go through the next round of processing the alternatives on the criterion next in importance, such as, say, the availability of a health spa on the hotel property. The process stops when one alternative is identified.

ELIMINATION BY ASPECTS The **elimination by aspects** (EBA) model, first proposed by psychologist Amos Tversky, is similar to the lexicographic model but with one important difference. The customer rates the attributes in the order of importance and, in addition, defines cut-off values. He or she then examines all alternatives first on the most important attribute, admitting for further consideration only those which satisfy the minimum cut-off level on this most important attribute. If more than one alternative meets this requirement, then the customer goes to the next step, appraising the remaining alternatives on the second attribute, delineating those that meet the minimum cut-off level on this attribute, and so on.[11]

In the potato chip example in Table 14.7, let us say that the customer considers, as before, fat as the most important criterion, and deems 2 grams as the maximum cut-off level. Using the EBA procedure, he or she will short-list Brands 1, 2 and 4, since they all meet this cut-off. Suppose the next most important criterion is price, with a cut-off level of $1.25. Of the short-listed brands, Brand 2 and 4 meet this second criterion. Suppose the next most important attribute is branded/generic with branded being the only acceptable brand. At this stage then, Brand 2 will be selected. In the pure lexicographic model, assuming the same importance ranking but with no cut-offs, Brand 4 would have been the choice. The reason is that only Brand 1 and 4 survive step 1 (examine fat content), and then in step 2 (examine price), Brand 4 has the lower price of the two.

Lonely hearts: desires as decision criteria

These decision rules can be, and usually are, applied to noncommercial decisions as well. For example, in seeking a date or a marriage partner, the individuals often use "looks" or "intelligence" as the most important criterion and use it in a lexicographic or EBA model.

HOW AND WHEN THE MODELS ARE USED

Several concepts shed light on how and when various choice models are used. These are processing by brand or by attribute, comparative features of various choice models, the two-stage choice process, rapid heuristics, and satisficing. In addition, as illustrated in the Window on Research box, decision-making practices are influenced by culture.

PROCESSING BY BRAND OR BY ATTRIBUTE   Customers making choice decisions employ various models according to the choice situation facing them. An important characteristic of these models is the manner in which the evaluation proceeds: one brand at a time or one attribute at a time (i.e., in Table 14.6 or 14.7, by rows or by columns). Conjunctive models entail considering one brand at a time with respect to all the attributes. The process of assessing one brand entirely before moving on to the second brand is called **processing by brands**. Note that the term *brand* is being used here to connote any alternative from which the choice must be made. Thus, the model is applicable to supplier choice as well as to choice of products and services.

In contrast to conjunctive models, the lexicographic and EBA processes entail **processing by attributes**, (i.e., processing all the brands simultaneously on one attribute at a time). This is simpler to execute than processing by brands. However, processing by brands allows a more thorough evaluation of brands than does processing by attributes. Furthermore, the lexicographic model is simpler to execute than the EBA, but the lexicographic loses the opportunity to purchase a brand that may be superior on the next set of attributes. In the mushroom example, lexicographic model would lead to selection of Brand 4, even though it is a generic brand; Brand 2, a superior brand for this customer

Decision Making by Chinese Customers in Montreal

The general process of decision making varies somewhat from one customer group to another. An important factor that makes the process different is the cultural background of the customer. For example, if you observe the buying behavior of immigrants in a country, you will notice differences between immigrants and natives, and also among immigrants from different cultures.

This is illustrated in a study of Chinese customers in Montreal. In this study, interviews were conducted with recent buyers of electronic equipment (e.g., audio systems, VCRs, televisions, and so on). The study found that the most notable cultural characteristic of this group of customers was the high value the group placed on thrift and the habit of saving. Correspondingly, buying by debt financing is generally disapproved in this group. Consequently, impulse buying of an expensive purchase was rare among the Chinese. Credit cards are used for convenience, not for credit; most Chinese customers pay off their entire balances monthly. This is in sharp contrast to North American customers, who usually finance their major purchases by credit.

This norm of not buying on credit makes every major purchase a three-stage process for Chinese customers: (1) budgeting for the purchase, (2) accumulating the savings, and (3) implementing the purchase. Information search takes on a different character during these stages. In the budgeting and saving stage, the search is lengthy, broad in scope, and leisurely. The customer is broadly "scanning the environment" rather than focusing on a specific aspect. The purpose of this search is to become familiar with the product or service category and various brands available in the market, to learn price points, to seek others' general impressions about various brands and features, and to decide on the amount they would like to spend. In the second stage, the search virtually stops, and the customer focuses on saving the amount needed. Finally, in the third, post-saving stage, which begins after the needed budget amount has been saved, the search is intense, short in duration, and directed at specific information about specific brands and models.

The study also observed some differences in the sources of information Chinese customers utilized. They distinguished between "factual" and "evaluative" information. They relied on salespersons for the former but not for the latter. Thus, they could ask the salesperson about the product features and other "objective" features, but for judgments about overall product quality, they sought independent sources like *Consumer Reports* and personal sources like friends and relatives. This general distrust of salespersons also made them rely much more on their own product inspection even for "objective" features. Thus, Chinese customers tended to search for product information in stores where they could browse without being approached by salespersons.

Because the implementation of the decision process is influenced by cultural background, it is important that marketers study the decision making process for customers in different countries, and for customers of different cultural backgrounds within the same country.

Additional information located at **http://www. io.org/ãdrews/ccamma/ccamma.html**

Source: Adapted from Kathleen Brewer Doran, "Exploring Cultural Differences in Consumer Decision Making: Chinese Consumers in Montreal," *Advances in Consumer Research* Chris Allen and D. John, ed. 21 (1994), pp. 318–22.

(because it is branded) gets eliminated simply because it happened to *not* be the lowest price brand.

COMPARATIVE FEATURES OF VARIOUS CHOICE MODELS The conjunctive, disjunctive, lexicographic, and EBA models are all *non*compensatory models, since the deficiency on one attribute is not allowed to be made up for by excess on another. An alternative may be eliminated in the first step for being only marginally inferior to an otherwise substantially better alternative on the second most important attribute (e.g., price

$1.05 compared to $.99); it doesn't matter that the eliminated alternative is much superior on all other attributes. The compensatory model eliminates the possibility of making such suboptimal choices.

The compensatory model is more burdensome to execute, however, because the customer has to consider several dimensions or attributes at the same time and somehow weigh them in his or her mind. Typically, therefore, the compensatory model is used sparingly and only for important decisions.[12] Most low-ticket items are likely to be chosen with the help of noncompensatory models. Thus, a customer may buy table salt based simply on a single criterion such as familiarity with the brand, or whether or not it is iodized, or perhaps on price alone. For example, a customer might consider all brands of salt to be basically the same, and might say "Let me buy the one with the lowest price." In this case, the customer is using a lexicographic model. Another customer buying an entree might use fat content as the important criterion and then either choose the one with the lowest fat content (thus employing a lexicographic model) or consider all entrees with fat content not exceeding 15 percent of total calories (and thus employing EBA). Calories per serving might then be used as second criterion, and, if need be, price as the third.

In terms of the three routine/limited/extended problem solving strategies, the compensatory model is likely to be used generally for extended problem solving. Noncompensatory models are likely used for limited and routine problem solving situations. Furthermore, noncompensatory models may also be used in the initial stage of an extended problem-solving decision situation, as explained next.

TWO-STAGE CHOICE PROCESS   For the more important decisions, a customer might first use a noncompensatory model and then, to further identify the choice, use a compensatory model. Customer researchers Bettman and Park have described customer decision process as a two stage process, termed **phased decision strategy**.[13] In the first stage, termed "alternative elimination stage," customers narrow down the set of alternatives for closer comparisons. In the second stage, termed "alternative selection stage" the smaller set of alternatives is further examined. The objective of the first stage is thus to identify the *acceptable* alternatives, whereas the second stage is meant to identify *the best*.

Since noncompensatory models are easier to execute, a large number of alternatives can be examined relatively quickly, particularly if processing is done by attributes rather than by brands. In the second stage, when only three or four alternatives remain, customers can more efficiently employ the compensatory model. Even here, if one or more attributes are matching across the alternatives, one simply ignores this attribute and applies the compensatory model on the smaller set of attributes. In this way customers can take advantage of the compensatory model to make an optimal decision without incurring the information-overload cost that would have accrued if all of the initially available large number of alternatives were to be processed by the compensatory model throughout.

RAPID HEURISTICS   For a common, repeat purchase of low-risk, low-ticket items such as shampoo, snacks, cereals, and other supermarket items, customers are unlikely to spend much time or effort. These purchases are perceived to be low-risk, low-involvement decisions. As such, hardly any information is examined, and brand choice is made by using a heuristic (simple rule of thumb). Examples of heuristics used for such repeat purchase items are "Purchase the known brand only"; "Purchase whichever brand is on sale"; "I saw my friend using this brand, so I too will purchase this one."

A study illustrating this was done by professor Wayne D. Hoyer of the University of Texas at Austin on U.S. customers; the study was later replicated on Chinese customers by the National University of Singapore professor Siew Meng Leong.[14] In these studies, customers were observed in a supermarket selecting a common, repeat purchase item (namely, detergent and shampoo) and later approached and asked the basis of their decision. In a subsequent experimental study, customers were given a product that could be examined by taste (namely, peanut butter in one study; cheese in another). Of the three brands presented to research customers, one was a well-known brand.

The researchers found that customers in the supermarket study spent very little time (less than 15 seconds) to complete their in-store decision, examined a small number of packages (about 1.5 on an average), made few brand comparisons, and looked at only a few shelf tags. In response to the question as to why they chose the brand they did, an overwhelming majority (approximately 95 percent) mentioned a single reason. This single reason, for the largest majority, was that "It worked better."

In the experimental study where customers were making a choice anew (since none of their usual brands were in the choice set), and where one of the three brands was known but the other two were not, customers overwhelmingly (97 percent) chose the known brand. Thus, "purchase the known brand" is a choice heuristic customers use most often, especially in a new choice task of a low-ticket, common, repeat purchase item. Not in vain, then, do advertisers spend considerable monies keeping their brands in the top-of-the-mind awareness of their target customers.

SATISFICING   No matter what decision model they use, customers as decision makers can never consider and appraise all of the alternatives exhaustively. Indeed, customers *do not* typically make the most optimal choice. As already pointed out, the use of lexicographic or EBA or other noncompensatory model might eliminate a brand from further consideration based on the first attribute even though the brand's other features could have made the brand more attractive overall. Yet customers are perfectly happy making a choice by noncompensatory models. This is a concept that Nobel Prize winner psychologist Herbert Simon calls "satisficing."[15] **Satisficing** refers to customer (or decision maker's) acceptance of an alternative that he or she finds satisfying, rather than pursuing the arduous search for the most optimal alternative there might be. Thus, even the ardent comparison shoppers finally give up and buy the product or service they find most acceptable from among those they have considered so far, even though they recognize that there might well be a slightly or even substantially better product or service or deal at the next store.

Step 4: Purchase

Once the customer has evaluated the alternatives, he or she makes the purchase. This at first appears a straightforward step, but even here customer behavior at times becomes intriguing. To understand this behavior, let us break down this step into three substeps as shown in the Figure 14.4. The first substep occurs when the customer identifies the most preferred alternative, based on the alternative evaluation process just described. In effect, the customer says, "Ok, this is the one I like and I prefer." The next substep is to form a purchase intent—a determination that one would buy that product or service. It is the act of giving self-instruction, like, "The next time I am in the market, I am going to buy it"; it is to make a mental note, to put it on the "to do" list, so to speak. The final substep is implementing the purchase. This entails arranging the terms of the transaction, seeking and obtaining the transfer of the title or ownership from the seller, paying for the product or service, and receiving possession of the product or of service commitment from the seller.

The first substep (choice identification) is the conclusion of a process where the customer's user role and his or her needs and wants as user become most salient. Although the payer's concern (e.g.,"would it be affordable") and buyer's concern (e.g., where to get

CUSTOMER BEHAVIOR AT THE PURCHASE STEP

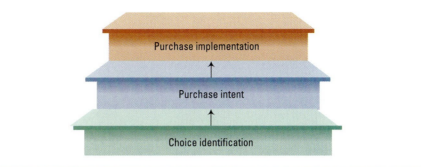

it) may also be taken into account, the emphasis is likely to have remained on the fit between the product/service and the performance and social/psychological values the customer seeks in the user role. In the second substep (purchase intent), the payer's concerns become most salient. If the payer is different from the user, a formal budget approval may be needed. The payer may have to assess whether the product or service is overpriced, whether the required cash or credit is available at this time, whether it sits well with established guidelines for allocating the budget over different categories of products or services, or whether it offers equity to other users (e.g., other members of the household, or other employees in the organization) who may have claims on the budget pool. Finally, the purchase implementation substep activates the buyer role and is influenced most by the concerns of the buyer. The buyer's market values ("convenience" and "service" values) become the determining forces. This may influence the store or supplier from whom the preferred item is bought, the day and time it is bought, how soon or late it is bought, and whether it is even bought. For example, a 13-year-old boy we know wanted to attend a space camp run by NASA. He called the camp organizers, got the brochures, identified the specific program he wanted to go to, and got his parents to agree to pay for the trip. The final task of putting together and sending the application was left to the older brother, who procrastinated until the deadline expired.

Even when the same person plays the payer, user, and buyer roles, the buyer role may hinder the implementation of the choice identified and approved by the other two roles. For example, a friend told us this personal story. She was watching "Meet the Press" (a Sunday weekly TV talk show in the United States), when she saw the advertisement for a vegetable patty that can be used in place of the beef patty to make a vegetarian hamburger. Being a vegetarian, she found the product appealing; however, it was not available in the store, but rather only by mail order from the company. She immediately called the toll-free number to order the product, but got a recording announcing that the order could be placed only on the weekdays. The next few days, she got busy and then she lost the phone number. The user was "stood up" (i.e., disappointed) by the buyer who had failed to come through with the task assigned to him or her. And the sale was lost because the marketer had been focused on the user needs only (offering a desirable and unique product), ignoring the buyer's needs (i.e., making it convenient to buy it anytime)!

Thus, as the above examples show, the customer journey from choice identification to purchase implementation does not always proceed in predictable ways. Sometimes, the purchase intention may not be implemented, as, for example, when a customer almost decides to join a particular weight-reduction program but somehow never gets around to actually doing it. But even if the purchase implementation eventually occurs, the customer journey may take a different route. Two factors can potentially "derail the journey": postponement or delay in implementation and deviation from the identified choice.

DELAY IN IMPLEMENTATION

Causes of delays in implementation occur throughout the customer decision process—from problem recognition through alternative evaluation to purchase. We discuss these here for convenience and because it is the purchase step that they ultimately delay. Two customer stories illustrate sources of delay in implementation. A few years ago, a college student bought a small used car, a Toyota MR2. The car served him well except when it snowed. His car, lightweight and rear-wheel drive, simply would not pull on the icy road. He decided (i.e., formed a purchase intent) that he would buy a four by four before the next winter. Well, the next winter came, and he struggled through it. As this book goes to press, he is still driving that old tiny car. What happened to the four by four he wanted to buy?

The second story pertains to a state university. This university had a contract with two computer suppliers, one for IBM compatibles and the other for Macintosh computers. These suppliers had agreed to offer preferred terms of purchase to faculty members who bought desktop computers for their personal use at home. Even though the computers were used at home, an important consideration in selecting a home computer was the compatibility with the computers at the office. Historically, the university provided faculty members the option to choose either computer (Mac or IBM compatible). Then, the new university president decided that the university would only support one platform and that it would be the IBM platform. Consequently, several faculty members had to modify their purchase intent of buying a particular model of Mac, which they had identified as their preferred choice, and undertake the evaluation process anew.

A recent consumer study by consumer researchers Eric A. Greenleaf and Donald R. Lehmann identified the reasons consumers give for delay in their purchase decisions. The study interviewed recent buyers of such products as home appliances, electronics, personal computers, clothing, furniture, sports equipment, and automobiles. The consumers were asked to describe the reasons that caused them to delay the decision in buying these products, and also the reasons or factors that subsequently caused them to "close the decision." These factors, along with their importance ratings in this study, are described in Table 14.8.

Delays in purchase implementations occur among business customers as well. One reason for such delay is a change in management—the new management may want to review all capital equipment procurement plans and/or redesign the procurement policies. Another possible reason is declining financial performance—if sales and profits fall below projected levels, then some capital equipment purchase plans may be put on hold. Finally, decisions may be delayed because of fourth-quarter syndrome—businesses typically postpone making major purchases until the last quarter of the accounting year; thus, purchase decision making may be delayed until the fourth quarter either to avoid committing money early in the year or because time pressure did not permit decision making earlier.

Understanding these reasons is important for marketers because it helps them facilitate the customer journey from problem recognition to purchase. By identifying the particular reason and the step where it has a delaying effect, marketers can work to overcome that barrier. Furthermore, marketers can implement separate actions directed individually toward the three roles of the user, payer, and buyer.

Table 14.8	REASONS FOR DELAY AND DELAY CLOSURE		
	REASON	MEAN IMPORTANCE	CUSTOMER ROLE
REASONS FOR DELAY			
	Time Pressure—Too busy to devote the time	3.91	User, payer, buyer
	Needed more information	3.43	User
	Couldn't afford at the time	3.19	Payer
	Not sure if needed the item	2.75	User
	Social and psychological risk if a wrong choice were made	2.70	User
	Felt another product at home would do	2.70	User
	Performance and financial risk if a wrong choice is made	2.65	User, payer
	Expected price reduction or product modification in the near future	2.52	User, payer
	Needed others' consent	2.41	User, payer
	Find shopping unpleasant	2.34	Buyer
REASONS FOR DELAY CLOSURE			
	Decided on another alternative	3.84	User
	Found the time	3.62	User, buyer
	Need had become passing	3.51	User
	Lower price became available	3.10	Payer
	Tired of shopping further	2.70	Buyer
	Found a good store	2.41	Buyer
	Was able to justify the expense	2.32	Payer
	Obtained the advice and consent I needed	2.14	User, payer
	Due to good word-of-mouth	2.01	User

Source: Reasons and means are from Eric A. Greenleaf and Donald R. Lehmann (1996).

DEVIATION FROM THE IDENTIFIED CHOICE

The second factor that may derail the customer purchase implementation is deviation from the identified choice. Several conditions may account for this. First, the preferred brand may be out of stock, thus forcing the customer to buy a brand different from the one identified. Second, new in-store information may reopen the evaluation process. Third, financing terms may render a purchase infeasible, forcing the customer either to abandon the purchase altogether or to substitute the purchase with a lower-level model or another brand available on preferred terms. These conditions may shift the relative impact of the customer roles. While the values of the user are most influential in the alternative evaluation phase, the values of the buyer (e.g., convenience of buying) or of the payer (e.g., the financing available) become influential at the purchase stage.

Step 5: Post-Purchase Experience

The customer's decision process does not end with the purchase. Rather, the experience of buying and using the product provides information that the customer will use in future decision making. In some cases, the customer will be pleased with the experience and will buy the same product from the same supplier again. In other cases, the customer will be disappointed and may even return or exchange the product. In general, as shown in Figure 14.5, the post-purchase process includes four steps: decision confirmation, experience evaluation, satisfaction or dissatisfaction, and future response (exit, voice, or loyalty).

Figure 14.5

STEPS IN THE POST-PURCHASE PHASE

Line diagram of postpurchase substages

DECISION CONFIRMATION

After a customer makes an important choice decision, he or she experiences an intense need to confirm the wisdom of that decision. The flip side is that he or she wants to avoid the disconfirmation. One of the processes that occurs at this stage is *cognitive dissonance*, discussed in Chapter 11, which is a postpurchase doubt the buyer experiences about the wisdom of the choice.

Methods of reducing dissonance and confirming the soundness of one's decision are seeking further positive information about the chosen alternative and avoiding negative information about the chosen alternative. Thus, customers reread product literature reviewing the brand's positive features, and avoid competitors' advertisements or negative information from others. They seek out friends to tell them about their purchase, hoping that their friends will validate their decision by praising the selected brand. Marketers can put this principle to use: After the purchase (say, during product or service delivery), salesmen can review with customers all the features of the product or service. Since customers are not likely to have considered all the product's features during the prepurchase information search, a comprehensive feature review during the postpurchase phase is likely to bring to customer attention a few positive features previously ignored, thus improving the perceived attractiveness of the product.

EXPERIENCE EVALUATION

Following purchase, the product or service is actually consumed. Marketers need to know whether customers consume it routinely or while consciously evaluating it. This depends on the level of enduring involvement in the product or service and the finality of the preference that caused this purchase.

Earlier in this chapter, enduring involvement was defined as the interest customers take in the consumption of the product or service on an *ongoing basis*. Of the hundreds of products and services we use in our lives, we use most of them routinely or mindlessly. We simply do not have the time or the motivation to think about them at the time of consumption. We notice them only if something does not work as expected. On the other hand, everybody is very enthusiastic about some products or services. In consuming these, we are conscious of the consumption experience, appraising and relishing it continually (e.g., wine drinking by wine connoisseurs). These then are the products and services that undergo conscious evaluation during use.

Secondly, customers buy some products and services on a trial basis, without making their preference final yet. These products, even if not of enduring involvement, are the ones that the customer is likely to be using with an eye to appraisal. Often, when customers receive free samples, they are not necessarily in an evaluative mode; therefore, they use them routinely, without consciously trying to register the product or service performance. Two things determine the productivity of free product sampling efforts. First, if the product or service's superiority is substantial and would be conspicuous in consumption, then it pays to sample; otherwise, free sampling might be a waste. Second, free samples should be targeted only to customers who are not satisfied with the current solutions. Because of their dissatisfaction, they would be actively appraising the sampled product or service.

SATISFACTION/DISSATISFACTION

Whether or not they actively evaluate a product or service during product use or consumption, users do experience the usage outcome. This outcome is characterized as satisfaction or dissatisfaction. Measuring overall satisfaction/dissatisfaction is easy. Customer researchers can simply ask, "How satisfied or dissatisfied are you with————(the product or service name)?"

What is more challenging is to understand *why* customers feel the way they do. There are two approaches to this challenge. One is to get the customer to rate a product or service on its various attributes. For example, a carmaker can ask the customer to rate his or her experience with a car on such attributes as handling, gas mileage, acceleration, braking, climate control, noisiness, and so on. Satisfaction or dissatisfaction with these product attributes can then be used to explain the customer's *overall* satisfaction or dissatisfaction with the product.

But this approach raises another question: What causes satisfaction or dissatisfaction with individual attributes? This question is successfully addressed by a theoretical approach to understanding satisfaction. Customer behavior scholars have proposed that satisfaction depends not on the absolute levels of performance on various attributes, but rather on how the actual performance compares with the *expected* performance. Thus, if the product or service experience fulfills prepurchase expectations, then satisfaction results. On the other hand, if the prepurchase expectations are not met, dissatisfaction results. According to this theory, therefore, satisfaction or dissatisfaction stems respectively from the confirmation or disconfirmation of our expectations (see Figure 14.6). The theory makes intuitive sense in our everyday experience. For example, we may find a

Figure 14.6

ROLE OF EXPECTATIONS IN SATISFACTION/DISSATISFACTION

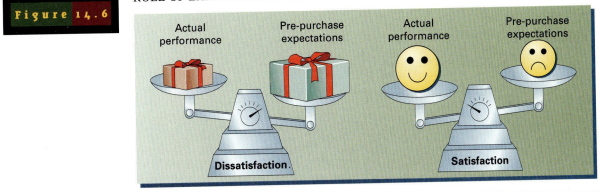

MEASURING SATISFACTION IN TERMS OF EXPECTATIONS

How did we do? How was our:

	FELL BELOW EXPECTATIONS	MET EXPECTATIONS	EXCEEDED EXPECTATIONS
Room appearance	O	O	O
Room cleanliness	O	O	O
Registration speed	O	O	O
Friendliness of staff	O	O	O
Room service promptness	O	O	O

particular level of cleanliness unsatisfactory in a Marriott hotel but quite satisfactory in, say, a Red Roof Inn. This is because our expectations about the Marriott are quite high compared to those we hold for the Red Roof Inn.

This theory of satisfaction has important implications for shaping expectations.[16] If marketing communications and other elements of the marketing mix (e.g., advertising, salespersons, price, appearance of the store, and so on) promise too much, they may create expectations that the product or service would almost surely fail to fulfill, thus risking customer dissatisfaction. Of course, if the expectations are too low, the sale may not result. The right strategy therefore ought to be to create realistic expectations and not over-promise, and to design the product or service so that the *realistic* expectations imply a performance level that the target market finds attractive enough to select the brand. To assess whether they are on target, marketers may use a measure of satisfaction such as the one illustrated in Table 14.9.

FUTURE RESPONSE: EXIT, VOICE, OR LOYALTY

Following the experience of satisfaction or dissatisfaction, customers have three possible responses: exit, voice, or loyalty.

EXIT If customers are dissatisfied with their experience with a brand, they may decide never again to buy the brand. This places them back to the start of the decision process the next time the problem recognition arises. They have to go through the arduous process of information search, alternative evaluation, and so on, all over again.

VOICE Dissatisfied customers may complain and then decide either to give the brand or marketer another chance or simply to exit.

What accounts for customers' tendency to complain or not complain? A customer's likelihood of complaining depends on three factors: dissatisfaction salience, attributions to the marketer, and customers' personality traits (see Figure 14.7).

■ Dissatisfaction salience—Not all dissatisfaction is salient (i.e., bothersome to customers). Generally small gaps between performance and expectations are ignored; moreover, even substantial gaps are not likely to be noticed if the product or service is trivial. Thus, importance of the product or service and the degree of performance-expectations gap determine dissatisfaction salience, which in turn determines the likelihood of customer complaints.

■ Attributions to the marketer—Customers make attributions about who is to blame for poor product or service performance. If customers blame themselves or circumstances, then complaining would not occur; on the other hand, if they attribute failure to the marketer, then they are likely to complain. Furthermore, if customers thought that the failure was not likely to

Figure 14.7

DETERMINANTS OF COMPLAINING

be repeated, they would be less motivated to complain. Finally, customers must also believe that the marketer is likely to take the corrective action; if they thought that redress from the marketer is unlikely, they may consider complaining a waste of effort.

- Customers' personality traits—Customers' personality traits play an important role in complaining. Customers differ in self-confidence and in their degree of aggressiveness/ submissiveness. Complaining requires self-confidence, and aggressiveness drives customers to assert themselves. These traits therefore lead customers to complain rather than meekly accept poor marketer performance.

Following the complaint, negative-word-of mouth is less likely and repatronage more likely if the complaint is successfully redressed. If the complaint is not successfully redressed, the negative word-of-mouth might in fact be further intensified beyond what it would have been had the customer not made the complaint in the first place. This occurs because, in addition to the dissatisfaction of product performance shortfall, now the customer experiences further dissatisfaction due to being given a "deaf ear." An important concept here is perceived justice. **Perceived justice** is customers' perceptions that they were treated with respect during the conflict resolution process, the policy and procedures followed were fair, and the decision outcome itself was fair.[17] When perceived justice seems not to have occurred, the hostility increases.

Research has found that customer complaint is actually good for the marketer. According to one research study, about 19 percent of the dissatisfied customers complain; of the complaining customers, a significant majority continue to buy the product or service, compared to those who are dissatisfied but do not bother to complain. Thus, complainers care enough to complain. Noncomplainers simply walk out, taking their patronage to a competitor.

As a marketer, which would you rather have: a customer who exits quietly or a customer who complains? When customers leave quietly, you will never know why. In con-

An Experiment in Marketer Response to Customer Complaints

Just to see the responsiveness of various car companies, an *Advertising Age* reporter wrote a complaint letter to the CEOs of 25 carmakers (both domestic and foreign). The letter read, in part:

> I was a big believer in your company's advertising when I bought my car late last year.... Now, a mysterious "clucking" sound is coming from the right-front wheel. The selling dealer hasn't been able to correct it.
>
> My warranty expires in two weeks, and I have a car I don't even know is safe to drive.... "Can you suggest how I can get my car out of this rut?"
>
> Under the old model of transaction selling, the letter will be sent to some clerk in the customer service department, unread in the CEO office, where a salesman would just smirk when he or she reads "My warranty expires in two weeks."

Mitsubishi was one of the companies that responded early; its reply letter claimed that the chairman had actually read the letter himself. Saab, Rolls-Royce, Volkswagen, BMW, and Volvo actually looked up the "presumed" customer's phone number in the phone book and left several messages and sent mailgrams persistently. The reporter notes: "In general, the imports were more prompt to respond than the domestics, and they used faster means (phone, mailgrams, rather than postal mail); and seven of the 25 companies failed to respond in any form! Bad customer service? Most assuredly. Bad customer retention practice? Absolutely."

Source: T. Kauchak, "A Little Service, Please!" *Advertising Age* (January 21, 1991), p. S-8. Reported in Terry Vavra, *Aftermarketing*, pp. 20–21.

trast, complaining customers are providing the marketer valuable feedback! Yet marketers discourage complaints when they do not provide convenient avenues of complaining and when customer service persons display an unwelcoming attitude toward complainers. This is a dysfunctional strategy for marketers. On the other hand, in customer-oriented companies top management understands the value of addressing customer complaints. See the box "An Experiment in Marketer Response to Customer Complaints."

LOYALTY   The third response is, of course, loyalty. Customer loyalty means the customer buys the same brand repeatedly. The concept of loyalty has been debated in the literature in various definitions of *brand loyalty*. First, brand loyalty can be defined simply as "the consistent repurchase of the same brand." This definition has two problems. First, in many product or service categories, it becomes useful for customers to buy an assortment of brands. This can happen because variety is desirable for some product consumption experiences. For example, eating the same cereal every day or eating lunch every day in the office cafeteria would not be satisfying. Or repeating the same brand of clothing every day, no matter how satisfying it is in itself, would become dissatisfying. This problem of variety can be handled by asking customers if the focal brand is consistently at least a part of the assortment the customer buys, if not an exclusive purchase.

The second problem with defining and measuring brand loyalty as a consistent repurchase is that one does not know if the consistent repurchase is merely due to convenience, is a routinization of the purchase decision, or reflects genuine preference for the brand. To overcome this uncertainty, some researchers have defined brand loyalty in attitudinal terms: the brand attitude underlying the repurchase. Only if a favorable brand attitude underlies repurchase is brand loyalty thought to exist. This topic is discussed more fully in Chapter 18.

Figure 14.8

RELATIONSHIP BETWEEN SATISFACTION/QUALITY AND LOYALTY

Source: Raymond E. Kordupleski and West C. Vogel, "The Right Choice—What Does It Mean?" AT&T, 1988.

Note: AT&T analysts used quality ratings as surrogate measures of satisfaction.

At first thought, one would think that if customers are satisfied, they would not switch brands. Thus, a satisfaction rating may be deemed to ensure loyalty. Recent customer research has shown however, that while customers are less likely to switch when they are satisfied than when they are not, being satisfied does not guarantee loyalty. One study showed that despite satisfaction, as much as 30 percent of customers were likely to switch suppliers.[18] Rather than being simply satisfied, being "highly satisfied" reduces potential switching behavior significantly. In a study by AT&T, 60 percent of satisfied customers (those rating service as "good") said they were very likely to repurchase. A much more impressive 90 percent of highly satisfied customers (those rating service "excellent") said they would repurchase (see Figure 14.8).

Several potential reasons explain why satisfied customers may still switch. First, customers report being satisfied with a brand , but they may also be satisfied with some other brands. The implication of this is that one should measure customer satisfaction with a brand *relative* to competitors' brands. The second reason is that the marginal utility of a repeated use may decline simply due to familiarity. The excitement of something new or a need for variety can drive brand switching. Finally, customers may expect to receive even greater value or satisfaction from some other brand. To understand and manage these possibilities, some marketers such as AT&T have adopted the measurement of relative value, in which they measure the customer-perceived value of their brand relative to competitors.

A COMPREHENSIVE MODEL OF CUSTOMER BEHAVIOR

The principles of decision making can be combined with principles from earlier chapters to create a broader model of customer behavior. Nearly three decades ago, then Columbia University professors John Howard and Jagdish N. Sheth proposed the general and comprehensive model of buyer behavior shown in Figure 14.9.[19] This model has four major components: Inputs (information sources), the mental processes of perceptions and problem solving, and outputs (attitudes and behaviors). The input component basically comprises the external sources of information. The perceptual processes concern how the information from the input component (i.e., external sources) is registered and coded by the consumer. The problem-solving process concerns how a purchase problem is recognized,

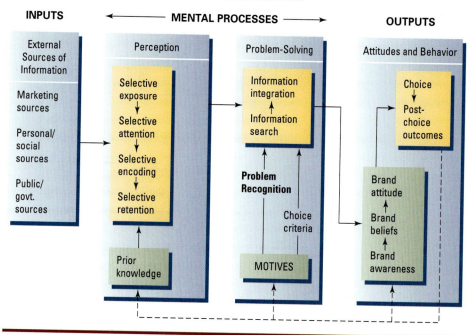

Figure 14.9

A COMPREHENSIVE MODEL OF BUYER BEHAVIOR

Source: Adapted from John A. Howard and Jagdish N. Sheth, *The Theory of Buyer Behavior* (New York: John Wiley & Sons, 1961).

and how this problem is solved using the information registered by the perceptual system. The outputs of this process are a set of cognitions about and evaluations of the various brands, which then lead to a choice and purchase decision, a purchase, and post-purchase behaviors.

The perception system is the gateway for all incoming information. Any information received from external sources is handled by the perception processes. That is, it is sensed (or registered), coded, and interpreted, in that order. These processes are influenced by prior knowledge, which includes expectations so that selective attention is given to incoming information, and there is biased interpretation of it.

In the problem-solving system, a purchase problem is first recognized. The problem recognition occurs due to an internal cue from one's motives in a state of unfulfillment, or from external stimuli evoking these motives. Examples of internal cues include hunger pangs, thirst, headache, and so on. Examples of external cues include the smell of coffee from a coffee shop in the mall, or an advertisement for hair transplant for a person who is feeling uncomfortable with his progressive hair loss. Once the problem recognition occurs, the problem-solving system either relies on prior knowledge and previously learned solutions or searches for new solutions through new information acquisition and its evaluation and integration.

The output of this information acquisition and integration process is certain beliefs, associations, and attitudes developed for the brand, all prelude to brand choice. Post-choice experience feeds back into the stock of knowledge the consumer builds over time.

INDIVIDUAL CUSTOMER DECISION MAKING AND THE THREE CUSTOMER ROLES

Table 14.10

CONCEPTS	USER	PAYER	BUYER
INDIVIDUAL DECISION MAKER	User in control of buying role as well; strong user values rule over payer/buyer values.	With someone else as payer, users tend to consume more; also user evaluation is less stringent.	Role convergence sometimes causes sacrifice in weak user values.
DECISION PROCESS Problem recognition	Users are the most frequent problem-recognizers.	Buyer dissatisfaction with service, convenience and personalization values can cause problem recognition. New delivery channels serve as solution stimuli to cause problem recognition by buyers.	Awareness of better price value from competitors causes payer role problem recognition.
Information search	Information pertaining to user values is sought.	Payer role seeks information about competitors' prices.	Inadequate buyer motivation to expend search efforts constrains user and payer desire for more information.
Search determinants: Perceived risk	User-felt risk causes more information search.	Payers willing to pay more to avoid user risks.	Buyers lean on trustworthy sources.
Involvement	User involvement may demand sacrifice in buyer/payer values.		Involved buyers do extensive information search.
Familiarity	User familiarity enables greater use of available information.		Familiarity lulls buyers into less search effort.
Time pressure	Users seek time-saving features in products/services.		Time pressure affects buyers the most who seek efficient exchanges.
Alternative evaluation	Users' values most important evaluation criteria.	For parity products (i.e., with user indifference), payers seek to maximize price value.	For parity products, buyer values become important criteria.
Decision models Compensatory Noncompensatory	Users participate actively. One or the other role may play a major role.	Payer value may be exercised through use of some noncompensatory model.	To minimize cognitive effort, buyers like to use noncompensatory model.
Functional/expressive product	For expressive products, users must participate in evaluation.		

(continued)

 INDIVIDUAL CUSTOMER DECISION MAKING
AND THE THREE CUSTOMER ROLES *(continued)*

CONCEPTS	USER	PAYER	BUYER
Purchase		Lack of agreement on financing may hinder purchase	This stage is most relevant to the buyer role.
Post-choice processes: Buyer's remorse/decision confirmation			Buyer role subject to remorse; seeks more favorable information toward decision confirmation.
Experience evaluation	Product use experience by the user role.		
Satisfaction	Determined largely by satisfaction of user values.		
Exit, voice, loyalty	User satisfaction leads to loyalty. Users spread word-of-mouth.		Loyalty simplifies buyer's task.
Complaint	User dissatisfaction motivates complaints.		Buyer aggressiveness determines if complaint will be made.

Individual Customer Decision Making and the Three Customer Roles

In this section, we pull together various concepts covered in the chapter and illustrate their relevance to the three customer roles. First, we talked about the setting of individual decision making. By definition, the user and buyer roles are played by the same individual, and often the payer role as well. Since buyer and user roles are combined in the same individual, the user has more control over what to buy and where. At the same time, if the user values are weak (i.e., the user is not highly motivated to get the best values, as happens for low-involvement products, for instance), then the buyer values take over (the buyer buys based on service and convenience). Thus, convergence of buyer and user role in the same individual may cause some sacrifice in weak user values. For example, if the individual feels too lazy to go out (a buyer role) to eat (a user role), he or she has to make do with a home-delivered pizza that may not be as good in quality and taste. Sometimes the payer role is separated, as in the consumption of public goods; with someone else as payer, the users tend to consume more as well as evaluate the product less stringently.

The three roles also come into play in the decision-making process stages: problem recognition, information search, alternative evaluation, choice or purchase, and post-choice experience. Although most products or services are bought in response to the problem recognition by the user role, the other two roles can also be the source of problem recognition. When the buyer values are violated—for example, when buyer doesn't get the prepurchase assistance, or a store employee is rude, or the store used to shop at becomes unfriendly, crowded, or otherwise inconvenient, the buyer recognizes the problem and looks for alternative means of buying the product or service. Furthermore, if a new means of obtaining the product or service becomes available (such as home delivery of groceries), the buyer's problem-recognition is triggered due to this solution stimuli. Payers recognize the problem when a competitor and brings home the point that they are paying too much for their current product or service. A case in point is the recent advertising campaign by LCI (a U.S. long-distance phone service provider), informing the users of competing long-distance phone services that these other companies round off to the next minute, causing the total call cost to be higher.

In the information-search stage, information is sought relevant to user and payer values. While some information is received without the buyer effort (e.g., information through advertisements), the information that requires visits to the store or going to the library, and so on, depends on the buyer motivation to undertake the effort. The buyer's values (i.e., his or her desire to limit the search effort) then constrain user and payer roles' desire to maximize its values. Buyers who enjoy browsing help the user role identify new solutions. Buyers who are comparison shoppers help the payer find the best price value. Various determinants of search (namely, perceived risk, involvement, familiarity, time pressure, and so on) also implicate the three roles differently.

Perceived risk generally necessitates search on brand features, the concern of the user role. To assure risk-free product or service for the user, payers may be willing to sacrifice on payer value. Buyers may want to limit consideration to suppliers they have come to trust in their interaction with them. Involvement with the product again emphasizes the user role, whose concern with getting the best product or service (in the case of high involvement) demands sacrifice in payer and buyer values, if necessary. High involvement again leads to extensive search. Buyers' roles can also vary in involvement. Some customers simply dislike shopping, while others enjoy it, reading product labels in the store, comparing products on features, and soon. Involved shoppers thus end up doing extensive information search. Uninvolved shoppers (i.e., buyers) would lead users to make do with less information. Familiarity with the product enables the user to more easily absorb the current information that the user comes across such as in advertising, but the buyer may feel less need to make the effort to "search" for new information. Time pressure is most relevant to the buyer role in the information-search stage and also in the purchase stage as the buyer would seek time-saving means of acquiring the product. Time pressure on users also is a factor and it will affect the performance criteria inasmuch as the users will seek time-saving features in products, such as ready-to-eat meals or faster cycle machines.

In the alternative evaluation stage, since the buyer is the same as the user, the market values the user seeks become the overriding criteria. Only in the case of parity products do the buyer's market values (e.g., convenience) become determinant so that the buyer buys whatever is convenient to buy. Furthermore, given user indifference to alternatives (which happens with parity products), the payer's concern with obtaining the best price value also becomes a prominent decision criterion. Decision models also implicate the different roles differently. Compensatory models require simultaneous consideration of various criteria, mostly comprising user values; therefore, users participate actively in the decision. Noncompensatory models generally emphasize one or the other of the three roles—for example, in seeking the lowest price as the sole factor (lexicographic model), the payer role is being given prominence. "Buy whatever is available" (another lexicographic rule) makes the buyer role the determinant. Functional versus expressive products also influence the interplay of the three roles. Expressive products can be evaluated only by the user, much more than is the case for functional products. For functional products, as a user you can specify the performance criteria, and then let the buyer role match the product or service against those criteria; in contrast, for expressive products, product evaluation against the desired social/emotional values can be done only by the user role, not the buyer role. Of course, users can subsequently routinize their choice by brand name for functional and expressive products alike and let the buyer simply execute it.

In the next stage, purchase, the values of the buyer and the payer become most important. Sometimes when the decision is made outside the store, or if the purchase cannot be executed as soon as the user decision is made, the buyer may delay buying the product or may fail to implement the decision, sometimes foregoing the purchase altogether. The payer value of best price and good financing or credit may sometimes hinder the purchase of the user's choice, for example when price negotiations fail. Clearly, the buyer skills in negotiating price and payment and delivery terms, and the payer's ability to receive credit or meet the payment terms block the purchase.

In the post-purchase stage, dissonance (or buyer's remorse) and the consequent decision confirmation are processes experienced by the buyer role. Experience evaluation is done by the user. Buyer and payer values received in the transaction are soon forgotten, but the user values persist. Satisfaction is largely determined by the extent to which the user gets the expected value during the product's use. Satisfactory user experience simplifies the buyer's task for the future—he or she can now simply execute the future purchases in the routine problem-solving mode. Favorable or unfavorable word-of-mouth ensues from satisfied or dissatisfied customers in their user role. Satisfied users display loyalty behavior; dissatisfied users seek exit from their current supplier and trigger the buyer role of finding a new source. If dissatisfied, the user role can feel enough anger to motivate a complaint, but the aggressiveness of the buyer role will determine whether or not the complaint is actually made.

The EBA model is most sensitive to the user, payer, and buyer roles. Whichever role has the opportunity to influence the decision uses EBA to emphasize its own value. If the customer is most concerned with user values, then the user role's market values become the first EBA criterion. On the other hand, if the customer's constraints as a payer or the buyer are insurmountable, then those roles' market values become the first EBA criterion. Thus, if the user value is most important, then the customer gets to buy his or her favorite brand, say, of clothing or computers. Thus, a popular or reputed brand name becomes the first EBA criterion. On the other hand, if the payer constraints are strong, then budget constraints or economic value (good value for the money) become the first EBA criterion. Finally, if the buyer role's constraint become the key decision influencer, then convenience or service values become the first EBA criterion. For example, if a customer is handicapped and is unable to go out, he or she is limited to ordering pizza from a pizzeria that offers home delivery, even though as a user he or she might prefer the pizza from another pizzeria.

In many developing countries, small villages have limited retail outlets, so people makes a periodic trip to the nearby city market, and a number of families in the village would request this person to make certain, broadly specified purchases on their behalf. This person plays the role of the buyer for his village friends and makes the purchase largely based on convenience and service value, rather than make the extra effort to go to yet another store in search of what may be a more fitting purchase for the user or payer. A similar situation occurs for residents of bordering countries. For example, the Islands of the Bahamas are only a short flight from Miami, the south coast city in the United States. Residents from the Bahamas visit Miami every couple of months and make many purchases for other members of family based on convenience (e.g., "I am not going to go to another store several miles away") and service (e.g., "Would the store ship this item to the Bahamas?"), using these market values of the buyer role as the first EBA criterion.

Summary

In this chapter, we studied customer decision making as a five-step process: problem recognition → information search → alternative evaluation → choice → post-choice. The customer decision problem begins with problem recognition. The problem recognition occurs due to an internal cue which comes from one's motives being in a state of unfulfillment, or from external stimuli evoking these motives. A typology of problems was suggested—namely, familiar-latent, familiar-vivid, novel-latent, and novel-vivid—and its marketing implications were discussed. Once problem recognition occurs, the customer (a) either relies on prior knowledge and previously learned solutions, or (b) searches for new solutions through new information acquisition and its evaluation and integration. In the information search stage, there are several determinants of information search, such as perceived risk, involvement, familiarity and expertise, and functional versus expressive nature of products.

Evaluation of alternatives entails use of compensatory and noncompensatory decision models. The latter include conjuctive, disjunctive, lexicographic, and elimination-by-aspects models. The outcome of these evaluation processes is the identification of a preferred brand and the formation of a purchase intent. Such purchase intent is then implemented by the actual purchase act, but it was suggested that the purchase act does not always occur as planned. Sometimes, substantial delays occur in purchase implementation, and at other times, the brand actually bought is different from the one planned, because of stock outs or new information at the time of purchase. In the post-choice phase, the processes of decision confirmation, satisfaction/dissatisfaction, exit, voice (complaining), and loyalty responses were discussed.

The individual purchasing behavior is determined by a person's individual characteristics such as demographics, personality, and motives (all discussed in previous chapters). This chapter focused on the process itself—how the individual buying behavior unfolds. Understanding this process should help you be aware of your own marketplace behavior in the future. And understanding the individual buying behavior is helpful to marketing managers, as reflected in the many applications and implications we outlined throughout the chapter. Ultimately, it behooves marketers to structure their offerings and their communications in a fashion that responds to and resonates with customers' decision processes.

Key Terms

Customer Decisions 518
Mental Budgeting 518
Customer Problem 520
Problem Recognition 520
Internal Stimuli 520
External Stimuli 520
Primary Demand 522
Secondary (Selective) Demand 522
Awareness Set 524
Evoked Set 524
Consideration Set 524

Marketer Sources 525
Advocate Sources 526
Nonmarketer Sources 526
Search Strategy 526
Routine Problem Solving 526
Extended Problem Solving 526
Limited Problem Solving 527
Systematic Search 527
Heuristics 527

Interattribute Inference 527
Evaluative Consistency 528
Other-Brand Averaging 528
Negative Cue 528
Perceived Risk 530
Purchase-Decision Involvement 530
Enduring Involvement 531
Ignorance paradox 534

Information Processing Mode (IPM) 534	Conjunctive Model 538	Processing by Attributes 541
Affective Choice Mode (ACM) 534	Disjunctive Model 539	Phased Decision Strategy 543
Information Overload 535	Lexicographic Model 539	Satisfcing 544
Compensatory Models 536	Elimination by Aspects 540	Perceived Justice 551
	Processing by Brand 541	

Review Questions

1. What is meant by mental budgeting? Explain how it affects customer behavior, and how marketers can utilize it.

2. What are the four types of problem recognition? Give two examples of each type.

3. What is meant by search strategies? Explain systematic versus heuristic search strategies. What factors influence the extent of search a customer would engage in?

4. Explain the following concepts, with two examples of each: (a) affective choice mode (ACM), (b) purchase-decision involvement, (c) information overload, (d) satisficing, and (e) ignorance paradox.

5. Explain the difference between compensatory and noncompensatory choice rules. Describe how the following choice rules work: conjunctive, disjunctive, lexicographic, and elimination by aspects.

6. What is meant by "phased decision strategy"? When do customers use it? How is it related to the concepts of processing by brand and processing by attribute?

7. How would you define "complaining"? What factors would determine whether or not a customer would complain?

Applications

1. Reflect on your customer behavior, drawing on examples from each consumption location where individual decision making can occur—at home, at work, in public places. Discuss which of the three customer roles and six customer values become more influential in different situations.

2. Reflect on how you might choose each of the following products or services:

   a. Graduate business schools.

   b. Restaurant for dinner with your spouse on your anniversary.

   c. Hotel for a business trip to Eastern Europe.

   d. Toothpaste during a business trip to an Asian country where none of your usual brands are available.

   e. A fax machine for your home office.

      For each, please indicate whether you will use:

      (a) a two-phase or a single-phase decision strategy.

      (b) a compensatory or a noncompensatory model, or both.

      (c) a heuristic, and what might this heuristic be.

3. Think again about each product or service in the previous question. Which sources of information in each category (e.g., internal, external, marketer, and nonmarketer) are you likely to utilize? Would some of these be more useful to you during the later rather than earlier stages in the decision process? Explain your answer.

4. Assume that you recently made these three customer decisions: (1) after evaluating three lawn-maintenance service companies, you just gave the contract to one of them; (2) you wanted to watch a movie on your hotel room TV and rented one out of the choice of two; and (3) at the restaurant, you debated briefly between iced tea and Coca-Cola and ordered iced tea. For which of these decisions are you likely to have experienced cognitive dissonance? Why or why not? What actions are you likely to have taken to reduce that dissonance? What can a marketer do, in each case, to help you overcome that dissonance?

5. What concepts does the attached advertisement for Kodak Camera utilize? Explain your answer. (Hint: The concept is covered in the present chapter. Further hint: more than one answer can be correct.)

Practical Experiences

1. You are intrigued by the concept of "mental budgeting" that you read about in this chapter. One issue that is nagging you is that the concept has been studied only in a Western country. You wonder if customers in other cultures set mental budgets and whether their mental budgets are as

This one is for you, the reader, to interpret. Not what it is selling (obvious), but rather what customer behavior concept it harnesses (not so obvious).

inflexible as reported here. To find out, you want to interview 5 customers from a different country (say, China) living in your country—for example, foreign students or employees. Prepare a discussion guideline for such interviews. Pay special attention to what happens for those instances of mental budgeting where the payer is a different member of the household than the user and/or buyer. Are mental budgets in such instances more flexible or less? Then, conduct the interviews and write your report, summarizing your findings. If you do not have access to foreign customers, then interview any five customers to find out to what extent they engage in mental budgeting.

2. Interview two customers on each of the following: (a) a recent major appliance purchase and (b) a recent supermarket product that was purchased for the first time. Query them on how they went about making their brand selection. Then identify for each the decision model they used, contrasting the two customers, as well as contrasting the two types of purchases for each customer.

3. Collect two or three advertisements for each of the four problem-recognition situations discussed in the chapter. If possible, identify one advertisement for each problem recognition directed at business customers.

4. Interview five customers about their most recent complaint (every consumer has complained one time or the other). Identify what led them to complaining in terms of the model of complaining presented in the chapter. Then try to assess how they felt after the complaint and whether it depended on how the complaint was resolved.

Notes

[1] Banwari Mittal, "Problem Recognition in Consumer Decision Making: How Marketing Can Help It," Unpublished Manuscript, 1996.

[2] See Shelley Chaiken, (1980) for a technical discussion of the terms heuristic versus systematic; and Furse, Punj, and Stewart (1984) for discussion of their use by consumers in one study; Shelly Chaiken, "Heuristic versus Systematic Information Processing and the Use of Source versus Message Cues in Persuasion," *Journal of Personality and Social Psychology* 39 (November 1980), pp. 752–66; David H. Furse, Girish N. Punj, and David W. Stewart, "A Typology of Individual Search Strategies among Purchasers of New Automobiles," *Journal of Consumer Research* 10, no. 4 (March 1984), pp. 417–31.

[3] Morris D. Holbrook, "An Audiovisual Inventory of Some Fanatic Consumer Behavior: The 25-Cents Tour of a Jazz Collector's Home," in *ACR* 14 (1987), Wallendorf and Anderson, pp. 144–49.

[4] C. Whan Park and V. Parker Lessig, "Familiarity and Its Impact on Consumer Decision Biases and Heuristics," *Journal of Consumer Research* 8 (September 1981), pp 223–30; James R. Bettman and C. W. Park,

"Effects of Prior Knowledge and Experience and Phase of Choice Process on Consumer Decision Processes: A Protocol Analysis," *Journal of Consumer Research* 7 (December 1980), pp. 234–48.

[5] Narasimhan Srinivasan and Brian T. Ratchford, "An Empirical Test of a Model of External Search for Automobiles," *Journal of Consumer Research* 18 (September 1991), pp. 233–42; also see Rajan Sambandam and Kenneth R. Lord, "Switching Behavior in Automobile Markets: A Consideration-Sets Model," *Journal of the Academy of Marketing Science* 23, no. 1 (1995), pp 57–65.

[6] Peter L. Wright, "The Harassed Decision Maker: Time Pressure, Distractions, and the Use of Evidence," *Journal of Applied Psychology* 59 (October), pp. 555–61; C. Whan Park, Easwar Iyer, and Daniel C. Smith, "The Effects of Situational Factors on In-Store Grocery Shopping Behavior: The Role of Store Environment and Time Available for Shopping," *Journal of Consumer Research* 15 (March 1989), pp. 4222–33.

[7] Banwari Mittal, "The Role of Affective Choice Mode in the Consumer Purchase of Expressive Products," *Journal of Economic Psychology* 9 (1988), pp. 499–524.

8 Jacob Jacoby (1984), "Perspectives on Information OverLoad," *Journal of Consumer Research* 4 (March 1982), pp. 432–35; Naresh K. Malhotra, "Information Load and Consumer Decision Making," *Journal of Consumer Research* 9 (March 1982), pp. 419–30; Naresh K. Malhotra, Arun K. Jain, and Stephen Lagakos 1982, "The Information Overload Controversy: An Alternative Viewpoint," *Journal of Marketing* (Spring 46) pp. 27–37; Naresh K. Malhotra, "Reflections on the Information Overload Paradigm in Consumer Decision Making," *Journal of Consumer Research* 10, no. 4 (March 1984), pp.436–40.

9 For a fuller discussion of these and other models, see James R. Bettman, *An Information Processing Theory of Consumer Choice* (Reading, MA: Addison-Wesley, 1979), pp. 173–228.

10 See Hillel J. Einhorn (1970), "Use of Nonlinear, Noncompensatory Models in Decision Making," *Psychological Bulletin* 73, pp. 221–30.

11 Amos Tversky, "Elimination by Aspects: A Theory of Choice," *Psychological Review* 79 (July 1972), pp. 281–99.

12 See Peter L. Wright, "Consumer Judgment Strategies: Beyond the Compensatory Assumption," in M. Venkatesan, ed., *Proceedings of the Third Annual Conference* (Chicago: Association for Consumer Research, (1972), pp. 316–24.

13 See, James R. Bettman and Michael A. Zins, "Constructive Processes in Consumer Choice," *Journal of Consumer Research* 4 (September 1977), pp. 75–85; James R. Bettman and C. Whan Park, "Effects of Prior Knowledge and Experience and Phase of Choice Process on Consumer Decision Processes: A Protocol Analysis," *Journal of Consumer Research* 7 (December 1980), pp. 234–48; Denis A. Lussier and Richard W. Olshavsky, "Task Complexity and Contingent Processing in Brand Choice," *Journal of Consumer Research* 6 (1979), pp. 154–65.

14 See Wayne D. Hoyer and Siew Meng Leong, "Consumer Decision Making for Common, Repeat-Purchase Products: A Dual Replication," *Journal of Consumer Psychology* 2, no. 2 (1995), pp. 193–208.

15 Herbert A. Simon, *Models of Man* (New York: John Wiley & Sons, 1957); also see, Peter L. Wright, "Consumer Choice Strategies: Simplifying versus Optimizing," *Journal of Marketing Research* 11 (1975), pp. 60–67.

16 Jagdish N. Sheth and Banwari Mittal, "A Framework for Managing Customer Expectations," *Journal of Market-Focused Management,* (1996), 1, pp. 137–158.

17 C. Goodwin and I. Ross, "Salient Dimensions of Perceived Fairness in Resolution of Service Complaints," *Journal of Satisfaction, Dissatisfaction, and Complaining Behavior* 2 (1989), pp. 87–92.

18 See Bradley T. Gale, *Managing Customer Value,* Free Press, 1994.

19 See John A. Howard and Jagdish N. Sheth, *The Theory of Buyer Behavior* (New York: John Wiley & Sons, 1961).

CHAPTER 15

After reading this chapter you should be able to:

Distinguish how families and households differ.

Identify types of families and households that people form as they journey through their family life cycle.

Explain how spouses influence each other in family buying decisions, including the factors that affect the roles of the husband and wife.

Describe the role that children play in influencing family purchases for their own use or for shared use in the family, including differences associated with a family's psychological makeup.

Summarize the role families play in children's marketplace socialization, that is, the way children acquire knowledge about the marketplace and skills to make choices of products and services.

Discuss how members of one family generation influence members of another generation with respect to family buying decisions.

Identify the mechanisms that exist for such intergenerational influence (IGI) to occur.

Describe how family members resolve the conflicts that arise when they attempt to influence one another within the same generation or across generations.

Household Customer Decision Making

The Subtle Art of Persuasion in the Store Aisle

It is Christmas time as we write this. Millions and millions of parents and grandparents around the world (especially in the parts of the world with a Christian majority) are buying toys for their children and grandchildren. Let us visit one of those toy stores, *Toys "R" Us*, located in a suburb of Manchester, England. There in the electronic toys aisle, we can see a child pester his mom to buy him that radio-controlled car. The 9 inch by 6 inch piece of sheet metal shaped like an Indy 500 car weighing less than half a pound costs £60 British. His mother would rather buy him a Lego set. It costs only £8 British. But money is not the only issue. Mom thinks the Lego set is "good for her child." If you stick around, you will eventually see the hassled Mom at the checkout register charging £60 on her credit card.

The same story is repeated in the clothing store, at the county fair, and in the supermarket. And, of course, there are other shopper groups—not just mother and child—each with its own separate "screenplay." Let us visit Marks and Spencer, a large supermarket chain store in Manchester, England. There, in aisle three are the Grants—Winston and Mary Beth, husband and wife. Winston is simply pushing the cart, quietly, disinterestedly, while Mary Beth is having a field day filling it up with whatever she chooses. Then, in aisle five are two adolescents in their early 20s, fussing over which potato chip to buy. The young lady wants the new fat-free potato chip, introduced in the United Kingdom recently by the U.S.-headquartered consumer-goods company Procter & Gamble. The young man is adamant that olestra, the new nonfat ingredient in the chip, is "not good for your body." Why is he so concerned? Is the young lady his wife? A girlfriend? Just a shopping pal? And how are they going to resolve their disagreement?

Introduction

Standing in a toy store and watching a child pester his mom to buy an expensive toy can be an interesting moment in the life of a student of customer behavior. Is the child going to throw tantrums? Is the mom going to give in or would she be able to persuade the child to buy another toy? And what about the Grants—in the supermarket, why is Winston so passive? Doesn't he care about how much it costs to fill that shopping cart? Is his wife Mary Beth the bread winner? Finally, what about the young couple arguing over olestra? Who is going to prevail—the one who pays for it or the one who is going to be the user? What conflict resolution strategies are they going to employ? You could stick around to find out.

But perhaps you should read this chapter first. It tells you about what roles husbands and wives, mothers and daughters, fathers and sons, and boyfriends/girlfriends play in influencing each other's marketplace choices. And about the various methods people use to resolve their differences over what to buy. In short, about how families and households buy.

The Importance of Studying Household Buying Decisions

Households are the basic unit of buying and consumption in a society. A **household** is a consumption unit of one or more persons identified by a common location with an address, such as the Rodrigues residence. While a number of customer decisions are no doubt made

Households are the basic unit of buying and consumption. Here, Goldstar is promoting its climate control electronics to one Italian family.

by individuals for their personal consumption (e.g., buying food during office lunch hour), the more significant decisions are made by individuals jointly with other members of their household, for joint use by the members of the household (e.g., food for family dinner, a kitchen appliance, and so on). In the decisions customers make in their capacity as members of a household, the decision processes become more complex, since these decisions must accommodate the diverse needs and wants of various household members. Increasingly, it is insufficient to appeal to customers in their individual capacity. Rather, the customer has to be addressed as a family member buying products and services within the family context.

Household decisions are important to study also because it is possible to separate the three customer roles: the user, the payer, and the buyer. In the individual buying

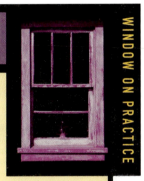

WINDOW ON PRACTICE

Families—The New Darlings of the Travel Industry

There was a time when Disney World, the San Diego Zoo, the Smokey Mountains, and Dollywood were hot favorites for families looking for vacations and fun. They still are. But other travel destinations and vacation marketers are vying for a piece of the action. Las Vegas, Club Med, and various cruise lines are all courting families. Joining them are such hotel chains as Hilton, Westin, Sheraton, and Hyatt—hotels that had so far catered largely to business travelers.

Why this attraction toward families by vacation marketers? Because the baby boomers have come of age and are now in middle age with children. No longer single or young couples, they are increasingly looking for family-oriented vacation destinations. The family vacation market is fast growing, accounting for some 20 percent of the total hotel/motel lodging business. At one time Club Med North America—a travel resort vacation service company—was largely dedicated to the singles market; by the middle of 1990s, half of its business came from families. Some cruise lines also have started sailing ships dedicated to families, such as the American Family Cruises, Carnival Cruise Lines, and Premier Cruise Lines' Big Red Boat.

Even Las Vegas, known as the gambling capital of the world, is now catering to families. The gambling casino properties are now building theme parks, virtual-reality video arcades, pirate ships. The idea is to keep the kids amused while Mom and Dad play the slot machines.

The values families seek are different from those sought by nonfamilies. They want activities that can be fun for children and adults together; they also want supervised activities for children so that parents can do their own things. Finally, they want a good economic value in the form of discounted fares and free room and meals for children, and so on. Increasingly, therefore, hotels and tour packages offer many supervised activities including baby sitting services.

While modifying the product and service to appeal to family vacationers is a positive market response, not understanding the user, payer, and buyer roles that different family members occupy can lead some marketers into trouble. Such was the case with one cruise line that sought a families segment of the travel business. Starting in 1994, the American Family Cruise promoted the line as a kid's dream at sea, offering a wide range of activities, including educational programs. The problem was that while the kids liked the experience, there was nothing much to do for parents as adults. There were no other adults without children, and no separate activities for adults alone. As a result, the American Family Cruise ship abandoned its program within the year for want of enough passengers. While the cruise line served the needs of children as users, it ignored parents as users. Since parents are also the payers and buyers, if their own needs as users are not met, they will not make the purchase no matter how well other users like the product.

Additional information available at **www.adage.com**

Source: Christie Fisher, "Kidding around Makes Sense," *Advertising Age*, June 27, 1994, p. 34. Jennifer D. Zbar, "Lessons Surface for Family Cruises," *Advertising Age*, August 15, 1994.

decisions, described in the preceding chapters, all three roles often merge in one person. When these roles separate, as they generally do in household buying behavior, the marketer has to appeal separately to different members of the households, differentiating the "selling appeal" according to the role the family member plays.

The separation of the three roles makes household buying behavior somewhat complex to track and influence. Moreover, these role allocations are dynamic. They vary from time to time, from one product to another, and from one family type to another. If a marketer wants to attract members of the family who would play the buyer role and the payer role to a product or service intended for shared consumption by the whole family, he or she will have to appeal to children as well as parents. It is important too that your product or service offer value to all family members, especially if parents are going to be the buyers and payers, whereas children are going to be merely users. The recent trend toward targeting families for vacation spots that were once the mecca for singles and couples only is a recognition of the importance of families.

However, some companies neglected the principle of providing value to *all* family members and courted failure (see the Window on Practice box). That is why it is important for a marketer to understand how an individual family changes over its lifetime, how households are changing in the aggregate, and how different members of these changing households make purchase decisions.

Families and Households

Years ago, a typical U.S. household would have been described as a nuclear family, consisting of a husband, wife, and 2.5 children. In 1970, married couples with children comprised 41 percent of all households in the United States. By 1995, such households had declined to 25.5 percent. At the same time, the proportion of single-parent households rose from 6 percent in 1970 to 9.15 percent in 1995.[1] Today's households display much more diversity.

To see this, consider the various forms a household can take. There are two types of household: family and nonfamily. See Figure 15.1. A **family** is a group of persons related by blood and/or marriage. Among the family households, four types are most common:

Figure 15.1

TYPES OF HOUSEHOLDS

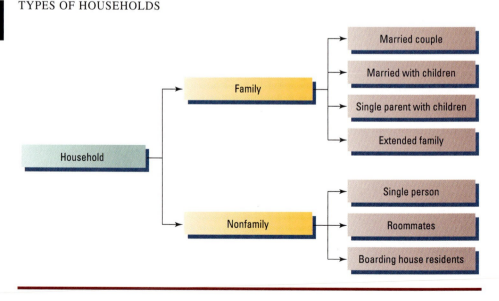

(1) married couples alone, (2) married couples with children, (3) a single parent with children, and (4) extended family, which may include parents, children's spouses, and/or grandchildren, and occasionally cousins. A **nonfamily household** is a household that does not contain a family. Among the nonfamily households are a single person living alone in a dwelling unit, roommates (two persons living in the same dwelling unit, including "persons of opposite sex sharing living quarters" (POSSLQ), a category used by the U.S. census, and boarding houses (three or more unrelated persons living in the same dwelling unit).

In 1995, of the 98.99 million households in the United States, 29.69 million were nonfamily and 69.30 million were family households. Among the nonfamily households, 24.3 million were single-person households. Among the family households, 25.64 million were couples with children; 11.5 million were one-parent (85 percent of them mother-only) families with children.[2]

The size of a typical family varies from culture to culture and from subculture to subculture. In some cultures, the family extends beyond the immediate nucleus to include cousins, brothers, and sisters. Even in the United States, the extended family was at one time the most common form of the family unit, including grandparents, cousins, and other relatives. Today, however, the "typical" family has changed dramatically.

The number of married couple families has decreased as a percentage of the total number of households from 75 percent in 1960 to 54 percent in 1995. As mentioned earlier, the proportion of families that comprise a married couple with children living at home also has fallen. However, the number of nonfamily households as a percentage of the total population has gone up from 26 percent in 1980 to 30 percent in 1995.[3] One key factor that affects the composition of households and changes in it is the family life cycle.

Family Life Cycle

The concept of **family life cycle** refers to the different stages a family goes through—starting from the time a person is young and single to the time he or she becomes a single, solitary survivor. As shown in Figure 15.2, the standard life cycle incorporates five stages: bachelor, couple, full nest, empty nest, and survivor.

A SIMPLIFIED FAMILY LIFE CYCLE

Figure 15.2

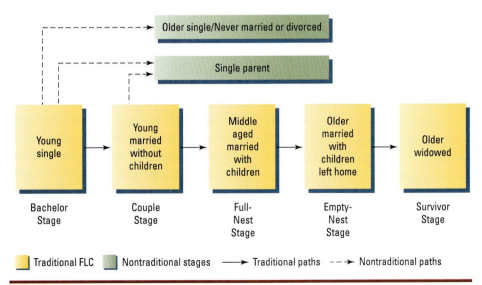

| Older single/Never married or divorced |
| Single parent |

| Young single | Young married without children | Middle aged married with children | Older married with children left home | Older widowed |

| Bachelor Stage | Couple Stage | Full-Nest Stage | Empty-Nest Stage | Survivor Stage |

■ Traditional FLC   ■ Nontraditional stages   ⟶ Traditional paths   ⇢ Nontraditional paths

This family life cycle has been adopted in consumer behavior as a standard description of family formation and dissolution. Of course, this or any other scheme cannot account for all the diverse paths a family may go through. For example, an early dissolution of marriage, splitting the family into two nonfamily households, or into single-parent families, is not explicitly included in the above scheme. Yet the scheme is useful for marketers to identify the changing needs of a family.

Some marketers respond to these changing needs by tailoring their product line to cover families through their entire life cycle. General Motors, for example, produces cars suitable for different life-cycle stages and then portrays itself as a car company that can serve the changing family needs through its entire life cycle.

Other marketers use the family life cycle to identify broad groups of customers whose spending patterns would likely differ from one another. They would then target a particular life stage, rather than all of them.

To further delineate the differences in the household consumption patterns more sharply, we suggest a slightly modified, and simpler, scheme of family life-cycle stages:

- *Stage 1: Start-up*—This consists primarily of singles and young, childless married couples. Their needs and consumption patterns center on setting up new households. The use of their discretionary income moves away (especially for married couples) from apartments, vacations, and leisure to the purchase of a home, automobiles, appliances, furniture, and all other related items needed for a young couple before the parenting stage or just entering it with a newborn.

- *Stage 2: Fully nested 1, 2, 3*—Each nest reflects the evolution of a growing family, moving from the first substage (first child is born) to the second substage (with children from the age of six to teenagers) to the third substage (with grown-up children still living at home). Consumption varies dramatically across these three substages. Major purchases like the home, furniture, appliances, and new car occur in the first two stages. The last substage is dominated by paying for the children's education and replacement of older items in the household.

- *Stage 3: Empty Nest 1, 2*—These two substages reflect a family more financially secure, due in main part to the children leaving the household and eliminating a financial drain on the parents. During the first substage, the empty-nest couples often invest in home renovations and spend a greater percentage of their discretionary income on vacations and leisure time activities. During the second substage, the head of the household may have retired, with a substantial loss of income. Financial outlays during this stage center on health care, with couples typically selling their house and moving into a smaller house or apartment.

- *Stage 4: Solitary Survivor*—With advancing age and with the death of the spouse, the solitary survivor's consumption behavior changes drastically. During this stage, the single survivor may or may not be working, and this transition entails significant changes in lifestyle. In all likelihood, the survivor will sell the family house, moving into a smaller condo or apartment. Discretionary income will be spent on vacations, leisure, and health care. Eventually, this person retires (if not already retired in the Empty Nest 2 stage). During this stage health care becomes a serious issue both because of the deteriorating health and because the employer-supported insurance is often terminated with retirement. Also of concern, especially to the solitary survivor, is the loneliness and the consequent immediate needs for affection and love from one's children.

CHARACTERISTICS OF THE LIFE-CYCLE STAGES

To further distinguish these four family life-cycle stages, we can characterize them along two dimensions: (1) needs and wants, and (2) resources (see Figure 15.3). As was described earlier in the book, needs and wants are determined by personal and environmental factors, and resources consist of time, money, expertise, and physical energy (effort).

The start-up family has limited resources but also limited needs and wants. The needs are limited because the family is small, and there are no children. Although the couple needs to set

Figure 15.3

THE CHANGING NEEDS AND RESOURCES OF A FAMILY

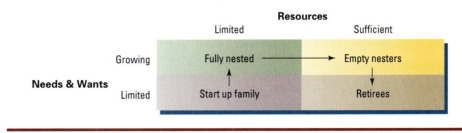

up a new household, they may either continue to live in a rented apartment, or buy a small home (called a "starter home"). Basic household necessities are generally received in wedding gifts or as loans from parents, and the couple typically "eases into the new home" slowly over the next several years. The resources are limited because one of the spouses may still be in college, or still trying to find a job in the new city. Even when both spouses are employed, they are typically on their first jobs at starting points of the salary scale. Although the couple might perceive this stage to be a time of struggle, the pressure on resources is nowhere as much as in the next stage; in retrospect, people come to refer to this stage as "the good old days." The principal guideline for marketers for appealing to customers in this stage is to offer basic versions of products, without the accompanying "bells and whistles."

In the fully nested stage, families begin to have children, and correspondingly the household needs grow rapidly, often faster than the resources. Families begin to make trade-offs between increasing their resources (for example, by having both spouses work full-time), or having one parent stay at home with the children and make do with reduced resources. If only one spouse works outside the home, the working spouse may try to bring in additional income through moonlighting (taking a second job) or simply working hard. The major drain on families in this stage is the expense of college education for their children. The exponentially rising needs with income resources lagging far behind may sometimes lead to a high degree of family dissension, including a divorce.

The typical purchases at this stage include buying a larger home, a larger car or a second car, appliances, clothes, and family vacations. This customer group is likely to be the largest segment for financial loans—for home mortgages; college loans; rolling credit on credit cards; or installment loans on appliances, cars, and furniture. Even though resources are constrained, major purchases are seen as investments so that families buy appliances, furniture, homes, and so on, that would last long and have the required features even if the cost goes up. Thus, adequately equipped, long-lasting, safe, and good performing products are sought at a good price rather than the basic versions. For consumer goods, store brands from established stores and economy packs become the favorite. Price value (lifetime costs rather than lowest initial cost) is likely to appeal to this group the most.

In the empty-nester stage, the kids have moved out of the home, and the family's needs begin to plateau, or even decline. However, at this stage, the grandchildren begin to enter into the household, but, fortunately, the resources are generally sufficient. Working spouses have more freedom to slow down in discretionary work habits, increasing their time resource. Experience and maturity make the couple wiser in dealing with family situations, expert at managing the family and household, and more efficient in spending time or effort or money.

With a surplus of time and money resources, the empty nesters may assume new family obligations, perhaps helping their children with a down payment for a home or with education for the grandchildren, thereby moving back, in effect, into a fully nested stage. Some adult children who cannot make it economically or are divorced or emotionally incapable of coping on their own may move back in with their parents. This return to the nest makes them members of the "yo-yo generation."

At this stage, the concern with price value will likely become less the factor in buying. Empty nesters may seek products with "bells and whistles" without concern for their real value. With time freed from taking care of children, empty nesters look to living a life they had postponed for so long—indulging in the comforts of life, buying, for instance, a big-screen TV, or a luxury car that they now plan to trade every two or three years. Also, due to an increase in discretionary time, more vacations, cruise trips, and so forth, become appealing to this group.

Finally, in the retiree stage, needs and wants decline, and the resources stay sufficient, as retirement income is available and equity builds up if there was adequate financial planning. The movement from empty nester to retiree is marked by divestment of resources so that there is a marked increase in "planned giving" to charities and foundations (especially by the affluent), and in establishing living trusts and estate planning. They also volunteer more time for social causes. Sometimes the retiree moves into the home of a child, especially if the spouse has passed away. The retiree then may become the baby-sitter in the family, freeing the time resource pressures on the young couple. Some retirees may, of course, move into nursing homes or into retirement communities.

LIMITATIONS OF LIFE-CYCLE MODELS

Models such as this have limitations. One is that these profiles represent the "average" or the "typical." Obviously, there are vast income variations within each of the four stages and, correspondingly, variations in what people buy and what values they seek. For example, an upper-income family in the full-nest stage will not be concerned with the economic value as much as our description above implies, but most of the families at this stage will be.

In addition, there has been no national or international survey of families aimed at documenting the consumption and spending patterns of families in these four stages. The profiles we described are based on our informed judgments and are offered here simply to illustrate how family life-cycle stages matter. We should view these profiles as tentative and illustrative, and, as students of consumer behavior and as marketers, we should be open to filling in more details as we observe and learn more about the evolving families in the United States and other cultures.

Nevertheless, the family life cycle is important because a family's basket of goods to be bought is intimately influenced by the life-cycle stage the family is in. This occurs because the needs and wants change accordingly. Equally important, the resources (in money, time, and physical energy) too are a function of the life-cycle stage.

Changing Nature of the Household

Several trends in household formation and types in the United States have special implications to marketers. These trends are the growth of ethnic households, single-parent households, and divorce and remarriage.

ETHNIC HOUSEHOLDS

According to the U.S. Census Bureau, the growth in the U.S. population in the 1990s will come primarily from people immigrating from other countries as opposed to people born in the United States. Much of this growth will come from African Americans, Hispanics and Asian Americans. The fastest-growing ethnic group in the United States is Asian Americans, most of whom are immigrating to the U.S. Already, these ethnic households spend well over $500 billion a year on products and services in every sector of our economy.[4] From food to clothing, to entertainment to telecommunications, ethnic households represent a growing market in the United States.

Each of these ethnic segments represents households that have very unique consumption patterns. For example, it is not uncommon to see larger extended families among these households, resulting in demand for larger package sizes. Also, larger family size necessitates the purchase of a large number of products and services in large quantities, thus putting a pressure on the payer. Accordingly, the economic and financing values become crucial. Subcultural group membership based on ethnicity serves a very dominant role in the shaping of values of customers and must be taken into close consideration by marketers. The growing size of the ethnic market in the United States is bringing about changes in the way marketers appeal to these households, from the use of spokespersons who come from similar backgrounds, to the language used on packaging, to a product assortment that more closely matches their needs and wants.

SINGLE-PARENT HOUSEHOLDS

Single parents represent another growing segment of households in the United States. In 1960, only 10 percent of American children lived with a single parent; by 1990, this percentage went up to 22 percent.[5] Single-parent families present a unique situation to marketers inasmuch as they represent the merger of the three roles of a buyer, payer, and user in a single person.

Convenience is an important consideration to this segment, since single parents must work to make a living and pay the bills. Time is another important resource, making home-shopping services an attractive way to shop for goods and services. The Peapod service in the Chicago area offers the possibility for customers to shop online from their home computer, and have groceries delivered. Services such as these will become an important marketing outlet for a whole host of product and service marketers.

DIVORCE AND REMARRIAGE

Divorces and remarriages are changing the nature of the household. The number of divorces has been increasing in the United States for many years. Preferences based on the previous marriage work their way into the new marriage if the divorcee remarries, or stays with them if they stay single. Divorced persons also have to take on new roles. The roles of payers and buyers, often different during marriage, merge in the same person following the divorce. A woman who stayed at home with the children when she was married suddenly becomes the new *payer* in her post-divorce household. Her buyer role may stay the same, but the choice of goods and services will probably be highly restricted due to new income constraints. Or the payer role may stay unchanged, but he or she would now have to assume a buyer role as well or to a greater degree, acquiring marketplace knowledge for the first time or anew. When men and women divorcees are compared, studies indicate that the men wind up with a higher income and women a lower income, creating a new set of financial limits and opportunities which change their purchasing habits dramatically.[6]

A related change that accompanies a higher divorce rate is a shrinking household size. These smaller households are often run by single parents.

Changing Customer Roles in the Family

Many forces are changing the pattern of customer roles in the family. Important among these are both spouses working, young adults as financial contributors, and individualism.

BOTH SPOUSES WORKING

Increasingly, in the United States and elsewhere in the developed, industrialized world as well, both the spouses are in employment, as we discussed in Chapter 8 as a trend in customer behavior. As more and more families move towards a dual-income status, the payer role is being blurred between the husband and the wife, with the wife assuming a copayer role. Also, with more women working, men are increasingly shouldering household chores, including buying supermarket items. In families where only the wife is the "bread winner," the husband takes on the lion's share of household chores, in effect becoming the homemaker.

When a husband shares household chores (as happens in many modern families), he is also sharing a user role on those items that hitherto were used by the wife alone (e.g., cleaning products); and the husband is sharing the burden of the buyer role as well. In the 1950s and 1960s, marketers never bothered to target cleaning products toward men. TV commercials typically showed the husband and children praising Mom for her choice of household as well as food products. Today, not targeting both genders for most products would be a marketing blunder.

When both spouses work, the household experiences more time pressure. The parents often delegate many routine shopping activities to teenagers or older children. A teenage daughter who comes home from school in the afternoon may find a shopping list her parents left for her. Thus, teenage (or older) children are increasingly playing the buyer role for the entire household.[7]

YOUNG ADULTS AS FINANCIAL CONTRIBUTORS

Increasingly children are taking part-time employment in their teenage years, thus having an income of their own. Moreover, there is a trend of adult children moving back into the parental home in order to save on expenses—the so called "yo-yo generation" (i.e., they go out of the family to live on their own and then come back to live with the parents). Because of these two phenomena, children are assuming the payer role, sometimes exclusively, sometimes jointly with their parents. Therefore, the selling appeals to teenagers have to emphasize not only the performance and social/emotional values (i.e., values of the user), but also economic, financing, facilitation, and personalization values, for example.

Indeed, in many families, children are being held financially responsible at a very early age. In one family we know, the child is only six years old. Like many U.S. families with children, this family would make a weekly trip to McDonald's. The six-year-old boy, Kiran, would always ask for a "happy meal" (one small hamburger, one small order of fries, one medium drink, and one small toy, costing $1.99 to $2.29). A few months ago, the family started giving him a weekly allowance of $10, out of which he must buy his own McDonald's meals and also save for any other major purchases of things he wants to acquire (e.g., a video game or the like). Guess what? Kiran doesn't buy McDonald's "happy meals" anymore. Instead, he buys a small hamburger and one order of small fries, and a medium or small drink piecemeal and pays $1.79 to $2.09. Yes, the savings are merely 20 cents or so. But Kiran has figured that the toy he got with the "happy meal" is not worth the 20 cents he needs to pay extra out of his own pocket. This is one more example of how customer decisions change dramatically when customers have to assume the payer role in addition to the user role.

INDIVIDUALISM

While the buyer and payer roles are becoming more spread out across various family members, and/or are being shared by multiple family members, a reverse trend is occurring with respect to the user role. In the past, a large part of household consumption was shared consumption, such as family dinner or the whole family watching the Ed Sullivan show (a very popular show on U.S. TV in the 1960s), or the wife/mother doing the whole family's laundry all at once. Today, consumption is becoming more individualized. Every member of the household has a different schedule, and each one fixes whatever they want to eat whenever they want to. Instead of the family dinner, now there is individual "grazing"—direct from the refrigerator (or a microwave oven) to the mouth, eliminating a table setting or common cooking. Both individuation and assumption of responsibility among teenage children is encouraged so that now children often do their own laundry, and, accordingly, may have their own preference of detergents. Every member of the household perceives, more now than before, his or her hair type to be different and has his or her own shampoo preference, for example. The concept of "the family car" is becoming alien as each adult member has a car of his or her individual preference. The cable TV offers multiple programming options so that different members prefer and watch different programs, thus necessitating a separate TV for each member of the house. There is a separate radio and a separate phone in every member's room, with design and aesthetics different according to individual taste. We would like to term these modern families, whose members want to structure their time and location independently of one another, as **roommate families**.

The marketing implications of more and more families becoming roommate families are profound, but remain under-researched. The "roommate families" would need larger refrigerators (in one family we know, even the milk is different for each member); more precooked frozen dinners; more individual-size portions; separate brands of coffee; separate TVs and entertainment systems; computers; and bathrooms filled with an array of shampoos, creams, deodorants, and other toiletries (a separate brand for each family member).

This picture of a modern family in a industrialized and advanced country contrasts sharply with that of families in underdeveloped, developing, or emerging nations. In the latter, family members eat meals together often cooked from scratch, watch a common TV show, eat the same breakfast cereal, patronize the same barber, use the same laundry detergent; there is even a "family shampoo." And it is not just because of a lack of resources (although that may be a factor too); there is much more *shared consumption* in the family. But even in these emerging countries, many families are becoming like their industrialized nation counterpart—allowing each member more individuation, and, in the process, acquiring the characteristics of "roommate families." To students of customer behavior and to marketers everywhere, the changing nature of families would be a fascinating phenomenon to study and observe, both within a country as well as across countries and across cultures.

While such individualism alludes to an erosion of shared living and of shared values in families, marketers may not assume that values have eroded irreversibly, if at all. First, in a large majority of the nations around the globe (most notably in Asia and the Middle East), families remain the epicenter of day-to-day living and consumption. Second, even in the industrialized nations such as the United States, after a decade or more of flirting with

Consumption as common ground: Common consumption in the family socializes children by developing early preferences.

individualism, freedom, and isolation, more and more people are looking to their families for emotional and economic support—either by seeking more committed long-term marital relationships or by the grown-up children moving back home with parents for greater financial well-being. At any rate, every society has a significant core population that cherishes family life and conducts everyday living within the family sphere. Marketers aware of this segment of families appeal to them by espousing the value of the family as corporate values.

The Family Decision-Making Process

Family decisions differ from individual decisions in two ways. First, the payer, buyer, and user roles are distributed across family members (the same family member may not have all three roles). In addition, these roles are shared by various family members (a single role may be jointly held by more than one individual). As an example of distributed roles, the husband may pay for the purchase of a diamond ring used by the wife, or a wife might

uted roles, the husband may pay for the purchase of a diamond ring used by the wife, or a wife might pay for as well as buy a gift of a necktie for use by the husband, or a single parent may buy cereals to be consumed by the child. As an example of the shared role, both spouses may do the actual buying or a product may be bought for shared family consumption or a parent and an adult child may jointly pay for a CD player the latter wants for his or her exclusive use.

The concept of joint payer role takes on an expanded meaning for married couples. If both spouses have income, then of course they literally share the payer role. But even when only one spouse is the earning member, spouses generally maintain common bank accounts, so they both typically have a vested interest in how the family money gets spent. Thus, even the non-earning spouse ends up sharing and being concerned with the payer role.

Given this distribution and sharing of the three roles among family members, how is the purchase decision process implemented? Specifically, who decides what to buy, when to buy, which brand to buy, and so on?

Steps in Family Buying Decisions

If you think back to a recent marketplace decision made in your family, you might recall that various members undertook various activities, en route to the final decision. Suppose that it was a family PC (personal computer) your family was considering buying. Tzvesti, your sixth-grader kid sister, first started asking for it—she was all excited about the computer they use at her school, with color graphics and all. She raved about how they could search an encyclopedia on the computer, and she wanted one at home. Your parents appreciated the educational value of a PC and decided to buy one. The task of finding out what kind of computer would be best for the family was left to you. You visited some local dealers in the college town that you live in, gathered the necessary information, and mailed it home to your parents.

Armed with that information, your mom and the junior visited some stores in your home town. They looked at some models. Mom found an IBM clone to be a good value. Your kid sister liked a Hewlett-Packard model better. Not able to agree, they sought intervention from Dad (who had kept out of the loop so far due to his heavy travel schedule). Dad recalled reading an article in a recent issue of *FamilyPC*; he dug out that article and reread it. Based on his reading, he thought that Hewlett-Packard was indeed a good buy, but that yet another model, Aptiva, would be even better—from the standpoint both of the graphics capability and value for the money. Mom suggested that they call you to see what you thought about this new model Dad had identified. You are in college, familiar with the latest in computers, and your parents value your opinion. Expect a call from them this weekend!

But right now, you are studying this book on customer behavior, and in the book you are reading about how families make decisions. You cannot help but see a pattern in the present decision your family is making and many others you and your family have made in the past. This pattern consists of some steps your family goes through in making major purchase decisions, and as you jot these down on your notepad, you realize how similar they look to the steps described in the next paragraph.

Based on research and observations, several consumer behavior and marketing scholars have identified and described the family buying process as consisting of the following steps.[8]

1. Initiation of the purchase decision.

2. Gathering and sharing of information.

3. Evaluating and deciding.

4. Shopping and buying.

5. Conflict management.

The first four steps are self-explanatory and are similar in interpretation to those described in the previous chapter. Therefore, these will be discussed here only briefly. The fifth step is particularly salient in all group decision making (and the family is a group). Therefore, that step will be discussed in detail in a later section.

Regarding the first four steps, although their meaning is self-evident and their basic operation similar to that in individual decision making, the actual dynamics are more involved. Different members of the family play different roles in the decision process. Thus, one member might initiate the purchase decision by making a product request. Another member of the family might collect information. A third member might evaluate and decide. Yet another member might make the actual product purchase. Finally, someone might take the responsibility of resolving any differences of preference and conflicts that may arise.

Such conflicts may arise before the decision is made, but may continue or may arise anew after the purchase. The interspousal or intrafamily influence can vary from step to step. One solution to avoiding conflict is to find a product or service brand that satisfies every family member's unique preferences. To simultaneously respond to unique interests of family members, marketers identify those features that, though different across family members, are not incompatible.

Throughout this process, different family members may influence the decision to varying degrees. Of particular interest to marketers is the influence of spouses and children.[9]

PATTERNS OF JOINT DECISIONS

Figure 15.4

| Autonomous decision by husband | Husband dominated decision | Syncratic decision | Wife-dominated decision | Autonomous decision by wife |

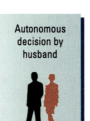
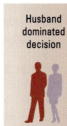

Husband-Wife Decision Roles

With regard to the roles of husband and wife, five patterns of relative influence are possible: (1) autonomous decision by the husband only; (2) husband-dominated decision; (3) syncratic decisions (equal role by both); (4) wife-dominated decision, and (5) autonomous decision by the wife. **Autonomous decisions** are decisions made independently by the decision maker. **Syncratic decisions** are decisions in which all play an *equal* role in making the decision (see Figure 15.4). It is naturally of interest to marketers to understand which pattern of decision making is prevalent for a specific product category or in a specific purchase situation.

In a study of 200 families, reported in 1979, for the purchase of three products (laundry washer, carpeting, television), the wife's influence was stronger for washers and carpeting, while the husband's was greater for televisions. But even for TVs, husbands reported more self-influence compared to wives, who reported more *joint* decision making. For each product, however, more families use joint decision making than autonomic decisions. The relative influence shifts during the decision stages. Generally, one spouse initiates the purchase consideration, but the process becomes more joint as the decision moves to advanced stages (of information gathering, and so on). Additional information is available at **http://retention.harrisblackintl.com** Although the study is two decades old, it provides a point of comparison. Has the pattern of relative influence between the spouses changed since then? In what manner?

JOINT DECISION PROCESS

Joint decisions are those in which more than one decision participant made the decision. When couples report they made joint decisions for a specific purchase, it is not easy to visualize exactly how each member participated to make it a joint decision. If you ask a couple who recently bought a home, "Who made the final decision?" chances are that their answer will be "both." If you ask them who influenced the decision more, the answer will be different. Each spouse is likely to say he or she influenced the decision more than did the other partner!

Consumer researchers consider these answers too simplistic and believe that the interpersonal dynamics of joint decision making is more complex. In fact, noted consumer researcher C. W. Park has termed joint decisions as a "muddling through" process. His study of home buying by couples revealed very interesting patterns of interpersonal dynamics among the spouses. Park studied the decision-making process for 45 couples soon after they had bought a home.[10] Among his findings:

- The similarity between the "decision plans" of the spouses is relatively *low*.
- When spouses agree on features that the product *must* have, this agreement on "must" features leads them to perceive that their decision plans are similar (even when they disagree on other

optional features). Contrarily, when there is disagreement on "must" features, spouses perceive conflict.

■ Individual spouses are more satisfied with some features of the product purchased than with others, and the features with which the spouses are satisfied differ between the spouses. Each spouse feels greater satisfaction with the feature whose inclusion was influenced more by that spouse.

■ Spouses agree more with each other on salient objective dimensions (e.g., number of bedrooms, presence of a swimming pool, and so on) than on subjective dimensions (the interior design, the amount of insulation, and so on).

■ Spouses grant each other certain role specialization with respect to the feature they are expert at or they should have a say about. Thus, a husband might be viewed by both spouses as an expert on insulation, but the wife on interior design. On these role-specialized features, spouses acknowledge the partner's relative influence. On other features, each believes he or she influenced the decision more than did the other partner.

To understand a couple's joint decision process, Park constructed a "decision plan net" as shown in Figure 15.5. A decision plan net is a tree diagram of the criteria that the decision maker will use and the sequence and manner in which he or she will use them.

These decision plans can be constructed at the outset of the decision process. For example, when a couple walks into a realtor's office, the realtor can ask each spouse questions about what kind of a house he or she is looking for, then construct the decision plan net. This tool can be used by salesmen for all high-ticket household items such as furniture, appliances, and so on. Understanding the separate decision plans of the spouses via this tool can then aid the salesmen in counseling the customers about alternatives that may satisfy both decision makers or in identifying early on what compromises would be called for.

Additional information is available at **www.pueblo.gsa.gov/housing.html**

Figure 15.5

DECISION PLAN NETS FOR A HUSBAND AND WIFE

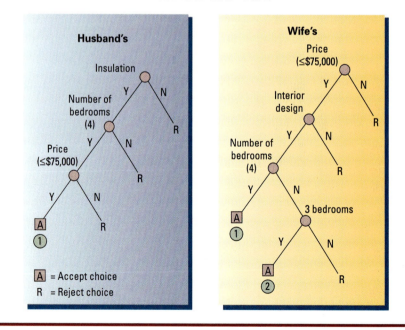

Source: C. Whan Park, "Joint Decisions in Home Purchasing: A Muddling-Through Process," *Journal of Consumer Research* 9 (September 1982), pp. 151–62.

FACTORS INFLUENCING INTERSPOUSAL INFLUENCE

Several factors affect the pattern of decision sharing among spouses. As shown in Figure 15.6, factors that have been identified include gender role orientation, wife's employment status, family life cycle stages, time pressure, purchase importance, and socioeconomic development level of the population group.

GENDER ROLE ORIENTATION Gender roles among spouses can be placed on a continuum of traditional-modern. The degree to which specific behaviors and norms are linked to a person's gender, rather than being shared across genders, is called **gender role orientation**. The traditional view is one of sharply dichotomous roles for the husband and wife, while the modern view is one of more sharing of responsibilities among the two sexes.[11] Modern gender role families would in general exhibit more joint decision making as well as wife-dominated or autonomous decisions made by the wife. In contrast, in traditional role families, more decisions will be husband dominated.

In studies from the 1980s, family decisions were found to be more joint and/or wife-dominated for household durables and housing purchases.[12] However, in the United States, there has been a blurring of gender roles in households. Wives are increasingly employed outside the home, and husbands are increasingly sharing housekeeping chores including buying everyday needs. Thus, there is a trend toward both merging of buyer, payer, and user role in the same person and sharing of a single role (e.g., payer) by both the spouses. Marketers need to keep an eye on these trends in role redistributions as the household changes because that determines what appeals should be targeted to which members of the household.

In general, even in traditional families, purchase decisions are domain specific. In many Asian, Middle Eastern, or other third-world countries, for example, cooking-related raw materials and kitchen supplies are the domain of women; likewise, certain aspects of engagements and marriage ceremonies are in women's domain. Accordingly, women decide what products need to be bought and in what quantities, although men go to the market to do the actual buying. Since many staple products do not carry brand names, brand decisions are not always pertinent in these third-world countries. One of the most

Figure 15.6

FACTORS THAT INFLUENCE INTERSPOUSAL ROLES

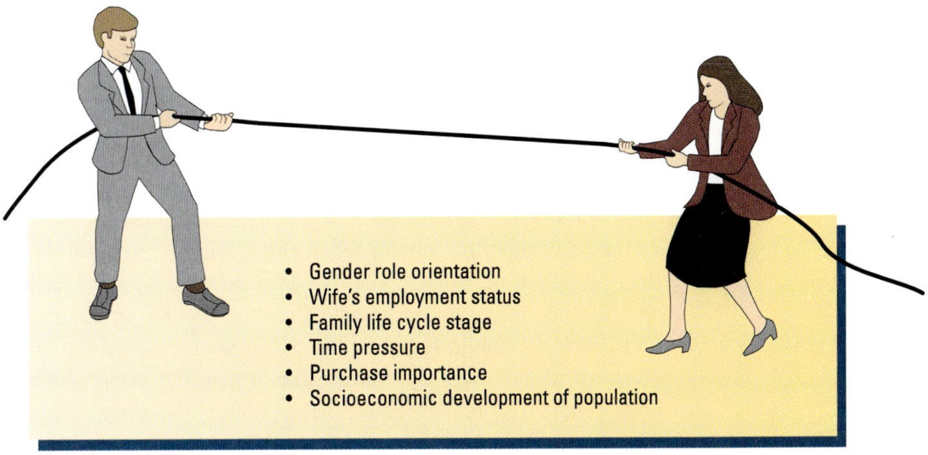

- Gender role orientation
- Wife's employment status
- Family life cycle stage
- Time pressure
- Purchase importance
- Socioeconomic development of population

fascinating aspects of family decision making is the variation in gender role orientation you find across diverse countries and cultures, and how this gender role variation influences interspousal decision sharing in different population groups.

WIFE'S EMPLOYMENT STATUS   The wife's employment status significantly influences gender-role orientation. In families where a wife is employed outside of the home, there is greater acceptance of her role in important family decisions. Not only does she make many decisions autonomously, but even in decisions historically the prerogative of the husband alone, the wife is often consulted. This occurs partly because the wife acquires greater recognition as a contributor to family finances. In addition, the greater exposure to the world outside of the home makes the wife more knowledgeable about a variety of products and services.

STAGE IN FAMILY LIFE CYCLE   Family life cycle has also been found to influence decision making in the families. Recently married couples tend to make more joint decisions; as the marriage ages, the chores become allocated along with the purchases that accompany those chores (e.g., grocery supplies for cooking, car wax for car washing, and so on) and get to be decided autonomously. However, the age of the marriage would tend not to affect important purchases. For important purchases, if the couple used joint decision making at the early stage of marriage, they would continue to do so during the later years of marriage.

TIME PRESSURE   Families with high time pressure tend to rely less on joint decision making, since autonomous or one-member dominated decision processes are generally perceived to be more time-efficient. However, such decisions may sacrifice effectiveness; the decision may not be optimal.

IMPORTANCE OF PURCHASE   Purchase importance refers to how important the family perceives the product to be. The importance of the purchase may stem from the financial outlay or from the centrality of the product to the individual—that is, whether the product is an important part of one's life. The more important the purchase, the more the decision making is going to be a joint one. One reason is that multiple members have a stake in a large expense (as it would affect everyone by draining family resources). Also, the members will have to live with the decision for a long time.

SOCIOECONOMIC DEVELOPMENT OF THE POPULATION   Gender role orientations and role specializations vary from one culture and country to another. Specifically, the culture of a country is related to the stage of socioeconomic development of the population. Thus, underdeveloped countries have a more traditional gender role orientation than do more developed countries. With development and the resulting modernization, urbanization, and concomitant increasing employment of women outside of the home, women's influence on marketplace decision making increases.

At least three factors account for the increasing role of women in modernizing societies: First, with modernization and urbanization, families become increasingly nuclear, as young adults take up jobs in urban areas, leaving their parents and grandparents behind in their rural homes. Nuclear family forms necessitate more sharing of all household responsibilities, including procurement of goods. Second, in advanced countries, with increasing dependence by the husband on the wife's supplemental income, husbands feel obligated to consult with their working spouses on at least the major purchases. Finally, smaller family units generate a greater egalitarianism among the sexes, which leads to more participatory decision making.

RELATIVE INFLUENCE OF SPOUSES IN HONG KONG FAMILIES

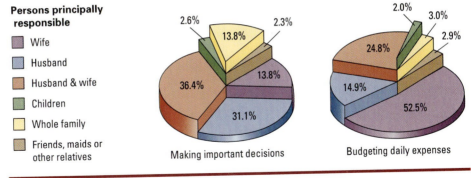

An example of how relative spousal influence in one country varies across product classes is presented in Figure 15.7. Based on a survey of Hong Kong nuclear families, Figure 15.7 shows that while important family decisions (which include nonmarket decisions) are made predominantly by husbands (31.1 percent) or jointly (36.4 percent), women alone make budgetary daily expense decisions in a majority of households (52.5 percent). Given this finding, a marketer would be well advised to direct his or her market communications toward both spouses.

This illustration about decision making in a Hong Kong family is merely a case in point. The larger lesson is that as students of customer behavior, we ought to be cognizant of the differences in household decision making behavior across different cultures and in different countries. As a marketer of a particular product category, in a particular culture and country, one of the first things you ought to do is to research family decision making for marketplace transactions in general, and for your product category in particular, and then base your marketing communications on that research.

Children's Influence in the Family Decision Making

Children as family members constitute an important target market for marketers of all household products. In 1990, U.S. children accounted for over $60 billion of direct spending and influenced over $380 billion of spending by other members of the family (see Table 15.1). Children's influence increases with age. In one study it was found that 21 percent of mothers of five to seven-year-olds yielded to their children's requests, while 57 percent of mothers of 11 to 12-year-olds yielded to children's requests.[13]

Children influence household buying in three ways. First, children influence household purchases by having individualistic preferences for products paid for and bought by

CHILDREN'S INFLUENCE IN FAMILY BUYING DECISIONS

AGE	DIRECT SPENDING	INFLUENCE ADDITIONAL SPENDING
4–11	$5b	$130b
12–19	55b	249b

Source: Sharon Kindel, "They May Be Small, But They Spend Big," *Adweek* (February 10, 1992), pp. 41–45.

parents (e.g., small children demanding particular toys or cereals). Second, children in their teen years begin to have their own money and become their own payers and buyers of items of self-use. A preteen child relies on his parents both to buy and to pay for the products he or she desires. However, a teenager, old enough to drive at the age of 16, is in a position to begin to buy and pay for products him- or herself, opening up a very valuable market to corporations selling a broad range of goods and services. Third, children influence their parents' choice of products that are meant for shared consumption (e.g., family vacation or home entertainment system), or even products used by a parent, by exerting expertise influence (e.g., by scorning an old-fashioned or no-name dress the mother might be considering buying for herself). The Window on Research box on page 589 describes summary findings of a research study on children's influence.

George P. Moschis, a marketing professor at Georgia State University, is one of the leading scholars who has studied the role children play in family decision making. One of his insights is that children's influence in the family decisions depends on whether the family has a "social" or a "concept" orientation. **Social-orientation families** are the ones more concerned with maintaining discipline among children, whereas **concept-oriented families** are those that are concerned with growth of independent thinking and individuality in children. Children from families with social orientation are less likely to make independent

Research Findings on Intergenerational Influence

WINDOW ON RESEARCH

Bank preference. A study from the 1970s found that 93 percent of college freshmen patronize the same bank as their parents.

Financial planning. The extent to which families preplan their financial goals and then act to fulfill those goals was found to be consistent over three generations studied.

Auto insurance. In one study, 40 percent of married couples had automobile insurance from the same company as the husband's parents. In another, 32 percent of adult men had the same auto insurance agency as did their fathers. This influence decreased with the age of adult children: 62 percent among men in their 20s fell to 19 percent among men 50 years or older.

Grocery items. In a study of 49 female college students and their mothers, brand preferences between mothers and their grown-up daughters were found to be more similar for grocery items with high brand-name visibility (e.g., toothpaste, facial tissues, pain reliever, and peanut butter) than for products with low brand-name visibility (spaghetti sauce, canned vegetables, coffee, and frozen juices). For high-visibility brands, 49 percent of mothers and daughters agreed on their brand preference, compared to only 31 percent agreement for low-visibility brands. There was also similarity on such choice rules (i.e., the rules-of-thumb con-

sumers employ to make their buying more efficient) as buying items on sale, brand loyalty, relying on others for advice or information, and prepurchase planning. Moreover, there was similarity in mothers' and their daughters' marketplace beliefs, such as "there is positive price quality relationship," "marketer-given information is useful," "advertising has positive value," and "private brands and sale merchandise are good value."

Additional information located at **www.usadata.com**

Sources: Elizabeth S. Moore-Shay and R. J. Lutz, "Intergenerational Influences in the Formation of Consumer Attitudes and Beliefs about the Marketplace: Mothers and Daughters," *Advances in Consumer Research*, M. Houston, ed., 15 (Ann Arbor, MI: Association for Consumer Research 1988), pp. 461–67; J. Fry, D. C. Shaw, C. H. von Lanzenauer, and C. R. Dipchard, "Customer Loyalty to Banks: A Longitudinal Study," *Journal of Business* 46, pp. 517–25; Hill, 1970; L. G. Woodson, T. L. Childers and P. R. Winn, "Intergenerational Influences in the Purchase of Auto Insurance," in W. Locander, ed., *Marketing Looking Outward: Business Proceedings*, (Chicago: American Marketing Association, 1976, pp. 43–49.

decisions and less likely to be involved in family decisions. Those with concept orientation are likely to have greater product knowledge. They are also likely to have a higher regard for their parents' opinion and a preference for objective sources of information such as *Consumer Reports*.[14]

Another way of classifying families is by how authority is exercised in the family. On this basis, *worldwide*, families can be classified into four types:[15]

1. **Authoritarian families**—The head of the household (mother in matriarchal and father in patriarchal societies) exercises strict authority on children, and children learn to obey their elders in all matters. Such families are found most in Asian societies. Although a culture of obedience to elders is considered to be a virtue, especially in Asian cultures, it does curb individuality among children and consequently their influence on family buying decisions.

2. **Neglectful families**—Parents are distant from their children, who are neglected in these families because the parent(s) place more priority on their individual affairs. Single-parent families risk this behavior most, some due to time pressure, others due to undisciplined lifestyle of the single parent, which engenders being irresponsible toward one's children. Of course, not all single parents neglect their children.

3. **Democratic families**—Every member is given equal voice. Most family matters are discussed among family members, especially those who would be affected by the decisions. Self-expression, autonomy, and mature behavior are encouraged among children. While opinions are sought from all affected members, the decision could be a joint one, or it could be exercised (or arbitrated) by the family head(s).

4. **Permissive families**—Children are given relative independence in conducting their own affairs, especially in their adolescent years. Unlike parents in the neglectful families, however, permissive parents closely watch children's interests and exercise of freedom.

The relative prevalence of these types differs across different countries, and their proportions would change in the same country over time. Also, families could have partial tendencies of more than one type.

Children's influence would obviously differ across these four types. It would be lowest among authoritarian families. In neglectful families, children would exercise no influence on parents' purchases. For products needed for their own use, however, they are likely to exercise relative autonomy, provided they have an independent source of income. If not, their resources would be rather limited, since the neglectful parent is unlikely to support most of their requests. In democratic families, children would share influence with other members. Finally, in permissive families, children would exercise relative autonomy for products for

Table 15.2

CHILDREN'S ROLE BY FAMILY TYPE

| | CHILDREN'S ROLE | | | |
| | FOR OWN-USE PRODUCTS | | FOR FAMILY-USE PRODUCTS | |
FAMILY TYPE	DIRECT CONTROL	SHARED INFLUENCE	DIRECT CONTROL	SHARED INFLUENCE
Authoritarian	Low	Low	Low	Low
Neglectful	High	High	Low	Low
Democratic	Moderate	Moderate	Moderate	Moderate
Permissive	High	Moderate	Moderate	Moderate

which they are the principal or sole user, exercising both the buyer and the decision-maker role. Depending on whether the product is for the children's own use or for shared use in the family, the degree of influence children will have in each of the four types of families is shown in Table 15.2.

Marketers can use this classification as a tool to understand family decision making in different countries. However, the classification has been studied in relation to family buying decisions only in one study, limited to preschoolers in one U.S. city.[16] The foregoing relationships between the four family types and children's relative influence are our intuitive judgments. Surely it would be interesting for us as students of customer behavior to study contemporary families in a variety of countries, cultures, and ethnic groups to see if the pattern of children's influence hypothesized here holds.

Learning the Customer Roles

Families are the first source of information about how to carry out the three customer roles. Parents and other respected elders teach children what to value and how to identify and pay for products that satisfy those values. Even as we become adults, we often seek the influence of family members with greater experience or expertise. Primary modes of learning customer roles are therefore consumer socialization and intergenerational influence.

Consumer Socialization

Consider these episodes:

- A single parent is clipping coupons on a Sunday afternoon. His 10-year-old daughter is nearby, helping her dad organize them—by product categories and by date of expiration. She makes a mental note: next time she sees a coupon in the paper, she will clip it and place it in these sorted envelopes.

- A mother is window shopping in a department store with her eight-year-old son. Suddenly, she begins to examine gym bags. She looks at one, puts it aside noticing its high price, loudly speaking her thought (as people generally do when they are with a "shopping pal"). The son points to another. "No, I am looking for one in black only," she says. Then she looks at another. The son "scoops out" yet another black bag. The mother looks at it briefly and rejects it, saying, "It doesn't have the pocket." "It does," says the son, pointing at the zippered pocket. "No, I mean a meshed pocket (i.e., the one made of net fabric)—like this other one does," says the mother. Then the dialogue proceeds as follows:

Son: Why is it made of a net?

Mother: To put your wet swimming suit in it.

Son: You can put it in the other kinds of pockets too.

Mother: Then it won't dry off.

Son: Why can't we dry it off at home?

Mother: We can. But if it is left in the bag for long, the bag will smell musty.

Son: It will?

Mother: Yes.

How do children learn to become consumers? By this we do not mean merely how they learn to consume. Rather, we mean how they learn all three roles of the customer—

preferring and deciding, purchasing, and using. How do they, in other words, become socialized to engage in marketplace exchanges? Socialized they do become, to an amazing degree. In one study, children 7 to 12 years old were found to possess strong brand preferences. And children who cannot yet read have been found to be able to recognize brand symbols, such as McDonald's arches and the Tony the Tiger mascot for Kellogg's Frosted Flakes.[17] Some observers believe that school and kindergarten children have had more experience with the marketplace than with arithmetic or writing!

Consumer socialization refers to the "acquisition of knowledge, preferences, and skills to function in the marketplace."[18] That is, consumer socialization occurs when one or more of the following are learned or acquired by children:

- preferences among alternative brands and products;
- knowledge about product features and the functioning of the marketplace; and
- skills in making "smart decisions," such as making price and product comparisons, discounting advertising and salesperson claims, and evaluating trade-offs across options (including the option "to buy or not to buy").

Learning and socialization are lifelong processes, continuing through a person's mature years. We focus here on childhood socialization, since that is when the first wave of socialization occurs and that is when the family has the greatest opportunity to influence the socialization process. Two factors play a role in consumer socialization of children: cognitive and environmental.

Cognitive factors are age-related mental abilities. Very young children, for example, are unable to discriminate between a TV program and a commercial and do not understand the persuasive intent of advertisers.[19] They are also driven by immediate perceptual features of the stimuli rather than by its substantive meaning. For example, a smaller glass filled to the top is judged to contain more juice than a larger but half-filled glass.[20] Cognitive development proceeds with age, and so does children's consumer socialization.

Environmental factors are socialization agents (sources of information and influence): mass media, peers, and family. Family has been the strongest influence on children's socialization in general, not just on their socialization as consumers.[21] As the child becomes older, peer influence grows, and the influence of family likely declines. In our experience, weakening of family influence with advancing years is less in Asian and third-world countries than in the more industrialized Western countries.

Children in industrialized countries are also greatly influenced by the mass media, especially television. In the United States, there is a rising trend of latchkey children (those who, returning home from school, use the housekey to enter their home because neither parent is home at that time). These children often pass their time alone by watching TV at home. This factor and increasing time pressure on parents have likely led to an increase in the influence of mass media. Moreover, the influence of mass media crosses global and cultural boundaries. TV is universal and ubiquitous, extending its reach even among rural residents in emerging countries. Thus, even in traditional societies of Asian and other third-world countries, children are well aware of Western fashions and other consumer goods.

LEARNING MECHANISMS

The socialization influence from parents to children occurs basically through the learning mechanisms described in Chapter 9: instrumental conditioning, modeling, and cognitive learning. These three mechanisms correspond to the three bases of reference-group influence (a topic covered in Chapter 6): utilitarian, value-expressive, and informational, respectively.

Instrumental conditioning refers to learning to do those things that are rewarded. In the early years of a child, parents control most resources and inculcate values through rewarding what they consider "good" behavior. Children learn those behaviors and the underlying values that receive rewards from their parents. Many of these behaviors and values are in the domain of consumption, such as what foods to eat and what items a child is allowed to buy with his or her allowance.

The second mechanism is modeling. Here children look up to their parents as role models and try to internalize and adopt their values, roles, aptitudes, and so on. Thus, for example, a child who watches a father dressing up in the morning in "office clothes" is quietly making plans to wear similar clothes one day.

The cognitive mechanism of learning toward socialization can occur at two levels: low involvement and high involvement. As described in earlier chapters, the low-involvement mode entails an undeliberated adoption of product choices simply because these products were used by one's parents and one became familiar with them while growing up. "Mom always bought Crisco oil or Morton salt, and it is not worth the hassle to figure out anew which brand to buy," the consumer might say. Thus, buying what "Mom always bought" becomes a decision-simplifying heuristic for a son or a daughter. At the high-involvement level, socialization influence can occur due to communication and education by parents about various brands or buying strategies. A mother might "educate" a daughter, for example, about what hygienic products are good, or when to use which of the several cough medicines she has in the family medicine chest.

Learning from the media can occur through cognitive and/or modeling processes. When a child sees an advertisement and becomes aware of the existence of the product, its features, where it is available, and so on, he or she is learning through the cognitive mechanism. Learning through the modeling mechanism occurs when a child observes product/brand use and identifies with desirable "models" in media programming and/or advertisements.

Learning from peers is predominantly via modeling. Occasionally it can be cognitive; peers can provide information. At times peers even use instrumental conditioning, rewarding by offering approval.

SOCIALIZATION OUTCOMES

Whether the socialization agents are the family or peers or the media, there are several possible socialization outcomes. First, children can simply "adopt" certain products and brands, simply by noticing them in use in the house or seeing them in advertisements. Reinforced by satisfactory use experience, they can then firm up preferences for these products and brands.

Children also can learn about desirable product features, alternative products, brands, stores, and other market options, and make this information a part of their stock of marketplace knowledge. Thus, children can learn, for example, that a particular toy is available at a particular store at a particular price, or that Sony Walkman comes in an attractive, neon-colored sports model, or that "Swatch" watches are cool, since they are worn by the coolest girls seen on TV and in the mall.

Finally, children can learn the knowledge and skills to make "smart choices." They can learn to clip coupons, do comparison shopping, and select items from mail catalogs. They can understand for example, that Wal-Mart offers a price guarantee so that one never needs to shop for price for items sold in Wal-Mart.

Intergenerational Influence

The **intergenerational influence (IGI)** of family members refers to the transmission of values, attitudes, and behaviors from one generation to the other.[22] In the context of customer behavior, IGI refers to the transfer of market values that ought to be important, of brand perceptions, and of brand decisions themselves (i.e., simply adopting the brand parents had been using). In studies done in the early 1970s as well as more recently in the late 1980s, such transfer of product and service preferences has been found for a range of products, including banks, auto insurance, grooming products, and supermarket items.[23] See the Window on Research box on page 584.

WINDOW ON RESEARCH

Children's Influence on Family Decisions

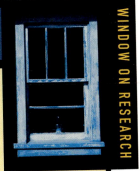

Consumer researchers Ellen Foxman, Patria Tanshuhaj, and Karin Ekstrom studied the role of adolescent children and found the following:

- Children (adolescents) had more influence for products for their own use.

- The greater the teenager's financial resources, the greater the influence he or she exercised.

- The greater the perceived knowledge, the greater the perceived influence.

- The greater the importance to the teenager of the product category, the higher the teenager influence.

- Teenager influence was higher in dual income families.

- Teenagers exercised more influence at the initiation stage than at the search and decision stage.

- Mothers attributed less influence to their children than did children themselves. This discrepancy was lesser between mothers and their daughters than between mothers and their sons.

In an extension of this research, consumer researchers Sharon E. Beatty and Salil Talpade collected new data and analyzed purchases of durables (TV, stereo, phone, and furniture) made for family use versus made primarily for the use by the teenager. Some of their findings were as follows:

- Financial resources of teenagers influenced only those durable purchases that were for the teenager's own use (as opposed to family use) and only in the purchase initiation stage, not in the search and decision stages.

- Children's product knowledge was influential only in the initiation of purchase consideration and only for products intended for teenager use. For family purchases, teenager influence was significantly enhanced with product knowledge but only in the search/decision stage and only for stereos (not for the other products investigated).

- Importance of purchase to teenagers affected their influence for both for-family and for-teenager purchases, and in both initiation and search/decision stages.

- When teenagers were the major users of for-family durables, they exercised more influence (than if they were not going to be the major user) in both initiation and search/decision stages.

- Children had greater influence in dual-income families than in single-income families; however, this influence was significant only for purchases made for shared family consumption. For purchases for their own use, children had influence alike in both single and dual-income families.

Additional information located at **www.aafcs.org**

Source: Adapted from Ellen R. Foxman, Patria S. Tanshuhaj, and Karin M. Ekstrom, "Family Members' Perceptions of Adolescents' Influence in Family Decision Making," *Journal of Consumer Research* 15 (March, 1989) pp. 482–91; and "Adolescents' Influence in Family Purchase Decisions: A Socialization Perspective," *Journal of Business Research* 18 (March 1989), pp. 159–72; also see George E. Belch, M. A. Belch, and G. Ceresino, "Parental and Teenage Child Influences in Family Decision Making," *Journal of Business Research* 13 (1985), pp. 163–76.

IGI can take place in two directions: forward (from parents to children) and reverse (from children to parents). Forward IGI can occur both when the child is young and lives with parents, and during adult years when the parents and grown-up children live in separate households. Typically, researchers have studied forward IGI during early childhood (that is, consumer socialization, the previous topic we discussed). In contrast, forward and reverse IGI during the adult years of sons and daughters has not been studied much.

REVERSE INFLUENCE

The *reverse influence* begins to occur as children grow up. In school and on the street, children are exposed to new knowledge and to new role models. Consequently, they begin to depend less on parents as role models or for guidance and begin to carve out their individual identity. In exercising their individual identity, when their preferences differ from their parents', they begin to influence what gets bought for family consumption, such as the type of home furnishings.

This influence can occur for two reasons. First, the offsprings begin to influence their parents' preferences and marketplace choices because on certain products children acquire greater knowledge and expertise than their parents, which their parents acknowledge. In these situations, parents may accept and indeed look to advice from their adult children about which brands are best to buy or what features or evaluative criteria to consider. Of course, this expertise-driven influence is not global but product specific, and can therefore occur in different directions for different products. For some products, adult sons and daughters might be considered experts; for others, parents might continue to retain their expertise credibility. Thus, a mother might look to her daughter for fashion advice, but the daughter might continue to look to her mother for advice on hygiene or on cooking. Likewise, a growing-up daughter or son might strongly influence the next kind of car the family buys, but he or she may seek parental advice on the purchase of a house.

The second mechanism of children-to-parent influence occurs due to what can be called "democratic justice." **Democratic justice** refers to a family norm in which each family member is given a voice in family decisions. Often parents accept the norm that family members should be allowed to develop their individual identities and be treated as individual citizens of the household, with an equal voice in family matters. In the popular American TV show *Cosby*, the father often calls for a "family conference" to resolve common disputes, with one vote by each member. Thus, in the purchase of common assets (e.g., car, furniture, and so on), many families may consider it legitimate to give youngsters a voice and thus allow them to influence parents' preferences. This influence can go beyond common assets. For products consumed by children exclusively (e.g., their own clothes or food) or primarily (the CD player and sound system), children are allowed to exercise their preference simply because parents grant children their democratic right to individuality.

Democratic justice as a mechanism of offspring-to-parent influence can cause tensions in a family. When the offsprings' preferences become incongruent with their parents' values, the value incongruence can be a source of conflict. Thus, if the offsprings want a different cereal or different sofa for the family room, or even a different color on the exterior of the house, these preferences may be granted as harmless since they violate no values. But when the offsprings want to buy, say, motorcycle clothing, or get a punk-style haircut, or turn a room into a discotheque, then it is likely to violate parents' sense of propriety and thus cause conflict. Secondly, when the offsprings' preferences make excessive demands on parents' resources, such as the former insisting on buying a $120 pair of Nike shoes, parents could view these demands as unreasonable and deny or at least resent them.

Both these sources of conflict are mediated, of course, by who controls the resources. If offsprings depend entirely on parents for financial support, then the rejection of the former's preferences is more likely. On the other hand, if they contribute to the family's financial resources, or at least earn part of their living, then parents are likely to allow more leeway. But the value incongruence does not disappear with resource sharing. As long as the offsprings are living under the same roof, parents may resent and are likely to attempt to change their sons' and daughters' counter-value purchases.

FAMILY CHARACTERISTICS THAT INFLUENCE IGI

Forward and reverse IGI are both influenced by family relationship and relative expertise across generations. **Family relationship** refers to the degree of mutual respect and trust between parents and their adult offsprings, and the harmony of relations and communication among them, in all areas of life (not just about products and shopping activities). Family relationship can be characterized as positive (harmony and mutual respect in the family) or negative (alienation, conflict, and mutual neglect). *Relative expertise* is the acknowledgement by the offsprings that parents possess expertise about a product (or, for reverse IGI, that parents acknowledge their offsprings to be experts).

Based on these two characteristics, four IGI states can occur (see Table 15.3).[24] When perceived expertise is high but the family relationship is negative, there will be disaffected IGI. This means the person acknowledges the soundness of the expert advice in principle but does not act upon the advice because he or she psychologically rejects the adviser. When perceived expertise is high and the family relationship is positive, there will be high IGI. Children and their parents will seek out and act on one another's advice. In contrast, when perceived expertise is low and family relationship negative, there will be no IGI. Finally, when perceived expertise is low and family relationship is positive, there will be discounted IGI, meaning the person receives the advice politely but discounts it as not being credible.

IGI ACROSS HOUSEHOLDS   A special case of IGI occurs when offsprings have formed their own households separate from parents. This can be termed "IGI *across* households."[25] Family members living under the same roof might make joint decisions simply as a way of life, but the physical distance between families in two households will not make joint decision making a natural thing to do. Furthermore democratic justice does not apply since the purchase under consideration is not for shared use among parents and offsprings, and no "justice" would be violated in not seeking everyone's opinion.

Why, then, does IGI occur across households? One reason is expertise. If grown-up offsprings still consider their parents experts on the purchase of a specific product (e.g., a

Table 15.3

INTERGENERATIONAL INFLUENCES (IGI)

		FAMILY RELATIONSHIP	
		NEGATIVE	POSITIVE
PERCEIVED EXPERTISE	HIGH	Disaffected IGI	High IGI
	LOW	No IGI	Discounted IGI

house, life insurance, stocks, and so on), they would turn to them for advice, despite household separation. Conversely, on matters where adult offsprings are perceived to possess expertise, parents will seek the former's advice. This is particularly likely to be the case for new technology products (e.g., computers, CD players, or even cars).

Another reason for IGI across households is lifestyle similarity between the generations. Illustratively, although a mother might perceive the daughter to be an expert on new fashions, if she perceives her daughter's lifestyle to be different from hers (e.g., she views herself to be a conservative professional and wears formal, conservative styles, while her daughter sports the "grunge look"), then she (the mother) is not likely to seek or accept her daughter's advice on clothing. But a mother returning to the workforce might appreciate her successful daughter's insights on what chic people wear to work.

The intergenerational influence can run across several generations. The reality of this influence is such that there is a certain "family-ness" to customer choices. Despite different demographics, such as age and race, this extended family depicts the kind of family identification of its members, which they display in the choice of clothing from Versace Couture.

Yet another factor, "resource control," refers to who finances the expense for the purchase under control. When parents finance the purchase, they would exercise IGI. If adult offsprings themselves finance their own purchase, even if partially, to that extent, forward IGI is reduced. On the other hand, if retired parents depend on their grown-up offsprings, then reverse IGI occurs. In each of these cases, the influence mechanism is reward/punishment. At the very least, the generation with the resource control can simply refuse to finance the purchase.

These three factors correspond closely with the three types of reference group influences we studied in Chapter 6: informational, identificational, and normative or instrumental. Informational influence occurs when the influencing agent provides useful information that guides, facilitates, or alters the choices the influence recipient makes. Instrumental influence occurs due to the ability of influence agents to reward or punish the influence tar-

Table 15.4

BASIS OF IGI ASSOCIATED WITH INFLUENCE TYPES

BASIS OF IGI	INFLUENCE TYPE
Perceived expertise	Informational
Perceived lifestyle similarity	Identificational
Resource control	Instrumental

get. This also includes what has been called "normative" influence—the expectations of significant others. Finally, identificational influence occurs when the influenced identifies with the influencer, viewing the latter as the role model and emulating his or her behavior (see Table 15.4). As mentioned earlier, for any of these influences to operate, there must also be a positive family relationship.

Conflict in Family Decisions

Family decision making may give rise to conflict, whether the customer roles are distributed among family members or shared by family members. Conflict among *distributed roles* arises when the user, payer, and buyer roles are played by different family members, and alternatives (such as brands) do not satisfy the goals (market values) of each. The conflicts arise due to differences in the perceptions and goals of the three different roles. Suppose the user (a child) wants a name-brand shoe (e.g., Nike), but that shoe is too expensive for the payer (a parent). Or if a payer (e.g., mother) likes the economic value warehouse clubs offer, but the teenage daughter who is responsible for the grocery buying chore for the family resents the inconvenience of warehouse clubs. In these cases, the alternatives (products, brands) that satisfy the goals of the player of one role leave unsatisfied the goals of players of the other roles.

Conflict due to *shared roles* arises when a single role is shared by multiple family members and their goals (market values) diverge. Consider a product intended for shared consumption in the family, such as a family car. Here, all the members of the family will be the users of the car. As users, however, they may differ on the functional values they seek from the car. The husband may want a high-performance car with a turbo engine, while the wife may want a car that is safe for small children in the family. If both these

Figure 15.8

CONFLICT DUE TO SHARED ROLES

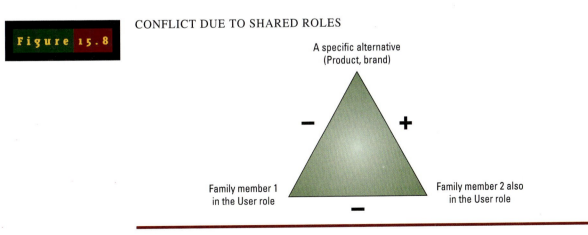

A specific alternative
(Product, brand)

Family member 1
in the User role

Family member 2 also
in the User role

user values can not be satisfied by a single solution or alternative, a conflict would occur (see Figure 15.8). Likewise, when both husband and wife play the payer role as they draw on common family funds, they may conflict on how much can be spent on home re-furnishing.

Types of Conflict

The conflicts that are inevitable if the family decision process entails joint decision making will arise if there is disagreement between family members either on goals (market values) or on perceptions (evaluation of alternatives). The nature of the conflict will differ according to whether there is disagreement in one or both of these areas (see Table 15.5). When values are in agreement but alternative evaluations differ, there is "solution conflict." A decision on where to take the family vacation would represent this conflict situation if everybody agreed that the vacation should be fun (goal agreement) but differed on whether Disney World or Cancun would be more fun. When both goals and perceptions diverge, conflict is *compounded*. This would happen in buying a condominium, for example, in a high-rise complex in Chicago, when spouses may desire different goals (e.g., the husband may want a city view and the wife may prefer a view of the lake) and also perceive two condominiums differently on a common goal (e.g., they may differ on which of the two condominiums they examined is more aesthetic).[26] When both values and evaluations converge across family members, there is no conflict; choice of many daily consumption items exemplify this setting. When goals diverge but perceptions of solutions are in agreement, there is "goal conflict." This occurs when the husband may want a stylish, youthful car but the wife wants a large, safe car.

Conflict Resolution

Four strategies of conflict resolution have been suggested by scholars: problem solving, persuasion, bargaining, and politicking (see Table 15.6). Problem solving entails members trying to gather more information, or to add new alternatives. When motives/goals are congruent and only perceptions differ, obtaining and sharing information (i.e., problem solving) often suffices to resolve conflicts. Persuasion requires educating about the goal hierarchy; the wife might argue how a safe and large car is in the best interest of the whole family since the car is needed to transport children. Bargaining entails trading favors (husband gets to buy a house with a den and the finished basement provided the car he buys is

Table 15.5

TYPES OF CONFLICT

		GOALS	
		CONVERGENT	DIVERGENT
PERCEPTIONS/ EVALUATIONS	DIVERGENT	Solution conflict (family vacation)	Compounded Complex, important purchases (home buying)
	CONVERGENT	No Conflict (daily consumption items)	Goal conflict (What to buy) (Product level conflict)

CONFLICT RESOLUTION TECHNIQUES

		VALUES/GOALS	
		CONVERGENT	DIVERGENT
	DIVERGENT	Problem solving	Politicking Bargaining
EVALUATIONS	CONVERGENT	No Conflict	Persuasion

one of his wife's preference). When goals and evaluations are so divergent that even bargaining is infeasible, politicking is resorted to. Here, members form coalitions and subgroups within the family and by so doing simply impose their will on the minority coalition.[27] Marketers can help household members resolve a conflict by aiding the problem-solving mode—they can provide additional information about alternatives. Such interventions are most feasible in interpersonal selling situations such as at the car dealership or with a real estate agent. Recent research has further focused on the interpersonal dynamics of how household members such as spouses influence each other in joint decisions. See the Window on Research box.

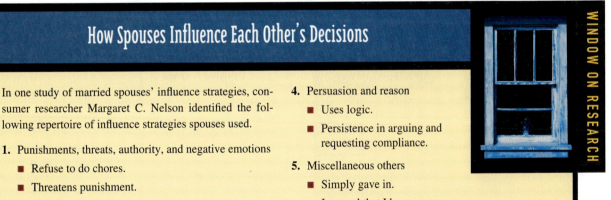

How Spouses Influence Each Other's Decisions

WINDOW ON RESEARCH

In one study of married spouses' influence strategies, consumer researcher Margaret C. Nelson identified the following repertoire of influence strategies spouses used.

1. Punishments, threats, authority, and negative emotions
   - Refuse to do chores.
   - Threatens punishment.
   - Becomes angry.
   - Questions spouse's right to disagree.

2. Positive emotion and subtle manipulation
   - Puts the spouse in a receptive mood.
   - Appeals to spouse's love and affection.
   - Promises to do something nice in return.
   - Acknowledges that it would be a favor.

3. Withdrawal and egocentrism
   - Denies affection, acting cold.
   - Clams up.
   - Looks hurt, sulks.

4. Persuasion and reason
   - Uses logic.
   - Persistence in arguing and requesting compliance.

5. Miscellaneous others
   - Simply gave in.
   - I argued that I knew more.
   - Compromise; meet in the middle.
   - Plead or beg.
   - Came up with a new solution acceptable to both.

Additional information available at **http://acr.web page.com**

Source: Margaret C. Nelson, "The Resolution of Conflict in Joint Purchase Decisions by Husbands and Wives: A Review and Empirical Test,"in *Advances in Consumer Research*, Michael J Houston, ed., 15 (1988), pp. 436–41.

A General Framework for Understanding Family Buying Decisions

It is useful to bring together the major topics covered in this chapter in an organizing framework. Figure 15.9 presents such a framework. Since we have already discussed most of the variables contained in this figure, we describe the model only briefly here.

Decision Process

The linchpin of the model is the decision process, which can be either autonomous (i.e., decision made by a single family member), or joint decision making. It is the joint decision making that distinguishes household buying from individual buying. The decision is joint if family members exercise any degree of influence during any of the stages of the decision process. These decision-process stages (not shown in Figure 15.9) are initiation,

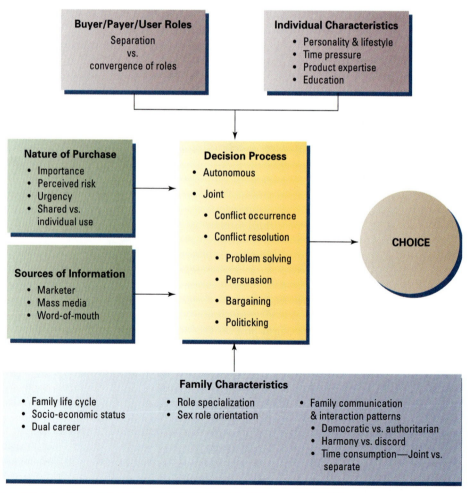

Figure 15.9 A FRAMEWORK FOR UNDERSTANDING FAMILY BUYING DECISIONS

information gathering, evaluation and decision, shopping and buying, and conflict resolution.

Conflict occurrence is a significant component of the decision process. The conflict may arise either because the family members do not agree on purchase goals and criteria or because they disagree on their perceptions as to which alternatives would best meet these goals and criteria. The conflict can sometimes be intense, clouding the entire decision process. It may be manifested in angry arguments and agonizing frustration with the "irrationality of the other members." Its resolution would typically follow one of the four strategies discussed earlier: problem solving, persuasion, bargaining, or politicking.

Influences on the Decision Process

The extent to which a decision process will be autonomous rather than joint, or vice versa, will depend on the nature of the purchase, separation of the buyer/payer/user roles, individual member characteristics, and family characteristics. And, of course, sources of information will influence the decision process. Different members may be exposed differently to different sources of information, and their individual perspectives and perceptual distortions make the decision process less or more involving and conflicting.

NATURE OF THE PURCHASE

CONSIDER THE NATURE OF THE PURCHASE   If the purchase is important and if there is high perceived risk associated with the purchase, then the decision will more likely be a joint decision. If the product or service is required urgently, then the time-consuming process of joint decision will be avoided in favor of autonomous decisions. Finally, if the product to be bought is for shared consumption among the family members, then the process is likely to be a joint one.

SEPARATION OF THE THREE ROLES   The extent to which the three customer roles are separated in a household will influence the customer decision. In some households, one spouse assumes all three roles, while in others spouses divide the role responsibility or jointly share each role. Likewise, the role of children varies from household to household, from one of being totally passive consumers to one where children actively influence what will be bought. Where the three roles do not converge in the same person, or where household members do not delegate their roles to others, joint rather than autonomous decisions are more likely, and consequently, conflicts too are more likely.

INDIVIDUAL CHARACTERISTICS

Among the individual characteristics, the first factor is whether any given individual in the family carries all three role responsibilities: buyer, payer, and user. If these roles converge in the same individual, then the decision making is likely to be autonomous. The more these roles are distributed across the family members, the more the decision process is likely to be a joint one.

Other characteristics of the individual are personality and lifestyle, time pressure, product expertise, and education. These influence both the extent of joint decision making, and the way in which the conflicts are resolved. Time pressure on one or more members will lead to less joint decision making. The member with greater time pressure is likely to delegate the purchase decision to the other members (i.e., those with less time pressure). If individual members have a lifestyle and personality that is individualistic rather than sharing and inclusive (i.e., a "me" rather than "us" personality), then autonomous decisions are more likely. Or if a particular decision has to be a joint one, then it is likely to be more conflict-laden (since members are less likely to be accommodative). Of course, product expertise of individuals will bring them more into family decisions. Finally, education will closely influence the interaction and the conflict management. Spouses and parents with more education will likely keep the conflicts manageable and solve them via rational arguments and persuasion, rather than by politicking.

FAMILY CHARACTERISTICS

One set of family characteristics that would impact the decision process includes family life cycle (FLC), socioeconomic status, and dual versus single career. Consider FLC: Newly marrieds have generally been found to use the joint process to a much greater extent than couples with aging marriages. Adolescent children begin to make more autonomous decisions for products for which they are the primary users. Socioeconomic status (SES) influences the extent of joint process and also how the conflicts may be resolved. Although there is no conclusive research evidence on this, for products meant exclusively for an individual member's use, the decision is more likely to be an autonomous one for both upper-class and lower-class (compared to the middle-class) households, but for different reasons. For the upper classes, budgeting and spending are not constrained, so the user will have the freedom to "just go ahead" and buy whatever he or she wants. For the lower SES families, the head of the household would typically exercise autonomous decisions regardless of who the intended user is. For products of shared consumption, the high SES families are likely to use joint process much more than low SES families. Note that this description is tentative, for want of concrete research data on this aspect.

A second set of family characteristics is the gender-role orientations and role specialization. In families where gender roles are traditionally oriented, there will be many more autonomous decisions. Also, with role specialization, purchases will tend to be assigned for autonomous decisions by those perceived to possess the most specialized knowledge of the topic. A related variable is dual versus single career in the family. In dual-career families, gender-role orientation is less likely to be traditional. Therefore, both spouses are likely to participate in major family buying decisions, making the decision process a joint one.

The last set of family characteristics comprises the communication and interaction patterns. Does the nominal head of the household govern and manage the family in an authoritarian or a democratic way? The decisions would be much more joint in the latter than in the former type of households. Furthermore, are day-to-day communications among the family members marked with harmony or with discord? The answer to this would affect whether influence attempts by one member will be accepted by other members, as we stated in discussing the intergenerational influence (IGI). Also, whether or not conflicts would arise in joint processes, and how conflicts would be resolved, would be closely influenced by democratic versus authoritarian management style and harmony versus discord in everyday communications within the family. Democratic and harmonious families are much more likely to use persuasion and problem-solving strategies than bargaining and politicking. Finally, whether or not the family members spend time together, or whether each does "his or her own thing," living, in effect, more like roommates than as a family would influence the decision process. The more family members share time and lifestyle, the more they are likely to engage in a joint decision process.

However, our description in this chapter of the family's customer behavior is founded

The Family Altar: The Nerve Center of Life for Chinese Customers

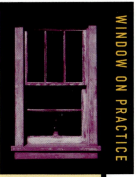

If you visit a Chinese home, you will see an altar located in the central room of the house, in front of the main gate or door of the house, and generally visible from the street. Intended to be open to public view, it is the gathering place in the house, including meeting with guests and visitors. The altar represents family ancestors as well as some animistic gods that many Chinese worship. On the left-hand side of the altar, there is an incense pot; to the right side are ancestral tablets representing various ancestors, including recent, immediate patrilineal forebears (e.g., a deceased grandfather or father). A household with one altar represents one family; a household with two altars represents two families; a household without an altar represents a family with its family altar located elsewhere (such as in the parental home). All members of the family worship at the altar and ask for favors such as good grades, a job, and so on. Members away from home visit their homes so that they may worship at the family altars.

In the Chinese culture, the family altar represents three properties: roundness, harmony, and fluidity. Roundness means there is continuity and relative comprehensiveness in the family—that is, the individual is part of a continuing whole comprising the ancestors, one's present family, and future family members yet to be born. Thus, the Chinese customer is nothing if not a representative of his or her family. The family face is always important to save, so much so that if a father were to die in debt, the children would take it upon themselves to pay off the debt to save the family's face.

The second characteristic, harmony, means that there is to be harmony in the family. When and if the family fights, it is considered a curse from the gods, whom the family then worships at the altar in the hope of restoring family harmony.

The third characteristic, fluidity, means that there is no heaven, no predetermined destiny; rather, life is made of luck and chance and the individual is free to explore his or her destiny. This last property gives Chinese culture a special twist: While family identity is important and nothing is to be done to violate its honor, the family members are free in their individual capacity to explore the world, to obtain material rewards, to become entrepreneurs, and so on.

With this backdrop, it is easy to understand some peculiarities of family consumption among the Chinese. Often, large Chinese families, comprising as many as 30 members from different generations, would go to a restaurant and linger on for several hours, relaxing, conversing, telling stories, and leisurely playing games of chance. These families would also go to a seaside house or resort on vacation and spend several days without so much as stepping out of their room or house. They have been spending time with the extended family, telling stories, enjoying conversations, and playing games of chance.

We don't know much else about family buying behavior among the Chinese for want of research and published studies in the discipline. It is clear, however, that the three properties of the family altar—roundness, harmony, and fluidity—cannot but exercise a pervasive influence on all family activities, including family decisions in the marketplace.

Additional information available at **www.china.com**

Source: Martin J. Gannon, "The Chinese Family Altar," *Understanding Global Cultures* (Thousand Oaks, CA: Sage Publications, 1994), pp. 323–37.

on research in North America. The Window on Practice box demonstrates an example of the wide-ranging cultural variations in family life that exist across the nations of the globe. Given such cultural and international variations, we invite students of customer behavior to deliberate over how the concepts described in this chapter would be adapted for families in other nations and in other cultures.

The Three Customer Roles and Household Decision Making

Nearly all of the concepts discussed in this chapter have relevance to the three customer roles. Some apply to all three roles; others acquire more or less salience depending on the role. These are outlined in Table 15.7.

Household Types

Households were classified into family and nonfamily types. In families the financial resources are generally pooled, and the earning members support the needs of the nonearning

Table 15.7 THE THREE CUSTOMER ROLES IN HOUSEHOLD CUSTOMER DECISION MAKING

ASPECT OF HOUSEHOLD DECISION MAKING	USER	PAYER	BUYER
Family and nonfamily households	■ In nonfamily households user and payer roles reside more likely in the same individual. ■ User values normatively influenced by nonuser family members.	■ In families where user and payer roles often separate, users need to persuade payers.	■ In nonfamily households, members may alternate buyer role across situations, but users may not surrender their choice decision responsibility.
Family life cycle	■ Members collaborate closely as each user also assumes the payer and buyer roles more in start-up families.	■ Payer role most strained in full-nest families	■ Buyer role most separated in full-nest families.
Family decisions	■ Users initiate and gather information about desirable alternatives.	■ Payers approve or disapprove category purchase.	■ Buyers often influence brand choices.
Children's influence	■ Very young children as users depend on parents as payers and buyers. ■ Adolescent children influence user decisions on products for common use.	■ Children on allowances look for price and value.	■ Teenagers assume purchase task, including brand decisions, for routine shopping and seek convenience value the most.
Consumer socialization of children	■ Observation of adults and mass media socialize children into becoming users.	■ Payer role socialization is the hardest to achieve. ■ Debt accumulation on credit card is a major concern of parents.	■ Accompanying parents on shopping trips socializes children into buying roles.
Intergenerational influence	■ Users values considerably influenced by and between the generations. Influence based on product expertise or taste.	■ Financial resources enable payers to influence user choices across generations.	■ Types of stores one shops at can be influenced by intergenerational influence.
Conflict resolution	■ User-user conflict on items for common use. ■ Usually resolved by problem solving (e.g., finding an acceptable alternative).	■ User-payer role separation principal source of conflict. ■ Often resolved by bargaining.	■ Buyers imposing their own user values can cause conflict.

members. Conversely, in nonfamily households, payer and user roles are more likely to reside within the same individual. The separation of user and payer roles often found in family households brings forth a need for users to persuade payers. Whenever payer and user roles are separated, the marketer needs to make the offering appealing not only to users but also to payers by offering good price and credit and financing values.

As regards the buyer role, in family households, either joint buying trips may be made, or role specialization, is likely to occur by product categories. In nonfamily households, in contrast, role specialization is less likely, and, instead, each member may take turns performing the buyer role for routine replenishment of common-need products (e.g., groceries). Other members may ask whoever is going shopping to also buy some items on their behalf, but in these cases, the item's make and brand are specified by the user. In families, in contrast, the buyer has much more leeway to exercise judgment in making brand choices. One implication of this is that if a marketer targets nonfamily households (other than singles living alone), the resulting divorce of the buyer role from any decision making would necessitate brand communications designed to shape brand choice outside of the store.

Also, user values are influenced much more by nonuser members in the family household compared to the nonfamily households. Since the nonuser members are not as involved emotionally in the user's product but they are involved as payers and buyers, they tend to emphasize performance value more. For example, a parent may argue with a teenager who wants to buy expensive Tommy Hilfiger jeans that the less expensive Levi's will serve the purpose just as well.

Household Life Cycle

Families in different stages of their life cycles share and shoulder the three roles differently. In start-up families, such as in newly married couples (whether young or old, whether first or second or third marriage), spouses do things together much more than in other stages of the family life cycle; consequently, there is much more joint discharge of the three roles in these families—except, of course, in cultures where gender roles are more sharply separated. Members collaborate more in carrying out the joint or respective roles; and furthermore, due to the new-found love and affection between them, there is greater empathy with each other's user needs and values. This sharing and empathy of the early couplehood returns with empty-nester families as older couples, bereft of the children to occupy their concerns, begin to do joint activities again. In the fully nested families, parental attention is focused on children's needs as users; strapped by resources outstripped by growing needs, parents shoulder payer and buyer roles willingly only for what they consider essential needs; for children's needs, driven more by their social and emotional needs (e.g., craving for expensive clothing or toys), parents are less accepting of children's demands.

It is in the full-nest families that the payer role is most strained. It is also in the full-nest families that parents are the busiest, and the buyer role is delegated to teenagers or discharged by one parent individually. Both convenience value (due to busyness) and financing value (due to resource shortage) become most sought in the full-nest stage.

Family Decision Making

As already mentioned, it is in families that role sharing is most likely; different members shoulder the customer role most suited to their skills and resources. Different family members also contribute to the decision differently, according to the role they shoulder. Individuals playing the user roles generally initiate the purchase request or need recognition and also gather information about available alternatives. Payers approve or disapprove the very idea of buying a specific product category (e.g., "no new TV this year"). Finally, buyers influence brand choices (e.g., which airline to fly on family vacation). Sometimes, buyers also act as gatekeepers for what brands and products are bought. For example, the buyer decides what brand of cereal to buy for the family.

Children's Influence

Children influence family purchases not only for products for which they themselves are users, but also for products meant for common use in the family (e.g., the family car). It is children's own tastes as users (i.e., social and emotional values) that they definitely want to impose on the parental choice of any product to be used in the common living areas, including such things as the color and style of furnishings.

In contrast to the user values, the payer values are not much influenced by children except when children are required to spend their own money (out of allowances) to buy something.

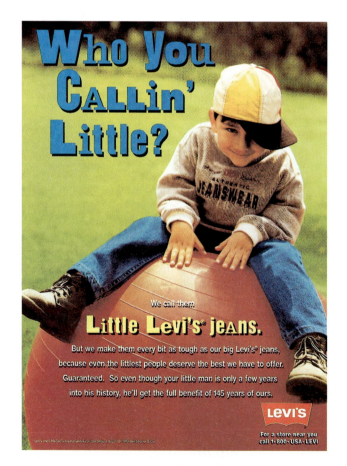

The parents are already your customers—have been all along since their adult years, wearing Levi's jeans. They will be happy to purchase one pair for their young children—only if you made them in child sizes. And, even more importantly, if you could appeal to their young children who will be playing the user role. Thus is born the brand extension, Little Levi's jeans.

Finally, children definitely influence the buyer values as teenagers increasingly assume the payer role for family groceries. As buyers, they sometimes even assume the brand decisions; and, moreover, more than their parents, they seek convenience value, buying the grocery item from the most convenient store, for example, or even from the neighborhood convenience store rather than the less expensive supermarket.

Consumer Socialization

Socialization of children as consumers is easy and natural in respect to the user role; children learn both by observation of consumption by parents and in the household and also from mass media and peers.

It is the payer role that is hard to socialize the children into and takes some judicious shaping (such as asking children to pay rent). Some banks now issue credit cards to children, and debt accumulation by these young customers is becoming a major concern to parents, especially when they co-sign the credit card application. Poor socialization into the proper payer role continues to afflict many customers in their adult years, who acquire things much beyond their financial means. Society as a whole needs to do a more effective job of socialization of children as prudent payers.

Finally, buyer role socialization also occurs relatively easily as children accompany parents on their shopping trips.

Intergenerational Influence

Obviously, tastes and preferences of customers as users influence other customers in the family across generations. Parents influence grown-up sons' and daughters' user values, even after they leave home, on products with which the latter have no experience whereas parents do; in turn, grown-up children, living apart from parents, influence parents' choices and user values on technological products or on current fashion trends and other innovations. Furthermore, in their payer roles, members of one generation influence the choices of other generations, in either direction, by controlling financial resources. Finally, buyer roles are also influenced in terms of selection of outlets—holiday gatherings where sons and daughters visit parents (or vice versa) are often occasions not only for social conversations but also for nondirected exchange of views on a variety of consumption-related topics, wherein choice of insurance companies, of stores, of new channels (e.g., banking by phone, or shopping by catalog, or shopping on the Internet) are discussed.

Conflict Resolution

Conflicts among family members are common even where the same member discharges all three roles. For example, if a teenage daughter buys an expensive pair of jeans for her own use and with her own money, the parent may frown on it as an instance of being "spendthrift." Of course, serious conflicts arise when multiple family members share the user role for the same product, such as products used in the common living areas—for example, what kind of pictures may be displayed in the living room. User-user conflicts are typically resolved by problem solving (e.g., by identifying alternatives that are acceptable to all members). In home buying, for example, spouses look for a house that is free from what we have called "the rejection-inducing dimension."

Next, user-payer role separation is the principal source of conflict, wherein payers exercise their power by ruling whether or not a particular product category would be bought. This conflict is often resolved by bargaining—for example, parents agree to buy their child something he or she wants in return for good performance in school. Among spouses, bargaining sometimes takes the shape of turn-taking in satisfying user wishes (e.g., "this season we go on vacation to where I want; next season you can have your wish.")

Finally, buyers are often in a position to control the brand choice—since they are the ones to implement the acquisition transaction—or their own user values, which can also cause conflict. For example, a teenager may buy household groceries from the corner store due to convenience, much to the dismay of more prudent shoppers that their parents might be. Or a homemaker may buy a generic or a store brand in accordance with her own user values or may not take the trouble to read nutrition labels, thus buying what other family members may consider inferior products. Such conflicts are generally resolved by persuasion.

Summary

We began this chapter with a discussion of the importance and challenge of studying household buying decisions. Principally, these decisions are complex because the user, payer, and buyer roles are shared among different household members. We then defined various types of family and nonfamily households and explained the movement of customers from one form of family to another due to a process of "family life cycle" (FLC). We described how the needs and wants of families at different stages of the FLC differ and why.

The family buying process was described as one in which different members of the family influence various stages of the decision process. Particularly, the relative influence of spouses in joint decision making was described as a "muddling-through process." The exact influence of either spouse was determined by such factors as gender roles, wife's employment status, family life cycle, time pressure, importance of purchase, and the socioeconomic development of the relevant population. Next, children's influence in family buying decisions was described. Children influence parental choices of products and services, as well as receive influence from parents in their own marketplace preferences. The latter process is captured in the concept of consumer socialization of children.

After childhood, the mutual influence of parents and children on each other continues into adult years of youngsters. This influence in either direction is termed intergenerational influence (IGI). IGI occurs because one generation (whether living in the same or a separate household) controls resources for another or has greater expertise than another or offers a power of identification over the other (i.e., the recipient of IGI identifies with the lifestyle and personality of the other generation and wants to be like its members).

Since family buying decisions are shared decisions with different members vying for influence and control, inevitably conflicts occur. We discussed various types of conflicts among the user, payer, and buyer roles. We also discussed four strategies of resolving these conflicts: problem solving, bargaining, persuasion, and politicking.

We then described a general framework for understanding family buying decisions. The model ties all of the preceding ideas and discussion together. The model views the choice as an outcome of autonomous or joint decision process with or without a conflict occurrence, which is then resolved by one of the four strategies. The decision process is affected by family characteristics (e.g., gender role orientation) as well as individual characteristics of various family members (e.g., their education). Also affecting the decision process are the nature of purchase (e.g., high risk or low risk) and sources of information utilized.

Finally, we identified three trends in households that change the character of family buying. These are the growing proportion of ethnic households, single parent households, and households with a history of divorce and remarriage. These changes in the American household reflect forces that will put continued pressure on the marketer to pay closer attention to who is using, buying, and paying for goods and services in households today.

Key Terms

Household 566
Family 568
Nonfamily Household 569
Family Life Cycle 569
Roommate Families 575
Autonomous Decisions 579
Syncratic Decisions 579
Joint Decisions 579

Gender Role Orientation 581
Social Orientation Families 584
Concept Oriented Families 584
Authoritarian Families 585
Neglectful Families 585

Democratic Families 585
Permissive Families 585
Consumer Socialization 587
Intergenerational Influence (IGI) 589
Democratic Justice 590
Family Relationship 591

Review Questions

1. How does a household differ from a family? How many different types of households have been identified to exist and what is their composition? Why is understanding the family and household composition important to the study of customer behavior?

2. Describe each stage of the modified family life cycle. How do these stages affect customer behavior and why should marketers be concerned about these different stages?

3. Describe the primary influences of customer socialization. Give a new example of each of these. Which influence is likely to be most dominant for the following products?

   a. Grocery/food items.

   b. Choice of a physician.

   c. Cosmetics and fashion clothing.

   d. Vacation spots.

4. Explain the concept of intergenerational influence (IGI). How is IGI related to consumer socialization? What similarities and differences exist between the two concepts? Give an example of each in comparing and contrasting the two.

5. Why does conflict arise in family customer decision making? What do families do to try to reduce conflict? What can companies do to help family members resolve their conflict?

6. You and a classmate are studying for your upcoming exam in consumer behavior. Your classmate missed part of the lecture on intergenerational influence and specifically the

discussion about the "yo-yo" generation. When you tell him that this will probably be on the test he says, "That's O.K. I already know a lot about this younger generation of kids and their desire to have toys just like the ones their parents used to play with." You sigh with frustration and then proceed to explain what "yo-yo" generation really means. What do you tell your classmate?

Applications

1. As demographic changes occur throughout the world, particularly as customer roles within the family change, marketers must keep abreast of these changes and alter their marketing strategies accordingly. Identify two or three changing customer roles within the family in your own country and give an example of what marketers ought to do in response to these changes.

2. The family buying decision process between spouses consists of several steps. Among them is the actual shopping and buying. We already know that the values important to the user are different than those that are important to the buyer and the payer, both involved in shopping and buying. For this step in the family decision buying process, what factors are likely to affect the pattern of decision sharing among spouses?

3. Review the chapter for various sources and mechanisms of intergenerational influence on household decision making. As a consumer yourself, think about the family or household you belong to (regardless of whether you are or are not currently living with your family members). Have you personally experienced IGI across households in your family? If you have, which mechanisms or sources of influence have been at work in your case? If not, explain why you might not have been susceptible to IGI.

Practical Experiences

1. Families have been classified into four broad types according to how different family members relate to one another (say, parents to children). Consider these four types and interview three of your friends, classmates, co-workers, acquaintances, and so on, from four different countries, and identify the extent to which these four types exist or do not exist in various cultures and countries. Furthermore, verify whether this classification of families has similar implications for family decision making in different countries.

2. Conduct an interview of children of the following age groups: (1) 7 years and younger, (2) between 8 and 13, (3) between 13 and 17. Ask them how they developed their preferences for their favorite brands of the following products and services:
   a. Breakfast cereal

   b. Sneakers

   c. Clothing

   d. Restaurants (fast food)

3. Contact a manager at any one of the following product-marketing companies: breakfast cereals, toys, personal care, home appliances, cooking products, athletic performance products, (e.g., sports goods) and clothing. Determine whether these companies utilize the concept of IGI and how they do it. If they do not currently utilize IGI, make a case for whether they should begin to utilize the concept and how.

4. As a follow-up to the research study conducted by consumer researcher C.W. Park, interview a couple who has recently made a large, expensive purchase (e.g., a home, a car, a piece of jewelry, and so on). The purpose of your interview is to be able to answer in your own words the

following questions:

  a. How similar or different were their decision plans?

  b. What "must" features did they have in common? Was there conflict in deciding these "must" features?

  c. Were individual spouses more satisfied on some features of the product than on others? What were they?

  d. Did spouses agree more with each other on salient objective dimensions (e.g., number of bedrooms, presence of swimming pool) than on subjective dimensions (e.g., the interior design, the type of landscaping)?

  e. Who was assigned role specification for what specific features and why?

5. Go to a movie theater that has many different movies playing simultaneously. Ask people as they are exiting the theater how they decided which movie they would see. In interviewing these customers, your purpose is to understand the following:

  a. Are they members of one family or a single household?

  b. Who made the decision to see this particular movie?

  c. Was there any disagreement on the choice of movie? If so, what was the nature of the disagreement? How was the conflict resolved?

  d. Finally, who influenced whom and how?

Compare your findings from people from one family or a single household versus your findings from people who are noncohabiting friends.

6. When people migrate into a new country, one of the first things they have to learn is how to go about acquiring the goods and services they need in the unfamiliar, new marketplace.

     Find three families who have come to your country from another country and one family from your home country. Ask them how they made their decisions about which products and brands to buy. Ask whether or not they were influenced by their parents' earlier education and socialization in terms of specific customer values. Finally, ask them whether they were influenced by any other agents (e.g., peers, the media, and so on) in their choice of certain types of products and specific brands. What differences exist across immigrant families from different countries? What differences exist between immigrant families and native-born families in terms of buying behaviors acquired from parents and from countries of past residence versus behaviors adopted anew in the new country?

Notes

[1] Based on U.S. government census estimates, obtained from the Internet Web site **http://www.census.gov/population/socdemo/ hh-fam/95his08.txt**; also see Gordon Green and Edward Welniak, "The Nine Household Markets," *American Demographics*, October 1991, p. 38.

[2] The U.S. Bureau of Census estimates drawn from the Internet site: **http://www.census.gov/population/socdemo /hh-fam/95**; also see U.S. Bureau of the Census, *Current Population Reports* (Washington, D.C.), 1992.

[3] U.S. Bureau of Census estimates drawn from the Internet site: **http://www.census.gov/population/ socdemo/hh-fam/95**

[4] McCarroll, "It's a Mass Market No More," *Time Magazine* (Fall 1993), pp. 80–81.

[5] Gordon Green and Edward Welniak, "The Nine Household Markets," *American Demographics* (October 1991), p. 38.

6 Frank Furstenbert and Graham Spanier, *Recycling the Family* (Thousand Oaks, California: Sage Publications, 1984).

7 "If Both Parents Are Breadwinners, Teenagers Often Are the Bread Buyers," *Marketing News* 21 (February, 1987) p. 5.

8 Jagdish N. Sheth, "Models of Buyer Behavior: Conceptual, Quantitative, and Empirical," in *A Theory of Family Buying Decisions*, (New York: Harper & Row), pp. 17–33.

9 Ibid.; Harry L. Davis, "Decision Making within the Household," *Journal of Consumer Research* 2 (March 1976), pp. 241–60.

10 C. Whan Park, "Joint Decisions in Home Purchasing: A Muddling-Through Process," *Journal of Consumer Research* 9 (September 1982), pp. 151–61.

11 Dennis L. Rosen and Donald H. Granbois, "Determinants of Role Structure in Family Financial Management," *Journal of Consumer Research* 10 (September 1983), pp. 253–58; Charles Schaninger and Chris T. Allen, "Wife's Occupational Status as a Consumer Behavior Construct," *Journal of Consumer Research* 8 (September 1981), pp. 189–96; Mary Lou Roberts and Lawrence H. Wortzel, "Role Transferral in the Household: A Conceptual Model and Partial Test," *Advances in Consumer Research* 9, (1982), pp. 261–66.

12 William J. Qualls, "Household Decision Behavior: The Impact of Husbands' and Wives' Sex Role Orientation," *Journal of Consumer Research* 14 (September, 1987) pp. 264–79.
    Elizabeth Moore-Shay and William L. Wilkie, "Recent Developments in Research on Family Decisions" *Advances in Consumer Research* 15 (1988), pp. 454–60.

13 Pierre Filiatrault and J. R. Ritchie, "Joint Purchasing Decisions: A Comparison of Influence Structure in Family and Couple Decision Making," *Journal of Consumer Research* 7 (September 1980), pp. 131–40.

14 George P. Moschis, "The Role of Family Communication in Consumer Socialization of Children and Adolescents," *Journal of Consumer Research* 11 (1985), pp. 898–913; George P. Moschis and Gilbert A. Churchill, "Consumer Socialization: A Theoretical and Empirical Analysis," *Journal of Marketing Research* 15 (1978), pp. 599–609; George P. Moschis and R.L. Moore, "Family Communication and Consumer Socialization," in W.L. Wilkie, ed., *Advances in Consumer Research*, 6 (Ann Arbor, MI: Association for Consumer Research (1979), pp. 757–59; George P. Moschis and L. G. Mitchell, "Television Advertising and Interpersonal Influences on Teenagers' Participation in Family Consumer Decisions," in R. J. Lutz, ed., *Advances in Consumer Research* 13 (Provo, UT: Association for Consumer Research 1986) pp. 181–86; George P. Moschis, A. E. Prahasto, and L. G. Mitchell, "Family Communication Influences on the Development of Consumer Behavior: Some Additional Findings," in R. J. Lutz, ed., *Advances in Consumer Research*, 13 (Provo, UT: Association for Consumer Research 1986), pp. 365–69.

15 Adapted from Conway Lackman and John M. Lanasa, "Family Decision Making: An Overview and Assessment," *Psychology and Marketing* 12 no 2 (March–April 1993), pp. 81–93; and from Les Carlson and Sanford Grossbart, "Parental Style and Consumer Socialization of Children," *Journal of Consumer Research* 15, no. 1 (June 1988), pp. 77–94.

16 Les Carlson and Sanford Grossbart.

17 Moschis and Moore 1982, Bahn 1986, and James U. McNeal, "The Littlest Shoppers," *American Demographics*, Vol. 14, No. 2 (February 1992), pp. 48–53.

18 Moschis and Churchill, 1978, Ibid.

19 Carole M. Macklin, "Do Children Understand TV Ads?" *Journal of Advertising Research*, 23, (1983), no. 1 pp. 63–70.

20 See Jean Piaget, *The Child's Conception of the World* (New York: Harcourt Brace, 1928).

21 Moschis and Moore; Scott Ward and Daniel Wackman, "Children's Purchase Influence Attempts and Parental Yielding," *Journal of Marketing Research* 9 (August 1972), pp. 316–19; G. W. Peterson and B. C. Rollins, "Parent Child Socialization," in M. B. Sussman and S. K. Steinmetz, eds. *Handbook of Marriage and Family* (New York: Plenum Press), pp. 471–507; Jan Møller Jensen, "Children's Purchase Requests and Parental Responses: Results from an Exploratory Study in Denmark," in Flemming Hansen, *European Advances in Consumer Behavior*, Vol. 2 (Provo, UT:

Association for Consumer Research, 1995), pp. 61–68. Sanford Grossbart, Les Carlson, and Ann Walsh, "Consumer Socialization Motive for Shopping with Children," *AMA Educator's Proceedings* (1988); Bonnie B. Reece, Sevgin Eroglu, and Nora J. Rifon, "Parents Teaching Children to Shop: How, What, and Who?" *AMA Educators' Proceedings* (1988) pp. 274–78; Les Carlson and Sanford Grossbart, "Parental Style and Consumer Socialization of Children," *Journal of Consumer Research* 15 (1988), pp. 77–94.

22 For an exhaustive annotated review of the literature in this area, see Reshma H. Shah, "Toward a Theory of Intergenerational Influence: A Framework for Assessing the Differential Impact of Varying Sources of Influence on the Preferences and Consumption Values of Adult Children," Unpublished working paper, University of Pittsburgh, 1992.

23 Ruby Roy Dholkia, "Intergenerational Differences in Consumer Behavior: Some Evidence from a Developing Country," *Journal of Business Research* 12, no. 1 (1984), pp. 19–34; Patricia Sorce, Philip R. Tyler, and Lynette Loomis, "Intergenerational Influence on Consumer Decision Making," *Advances in Consumer Research* 16 (1989), pp. 271–75.

24 See Shah (1992) for an annotated review of the literature covering the origins of IGI's from parent to child; D. Riesman and H. Roseborough, "Careers and Consumer Behavior," in *Consumer Behavior, Vol. 2: The Life Cycle and Consumer Behavior*, in L. H. Clark (Ed.), New York, NY: New York University Press, 1995.

25 This section is adapted from Reshma H. Shah and Banwari Mittal, "The Role of Intergenerational Influence in Consumer Choice: Toward an Exploratory Theory," eds. Merrie Brucks and Debbie MacInnis, *Advances in Consumer Research* (Provo, UT: Association for Consumer Research, 1997), pp. 55–60.

26 An interesting conceptual framework with a description of group decision-making processes in conflict situations is found in Kim P. Corfman and Donald R. Lehmann, "Models of Cooperative Group Decision-Making and Relative Influence: An Experimental Investigation of Family Purchase Decisions." *Journal of Consumer Research* 14 (June 1987), pp. 1–13, also see Rosann L. Spiro, "Persuasion in Family Decision Making," *Journal of Consumer Research* 10 (March 1983), pp. 393–402; and Daniel Seymour and Greg Lessne, "Spousal Conflict Arousal: Scale Development," *Journal of Consumer Research* 11 (December 1984), pp. 810–21.

After reading this chapter you should be able to:

Compare and contrast business buying and household buying.

Identify ways to classify business customers.

List the steps in the business buying process.

Describe characteristics that influence this process.

Define buying center and discuss how that concept helps explain the buying decisions of businesses.

Summarize how conflicts among decision makers are resolved.

Describe new developments in organizational purchasing.

Compare and contrast government and businesses as buyers as well as the buying processes of each.

Identify the steps in the government procurement process and major regulations governing government buying.

Explain how governments use procurement as a tool of social policy.

Business and Government Customer Decision Making

Airbus or Boeing? Which Plane Would Your Company Buy?

December 19 of last year was both a happy and a sad day for Airbus Industries, a European consortium, and the maker of commercial airplanes. On that day, Swissair awarded to Airbus a contract to buy 15 planes—six A330-20 to be delivered in 1999 and nine A340-600 for delivery in 2002. What is interesting here is the fact that Swissair had been a customer of rival U.S.-based Boeing for the past 26 years. Swissair is replacing its old fleet of Boeing 747s with Airbus's 378-seat A340-600 jumbo jets.

On the same day, however, Airbus lost two business deals to rival Boeing. First, El Al Israel Airlines announced that it was buying its next fleet of five planes from Boeing to be delivered in 1999. And, second, Turkish Airlines signed an agreement to buy 26 Boeing 737-800 aircrafts. In both the deals for Boeing, the U.S. government seemed to have applied its influence. The U.S. government gives Israel $3 billion a year in foreign aid and consequently was able to exercise considerable influence on state-run El Al Airlines, although a company spokesperson attributed the decision to a 6 percent discount offered by Boeing. As for the Turkish Airline, Turkey was desperately seeking closer ties with Washington, following its recent exclusion from the European Union. In fact, the Turkish Airline contract was signed at the White House, with Turkish Prime Minister Mesut Yilmaz and U.S. vice president Al Gore looking on! Such is the dynamics of purchase decisions by business and government customers.[1]

Introduction

In selling to business and government customers, one thing becomes immediately clear. The decision processes of business and government customers differ vastly from those of the individual and household customers. The challenge of marketing to organizational customers therefore is to understand the decision-making process of organizational customers as end users, payers, and buyers. These customers include business and government customers, as well as institutions (both private and public) such as universities, hospitals, religious groups, and charitable organizations, which purchase products and services for use by their employees, members, or clients.

(In contrast, resellers, such as distributors and retailers, generally take on only the roles of buyers and payers. Therefore, we cover the reseller's buying behavior separately in Chapter 17.)

In the present chapter, we examine the roles and processes entailed in organizational buying, first for business firms and then for government. We begin by describing the types and general buying behavior of business customers. Then the chapter discusses the components of the business buying process, including the steps in, influences on, and participants in the process. We also discuss how decision makers in this process resolve conflicts. The section on business buying closes with a summary of some trends that have been changing the nature of this process. The next part of the chapter covers the buying behavior of government. It explores ways in which business buying behavior and government buying behavior differ from and resemble one another. It describes procedures and regulations that characterize government buying, as well as challenges and rewards of doing business with the government. Finally, we explore developments in government buying.

Business Buying Behavior

A **business** is a licensed entity engaged in the activity of making, buying, or selling products and services for profit or nonprofit objectives. This definition considers any organization that makes and sells something to be a business. As customers, businesses buy products or services to provide value for their customers, employees, or owners (i.e., the key stakeholders). For example, the purchasing department buys raw materials, components, supplies, support services, and machinery to fulfill the needs of its employees related to their jobs. Many business firms view their purchasing departments as "value centers"— their charge is to constantly strive to create value for the firm, by finding sources of better products at lower total costs.

Marketers have developed different ways of serving household and business customers, in part because of differences in the behavior of these two customer groups. Business buying typically differs from household buying in several key ways: greater specialization of roles, more formalization of the buying process, more formal accountability for decisions, greater internal capabilities, and more complex requirements (see Table 16.1).

Specialization of Customer Roles

As we explained in Chapters 14 and 15, individual buying requires that the three customer roles—payer, buyer, and user—be combined in a single individual, whereas in household buying decisions, these roles may be held by a single person or distributed among various family members. Such role specialization is even more marked in business buying. Thus, even more

	COMPARISON OF HOUSEHOLD AND BUSINESS BUYING	
Table 16.1		

CHARACTERISTIC	HOUSEHOLD BUYING	BUSINESS BUYING
Specialization of customer roles	Combined or slightly specialized	Moderately to very specialized
Formalization of the buying process	Informal	Slightly formal (small businesses) to formal (large businesses)
Accountability for decisions	Usually not formally measured	Strict measures
Internal capabilities	Weak	Weak (small businesses) to very strong (large businesses)
Complexity of requirements	Little complexity	Operational and strategic complexity

than in the household buying, the three roles separate out. An exception to this pattern is a one-person entrepreneur, who makes decisions equivalent to individual decision making.

Formalization of the Buying Process

Business buying is formalized with respect to policy, procedures, and paperwork. Generally, businesses have written policies and rules to guide the solicitation of price quotes, preferential treatment to a certain class of vendors (e.g., minority businesses), and the way the decisions are to be made in the buying firm. They prepare and sign detailed contracts that specify the obligations of each party. This degree of formalization is rare in family buying behavior.[2]

The degree of formalization may vary from business to business. Small business firms tend to be less formal and, therefore, similar to household buyers. This occurs often because small companies tend to be owner-managed businesses (OMBs). At the other extreme, regulated industries (telecommunications and utilities) and government organizations tend to have more formal policies, procedures, and paperwork. Large business customers tend to be somewhere in the middle.

Accountability for Decisions

Unlike household buying, business buying holds accountable those who are in charge of paying and buying. This results in more formal evaluation of and feedback on these purchase decisions. There are also internal and external audits of the buying process to ensure that value obtained through procurement is maintained and enhanced by the decision makers.

This greater accountability in business arises because ownership is divorced from management, and buying is divorced from usage. Therefore, business buying encourages formal supplier ratings and scorecards as well as constant feedback and communication to its suppliers.

Internal Capabilities

More often than households, business customers are capable of producing certain items in-house rather than buying them from others. This capability requires business customers to analyze the economics of the "make versus buy" options. Even when the decision is to buy rather than make, the internal capability to make the product gives the buyer clout

Business buying is different from household buying.

among potential suppliers. Thus, sellers to business customers cannot forget that the customer can become a competitor by self-producing the item rather than buying it.

Complexity of Requirements

Business customers have both operational and strategic complexity of buying behavior. Operationally, the number of employees who participate in the buying process, often from several locations, adds complexity. Further complexity results from the need to adhere to government rules and regulations related to reciprocity of buying and selling to one another. Finally, many business buying decisions involve multiple authority and expertise levels, making the process even more complex.

Additionally, procurement is often a strategic function. It is often the single largest cost center to a business organization. This cost center is responsible for buying both capital goods and materials, so the risks associated with failure are enormous. For example, the purchase of a wrong chemical in a product can create a significant health hazard in processed foods or drugs. Or, as another example, buying a network computing system that turns out to be unreliable can shut down operations in such major businesses as airlines, health care, and banking. Because the risks associated with unsound procurement are high, organizations view it as a strategic function.

Components of the Business Buying Process

With purchasing being such a significant and complex function, all but the smallest organizations have formal systems for carrying it out. These systems, called procurement systems, have several components, shown in Figure 16.1: nature of the purchase, organizational characteristics, buying center, rules and procedures, and a decision process. These components also exist in small businesses, but tend to be simpler and less rigidly defined. By determining the way the components fit together in a particular business, marketers can describe the business's customer behavior.

Nature of the Purchase

The way an organization makes a purchase decision depends to a large degree on the nature of the purchase. This nature is defined by the buyclass (type of purchase need); the significance of the decision in terms of perceived risk, importance, and product complexity; and the time pressure faced by the decision makers.

BUYCLASS

For an individual, purchase needs may require routine problem solving, limited problem solving, or extended problem solving. Similarly, businesses have three types of procurement needs, or **buyclasses**: straight rebuy, modified rebuy, and new task.

A **straight rebuy** is a need that has been processed and fulfilled before. It is for an item that is needed repeatedly and has been bought before. Examples include shop supplies (e.g., lubricants), worker uniforms, and office stationery. Moreover, the outcome has been satisfactory, and the total costs are low so there is no need to reopen the supplier search process. The gains in savings from a new search and a fresh decision are unlikely

Figure 16.1

COMPONENTS OF THE BUSINESS BUYING PROCESS

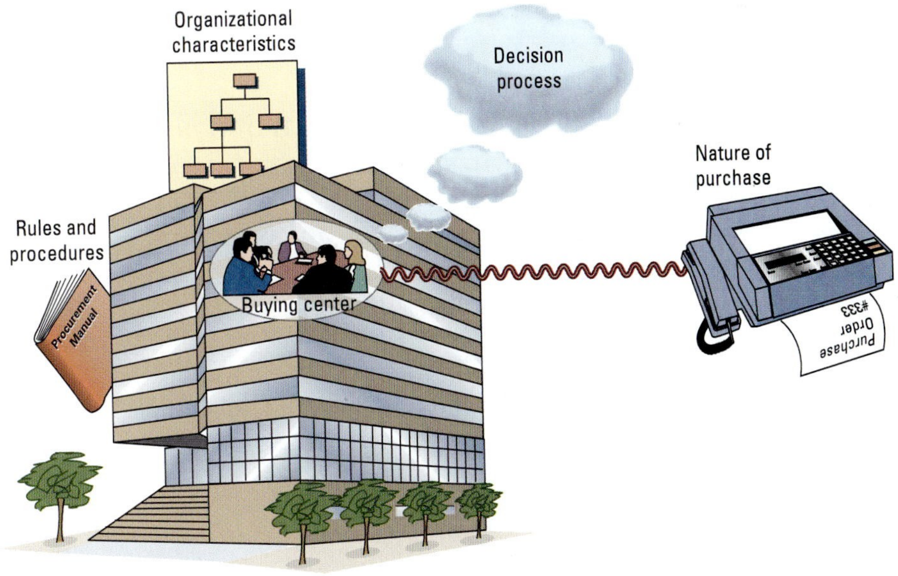

to be significant, and at any rate unlikely to outweigh the costs of the effort. Thus, the business simply places the order with one of the past suppliers. For these items, businesses often negotiate an annual purchasing agreement. They may computerize procurement of straight rebuys, perhaps reordering these items automatically.

A **modified rebuy** represents a need that is similar in broad nature to the previously fulfilled needs, but entails some changes either in design/performance specifications or in the supply environment. For example, the organization has bought sheet metal before, but of a different gauge (i.e., thickness) than needed now. Or the firm wants to buy some more desk-top computers; although the firm has bought these before, it wants to re-examine the latest technology available. Or the consultant services it bought last time were good, but the firm's executives wonder if a better consulting firm might exist. Or, finally, a new supplier of high reputation has entered the copier market, and the firm desires to evaluate this new supplier for its next purchase of copiers.

New task purchases pertain to those needs that are new to the organization. A purchase of this item has never been made, and indeed the need has never been experienced before. Therefore, there is considerable uncertainty about the design/performance requirements, which are still being assessed. Also, suppliers may not already be on the company list, and at any rate new suppliers may need to be added and all suppliers may have to be appraised anew.

The concept of buyclass is important because the purchase process is different across the three buyclasses (see Table 16.2). On a continuum of straight rebuy to modified rebuy to new task, the more the purchase is of the new task type, the more the buying group:

- Perceives the need for information.
- Is large.
- Is deliberative and patient.
- Is concerned with finding a good solution.
- Underplays low price and assured supply as evaluation criteria.
- Will consider new suppliers.
- Will value the influence of technical persons, relative to the influence of buying agents.[3]

Table 16.2

BUYING BEHAVIOR ASSOCIATED WITH BUYCLASSES

BUYCLASS	DESCRIPTION OF NEED	BUYING CENTER SIZE	INFORMATION SEARCH
Straight rebuy	Item is frequently needed and has been satisfactorily bought before	Very small; ordering may even be automated	Brief or nonexistent; new suppliers rarely considered; technical expertise rarely sought
Modified rebuy	Need is broadly similar to one that has been fulfilled before but requires some change in specifications or the supply environment	Moderate	Some information is gathered; new suppliers may be considered; technical experts may have input into decision
New task	Need is completely new to the organization	Large	Extensive; new suppliers often considered experts usually have major input into decision

PERCEIVED RISK, IMPORTANCE, AND COMPLEXITY

Each type of purchase involves a different level of perceived risk, importance, and complexity for the decision maker. Business customers use information such as the type of purchase to estimate risk, importance, and complexity. Then they adjust their decision-making strategy accordingly.

Perceived risk refers to the expected probability that the purchase may not produce a satisfactory outcome. It is a product of two factors:

1. The degree of uncertainty that a choice may be wrong.

2. The amount at stake should a wrong choice occur.

Uncertainty stems from the absence of prior design/performance specifications and from lack of experience with potential suppliers. Thus, new tasks have the most uncertainty, and straight rebuys the least. Amount at stake is the financial loss or performance loss from a sub-optimal choice. Financial loss depends on the purchase price in absolute terms (the more expensive the purchase, the greater the financial loss) as well as from a less advantageous price (the supplier chosen may not be the best-priced supplier). Performance loss comes from the product not performing to standards, which may, in fact, cause systemwide damage (e.g., a chemical ingredient of lesser purity than required might damage the processing equipment).

The **importance of purchase** is a combination of the amount at stake and the extent to which the product plays a strategic role in the organization. The higher the amount at stake, and the more strategic the product's role, the more important the purchase. Thus, a large fleet of transportation vehicles might cost more than, say, a communication network; yet the latter might be viewed as a more important purchase due to its strategic role in equipping the customer firm for the information age.

Complexity refers to the extensiveness of effort it takes to comprehend and manage the product during its acquisition. Complexity has two dimensions: (1) the number of performance dimensions, and (2) the technical and specialist knowledge required to understand those dimensions. Thus, a single dimensional product like a chemical is simpler

"Chairs that heighten your productivity"—Haworth heightens the perceived importance *of its product for business customers.*

than a multidimensional item like a personal computer (even though the risk might be greater with the purchase of a chemical than with that of a computer). Office furniture is less technical than surgical sutures. The latter require more specialist knowledge to understand the design/performance characteristics and the supplier information.

As the foregoing examples suggest, importance, complexity, and perceived risk are often related, but not always. Together, these influence how extensive and involved the purchase decision process will be. As perceived risk increases, more individuals will participate in the decision; decision makers will deliberate more; a wide range of information sources will be consulted; product quality will be emphasized over price; and conflict and role stress among decision makers will increase. See the Window on Research box, which summarizes the findings of 25 years of research on perceived risk and organizational buying.

What Perceived Risk Does to Business Buying Behavior

WINDOW ON RESEARCH

Over the past quarter century, researchers have studied extensively the impact of perceived risk on buying behavior. Their findings have supported the view that when business customers perceive high risk, they adjust their buying behavior to protect themselves and their organizations.

For example, with higher perceived risk, the buying group (center) becomes more complex. That is, more people are involved in the purchase decision throughout the purchase process, and they are drawn from a greater variety of departmental and/or organizational interests. Additionally, buying center participants will generally be of higher organizational status and authority; if not, the buying center will not have authority to make the final purchase decision. Instead, its function will be to (1) gather and evaluate relevant information, and (2) make recommendations to upper-level management.

Participants in a high-risk purchase decision process are more educated and experienced in their area of expertise. Also, since the purchase decision is important, participants are motivated to expend greater effort and deliberate more carefully throughout the purchase process.

High-risk decisions favor sellers who offer proven products and solutions. Product quality and after-sale service will be of the utmost importance. Price will be considered only after product and service criteria have been fully met. If (after careful scrutiny) two or more sellers appear equally capable of satisfying purchase requirements, price will play a dominant role in the purchase decision.

Information search is active, and a wide variety of information sources are used to guide and support the purchase decision. Buying center participants may rely more heavily on impersonal, commercial information sources (e.g., trade publications, sales literature) during the earlier stages of the decision process. As the procurement decision progresses, personal, noncommercial information sources (e.g., consultants, other organizations that have already made similar purchases) may become more important.

Within the buying firm, conflict between buying center participants increases. One reason is that more departments (through their representatives) are involved in the purchase decision. Also, since the purchase outcome is important, buying center participants will be reluctant to make concessions without some form of reciprocal reward. Therefore, buying center participants will most likely use a "bargaining" (tit for tat) negotiation strategy.

Role stress among decision makers increases. One cause is the size and complexity of the buying center, resulting in greater conflict among participants with differing perspectives and motivations. Also, in a highly visible (important) purchase where the outcome is uncertain, the chances of making a "wrong" decision and the associated consequences of a "wrong" decision intensify participant stress.

Source: Wesley J. Johnston and Jeffrey E. Lewin, "Organizational Buying Behavior: Toward an Integrative Framework," *Journal of Business Research*, 1996, 35 (January), pp. 1–15. Additional information available at **http://www.mcb.co.uk/cgibin/journal1/jbim**

TIME PRESSURE

Customers behave differently when they are under time pressure. Time pressure refers simply to how urgently the item is needed. When the item is needed urgently, the purchase decision will tend to short-circuit the usual process, make the process less deliberative, and give more direct role to the user/requisitioner.

Organizational Characteristics

Four organizational characteristics of the customer firm affect buying behavior: (1) size, (2) structure, (3) purchase resources, and (4) purchase orientation.

SIZE

The size of the business determines not only the customer's potential dollar volume, but also the sophistication of its buying process. Small business organizations behave more like a family in their buying behavior; entrepreneurial firms usually consist of a one-person purchasing group and thus resemble an individual buying decision. Large organizations, in contrast, have larger buying groups and more formalized procedures.

STRUCTURE

A business's structure refers to the number of departmental units, geographical locations over which the units are spread out, and its degree of centralization. The more departments a business has, the larger the buying group and more prolonged the buying process is likely to be. Multilocation buying firms create more complexity for the seller than single locale firms. For example, a firm selling construction equipment may have to visit the administrative headquarters of a construction firm as well as its construction site managers.

PURCHASE RESOURCES

Purchase resources refer to the availability of professional buyers and the extent to which the purchase office is staffed with the required type and number of experts as well as equipment (e.g., computerized supplier information system). Generally, large and professionally managed (as opposed to owner-managed) firms would have better resourced purchasing departments.

When purchasing departments are staffed with well-qualified personnel, the vendor evaluation is more formal as well as rigorous. Staff shortage leads to less well-evaluated decisions and greater reliance on current vendors because there is not enough time available to entertain and appraise proposals from new vendors. Furthermore, when purchasing departments lack the necessary personnel with requisite technical skills, complex or technical purchasing tasks may be outsourced to external consultants.

PURCHASE ORIENTATION

The organization's purchase orientation refers to its purchasing philosophy along a continuum from viewing purchasing simply as an administrative function that finds the most economical sources of materials needed as and when they are needed to viewing it as a strategic, managerial function whose goal is to add value to the organization's ability in turn to offer better value to its customers. As a strategic function, purchasing is engaged in several key activities:

- Scrutinizing make versus buy decisions—it questions the very need to buy something, or even whether rather than buying an intermediate product and then converting it into a final marketable product, it may not be better to buy the whole thing.
- Continually finding better products, materials, and technology.
- Developing long-term sources of supply and building relationships with the suppliers.

These two ends of the continuum may be referred to as reactive and proactive buying, respectively.

The Buying Center

In all but the smallest organizations, purchase decisions are handled by a formal or informal **buying center**—a multifunction, multilevel internal organization that is responsible for the centralized purchasing function. The buying center represents a subset of *roles* within the organization who participate in the buying process. Several roles have been identified:

- *User*—This is the user department who would use the product to be purchased by an organization.

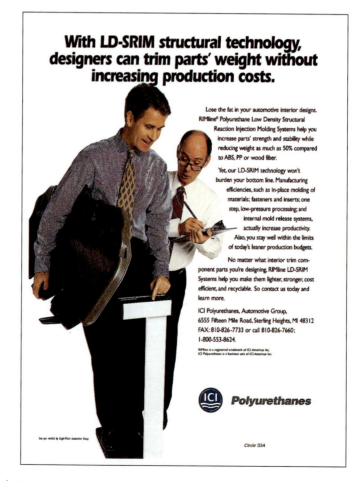

In selling to business customers, marketers address the concerns of multiple roles in the buying center—shown here are user and payer concerns.

- *Buyer*—The buyer, alternatively called purchasing manager, purchasing executive, and so on, has the formal authority to execute the purchase contract and place a purchase order.
- *Analyzer*—One who performs technical analysis of suppliers by using such tools as cost analysis, value analysis, and so on.
- *Influencer*—By their expert advice, these role holders influence the evaluative criteria and supplier ratings and/or the final decision itself. Typically, these are design engineers and external consultants.
- *Gatekeepers*—They regulate the flow of information from suppliers to the other members of the buying center. They permit or deny salespersons access to design and user departments or to other executives.
- *Decider*—The deciders make the final decision. This role may be played by a formal buying committee, or by the CEO, CFO, or purchasing executive alone. Sometimes, the user and engineering departments short list and rank the suppliers, and then a high-level executive who may or may not be a member of any buying committee makes the final decision.

The buying center roles (user, influencer, etc.) are roles, not titles or persons (except that the roles of "user" and "buyer" are also the names of the positions). An individual may play multiple roles, such as influencer and gatekeeper. Although various executives may play a crucial role in the buying decision, personnel from three departments are typically involved more extensively: purchasing, manufacturing, and quality control.

"Buying center" is a concept and should not be confused with buying committees many organizations may have. When buying committees exist, persons other than those on the formal committee may influence the decision and are therefore deemed to be a part of the buying center concept. When buying committees do not exist, buying centers still exist as "virtual groups"—they may have not been appointed but do operate inasmuch as various individuals spread throughout the organization play some role in some specific purchase. Conceptually, different buying centers come into being for individual purchases.

That buying center is a concept is precisely its merit. The concept tells us that a salesperson must look beyond the formal buying committees and/or formal titles, and seek to identify the members who are playing various roles of the buying center concept.

Rules and Procedures

Businesses generally set up elaborate policies (e.g., favor a minority supplier), rules (e.g., purchase needs must be consolidated for the entire organization), and procedures (e.g., minimum number of bids required). The degree of formalization and decision freedom varies from buyer to buyer. If the buying firm is less obligated to adhere to prescribed rules and procedures, a business marketer has a lot more freedom to innovate and add value to offerings and educate the buyer about it.

Decision Process

Like individual and household buying decisions, organizational buying decisions entail a multistage process. Business buying decisions comprise the following stages:

- Need assessment—Deciding the technical and performance specifications for the needed item.
- Developing choice criteria—Identifying supplier selection criteria.
- Request for proposals (RFPs)—Calling for proposals by publishing requests for quotes (RFQs) and inviting suppliers to submit bids. Additional suppliers are actively solicited if

adequate suppliers are not already on the list. For suppliers who submit proposals, additional information is collected about their capabilities and past performance. This information comes from suppliers themselves and, importantly, from other independent sources such as consultants, trade associations, word-of-mouth, and formal rating reports from independent sources.

- Supplier evaluation—Rank-ordering vendors. Some negotiations may occur toward reconciling differences both on technical aspects and on price variations among various bidders or suppliers.
- Supplier selection—Awarding the contract or placing an order.
- Fulfillment and monitoring—Monitoring for smooth fulfillment in a timely fashion and to the satisfaction of the buyers and users.

These steps are similar to individual decision making except that there is a lot more formal analysis as well as use of more structured procedures. The Window on Research box on page 624 describes the buying process customer researchers found in their study of business purchases of items purchased on a long-term contract and on a repeat purchase basis.

Various roles in the buying center participate more in some stages than others (see Table 16.3). Generally, users exercise more influence at the need assessment and choice criteria stages; buyers shoulder the major responsibility at the RFP, supplier search, and fulfillment stages; analyzers help most at the supplier evaluation stage; influencers, at supplier evaluation and selection stages; and decision makers, at the vender selection stages. Gatekeepers, of course, would be active throughout, depending on the inflow of information, influence, and salesperson communications, all vying for the decision makers' attention. However, the exact pattern of influence each member exercises at each decision stage varies from case to case.

It is the task of a business-to-business salesperson and marketer to identify and map this pattern for each business client individually. According to a recent survey reported in *Purchasing* magazine, engineering and technical staff participate more during the need identification and specification generation stages, whereas purchasing agents/managers participate more in the later stages of identifying the sources of supply and evaluating and choosing them (see Table 16.4).

Table 16.3

VARYING INFLUENCE OF BUYING CENTER ROLES

BUYING CENTER ROLES

	USER	BUYER	DECIDER	ANALYZER	INFLUENCER	GATEKEEPER
Need assessment	√√		√		√	
Vendor search		√√	√√		√√	√√
Choice criteria	√	√		√	√√	
RFP		√√				
Supplier evaluation				√√	√√	
Selection	√	√	√√	√	√	√√
Fulfillment/monitoring	√√	√√				

√ Influence
√√ Strong Influence

PARTICIPATION OF FUNCTION IN VARIOUS DECISION STAGES

Table 16.4

DECISION STAGE	ENGINEERING	PURCHASING	PRODUCTION	MARKETING	TOP MANAGEMENT	OTHER
Recognize need for materials or components to go into finished product	82	53	40	32	27	4
Decide what materials or components will be used, and agree on performance specs	89	41	23	27	17	3
Investigate and evaluate potential suppliers who can meet these specifications	47	85	15	11	15	1
Choose suppliers for the initial buy	48	81	11	7	7	3
Choose suppliers for repeat buys	20	87	17	4	8	1

Note: The above findings are based on a survey of design engineers. Numbers are percent of respondents indicating participation.
Source: "Purchasing Pros Do Select Suppliers—Really," *Purchasing,* April 3, 1997, p. 22.

PROCUREMENT COSTS

In business buying, when decision makers weigh costs, they consider the total costs of a purchase. The total costs are more than the purchase price, sometimes significantly higher. These costs consists of acquisition costs, possession costs, and usage costs. These three component costs consist of the items listed in Table 16.5.

As a business-to-business supplier, a firm should understand and know these costs for a specific customer, then design market offerings in a way that reduces the customer's total costs, rather than just the selling price. A marketer can even use this as a selling tool to educate the customer about how, for example, his or her price may appear disadvantageous, but the total costs are lower than the competitor's and thus offer the buyer better value. Buying centers that view themselves as a "value center" for their firm are concerned most with the total costs and net value, rather than just the quoted price.

For example, if a machine from vendor A costs $800 to buy but consumes electricity costing $200 a year, and another comparable machine from vendor B costs $900 but consumes only $50 worth of electricity, then the total cost is lower for make B. Vendor B should educate the prospective customer about the total lower cost of its offering.

COMPONENTS OF A BUSINESS CUSTOMER'S TOTAL COSTS

Table 16.5

ACQUISITION COSTS	POSSESSION COSTS	USAGE COSTS
Price	Interest cost	Field defects
Paperwork cost	Storage cost	Training cost
Shopping time	Quality control	User labor cost
Expediting cost	Taxes and insurance	Product longevity
Cost of mistakes in order	Shrinkage and obsolescence	Replacement costs
Prepurchase product evaluation costs	General internal handling costs	Disposal costs

Source: Frank V. Cespedes, "Industrial Marketing: Managing New Requirements," *Sloan Management Review,* Spring 1994, MIT.

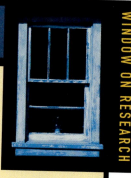

How Businesses Award Long-Term Contracts for Repeat-Purchase Items

To study the process of selecting a vendor for long-term contracts, customer researchers Niren Vyas and Arch Woodside interviewed managers in six buying firms. Among the 18 products included in the study were corrugated boxes, metal bars, rubber gaskets, fuel oil, electric cables—a sample of all three buyclasses.

Based on their study, the researchers described the vendor selection decision as comprising five steps:

1. *Identifying the suppliers*: For straight rebuy and modified rebuy items, the buyer firm already had a list of potential suppliers. For "new task" items, potential suppliers were identified from prior experience, advice from design engineers, and trade journals.

2. *Qualifying the suppliers*: Buyers assessed suppliers on such factors as capacity, location, manufacturing facility, and financial resources—judged from brochures, salesmen-supplied information, and plant visits. To qualify suppliers, buyers applied conjunctive decision rules (a "list of required minimums"). Some buyers had a policy of including minority suppliers in the list even if this necessitated relaxing some criteria.

3. *Inviting bids*: The buyers issued RFQs (requests for quotations), which detail the design specifications and product performance criteria. The specifications are generated by design and production engineers, based on their technical need and their knowledge of what is available. Buyers preferred to have at least three bidders. If the list of qualified suppliers was long, the conjunctive decision rule was made more demanding (i.e., "the required minimums" were raised). If this step left more than three bidders, buyers tried to eliminate other suppliers with a lexicographic rule (i.e., eliminate the supplier with the least-attractive value on the most desirable criteria).

4. *Bid evaluation*: Bids are evaluated on both technical and commercial criteria. Commercial evaluation, done by the purchasing department, entails checking payment terms, price escalation, labor contracts expiration dates, shipping terms, and so on. Technical evaluation was done by user departments and design engineers, generally without the price information so that the technical evaluation was unbiased. A chief goal was to determine the amount of price premium to allow suppliers for superior quality and service. None of the firms used a formal evaluation system, so the price premium decision was simply an intuitive judgment by the buying center.

5. *Bid selection*: If only one bid was received, buyers started immediate negotiations with the bidder on price and delivery schedule. With multiple bids, the first decision was whether to patronize more than one supplier. Buyers often preferred the bargaining advantage of two (or more) suppliers. Factors that affected the final selection were successful experience with a bidder, supplier reputation, and location of the service organization. These factors were weighed against the quoted price in a compensatory decision rule (i.e., the lack of one factor is compensated by superiority on others). The lowest bidder was often selected, but bidders with as much as 6 percent price premium over the lowest bidder were sometimes awarded the contract. When multiple suppliers were selected, the current supplier was given more than 50 percent of the annual order.

Source: Adapted from Niren Vyas and Arch G. Woodside, "An Inductive Model of Industrial Supplier Choice Process," *Journal of Marketing* 48 (Winter 1984), pp. 30–45. Additional information available at **http://www.ama.org/pubs/jm**

PSYCHOLOGY OF DECISION MAKERS

The decision-making process is primarily driven by two psychological processes occurring in the decision makers: (1) their expectations and (2) their perceptual distortions.

EXPECTATIONS One factor that sets organizational decision making apart from individual and household decision making is that the various members of the buying center tend to have a set of differential expectations. Their expectations are influenced by their background and their satisfaction or dissatisfaction with past purchases.[4]

The background that shapes expectations comprises educational and work experiences. Since different individuals have different backgrounds, their expectations differ. Persons with different technical backgrounds emphasize different decision criteria (e.g., engineers focus on technical factors and buyers focus on price factors). Expectations are created also by role orientations. Thus a buying agent who views her or his role primarily as one of managing the purchase budget expects the buying decisions to proceed in one way; in contrast, a buying manager who views her or his role as more proactive (rather than reactive) would expect the purchase decision to be made more deliberatively and with long-term interests.

The second source of individual expectations, satisfaction with prior buying experiences with suppliers, focuses on the price and quality of previously purchased products. Those who experienced satisfactory outcomes will tend to expect the existing suppliers to be more qualified for the future purchase as well. Prior experience might also be used to generalize from limited evidence. A buyer might expect, for example, that CPA firms are not a good source of management consultancy or that small businesses cannot supply sophisticated computer components.

PERCEPTUAL DISTORTIONS   Business customers, like individual consumers, encode incoming information selectively (attending to some and ignoring other information) and in a biased manner. This tendency is called selective perceptual distortion. Expectations play a major role in selective perceptions. Thus, some buying center members might expect that only engineers are able to understand product specifications; they might then discount as unreliable any information that salespeople provide, assuming they do not have an engineering background. Such a premise might be entirely misguided, but the resulting perceptual distortion might cost a supplier an order.

CONFLICT AND ITS RESOLUTION

When expectations of various members in the buying center differ, conflicts arise. These may concern either the relative weight of the evaluative criteria or the rating of different suppliers on these criteria. Given their perspectives, some buying center members may give more credence to some information than to other information.

When conflicts arise, they may be resolved in the four different ways introduced in Chapter 15: problem solving, persuasion, bargaining, and politicking.[5]

Problem solving is a rational approach to conflict resolution. It entails a search for more information, further deliberation on the new information, and possibly consideration of new suppliers. If the conflict is due to disagreements on what is to be expected from the suppliers and their products, then the conflict will likely be resolved in the problem-solving manner.

Persuasion, also a rational method of conflict resolution, is used when there is a disagreement on specific criteria for supplier evaluation (but overall agreement on what is to be expected of them). Resolution comes by some members demonstrating how the other person's position will lead to suboptimal outcome on overall goals. In this method, additional information is not gathered, but further deliberation among existing parties continues, and may even proceed to the inclusion of an outside party to resolve the conflict.

When the difference between the buying parties centers on basic goals and objectives, the conflict resolution method shifts from a rational orientation to **bargaining,** which hinges on distributive justice for all. This method is quite common in the case of a new task purchase. Resolution begins by a recognition and acceptance of differences in goals of dissenting members. Thus, no one attempts to change these goals. Rather, the dissenting members negotiate give and take. Ultimately, and generally, one party winds up making the decision in return for granting some favor to the others in the future.

In **politicking,** resolution comes from back-stabbing techniques and centers on the use of an efficient, nonrational approach to dealing with conflicts. Members form partisan coalitions and then "manage" the decision with behind-the-scenes maneuvering. Politicking is used if the disagreement stems from the *style* of decision making used in the process. This often centers on personalities as opposed to substance and is the result of personal hostilities between people who are able to vent their anxieties or dissatisfaction with some members in a professional setting. The organization suffers when this method is used, as decisions either get delayed or are resolved in a manner not consistent with the overall goals and objectives of the organization.

A Comprehensive Model of Organizational Customer Behavior

To bring together the individual components of the business procurement system, we can diagram a comprehensive model of organizational buyer behavior, such as the one in Figure 16.2. This diagram unites concepts from several theoretical models in a simplified form.

Figure 16.2

A COMPREHENSIVE MODEL OF ORGANIZATIONAL CUSTOMER BEHAVIOR

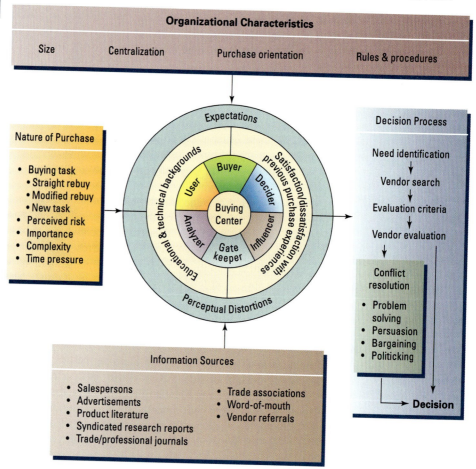

As Figure 16.2 shows, the nature of purchase and organizational characteristics (including rules and procedures) influence the structure of the buying center—whether a formal buying center exists, how many members it has, who its members are, what its charge may be, and so on. The buying center is constituted within the framework of buying policies, rules, and procedures (which are determined by the organizational characteristics), and the buying center in turn influences these by interpreting, implementing, and/or deviating from them. Decision process is influenced by the buying center as well as by the policies, rules, and procedures. Sources of information form an input at the supplier search stage of the decision process. This input is routed, of course, via the gatekeeper and is filtered through the perceptual distortion processes of the buying center members. Conflicts may occur at the supplier evaluation and selection stage, and if they do, they are resolved by one of the four methods described earlier.

One factor not shown in the figure is the macroenvironment. It consists of the economic, political, legal, cultural, technological, and marketplace (i.e., suppliers and competitors). These envelop the entire buying system. For example, legal restrictions might exist against seeking foreign sources of supply. Economic uncertainty might engender shortage or surplus of certain products. The marketplace may offer no current suppliers so that a new supplier may have to be commissioned expressly, making competitive bidding irrelevant. Technology that suppliers use to offer product information (e.g., Internet) or one that buyers require (e.g., electronic ordering) might render some suppliers or buyers unsuitable for each other. And certain suppliers or supplier cultures (especially involving cross-national dealings) might mandate certain styles of negotiations (e.g., misrepresenting information) unacceptable. Thus, the entire procurement system is facilitated and constrained within the framework of the macroenvironment surrounding it.

The Future of Business Buying Behavior

In practice, the purchasing function in the future will see two strategic shifts: (1) a shift from a transaction orientation to a relational orientation, and (2) a shift from domestic to global sourcing (see Figure 16.3).[6] The shift from transaction to relational refers to a change in buying practice wherein customers seek to maintain the same supplier rather than seek new bids from vendors every time a specific product or service is needed. The shift from domestic to global sourcing refers to buyers not being restricted to suppliers in close geographic proximity or to domestic suppliers. The reason for this because of the lessening trade restrictions between nations. Consequently, the role, processes, and strategies of the procurement function will be altered dramatically.

Forces for Change

Several forces are responsible for these shifts in the procurement strategy of business customers:

- Global competitiveness.
- The total quality management (TQM) philosophy.
- Industry restructuring.
- Technology enablers.

Figure 16.3

STRATEGIC SHIFTS IN PURCHASING

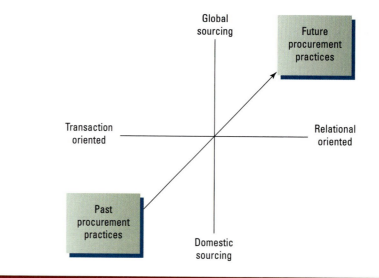

First, global competitiveness is heightening the pressure to reduce costs of production, and one significant avenue to cost reduction is establishing a partnership relationship with suppliers to jointly explore cost-cutting measures in the products and services that the business customer firm buys. Second, the TQM philosophy adopted in organizations has brought home the point that quality of finished products is dependent on the quality of input materials. This means the firm's purchasing has to become more quality oriented. Third, as companies merge and get acquired on a global basis, the purchasing departments of the resultant global companies are becoming more centralized, buying for the entire conglomerate from the headquarter procurement office; moreover, because the total conglomerate is now a global firm, the procurement is based on global sourcing (i.e., finding a vendor anywhere in the world). Finally, information technology has changed the buying process, such as the electronic data interchange (EDI) that makes ordering automatic and more efficient.

Forecasted Changes

The above-mentioned four forces will bring about significant changes. These include making procurement a core competency, treating suppliers as partners, considering cross-cultural values, and focusing more on procurement of services.

PROCUREMENT AS A CORE COMPETENCY

In industries where the supply function is strategically critical, companies will focus on creating a core competency on supply side management. That is, for these firms, their competitive advantage would stem from the fact that, among other things, their procurement is more cost-effective. The buying center structure and processes will be replaced with cross-functional teams whose sole purpose will be to maintain a good working relationship with the key suppliers used by the organization. See Eli Lilly's procurement reforms in the Window on Practice box.

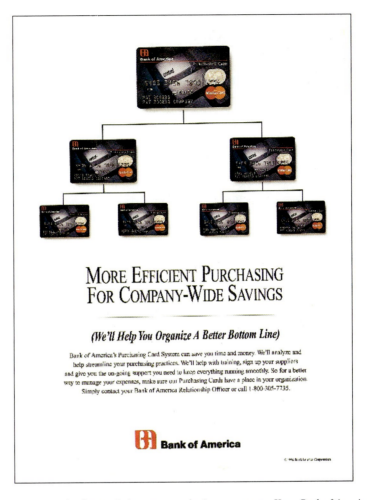

Efficiency in procurement is of strategic importance to business customers. Here, Bank of America offers this benefit to its business customers.

SUPPLIERS AS PARTNERS

Suppliers will be treated less as suppliers and more like partners. This will call for a greater degree of commitment and trust on the part of the supplier organization as they begin to work together in a new relationship.

As customers form partnerships with their suppliers, they will use fewer suppliers and make greater investments in the training, capital, and know-how with the ones being used. It will not be profitable to build and maintain relationships with all suppliers. Performance measures that quantify supplier relationship equity will be developed. These will then guide the firm in becoming selective in building relationships with suppliers. (This topic is discussed in Chapter 19.)

CROSS-CULTURAL VALUES

Business buyers will increasingly rely on "global sourcing." As it becomes evident to organizations that buying and selling practices differ widely across the globe, there will be a big push to better understand cross-cultural values, which differ widely from culture to culture. For example, what is considered a legitimate agency fee in one country is considered a bribe in another. Likewise, reciprocity, or doing business with family members or

Eli Lilly & Co.: The New Face of Purchasing

Eli Lilly & Co. is a pharmaceutical company based in Indianapolis, Indiana, with global R&D efforts and with 1996 sales of $7.35 billion. In a recent year, it spent approximately $2.25 billion (on sales of $6.79 billion) for raw materials and supplies. Five years ago, the company's profits were falling, and in search of cost-saving opportunities, the company identified its purchasing process as an important avenue.

Lilly divides the entire procurement cycle into two distinct phases: upstream and downstream. Upstream activities require an understanding of global markets in the materials we buy, identifying quality sources, developing clearly defined specifications, and negotiating relational terms of doing business. Downstream activities are ordering, receiving, and payment.

Lilly's purchasing organization had been decentralized, with 60 to 70 percent of its time and efforts devoted to downstream activities, which are basically just "transactions." Lilly reorganized the purchasing function to make it more centralized and to automate many downstream activities. Following this reorganization, purchasing spends only 20 to 30 percent of its time on downstream activities, freeing most of its time for upstream activities, or "strategic sourcing."

One way Lilly reduced time on transactions was by issuing "procurement cards" to employees in the user departments. Any employee who has been preapproved by the budgeting authority can simply use the card to make the necessary purchase. The card is now used for 25 percent of purchases, mostly small orders amounting to 2 percent of the total corporate procurement budget. The buyers in corporate purchasing are therefore able to use their time more productively. "Our goal is to have purchasing professionals involved when they can add value," says Andy Wiesman, Lilly's manager of procurement for the U.S. affiliates. "If they can't add value and are only a step in the process, we'd like to automate that process or place it in the hands of the user, either by delegated buyer status or procurement card."

Under strategic sourcing, the company began adding global sourcing managers. These managers, organized around major product groups (e.g., chemicals), developed databases that offered a global view of the market and identified optimal sourcing decisions. One outcome of this has been the reduction in the number of suppliers, reducing MRO (maintenance, repairs, and operating supplies) suppliers, for instance, from 2,000 to 20! In the first two years of reorganization, the company saved 8 percent on the total procurement budget.

Additional information available at **http://www. lilly.com**

Source: Cheryl Cullinan Lewis, "Purchasing Turns Strategic at Lilly," *Purchasing*, April 3, 1997, pp. 34c12–34c16.

---

with politically connected individuals, might be viewed as providing a sense of trust and commitment in one culture, but be considered nepotism and an unethical act in another. Understanding these value differences will become a necessity as companies begin partnering with businesses from countries all over the world.

Cross-national rules, which regulate the economic practices of companies, also differ widely from one country to another. Organizations will need to educate themselves in the areas of ownership, management control, and coproduction practices in relation to these cross-national rules.

SERVICE PROCUREMENT

Many activities that used to be done by employees are being outsourced: janitorial services, building security, recruitment, legal services, computer network and data management, payroll, and so on. To fulfill this need, new businesses are emerging around these niches. However, knowledge of services procurement currently is limited. As organiza-

Superior product performance .

Cost-effective materials management services

tions begin to outsource more and more internal services, and as suppliers compete to get that business, there will be a greater need to understand services procurement. For example, because it is difficult to standardize services across suppliers, and because it is difficult to measure service quality objectively (as can be done for physical products), firms buying these services will have to develop methods for evaluating service suppliers and monitoring their performance.[7]

Government Buying Behavior

Governments are legal entities empowered to organize and govern people, processes (e.g., free trade), and infrastructure (e.g., highways) by the resources and compliance mechanisms they possess as kings and monarchs, dictators and elected presidents, prime ministers, and governors, the military and the civil service, along with the many democratically elected or administratively appointed bodies (e.g., parliament, congress, assembly, or the city council).

In every country, the government buys a lot of products and services. In most countries, in fact, it is likely to be the single biggest buyer. It buys heavy equipment, appliances, jets, road vehicles, ships, telecommunication equipment, food grain, prepared food, clothes and uniforms, scientific equipment, maintenance parts, supplies, camping equipment, power boats, paper, furniture, janitorial supplies, landscaping, transportation, and communication services, to name a few. It buys at every level: national, state, city, and village level.

The U.S. government's annual purchasing budget is over $200 billion, more than that of any other government in the world—or any other corporation, for that matter. A considerable share of government purchasing is done by the Department of Defense (DOD). Some businesses are totally dedicated to supplying to the DOD. Another major U.S. government purchasing agency is the General Services Administration (GSA)—a central management agency in the federal government. Its mission is to provide expertly managed space, equipment, supplies, services, and solutions, at the best value, to enable federal employees to accomplish their missions. For and on behalf of various federal government agencies, GSA negotiates contracts with and buys products and services from the private sector worth about $40 billion annually.

Government as a Customer

Doing business with the government represents a huge opportunity for businesses; many, in fact, exist solely as government suppliers. But selling to the government is nothing like selling to private corporations. The expense-account lunches, polished sales presentations, and personal charm have no place in government marketing. To sell to government, you have to be a ruthlessly low-cost producer/supplier, monitor quality and delivery tightly, observe the discipline to follow all the rules and regulations, withstand the burden of enormous paperwork, and be a good business person.

Its large-order size gives government clout over potential suppliers; and its rule-making powers give it the authority to dictate the terms of trade with its suppliers. The federal government, unlike a business customer, is a sovereign power and determines the conditions under which business is conducted. Not only is the government the sole buyer for many items, but it can even pass laws that influence purchasing transactions. For example, the government has passed laws that give it the right to examine the records of its suppliers. These and other characteristics make government a customer worthy of special study.

Government Buying Procedures

Governments typically follow well-specified and rule-driven buying procedures. As an example, we describe the procurement process for the U.S. federal government. Government buys in two basic ways: direct purchase and competitive procurement.[8] In the **direct purchase** method, usually adopted for orders costing up to $25,000, the government buyer may simply call a few suppliers or send a written request for quotation (RFQ), and then place an order with one of the firms so contacted, usually on the lowest quote basis.

In the **competitive procurement** method, there are, in turn, two approaches: invitation for bid (IFB) and request for proposal (RFP). In an **invitation for bid** (IFB), the government specifies the item being sought exactly and invites sealed bids. The bidders, who are called "offerers," must supply exactly the same item (with no modifications or substitutions) and quote a price. The bids must be received by the deadline, and then they are opened in public at a pre-announced time and place. The lowest bidder that meets the requirements of the IFB is awarded the contract. To get an invitation to bid, you must register yourself by filing a form called *Solicitation Mailing List Application.*

The government uses the **request for proposal** (RFP) method when it doesn't exactly know what it wants, or what might become available, and/or when it wants to negotiate a contract (hence, it is also called a "negotiated bid"). An RFP is likely to be issued when the product or service is new, complex, and/or entails large sums of money. RFPs are reviewed and evaluated by a team of experts behind closed doors and the decision communicated to individual submitters. Quoted price is important but not the only determining factor, and the final specifications and price are arrived at only after a series of consultations and negotiations with individual offerers.

FEDERAL ACQUISITION REGULATIONS (FARS)

Whether by bid or by RFPs, all government procurement has to comply with **Federal Acquisition Regulations** (FARs), procurement regulations that all agencies of the government have to follow. In addition, the Department of Defense has its own regulations called **Defense Acquisition Regulations** (DARs). The bid document will refer to particular FAR or DAR numbers, and the bidder has to become aware of what these specific regulations are. Upon request, the contracting office will make a full text of the relevant FARs available to the bidders.

INVITATION FOR BID PROCEDURE

All bid opportunities are published in *Commerce Business Daily* (CBD), along with the name of the contracting officer. Suppliers on the government's mailing list receive a bid document in the mail, but others may request it upon learning about the opportunity in the CBD. The cover letter on the bid document spells out whether it is an open bid or restricted to a certain category of bidders such as "set aside" for small businesses.

Government is obligated to offer equal access to all potential sellers for its purchase needs. To achieve this goal, government maintains a computerized list of potential vendors and contractors; to get on the list, vendors must register by filing a form that elicits some basic information about the firm. The applicant firm's goods and services are then keyed into a computer file for easy retrieval.[9]

BID SPECIFICATIONS

Government entities attempt to develop clearly written specifications. At first notice that something is needed, the purchasing officials contact the user department. The

The U.S. government's GSA (General Services Administration) is one of the few largest procurement organizations in the world.

specifications are developed to accommodate a broad range rather than a narrow one so that as many vendors are able to respond as may meet those broad specifications. Occasionally, if a vendor has improved a product, the specifications might be developed with the improvement in mind, even though only one firm may be able to fulfill those specifications. Sometimes, the bid specifications are given indirectly, by citing a manufacturer whose product is judged to meet the entity's requirement. Sometimes the bid specifications also allow the bidder to offer an "equal" product; in that case, vendors are free to suggest an alternative product or service that would meet the same need. Figure 16.4 presents an example of a bid specification.

For products and services that are needed repeatedly, the government has established standard specifications. These are available in the following forms:

■ Federal specifications—For such routine products as paper clips, motor oil, or janitorial services, the government has established standard specifications that define physical or performance technical requirements. Available from the General Services Administration (GSA), all federal government agencies are mandated to follow it.

■ Commercial item descriptions (CIDs)—These are used to describe the specifications for a commercially available item. The government may sometimes simply refer to the item by its make and model number, such as Acme Model 1000 yard blower and vacuum. Bidders are expected to provide an equivalent product. See Figure 16.4 for an example.

Figure 16.4

COMMERCIAL ITEM DESCRIPTION

SAMPLE BRAND OR MANUFACTURER S REFERENCE

The City of _____ has determined that the *(name of brand, model name, or number)*, manufactured by *(name and address)* meets these specifications. This manufacturer s reference is not intended to be restrictive but descriptive of the type and quality the City of _____ desires to purchase. Quotes for similar manufactured items of like quality will be considered if the bid is fully noted with the manufacturer s brand name and model. The City of _____ reserves the right to determine products of equal value. Vendors will not be allowed to make unauthorized substitutions after award is made.

SOURCE: "Stephen Cole, Improving the Purchasing Function," *Government Finance Review*, February 1996, pp. 23–27.

- Military specifications—Items required by the Department of Defense are described in military specifications (Mil-Spec). There is also a military specification that specifies what a military specification should look like! Numbered as MIL-STD-490, it is of benefit to bidders because it tells where to find what element of specifications.

For nonroutine items for which no standard specification already exist, the government specifies the item in purchase descriptions or a statement of work. The purchase description identifies the physical and performance characteristics the item must meet. The statement of work tells how the government wants a particular work performed.

CONTENTS OF THE BID DOCUMENT

Because FARs govern the content and preparation of the bid document, all bid documents are structured according to the Uniform Contract Format (UCF). It is useful for us to peruse this format (in Table 16.6) because it highlights the government's decision considerations. The form consists of four parts:

- *Part I—The Schedule*. Section A, Solicitation/Contract Form, seeks basic information about the bidder. Section B describes the item and seeks a price quote from the bidder. Section C describes in detail the work the bidder is required to perform (for example, how the item should be painted). Section D provides detailed instructions on how the items should be packaged and marked to prevent damage in shipping and handling. Section E specifies the level of quality the government wants, the quality inspection system the offerer must maintain, and how the government itself plans to inspect quality. Section F tells when you will have to deliver the goods. Section G, Contract Administration, gives the contracting officer's name and address. Section H outlines special requirements such as an insurance requirement, information on any parts that may be allowed duty-free entry, or any parts the government will supply.

- *Part II—Contract Clauses*. This is a list of all the FARs that apply to the specific bid. These clauses may pertain to prohibition against kickbacks, equal opportunity, affirmative action or

Table 16.6

UNIFORM CONTRACT FORMAT

SECTION	TITLE
Part I—The Schedule	
A	Solicitation/Contract Form
B	Supplies or Services and Price/Costs
C	Description/Specifications/Statement of Work
D	Packaging and Marking
E	Inspection and Acceptance
F	Deliveries or Performance
G	Contract Administration Data
H	Special Contract Requirements
Part II—Contract Clauses	
I	Contract Clauses
Part III—List of Documents, Exhibits, and Other Attachments	
J	List of Attachments
Part IV—Representations and Instructions	
K	Representations, Certifications, and Other Statements of Offerors or Quoters
L	Instructions, Conditions, and Notices to Offerors or Quoters
M	Evaluation Factors for Award

The Uniform Contract Code, as stipulated in the Federal Acquisition Regulations, governs the structure of most bids.

Source: Clinton L. Crownover and Mark Henricks, *Selling to Uncle Sam: How to Win Choice Government Contracts for your Business* (New York: McGraw Hill, 1993), p. 56.

small business concerns, drug-free workplace, or Buy American Act. The bidder is supposed to read the FAR in its entirety (not provided with the bid document) and ensure compliance.

- *Part III—List of Documents.* Basically, it is a list of all the documents attached to the bid.

- *Part IV—Representations and Instructions.* Section K requires the bidder to certify such things as (a) the bid price has been determined independently without conferring with other bidders, (b) whether an outside consultant was retained for bid preparation, (c) that you have not violated the Federal Procurement Policy Act, (d) your federal tax identification number, and so on. Section L gives specific directions on filing the bid; its purpose is to ensure that all essential information is included and at the same time to prevent unnecessary details. Section M details the evaluation criteria, which signal what the government thinks is important. Generally, the ultimate judgment the government makes is summed up in a phrase the government often uses, namely, "lowest responsive, responsible bidder."

THE ACQUISITION TEAM

Generally, the government sets up an acquisition team, drawing individuals from various departments such as engineering, contract administration, supply support, training, human factors, quality assurance, and so on. This team is the one that prepares the bid document. There is a designated contact person to clarify any queries the bidder may have. This person acts as a gatekeeper for all information from and to the bidders.

PREPROPOSAL CONFERENCE

On some occasions, the government holds a preproposal conference after the solicitation has been issued but prior to the bid submission due date. Bidders are asked to submit the

CONTRACT PRICING PROPOSAL COVER SHEET (SF 1411) FOR CERTIFYING PRICING DATA

Figure 16.5

CONTRACT PRICING PROPOSAL COVER SHEET	1. SOLICITATION/ CONTRACT/MODIFICATION NO.	FORM APPROVED OMB NO. 3090-0116

NOTE: This form is used in contract actions if submission of cost or pricing data is required. *(See FAR 15.804-6(b))*

2. NAME AND ADDRESS OF OFFEROR (include ZIP Code)	3A. NAME AND TITLE OF OFFEROR'S POINT OF CONTACT	3B. TELEPHONE NUMBER
	4. TYPE OF CONTRACT ACTION *(Check)*	

4. TYPE OF CONTRACT ACTION *(Check)*	
A. NEW CONTRACT	D. LETTER CONTRACT
B. CHANGE ORDER	E. UNPRICED ORDER
C. PRICE REVISION/ REDETERMINATION	F. OTHER *(Specify)*

5. TYPE OF CONTRACT (Check)
☐ FFP   ☐ CPFF   ☐ CPIF   ☐ CPAF
☐ FPI   ☐ OTHER *(Specify)*

6. PROPOSED COST ($A \cdot B \cdot C$)		
A. COST	B. PROFIT/FEE	C. TOTAL
$	$	$

7. PLACE(S) AND PERIODS(S) OF PERFORMANCE

8. List and reference the identification, quantity and total price proposed for each contract line item. A line item cost breakdown supporting this recap is required unless otherwise specified by the Contracting Officer. *(Continue on reverse, and then on plain paper, if necessary. Use same headings.)*

A. LINE ITEM NO.	B. IDENTIFICATION	C. QUANTITY	D. TOTAL PRICE	E. REF.

9. PROVIDE NAME, ADDRESS, AND TELEPHONE NUMBER FOR THE FOLLOWING *(If available)*

A. CONTRACT ADMINISTRATION OFFICE	B. AUDIT OFFICE

10. WILL YOU REQUIRE THE USE OF ANY GOVERNMENT PROPERTY IN THE PERFORMANCE OF THIS WORK? *(If "Yes," identify)* ☐ YES ☐ NO	11A. DO YOU REQUIRE GOVERNMENT CONTRACT FINANCING TO PERFORM THIS PROPOSED CONTRACT? *(If "Yes," complete Item 11B)* ☐ YES ☐ NO	11B. TYPE OF FINANCING *(√ one)* ☐ ADVANCE PAYMENTS ☐ PROGRESS PAYMENTS ☐ GUARANTEED LOANS
12. HAVE YOU BEEN AWARDED ANY CONTRACTS OR SUBCONTRACTS FOR THE SAME OR SIMILAR ITEMS WITHIN THE PAST 3 YEARS? *(If "Yes," identify item(s) customer(s) and contract number(s))* ☐ YES ☐ NO	13. IS THIS PROPOSAL CONSISTENT WITH YOUR ESTABLISHED ESTIMATING AND ACCOUNTING PRACTICES AND PROCEDURES AND FAR PART 31 COST PRINCIPLES? *(If "No," explain)* ☐ YES ☐ NO	

14. COST ACCOUNTING STANDARDS BOARD (CASB) DATA *(Public Law 91.379 as amended and FAR Part 30)*

A. WILL THIS CONTRACT ACTION BE SUBJECT TO CASB REGULATIONS? *(If "No," explain in proposal)* ☐ YES ☐ NO	B. HAVE YOU SUBMITTED A CASB DISCLOSURE STATEMENT *(CASB DS 1 OR 2)*? *(IF "Yes," specify in proposal the office to which submitted and if determined to be adequate)* ☐ YES ☐ NO
C. HAVE YOU BEEN NOTIFIED THAT YOU ARE OR MAY BE IN NONCOMPLIANCE WITH YOUR DISCLOSURE STATEMENT OR COST ACCOUNTING STANDARDS? *(If "Yes," explain in proposal)* ☐ YES ☐ NO	D. IS ANY ASPECT OF THIS PROPOSAL INCONSISTENT WITH YOUR DISCLOSED PRACTICES OR APPLICABLE COST ACCOUNTING STANDARDS? *(If "Yes," explain in proposal)* ☐ YES ☐ NO

This proposal is submitted in response to the REP contract, modification, etc., in Item 1, and reflects our best estimates and/or actual costs as of this date

15. NAME AND TITLE *(Type)*	16. NAME OF FIRM	
17. SIGNATURE		18. DATE OF SUBMISSION

NSN 7540-01-142-9845   1411 101   STANDARD FROM 1411 (IC 83)
                                                                     Produced by GSA

U. S. GOVERNMENT PRINTING OFFICE : 1984 0 - 437-443

Source: Clinton L. Crownover and Mark Henricks, *Selling to Uncle Sam: How to Win Choice Government Contracts for your Business* (New York: McGraw Hill, 1993), p. 141.

questions in writing before the date of the conference. The conference is not only an occasion to clarify technical details, but also an opportunity to see the members of the acquisition team face-to-face and to observe any concerns specific members may have.

THE PROPOSAL

The proposal is in two parts: technical and price. **Technical proposals** contain all the technical details of the offer. The government requires the technical proposal to be structured according to strict guidelines, set forth in section L of the bid document.

The government prohibits any reference to price in the technical proposal because the technical and price proposals are evaluated by two entirely independent committees. Strict guidelines also include such mechanical requirements as the number of copies to be submitted, the type font to be used, the page size, and the type of binder.

The proposal document itself can run into more than a hundred pages. Organized in different sections, it seeks complete details on all aspects of the company's proposed effort: history of past government contracts, quality program, reliability and maintainability documentation, engineering details, manufacturing details, management organization and personnel, logistics, and cost data along with supporting rationale.

The **pricing proposal**, which is also made using a specific government form, contains the cost data and the offered price. The proposal entails certifying current cost and pricing data for each line item. See a sample form in Figure 16.5. The bidder must also provide supporting documents for each cost component, such as labor estimates and subcontractor quotations. Certain conditions, detailed in relevant FAR, may allow the bidder an exemption from submitting certified cost or price data.

AWARDING THE CONTRACT

Contracts are awarded in two forms:

1. **Annual purchasing agreements** (also called blanket purchase agreements) are agreements established with specific suppliers that allow the governmental entity to purchase small items covered under the agreement throughout the year without having to follow the normal purchase procedure every time. Typical items covered are office supplies, fuel for vehicles, maintenance supplies for equipment and buildings, janitorial supplies, employee uniforms, and so on. These agreements can be made with a single or with multiple vendors. In the multivendor agreement, the government entity needing to purchase an item contracts the primary vendor first. If the primary vendor is unable to supply, the entity should then contact the second supplier on the list. Vendors who agree to participate in this program are required to maintain a certain level of stock.

2. **Maintenance/labor agreements** are signed to obtain a maintenance service throughout the year on an as-needed basis. Generally, only the hourly rate is determined, not the total job cost. The number of hours required for job completion is left undetermined; for this reason, the government entity keeps a close eye on the project so that the contractor does not stretch the hours spent on the job.

Generally, the vendor with the lowest cost whose product would meet the agency's need is awarded the contract. The costs are computed by including both the initial purchase price and the maintenance costs.

Procurement by State Governments

State governments are, collectively, responsible for a huge procurement budget. Each state has its own guidelines for doing business. Many states now have vendor information available on their Internet Web site. For example, the State of Kentucky has a Web site

Figure 16.6

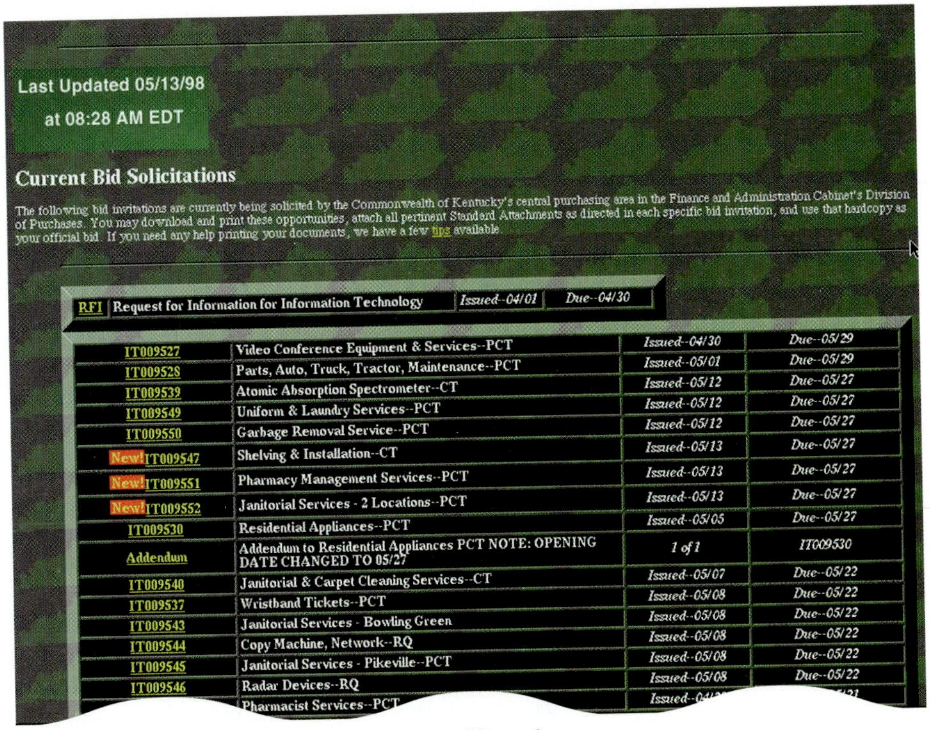

Last Updated 05/13/98
at 08:28 AM EDT

Current Bid Solicitations

The following bid invitations are currently being solicited by the Commonwealth of Kentucky's central purchasing area in the Finance and Administration Cabinet's Division of Purchases. You may download and print these opportunities, attach all pertinent Standard Attachments as directed in each specific bid invitation, and use that hardcopy as your official bid. If you need any help printing your documents, we have a few tips available.

RFI	Request for Information for Information Technology	Issued--04/01	Due--04/30
IT009527	Video Conference Equipment & Services--PCT	Issued--04/30	Due--05/29
IT009528	Parts, Auto, Truck, Tractor, Maintenance--PCT	Issued--05/01	Due--05/29
IT009539	Atomic Absorption Spectrometer--CT	Issued--05/12	Due--05/27
IT009549	Uniform & Laundry Services--PCT	Issued--05/12	Due--05/27
IT009550	Garbage Removal Service--PCT	Issued--05/12	Due--05/27
New! IT009547	Shelving & Installation--CT	Issued--05/13	Due--05/27
New! IT009551	Pharmacy Management Services--PCT	Issued--05/13	Due--05/27
New! IT009552	Janitorial Services - 2 Locations--PCT	Issued--05/13	Due--05/27
IT009530	Residential Appliances--PCT	Issued--05/05	Due--05/27
Addendum	Addendum to Residential Appliances PCT NOTE: OPENING DATE CHANGED TO 05/27	1 of 1	IT009530
IT009540	Janitorial & Carpet Cleaning Services--CT	Issued--05/07	Due--05/22
IT009537	Wristband Tickets--PCT	Issued--05/08	Due--05/22
IT009543	Janitorial Services - Bowling Green	Issued--05/08	Due--05/22
IT009544	Copy Machine, Network--RQ	Issued--05/08	Due--05/22
IT009545	Janitorial Services - Pikeville--PCT	Issued--05/08	Due--05/22
IT009546	Radar Devices--RQ	Issued--05/08	Due--05/22
	Pharmacist Services--PCT	Issued--04/	

A bid solicitation form posted on Website of the state of Kentucky

that allows vendors to view and download current bidding opportunities, view the directory of buyers by commodity type in the Division of Purchases, and a listing of all of the state agency price contracts. The State of Wisconsin has a Web site, called VendorNet, which even allows vendors to register online.

Similarities between Government and Business Procurement[10]

Government spending, especially at the federal level, involves large amounts of money, complex procedures, and red tape in even the smallest purchase. However, there are some parallels between business buying and government buying.

BUYCLASS PARALLEL

In business buying, the purchase task was classified as straight rebuy, modified rebuy, and new task. In government, the buying tasks can be viewed as nondevelopmental, modified nondevelopmental, and developmental. These classifications are based on the level of analysis and the degree of buyer attention they require. Generally speaking, buying decisions for both business and government buyers involve either repetition of a previous purchase, some variation of a previous purchase, or a new purchase situation.

Nondevelopmental buying tasks occur when the need is not a new one. The same material/service has been procured before and can, in fact, be procured simply off-the-shelf, following well-established procedures. Also, awarding the contract to the lowest bidder happens most in this task compared to the other two buyclasses.

Modified nondevelopmental tasks are those in which products of known configurations need to be fitted to the need at hand. This task may require a two-step submission of proposals. First, only technical proposals may be solicited (without price information);

and only those suppliers judged to be capable of meeting the technical needs (who are able to "custom-fit") may be asked to submit a detailed bid.

For new developmental tasks, the procurement process is more involved and requires more interfacing with prospective suppliers (as it does in the new buy tasks in the private sector). Prospective suppliers need a lot more information and interaction with the buyer organization to understand the purchase need and to develop the technical proposal. The submission of a technical proposal is almost always separated from (and generally precedes) the price proposal. Subsequently, negotiations are required with all bidders whose bids are within the competitive range. Price is often not the most important factor, and bidders have the opportunity to submit a revised bid. New developmental tasks are implemented as "negotiated purchases," and here the governmental agency generally has the same freedom as a purchasing agent in the private sector. Sometimes, a large contract for a major, unprecedented need (e.g., a new weapon system) may be awarded based on negotiations with a "sole-source," after the source has been identified and qualified as technically competent and most equipped to codevelop the product specifications and fulfill the project needs.

BUYING STEPS PARALLEL

The steps in the buying process for business and government buying are listed in Table 16.7. Except for some difference in nomenclature, the steps are similar. Both processes begin with the definition of a need and must make those needs known to interested suppliers and invite them to develop offers and bids. Next, a selection process takes place, with some kind of follow-up after the order is placed.

Some details of these steps differ, though. In government, often the need for materials is so high in volume, diversity, and complexity (even for nondevelopmental purchases), that a simple need identification takes the character of a plan. Besides, funding must be identified and/or sometimes sought through an arduous and long-drawn legislative or electoral process. For example, in 1995, the city government of Cincinnati identified a need to build a new stadium; however, the funding sources remained unclear for several months, so in March 1996, a public ballot was conducted on a proposal to raise local tax by 0.5 percent.

Following the need identification and funding encumbrance, requests for proposals (RFPs)—called RFQs in corporate buying—are issued and published in *Commerce Business Daily*. Competitive bidding receives more emphasis in government than in the private sector, but, in both sectors alike, the contract does not have to go to the lowest bidder. Government law requires that an award be made to that supplier whose bid is most *advantageous* to the government, with price and *other factors considered*. Despite

Table 16.7

COMPARISON OF BUYING PROCEDURES BETWEEN BUSINESS AND GOVERNMENT

BUSINESS	GOVERNMENT
STEP 1: Need identification	Need planning and funding
STEP 2: Request for quotations	Request for proposals
STEP 3: Supplier evaluation/selection	Bid selection
STEP 4: Finalization of price and delivery terms	Bid negotiation
STEP 5: Placement of order	Contract award
STEP 6: Follow-up and expediting	Contract administration

this provision to weigh nonprice factors, the tendency in government has been to select the lowest bidder.

Bid negotiations take the form of further streamlining of the terms of mutual obligations. The awarding of the contract in the government is equivalent to the placing of an order in the private sector. Finally, in both business and government sectors, order fulfillment, progress in project completion, and compliance with the terms of purchase are under constant monitoring and enforcement.

PROCUREMENT MANAGEMENT GOALS PARALLEL

Both business and government buyers pursue the same objectives in managing their procurement responsibilities and in reaching their supplier decisions. Both exist to fulfill the material needs of their user departments, seek to develop competent and reliable sources, must procure at prices most advantageous to the buying organization, must minimize inventory costs, and encourage competition for their business.

How Government Customers Differ from Business Customers

While there is similarity on the goals and the overall nature of the procurement task between the business and government sectors, there are also a number of differences. These differences arise mainly in how the tasks are *procedurally* implemented. (See Table 16.8 for some major examples.)

SIZE OF THE AVERAGE PURCHASE AND STANDARDIZATION

It is commonly known that weapons and space systems are among the most costly and complex items in existence. In the private sector, nothing compares in cost, other than perhaps large construction projects or the development of commercial aircraft. But even for simple supplies such as stationery, the order size is generally larger than most private

Table 16.8

GOVERNMENT CUSTOMERS VERSUS BUSINESS CUSTOMERS

	GOVERNMENT	BUSINESS
Largest, most standardized purchases	☑	☐
Most heavily regulated purchases	☑	☐
Solicitation of sellers	☑	☐
Public information available about past and future purchases	☑	☐
Greater diffusion of authority in the buying center	☑	☐
Most paperwork	☑	☐
Greater stability	☑	☐
Concern for efficiency	☑	☑
Global expansion and purchasing	☑	☑

decision making, and the purchasing manager or the user department who may jointly make the supplier selection also authorizes payments. Thus, in the private sector, there is much less diffusion of authority, perhaps because there is less need for checks and balances.

PROCEDURAL DETAIL AND PAPERWORK

Finally, there is the inevitable paperwork, substantially more voluminous in government than in business procurement. The U.S. government's "invitation for bids" form consists of 13 administrative sections, with typically more than 100 pages. Then there is need for strict adherence and legendary red tape. For example, if a bidding application contains a substantive error, it must be rejected.

Private contractors have often complained, despite help from the Small Business Administration who assists in bid preparation, that it takes as much as one year by a large contingent of staff to digest and follow all the instructions and the required paperwork. The product specifications tend to be exhaustive. For example, the description of oatmeal chocolate chip cookies procured by the defense department runs into 15 pages! These detailed specifications give the government ample ground to reject suppliers found unqualified.[11]

The Travails and Rewards of Selling to the Government

When faced with all the rules, regulations, and mountains of paperwork required in government contract bidding, it is easy to be discouraged. Certainly, the effort is enormous, and an army of personnel is kept busy for several months both before and after the bid submission. But rather than fret about and decry the government procurement processes, including its massive paperwork, marketers and students of customer behavior ought to develop an appreciation for its idiosyncrasies.

RATIONALE FOR THE COMPLEXITY OF GOVERNMENT PROCUREMENT

Although many of the practices need reform, and indeed just such a reform debate is under way, many of the quirks and nuances in government procurement stem from the responsibilities and obligations of public policy and public expenditures. Many public projects (of the developmental tasks type) are still in the evolutionary phase of planning at the time of bid solicitation; with final configurations still unknown (e.g., the mission for Man in Space), the process of "need identification" and its articulation can be prolonged.

Furthermore, public procurement is funded by taxpayers' money, and it is only proper that the money be spent wisely. To ensure this, the U.S. Congress has mandated a system of checks and balances. In fact the separation of subtask execution and diffusion of authority described above is a meticulously designed mechanism with much merit, and the system of checks and balances reduces misuse of authority. Wide-ranging scrutiny, including that done by the general public via open access to information, is almost a necessity given the public source of funding.

Most important, government has the responsibility to implement its procurement function in a socially responsible way. Since its procurement budget constitutes a huge resource, it is proper to leverage it to advance socioeconomic policy at the same time that a business function of procurement is executed. Thus, it is not unreasonable to demand that its contractors, and subcontractors in turn, adopt socially desired hiring practices, adopt pro-environment measures, and in general demonstrate good corporate citizenship behavior.

Finally, the rules require detailed paperwork so that everything is in writing. This helps to protect the government as well as the bidder. The government cannot exploit the bidder by requiring anything more than what was agreed to in mountains of documents. If the government requirements change during the contract work, the bidder can usually profit from it by renegotiating the extra work.

BENEFITS OF SUPPLYING THE GOVERNMENT

Although there is room for reform, an appreciation of the background philosophical factors that frame government procurement will help marketers seeking the lucrative business of massive government contracts. As a source of business, many would find it a desirable opportunity despite the hassle. Consider some of the unique benefits of doing business with government:

- *Stability*—The economy affects private businesses much more than government. Government buys in bad as well as good economic times. Sometimes government purchasing is even countercyclical, increasing during bad economic times. For example, policy makers may want to inject more money into the economy or to support food supplies and housing to segments of the population recently or temporarily made poor by bad economic times. Thus, doing business with the government gives a contractor stability.

- *Security*—As a customer, government has the best credit in the world. Suppliers to a stable government such as the United States don't even have to ask for credit references. Sometimes, the government will even pay part of the costs in advance as progressive payments.

- *Size*—Government buys a lot of things and buys them in large quantities. Hundreds of businesses, including some of the biggest, such as General Dynamics, McDonnell Douglas, IBM, and Exxon, came into existence and continue to be supported by government contracts.

- *Breakthrough R&D Work*—Some government contracts entail funding the development of new technology and new applications, which can be later utilized for wider commercial applications. Teflon nonstick cooking surfaces and Tang instant breakfast were developed for the U.S. government's space program.

- *Challenge*—The government is a stickler for cost efficiency and performance specifications. (The story about the $600 toilet seat bought by the Department of Defense is often told only because it is rare.) Satisfying the government requires total quality management, mastery of details, an ability to plan long term, and perseverance to do the job (including the daunting paperwork) right. There can be no better training ground than this. If a business firm can successfully do business with the government, it can compete anywhere else!

Future of the Government as Customer

Just as corporate America is going through changes in its purchasing function, so too government procurement is experiencing pressures to change. The resulting changes include downsizing and restructuring, globalization, and economic pragmatism.

Downsizing and Restructuring of the Government

As businesses have improved efficiency through downsizing and restructuring, people are demanding that their governments do the same. As a payer, the government is becoming more cost-conscious. Consequently, it is more concerned about fraud, waste, and mismanagement. Governments at all levels have responded with efficiency improvements of many kinds.

Government owned prisons are customer for a number of products and services.

One of the most basic tactics, of course, is downsizing. Most notably in the United States, the Department of Defense has seen its annual budgets cut by half over the past decade. Under pressure to reduce costs, the Pentagon is not only buying less, but also streamlining its supplier pool by restricting negotiations to fewer suppliers. Cutbacks are not limited to defense but extend to health care, education, human services, and scientific and regulatory agencies. U.S. government agencies such as the National Aeronautics and Space Administration (NASA), the National Science Foundation, and the National Institutes of Health have come under tremendous budget pressures. Welfare programs have been scaled back, and government purchases of health care have shifted from fee-for-service providers to managed care.

PRIVATIZATION AND OUTSOURCING

One way governments are getting by on reduced funding is through combinations of privatization and outsourcing. Privatization involves converting government operations into private businesses. In many European, Latin American, and Asian countries, industries such as telecommunications, railroads, airlines, television, and postal services have been privatized. In the United States, privatization is extending to primary and secondary education, prison systems, military bases, highways, transit systems, museums, and parks and recreation bureaus.

Outsourcing, in contrast, involves contracting with private businesses for the handling of certain tasks. Organizations gain overall efficiency by outsourcing activities that are beyond their areas of expertise. Government agencies have outsourced such functions as cafeteria operations, barber shops, and even such critical operations as research and spacecraft.

ACQUISITION REFORM

Along with saving money, restructuring is aimed at reducing suppliers' frustration with government red tape. In the United States, achieving these goals has been the object of the Clinton administration's policy of "reinventing government." This program of restructuring includes the goal of saving $22.5 billion by simplifying the procurement process.

Some changes being considered as part of acquisition reform include exempting items currently available in the marketplace from the thicket of laws governing major purchase contracts. For relatively small purchases of currently available items, a government procurement officer could buy in the private marketplace, rather than undergoing the lengthy bidding procedure. Acquisition reform will also likely require greater use of electronic communication and ordering. The overall objective is to cut red tape and make it easier for suppliers to do business with the government.

Globalization

The government sector enterprises are becoming global. For example, the Army and Air Force Services or PX stores are worldwide in scope. The services are among the top 10 retailers in the U.S. and more global than other retailers such as Sears and Wal-Mart. Similarly, the Internet is a government network operated by the Advanced Research Programs Agency (ARPA), and the Weather Satellite is operated by the government.

Many government agencies are looking for expansion to global markets. Examples include the defense department and several civilian agencies such as the CDC.

Economic Pragmatism

Governments are reducing their emphasis on social objectives as a component of procurement. Buying decisions are governed less by concern for affirmative action, minority enterprises, subsidized education, fellowships, U.S. aid programs, foreign aid, and investment in world agencies such as the United Nations, IMF, and the World Bank. Rather, governments are becoming rigorous in ensuring that procurement decisions are economically sound.

As the source of global dominance has shifted since the Cold War from military might to economic prowess, the importance of the Secretary of Defense and the State Department is being replaced by the increasing importance of the Secretary of Commerce and the Secretary of the Treasury. Just witness the strides that Japan has made in world dominance due to its global economic reach. Conversely, the global power of Russia and the other former USSR entities has been hurt by internal strife and a shift in political ideology from socialism to capitalism.

Business and Government Customer Decision Making and the Three Customer Roles

Various concepts discussed in this chapter have relevance to the three customer roles. In the chapter, several unique aspects of business customer decision making were identified. Important among these are greater role specialization, formalized process, accountability, internal capabilities, complexity, buyclass, buying center, decision process, and conflict resolution process. Each has implications for one or more of the three customer roles.

Much more than for household customers, it is for business customers that the three roles are often most separated. Business buying requires specialist knowledge to evaluate each of the six market values, and for this reason assigns the user, payer, and buyer roles to different individuals. Users focus on technical performance evaluations, payers focus on organizationwide budget allocations, and buyers specialize in buying tasks, especially finding and appraising alternative sources. To ensure that maximum user values are obtained at lowest total costs, organizations lay down rules that each role holder has to follow. Users have to seek budget approval from payers and submit a formal requisition, payers use sound budgeting practices, and buyers ensure that vendor selection follows the stipulated process. Each role holder is accountable for his or her part in the job—users for ensuring correct specifications for maximum performance value; payers for not overspending, and buyers for making the procurement more efficient and effective. Internal capabilities are relevant for all three roles—users may produce the item in-house; payers with deep pockets can gain more favorable terms from suppliers; as to the buyer role, if the buyer is not adequately skilled, the procurement itself may be outsourced.

Complexity makes both user and buyer tasks more demanding as ensuring the fit with requirement becomes crucial. For complex purchases, buyers may need to coordinate with multiple suppliers for complementary portions of the job. Buyclass affects all three roles. Users may automate the requisition process for straight rebuys, but for new tasks, they would need to generate product specifications perhaps for the first time. For straight rebuy, the budget is easily approved or earmarked; but for new tasks payers may have to juggle money, including raising new capital. Scarcity of funds, or greater merit of other demands, may lead payers to deny a user request for an item. For rebuys, buyers rely on current suppliers, routinizing the purchase process; at the other end of the continuum, for new tasks, buyers need to go through an extensive process of identifying all qualified vendors and then sifting through them, bringing professional buying skills and talents to bear on the process.

Buying center is a concept unique to business buying, and it is founded on the very idea that the three roles may be, as they often are, separated and allocated among different personnel. Payers (such as senior management) often play the decider role, while buyers bring vendors and users together for exploring technical fit.

In the decision process, each role plays a more or less significant part as Table 16.10 shows. Generally, users are most active at the need specification and vendor screening stages, payers at the decision stage, and buyers throughout for coordinating the entire process. Conflicts may arise among users or among buyers or among payers, if each of these roles is itself shared among more than one individual. Conflicts may also arise among the three roles. Buyers may want to keep certain vendors out of the process, for example, while users may insist on certain preferred vendors. Sometimes they may design product specifications to ideally suit only a particular supplier. Payers may be driven unduly (or may be seen to be driven) by price considerations, constraining optimal choices for users.

The customer decision process for government buying also affects the three roles differently. Some of the unique aspects of government buying are RFPs, bid evaluation, acquisition team, acquisition reform, and so on.

In government procurement, user specifications are extensive in seeking RFPs. Bid evaluation is handled in two independent parts: technical evaluation and price evaluation. Users play a dominant role in the former while costing experts in the buyer department handle the second part. Each is accountable for his or her part, and thus each task is handled more rigorously. The acquisition team itself comes from different departments and

Table 16.10 BUSINESS AND GOVERNMENT CUSTOMER DECISION MAKING AND THE THREE CUSTOMER ROLES

CONCEPTS	USER	PAYER	BUYER
BUSINESS CUSTOMERS DECISIONS: UNIQUE ASPECTS			
Role specialization	Users focus on performance value evaluation.	Payers focus on budget allocations.	Buyers, often separate from users and payers, specialize in buying task.
Formalized process	Users submit a formal requisition and technical specifications.	Payers use sound budgeting practices.	Buyers follow well-laidout policies and processes.
Accountability	Users accountable for correct specifications.		Buyers accountable for professional buying.
Internal capabilities	User capabilities may lead to in-house production.	Strong financial position can gain favorable terms for suppliers	Buyers with low skills may draw on external advice.
Complexity	Need identification may be an extended process.		Buyers may need to coordinate with multiple suppliers.
Buyclass	Users may automate the requisition for rebuys.	For new task buys, payers may have to juggle money.	Rebuys may be routinized and automated. New task buys would require professional talents of buyers.
Buying center	Buying center brings all roles together.	Payers often are the deciders in the buying center.	Buyers bring vendors and users together.
Decision process	Users most active at the specification and vendor screening stage.	Payers most active at the decision stage.	Buyers active throughout the decision process.
Conflict resolution	Three roles often in conflict.	Payers often overly concerned with cost minimization.	
GOVERNMENT CUSTOMER DECISIONS: UNIQUE ASPECTS			
RFPs	User specifications are extensive in RFPs.		Buyers act as gatekeepers.
Bid evaluation	Users conduct technical evaluation.	Payers engage in cost evaluation of the bid.	Buyers coordinate and intensely participate in price evaluation.
Acquisition teams	Users play important role on acquisition teams.		Buyers handle principal responsibility for acquisition.
Acquisition reforms	Greater authority to users for direct purchase.	With rising concern with waste, payers would have to do budget allocations more conscientiously.	Buyers' job made more efficient.

thus from all three roles. Acquisition reform in the U.S. government will simplify the buying process, raising the dollar threshold for adopting routinized buying procedure, and giving greater authority to user departments for direct purchase. This will simplify the buyer task and also give more flexibility to users who will need less lead time to order. As public concern with government waste rises, payers would have to become more cautious in ensuring judicious use of available budgets.

Summary

In contrast to household buying, the customer behavior of a business involves greater specialization of customer roles, a more formalized buying process, greater accountability for decisions, more sophisticated internal capabilities, and more complex requirements.

The business buying process has several components: the nature of the purchase, organizational characteristics, a buying center, rules and procedures, and a decision process. The nature of the purchase is defined by the buyclass (straight rebuy, modified rebuy, or new task); perceived risk, importance, and product complexity; and the time pressure faced by the decision makers. A business customer spends the most time and effort investigating a new task purchase, and/or purchase that involves relatively great perceived risk, importance, and complexity. In contrast, time pressure will shorten the decision process and increase the impact of the user's input.

Buying behavior is also affected by four organizational characteristics of the customer: size, structure, purchase resources, and purchase orientation. Small organizations behave more like individuals or households, whereas large organizations use more formalized buying procedures. Structure refers to the number of departments in the organization, where they are located, and how centralized they are. Organizations with many departments in multiple locations engage in more complex buying behavior. Purchase resources are the organization's professional buyers and ordering equipment. Purchase orientation is the organization's purchasing philosophy, ranging along a continuum from viewing purchasing as an administrative function to viewing it as a strategic one. A purchasing department with a strategic role is more active in the decision-making process.

The buying center is a multifunction, multilevel internal organization responsible for the centralized purchasing function. Rather than a department or committee, it is a concept, defining the variety of roles involved in a purchase: user, buyer, analyzer, influencer, gatekeeper, and decider. A successful seller to businesses identifies the people in the organization who play each role in a particular purchase decision and addresses the needs associated with each role.

Most businesses set up policies, rules, and procedures that limit the decision criteria and decision process.

Business buying decisions take place in several stages: need assessment, developing choice criteria, request for proposals (RFPs), supplier evaluation, supplier selection, and fulfillment and monitoring. These steps involve more formal analysis than in the typical household buying decision. Total procurement costs, rather than price alone, are an important factor in most business buying decisions. The decision process is primarily driven by buyers' expectations and perceptual distortions. Conflicts are resolved through some combination of problem solving, persuasion, bargaining, and politicking.

In the future, business buying behavior will shift from a transaction orientation to a relational orientation, and from domestic to global sourcing. Forces behind these changes include global competitiveness, the total quality management philosophy, industry restructuring, and new technology. Businesses will respond to these forces by making procurement a core competency, partnering with suppliers, learning cross-cultural values, and learning more about services procurement.

Government is a major customer in every country. Governments are powerful customers because their orders are large and their power to make and enforce laws gives them substantial control over the buying process. In the United States, the federal government buys through two highly structured processes: the direct purchase method and competitive procurement. Marketers to the federal government must operate within the strict guidelines of these procedures. State governments are also sizable customers. Each state has its own guidelines for marketers to learn and follow. Many of the details are available on the states' Web sites.

Government procurement and business procurement resemble each other in terms of buyclasses, buying steps, and procurement management goals. However, government buyclasses are called nondevelopmental, modified nondevelopmental, and developmental. Also, the government process may be more formal. In other ways, government procurement and business procurement differ. Government purchases tend to be larger and more standardized. They involve more legal restrictions and compliance reviews. Unlike businesses, governments must solicit suppliers widely. Government purchases also involve open access to information, greater diffusion of authority, and more paperwork. Nevertheless, selling to the government offers the advantages of stability, security, size, access to breakthrough R&D work, and a quality-inspiring challenge.

The government's role as customer is undergoing change. Governments are increasingly engaged in downsizing and restructuring, which may include privatization, outsourcing, and acquisition reform. Government buying behavior increasingly takes place on a global scale. Finally, governments are placing more weight on the goal of economic pragmatism.

Key Terms

Business 612	Persuasion 625	Federal Acquisition
Buyclass 615	Bargaining 625	Regulations 633
Straight Rebuy 615	Politicking 625	Defense Acquisition
Modified Rebuy 616	Governments 632	Regulations 633
New Task 616	Direct Purchase 633	Technical Proposals 638
Perceived Risk 617	Competitive Procurement	Pricing Proposal 638
Importance of Purchase 617	633	Annual Purchasing
Complexity 617	Invitation for Bid 633	Agreements 638
Buying Center 620	Request for Proposal	Maintenance/Labor
Problem Solving 625	633	Agreements 638

Review Questions

1. What factors distinguish business customers from household or individual customers? In providing your responses, give an example of a business customer for each factor that you identify.

2. How do organizational characteristics affect buying behavior? Why is it important for marketers to consider these organizational characteristics in their efforts to appeal to business customers?

3. Why would conflicts arise in organizational buying decisions? When conflicts do arise, what are some ways in which organizational members can attempt to resolve them?

4. Besides the many differences between government customers and business customers, there are parallels or similarities between the two. Identify three parallels. In your opinion, are the two groups more similar or more dissimilar?

5. Briefly describe the steps in the federal buying process, identifying any adaptations the government makes according to the size of purchase.

6. What is a Federal Acquisition Regulation? What are some of its important provisions?

CHAPTER 17

After reading this chapter you should be able to:

Define the types of intermediary customers: resellers, buying groups, and affinity groups.

Describe a model of how resellers buy, including factors that influence their merchandise buying decisions.

Summarize the concept of channel partnership, how it works, and why resellers desire partnerships with their suppliers.

Identify the bases of relative power between resellers and their suppliers.

Discuss the role of resellers own marketing strategy in their merchandise and vendor decisions.

Explain membership buying groups, how they function, and how manufacturers and suppliers adapt their marketing mix to appeal to membership buying groups.

Intermediary Customer Decision Making

Gordon Franklin is a buyer in the men's department at Rundel's Department Stores Company. Rundel's is a one-city operation with one store downtown and four stores in suburban locations. Being the smallest division of its holding company, Urban, Inc. (which operates four other department store companies with 340 stores nationwide), Rundel's is encouraged to be innovative in its merchandising practices. "If a new product or concept has to fail, let it fail here—on a smaller scale," argue Urban executives. Accordingly, Rundel's is more innovative in its buying and merchandising programs than an average department store. And Gordon is the most innovative of all the buyers at Rundel's.

Six years ago, when he joined his present position, he started stocking men's jeans, a successful decision that now accounts for 19 percent of all sales in Rundel's men's department. The store depends on Levi's, Farah, and a lower-priced supplier of unbranded jeans as its three main sources. But it also buys from a few other suppliers, such as Davis. Davis is actually a manufacturer of name-brand jeans with a nationally known brand name, and although Davis's jeans had a significant presence at Rundel's, Davis was never viewed as a major source. Moreover, Rundel's had deemphasized Davis jeans over the last three years because Davis had not kept up with fashion trends in jeans design.

Stung by declining sales of its brand nationwide, Davis had recently started a major effort at recapturing the market. By hiring a well-known fashion designer, it created contemporary designs well liked by consumers in new-product acceptance research the company has done. In fact, even loyal customers of Levi's jeans expressed a desire to buy Davis's new jeans if they became available in the market. Armed with this market research finding, Sue Anderson, Davis's sales manager made a presentation to Gordon Franklin, seeking a "major supplier source" status. Eager to be innovative, Gordon agreed to the request, provided that Davis offer a vendor program with these components: (1) a guaranteed order fulfillment within two weeks, (2) a guaranteed markup of 48 percent, and (3) Davis cooperative advertising support to include 60 percent of all newspaper linage costs.

Sue Anderson knows it is much more than what other suppliers in the industry offer. And she knows that guaranteeing a two-week order fulfillment time itself will add to the company's costs significantly. Yet she also knows that no matter how well consumers like the new design, it is useless unless resellers carry it. She is determined to be a main source of jeans for Rundel's[1]

Introduction

Resellers like Rundel's Department Store play a critical role in enabling end-user customers to acquire products and services. As Sue Anderson of Davis Jeans Company realizes, even if a product or service package is attractive or appealing for the end-users, manufacturers must appeal to and satisfy resellers as customers or the product probably will not sell. Manufacturers often focus their activities on producing the product (or designing the service package), relying on intermediaries to bring the product or service to end-user markets. These intermediaries bridge the gap between manufacturers and end-user markets, and in their reseller role they themselves assume the marketer role for the product or service. However, they also play the customer role vis-à-vis the manufacturers. Therefore, manufacturer/marketers themselves have to understand the customer behavior of intermediaries.

Principles and concepts covered so far for other classes of customers (namely, individuals, households, businesses, and government) also apply to intermediaries—intermediaries have perceptions, motivations, and attitudes; they follow the decision steps from need recognition to alternative evaluation; and they experience post-decision satisfaction/dissatisfaction and recycle and adapt their prior choices. However, because intermediaries are themselves marketers, these decision processes and considerations take on additional characteristics. Accordingly, marketers must understand their specific motivations, the benefits and terms of business, and consequently the market values that intermediaries seek. Exploring these topics is the purpose of this chapter.

The chapter discusses three types of intermediaries—resellers, buying groups, and affinity group buyers—in three separate sections. First, we define resellers and describe a model of their merchandise buying decision making. Next, we describe the concept of channel partnership and the benefits resellers obtain by entering into a partnership with their suppliers. The concept of power in reseller dealings with suppliers is discussed next, followed by a discussion of how resellers' own marketing strategies influence their buying decisions. In the second section, we describe what buying groups are and how they function in their role as resellers as well as customers themselves. The final section explains affinity groups, including why and how marketers engage affinity groups as customers.

Resellers as Customers

A **reseller** is a licensed business entity that buys someone else's products and services, adds some value for the customer, and sells them to other customers who may themselves be resellers or end users. Typically, a reseller is more involved with creating value for the buyer, whereas a manufacturer of products is more involved with creating value for the user. As described in Chapter 3, the values sought by the customer in his or her buyer role are service, convenience, and personalization; and a reseller creates these values by creating time and place utilities (i.e., by making the product or service available at a time and a place desired by the customer). Often, however, resellers create values relevant to the user role also, for example, when a jewelry store sizes a ring, or when a clothing store does alterations; furthermore, sometimes the store name itself adds prestige to the product, thus giving the user social and emotional value. Resellers also tend to add value for the payer role, by offering price value (e.g., buying in large quantities and passing on the savings to customers) and by offering credit and finance values.

Since most consumer products tend to be sold through resellers, resellers are very important customers for the manufacturers of consumer durables (such as appliances, automobiles, and consumer electronics) and for consumer nondurables (such as grocery products, drugs and household products, and supplies). Resellers also serve business markets for components, office equipment, and supplies: for example, U.S. retailers Staples, Office Max, and Office Depot.

There are many different types of resellers, selling a wide variety of goods and services, from food to clothing to electronics to hardware. The reseller types are wholesalers, distributors, agents and brokers, retailers, and value-added resellers (VARs). Among the retailers, the major types include specialty stores, department stores, supermarkets, convenience stores, superstores, hypermarkets, and so on (see Table 17.1).[2]

Table 17.1

MAJOR TYPES OF RESELLERS

	WHOLESALERS
Merchant wholesalers	An independently owned business that is primarily engaged in buying, taking title to, usually storing and physically handling goods in large quantities, and reselling them to retailers in smaller quantities.
Distributors	A type of wholesaler especially in lines where selective or exclusive distribution is desired; resells generally to other manufacturers.
Agents	A business unit that negotiates purchases, sales, or both without taking title.
Brokers	A middle man who acts as a go-between for buyers or sellers. Does not take title or physical custody of goods.
	RETAILERS
Retailer	A merchant who is engaged in selling primarily to the end consumer.
Value-added resellers	Retailers who buy a product from a manufacturer or wholesaler and then add their own component (self-produced or bought from another manufacturer) so that the final product is more valuable to the end user than the individual component or unassembled product.
Supermarkets	Stores that carry food and nonfood products to meet consumers day-to-day household maintenance needs. Wide assortment of items sold on low-margin, high-volume, self-service basis.
Convenience stores	A relatively small store in residential neighborhoods offering limited products at extended convenient hours.
Department stores	Large stores that carry several generally durable goods and services such as clothing, furnishings, small appliances, a hair salon, interior decor, and so on, each in a separate department.
Discount stores	Stores that sell general or specialty (e.g., electronics) name-brand merchandise at a regularly deep discounted low price.
Specialty stores	Stores that carry a narrow product line with a deep assortment in it (e.g., appliances only, or electronics only, or shoes only).
Hypermarkets	Very large stores that are a combination of supermarket, discount, and drug store, carrying routine purchase as well as durable goods, and operating on warehouse retailing principles such as bulk display, minimum service, and low price.

Source: Prepared by authors based on Peter D. Bennett, ed., *Dictionary of Marketing Terms*, 2nd ed. (Chicago: American Marketing Association, 1995).

How Do Resellers Buy?

Resellers are in the business of acquiring and reselling products that their customers need. In theory at least, reseller decisions about what to buy should therefore be straightforward—they should buy whatever products and brands are in demand by their customers that they can obtain at a desirable trade discount (i.e., a markdown from the selling price that leaves them enough profit). But rarely are reseller decisions so straightforward. After all, they have a limited amount of physical space in the store, so they must limit the number of brands they can carry in any product category. And for a given product category, there are a number of suppliers, all vying to get into the stores. Not only do suppliers' product offerings differ, but they also differ greatly in the way they do business, the terms and conditions of trade they offer, the support services they offer, and the reseller effort they demand. Resellers must therefore make their merchandise buying decisions with great care.

A marketer selling to resellers should understand the factors that go into the reseller's decision making. Figure 17.1 shows a model that identifies the major components of resellers' buying decisions.[3] According to this model, a number of factors influence the buyer decision-making unit (DMU). The DMU responds with a choice of supplier and merchandise. This choice leads to the experience of satisfaction or dissatisfaction, which provides feedback for future decisions.

FACTORS THAT SHAPE RESELLER DECISIONS

A reseller's buying behavior is a function of several factors. In Figure 17.1, which ties these factors together, there are three major categories of factors: (1) merchandise requirements, (2) supplier alternatives, and (3) situational characteristics. These factors influence the decision process by members of the decision-making unit. Merchandise requirements

Figure 17.1

A MODEL OF RESELLER MERCHANDISE BUYING BEHAVIOR

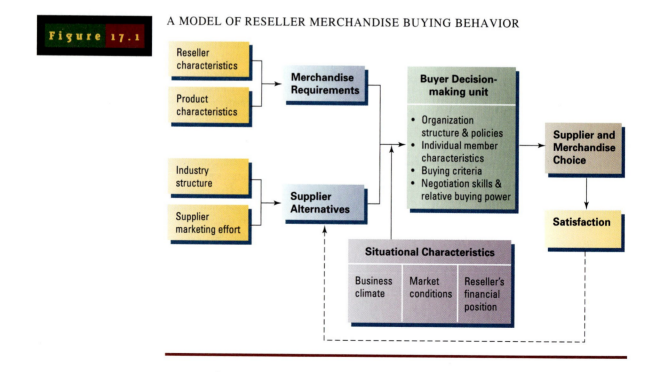

and supplier alternatives are antecedents, or primary determinants, of the decision process. Without them, the need for decision making does not even arise. Situational characteristics are "moderators"—they moderate or modify the process set in motion by the first two factors.

MERCHANDISE REQUIREMENT   As is true with any decision making (whether by household or business customers), at the heart of the decision process and outcome are the resellers' buying motives and their associated purchase criteria. A successful retailer can assess customers' needs/wants and then properly translate them into merchandise requirements. Merchandise requirements vary from reseller to reseller, according to reseller characteristics and product characteristics.

Reseller characteristics include the size of the organization, the type (e.g., discount versus department store), and the location of its outlets (national, regional, or local). Resellers also vary on management philosophy. For instance, some resellers are more financially oriented, while others are more merchandise driven. The former buy primarily based on financial outcomes of a specific transaction, while the latter buy based on merchandise quality and need. Another reseller characteristic is the reseller's positioning and market niche. A reseller that has positioned itself as a reseller of name-brand products at value prices is going to buy based on opportunistic sale of excess inventory by name-brand manufacturers of established products. In contrast, an upscale specialty store will be seeking unique and innovative merchandise without price constraints.

Even for the same reseller, the buying process will vary from one product line to another. For example, Sears will have different requirements for its automotive and clothing divisions due to the nature of the product differences. In the automotive division, product quality, warranty, technical advice, ease of reclaiming the cost of repair work redone due to defective parts, and lead time for supplying parts at short notice would be important. For the clothing division, product quality, price, credit, and annual delivery schedule might be more important.

SUPPLIER ALTERNATIVES   Obviously, an important factor in reseller buying decisions is the availability of a number of suppliers. This, in turn, depends on industry structure and supplier marketing efforts.

Industry structure is the level of competition in the specific industry sector. Table 17.2 identifies the nature of resellers' decision for each of the types of industry structure: monopoly, oligopoly, monopolistic competition, and pure competition. In a monopolistic industry, there is only one supplier, so the reseller's buying decision concerns not the choice of supplier but whether or not to carry that product (such as prescription drug Rogaine for hair regrowth from the Upjohn Co.). In oligopolistic competition, where there

Table 17.2	RESELLER DECISIONS ASSOCIATED WITH TYPES OF INDUSTRY STRUCTURE	
INDUSTRY STRUCTURE	DEFINITION	RESELLER DECISION
Monopoly	Industry with one supplier	Whether or not to carry the supplier's product
Oligopoly	Industry with few suppliers	Which supplier offers the best terms
Monopolistic competition	Many suppliers serving specialized niches	Which supplier line or product to carry
Pure competition	Many suppliers offering essentially the same product	Which supplier from among a possibly overwhelming array of choices.

are only a few suppliers, as in the steel industry, the reseller has more negotiating opportunity. In monopolistic competition, many suppliers carve out special product niches and monopolize within the niche; for example, there are hundreds of software suppliers, but they specialize in specific applications. The reseller decision therefore concerns the product line (or specific product) to carry, rather than the supplier choice. Finally, in the competitive industry structure, the reseller has a wide choice of suppliers. The variety and abundance of suppliers may, in fact, become confusing and time-consuming to sort. Often, therefore, some supplier industries may operate on exclusive reseller contracts, such as car dealerships and service franchises.

When there is brand proliferation due to intense competition from a large number of suppliers, resellers generally prefer pioneer brands over follower brands. **Pioneer brands** are those that are the first to enter the market and have significant advantage over existing substitute products. Resellers prefer the pioneer brands over follower brands even when these follower brands are just as good. The reason is that the success of follower brands generally comes at the expense of pioneer brands, so follower brands will cannibalize the sale of established pioneer brands (which are first-to-market). Because reselling follower brands would require allocation of shelf space to multiple brands, this will reduce category sales per unit of shelf space.[4]

The mere existence of suppliers is not adequate; what matters is whether or not the suppliers offer the kind of support the reseller requires and the marketing effort the suppliers are undertaking to make themselves appealing to the reseller. Some suppliers limit their reach to domestic markets and are therefore unappealing to foreign resellers, or to multinational resellers who need international availability of merchandise. Other suppliers, even if offering international service, are excluded from the consideration set due to their poor corporate image or poor country-of-origin image. For example, many well-qualified suppliers from third world countries are simply excluded due to poor country image, while suppliers from Japan and West Germany benefit from their positive country image.

Beyond global access and country and corporate image, the suppliers' marketing efforts in terms of support services they offer to resellers become a significant consideration. Some suppliers will offer only standardized merchandise with no support services. Others will offer a full slate of services such as technical advice, reseller staff training, missionary selling to end users (where the supplier salespersons will call on end users to educate them about the product and then direct them to resellers to place orders when needed), inventory and logistic support, and promotional support. Many suppliers have dedicated teams to manage the total relationship with the reseller. For example, Coca-Cola Company treats McDonald's as a major national account with an entire multifunctional team in place to respond to McDonald's needs as a reseller of Coca-Cola beverages.

Thus, supplier availability and access (determined by industry structure) as well as supplier attractiveness (determined by marketing efforts of various suppliers) in combination determine the supplier alternatives for the reseller.

SITUATIONAL CHARACTERISTICS Along with supplier alternatives and merchandise requirements, resellers' decisions are influenced by situational characteristics. Figure 17.1 identifies three key characteristics: (1) business climate, (2) market conditions, and (3) reseller's financial position.

Business climate refers to the condition of the national or international economy at the time of the purchase decision—an environmental context factor discussed in Chapter 5. The national or world economy might be going through a recession or inflation, and the interest rates might be low or high. During the recession, the reseller is likely to seek a supplier willing to sell smaller quantities. During an inflationary period, when the interest rates are high, resellers will be looking for liberal credit rates or for **consignment buying,**

an arrangement wherein the reseller receives the title and pays for the merchandise only after it is in turn sold to the end user.

Market conditions refer to unpredicted events causing a shortage or surplus of supply or changes in access to markets. For example, a labor strike at a major supplier, a drought causing crop failure, a political coup in a foreign supplier country, a trade embargo, and so forth, all represent market conditions that change the degrees of freedom the reseller has as a buyer.

The reseller's financial position represents its current profitability and liquidity position (i.e., availability of cash), and it varies from one business cycle to another. A reseller that is highly profitable but has low liquidity is likely to lean toward long-term contracts with better credit terms. On the other hand, if the reseller is not profitable but does have good liquidity, it is likely to seek large quantities at near-cost prices. In general, the healthier (more profitable and more liquidity) the financial situation a reseller is in at the moment, the more aggressively he or she is going to buy (i.e., encourage more suppliers to offer competitive pricing and negotiate very hard).

THE DECISION-MAKING UNIT (DMU)

The decision-making unit consists of those reseller personnel who participate in buying decision making and who have the authority to make the decision. DMU is a more general term—it may consist of a single individual, or two managers, or top management, or a committee. The buying center, discussed in Chapter 16, is a specific DMU, comprising members from diverse departments playing specific roles. The exact composition of the DMU varies from reseller to reseller. In general, it depends on whether the reseller organization is an independent owner-operated small store (such as the one you may find in

Figure 17.2

DECISION-MAKING UNIT CHARACTERISTICS
THAT INFLUENCE PURCHASE DECISIONS

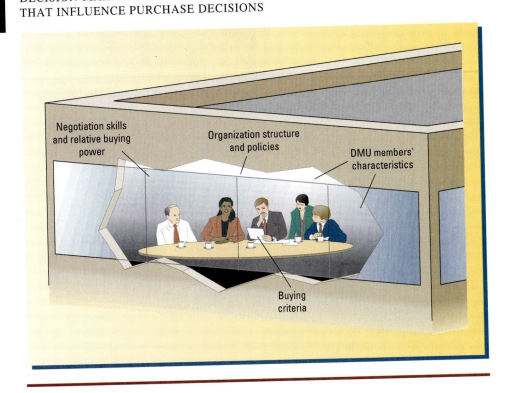

your neighborhood that sells, say, fresh fruits and vegetables only, or fresh fish only), a large professionally managed store (such as Harrod's of London or Robert's Grand in the United States), or a chain store such as Target, Kroger, Kmart, or Pier 1 Imports in the United States, Sainsbury's or Marks & Spencer in the United Kingdom, or Carrefoure in France, and El Corte Inglés in Spain.

The way the DMU makes decisions varies according to the organization's structure and policies, the DMU members' characteristics, the buying criteria, and the buyer's negotiation skills and relative buying power (see Figure 17.2).

ORGANIZATION STRUCTURE AND POLICIES   Resellers differ in their purchase organization. In multiunit reseller chains (such as a chain store company with a number of stores), the purchasing function may be left to each store, or it may be centralized. In this centralized purchasing unit, or even in the decentralized, store-by-store purchasing units, the decision makers may comprise members from other specialties such as finance, sales, and so on, or the purchase authority may rest with a purchase task specialist.

DMUs may also differ on purchase policies. For example, some resellers have a policy of buying from domestic producers only. Others enforce certain supplier practices

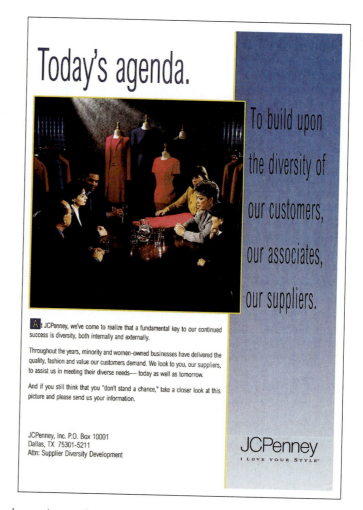

Business customers have various purchase policies. Here JCPenney promotes its policy of encouraging minority and women-owned suppliers.

(e.g., child labor laws, environment-friendly resource conservation, and so on). Another policy is to buy on consignment only.

INDIVIDUAL CHARACTERISTICS OF THE DMU MEMBERS   The characteristics of the individual DMU members include their educational and technical backgrounds, their level of expertise, personalities, and their motivations. These factors, discussed for business buyers in Chapter 15, influence the reseller buyer's need for information and advice (how much and what kind), evaluation criteria, and preference for modes of interaction with supplier personnel.

BUYING CRITERIA   Resellers also differ in buying criteria. These refer not just to merchandise-specific requirements but also to vendor evaluation criteria. Vendor evaluation criteria refer to relative emphasis on such vendor attributes as delivery lead time, quality assurance, and willingness to customize delivery and lot sizes.

NEGOTIATION SKILLS AND RELATIVE BUYING POWER   Buyers differ in their aptitude for negotiating the terms and conditions of purchase. The actual supplier choice is influenced by how hard the reseller bargains for favorable terms, and, correspondingly, how far suppliers are willing to offer various terms of sale. Generally, once the merchandise is relevant and acceptable, the supplier choice is affected strongly by the terms and conditions the supplier is willing to accede. The negotiation process and outcome are influenced by negotiating skills of the two parties and the relative power between them (discussed later).

SUPPLIER AND MERCHANDISE CHOICE AND SATISFACTION

Once the DMU makes the supplier selection, it delivers the purchase contract to the supplier. The resellers then monitor the supplier performance in supplying according to the contract. They evaluate both the quality of merchandise and the service support. If supplier performance is up to or above expectations, satisfaction results; if the performance falls below, dissatisfaction ensues. The satisfaction or dissatisfaction feeds back into the criteria related to supplier alternatives, thereby influencing future decisions.

What Do Resellers Desire from Suppliers?

When resellers agree to do business with suppliers, they want the reseller to fulfill certain obligations. Obviously, resellers want the merchandise to be of the desired quality. But they want more. Specifically, among the other services or support that resellers desire are freedom to price and promote the merchandise; adequate trade margins; protection from undue competition; adequate advertising, merchandising, training, and information support; and efficient order fulfillment.

FREEDOM TO PRICE AND PROMOTE THE MERCHANDISE

Resellers as customers of manufacturers want freedom to price their merchandise in line with their own goals and interests; they tend to reject manufacturer control over the price to end-user customers. In most circumstances in the United States, manufacturers' attempts to dictate a reseller price are illegal under the **Robinson Patman Act**—the act prohibits reseller price maintenance practices since such practices would erode free competition. Manufacturers are entitled to demand an end-user price maintenance, however, if the merchandise is sold on consignment. They also may attempt to influence the reseller price by printing a suggested retail price on the package. Even in these circumstances though, resellers generally wish to retain some control over their pricing practice.

A related issue is the participation in manufacturer-dictated sales promotion schemes. Resellers desire freedom from pressure to implement supplier-designed promotion

WINDOW ON RESEARCH

How Japanese Supermarkets Buy

Do Japanese resellers desire to do business with the United States and other foreign manufacturers and suppliers? What factors influence their supplier selection? And, what kind of business relationships do they seek with their suppliers?

To answer these questions, an international team of marketing professors (Frank Alpert, Michael Kamins, Tomoaki Sakano, Naoto Onzo, and John Graham) surveyed 107 buyers of different product groups in Japan's 16 largest supermarkets. Based on the survey data, in-depth interviews, and personal observations, the researchers concluded that Japanese supermarkets exhibit the following buying behavior:

■ *Preference for pioneer brands*—The preference for pioneer brands over follower brands is even more marked among Japanese supermarkets than among their U.S. counterparts. One reason is that shelf space is scarce in Japan, where most stores are small. Also, Japanese pioneer brands generally keep on improving (due to the Japanese business philosophy of *kaizen*, continuous improvement), so the follower brands are seldom able to catch up. Finally, because the Japanese market is geographically compact as well as more homogeneous in terms of consumer tastes, market penetration of pioneer brands is quick and complete, leaving little room for follower brands.

■ *Loyalty to established suppliers*—Japanese cultural norms encourage loyalty and long-term relationships with suppliers. Specifically, the norm of *amae*, or "indulgent dependency," guides Japanese to seek and value relations of mutual dependence. The norm of *giri-ninjo*, meaning "obligation and compassion toward others," keeps Japanese wanting to return favors from channel partners. And the "good of the group over the individual" norm discourages self-centered and opportunistic behavior in relationships with suppliers. Because developing long-term relationships takes time and effort, resellers don't encourage new suppliers, which further reinforces their loyalty to established suppliers.

■ *Preference for caring interaction style*—Some researchers have proposed two broad types of interaction styles: principled and caring. In the principled interaction style, the supplier basically follows the rules, even when such rules may lead to the reseller-customer's dissatisfaction. In the caring interaction style, the supplier would go to great lengths to take care of the customer's requests. For example, if a reseller wanted more merchandise than usual during a specific period, and if supplying that quantity required overtime production, a principled supplier would not accommodate this request, whereas a caring supplier would. Of these two interaction styles, Japanese supermarkets preferred the caring style.

■ *Preference for large suppliers*—Japanese resellers preferred large suppliers because they perceived them to be more stable and likely to be around for a long time. Larger suppliers were also perceived to have adequate resources to serve their needs.

■ *Preference for domestic suppliers*—Japanese resellers preferred domestic rather than foreign suppliers, but not because of antiforeign sentiment. Rather, they perceived Japanese product quality to be superior to that from foreign suppliers. Also, Japanese suppliers were already established as suppliers, and loyalty precluded encouragement to other suppliers. Finally, the interaction style of foreign suppliers tended to be principled rather than caring.

Source: Frank Alpert, Michael Kamins, Tomoaki Sakano, Naoto Onzo, and John Graham, "Retail Buyer Decision Making in Japan: What U.S. Sellers Need to Know," Report No. 95-108 (Cambridge, MA: Marketing Science Institute, 1995). Additional information available at **http://www.japan-guide.com/e/e2073. htm**

policies. Resellers want to use their shelf space for stocking items they believe will move fast, rather than stocking items the manufacturers want to promote. The flip side of the coin is that resellers desire, rather than dislike, some kinds of promotions—the promotions that would increase their sales; manufacturer attempts to block such promotions are then met with reseller opposition.

A case in point is Procter & Gamble's adoption of the everyday low pricing (EDLP) practice in the early 1990s. Prior to this practice, the company offered consumer promotions featuring discounted price, or special bonus product offers from time to time. EDLP eliminated these promotions in favor of a slightly reduced price now available on a permanent basis. However, retailers had become so used to promotional allowances on established P&G brands that they saw P&G's new pricing policies to be counter to their own interest; some even threatened to drop P&G products from their merchandise assortment. P&G held its ground, and most retailers continued to carry (or resumed carrying) P&G products. P&G took pains to explain its rationale to its resellers: EDLP results in new efficiencies by eliminating unevenness in production runs and resultant inventory build-ups. Such educational efforts, and its strong brand standing, earned P&G its resellers' continued participation in the distribution chain. At the same time, the case underscores the general desire among resellers to be in control of how much promotion they want to run, when, and for which products.

ADEQUATE TRADE MARGINS

Resellers desire adequate profit margins for their effort and investment. They sell many products at manufacturer-suggested list prices, even in situations where they are not obligated to maintain the manufacturer suggested price. In these situations, obviously, the resellers want the trade discount from the list price to be adequate to allow the reseller to cover his or her costs of operation and adequate profit. But even in situations where the reseller sets his or her own price, competition dictates the final price, and resellers desire the trade margins to be adequate at these going prices.

Many resellers work on a fee basis, especially in the service businesses (e.g., insurance, stock brokerage, or travel agency). In these instances, resellers desire an adequate fee; suppliers are of course interested in minimizing this fee, which is a cost to them. The acceptable solution is to ensure that fee is based on effort rather than mere sales volume. An example is travel agencies that sell airline seats. Historically, travel agents have received 10 percent of the ticket price as their commission. Many U.S. airlines are redesigning the fee structure: for example, Delta Airlines allows a maximum of $50 as a flat fee. Since the effort to book a travel itinerary is the same regardless of the ticket price, it makes sense to reward the travel agents on a flat fee basis rather than as a percentage of the ticket price.

For other resellers who handle physical goods, a recent practice is activity-based trade discounts. The price charged to the reseller is broken down as the basic merchandise price for the physical product plus fees for additional services according to the cost of these services. Thus, if a reseller orders a truckload, the supplier saves on part-truckload costs of transportation and passes on these savings. If the reseller does not need merchandise display assistance, then the reseller is not charged for this service. This **activity-based costing** (ABC)—in which trade discounts and fee are based on specific services the reseller asks of the supplier—allows resellers to make a profit commensurate with their value-adding effort.

PROTECTION FROM UNDUE COMPETITION

Each reseller wants to be able to sell a manufacturer's or supplier's brand without undue competition. This competition can come from the manufacturer selling the merchandise to too many other resellers, selling the merchandise to off-price resellers, and engaging itself in direct selling to end users.

For any product, the manufacturer has to decide the desired **distribution intensity**— the number of outlets at which a product is available in any market. Three distribution intensities are possible: **exclusive** (only one reseller offering the product in a particular market), **selective** (only a few resellers offering a product), or **intensive distribution** (offering the product through as many resellers as possible in order to make it conveniently available). A manufacturer has to select the distribution intensity and also decide how many resellers are needed to implement the desired intensity. For example, with exclusive distribution, how should the territory be demarked to delineate a single market? The reseller would like its territory defined as broadly as possible. The manufacturer wants to ensure that its products are available to end users without inordinate inconvenience that a broad territory would cause because customers would have to travel larger distances or wait longer for the reseller to service individual end-user's needs. The reseller needs to be educated on the need to have enough resellers to serve the end-user customers effectively.

A specific case arises when markets develop so that a single reseller can no longer serve a market that it once adequately served. For example, one automobile dealer or one McDonald's franchise might have been sufficient in a town when it was small; with population growth, the town might have grown too large for one dealer. Even so, the dealer might not be agreeable to having another dealer in the area. One solution to this dilemma is to motivate the dealer or reseller to open a second store in the area.

The second source of competition that the reseller wants to avoid is from off-price resellers. For example, specialty stores (Structure or American Eagle—U.S. retailers of casual clothing) and upscale department stores (such as Bloomingdale's or Neiman Marcus in the United States and Harrods of London) would like their suppliers to *not* make the same merchandise available to discount stores (such as Target or Kmart) and off-price de-

Louis Vuitton. Writing

Louis Vuitton luggage and accessories are sold only in exclusive Louis Vuitton shops in London: Mayfair, 149 New Bond Street • Knightsbridge, 198/199 Sloane Street The City, 7 Royal Exchange, Cornhill • Harrods, Ground Floor, Knightsbridge. For more information, please call: 0800 393 304.

LOUIS VUITTON

Louis Vuitton prides itself on its use of very selective distribution.

signer stores (such as TJ Maxx, a clothing store in the United States). To minimize competition of this sort, manufacturers generally restrict the availability of a brand in its initial years; discount and other retailers have access to the brand only after it has been around for a few years. Generally by that time new line extensions are brought out, and these newer brand extensions are again restricted, limiting access to the full-price resellers. In addition, manufacturers may offer discount or off-price resellers only irregular or excess merchandise, often with the brand label disfigured. Finally, manufacturers bring out brand variations, with differences in features and price to match the reseller image. A good example of this strategy is Seiko Watch Co., which sells three different brands through different channels: Pulsar, selling for $75 to $200 through mass merchandisers; Seiko, selling for $150 to $400, mostly through the high-end discount merchandisers; and Lassale, selling for $450 to $650 through jewelers, other specialty stores, and upscale department stores. Since each type of reseller caters to different categories of end users or household customers, the resellers are agreeable to this strategy.

The third source of competition for the reseller is from the manufacturer itself, which may want to deal with large end users directly. The logic here is that it is not efficient for some end users to buy from the reseller; rather they need to deal directly with the manufacturer. This can happen when the customer is nationwide or global, and the resellers are local. In some cases, resellers may be unable to provide the volume or technical assistance needed by specific end users. Or the end users may not need the value that resellers add. For instance, resellers stock the merchandise until customers need it, but some large customers provide their own warehouse, so they don't want to pay for the cost of warehousing inevitably included in resellers' price. One such large customer is the U.S. government's General Services Administration (GSA), whose requirement is for large quantities of products, and which has its own warehouse to stock merchandise until its own internal end users requisition it. GSA wants to deal directly with manufacturers. Resellers are generally agreeable to such direct dealing by the manufacturer if they understand that to be the most efficient and sometimes the only feasible way.

In many cases, a good compromise is to assign the warranty work or installation and training tasks to the local reseller for those end users to whom the company has sold directly. Resellers are agreeable to this solution since they save on the cost of selling effort and yet retain the after-sales business from these customers. For example, IBM sells its computers direct to some large end users, but redirects their installation, training, and maintenance work to local resellers.

SUPPORT FROM MANUFACTURERS

Resellers desire support from manufacturers on many aspects of business:

- *Training*—Resellers want manufacturers to train their (resellers') employees in product knowledge, demonstration, technical applications, and store operating procedures. This desire is often compatible with manufacturers' own goals: to maintain a high quality of service to end-user customers, some manufacturers require reseller personnel to be trained and certified and periodically recertified.

- *Advertising and promotion*—Resellers also desire manufacturers to advertise and promote the merchandise to end users both nationally as well as in their local markets. They also desire trade allowance for local advertising wherein the reseller would advertise both its store as well as specific merchandise.

- *Merchandising*—Merchandising support can range from the supplier or distributor personnel taking care of shelf stocking and stockkeeping to giving advice to store salespersons on how the merchandise presentation can be made attractive.

Dole Food Company offers its resellers all the support they need.

■ *Information*—Resellers look to manufacturers to keep them abreast of new developments in the market and to share information that the manufacturer's market research department may have collected on trends in reselling. This last requirement is actually mutual—resellers too have intelligence about local markets that manufacturers want to know. This mutual need calls for reciprocal sharing of information.

EFFICIENT ORDER FULFILLMENT

Finally, resellers want quick order fulfillment, as was demanded by Rundel's department store in the opening vignette. Most resellers want to minimize their inventory carrying costs. Not only do resellers want to minimize the amount of inventory they carry; they also want to avoid stockouts. In fact, the benefits of efficient order fulfillment are valued so much that resellers are seeking channel partnerships.

Channel Partnerships

Suppose you are a producer of electronic equipment, such as direct satellite TV antennas, selling them to electronic equipment stores, who then sell them to end users. To maximize your profit, you could always attempt to squeeze the maximum price out of your dealers; dealers in turn could try to squeeze out the lowest price from you. As each party tries to influence the other and each resists such attempts from the other, the interaction could become adversarial. Such interactions do not pay. Increasingly, resellers as well as suppliers are engaging in more cooperative behavior by entering into channel partnerships.

A **channel partnership** is a relationship between a reseller and a supplier in which these two parties agree on objectives, policies, and procedures designed to further each other's business.[5] Channel partnerships differ from the franchise system (e.g., McDonald's or car dealerships) in that franchising is based on nonexclusive supply agreements: each party has the freedom to deal with other suppliers/resellers. As an example, in early 1993, Kmart initiated a program of "Partnership in Merchandise Flow" with more than 300 suppliers (some of them direct competitors).[6]

The partnership differs from the traditional approach. In the traditional approach, each party tries to serve its own interest, even if it comes at the expense of the other. For example, the manufacturer or supplier wants to maximize its sales volume at the highest price; the reseller, on the other hand, wants to negotiate the lowest price possible. These two goals often made the two parties behave like adversaries. In contrast, in the partnership approach, the goal is to maximize the profits for the entire supply chain system, which consists of the supplier and the reseller.

This is done by minimizing the cost and ensuring maximum availability of the item for the reseller's customer. That is, the goal changes to ensuring that the right product is at the right place at the right time with minimum cost of carrying the inventory. Achieving this goal requires joint management of inventory flow: hence the need for partnership.[7]

Marketing to resellers entails more than selling just the product. Ambassador Card Co. offers its reseller customers help in store design and management.

Areas of Cooperation

At a minimum, most channel partnerships engage in and benefit from improving the inventory management and stock replenishment processes. Some partnerships extend their cooperation beyond order replenishment to cover other activity areas, such as new-product development, category management, and joint marketing.

MANAGEMENT OF INVENTORY FLOW

As resellers have figured the high costs of keeping a large amount of inventory, management of inventory flow has become their single most important concern. More and more resellers are therefore seeking (and receiving) inventory management support. The support may involve some form of "quick response" or "efficient consumer response." **Quick response** refers to suppliers offering fast product replenishment to resellers. This practice was first used in the mid-1980s by the association of domestic textile and apparel producers as a competitive weapon against apparel imports. Taking advantage of their domestic location, they promised to offer resellers a superior stock-replenishment service.

This practice was termed **efficient consumer response** (ECR) by the food industry. The goal of ECR was for the food supplier and reseller, such as supermarkets, to work together to bring better value to the grocery consumer. In this approach, food suppliers design a distribution system that simultaneously (a) avoids stockout at the grocer and (b) minimizes the cost of carrying inventory in the entire channel. This entails various action components such as (1) the food supplier is linked with store-shelf inventory data that is updated immediately as customers buy food items from the store, (2) producing food based on real-time food store sales forecasts, (3) relocation by the supplier of warehouse

Procter & Gamble appeals to resellers by its "floor-ready" packaging.

facilities closer to food stores and design of food trucks so they, too, serve as storage and miniwarehouses (e.g., the trucks are equipped with a cold storage facility). These actions together minimize the inventory costs throughout the system, and the supplier is able to pass on the savings to resellers, and through them to the consumer. Both resellers and consumers get better value in terms of lower prices and merchandise availability (due to reduced stockouts).

As far back as the mid-1980s, retailers and their suppliers began to work together to share information and technology in an effort to improve their relationship. By late 1993, department stores, discount houses, specialty retailers, and others had developed very effective channel partnerships. Reseller customers in the partnership desire and obtain such additional benefits as obtaining merchandise "floor ready" (ready to display on the sales floor as the task of ticketing the merchandise is shifted to the supplier) and reducing control steps in the process because of greater trust among the partners.

Excellent examples of companies that have successfully created a channel partnership are Wal-Mart and Procter & Gamble, which initiated a partnership in 1985. They began to use information technologies to improve the efficiency of merchandise flows to ensure that Wal-Mart shelves are always adequately stocked without excess inventory. Through the use of electronic data interchange (EDI), which hooks computers together via telephone lines to swap information, P&G's on-time deliveries to Wal-Mart improved significantly, and at the same time, **inventory turnover**—the number of times the inventory is completely restocked during a given year, which is an index of inventory

Electronic Partnering: The Case of Cedar Works

WINDOW ON PRACTICE

In 1990, Wal-Mart told Cedar Works, the then $4 million manufacturer of aromatic bird feeders and mailboxes, that it had to start taking orders and sending invoices online. The company's experience with information technology at the time went no further than two stand-alone Macintosh computers. Nevertheless, Cedar Works' owners were enthusiastic about mastering whatever technology was necessary to keep a big customer happy. Today, Cedar Works is an $18 million company, online with no fewer than 10 major retailers, including Home Depot Inc., Target Stores, and Nature Co. Inc. Roy Williams, one of Cedar Works' owners and its vice president, says it's been a win-win situation. "We've improved cash flow and customer satisfaction," notes Williams. "And even if we were losing money, customer satisfaction alone might justify being online."

Whether companies are ready or not, the age of electronic partnering has arrived. For many that will mean replacing conventional order-taking, shipping, and invoicing processes with electronic data interchange (EDI) systems.

Large companies and companies that serve consumers may be able to pick and choose when and with whom they set up EDI relationships. But growing companies that supply large organizations aren't likely to have much say in the matter.

Giant retailers, big manufacturers, and the U.S. government are pushing EDI harder than ever. That's because they can save millions with EDI by placing and processing orders faster and more accurately. In addition, by sharing critical point-of-sale, inventory, and forecasting information with suppliers, large companies can carry smaller inventories and yet not be stocked out too frequently. Additional information available at **http: //www.ediconnection.com**

Source. Joshua Macht, "Are You Ready for Electronic Partnering?" *Inc. Technology*, no. 4 (1995), pp. 43–51.

efficiency—increased notably. To manage this partnership, P&G assigned a separate team to the Wal-Mart account, and even relocated some of its staff near Wal-Mart's purchasing office. It is this level of commitment to reseller that helps build partnership.[8] Wal-Mart has found its electronic partnering with P&G to be so useful in terms of procurement efficiency that it began seeking similar partnerships with other suppliers, as the accompanying Window on Practice box on page 671 shows.

AUTOMATING STOCK REPLENISHMENT

Using digital technology, resellers who participate in a channel partnership are able to automate the stock-reordering process as follows. With conventional (nonautomated) order placement, the reseller transmits a replenishment order to the supplier by mail, phone, fax, or E-mail; the supplier has to reenter the order in its records for order processing. In contrast, with digital technology, the item sold is scanned at the checkout register, and the remaining stock is instantly updated. The stock is compared to model stock quantity. **Model stock quantity** is the number of units needed to cover the expected demand at a prespecified percent of the time (usually 95 percent), between the order placement and receipt of merchandise. Since this elapsed time depends on the supplier's response time, the model stock determination requires joint planning by the supplier and reseller. Research has shown that a well-designed model stock yields considerably higher rates of inventory turnover than traditional, nonautomated order placement and replenishment methods. Thus, model stock-based automated replenishment is a key benefit of channel partnership.

Resellers may use varying degrees of automation for stock replenishment:

- *Preparing replenishment orders*—Resellers prepare the replenishment order and then transmit it to the supplier via EDI. Even though the resellers themselves prepare the order, they may still provide ongoing access to the supplier to their point-of-sale (POS) data to enable the supplier to plan their production schedule.

- *Reverse purchase order*—The suppliers prepare the electronic purchase order (based on the model stock and the POS data transmitted from the reseller to the supplier) and send it to the reseller for reseller review and approval, with any modifications if necessary.

- *Supplier-managed replenishment*—Resellers give the supplier a blanket authorization to prepare and ship orders based on POS and stock information transmitted from the store direct to the supplier through an EDI system. This saves the reseller the order preparation task and thus reduces buying costs. A prime example of this arrangement is the partnership between Wal-Mart and Procter & Gamble, described earlier.

NEW-PRODUCT DEVELOPMENT

Some resellers want to be involved in the new-product development process both in generating specifications and in facilitating market tests of products. For example, apparel resellers allow manufacturers access to their customers for testing new design concepts. For new products with long gestation time, resellers participate in R&D to assure themselves a guaranteed source, sometimes on an exclusive basis. For example, developing new strains of produce may take as much as six to eight years and a lot of money. Many supermarkets in the United Kingdom and Europe have collaborated closely with fruit producers in New Zealand to develop new strains of kiwi fruit.[9]

CATEGORY MANAGEMENT

Some resellers partner with suppliers on **category management,** the merchandising decisions intended to maximize reseller profits on an entire product category (e.g., diapers, bakery goods, or soft drinks). The reseller gives the leading supplier for a product category responsibility to study demand patterns and recommend ideal assortments and shelf-space allocations, including merchandise from competing suppliers.

JOINT MARKETING

Some resellers may request or accept supplier collaboration in selling to key new accounts (end users). This cooperation can also take the form of the marketer undertaking a direct marketing effort to selected groups of the reseller's customers such as senior citizens. Resellers and their suppliers may also develop in-store promotions; these differ from promotion schemes imposed unilaterally by manufacturers or resellers' use of self-designed promotions that run counter to manufacturer's desired product image (e.g., price promotions on designer clothing).

Power in Relationships with Resellers

One factor that deeply influences the partnership relationship in a channel is the relative power between the two parties. **Power** in a reseller and supplier pair is the ability of one party to influence the decisions of the other. For example, if a reseller can influence a manufacturer or supplier to modify quality assurance processes, or to assume the task of placing tags on merchandise so the merchandise is floor- or shelf-ready, then the reseller has exercised power over the supplier. On the other hand, if a manufacturer/supplier can influence a reseller to alter shelf-space allocation in favor of the supplier, then the supplier has exercised power. Both parties can exercise power—resellers can influence some decisions of suppliers, and suppliers can influence other decisions of resellers.

BASES OF POWER

Power comes from the relative resources a party controls. A manufacturer with a strong brand has power due to the end-user appeal of the brand. A reseller with a loyal following of customers commands power over suppliers because it offers access to markets the manufacturer desires. These resources that enable power to be exercised are termed **power bases or sources of power**.

Work on bases of power in human interaction has been pioneered by sociologists John R. P. French and Bertram Raven.[10] Based on their pioneering work, marketing scholars have identified five bases of power in distribution channels: reward power, coercive power, legitimate power, referent power, and expert power (see Table 17.3).[11]

REWARD POWER   A channel member's reward power arises from the ability to give the other party something of value contingent upon certain favorable activity by the latter. Thus, resellers can promise manufacturers access to scanner data in return for expedited delivery schedule. On the flip side, manufacturers can offer large sums of advertising money in return for being made the primary supplier. Some of the key rewards resellers value and seek are cooperative advertising money, expedited shipments, special price deals, enhanced trade allowances, training and joint marketing support. In turn, resellers have the following rewards at their command: primary supplier status, preferred merchandising display, point-of-sale (POS) support, special emphasis in personal selling.

COERCIVE POWER   Coercive power consists in a channel member's ability to punish the other for failure to undertake the desired activity. Thus, manufacturers/suppliers can threaten to drop the reseller if the latter did not carry out the company's policies. Resellers can likewise threaten to boycott a particular manufacturer's merchandise if the

Table 17.3 POWER BASES IN DISTRIBUTION CHANNELS

POWER BASE	SOURCE	EXAMPLES
Reward power	Ability to give the other party something of value contingent on the other party's behavior	Resellers providing access to scanner data in exchange for favorable delivery schedules; manufacturers providing advertising money in exchange for being made primary supplier
Coercive power	Ability to punish the other party for failure to undertake a desired activity	Resellers boycotting a manufacturer's merchandise if it requires a slotting allowance; manufacturers dropping a reseller if it does not participate in a sales promotion
Legitimate power	The belief of one party that the other has a right to make demands or influence decisions	Resellers that handle products on a consignment basis, accepting the manufacturer's right to set prices; manufacturers accepting resellers' right to set prices when they take title to the products
Referent power	One party's identification with and attraction to the other	Resellers' desire to carry products and brands that fit their desired image; manufacturers' desire to have their products placed in stores with the desired image
Expert power	One party's possession of knowledge valuable to the other	Resellers needing training to handle technical products; manufacturers wanting insight into how customers make buying decisions in the store

latter doesn't alter some undesired selling practice. For example, when the news broke of some brands of clothing being manufactured in sweat shops in third world countries under despicable conditions of child labor and low wages, some retailers announced their intentions to drop the brand until manufacturers improved their labor practices.

LEGITIMATE POWER   Legitimate power resides in the belief of one party that the other party has the "legitimate" right to demand or influence decisions. For example, if a reseller handles some merchandise on consignment basis (where the reseller acquires ownership of and pays for the item only after it is sold to the end user), he or she would consider it a legitimate demand from the supplier that the item be priced at a certain price. In other settings, where the reseller obtains title to the merchandise received from the supplier, he or she has the legitimate right to price that merchandise.

REFERENT POWER   Referent power results from the fact that one party identifies with the other and finds the other an attractive business partner. In effect, the reseller views the manufacturer or supplier (or vice versa) as offering the merchandise ideally suited to his or her own image of self. Thus, Bloomingdale's or Harrods would like to carry Ralph Lauren's line of clothing, but not a brand from an unknown supplier. Resellers and suppliers may also identify with each other when they adopt the same philosophy of business or share a social cause (e.g., environment, or good labor practices) or adopt the same strategy such as a strategy of low cost or of differentiation.

EXPERT POWER   Expert power comes from one member possessing special knowledge valuable to the other party. For technical products, generally, the manufacturer has more knowledge and resellers depend on them for technical training. Similarly, resellers often have intimate knowledge of their customers' behavior, and this expertise is valued by manufacturers.

THE EXERCISE OF POWER

As already mentioned, power is never completely unilateral. Rather, each party exercises some power. The negotiations and dealings among the parties are inevitably shaped by the perceptions of relative power (and the source of a specific power), and their long-term relationship is based on the history of exercised power.

Moreover, power shapes relationships and dealings by its very existence, even when it is not exercised. This is specifically true for negative power (coercive power). If one party possesses a specific power (such as coercive power), the other's mere awareness of it elicits the desired cooperative behavior. One key skill of channel partners is therefore to be able to correctly read the degree of relative power the other party has. Manufacturers and suppliers have to be cognizant of the sources of power resellers possess.

The Role of Reseller Strategy

For business firms in general, business strategy scholar Michael Porter has identified three strategies: market niching, low-price strategy, and differentiation.[12] Market niching refers to tailor-making one's market offering to the needs of a small segment of customers. In the low-price strategy, a firm competes by a low-cost advantage, assuring customers a below

Target Stores' "low price, good value" marketing strategy influences its own choice of suppliers.

going-rate price. In differentiation, the firm competes by offering better product quality. Resellers too adopt one of these strategies. For example, Limited and Banana Republic stores use a niche strategy in clothing; Pier 1 Imports in home furnishings; natural or organic food stores use market niching for those products. Kmart, Big Lots general merchandise store, and warehouse clubs use a low-price strategy. Examples of the differentiation strategy include Bloomingdale's department store, Victoria's Secret (a store chain for women's lingerie), and Lens Crafters (an eye glass store chain), which differentiate themselves on the basis of product quality, merchandise assortment, and/or customer service.

Scholars in distribution channel management have argued that resellers' competitive strategies determine what kind of manufacturer/supplier they select to do business with and also what kind of relationship they want to have with the supplier. For example, based on a study of hardware dealers in the United States, marketing professors F. Robert Dwyer and Sejo Oh state, "There is no question that the principal wholesaler plays a significant role by orchestrating, enabling, and magnifying key aspects of the [reseller customer's] strategies."[13] The support that manufacturers and suppliers are able to offer must be compatible with the merchandising strategy the reseller has adopted. (For details, see the Window on Research box.)

How Resellers' Strategy Shapes Their Interaction with Manufacturers

WINDOW ON RESEARCH

Marketing professors Gerald E. Smith, Meera P. Venkatraman, and Lawrence H. Wortzel have done research on reseller preference for manufacturer-suppliers, depending on a match between the strategies of the two parties. They first propose a typology of strategies, which comprises a differentiation strategy and a price-centered strategy. Manufacturers' using a merchandise differentiation strategy focus on offering superior products, introducing new products with the latest technology or features, and investment in creating strong brand reputation. Price-centered manufacturer strategies are of two types: (a) low-price-enabling activities—quantity discount programs and frequent price promotions; and (b) price maintenance actions—policies instituted to avoid price wars, retaliation against dealers who undercut others, and efforts to maintain and control resellers' prices. Analogously, resellers pursue either a merchandise differentiation strategy or a low-price strategy.

To examine the role of each party, Professors Smith, Venkatraman, and Wortzel surveyed 120 resellers (who were independent television retailers). The survey questions were designed to find out the retailer's own marketing strategy and the kind of manufacturer/supplier support they seek and the manufacturer/supplier activity they like and dislike. Their findings were as follows:

Resellers who pursue a low-price strategy would value manufacturers that offer low-price-enabling activities over those that offer merchandise differentiation activities. Such resellers would avoid doing business with manufacturers/suppliers who pursue price maintenance actions. The converse is the case for resellers that pursue a merchandise differentiation strategy; they will value manufacturers offering merchandise differentiation activities.

Furthermore, resellers pursuing a merchandise differentiation strategy will look to the manufacturer to enable them to pursue their strategy; in comparison, low-price resellers consider their own actions (rather than the manufacturer's) to be more relevant and valuable in pursuing their strategy.

Source: Gerald E. Smith, Meera P. Venkatraman, and Lawrence H. Wortzel, "Strategic Marketing Fit in Manufacturer-Retailer Relationships: Price Leaders versus Merchandise Differentiators," *Journal of Retailing*, 71, no. 3, pp. 297–315. Additional information available at **http://haas.berkeley.edu/~jr/**.

Buying Groups

Suppose you were a small independent poultry farmer; how would you buy chicken feed, for instance? You could buy it from a pet food store and pay an exorbitant retail price; or you could buy it from the chicken feed salesman who comes calling on you to sell the chicken feed of an out-of-town factory. As an independent farmer, you depend on this supplier for your needs—and you don't have much clout. Now, suppose that instead of buying your requirement of chicken feed on your own and by yourself, you joined your neighbor, also a chicken farmer, and the two of you then joined your neighbor's neighbor, also a chicken farmer, and then the three of you joined with another chicken farmer at the other end of the town. You would now have some clout, and you will be able to demand the terms of sale most suitable to you.

This is the genesis and the rationale of what are known as buying groups. **Buying groups** are organizations in which individual customers form an entity authorized to pool the needs and requirements of its members in order to obtain the economies of scale in buying and other favorable terms of sale from the seller.

Group Buying by Organizations

Buying groups first emerged in the agricultural sector, where farmers formed collectives to buy farming items, such as seed and fertilizer, in bulk (at a much lower price) and then redistribute these among themselves. This type of buying has also been referred to as *co-operative buying*.

Today, the practice is widespread among supermarkets, drug stores, department stores, and even some institutional buyers such as hospitals. Among the supermarkets are IGA stores in the United States, whose name is an abbreviation for Independent Grocers Association. Similarly, in the drug store sector, smaller independent drug stores have begun to form buying groups, purchasing their products from the same manufacturers.

This pattern of buying has also been very prevalent in the department store sector, where, after the emergence of the chain stores, independent retailers realized that they didn't have the volume necessary to buy at low prices. As a result, the independent stores merged to form what is referred to as Federated Stores, which is basically a buying group. For example, Macy's and Rich's department stores, part of the Federated group, buy all their merchandise together, a fact that a household customer may not even be aware of. Another important sector where buying groups are playing a key role is the health-care sector. Hospitals are forming alliances with centralized purchasing, working in effect as a buying group.

Christian Purchasing Network: A Buying Group for America's Churches

Churches need a lot of products they buy from the commercial market: steeples, pews, lecterns, chairs and other furniture, copiers, fax machines, audio-visual equipment, and so on. How do they buy these products? They could search for individual products from individual suppliers, locate a suitable supplier, and then buy just what each church needs individually. Alternately, they could buy from a single-source supplier who acts as a buying group on their behalf. This is exactly what some 12,000 U.S. churches in and around Sarasota have done. For all their needs, they depend on a buying group called Christian Purchasing Network (CPN).

CPN started in 1989, when representatives of two Pentecostal denominations asked Tom McElheny, a consultant with an MBA and a doctorate in education, to study the feasibility of a purchasing network, and subsequently to start a company that would serve the two denominations with the purchase of durable goods. Today, CPN's annual sales are $19 million. McElheny knows that the total budget for the nation's 400,000 churches exceeds $100 billion a year, of which $30 billion is spent on hard goods and services—a large market to tap.

One characteristic of customers in this market is that churches don't have large capital, but they have good cash flow. CPN therefore arranges sales on a lease-purchase basis. CPN does not keep inventory of goods it sells. Rather, it arranges the sale by acting as an intermediary between manufacturers and church customers. These in-dustry-leading companies would rather not sell on a church-by-church basis; CPN provides them access to America's church market. CPN is designated as the preferred provider to the church market and gets a commission, and the churches get a price break. CPN has entered into contracts with such suppliers as office equipment maker Lanier Worldwide, Inc., and alarm system company ADT Securities System as their exclusive buyer group for churches.

CPN is a for-profit company and operates as such. It guarantees satisfaction of its church customers. It has a sales force looking for leads on any churches that may need something it can sell. It even seeks endorsements from its satisfied customers to attract other customers. But it is a business with compassion and religious fervor. It donates 10 percent of its profits to various church denominations. And its debt collection letter begin with a message from the Scriptures: "Every workman is due his wages."

Source: Michael Pollick, "Purchasing Firm Commands Bully Pulpit: When Churches Need Pews, Bibles, and Other Accessories, They Don't Rely on Divine Inspiration; They Rely on the Christian Purchasing Network," *Sarasota Herald Tribune*, Business Weekly section, June 30, 1997, p. 11. Additional information available at **http://www.christianet.com/cpn/**.

The economies of group buying are so attractive that the practice has spread to all types of organizations—bookstores, schools, police, NFL teams. For example, all of the teams in the National Football League have a centralized procurement department to buy helmets, jerseys, shoes, and so on. This results in huge savings. Public services such as police and ambulances do the same thing. For example, in the Los Angeles area, there are approximately 200 jurisdictions, each with its own budget; however, they all band together as a group when it comes to buying automobiles. So even though one jurisdiction may need to buy only two cars in a given year, by being part of a buying group and being among an order for 30,000 cars for all of the jurisdictions, the precinct gets a very favorable price negotiated with General Motors. In response to this type of buying, GM gets one standardized paint, which is black and white in California, and offers even lower prices to the jurisdictions by using a single color for all of the police cars. So both the local police and highway patrol cars look the same in California. Even many churches buy their requirements through a buyer group, as the accompanying Window on Practice box shows.

Membership Clubs

In consumer markets, people in small towns form informal buying groups when they take turns going to the nearby city to make purchases for many families at once. Traditionally, families have not charged each other for this service, but the activity has become institutionalized, and the resulting organizations charge for the service.

Buying groups of consumers are more formally organized as membership clubs. **Membership clubs** (also known as wholesale clubs) are buying organizations that buy in large quantities and then act as resellers to their members, who can be household or business customers or other, smaller, resellers. In the United States, the two largest membership clubs are Sam's and Costco; the total club industry sales are in excess of $40 billion.[14] By 1992, more than 21 million people held membership cards in U.S. wholesale clubs. And, according to one recent estimate, one-third of the membership club shoppers operate small businesses and are relatively upscale.

The major appeal of a membership club is price (see Figure 17.3). In a study sponsored by the Food Marketing Institute and conducted by McKinsey and Co. and Willard

REASONS FOR SHOPPING AT A WHOLESALE CLUB
VERSUS ANOTHER GROCERY OUTLET

*To be read: 74.9% of shoppers with a store preference for a wholesale club choose that store because of price.
Source: Based on a study of 2,117 shoppers carried out by MA*RT Consumer Intelligence System, Impact Resources Inc., reported in Robert E. O'Neill, "Competition," *Progressive Grocer*, May, 1992, pp. 61–78.

Bishop Consulting, it was concluded that membership clubs were able to sell the same grocery products for 26 percent less than grocery stores. In addition to low prices, membership clubs offer other advantages to customers. By charging a fee to enter the store, the clubs limit the number of people shopping in the store, and discourage convenience shoppers (which is why you won't find any express lanes there). To some shoppers, the membership clubs also offer a sense of novelty.[15]

The buyer behavior of membership clubs differs from conventional supermarkets primarily in that they want to exercise their buying power and negotiate deeply discounted prices. Their needs may also differ in terms of package sizes. Typically wholesale clubs require special display carton/tray packaging, special unit packaging/size, and/or special palletizing. Manufacturers can offer attractive prices due to economies of scale from bulk packaging and shipping the product from the factory directly to the store; the wholesale club's orders typically make up a truckload. This saves on transportation, warehousing, and inventory costs.

Membership clubs cannot succeed without the help of the manufacturer. Although many manufacturer marketing programs are common to wholesale clubs and traditional supermarkets, there are some programs tailor-made to benefit the wholesale clubs. To serve the needs of wholesale clubs, some manufacturers offer such extra added-value programs as special displays, in-store demonstrations, corporate volume purchase incentives, and special terms of payment.[16] For an example of the needs and strategies of a membership club, see the Window on Practice box.

Sam's Targets Business Customers

WINDOW ON PRACTICE

Sam's, the industry leader in the warehouse wholesale club business, experienced a lackluster performance in the recent past, due to increased competition as well as a generally depressed economy. To gain some lost ground, Sam's redirected its energies to its core customer group—office managers, convenience store operators, and other small businesses that buy from warehouse clubs for re-selling to the general public. Businesses have always accounted for a majority (about 70 percent) of clubs' sales. Sam's targets these small businesses sector by sector—medical, janitorial companies, hotel/motel operators, and so on, selling them such products as wheelchairs, floor strippers, and sheets and towels.

Sam's has also adopted direct marketing. It has landed more than 10,000 new accounts from schools, governments, and business corporations. Many of the products sold to these large customers are delivered direct from manufacturers (i.e., Sam's own supplier sources).

In its own buying practice, Sam's is looking for even greater value. It set up a new buying group to find what it calls "treasure hunt items"—high-ticket items such as jukeboxes and grand pianos at bargain prices—that it targets to upscale household customers. For other items, it uses its large-volume clout to obtain the best prices available in the market. This enables it to offer merchandise at a 30 to 50 percent lower price than its competitors (other wholesale clubs).

Source: Wendy Zellner, "Why Sam's Wants Businesses to Join the Club," *Business Week*, June 27, 1994, pp. 48–49. Additional information available at **http://www.samsclub.com/**.

Affinity Customer Groups

Suppose in your mail one day you find the following offers from various marketing firms:

- One letter is from your alma mater's alumni association president, introducing a Visa credit card with your alma mater's seal. The letter suggests that the Visa company will make a donation to the alumni association and that you should be proud to own a Visa with your alma mater's seal.

- Your monthly bank statement has an insert advertisement offering you a selection of merchandise (such as a watch, a small am/fm radio, or a briefcase) at a special price for cardholders only.

- Another letter, from a life insurance company, offers you a special insurance policy as a member of the American Marketing Association (AMA). The insurance company got a membership list from the AMA and claims to have designed a policy specifically for AMA members.

What do these three market offers have in common? It is that you received each because you are a member of a group. The marketer decided to take advantage of (and give you an advantage based on) your affiliation with that group. Each offer is an example of what marketers call "affinity marketing."

Affinity Marketing

Writers on this topic have defined **affinity** as "an individual's level of cohesiveness, social bonding, identification, and conformity to the norms and standards of a particular reference group."[17] **Affinity marketing** has been defined as "a strategy used by vendors of goods and services to offer special incentives to association members in return for their endorsement."[18] A more recent definition refers to it as "a unique exchange process, in which value-expressive products and services are marketed to reference groups with cohesiveness, common interests, and/or values, usually in return for the group's endorsement, as marketing leverage to its individual members of constituency."[19]

The second definition draws on "affinity" much more intensely than does the first one and is, for that reason, more restrictive. First, it calls for value-expressive products and services, meaning products and services that express some value held dear by the group, such as an environmentally friendly product to an environmental group, or a religious product to a religious association. Second, the definition also requires the nature of the group to be such that its members are bound by some values and common interests, in the case of MADD (mothers against drunk driving), or Sierra Club (an environmental group).

Many affinity programs satisfy neither of these two conditions: for example, when as a frequent-flyer club member of an airline you receive an offer of special rates for long distance calling, the market offering neither expresses any value of the group, nor are you (and other frequent-flying club members) bound to the club with any emotional, value-based or common interest based ties. Rather, the offer is no more than an instance of target marketing with the distinction that it has received the endorsement of the group of which you are a member.

The Christian Purchasing Network (CPN), discussed earlier, is a good example of affinity marketing. Besides selling to churches, CPN targets individual church members for many products and services. As a church member, you get a special discounted price, and your church will receive a donation. CPN has even arranged for church members to obtain mortgage financing from PHH Corp., a real estate holding company as well as a mortgage banker. For PHH, affinity marketing is nothing new. It has been selling affinity

AAA, American Automobile Association, acts as an affinity group for a variety of products and services, such as a dining club membership, promoted here.

mortgages to members of the United States Automobile Association (USAA). USAA has about 3 million members, and PHH provides them with nearly $1.8 billion in home mortgages annually. CPN is aiming at 160 million Christians through its affinity programs.[20]

The most important element of affinity group marketing is obtaining the endorsement of groups of which the target customers are members. The members of these groups are the final recipients of the marketers offering, but they are actually the second-tier customers. The first-tier customer is the group or association's management—they had to be sold on the idea. On the members' behalf, therefore, they are acting as a buyer group. Accordingly, what is in it for them? With this question in mind, we examine the nature and functioning of affinity customer groups more closely.

Types of Affinity Groups

There are five main types of affinity groups: professional, social, common-cause, demographics-based, and marketer-generated.[21]

PROFESSIONAL AFFINITY GROUPS

Practitioners of a profession may form a professional affinity group to advance the profession's status and to facilitate individual professionals' practice of the profession. Members join the group, usually with a membership fee, to advance their individual careers, improve their status, network with other professionals, and generally heighten their identity and visibility in the profession. The American Marketing Association is an example of a professional group with a large, worldwide membership comprising marketing managers and marketing professors.

SOCIAL AFFINITY GROUPS

Individuals with common interests (usually unrelated to school or work) may form a group. Examples of these social affinity groups include neighborhood groups, PTAs (parent-teacher associations), bridge clubs, and bowling groups. Social groups are characterized by a high degree of social bonding that comes with the members' shared interests.

COMMON-CAUSE AFFINITY GROUPS

Some groups get formed to promote a socially desirable cause, such as prevention of drunk driving, promotion of certain religious values, or eradication of racial prejudice. The primary motivation for group members is the commitment to the group's mission and identification with the group's values. Examples of these common-cause affinity groups include political and religious groups, such as the Christian Coalition and the many political action committees, and Greenpeace (an environmental group).

DEMOGRAPHICS-BASED AFFINITY GROUPS

Some other groups are formed on the basis of common demographics such as age, religion, or ethnic heritage. The purpose of these demographics-based affinity groups is to promote interests common to the demographic group. The American Association of Retired Persons (AARP) is a prime example of age-based groups. In many communities, there are teen clubs, women's clubs, the Jewish center, or the Panhellenic group (for persons of Greek ethnicity).

MARKETER-GENERATED AFFINITY GROUPS

Finally, there are groups created by marketers themselves. These marketer-generated affinity groups include groups with special interest in a specific product—thus Harley Davidson (a U.S. manufacturer of motorcycles) has formed a Harley Owners Group (HOG). Similarly, Saturn car company and Nintendo (an electronic game company) have formed their own groups of product users. Many business firms now issue a membership card to their frequent customers, and these enrolled members then become an affinity group for other marketers.

Other marketer-generated groups are simply all the customers of a particular company. Thus, all American Express Card holders are automatically "card members"; the bank you do business with considers you a member of the bank's customer group. And, of course, you are a member of your fitness club, your sports club, even your magazine subscriber group. Marketers of diverse products could target you as a member of one of these groups. For example, a marketer of vitamins or natural herbal therapy products could send a mailing to a fitness club's members, offering them special membership price.

Affinity Strength

Groups are not equal in the affinity among members (i.e., in the degree of group cohesiveness and bonding individual members feel with the group and with one another). The degree of affinity of a group can be characterized along three dimensions: active/passive participation, level of socialization, and value identification. Other things being equal, affinity strength is presumably higher for groups that are more active than passive, provide opportunities for social interactions among members, and are centered around a value-based mission and strong identification among members (see Figure 17.4).

ACTIVE VERSUS PASSIVE PARTICIPATION

Some group memberships are based on members' active participation, while others require merely the passive enrollment of members. Examples of the former are PTA groups, the groups of volunteers for a social cause, various protest groups, and so forth. Passive enrollment groups include magazine subscribers, bank customers, or being on the mailing list of a local merchant. No group activities are required of (or indeed provided for) these members. But even among the active groups that offer group activities, individual members may choose to play either an active or a passive role.

LEVEL OF SOCIALIZATION

Some groups' activities entail face-to-face interaction among members, while other group activities, even when members participate actively, do not entail face-to-face interactions. Thus, environmental group members may actively participate in the group's activity (e.g., fund raising, writing to their congressman, promoting the cause among their work groups, and so on), but there may be few opportunities of social interaction among members. Purely social and local groups (e.g., bridge groups) score higher on this dimension than other groups.

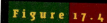 **Figure 17.4**

DIMENSIONS OF AFFINITY STRENGTH

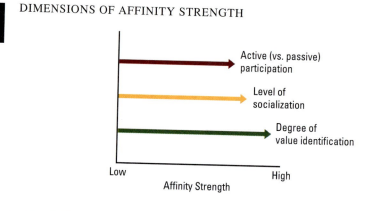

VALUE IDENTIFICATION

The group's value identification is the extent to which members are bonded by common group values and identify strongly with the group, taking pride in their group membership. Cause-related groups score high on this dimension, but other groups can vary from low to high as well. Thus, college fraternity groups (a type of social group) elicit a much higher identification and pride from their members than, say, bingo groups. Alumni are often proud of their alma mater and feel strong identification. Similarly, many ethnic groups elicit strong identification from their members.

Affinity Group Buying Motivations

Exchanges in affinity groups involve three parties: the affinity group organization, individual members, and the affinity marketer. For affinity buying to work, each party must benefit from the exchange. Each party receives different benefits from participating in an affinity group buying program. Table 17.4 summarizes these benefits.

BENEFITS TO THE AFFINITY MARKETER

The affinity marketer (i.e., the firm courting the affinity group) derives several benefits from targeting an affinity group. First, it gains access to the affinity group members with a single point of contact. Suppose an affinity group has 100,000 members; the marketing firm needs to negotiate a deal on behalf of these members only with a single DMU (decision-making unit) in the affinity group's executive body at the headquarters. It gains the names and addresses of all the members through the group's headquarters. Alternatively, it needs to direct its offering package only to the headquarter group, which would then communicate the offering to its members. Second, since the affinity group members share some common interest (such as the members of a theater group share a high level of interest in literature and drama), a market offering can be customized according to that shared interest. For example, the theater group members may be offered a CD collection of plays of interest to them. The large size of the group allows economies of scale in customization. Third, because the offering is now customized, the brand of product or service becomes differentiated from other noncustomized competitor offerings. Finally, the marketer's promotional costs are reduced; this reduction occurs because the affinity group promotes the program as part of its own regular member communication program (e.g.,

Table 17.4

BENEFITS OF AFFINITY MARKETING TO EACH PARTY

AFFINITY MARKETER	AFFINITY GROUP ORGANIZATION	INDIVIDUAL MEMBERS
Access to a customer group	Financial gains from shared incentives	Better value from the enhanced benefits package
Opportunity to customize offering on a large group basis	Publicity and promotion	Risk shifting in "brand" decision—implied reference group support
Meaningful brand differentiation	Enhanced image through corporate association	Satisfaction from contribution to their affinity group
Reduced promotion costs due to shared publicity vehicles	Better value for members	Pride in displaying the group's logo

monthly newsletter or the playbill of a theater performance), or incorporates it in its own offerings or in its own distribution outlets (e.g., the theater displaying the CDs in its lobby, or even selling it at the in-theater shop during the intermission).

BENEFITS TO AFFINITY GROUP ORGANIZATION

The affinity group organization also benefits in a number of ways. First, clearly there is some financial incentive for the organization—typically, the marketer would offer a share of profits to the group. Second, the group gets added publicity and promotion of its own cause. For example, Salant Menswear Group, California, has teamed up with World Wildlife Fund (WWF) to market ties carrying various wildlife designs. When people wear the tie, others notice and talk about it, thus giving WWF much-valued publicity. Third, sometimes the affinity marketer has high social prestige, and association with such marketers gives the affinity organization a better image. For example, if AARP (American Association of Retired Persons) agrees to lend its name to say, Kennedy Center for the Performing Arts, or the Kiwanis International sponsors a special exhibit at the National Gallery of Art in London, the image of the AARP or Kiwanis International is enhanced. Finally, the organization benefits as much as it enables or facilitates a better value offering to its members. The organization's first priority is to its members, and even if no other benefits were to accrue from a specific affinity program, its role is in serving as a conduit for its members to the benefits that the marketer's special value offering delivers.

BENEFITS TO INDIVIDUAL MEMBERS

Individual members benefit as well from an affinity program. First, they obtain better value from the affinity marketer's offering, which has been customized precisely to offer better value. For example, if the theater members were to build a collection of CDs of their interest, they would have to expend much time and money on their own. Second, the endorsement of the affinity group management can serve as a seal of quality, both in terms of the physical quality of the merchandise (e.g., the sound quality on CDs) as well as the quality of the nonphysical component of the offering (e.g., the content of selections on CDs). Consider, for example, a parent buying a children's story on audio cassette; if a church group has sponsored it, then the parent can rest assured that there would be no risk of the cassette containing improper material for the child. Thus, the member, in effect, shifts the risk in brand decision to the affinity organization's management. Third, the affinity-based purchase gives the member customer an implied reference group support from other members. The theater group member would feel comfortable, for example, in the knowledge that other members of the group would be buying the same collection. Fourth, members feel a sense of contributing to their organization by buying the affinity merchandise. For example, if members know that part of the profits will go to their organization, they feel good in making their contribution to the organization's cause. Finally, if the merchandise carries the organization's logo, as it often does, members may feel proud to display that logo. For example, a Visa card with your college seal on it can be a source of immense satisfaction to many graduates. It is important to note that an affinity offering has to offer at least one of these benefits in order to succeed; without it, there is no point to the affinity marketing program.

Marketing Programs for Affinity Groups

Affinity group marketing programs are distinguished from other types of marketing by their essential elements: a third-party endorsement, a shared incentive, and an enhancement package. The market offer received by group members has been first approved by and endorsed by the group's management or leader. This third-party endorsement gives the offer credibility. The endorsement may be explicit (when the group leader writes the cover letter) or implicit (it is understood that the offer is issued with leadership approval). Members tend to view such communications with a less negative (often actually positive) mind-set than is typical with other direct marketing.

Furthermore, the market offer to members includes an incentive that members value not as an individual benefit but as a contribution to the group's common cause or common resources. The affinity marketer typically contributes part of its profit to the group or to a cause valued by the group. For example, a credit card company may choose to contribute some funding to your alumni association.

The third essential element in affinity market offerings is an enhanced benefit package for the members. The market offering is packaged to suit the needs typical of the group's members. A similar package is either unavailable in the market or more expensive; accordingly, the affinity marketer's offer is more valuable to the individual member than other available options. For example, members of the Canadian Automobile Association (CAA) can get discounts at a number of hotels, motels, and car rental companies.[22]

Intermediary Decision Making and the Three Customer Roles

In this section, we illustrate the relevance of various concepts covered in the chapter to the three customer roles. Table 17.5 presents an overview.

If one considers the entire chain from manufacturer to the household consumer, it is customary to think of the end user as the user, and the intermediary reseller as the buyer. For example, a supermarket can be viewed as a buyer for households in its market area. However, the thrust of our discussion here is to view the reseller as a customer of the manufacturer/supplier, and in that role, all three roles of the customer apply to the reseller. Thus, the reseller organization itself plays all three roles vis-á-vis the manufacturer. Generally, the store department in which the merchandise is displayed and which is responsible for its sale is the user department. The formal buying department or buyer for the store is playing the buyer role, and the payer role belongs to someone responsible for financial planning and control. Various aspects of the reseller customer decision making apply, therefore, to these three roles in varying degrees.

First consider the reseller decision-making model. Among the important factors considered in this model are merchandise requirement, supplier alternatives, situational characteristics, DMU, and buying criteria. Merchandise requirements reflect the user department's needs and are relevant only to the user role—for example, in a department store, whatever the store floor managers want to feature the next season becomes the merchandise requirement. Availability of supplier alternatives affects both user and buyer roles. Users can exercise greater choice of merchandise if there are a lot of alternative suppliers; likewise, buyers get a choice of many vendors. Among the situational characteristics, the reseller's financial condition bears on the payer role; payer affordability increases with good financial condition. Merchandise buying DMUs differ from reseller to reseller, in that users may or may not be included in it, and if included, their role may also vary. Accordingly, the buying criteria may also vary. If users are included and are accorded importance, then the merchandise-related information will be valuable to DMUs, and a vendor with superior merchandise value would be able to mold initial merchandise specifications; if users are relegated to a peripheral role, then vendor attributes and financial terms of sale

Table 17.5 INTERMEDIARY CUSTOMER DECISION MAKING AND THE THREE CUSTOMER ROLES

	USER	PAYER	BUYER
A. RESELLER			
A Reseller Decision Model			
■ Merchandise requirement	■ Merchandise requirements reflect user dept.'s needs.		
■ Supplier alternatives	■ Availability of supplier alternatives gives users more choice of merchandise.		■ Supplier alternatives offer buyers more choice of vendors.
■ Situational characteristics		■ Reseller's financial condition reflects buyer resources.	
■ DMU	■ User inclusion and role in the DMU varies from reseller to reseller.		■ Professionalism of buyers varies from reseller to reseller.
■ Buying criteria	■ Users influence merchandise specifications.	■ Payers influence desirable credit terms.	■ Buyers develop criteria related to desirable vendor attributes.
What Resellers Seek			
■ Freedom to price	■ Pricing freedom gives users freedom to "use" the merchandise as they see fit.		
■ Adequate trade margins		■ Payers want to return on their investment.	
■ No undue competition	■ Removes user constraint on selling merchandise on value rather than on price.		
■ Manufacturer support	■ Helps users sell merchandise.		■ Avoids buyer hassle of obtaining the needed support from elsewhere.
■ Efficient order fulfillment	■ Users want to avoid stockouts.		■ Buyers want to automate replenishment.
B. BUYING GROUPS	■ Wholesale clubs are similar to resellers in regard to user, payer, buyer roles.	■ Price value is the principal reason for buying groups to operate.	■ Buyer sophistication varies, with wholesale club at the high end and local consumer groups at the low end.
	■ For cooperatives, end users/consumers also play the user role.		
C. AFFINITY GROUPS	■ Members are the users, and they derive various benefits from affinity programs (e.g., better merchandise value, and pride of contributing to the organization's cause).	■ Payer role is basically played by members, and price value to them should be considered.	■ Organization executives act as buyers who negotiate the deal.

are likely to dominate. In setting the buying criteria, merchandise specifications come from users, payers influence the desired credit terms, while buyers play a dominant role in developing criteria for desirable vendor attributes. Of course, the professionalism of buyers varies from reseller to reseller; large chain stores would have highly qualified buyer staffs at the chain's headquarters. A small local store may not be able to afford a buyer with special buying skills.

Another important topic we covered about resellers concerned what resellers seek from manufacturers. These include freedom to price the merchandise as one sees fit; adequate trade margins; no undue competition; manufacturer support in advertising, merchandising, and training activities; and efficient order fulfillment. These areas too are sought more or less by the three roles. Basically, user departments (i.e., sales floor managers) seek freedom to price the merchandise at a level they deem fit. User departments also seek protection from undue competition so they themselves don't have to resort to price-based marketing. They also seek manufacturer support for training, merchandise advertising, and in-store display. Finally, user departments value efficient order fulfillment, since they want to avoid stockouts.

For payers the most relevant consideration is adequate margins so that they may recover their investment in the merchandise. Finally, the buyer role of resellers also values adequate manufacturer support. Without such support from the manufacturer, the buyer department would have to obtain the support services from other vendors, which is a hassle. Buyers also want automatic order fulfillment so that the tedious task of reordering the merchandise is avoided or minimized.

The second type of intermediaries is buying groups. One type is wholesale clubs, and they are similar to resellers in respect of the three roles, so we shall not discuss them separately. Other types are cooperatives such as consumer credit unions or informal groups of friends and neighbors who might pool their buying needs and resources. For these groups, the end users play an active role as users, in generating merchandise requirements. For these consumers and end users, price value is the principal reason for forming the buying group, so the payer role is clearly very important. In regard to the buyer, that role is played by someone in the co-op or the informal group designated to carry on the buying task. Thus, buyer sophistication would vary widely, with wholesale clubs at the high end, where professionals are hired as buyers, and informal groups at the low end of buyer sophistication.

Affinity groups are the third type of intermediaries. Here, the user role clearly belongs to the affinity group members. In buying from an affinity program, they derive various user benefits. They might get better value merchandise in terms of performance; risk reduction due to the endorsement by the affinity organization also contributes to the performance value users seek. Pride of contributing to the organizational cause and opportunity to display affinity group membership via the affinity marketer offerings (which typically carry the affinity group's logo) give users some social and emotional values. Better value in the form of lower price gives value to the payer role, which is also played by the members. Finally, the buyer role is played by the affinity group's organization who negotiates the deal. The organization's policies about what kind of affinity merchandise to solicit and/or endorse and the executive's negotiation skills will influence the decision on any affinity program proposal.

Summary

In this chapter, we described the customer behavior for three types of intermediaries: resellers, buying groups, and affinity groups. No matter how much household customers want a manufacturer's product, it won't get sold unless intermediaries first buy it for reselling purposes. Resellers (wholesalers and retailers) make their decisions as customers based on several factors. We described these factors in a model of reseller decision making. They are merchandise requirements, supplier alternatives, and situational characteristics. Merchandise requirements of different resellers differ due to both reseller characteristics (e.g., size and type of reseller) and product characteristics (e.g., perishable, bulk, and so on). Supplier alternatives influence the decision because the availability of suppliers with competitive terms offers resellers more degrees of freedom in supplier choice. Finally, situational characteristics such as business climate, market conditions, and the reseller's financial position also influence reseller buying decisions. These external factors interact with internal factors such as the characteristics of the decision-making unit (DMU) itself, organizational policies, and the buyer's negotiation skills.

Next, we described what resellers desire from their suppliers. They desire freedom to price and promote the merchandise as they see fit; adequate trade margins; protection from undue competition; adequate advertising, merchandising, and training support; and efficient order fulfillment. To make the merchandising buying function more efficient, many resellers seek partnership arrangements with their suppliers. In partnerships, resellers and their manufacturers/suppliers stop the conventional practice of trying to squeeze the maximum benefit from each other; instead they cooperate to maximize the profits of both the parties by making sure that the right merchandise is at the right place at the right time. Quick response and efficient consumer response are supplier programs to ensure that inventory carrying costs are minimized throughout the channel.

Whether or not resellers deal with their suppliers under partnership arrangements, each party inevitably exercises certain power over the other. The power stems from five power bases: reward, coercion, legitimacy, referent, and expert power. Either party may command one or more of these, counterbalanced by the reciprocal flow of power between them. These bases were explained as to their nature and role in reseller buying behavior. Finally, we discussed the role of resellers' own marketing strategy in their preference for manufacturer activities. Broadly, two strategies are available to each party: differentiation of merchandise and low price. We described research that shows that resellers who themselves adopt a differentiation strategy prefer to deal with a supplier who has adopted the same strategy and resist suppliers who want to engage in price discounting. On the flip side, resellers using low-price strategy in respect to their own end-user customers in turn seek suppliers who follow the low-price strategy themselves, because that enables them (the resellers) to offer low prices to their customers.

The second group of intermediary customers we discussed was buying groups—organizations formed to pool the needs and resources of their members in order to buy in large quantity and obtain economies of scale. Buying groups are prevalent among retailers (e.g., Independent Grocers Associations), wholesalers (e.g., Sam's wholesale club), institutions (e.g., hospital buying group, church buying groups), and individual household customers (e.g., employee credit unions). Buying groups' customer behavior has some specific characteristics: for example, they seek deep quantity discounts and special packaging (e.g., pallet size).

Finally, we discussed affinity groups as the third type of intermediaries. Affinity groups are membership clubs and associations that form the group to pursue some interest other than buying as a group (e.g., the Rotary International Club). Marketers seek the endorsement of the group and then direct their offering to group members at special terms. There are three parties to this type of exchange: the marketer, the affinity organization, and its members. All three benefit from an affinity marketing program. The marketer benefits by getting access to a customer group with shared interests, having the opportunity to customize the offering and meaningfully differentiate it from the competition, and by receiving a reduction in the costs of program promotion due to shared activities. The affinity organization benefits from financial gains, increased publicity, enhanced image (if the marketer is a prestigious one), and most importantly, by being able to offer its members better value. Members themselves benefit, of course, from getting the better value. But they also benefit from reduced risk because of the organizations' endorsement, and by gaining implied reference group support, an opportunity to contribute to their organization and its cause, and by being able to display their membership status or support for the organization.

In the last section, we pulled together concepts and illustrated their application to the three customer roles. Marketers selling to intermediaries must look at them not only as buyers but also as users and payers. They must then strive to respond to the needs and motivations of each role if they are to succeed.

Key Terms

Reseller 656
Pioneer Brands 660
Business Climate 660
Consignment Buying 660
Market Conditions 661
Robinson Patman Act 663
Activity-Based Costing
(ABC) 665
Distribution Intensity 665

Exclusive Distribution 666
Selective Distribution 666
Intensive Distribution 666
Channel Partnership 669
Quick Response 670
Efficient Consumer
Response (ECR) 670
Inventory Turnover 671
Model Stock Quantity 672

Category Management 672
Power 673
Power Bases, or Sources of
Power 673
Buying Groups 677
Membership Clubs 679
Affinity 681
Affinity Marketing 681

Review Questions

1. The chapter describes the role of resellers in providing customer value. Who is a reseller and what value does a reseller provide to end users?

2. Reseller buying behavior is affected by a number of factors. What are these? Explain each briefly.

3. What do resellers expect and desire from manufacturers? Identify at least four expectations and briefly explain each.

4. What is a buying group? What benefits do customers get when they buy as a member of some buying group? Explain your answer briefly.

5. When manufacturers and resellers deal with each other, one party exercises its power over the other to get the other's cooperation. What are the various bases of power? Explain each briefly, giving an example.

6. Define affinity groups and affinity marketing. Give two examples in which customers buy as members of an affinity group. Briefly discuss what benefits they might get by buying as a member of the affinity group.

Applications

1. Your friend has missed class again. You tell her that the topic dealt with membership clubs. Your friend gets very excited and tells you all about her adventures at a club the previous evening. You shrug your shoulders and proceed to correct her perception; you tell her what the lecture was all about. What would you tell her?

2. Compare and contrast the competitive intensity for the following makes of automobiles: (1) GM's Saturn, (2) Mercedes, (3) Lamborghini. How will the dealers or resellers of these automobiles be protected by their manufacturers from undue competition?

3. How has EDLP (everyday low pricing) affected the relationship between manufacturers and resellers? Likewise, how has EDI (electronic data interchange) affected the way resellers want to do business with their suppliers?

4. What are the advantages and disadvantages of channel partnership? Why are partnerships between manufacturers and resellers on the rise in the United States? Do you believe that partnerships will flourish in the new millennium, or will partners suffer from channel conflict and unattained goals? Why or why not?

Practical Experiences

1. Visit with a buyer/buying department manager of (1) a local department store, and (2) a local supermarket. Interview the person to understand his or her merchandise buying behavior.

2. Interview an affinity group manager (e.g., AARP executive director or Rotary Club International). Query him or her about a recent program in which a marketer promoted some merchandise through this affinity group. Describe, from the affinity group manager's point of view, what the advantages and disadvantages of participating in this program were.

3. Select two stores in the same product category, but with vastly different store strategies of doing business. Interview the buying department manager to identify what the store expects from its suppliers. Synthesize these two separate interviews and comment on whether or not a reseller's own marketing strategy affects the way that reseller wants to deal with its own suppliers.

Notes

1. Adapted from the case "Rundel's Department Store," in Donald J. Bowersox and M. Bixby Cooper, *Strategic Marketing Channel Management* (New York: McGraw-Hill, 1992), pp. 125–129.

2. Philip Kotler, *Marketing Management: Analysis, Planning, Implementation, & Control*, 7th ed. (New York: Prentice-Hall, 1991), pp. 537–48.

3. Jagdish N. Sheth, "A Theory of Merchandise Buying Behavior," Faculty Working Paper #706, University of Illinois, August 29, 1980.

4. Frank Alpert, Michael Kamins, and John Graham, "An Examination of Reseller Buyer Attitude toward Order of Brand Entry," *Journal of Marketing* 56 (July 1992), pp. 25–37.

5. Robert D. Buzzell and Gwen Ortmeyer, "Channel Partnerships: A New Approach to Streamlining Distribution," *Marketing Science Institute Report*, No. 94–104 (Cambridge, MA: Marketing Science Institute).

6. Ibid.

7. See for further description, F. Robert Dwyer, Paul H. Schurr, and Sejo Oh, "Developing Buyer-Seller Relationships," in *Journal of Marketing*, 51 (April 1987), pp. 11–27.

8. Buzzell and Ortmeyer, "Channel Partnerships."

9. Based on Richard Brooks, "Recent Changes in the Retailing of Fresh Produce: Strategic Implications for Fresh Produce Suppliers," *Journal of Business Research* 32 (1995) pp. 149–61.

10. See John R. P. French, "A Formal Theory of Social Power," *Psychological Review*, 1956, p. 184-; John R. P. French and Bertram Raven, "Bases of Social Power," in *Studies in Social Power*, ed. Durwin Cartwright, (Ann Arbor: University of Michigan, 1959), pp. 154.

11. See Frederick J. Beier and Louis W. Stern, "Power in the Channel of Distribution," in *Distribution Channels: Behavioral Dimensions*, ed. Louis W. Stern, (Boston, MA: Houghton Mifflin, 1969), p. 101.

[12] Michael Porter, *Competitive Advantage* (New York: Free Press, 1985).

[13] F. Robert Dwyer and Sejo Oh, "A Transaction Cost Perspective on Vertical Contractual Structure and Interchannel Competitive Strategies", *Journal of Marketing* 52, no. 2 (April 1988), pp. 21–34.

[14] Robert E. O'Neill, "Competition," *Progressive Grocer* (May, 1992), pp. 61–78.

[15] Ibid., p. 70.

[16] Ibid., p. 72.

[17] See Bart Macchiette and Abhijit Roy, "Affinity Marketing: What Is It and How Does It Work?" *Journal of Services Marketing* 6, no. 3 Summer 1992, pp. 47–57.

[18] Ibid.

[19] Ibid.

[20] Michael Pollick, "Purchasing Firm Commands Bully Pulpit: When Churches Need Pews, Bibles, and Other Accessories, They Don't Rely on Divine Inspiration; They Rely on the Christian Purchasing Network," *Sarasota Herald Tribune*, Business Weekly section, (June 30, 1997), p. 11.

[21] For a more complete discussion of the five major sources of affinity marketing, see Bart Macchiette and Abhijit Roy, "Affinity Marketing: What Is It and How Does It Work?", *Journal of Services Marketing*, Vol. 6, No. 3, Summer (1992), P. 47–57.

[22] See Macchiette, Bart and Abhijit Roy, "Affinity Marketing: What Is It and How Does It Work?" *Journal of Services Marketing*, 6, no. 3, Summer 1992, pp. 47–57.

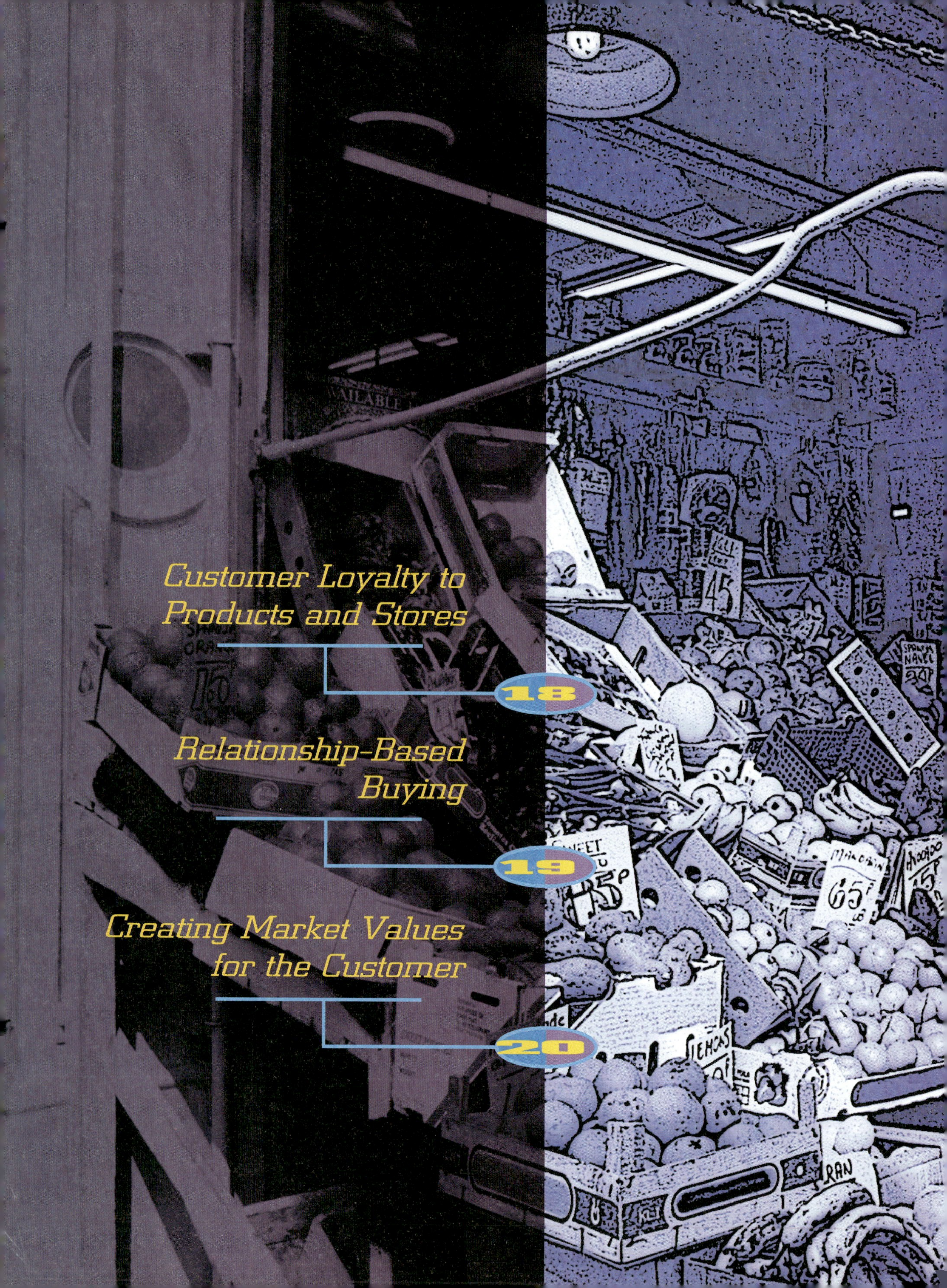

part five

Customer Focused Marketing

CHAPTER 13

After reading this chapter you should be able to:

Define what brand loyalty is, and describe the factors that determine it.

Discuss the concept of brand equity, identifying its components.

Explain how customers decide on which stores to shop and how their shopping behaviors are affected by environmental factors in the store.

List and describe various shopping motives.

Summarize the factors that influence customers' store loyalty.

Describe the concept of one-stop-shopping (OSS) and explain why

A DIFFERENT KIND of COMPANY. A DIFFERENT KIND of CAR.

Customer Loyalty to Products, Brands and Stores

A Woodstock for Saturn Lovers

In the summer of 1994, about 25,000 men, women, and children gathered in a celebration in Spring Hill, Tenn. There was music, a barbecue, a visit to Opryland, and a tour of an automobile factory. The crowd was diverse, but they had one thing in common: they all drove the same car, a car carrying the Saturn logo.

They came from far and wide. Some came with enthusiasm, proud to be owning the car they did. They called it "homecoming," implying that the Saturn factory was their home. They came, because their company, the company that makes their car, sent an invitation. They had been invited to tour the factory, to meet company executives, to see other Saturn owners—and, importantly, to have fun. It was the Woodstock of 1994!

To cultivate such zealousness among its customers, Saturn goes to great lengths in the way it treats them. To begin with, Saturn has a no-haggle pricing policy. Its salespersons are salaried rather than commissioned, so its dealerships put less pressure on customers. When a customer buys a Saturn, all of the dealership staff celebrate the customer's decision by gathering around the car and chanting as the customer drives off. The customers later get a Polaroid photograph of this ceremony.

Saturn's advertising and marketing reinforce that bond by focusing not just on the product and its features—as other automakers tend to do—but also on the people who make and sell it, and the place from which it originates. Periodically, dealers hold barbecues for their buyers and free clinics to educate them about their cars. Says one Saturn owner, "It's such a friendly atmosphere, I look forward to going to the dealership."

Indeed, many Saturn owners call themselves groupies, fanatics, even members of a cult.

Source: Adapted from James Bennet, "Saturn Invites the 'Family' to a Party," *New York Times*, June 20, 1994, Late Edition, Section D, p. 1.

the customer perceives all the brands to be more or less the same and buys this one merely out of inertia. If the other brands were to offer a price deal, the customer might easily switch. To move this customer into the "loyalty" quadrant, the marketer would have to strengthen the customer's perception of the brand's image.

Finally, in the quadrant with high attitude and low behavior, the customer has latent loyalty. He or she likes the brand but has been unable to buy it; perhaps the price is too high or the customer lacks access to the brand or the store. Here, the marketer needs to tap into this hidden potential market by lowering whatever barriers prevent customers from buying this desired brand.

A Model of Brand Loyalty

What makes a customer brand-loyal? Several factors induce brand loyalty; others work against it. The degree of brand loyalty is the net outcome of these positive and negative factors (see Figure 18.2).

Contributors to Brand Loyalty

As shown in Figure 18.2, several factors contribute to brand loyalty. The three major contributors are the perceived brand-performance fit, social and emotional identification with the brand, and habit combined with a long history of using the brand.

Thus, favorable brand attitude and brand loyalty result primarily from the satisfaction of user values. As described in Chapter 3, user values fall into two categories: (1) performance and (2) social and emotional identification.

A MODEL OF CUSTOMERS' BRAND LOYALTY

Figure 18.2

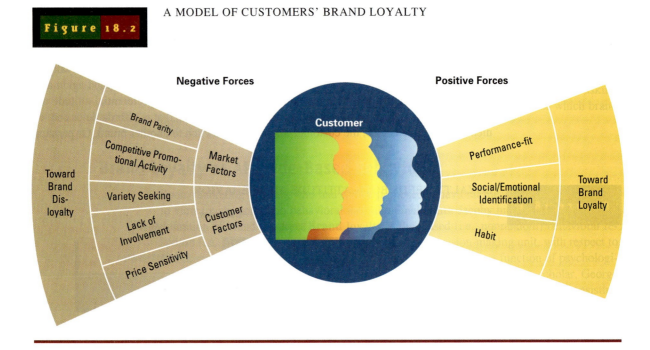

PERCEIVED BRAND-PERFORMANCE FIT

Basically, customers like brands that meet their needs and wants well. If they have a positive usage experience, customers want to seek that reward again.

Brands differ not only in the quality of their performance (e.g., how well a shampoo cleans hair, or the reliability of a network communication system) but also on specific performance dimensions (e.g., shampoo that gives hair body versus the one that eliminates dandruff, or a network's data capacity, transmission speed, and portability). Furthermore, customers have different needs for specific performance features (e.g., shampoo for oily, dry, or thick or thin hair; speed versus data volume in a network). Consequently, brand loyalty depends not merely on whether a brand does what it is intended to do but on the degree of fit between the customer's specific performance requirements and the brand's performance capability.

In Healthcare Services, Caring Matters More Than Cure

Recently, we surveyed a national consumer panel in the United States, to assess their commitment to their health-care providers—specifically, three categories of health-care professionals (physicians, dentists, and pharmacists) and three health-care institutions (public hospitals, private hospitals, and hospitals with religious affiliations). In the survey, we asked consumers, "Would you switch providers to get better products and services?"

Based on this question, we computed the percentage of respondents who said that they would switch. Potential switching rates ranged from 18 to 24 percent for health-care professionals, with dentists receiving the lowest switching rate of 18 percent. Among the hospitals, the switching rate was higher for public (34 percent) than for private (30.2 percent) and religious (28.3 percent) hospitals.

Consumers also answered two questions relating to their perceptions of quality: (1) rating of the quality of service these professionals and institutions provided, and (2) the rating of the *way* they provided the service—each rated on 0–10 scale where 10 meant "excellent." We termed these ratings the "quality of cure" and the "quality of caring," respectively.

What did we find? First, potential switching rates were strongly correlated inversely with the perceived quality for all six services. For example, among those who rated the quality of physician service as low, 84.8 percent were willing to switch physicians. As quality levels rose, this percentage fell—dropping to only 3.6 percent, for

physicians. The response patterns for the other five services were similar.

To identify what mattered more, the cure or caring quality, we divided the entire sample into four groups, based on whether their rating of each measure was high or low. As Figure 18.3 shows, for each health-care provider, when both dimensions of quality were scored low, the switching propensity was high. And, not surprisingly, the switching propensity was much lower when both measures of quality were scored high. But what happens if both measures of quality are adequate, and only one is then improved—which measure of quality will have the larger impact? According to our results, improving the caring dimension did more to reduce the propensity to switch than did improving the cure dimension.

These results imply important lessons for health-care professionals and marketers. To satisfy and retain clients, the service quality has to be in the top two boxes (i.e., 9 or 10 on a 0–10 scale). This is where the loyalty rates of 80 percent or higher are seen. Furthermore, although quality of "cure" and "caring" both matter, quality of "caring" pays off immensely in winning customer loyalty.

Source: Jagdish N. Sheth and Banwari Mittal, "The Health of the Health-Care Industry: A Report Card from American Consumers," *Marketing Healthcare Services*, Winter 1997, pp. 29–35.

brand and predisposition to buy it. In comparison, brand equity is based more on specific brand associations and a consideration of the value those associations represent. Thus, the emphasis in studying brand equity is on the brand associations and value.

Components of Brand Equity

What considerations underlie customer perceptions of brand equity? This question was answered recently in a study by marketing professors Walfried Lassar, Banwari Mittal, and Arun Sharma.[9] They identified five dimensions of brand equity:

1. *Performance*—a customer's judgment about a brand's fault-free and long-lasting physical operation and flawlessness in the product's physical construction.

2. *Social image*—the consumer's perception of the esteem in which the consumer's social or reference groups hold the brand.

3. *Value*—the brand's perceived utility relative to its costs, based on a comparison of what is received with what is given up.

4. *Trustworthiness*—the customer's trust the brand has won—trust that the brand will maintain its strengths, and that it will not compromise its quality or otherwise take advantage of its customers. An example of a trust-failure is the press story a few years ago about Sears automotive shops doing unneeded repairs on cars; this story detracted from Sears' brand equity.

5. *Identification*—the degree to which customers identify themselves with the brand, or feel some attachment to it. In effect, consumers would say that it is their brand; it is the kind of brand they would be happy to be associated with. Often, identification occurs because the brand is associ-

Versace: extending the brand from high fashion clothing to high fashion home furnishings.

ated with things, persons, ideas, or symbols we find engaging. In particular, celebrities and role models are often used to develop identification. For example, country music stars hold a special identification appeal for a growing population of Americans. (See the Window on Practice box, "Consumer Products Go Country.")

In many cases, brand identification springs from the social policy the brand's makers promote (e.g., diversity in hiring, environmental friendliness, and so on). Benetton has long employed shocking images of social issues (e.g., AIDS research, racial harmony); it hopes to generate bonds of identification among its core customers in whom such images strike an emotional chord. Identification suffers when the brand marketer adopts some policy that goes against the value system of its customers. Currently, Denny's Restaurant chain has come under fire for discriminating against minority customers in some of its restaurants; while these are isolated incidents by independent restaurant franchisees, the costs in customer goodwill are substantial. Denny's stands to lose patronage not only from minority customers, but also from other customers who abhor discriminatory practices.[10]

Marketers can measure the components of brand equity by seeking customer ratings of brands on these aspects. Table 18.2 shows a sample measurement scale. Brand equity will be highest when the brand scores well on all five components. Managers can identify which components are weak, and work to improve those aspects of the brand. Thus, measurement of these components helps managers to map their own brands vis-à-vis competitors, then take action to improve the deficient component.[11]

Consumer Products Go Country

WINDOW ON PRACTICE

Many marketers are drawn to the strong loyalty country music lovers show toward the country music lifestyle and country music stars. "The country listener is loyal to the lifestyle and the music," says Lisa Decker, general sales manager at KMPS Country 94.1 in Seattle, the number one country music station among listeners 25 to 54 years old. "You tell them to do something and they do it. They're not lemmings, but they trust those associated with the music impeccably."

Recently, Frito-Lay launched a national ad campaign for its new Fritos Texas Grill corn chips, featuring Reba McEntire, a country music star. The campaign, kicked off during the Academy of Country Music Awards on NBC, featured a toll-free number for viewers to call for a free product sample. Also featured was a supermarket sweepstakes to offer a trip to Texas to attend a barbecue and a concert by McEntire.

Other companies are also climbing onto the country music stars' popularity. Fruit of the Loom sponsored the tours of two country music stars, Alabama and Alan Jackson, along with All-Star Countryfest, a one-day concert at the Atlanta Motor Speedway featuring a number of additional country music stars. To get tickets for the concerts, consumers had to send in UPC symbols from Fruit of the Loom products. Over 200,000 fans are estimated to have responded.

Other recent promotions linked with country music include Maxwell House, Country Time, and Tombstone. Maxwell House, a brand conceived in Nashville, ran a contest searching for America's number one music fan. Country Time offered a compact disc sampler of some of country music's best. Tombstone Pizza Co. gave away a tour poster by mail, and Oscar Mayer organized talent search auditions.

Source: Adapted from Chad Rubel, "Marketers Goin' Country in Search of Brand Loyalty," *Marketing News* 30, no. 13, June 17, 1996, p. 1. Additional information available at:
http://www.kmps.com
www.fritolay.com
www.countrycomfort.com

ILLUSTRATIVE MEASURES OF COMPONENTS OF BRAND EQUITY

State your opinion on the following statements by rating them 1 through 5, where 1 means strong disagreement and 5 means strong agreement:

Performance
P1 From this brand of television, I can expect superior performance
P2 During use, this brand of television is highly unlikely to be defective
P3 This brand of television is made so as to work trouble free
P4 This brand will work very well

Social image
SI1 This brand of television fits my personality
SI2 I would be proud to own a television of this brand
SI3 This brand of television will be well regarded by my friends
SI4 In its status and style, this brand matches my personality

Value
V1 This brand is well priced
V2 Considering what I would pay for this brand of television, I will get much more than my money's worth
V3 I consider this brand of television to be a bargain because of the benefits I receive

Trustworthiness
T1 I consider the company and people who stand behind these televisions to be very trustworthy
T2 In regard to consumer interests, this company seems to be very caring
T3 I believe that this company does not take advantage of consumers

Attachment
A1 After watching this brand of television, I am very likely to grow fond of it
A2 For this brand of television, I have positive personal feelings
A3 With time, I will develop a warm feeling toward this brand of television

Source: Walfried Lassar, Banwari Mittal, and Arun Sharma, "Measuring Customer-Based Brand Equity," *Journal of Consumer Marketing* 12, no. 4, (1995), pp. 11–19.

Store Choice

Which grocery store do you shop at? Do you shop there regularly or occasionally? Do you shop there exclusively, or is it just one of the several grocery stores that you shop at? Why do you shop there rather than at other stores? Why is it the store you shop at most frequently? Are there other stores in the area? Are they less convenient? More expensive? Less friendly? Or what? And what about the clothing store, the hardware store, or the appliance store? Do you have a favorite store in each of these categories?

These questions are important to any store owner. Owners want to get you to shop at their stores, again and again in preference over other competing stores. In other words, they want you to become their loyal customers. Therefore, they need to understand customers' shopping behavior—how customers decide where to shop, as well as factors that influence customers' store loyalty.

How Customers Shop

A typical customer generally has the option of three or four general merchandise stores to shop at; for supermarket items, the choice may even extend to 10 stores. How does the customer choose the store to shop at? As every store manager will tell you, the number one factor in store choice is location. This, in fact, was also the conclusion of a survey of about 10,000 supermarket shoppers conducted by *Consumer Reports*.

But location is a relative criterion, not an absolute one. That is, customers do not always go to the nearest store, even though they want to minimize the travel distance. Sometimes, they will go to a distant store, if they get better quality or selection or price. Merchandise quality and price were the second and third criteria in the *Consumer Reports* study. In actuality, customers do not choose a store on the basis of a single factor, or do not always value various factors in a specific priority order. Rather a dynamic *interplay* of factors influences their choice.[12]

To understand this dynamic interplay, let us consider the supermarket shopping behavior of a family we shall call the Brown family. The Browns live in a suburb of a U.S. metropolis, near two supermarkets—Kroger, two miles to the south, and Thriftway, one and a half miles to the north (both are big supermarket chains with stores in a number of U.S. cities). The nearest convenience stores are a Speedway gas station at a main-road crossing about half a mile to the northeast, and an Ameristop at about the same distance but slightly off the main road.

The Browns rarely shop at the convenience store except for gas. Their most frequent gas station is Speedway, where they occasionally buy milk when they run out of it and it is not convenient to visit the supermarket. They never shop at Ameristop. They divide their main food shopping between Thriftway and Kroger, shopping more often at Kroger because it is on Mrs. Brown's way to work. Also, it offers a "double coupon" feature. They shop Thriftway every week or so to take advantage of price specials. They visit Kroger about once a week for a major shopping trip, when they buy the bulk of the weekly requirements, and once a week for a "filler trip" to buy only a few items. In some weeks, they split the major shopping between Kroger and Thriftway to take advantage of price deals at each store.

The Browns also shop for food at a few other stores. About one and one-half miles beyond Thriftway is a new store, Meijers, which is a *supercenter*, a store that sells food as well as apparel and hard goods (small appliances, electronics, and so on). Although it is farther, the Browns shop there once in two to three weeks; this would be their major shopping trip, and they typically spend substantially more than at Kroger. There is also Sam's Warehouse Club (about five miles west) and Bigg's, a warehouse store, about eight miles west, but the Browns never shop at either. Even though the Browns visit the nearby mall (about half a mile from the Bigg's store), they never consider food shopping and mall shopping as a single trip. Finally, about 10 miles to the northeast, there is Jungle Jim, a store that features exotic vegetables and international food items. The Browns shop there about every two months because they enjoy the merchandise variety. They consider the trip an excursion—a combination of purchasing and excitement of browsing through the exotic products.

THE INTERPLAY OF DECISION CRITERIA

Although no two families are alike in their food shopping (and shopping for other products), the Brown family illustrates the sort of interplay of factors that influence a customer's store choice:

- Distance is an important consideration, but it is not always measured from home or in kilometers/miles; rather it is measured by convenience, such as whether it is on the way to work and on or off the main road or main commuting route. Moreover, small differences in distances are ignored, so that a slightly farther store may be chosen on occasion even without any other advantage. In fact Weber's Law and the related concept of "just noticeable difference" (JND) which we discussed in Chapter 9 in respect to customers' price perceptions, apply to store distances as well: some stores that are only slightly farther than the nearest may not even be perceived as being farther (particularly if they are not on the same linear path). Moreover, even among the distance differences that are perceived, some small differences might be considered negligible as trade-offs with other store features.

- If two or more stores are equally convenient from a distance standpoint, then other factors (quality, assortment, and price) influence the store choice. If these other factors are significantly inferior at the nearest store, then a distant, less convenient store is likely to be chosen for regular shopping. The most convenient store may continue to be chosen, however, for filler trips.

- A typical customer does not limit food shopping to just one store. Rather, customers have a repertoire of stores, with one store shopped most frequently and regularly. For example, an average American household makes an average of 2.2 visits per week to a supermarket. However, for a majority of households (over 80 percent), only one visit is made to their most preferred supermarket. Thus, a majority of American households rely on more than one food store for their food needs.[13]

- If there are stores that specialize in quality, assortment, or price deals, these stores are likely to be included in the repertoire of stores. They will be visited despite the locational disadvantage, but on a special occasion rather than a regular basis.

The most important point is that customers have a repertoire (i.e., assortment) of stores. This concept is analogous to the "consideration set," or preference set, discussed in Chapter 14. Customers have consideration sets and preference sets not only for brands but also for stores. They limit their shopping to these stores. The choice of a specific store from the repertoire is based on the exigencies of the specific situation—for example, is this an emergency, a major shopping trip, or a filler trip? Is one of the stores in the repertoire running a price special, and so on?

As shown in the flow chart of the decision process in Figure 18.4, a store decision begins, but often does not end, with distance considerations. (The flow chart is an attempt to assemble a reasonable description of the process as inferred from a number of unrelated studies, existing marketing literature, and the authors' own customer observations and intuitive reflections.[14] To understand the store choice process for a particular clientele, marketers and researchers must conduct specific studies in their trading area.)

CHOICES BASED ON NONLOCATIONAL CRITERIA

The previous description mainly contrasts location and nonlocation as choice criteria. How do customers choose among the other factors, namely, quality, assortment, and price? The answer is twofold.

First, as we saw in the case of the Brown family, if the store offers a substantial advantage on any one of these factors, it may be included in the repertoire. If different stores offer one each of these advantages, they all may be included in the repertoire, although for occasional shopping only.

Second, if all the stores offering price or quality or assortment were conveniently located, convenient enough for the customer to make each a regularly shopped store, customers might select the store with the advantage they value most. While some customers may patronize each type of these stores to regularly take advantage of each of these three factors, most customers would value one advantage more than others and choose the store with that advantage as their regular store.

A FLOW CHART OF CUSTOMERS' STORE CHOICE DECISION PROCESS

Figure 18.4

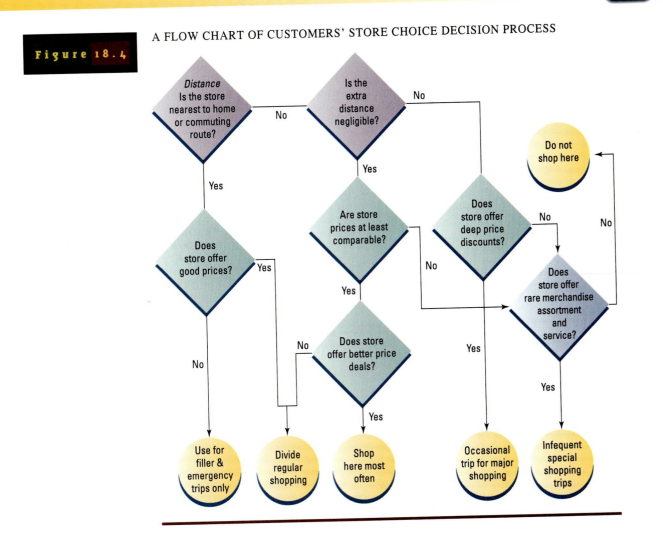

This last point is important in understanding how stores differentiate themselves. They differentiate themselves first on price, or assortment, or merchandise quality. These serve as the basis of the first tier of store classification: Supermarkets tend to offer medium levels of merchandise and assortment at moderate prices, at levels considered acceptable by the mass market. Some supermarkets such as Food Lion and supercenters such as Meijers, feature low prices more than do other supermarkets. Warehouse stores offer limited selection but very attractive prices. Specialty stores, such as Jungle Jim or H-E-B Marketplace in San Antonio, Texas, focus on merchandise selection and assortment.

Some supermarkets such as Harris-Teeter make fresh produce their stores' special focus. Such differentiation strategies work by a process of customer **self-selection**—customers self-select themselves to be the customers of the store that offers the advantage they seek.[15]

Three other factors also play a role: (1) service—the courtesy and helpfulness of store personnel; (2) in-store display—the ease of finding the merchandise; and (3) atmospherics—the pleasantness of the ambiance (e.g., the lighting, the appearance, the music, and in general, the cheeriness or the gloominess of the store). These factors are generally used, however, as

BonMart, a store chain in Israel, differentiates itself on price value.

second-tier factors: that is, they help in choosing the store from among those that offer similar price, assortment, and quality. When these first-tier factors are equalized, customers are likely then to choose a store that offers one or all three of the second-tier advantages.

Publix, a U.S. store chain in the South, emphasizes service with its motto "Where Shopping Is a Pleasure." Among other things, employees carry customers' shopping bags to their cars, something that South Florida customers (many of them elderly) value. Stew Leonard's Dairy Store in Norwalk, Connecticut, is famous for store atmospherics. Shopping there is fun for the whole family: it features, supposedly, the single largest bakery store in the world. Then there is the mechanical mooing cow; there are animal characters in costume; there is even a petting zoo right in the parking lot of the store!

Planned, Unplanned, and Impulse Buying

Once a customer selects and visits a store, the marketer's next concerns are whether he or she buys something and what he or she buys. These decisions are influenced by whether the customer engages in planned, unplanned, or impulse buying.

Consider your own shopping behavior: Do you always buy something when you visit a store? Do you buy exactly what you had intended to buy, something different, or something you hadn't even thought of buying? And what factors determine this? These questions are important and have been studied by some marketers.

All products that customers buy in the store can be classified as planned, unplanned, and impulse purchases. **Planned purchases** are those that the customer had planned to buy before entering the store. **Unplanned purchases** are those the customer did not intend to buy before entering the store. The customer need not have specifically decided not to buy those products; the customer may have simply not thought about those products.

Shopper's Stop in Bombay (India) is open every day (including Sunday—a rarity in India) to appeal to impulse shoppers.

Unplanned purchases can be of three types:

1. **Restocking unplanned purchases** are items the shopper had not thought about buying at the time but has been using regularly. He or she buys it due to an in-store display or special deal, and so on, knowing that the item will be needed in the future.

2. **Evaluated new unplanned purchases** are those the customer needs which had not been recognized prior to this purchase occasion. These may either be products not already in use by the customer (e.g., a cellular phone), or products in use already and not in need of a replacement yet. The customer simply decides to buy additional units to expand the collection (e.g., wardrobe, one more TV set in the house) or to get extra features in newer units (high-definition television).

3. **Impulse purchases** are the extreme kind of unplanned purchases—items bought spontaneously and completely unpremeditated. The customer buys in response to feeling a sudden urge to buy something. These purchases are made quickly and without an evaluation of need.[16]

The best way to study planned buying is to observe the use of shopping lists. According to a recent Gallup study, about 55 percent of supermarket shoppers use a shopping list. However, the use of shopping lists does not rule out unplanned buying. One reason is that the use of unplanned buying depends on how exactly an item is written down on the shopping list. A person may write only the general item type (e.g., entree), a specific product category (frozen pasta), or a specific brand (Sara Lee). Thus, there can be degrees of unplanned buying. Second, even when the product or brand is specified, customers may

Determinants of Store Brand Acceptance

What leads customers to buy store brands? This important question was investigated in a study of supermarket shoppers by marketing professors Paul S. Richardson, Arun K. Jain, and Alan Dick. They surveyed a sample of 582 grocery shoppers about their acceptance and purchase of store brands in 28 product categories (e.g., bacon, soups, juices, frozen vegetables, paper towels, laundry detergents, and so on). Their findings were the following:

- Among the demographic characteristics, family size and income were correlated with store (private) brand buying behavior, but education level and age were *not* related. Larger households were more likely to buy private brands, as were lower income households.

- Among beliefs and psychological variables, shoppers' familiarity with store brands, perceived value for money, perceived quality differential between national and store brands, and perceived risk affected store brand buying. Shoppers familiar with store brands and believing that store brands give you good value for the money were more likely to buy store brands, but if they perceived risk of poor quality (a perception that was aided by lack of familiarity), then they were less likely to buy store brands.

- The personal trait of "intolerance for ambiguity" (i.e., discomfort in uncertain situations) acted against private brand acceptance.

Another recent study of 1,000 grocery shoppers in the United Kingdom, by professor Ogenyi Ejye Omar of the School of Retail Studies, The London Institute, has shed some light on this question.

Generally, national food brands were perceived as superior to store brands in terms of quality, packaging, consistency, and image, but lower on "good value for money."

The store brand shopper had slightly less formal education, was young, likely to be a female between 18 to 24 years of age, had at least one to two children living at home, had a larger family, had lower socioeconomic status, lived mainly in rented accommodations, and tended to be thrifty and more adventurous.

The store brand shopper shops frequently and longer, ostensibly striving for the best price and value for money. In contrast, national brand shoppers prided themselves on shopping for food quality, good product packaging, and good product design and appearance.

Source: Paul S. Richardson, Arun K. Jain, and Alan Dick, "Household Store Brand Proneness: A Framework," *Journal of Retailing* 72, no. 2 1996, pp. 159–85; Ogenyi Ejye Omar, "Grocery Purchase Behavior for National and Own-Label-Brands," *Service Industries Journal* (January 1996), 16 no. 1, pp. 58–66.

Additional information available at **http://www.luc.edu. www.buffalo.edu.**

THE "HOW" FACTOR

Store loyalty also depends on how favorable the shopping experience is in a particular store. This "how" factor includes ease of merchandise selection, in-store information and assistance, convenience, problem resolution, and personalization.

EASE OF MERCHANDISE SELECTION A store's merchandise selection ease refers to how easily and effortlessly customers of the store select products. This depends on several features: layout of aisles and shelf displays, shelf tags, product information cards, and signage. Merchandise should be arranged for easy access and for easy interbrand comparisons. According to some reports, until recently, customers complained about the tall shelves in Toys "R" Us stores; customers, especially short and elderly customers, found it difficult to reach the merchandise for inspection. Similarly, correct price and brand shelf tags should allow easy evaluation, and comparable size and quality brands (including store brands) should be placed side-by-side for easy comparison. Store signage should be visible from throughout the store to locate the aisles and shelf facings. Finally, items should not be out of stock.

These actions make it easy for the customer to make his or her product selection efficiently and effortlessly. This ease, in turn, positively influences a customer's decision to patronize the store regularly.

IN-STORE INFORMATION AND ASSISTANCE   By in-store information and assistance, we mean the availability of credible information about the merchandise and salesperson assistance in shopping. Merchandise selection ease provides efficiency in the self-selection of items, and most stores in the Western world are organized for self-selection. But beyond self-selection, customers sometimes need information and assistance from salespersons (for example, to see a product demonstration). If customers find that salespersons are not easily available or they are not knowledgeable or fair and impartial in their advice, then it detracts from their buying efficiency or effectiveness. On the other hand, the availability of salespersons who are knowledgeable and credible and trustworthy makes the store attractive for customers to patronize it.

CONVENIENCE   Customers also want convenience, or ease in getting to the store and getting out of it once the merchandise selection is completed. This translates into ease of reaching the store location, parking availability, and quick checkouts.

Location has always been a critical variable in a store's success. Generally, a supermarket attracts customers from up to a five-mile radius, and a department store or a mall from up to 15-mile radius area. The location therefore basically determines who would choose to shop there regularly. Convenient parking is also a consideration in store preference, particularly for older consumers.

Once a customer has completed his or her product selection, nothing is more important to the customer than to be able to check out and go home as soon as possible. Quick checkouts therefore become another important component of convenience. All else being equal, customers like to patronize stores that are convenient to access.

PROBLEM RESOLUTION   When they need problem resolution, or remedy for mistakes or oversights, customers want this service to be easy and hassle free. The most typical problems are the need to return or exchange the merchandise. Stores that have a liberal return policy that allows customers to return unused merchandise within reasonable time, or that will repair or replace the faulty merchandise within reasonable time, even beyond the warranty period, are likely to earn customers' repeat patronage.

Suppose you buy a shirt and its color fades after a few washes; you would expect the store to take it back, wouldn't you? Many stores are known to accept defective merchandise. As another example, suppose you bought a television from a store and it had a 90-day free labor and parts warranty; suppose the TV stopped working on the 91st day. Again, you would expect the store to fix the TV free of charge since it is only one day beyond the warranty expiration. However, some stores would do it, while some would not. Customer loyalty is likely to be greater toward the former group of stores.

PERSONALIZATION   By personalization, we mean positive employee behavior toward customers. Customers expect store employees to be pleasant and courteous in their interaction and eager to help customers during their shopping. Stores differ greatly on this dimension. Stores that hire employees with poor interpersonal skills and low aptitude for socialization with customers are likely to earn less loyalty from their customers.

5. What is one-stop-shopping (OSS)? What are some of the benefits that customers seek in OSS? Is there any downside to OSS? If so, what is it? Illustrate by examples.

Applications

1. Well, it happens again. Your classmate has missed the class when the topic of "atmospherics" was discussed. Your friend feels he already knows a lot about the topic because he regularly watches the weather channel on TV. You tell him to slow down, and then you proceed to tell him what the topic of atmospherics is really about. What would you tell him?

2. As a store manager, you just read the model of store loyalty described in this chapter. You are excited because you believe you have found the key to making your customers loyal to your store. Briefly outline your action plan.

3. Identify any five brands to which you are loyal. Discuss why you are loyal to those brands, using the explanation offered in this chapter.

4. Why do you shop? Is it purely a purchasing activity, or are there other motives? Apply the model of store loyalty to yourself and discuss which "what" and "how" factors apply to your own behavior. For the following items, map out your own shopping motives: (a) clothing, (b) music, (c) coffee/tea, (d) books, (e) electronic equipment, and (f) haircuts.

5. You just read the section on brand equity discussed in this chapter. As a brand manager of (1) a consumer packaged goods company or (2) an automobile insurance company, you make it your goal to strengthen your customer-based brand equity considerably over the next five years. Outline your plan of action.

Practical Experiences

1. Interview five household customers to understand their store choice process for supermarkets. Flow chart their store selection process similar to the flow chart shown in the chapter.

2. Interview three customers to understand whether they are store loyal and query them further to explain why they are or are not. Do this study for (1) supermarkets and (2) clothing stores.

3. Interview two business customers to understand their loyalty to (1) a document-delivery services and (2) office supplies stores.

4. The chapter describes five segments of customers based on their loyalty. Interview five customers to identify which segment each of them belongs to, if any.

5. Interview two customers who do not buy store brands and two who do. Synthesize your interviews to describe customers' perceptions of store brands and what explains whether or not customers would consider any store brands.

Notes

1. Reported in John A. Quelch and David Harding, "Brand versus Private Labels: Fighting to Win," *Harvard Business Review*, January–February 1996, pp. 99–109. For classical literature on brand loyalty, where these measures are developed, see R. M. Cunningham, "Measurement of Brand Loyalty," *The Marketing Revolution*, Proceedings of the Thirty-Seventh Conference of the American Marketing Association, Chicago: American Marketing Association, 1956, pp. 39–45.

2. Jacob Jacoby and Robert W. Chestnut, *Brand Loyalty Measurement and Management* (New York: John Wiley & Sons, 1978), p. 2.

3. See Alan S. Dick and Kunal Basu, "Customer Loyalty: Toward an Integrated Conceptual Framework," *Journal of the Academy of Marketing Science* 22, no. 2 (1994), p. 101.

4. See Sharon Beatty and Lynn Kahle, "The

Involvement-Commitment Model: Theory and Implications," *Journal of Business Research*, Vol. 6 (30, 149–168.

[5] See Banwari Mittal, "An Integrated Framework for Relating Diverse Consumer Characteristics to Supermarket Coupon Redemption," *Journal of Marketing Research,* 31, Nov. 1994, pp. 533–544.

[6] David A. Aaker, *Managing Brand Equity* (New York: The Free Press, 1991).

[7] Reported in Synn B. Upshaw, *Building Brand Equity: A Strategy for Success in a Hostile Marketplace* (New York: John Wiley & Sons, Inc. 1995), p. 16.

[8] See Kevin L. Keller, "Conceptualizing, Measuring, and Managing Customer-Based Brand Equity,"*Journal of Marketing* 57 (January 1993), pp. 1–22.

[9] Walfried Lassar, Banwari Mittal, and Arun Sharma, "Measuring Customer-Based Brand Equity," *Journal of Consumer Marketing* 12, no. 4, (1995), pp. 11–19.

[10] For further reading on 'bonds of identification,' see C.B. Bhattacharya, Hayagreeva Rao, and Mary Ann Glynn, "Understanding the Bond of Identification: An Investigation of Its Correlates Among Art Museum Members," *Journal of Marketing,* Oct. 1995, Vol. 59, #4, PP. 46–57.

[11] For further reading, see Kevin L. Keller: Wagner A. Kamakura and G.J. Russell, "Measuring Customer Perceptions of Brand Quality with Scanner Data: Implications for Brand Equity," *Report Number 91–122* (Cambridge, MA: Marketing Science Institute). Pierre Francois and Douglas MacLachlan, "Ecological Validation of Alternative Customer-Based Brand Strength Measures," *International Journal of Research in Marketing* 12 (1995) p. 322; R. Kenneth Teas and Terry H. Grapentine, "Demystifying Brand Equity," *Marketing Research* 8, no. 2, (Summer 1996), pp. 25–29.

[12] An excellent reader on American consumers' supermarket shopping behavior—a source that has richly informed our own description here is by Barbara E. Kahn and Leigh McAlister, *Grocery Revolution: The New Focus on the Consumer* (Reading, MA: Addison-Wesley, 1996).

[13] Ibid., p. 96.

[14] For further reading, see Dennis W. Rook, "The Buying Impulse," *Journal of Consumer Research* (September 1987), pp. 189–99;

Easwer S. Iyer, "Unplanned Purchasing: Knowledge of Shopping Environment and Time Pressure," *Journal of Retailing* 65 (Spring 1989), pp. 40–57.

[15] Art Thomas and Ron Gardland, "Supermarket Shopping Lists," *International Journal of Retail and Distribution Management* 21, no. 2 (1993), pp. 8–14; Also see Susan Spiggle, "Grocery Shopping Lists: What Do Consumers Write?" in Melanie Wallendorf and Paul F. Anderson eds., *Advances in Consumer Research* 14, (Provo, UT: Association for Consumer Research, 1987), pp. 241–45.

[16] Rook, "The Buying Impulse."

[17] Thomas and Gardland, "Supermarket Shopping Lists."

[18] See, C. Whan Park, Easwer S. Iyer, and Daniel C. Smith, "The Effects of Situational Factors on In-Store Grocery Behavior: The Role of Store Environment and Time Available for Shopping," *Journal of Consumer Research* 15 (March 1989), pp. 422–33.

[19] Quoted in Kahn and McAlister, p. 123.

[20] Ronald E. Milliman, "Using Background Music to Affect the Behavior of Supermarket Shoppers," *Journal of Marketing* 46, no. 3 (1982), pp. 86–91.

[21] For further reading on the effect of store atmospherics on customer shopping behavior, see Robert J. Donovan, John R. Rossiter, Gilian Marcoolyn, and Andrew Nesdale, "Store Atmosphere and Purchasing Behavior," *Journal of Retailing*, 70 (3), pp. 283–94, 1994.

[22] For some research literature on this topic, see Edward M. Tauber, "Why Do People Shop?" *Journal of Marketing*, 36 (october), 1972, pp. 47–8. Danny Bellenger and Pradeep K. Korgaonkar, "Profiling the Recreational Shopper," *Journal of Retailing*, 56, 3, 1980, pp. 77–92; and Barry J. Babin, William R. Darden, and Mitch Griffin, "Work and/or Fun: Measuring Hedonic and Utilitarian Shopping Value," *Journal of Consumer Research*, 20 (March 1994), pp. 644–56.

[23] See Peter N. Bloch, Nancy M. Ridgway, and Scott A. Dawson, "Shopping Mall as a Consumer Habitat," *Journal of Retailing* 70, no. 1 (1994), pp. 23–42.

[24] Based on a report in *Chicago Tribune*, June 23, 1996, Business Section, p. 1.

After reading this chapter you should be able to:

Define relationship-based buying, and explain why it is important to marketers.

Identify customer motivations to engage in relationship-based buying.

Describe a model of relationship-based buying in terms of the determinants of relationship-based buying and its consequences.

Discuss the concepts of trust and commitment, including their role in relationship-based buying.

Describe the determinants of trust and commitment by household and business customers.

Define reverse marketing, and discuss why buyers would want to persuade sellers to do business with them.

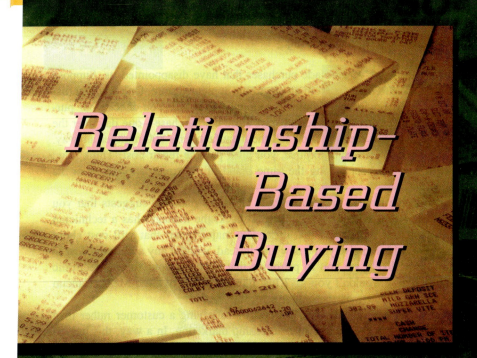

Relationship–Based Buying

Book Us Every Year for the Rest of Our Lives!

When more than a hundred passengers took off in a chartered flight from New York to a Club Med resort in Cancun, they had no idea what they were in for. The flight was 10 hours late. Consequently, the food had run out early, as had beverages. The landing at Cancun at 2 A.M. was so hard that oxygen masks dropped from above the seats, and luggage tumbled on passengers below. Passengers considered their vacations ruined even before they had begun. In fact, a lawyer among the passengers was collecting names of others for a possible class-action suit—until he and the others came upon a show put on at the terminal by Sylvio de Bertoli. De Bertoli was Chef de Village for Club Med, legendary for keeping his guests happy. When he heard of the plane's late arrival, he decided to put on a "welcoming party." He took half his staff to the airport, where they greeted each passenger personally, handled their baggage, gave them a friendly ear, and apologized profusely for the inconvenience. When passengers arrived at the village, welcoming them was the rest of the staff and a lavish banquet, complete with champagne and a mariachi band. The staff had even rallied other guests to join the party, which lasted until sunrise. Not only had the guests forgotten and forgiven the nightmarish flight; they thought this was the most fun they had had in their lives!

At that time if a customer researcher had asked them, "Would you like to take a Club Med vacation again?" their reply most likely would have been "Book us every year for the rest of our lives!"[1]

This requires understanding about what motivates customers to engage in relationship-based buying. We integrated these motivations in a model of relationship-based buying. In this model, two groups of factors constitute the motivations: (1) cost-benefit factors that comprise search costs, risk reduction, switching costs, and value-added benefits, and (2) sociocultural factors that comprise early socialization, reciprocity, networks, and friendships. These antecedent factors result in supplier-customer relationships that are characterized by commitment and trust. The outcome of these relationships is customer loyalty to the supplier, increased buying, willingness to pay more, favorable word-of-mouth, and customer equity or goodwill.

Next, we discussed aftermarketing, the marketing efforts directed at the customer after the sale is made. It includes activities designed to keep customers satisfied after the purchase. A program of aftermarketing entails several steps. These include maintaining a customer information file, identifying customer contact points, analyzing informal feedback, conducting satisfaction surveys, managing communication programs, hosting special events for customers, and auditing and reclaiming lost customers.

Next we discussed relationship buying and selling in business markets. The process of relationship buying in business markets was captured by the Industrial Marketing and Purchasing (IMP) group (a group of business researchers in Europe). In the IMP model, three key factors are recognized, namely, transaction-specific investments/adaptations made to meet the need of a specific customer, power dependence that reflects the dependence of one partner on the other, and role formalness that indicates how personal or impersonal the interactions between the partners are.

Following this, we identified a set of reasons for relationship development in business buying. These reasons include business customers' need to assure long-term supply, to reduce the cost of transactions, and to pursue quality and cost-reduction goals.

Next we described the determinants of trust and commitment, identified earlier as key elements of business relationships. Business customers trust their suppliers when suppliers make partner-specific investments, strive for mutual goals, offer open communications and product support, and avoid opportunistic behaviors. Conversely, suppliers also need to trust their customers, and this trust depends on customers adopting a single-source policy and engaging in data sharing and nurturance.

We also discussed reverse marketing, or developing and nurturing suppliers. Reverse marketing is needed when future needs would not be met by existing suppliers, when specific but unprepared suppliers need to be patronized, when certain environmental policies need to be promoted, when vendors need quality assurance support, or when a program of cost reduction is needed.

The last topic was supplier-customer partnering—the establishment of partnership-like relations with one's customers or one's suppliers. Four sets of factors encourage business firms to engage in supplier partnering: competitive intensity, pressure on market prices, high concern with quality, and the availability of enabling technology. Reviewing the emerging trends, we suggested that future business buying will increasing be relational and based on a strategic plan for supplier development.

Key Terms

Relationship-Based Buying 737	Perceived Risk 739	Trust 744
Switching Costs 740	Reciprocity 743	Commitment 745
	Networks 743	

Review Questions

1. What is relationship-based buying? Why would customers like to engage in it? Give two examples of household customers and two examples of business customers who have adopted the practice of relationship-based buying.

2. What are the two categories of customer motivations discussed in the chapter that explain relationship-based buying?

3. Define the concepts of trust and commitment. What role do they play in relationship-based buying?

4. What benefits occur to a company whose customers have decided to do business with it on a relationship basis? Explain each briefly.

5. Perceived risk and switching costs are advanced as two determinants of relationship-based buying. Explain how these two factors together work to promote or discourage relationship-based buying.

6. What is reverse marketing? How does it help companies, both the customer and the marketer? Is this something that marketers should really be concerned with? Why or why not? Give three examples of companies that practice reverse marketing.

Applications

1. Your friend, who has always had a lot of girlfriends, decided to skip the class on the topic of this chapter. He figured he has no trouble with relationships and doesn't need a lecture to tell him how to go about them. You quickly let him know that the concept of relationship here deals with buyers and sellers, not girlfriends and boyfriends. And that much more goes into building relationships with customers than with friends. How would you explain the chapter's main theme to him?

2. The chapter describes the perceived risk/switching costs model of relationship buying. Based on this model, identify for each of the following businesses what a company can do to encourage relationship-based buying by its current customers: (a) a credit card company, (b) a long-distance phone company, (c) a supermarket, (d) a package-delivery company such as FedEx for its business customers, and (e) a health insurance company dealing with employers as customers.

3. Trust and commitment are advanced as two essential ingredients in relationship-based buying. Write your boss a memo, outlining all the actions your company can take to improve its trust and commitment scores with its major customers.

4. A friend has just graduated from college in liberal arts; a company has offered him a job as an assistant to the director of purchasing. He is wondering how it relates to marketing, his main interest. Unlike him, you took a class in customer behavior where the strategic role of procurement was emphasized and such developments as supplier partnering and reverse marketing were discussed. Would you advise your friend whether or not the job he is

offered is a marketing job? How would you explain to him the significance of his job to a career in marketing?

5. How does the IKEA box in the chapter represent a case of reverse marketing? What does each party gain from this relationship?

Practical Experiences

1. Think about your own experiences as a customer, or the experiences of your company as a customer. Think of five or six companies that you (or your company) do business with as a customer. What does the company do or not do to encourage or discourage you from relationship-based buying from it? Make a list, and compare it across the companies you have considered.

2. Contact two companies. One of them should be known for building and maintaining long-term relationships with buyers and one that is notorious for transactional relationships. Talk to a marketing person within each of the companies and ask him or her to describe the advantages and disadvantages of his or her relative positions. Now, find two people who consume the products and/or services of these companies. Ask them how satisfied they have been with their overall experiences with these companies. Report on any similarities and/or differences.

3. Contact the purchasing director of a company, and interview him or her to identify if the firm engages in any one of the following: (a) supplier partnering, (b) reverse marketing or supplier development, or (c) long-term contract buying. Query him or her about (1) the advantages and disadvantages of this manner of dealing with its suppliers, (2) how the firm goes about establishing this relationship, and (3) what each partner does to satisfy and maintain the commitment of the other.

Notes

1. Adapted from Christopher W.L. Hart, James L. Haskett, and W. Earl Sasser, Jr., "The Profitable Art of Service Recovery," *Harvard Business Review*, July–August 1990, pp. 148–156.

2. Adapted from, Jagdish N. Sheth and Atul Paravatiyar, "Relationship Marketing in Consumer Markets: Antecedents and Consequences," *Journal of the Academy of Marketing Science* 23, no. 4 (Fall 1995), pp. 255–71.

3. James C. Anderson, Hakan Hakansson, and Lars Johanson, "Dyadic Business Relationships within a Business Network Context," *Journal of Marketing* 58 (October 1994), pp. 1–15.

4. Ingmar Bjorkman and Soren Kock, "Social Relationships and Business Networks: The Case of Western Companies in China," *International Business Review* 4, no. 4 (1995), pp. 519–35.

5. For further discussion, see Banwari Mittal, "Trust and Relationship Quality: A

Conceptual Excursion," in Atul Parvatiyar and Jagdish N. Sheth (eds.), *The Contemporary Knowledge of Relationship Marketing* (Atlanta, GA: Emory University, Center for Relationship Marketing, 1996), pp. 230–240. Also see Jagdish N. Sheth and Banwari Mittal, "A Framework for Managing Customer Expectations," *Journal of Market-Focused Management* 1, no. 2 (1996), pp. 137–158.

6. See Wilson 1995; Dwyer, Schurr, and Oh 1987; Moorman, Zaltman, and Deshpande 1992).

7. Terry G. Vavra, *Aftermarketing: How to Keep Customers for Life through Relationship Marketing*, 2nd ed. (Chicago: Irwin Professional Publishers, 1996), p. 22.

8. Philip Kotler, *Marketing Management*, (Upper Saddle River, NJ: Prentice Hall, 1997), p. 12.

9. IMP Group, 1982, "An Interaction Approach," in H. Hakansson, ed.,

International Marketing and Purchasing of Industrial Goods (John Wiley & Sons, Chichester).

10 For additional perspectives, see Neeli Bendapudi and Leonard Berry, "Customers' Motivations for Relationships with Service Providers," *Journal of Retailing* 73, no. 1 (1997), pp. 15–37.

11 Adapted from Michael R. Leenders and David L. Blenkhorn, *Reverse Marketing: The New Buyer-Supplier Relationship* (Free Press, 1996), pp. 164–170.

12 Ibid., p. 2. See, Alan J. Magrath and Kenneth G. Hardy (1994), "Building Customer Partnering,"*Business Horizons*, January–February, pp. 24–28.

13 Ibid., pp. 136–37.

14 See, Alan J. Magrath and Kenneth G. Hardy, "Building Customer Partnering,"*Business Horizons*, January–February 1994, pp. 24–28.

CHAPTER 20

After reading this chapter you should be able to:

Define the two dimensions of value delivery, namely effectiveness and efficiency.

Specify various tools with which businesses offer specific market values to customers.

Describe how to determine dimensions of customer values.

Discuss how to assess customer perceptions of how well various tools are delivering the value they were intended to deliver.

Explain how businesses can appraise customers' happiness with the firm so that they learn how successful they are in satisfying customers.

Creating Market Values for the Customer

And Then There Was This Value Oasis for Belgian Customers

Brussels—a small gem in the middle of Europe. For centuries a major trading center, it is today also the headquarters city of the European Union and the North Atlantic Treaty Organization (NATO).

But despite its key role in world commerce and politics, Brussels was once a kind of wilderness for the movie theater industry. The business had already been in decline for two decades, and after the advent of VCRs and cable TV in the 1980s, people went to the movies even less. The average Belgian's movie-going dropped from eight times a year to barely two. Movie theaters were closing by the minute. Others managed to survive by converting into multiplexes, with as many as 10 screens, expanded food services, and increased show times. But customers continued to give the movie industry a cold shoulder.

Then Kinepolis came on the scene. Created by Bert Claeys, a movie-theater-operating company in Belgium, Kinepolis was a new concept in movie theater entertainment: the world's first megaplex. Located just outside of Brussels, it boasted 25 screens that measure 29 meters by 10 meters, 7,600 roomy seats, and state-of-the art sound and projection equipment. Moreover, parking was free, and the ticket price was lower (due to the low cost of land outside of the city). In short, Kinepolis offered the residents of Brussels an unparalleled movie-going experience.

Within a year, Kinepolis captured 50 percent of the market share in Brussels. Belgians fondly refer to the experience of visiting this megaplex as "an evening at Kinepolis."

Source: Adapted from the report in W. Chan Kim and Renée Mauborgne, "Value Innovation: The Strategic Logic of High Growth," *Harvard Business Review*, July–August 1992, pp. 103–12.

Introduction

The reason Kinepolis became such a hit with Belgian customers is that it gave them a radically superior market value: a good price, coupled with an unprecedented viewing experience in the Kinepolis's large theaters, with their comfortable seating. Other examples of value innovation abound: Barnes and Nobles bookstores are large theaters complete with coffee shop and music room; British Airways offers showers in the arrival lounge; Nordstrom's salespersons keep an eye out for merchandise that may be of interest to specific customers; L.L. Bean will gladly refund merchandise returned anytime during its lifetime, no questions asked; Southwest Airlines' cabin crew will announce a garage sale in the destination city.

These companies demonstrate the essence of marketing: to create value for customers. What underlies their ability to offer outstanding value? How can other marketers create market values for their customers?

To answer these questions, we begin this chapter by discussing the two dimensions of value delivery, effectiveness and efficiency. Following that, we present specific management tools that would enable firms to deliver market values to customers. These tools are specific to individual values the firm might wish to strive for. The next section deals with a measurement strategy. Our discussion dwells first on a method of determining customer values; it then suggests measurement statements to assess how well various value-delivery tools are doing their job, from the customers' viewpoint. In the final section, we return to the opening theme of the book—namely, customer orientation—and the firm's ultimate goal of keeping customers happy. We conclude by suggesting a measurement tool that tells the firm just how happy its customers are.

Value Delivery

As defined in Chapter 3, value is what customers seek in products, services, and suppliers.[1] It stems from a product's potential to satisfy a need or want of the customer. The fulfillment of a customer's need or want is called value delivery.

Dimensions of Value Delivery

Value delivery has two dimensions, effectiveness and efficiency. **Effectiveness** is the ability of the product or service to meet the customer's needs and wants. **Efficiency** is minimal cost to the customer, measured in money, time, and physical effort to receive that value. The less a product or service costs, the more efficient it is from the customer's point of view.

If a marketer's offering fulfills a customer's needs and wants very well, and if in obtaining and using that offering, the customer has to expend as few resources (time, money, and physical effort) as possible, then both efficiency and effectiveness are being simultaneously harnessed to achieve the *best value* for the customer (see Figure 20.1). For example, if the marketer offers the customer a better product (which implies higher effectiveness) at a lower price or at greater convenience (i.e., at a higher efficiency), then the marketer has created the best possible combination. However, if a company can offer a better product but only at a higher price, or if it charges a low price but cannot offer good quality at that price, then the accrued value is only partial. Therefore, the ideal goal of a marketer ought to be to leverage *both* effectiveness and efficiency to deliver the best value.

DIMENSIONS OF VALUE DELIVERY

Figure 20.1

There are many examples of companies offering both effectiveness and efficiency in delivering customer value. For example, the Toyota Camry is a high-quality car sold at a relatively low price. Mass merchandise catalog companies, such as L.L. Bean or J. Crew, offer customers better-known, branded products (effectiveness) with the convenience of shopping from home (efficiency). Some airlines offer customers very good flight schedules (effectiveness) at competitive prices, available 24 hours a day, seven days a week through credit card usage over the telephone (efficiency).

In the business-to-business service markets, Federal Express offers a value both via effectiveness and efficiency. It offers effectiveness by satisfying customer need for on-time, guaranteed delivery of time-sensitive documents and packages. On the efficiency

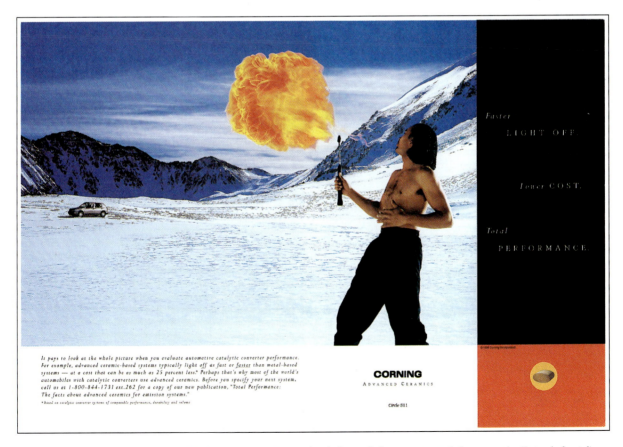

Corning promotes performance and 25% less price as customer values in its catalytic converters made from ceramics (instead of metal).

side, it conserves the customer's time and effort resources via its pickup service and via giving customers computer software so they may process the shipping themselves.

However, its price value is no better than its competitors'. Business firms also offer efficiency value to customers by providing access via the Internet so that customer effort in interacting with the firm is minimized. Firms that offer electronic document delivery such as a database or an article from a journal offer both effectiveness and efficiency—having the information on electronic medium allows customers to use that information more effectively, for example, via word search, or cutting and pasting, moving the text around, enhancing the graphs and photos, and so on. Also the customer effort is minimized (saves the effort to get it by mail, or to go to the library, and so on).

Tools for Creating Customer Values

To offer various values to the customer, marketers need to incorporate certain attributes and elements in their offerings. For example, to offer convenience as a value, marketers have to incorporate certain time- and effort-saving mechanisms in the product or in the manner in which customers can purchase that product or service. As described in Chapter 3, different types of value are sought by the user, payer, and buyer roles. Users seek performance value and social and emotional values. Payers want price value and credit and financing values. Buyers desire service value and convenience and personalization value. Offering each of these market values requires certain marketing tools, summarized in Table 20.1 and described in the following sections.

TOOLS FOR CREATING MARKET VALUES

USER VALUES	PERFORMANCE	SOCIAL	EMOTIONAL
	■ Quality improvement ■ Innovations ■ Mass customization ■ Warranties and guarantees	■ Price exclusivity ■ Limited availability ■ Social image ads ■ Exclusive offerings	■ Emotional communications
PAYER VALUES	PRICE	CREDIT	FINANCING

	■ Low price from
	  lower margins
	■ Low price from
	  increased productivity
	  (achieved through
	  economies of scale,
	  modernized plant,
	  automation, business
	  process reengineering)
		■ Acceptance of
		  credit cards
		■ Offering of own
		  credit card
		■ Deferred payment
			■ Leasing
			
			■ Customized financing

BUYER VALUES	SERVICE	CONVENIENCE	PERSONALIZATION

	■ Product display and
	  demonstration
	■ Knowledgeable
	  salespersons
	■ Responsiveness
	■ User support and
	  maintenance service
		■ Convenient
		  point-of-access
		■ Automated transaction
		  recording
			■ Personal attention
			  and courtesy

Creating Market Values for Users

The user is primarily concerned that the product or service perform as desired and that its use delivers social and emotional benefits.

Performance Value

The user obtains the universal value of performance when the product or service delivers its physical performance better than competing alternatives do, and when the product performs that way consistently without failure. Physical performance stems from the physical composition of the product. As such, it is directly linked to product attributes and to product quality. More specifically, firms can offer superior performance value by adopting four tools: quality improvement, product innovations, mass customization, and warranties and guarantees.

QUALITY IMPROVEMENT

Companies can offer better performance value by building quality in their products. Many firms aim for "zero defects"—eliminating product failures completely. The automobile industry is an illustrative case. As late as the early 1980s, the U.S. automobile industry offered cars that, with few exceptions, broke down frequently. Japanese cars became the choice of many consumers simply because they were more reliable. In the late 1980s to early 1990s, the U.S. car industry turned to building quality in their cars and, consequently, regained some of the lost market share. In fact, Saturn was created by General Motors simply to build a quality car company from scratch—free from the legacy of poor quality its parent company, in the eyes of many consumers, has been afflicted with.

FedEx Quality Improvement Program

WINDOW ON PRACTICE

Quality has been a top priority at Federal Express right from the outset. It achieved, for example, 99 percent levels of reliability on its on-time delivery. Yet FedEx was not satisfied, for it realized that a 99 percent on-time delivery would still leave a lot of customers (those affected by the 1 percent error rate) very irate. So it began a program of "zero failures," counting errors in absolute numbers rather than as percentages.

The company developed a Service Quality Index (SQI), computed daily, based on errors in 12 different delivery events weighed by the seriousness of the error that was reflective of the amount of aggravation caused to customers. For example, missing a promised delivery date generated five points, compared to one point when a customer requested that an invoice be adjusted. If *everything* went wrong, the SQI daily score would be 40 million.

In 1988, when the program was established, the estimated SQI score was 152,000 points per day. The company set its first goal at holding this level (which actually implied a 20 percent improvement, given forecasted growth in package volume of 20 percent). FedEx's employees surpassed this goal, with the actual 1989 SQI score at 133,000 points. Accordingly, the company's profit goals were reached too. This level of attention to detail in its quality program has enabled FedEx to offer its customers unparalleled performance value.

Source: Christopher H. Lovelock, "Federal Express Quality Improvement Program," Case 44, in Christopher H. Lovelock and Charles B. Weinberg, *Marketing Challenges: Cases & Exercises* (New York: McGraw Hill, 3rd ed., 1993), pp. 545–558. Additional information available at **http://www.federalexpress.com**

In the services industry, firms can improve the quality of their offering by hiring well-qualified service staff and then by continually training and retraining them. An example of consumer service in which quality is very critical to the customer is surgical procedures. The patient wants to be absolutely sure that the procedure will be carried out with expertise and dependability. Hospitals can offer the desired performance value by hiring qualified and skilled surgeons and nursing staff, and by acquiring high-quality equipment and by keeping the operating room meticulously sterilized.[2] For an example of a service firm committed to zero defects, see the Window on Practice box on page 775.

INNOVATIONS

Firms can also increase the performance value of their offerings by designing new features in products and/or services. Consider VCRs that enable slow-motion viewing, cassette recorders that feature voice-activated recording, automobiles equipped with antilock braking devices, aqua-tread tires that do not slip on wet pavement, detergents that clean in cold water, and hotels that offer in-room fax service. Today we take them for granted, but when they first appeared, each added to the performance value derived by the user. Current examples of innovations are automobiles equipped with navigation devices (an electronic map that shows where you are and gives directions to the desired destinations), a great value to rental car customers driving in unfamiliar cities; computers that convert voice into written text; software that allows manipulation of photographic images; many Internet-based information sources; and new antidepressant medications.

Philips/Magnavox displays its innovation—a palmtop that gives you "anytime, anywhere" product usability.

R & D LEADS TO MORE SALES FROM NEW PRODUCTS

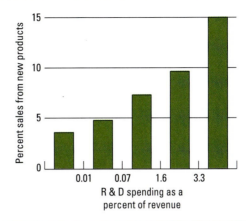

Source: Bradley T. Gale, *Managing Customer Value* (New York: Free Press, 1994), pp. 202–3.

Companies that focus on innovation have a culture of innovation. One of the most innovative companies in America is 3M Corporation. To foster its climate of innovation, 3M is reported to have the following work rules: (1) Twenty-five percent of each division's revenue should come from products that did not exist five years ago. (2) Researchers are encouraged to spend up to 15 percent of their resources on unassigned projects of personal interest. Other innovative companies are Microsoft and Intel, where products are being constantly upgraded by their newer versions every 18 months or so.

Innovative companies also spend more on R&D. PIMS (Profit Impact of Marketing Strategies) is a program of data gathering and analysis, which analyzes about 3,800 business units on about 200 pieces of data to identify strategy factors that determine business profitability. An analysis of firms in the PIMS database found that R&D investment leads to more sales from new products (see Figure 20.2). Furthermore, the proportion of sales from new products was positively correlated with the gains in market share.[3] See Figure 20.3.

NEW PRODUCT ACTIVITY LEADS TO GAINS IN MARKET SHARE

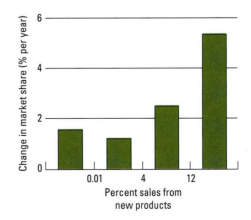

Source: Bradley T. Gale, *Managing Customer Value* (New York: Free Press, 1994), pp. 202–203.

MASS CUSTOMIZATION

The third tool for improved performance value is **mass customization**, the offer of customized products to individual customers without raising the price due to customization.[4] Motorola, for example, offers 20 million varieties of pagers and assembles them after it receives the customer order from one of its salespersons in the field who transmits the order from a laptop. Similarly Hewlett-Packard offers customized products to its business customers. This is made possible mainly by producing the product in modules and then assembling the product from these modules at the last step in the supply chain—such as at the distributor warehouse.

The first customers to benefit from mass customization were organizations because their orders tend to be relatively large. However, advances in automation and information processing have enabled mass customization to meet the needs of consumers. As detailed in the Window on Practice box, Levi Strauss will even customize a single pair of jeans.

WARRANTIES AND GUARANTEES

To alleviate customer apprehensions of possible product failures, companies also offer warranties or guarantees. Whereas warranties offer certain insurance by the manufacturer that specific product features will perform as promised, guarantees are offered by the stores that sell the product. Sears, for example, offers a satisfaction guarantee that gives customers the opportunity to return a product if they are not satisfied with it. L.L. Bean offers a lifetime warranty—you can return its merchandise if it proves unsatisfactory, no matter how long ago you bought it. In business-to-business markets, companies like Caterpillar and Boeing are well known to offer outstanding warranties.

One service company that offers unmatched performance value is the Miami based "Bugs" Burger Bug Killer (BBBK), which provides a "zero-defect" exterminating service. This zero-defect performance is backed by, and is reflected in, its extraordinary per-

---

Blue Jeans for You Alone

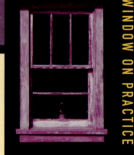

If you walk into the Original Levi's Store in Cincinnati, Ohio, you will be greeted by a sales clerk with a measuring tape in hand and a personal computer (PC) on a nearby desk. He will take your measurements, feed the data into a computer, make final adjustments to the blueprint of a pair of jeans that pops up on the PC screen, push the "transmit" key, give you a receipt for the $40 you paid, and send you home. Forty-eight hours later, the jeans arrive at your home, delivered by FedEx! The jeans must fit you like a glove or you can return them for a full refund.

This is how it works: The PC in the retail store transmits the data to the Levi's factory in Tennessee. There, the computer data are received directly by a robotic tailor who cuts a bolt of denim precisely to the customer's measurements. Usually, the jeans are shipped back to the store in three weeks, but for a slight extra charge, customers have the option of receiving them within 48 hours. The service is a blessing to women, many of whom have difficulty finding jeans that fit them. When the service was introduced for women's jeans in the Cincinnati store, sales went up by 300 percent compared with the same period the previous year.

Source: Adapted from Glenn Rifkin, "Digital Blue Jeans Pour Data and Legs into Customized Fit," *New York Times*, November 8, 1994, pp. A1, D8. Additional information available at **http://www.levi.com**

formance guarantee. Customers don't pay a dime unless they are satisfied that the company has successfully destroyed all pests and breeding and nesting places. Should "defects" be found later, the company refunds the last 12 month's service fee and pays for service by a competing firm for one year. Should a guest in a hotel or restaurant serviced by BBBK find a bug, the company would pay for the guest's meal or room and offer a free gift for a future meal or room. The company charges about four times the market rate, and customers who value performance and quality happily pay it.[5]

Social and Emotional Values

The personal values that satisfy customers' wants are the social and emotional values. These are neither engineered in the product nor delivered via better service. Rather, they are created by association with other desirable objects, persons, situations, or symbols.

Social values are derived from the association of a product with one or more social groups in society. These groups may be defined in the basis of demographic, socioeconomic, or cultural-ethnic characteristics and tend to be defined in the customer's mind as either a positive or negative stereotype. For example, the stereotype of a rich person driving a Cadillac may be perceived to be a positive stereotype by some and negative by others.

Marketers offer social and emotional value through prestige pricing, limited availability, social-image-based marketing communications that focus on association with desired persons or objects or symbols, and new exclusive offerings. Emotional value is also deliverable by emotional advertising.

PRESTIGE PRICING

Pricing a product high enough so that only a few customers can afford it ensures that the product will be sold in limited target markets. Ubiquitous availability and universal use of a product detracts from its exclusivity. High price itself leads to prestige, which is further fueled by limited penetration in the mass market. Marketers seeking to offer customers this value would not then seek to simultaneously offer price value. High-priced cars such as Lotus, Rolls Royce, and Lamborghini; watches such as Rolex and Concorde; and pens such as Mont Blanc all give their owners social prestige.

LIMITED AVAILABILITY

Related to exclusive pricing is the strategy of limited availability. Many products are offered in limited editions and quantities and for this reason acquire social value for their owners. Examples include the Cobra limited edition of Ford Mustang; or First Day postage stamps, which are bought by customers on the first day of issue; rare pieces of art such as original Rembrandt or Van Gogh paintings, and so on.

SOCIAL-IMAGE-BASED MARKETING COMMUNICATIONS

Much of the social and emotional value stems from marketing communications that associate the product or service with certain social symbols and feelings. Thus, Nike athletic shoes are depicted as suited to the serious athlete, while Air Walk is for the young and trendy. Elizabeth Taylor's Passion perfume is for the successful, mature woman, while Tommy Boy or Tommy Girl colognes are for teenagers and adolescents.

These communications stem, not just from advertising, but other elements of the marketing mix. Thus, a product design could convey a sleek, modern image or traditionalism; it could be gaudy or subtle, signifying poor or refined taste. Price also communicates social exclusivity. Place has social image associated with it, such as a location in a business district or in a run-down strip mall. Moreover, social observations on the street about who is using a product or service also communicate its social value. Loss-leader pricing is one specific approach within the lower-margin strategy category. Stores typically offer a few selected items at a very low price, sometimes below cost, to attract customers. They take a loss on these items in the hope of making more profit on other items that the customers buy.

NEW EXCLUSIVE OFFERINGS

The fourth avenue to delivering social and emotional value is expanded product offerings that already possess social or emotional value for a segment of customers. For example, Budget Rental Car Company was the first one to recognize the opportunity and to offer luxury cars, like the Lincoln. Today, Budget is the only company that offers Jaguars—a car that connotes a great social value to many consumers.

EMOTIONAL COMMUNICATIONS

Many of the tools that create social value also create emotional value. The feeling of exclusivity of ownership, for example, gives some people an emotional uplift. But a more direct route to engendering emotional value is the use of **emotional communications**—

Love

Sight Mercedes-Benz showcases its famous logo on a candy, hoping this emotional communique will evoke "love" in its customers.

communications that evoke some emotional experience in the viewer or reader. Valentine's Day gifts like flowers, candy, and diamond jewelry are sold as symbols of love, and much of the emotional symbolism is communicated to customers by marketing communications. **Social cause marketing**—programs that promote social causes such as race unity—arouse strong emotional bonds of identification among many viewers. For example, Benetton uses very vivid images of social causes such as race harmony and AIDS research to establish such an emotional bond with its target customers who generally can be characterized as "global youth"—broad-minded youth with awareness of global issues. A car dealer of U.S. cars in Michigan gives out American flags on the Fourth of July and urges people to buy American.

One legendary commercial that is the epitome of emotional advertising is by the Coca-Cola Company: In the ad, a child offers a bottle of Coke to Mean Joe Greene, a football star. After initially declining, the football player finally accepts the Coke at the child's insistence. The child watches his hero gulping the beverage; and the football star is so moved by the child's gesture, and perhaps so delighted by the thirst-quenching beverage, that he tosses his jersey to the grateful child. This advertisement was so successful in generating the desired emotions in viewers that it was used worldwide.

Creating Market Values for Payers

The types of value most important to payers involve low-cost and ease of making payments. Thus, marketers' tools to create value for payers include keeping the cost of purchasing and using the product low and offering services that are helpful to payers.

Price Value

The price value represents the relative affordability of the product or service to the customer. It is the degree of economic sacrifice the customer has to make to purchase the product or service.

As discussed in Chapter 3, affordability is a function of buying power and prices. Buying power depends on the buyer's disposable income. Price comprises both the initial purchase price and the cost of maintaining the product usage-ready or the cost of using the product. The concept of "lifetime cost" or "life-cycle costing" is supposed to capture these two components. Marketers of initially high-price items need to draw customer attention to the life-cycle cost of their offerings.

Take a refrigerator, for example. The cost of electricity and maintenance over the 12 years it is likely to last is estimated to be as much as 65 to 70 percent of the total cost of using the product. In other words, the initial cost is only approximately 30 percent of the total cost. With such a product, affordability goes beyond the initial cost and must include the cost of upkeep and maintenance over the product's life. One way in which companies are sensitizing customers to this notion of life-cycle costing is by attaching energy guide tags to the front of appliances in stores.

While affordability is a characteristic of the customer (which the marketer cannot alter), price is an element of the marketing mix, and the marketer can do something about it. Companies that want to differentiate themselves on this value are constantly striving to offer the product or service at a lower price. To reduce price, companies can opt for two approaches: (1) accept lower margins, and/or (2) reduce their own costs of production by improving productivity.

LOW PRICE FROM LOWER MARGINS

The **lower-margin approach** consists of selling at a low-profit margin to attract customers. Many firms use this approach, cutting their prices below the competitors' price to attract the competitors' customers. Long-distance phone companies that are not the market share leaders (e.g., MCI and Sprint) have used price as a competitive weapon to take share away from the market leader. Similarly, smaller airlines, such as the now defunct People's Express and currently successful Southwest Airlines, offer extremely low fares. These companies offer limited schedules; the national airlines attempt to match fares on the routes these smaller airlines operate.

The lower-margin approach is often the outcome of a *strategic insight*. That is, some companies simply figure out the "right formula" that enables them to offer the required price value. Budget Rental Car Company performed an analysis of its costs and car-usage pattern and figured out that it can profitably offer "unlimited mileage," a practice the company then pioneered. Likewise, Texas Instruments decided to sell its electronic calculators with a low-price strategy because it foresaw the potential drop in production costs that would result from the "experience learning curve."[6]

LOW PRICE FROM INCREASED PRODUCTIVITY

The second enabler of lower price is the **increased-productivity approach,** in which a firm strives for a lower cost of production. Higher productivity makes individual firms or whole industries more competitive by enabling them to offer better economic value to the customer. A case in point is Compaq, which had been losing in sales and market share for years. In 1992, following a major restructuring effort designed to sharply hike productivity, it was able to cut prices, offering customers good economic value on its computer products, which were already known to be high in performance value. By 1994, the company's revenues had doubled, making it no. 1 in the PC business with a 13 percent market share. What is more, despite a price cut, its profits increased fourfold.[7]

To lower production costs, companies can choose from among several strategies. They can develop economies of scale, use modernized plants that operate more efficiently, automate processes, and use business process reengineering.

ECONOMIES OF SCALE   Economies of scale occur when larger volume leads to lower per-unit costs. This happens both because larger production units may run more efficiently and because they distribute fixed-cost overheads over a larger number of product units. High-volume firms can also negotiate more favorable prices from their suppliers, which then reduces their cost of production or of acquisition of resalable items. Wal-Mart, for example, is able to negotiate long-term contracts with its suppliers on favorable terms because of the size of its purchases.

One of the key findings of the PIMS study referred to earlier also confirms the role of the economies of scale. The PIMS study found that market share and profitability are strongly related. The reason, as the authors explain, is that the larger shareholders produce and operate on a large scale and thus obtain a lower cost due to economies of scale. This reduced cost allows them both a higher margin and a capability to offer better price value to customers.[8]

MODERNIZED PLANT   Outdated plant and equipment run inefficiently, and any modernization of plant reduces production costs. The casebook *Marketing Challenges* describes a company in Vancouver that produced skylights, whose modernized plant gave it a 20 percent cost advantage over Columbia Plastics, a manufacturer of skylights in Seattle. This cost advantage gave the Vancouver firm the ability to offer better economic value to Columbia's customers, stealing substantial business from the latter.[9]

Furthermore, the adoption of better substitute technologies may enable better cost structures. Thus, use of plastic and fiberglass as a substitute for metal components in such wide-ranging products as automobiles, chemical tanks, plumbing piping, boats, and rocket combustion chambers has enabled various pioneering companies to differentiate themselves by offering their customers better price value.

AUTOMATION Many companies have reduced costs through automation, the use of technology and machines to substitute, partly or wholly, for human labor that would otherwise be required to perform a task. Automation may simply make an employee's work more efficient, or it may remove the need for an employee to personally attend to the customer.

As an example, consider a warehouse automation program at Kinney Drugs, a drug retail chain store headquartered in New York. The overall warehousing process under the newly automated system uses bar codes to track all inventory from the time it arrives to outgoing shipment. Radio frequency (RF) computer terminals match the purchase order upon inventory arrival, assign a unique bar coded number, which is then easily tracked and managed so that arrivals are available immediately for outshipping without first going to a central inventory area (i.e., arrivals can be "cross-docked" immediately). The outgoing shipment order is itself automated by an EDI (electronic data interchange) system that links the warehouse to retail drug stores, where the inventory movement data are generated and fed back to the warehouse. Such automations not only increase productivity but they also reduce errors.[10]

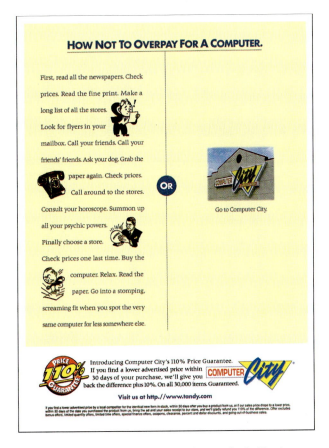

Computer City assures a good price value in this ad.

Examples of the automation of the encounter with the customer include the use of ATM banking machines, voicemail in companies, or automatic checkout on the TV screen in many hotels. Also, electronic commerce is the latest in business's attempt to automate customer information services and sales transactions. Business Web sites offer information, searchable by the user, based on his or her specific information needs. Because users self-navigate, it saves company costs over a human agent providing information. Not only do these procedures reduce a company's cost of serving its customers, but sometimes they also save customers time and hassle and thus offer convenience value.

BUSINESS PROCESS REENGINEERING   The objective of business process reengineering is to design entire business processes (e.g., order-fulfillment process, equipment installation process, new-product development process) to make them more efficient. Reengineering differs from simple quality upgrade or continuous improvement. Rather than merely improving it, **reengineering** redesigns a process starting from a blank slate. The objective is to reduce the **cycle time** (the total time it takes for the entire production and/or delivery task to be completed), the amount of labor input, and the component and processing costs.[11]

For example, McDonnell Douglas Corp., bought by Boeing, Inc. in 1997, undertook a program of reengineering for the assembly of the C-17 military cargo plane. The C-17 plane was a new type of airlifter to support the military's Rapid Deployment Force and was initially ordered in 1980. Subsequent funding was erratic, and changing military goals made timely and efficient development and production difficult. The company man-

---

Reengineering at Taco Bell

WINDOW ON PRACTICE

In the late 1980s, Taco Bell embarked on a major reengineering effort. In many fast-food restaurants, the cost of food that a customer gets is about 25 cents of every dollar the customer spends; the rest goes into operations and marketing. Taco Bell turned this around. It did some customer research and found that what customers wanted was good food, served in a clean environment and at an affordable price. To increase the value food customers get for every dollar they spend, Taco Bell cut down costs by simplifying both the management process and the operations. The company eliminated entire layers of management and gave restaurant managers more responsibility. To reduce operations costs, the company redesigned the restaurant building. It cut down the kitchen area from 70 percent to 30 percent, increasing the customer area to 70 percent, doubling the seating capacity. To accomplish this, the company implemented the concept of K-minus (i.e., kitchenless restaurant). Now all cooking is done in central commissaries, from which food is delivered to individual restaurants that now focus on serving the customer rather than cooking the food ingredients.

The gains from this effort are best described in the words of John E. Martin, the company's CEO, who led the effort:

> This has also doubled our productivity. Today, our peak capacity is $1,000 per hour (compared to $400 per hour before the reengineering effort), and our average customer pricing has gone down by about 25 percent!

Adapted from Michael Hammer and James Champy, "One Company's Experience—Taco Bell," *Reengineering the Corporation* (New York: Harper Collins, 1993), pp. 171–81. Additional information available at **http://www.tacobell.com**

aged to meet the required delivery schedule but only at substantial cost overruns. Under the U.S. Air Force's contract, however, its price was firm, so McDonnell Douglas had to reexamine and reengineer its processes. Two years into reengineering, the Drivematics team (the unit assigned to explore reengineering first) had produced dramatic results. It had cut work time on assembly of the wing skin on a pair of wings by 75 percent, and the time spent in correcting mistakes on this part of the job had plunged from 8,625 hours to 611 hours. The company estimates that reengineering this procedure alone saved $1 million per plane.[12] To learn how another firm (Taco Bell) used reengineering to help it offer more value to payers, see the Window on Practice box.

Credit and Financing Values

Payers seek credit and financing values because they improve affordability by creating deferred payments or providing credit. Specifically, credit value is delivered in several ways:

- Sellers may accept credit cards issued by third parties or banks.
- Sellers may issue their own credit cards or give credit by other instruments (e.g., a small store might give a credit voucher that the customer signs as proof of having received credit).
- Sellers may allow a delayed or deferred payment, such as in "90 days same as cash" schemes utilized by many vendors.

Offering credit was a pioneering strategy adopted by Sears, which on top of their promise of "satisfaction guaranteed," always offered financing arrangements enabling customers to charge their purchases. Sears had credit cards available to customers long before any other major retailer did, reaching almost 40 million households.

Financing goes beyond simple credit and involves specific payment schedules designed for a customer or for a group of customers. Leasing is one such system of financing. Another means is customized financing offered by many companies especially to business customers of capital equipment. Lucent Technologies, formerly AT&T Network Systems, which manufacture telephone equipment such as switches, cable, and transmission equipment, has created a financing feature that enables customers without the necessary capital to quickly modernize their telephone networks.

Leasing not only helps as a mechanism to defer large cash outlay, but may offer tax advantages to both individuals and companies. Some companies have leasing subsidiaries or divisions. One of these, GE Capital, offers customers affordable options to finance their purchases. GM has reaped great benefits from its leasing program on the Cadillac Seville. Even though a Seville may cost close to $55,000, it can be leased for approximately $500 per month. After 24 months, the user walks away with the automobile at a price that may even be lower than the depreciated value of the car. Business customers of manufacturing equipment also find leasing to be an attractive option. Currently, the equipment leasing business is estimated to be about $150 billion. In addition to the financing value received from leasing, customers also receive enhanced performance value: leasing avoids technological obsolescence, which is an important concern in purchases of computers and telecommunications equipment.[13]

Financing is possible for both services and products and for consumables and durables. For example, dental care costs may add up to thousands of dollars, which becomes a significant burden on customers lacking dental insurance. Recognizing an opportunity, some dentists have begun to accept credit cards or installment payments from patients. By doing this, dentists provide a financing value and make themselves more attractive than their fellow dentists who do not offer financing.

Creating Market Values for Buyers

In general, buyers are looking for good service before and after they make their selections. In addition, they want their purchases to be convenient—not too time-consuming and in a time and place that fits their schedule.

Service Value

Whereas the performance value is built into the product or service by the manufacturer or the service designer (economists call this **form utility**), the service value is created by the distribution system. Customers receive service value during pre-purchase and post-purchase phases of product or service acquisition.

PRE-PURCHASE SERVICE

During pre-purchase, a buyer needs product information and help in assessing the fit between customer needs/wants and what the product/service delivers. Marketers in general, but retailers in particular, are generally expected to offer these values, and retailers who offer them in a superior way can differentiate themselves from their competitors. Marketers can offer this value by having the product on display or ready for demonstration and/or for trial use, and by hiring knowledgeable and responsive salespersons who can answer customer questions. For an example of the importance of service value, see the Window on Practice box.

Should Service Be Job One?

The automobile industry illustrates the business impact of service value in both pre- and post-purchase phases. When Ford Motor Company came out with the slogan "Quality Is Job One" and worked on improving the performance value of its models by making them more reliable, dependable, and predictable, they were very successful at selling some of their more popular models, like the Taurus. In fact, the Taurus became the best-selling automobile for a period of time. Unfortunately, it was never rated very high in the J.D. Power and Associates survey of customer satisfaction. Why does a product appeal to customers but fail to satisfy them when they buy it?

Customer satisfaction depends, ultimately, on both product quality and dealer service. Ford's problem was that although the product quality was now perceived to be high, dealer service was still inadequate. In other words, from a customer's viewpoint, quality cannot stop at the manufacturer, but must continue with the service delivered by the dealer. On the other hand, customers rate Japanese companies like Honda, Toyota, and Nissan the highest on both dimensions of product quality and dealer service.

GM has taken just the opposite approach, emphasizing the dealer service, and not investing in manufacturing to produce a high-quality product. Companies like Hyundai and Yugo have emphasized only price, so customers perceive them as companies that emphasize neither dealer service nor product quality.

Additional information available at **http://www.carsandculture.com**

WINDOW ON PRACTICE

PRODUCT ON DISPLAY OR DEMONSTRATION Although a number of alternative forms of *non*store retailing (e.g., telemarketing) have come into existence, retail stores continue to have their appeal, foremost because of their "merchandise on display" utility. For some customers, there is nothing like being able to walk into a store and see, touch, and feel the merchandise. Stores that showcase their wares better (for example, with life-size models, reality-enhancing props, and attractive lighting) would have an edge—other things being equal—over their poorly merchandising competitors. Industrial distributors offer similar value by offering the product for demonstration. Trade shows are an effective means of displaying product developments, as are fashion shows for clothing. Even catalog marketers recognize the service value of product displays, so they use high-resolution photographs of goods in their catalogs.

Another tool marketers can use to offer service value is having the product available in trial sizes. In supermarkets, new food items are offered as "taste samples." A test drive of a car offers similar service value. Various kinds of subscriptions and memberships, offered free for the first month, are instances of service value to the purchase decision maker. Similarly, shoe stores offer the customer an opportunity to take the shoes home, try them for a week or a month indoors, and return them if they do not fit; this offers service value to the customer. This service value in product trial is unavailable to you when you are a tourist; as a tourist you will generally not consider buying products that you want to have the option of returning later if they "do not fit."

KNOWLEDGEABLE SALESPERSONS The second resource that marketers can use and offer to customers is product knowledge. Retail store salespersons and other salespersons vary greatly in the degree of competence and product knowledge they possess. Salespersons at a discount store tend to be substantially less knowledgeable about their products than those at a specialty store. Professional photographers, for example, would prefer to patronize specialty camera shops than discount stores; likewise, those who play any game seriously (rather than leisurely) would prefer to shop at specialty sporting goods stores.

Professional, knowledgeable salespersons help not only by offering better product knowledge, but also by assisting the customer in choosing a product that would fit his or her (customer's) needs and wants better. Clothiers with personal service, for example, would assist the customer to choose "the right suit"; such personalized advice is simply unavailable at large department stores. Likewise, a computer company's salesperson helps the customer figure out which equipment and options would meet his or her needs better. Insurance salespersons can distinguish themselves by taking the time to assess a customer's needs and recommending an insurance product accordingly. Financial asset managers, stock brokers, and other bank officers can likewise distinguish themselves from their competitors by offering up-to-date information and advice about their products and services.

SERVICE IN THE POST-PURCHASE PHASE

Generally known as after-sales service or after-sales product support, service in the post-purchase phase refers to all the assistance a marketer can provide to maintain the product use-ready. This service value accrues inasmuch as it enables the user to derive the maximum utility from the product or service. Two specific avenues are available to marketers for this service: product-use advice and product maintenance.

PRODUCT-USE ADVICE AND SUPPORT Consumers often need assistance in using the product, and marketers who offer this assistance differentiate themselves from their competitors. Thus, companies have toll-free technical assistance lines, especially for technical products like personal computers. In 1993, General Electric Co. commissioned a

IBM promises its business customers network solutions that will satisfy the customer firm's own customers in turn.

state-of-the-art customer advice facility it calls the Customer Answer Center. The service representatives who answer customer questions on its toll-free phone lines are equipped with online product information as well as an instant display of customer records. This helps them resolve customer problems efficiently and efficaciously. The center receives about two million calls a year, and the company has experienced a significant increase in customer satisfaction since the center began.

Note that the quality of user advice is a user value; but ease of obtaining it is a buyer value. For example, if user support is not part of the original seller's offering, then the buyer has to procure it from elsewhere. Thus, service value for the buyer is obtained when user support and maintenance support (discussed next) are available to the buyer along with the original item's purchase.

PRODUCT MAINTENANCE Perhaps the most significant service value accrues from the product maintenance service the marketer offers a customer. If a car breaks down, the customer wants it repaired quickly and without any inconvenience. It is for this reason that Lexus gives the customer a loaner car during the repair period.

Product downtime can be immensely consequential in business products, such as computers, copiers, and communication networks. Xerox realized the importance of minimizing the downtime on its office equipment and set up an infrastructure—an army of 12,000 service reps—so that its service reps could reach any customer's location within the whole

United States within 30 minutes. This outstanding service value (along with the performance value of its improved equipment) made Xerox the preferred supplier for many new customers. The company experienced the greatest growth rate of the past 10 years.

In the service industries, the core product itself is service (e.g., haircutting for a hair salon, access to special channel broadcasts for cable TV companies). How good this core product is constitutes the performance value. The manner in which this core product is delivered constitutes "service value" in our values framework. The cable TV industry was the subject of very high consumer complaints during the late 1980s to early 1990s. These complaints focused on the poor quality of signals (i.e., poor performance value), the service being overpriced (i.e., poor economic value), but most importantly, its poor responsiveness to consumer complaints (i.e., poor service value). The cable industry had ignored consumer concern for a long time, but from 1993 to 1995, it faced the prospect of losing its monopoly (regulators were increasingly permitting a second cable operator to start operating in what had hitherto been an exclusively licensed territory); consequently, it turned to repairing its poor image with consumers. It worked to improve its servicing of a customer's request and began to offer service guarantees.

Gearing a firm to deliver superior service value to customers is actually what differentiates a manufacturing-driven company from a marketing-driven company. Generally, manufacturers are concerned with producing the right products in the right quantities at the right time and at the right cost. They see marketers as having little understanding of their role in the corporation. In a manufacturing-driven company, everything is done to ensure low costs and a smooth production process. Simple products, narrow product lines, and high-volume production are the goals of a manufacturing-driven firm. In contrast, a marketing-driven firm will be more concerned with satisfying customers' needs.[14] The importance placed on service value forces companies to move from a manufacturing to a marketing-driven mentality.

Convenience Value and Personalization Value

As described in Chapter 3, convenience and personalization values accrue from being able to obtain a product or service in a hassle-free and socially pleasant exchange with delivery personnel. Similar to the social and emotional values, it represents an influence on the customer's "wants." It is something that is preferred, not needed.

CONVENIENT POINT-OF-ACCESS

To deliver convenience value, firms can provide convenient points-of-access. They can locate the distribution and retail facilities conveniently and keep them open 24 hours. Banks now have branch locations inside supermarkets, and many banks offer Saturday and Sunday banking services. Domino's distinguished itself by offering convenience value through home delivery of pizzas, a pioneering practice that made a significant dent in market leader Pizza Hut's market share. Ultimately, to remain competitive, Pizza Hut had to offer home delivery as well. Supermarkets offer this value by ensuring short checkout lines and by delivering the groceries to a customer's car. Some clothiers will alter a suit, press it, and deliver it to a customer's home. Companies like Office Depot will deliver office products over a minimum purchase price to a customer's home. Many fast-food restaurant chains such as Taco Bell, McDonald's, and Burger King have increased their sales by going beyond their free-standing traditional store design, and opening small-scale service counters at such diverse locations as schools, corporate cafeterias, shopping malls, and airports, and, for Taco Bell, even within gas stations.

Britain's First Direct Bank offers its customers convenient access—a buyer value.

Some companies sell in the customer's home or office. Banking by phone, computer, and Internet is such an instance of convenience. This service is so much valued by a segment of British customers that a British bank works exclusively as a "banking-by-phone" bank.

AUTOMATED TRANSACTION RECORDING

Automation is a significant means of offering convenience. Automation such as at ATMs for banking and telephone-based automated response systems such as the one used by banks, document shipping companies such as FedEx, and customer service departments of many companies offer convenient access. They also offer convenience by automating the transaction so it is not held up by the unavailability of service employees. Selected supermarkets are testing a device that the customer uses to scan each item as he or she places it in the shopping cart; this would eliminate the need for checkout lines altogether. Similarly, many gas stations are equipped with a credit card reader right at the pump. This "pay at the pump" feature is a source of great convenience value, especially to customers with small children in the car, who may be apprehensive about leaving the car unattended.

COURTESY

As explained in Chapter 3, personalization value accrues from sales and service employees treating customers with courtesy. Thus, checkout clerks who are courteous to a customer are offering service value. This avenue of offering service value is especially important in service businesses. A car rental agent, hotel registration clerk, airline ticket agent, or a waiter or waitress who shows courtesy in dealing with the customer is offering a service value, and this can be an important differential advantage for service firms.

Measuring Value Delivery

With so many tools available for delivering customer values, marketers must make sure their organization is delivering the values their target markets most desire—and that customers are aware it is doing so. The effective way of ensuring this is with the basics of marketing management: (1) find out what customers want, (2) organize to deliver those values, and (3) measure how well, in customer perceptions, those values have been delivered.

To identify the specific benefits and processes customers want on each of the six values, the marketer would conduct customer research. A blueprint for conducting this research is presented in the Window on Research box.

WINDOW ON RESEARCH

Process for Determining Customer Value

Robert B. Woodruff, marketing professor at the University of Tennessee has done research with a number of firms, helping them identify a process for determining exactly what value means to customers of a specific product or service. As a basis for this process, he defines Customer Value as "a customer's perceived preference for and evaluation of those product attributes, attribute performances, and consequences arising from use that facilitate (or block) achieving the customer's goals and purposes in use situations." Thus, customer value includes customer perceptions at three levels:

1. *Attribute performance*—whether the product has the desired attributes and attribute performances.

2. *Attribute consequences*—whether using the product has the desired consequences.

3. *Goals pertinent to attribute consequences*—whether the consequences of using the product help the customer meet his or her goals.

If using the product meets each of these desires, the result is satisfaction in that area.

To measure a customer's overall satisfaction with the received value, the marketer would assess satisfaction at all three levels. For example, for Healthy Choice frozen entrees, attribute performance might be that "fat content is low"; a related consequence could be "it will keep blood cholesterol level low." Customer goals would be "staying healthy." To assess customer value for Healthy Choice, then, marketers would have to assess how well the brand meets the performance, consequences, and goals levels.

How can managers use this process to form a strategy to enhance customer value? As shown in Figure 20.4, the marketer begins by conducting research to learn which values at the three levels (performance, consequence, and goals) customers desire. Further research, combining customer interviews with management intuition, would then narrow the list to the most important of those values. Further surveys would assess the firm's delivery of those important values—how well the firm is satisfying those values. The final step is not a measurement but a diagnostic analysis; managers must identify causes of the value delivery gap and possible corrective actions. All these steps should be informed by a futuristic perspective—what are the customers likely to value in the future?

Additional information available at **http://www. healthychoice.com**

Source: Robert B. Woodruff, "Customer Value: The Next Source for Competitive Advantage," *Journal of the Academy of Marketing Science* 25, no. 2 (1997), pp. 139–153.

Figure 20.4

A PROCESS FOR DETERMINING CUSTOMER VALUE

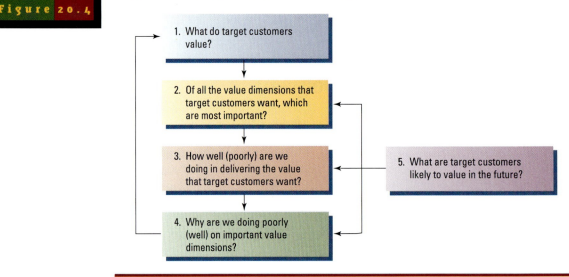

That model focuses on value assessment related to product use. We can also apply this type of evaluation to the purchase and payment situations. In keeping with the three customer roles, a complete assessment should include customer values in using, paying for, and buying the product.

Once the values are identified, an organization has to organize efforts and strategies to deliver these values. This may require substantial investment in equipment, technology, and human resources. The principal action strategies have been described in the chapter.

As these strategies are implemented, they need to be appraised to determine whether implementation is progressing as planned and whether the strategies are effective. One means of appraisal is internal audits, in which a cross-functional team of managers could rate the various processes. For example, for reengineering the process (which helps deliver price value), managers should assess the degree to which the reengineering project has been implemented, as well as the extent to which reengineering has improved productivity and lowered costs.

Some of these processes are not visible to customers, so customer input cannot be used to assess progress; for example, the reengineering process itself is not visible to customers, nor are customers concerned about *how* a firm manages to deliver specific values. For these internal processes, management's own assessment is the only option. However, the outcome of these processes, as delivered to customers, is visible to customers and indeed experienced by them as six market values. Therefore, marketers should solicit customer appraisal of these experiences.

To do this, marketers should assess the firm's success both in satisfying the six values and in using value-creation tools in a way that customers experience and appreciate. They can make both assessments by asking customers to rate statements about the product and the firm. Thus, to measure success in satisfying the six values, the marketer can use statements such as the ones given in Chapter 3. For example, to measure the performance value of a Saab automobile, customers can be asked to rate their degree of agreement with the statement "My Saab gives me good gas mileage"; to measure the price value, they can rate the statement "This brand at this price is a good bargain."

SAMPLE QUESTIONS FOR MEASURING CUSTOMER PERCEPTIONS OF VALUE DELIVERY PROCESSES

Figure 20.5

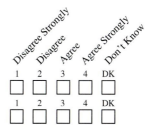

USER VALUES	Disagree Strongly (1)	Disagree (2)	Agree (3)	Agree Strongly (4)	Don't Know (DK)
PERFORMANCE VALUE PROCESSES					
Quality improvement					
The quality of this firm's products and services is superb.	☐	☐	☐	☐	☐
The quality of this firm's products and services has been improving continuously over the last several years.	☐	☐	☐	☐	☐
Innovation					
The firm has consistently introduced breakthrough designs and new technologies in its products/services.	☐	☐	☐	☐	☐
The firm's current products represent significant advances over their earlier versions of a few years ago.	☐	☐	☐	☐	☐
The firm's products/services are one step ahead of what the competition offers.	☐	☐	☐	☐	☐
Customization					
The firm is able to offer me individually customized products and services.	☐	☐	☐	☐	☐
The firm's products and services are available in a large variety and with options so that I can have the kind of product/service I like.	☐	☐	☐	☐	☐
I can purchase a custom-made product from this firm without sacrificing timeliness.	☐	☐	☐	☐	☐
Warranties and guarantees					
The firm offers one of the best warranties in the industry.	☐	☐	☐	☐	☐
The firm truly follows a "no questions asked" full-refund policy.	☐	☐	☐	☐	☐
SOCIAL VALUE					
Price exclusivity					
The firm prices the product/service high enough to maintain its exclusivity.	☐	☐	☐	☐	☐
The product/service's price gives me a special satisfaction of possessing an exclusive, not-too-common product/service.	☐	☐	☐	☐	☐
Limit availability					
The firm makes its products/services available too widely.**	☐	☐	☐	☐	☐
I like the fact that the product/service's distribution is restricted.	☐	☐	☐	☐	☐
Social image ads					
Advertisements for the product/service show the product in association with people and images that I find appealing.	☐	☐	☐	☐	☐
Exclusive offerings					
Over time, the firm has extended its product line to include other prestigious brands.	☐	☐	☐	☐	☐
EMOTIONAL VALUE					
Emotional communications					
I can personally identify with the social causes that the firm promotes in its communications.	☐	☐	☐	☐	☐
When I view the firm's advertisements, I can visualize the wonderful emotional experience I will have using the product.	☐	☐	☐	☐	☐

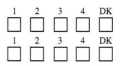

(continued)

Figure 20.5 SAMPLE QUESTIONS FOR MEASURING CUSTOMER PERCEPTIONS OF VALUE DELIVERY PROCESSES *continued*

	Disagree Strongly	Disagree	Agree	Agree Strongly	Don't Know

PAYER VALUES

Price value

Over time, this firm has consistently offered me better price value for its products/services.

| 1 | 2 | 3 | 4 | DK |

Compared with three years ago, the firm is offering me better products without raising the prices.

| 1 | 2 | 3 | 4 | DK |

I think that the firm cares about reducing my costs without sacrificing what I get from its products/services.*

| 1 | 2 | 3 | 4 | DK |

Credit

The firm offers liberal credit terms.

| 1 | 2 | 3 | 4 | DK |

The firm offers interest-free deferred-payment plans.

| 1 | 2 | 3 | 4 | DK |

Financing

The special financing plan the firm offers suits my needs very well.

| 1 | 2 | 3 | 4 | DK |

Over the years, the firm has customized its financing options for my needs.*

| 1 | 2 | 3 | 4 | DK |

BUYER VALUES

SERVICE VALUE

General

Over time, the firm has made it increasingly easy for me to do business with it.

| 1 | 2 | 3 | 4 | DK |

Product display

The firm makes it easy for me to inspect the product and see it working before deciding to buy it.

| 1 | 2 | 3 | 4 | DK |

Knowledgeable salespersons

This firm's employees seem to have been well screened and trained for their jobs, and I find them very knowledgeable about their products/services.

| 1 | 2 | 3 | 4 | DK |

User support

If users of this product need help in operating or using the product, they can easily receive advice from the firm.

| 1 | 2 | 3 | 4 | DK |

Maintenance support

It is easy to obtain the required maintenance to keep the product always ready for use.

| 1 | 2 | 3 | 4 | DK |

Responsiveness

The firm welcomes complaints and tries to do whatever it takes to win a customer over.

| 1 | 2 | 3 | 4 | DK |

CONVENIENCE

Points of access

I find the firm's products and services conveniently located.

| 1 | 2 | 3 | 4 | DK |

I can access the firm anytime from anywhere I like.

| 1 | 2 | 3 | 4 | DK |

Over past few years, the firm has considerably expanded the ways I can obtain its products/services.

| 1 | 2 | 3 | 4 | DK |

Automated transaction recording

Employees who record the transaction seem to be well equipped with technology to complete my transaction efficiently.

| 1 | 2 | 3 | 4 | DK |

Figure 20.5

SAMPLE QUESTIONS FOR MEASURING CUSTOMER PERCEPTIONS
OF VALUE DELIVERY PROCESSES *continued*

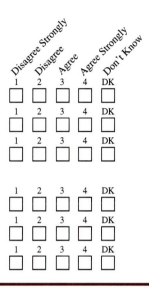

BUYER VALUES *(continued)*	Disagree Strongly	Disagree	Agree	Agree Strongly	Don't Know
	1	2	3	4	DK
The firm has the system and technology in place that makes it very easy for me to obtain its products/services.	☐	☐	☐	☐	☐
This firm seems to have organized its various departments, operations, and procedures to maximize customer convenience.*	☐	☐	☐	☐	☐
I find it very convenient to complete the transactions with this firm using its self-service technology.	☐	☐	☐	☐	☐

PERSONALIZATION

Personal attention

The firm's employees are very polite, courteous and pleasant.	☐	☐	☐	☐	☐
The firm's employees and managers consider no other activity more important than to attend to a customer like myself.	☐	☐	☐	☐	☐
The firm's employees seem to show an understanding of my perspective and treat me as a person so that I feel very happy dealing with them.	☐	☐	☐	☐	☐

*These items may be especially useful for business customers.

**The item should be reverse scored so that disagreement is given the higher value on the scale.

Marketers can also measure how well the various tools are delivering specific values they were purported to deliver, and whether the firm has been able to improve value delivery over the years. Marketers can do this by having customers rate statements such as those in Figure 20.5. These statements are illustrative and may not all apply to every company. Some are especially suitable for business-to-business customers, and others are general but may still need adaptation to specific product/service situations. As a marketer, you would use them as a basis for thinking about how they apply to individual situations, and for researching their utility in improving your firm's ability to deliver customer values.

Fulfilling the Business Purpose by Delivering Customer Value

Research into value-delivery processes helps marketers focus on what should be their fundamental business purpose: to make the customer happy.

Addressing that issue returns us to the theme with which we started the book. Josh played by Tom Hanks, the hero in our opening story in Chapter 1, epitomized customer orientation, but he did so by virtue of being the customer himself. Most marketers don't have that luxury. Rather, by applying the concepts in this book, managers learn about customers and their behavior with respect to the various market values they seek. The tools we presented in this chapter are supposed to deliver those values. The ultimate goal of implementing these value delivery tools is to make the customer happy.

ASSESSMENT OF THE CUSTOMER'S FINAL JUDGMENT

Please rate the following statements on a 0–10 scale where 0 means you disagree entirely, and 10 means you agree wholeheartedly.

Disagree   Agree
Entirely   Wholeheartedly

0   5   10

- The firm understands my needs and preferences well.
- I can trust the firm not to take advantage of me as a customer.
- The firm values and shows its appreciation for my business.
- The firm takes specific actions to keep me as a customer.
- I can identify myself with the firm's products and its actions.
- The firm can count on me as its supporter.
- I enjoy dealing with the employees of this firm.
- I love this firm's products.
- I love to do business with this firm.
- I expect to continue my relationship with this firm for a long time.

    As we proposed in Chapter 1, the purpose of the business is to satisfy a customer. In this context, General Electric Company's vision of itself, excerpted in Chapter 1, is worth repeating:

> Customers are . . . the lifeblood of a company. Customers' vision of their needs and the company's view become identical, and every effort of every man and woman in the company is focused on satisfying those needs.[15]

We would paraphrase GE's assertion slightly: *Happy* customers are the lifeblood of a company. Therefore, a firm must do everything feasible to make and keep its customers happy—so happy, in fact, that customers delight in doing business with the firm.[16] They take pride in the company's existence and in its actions; and rather than just draw on its resources, they are eager to support it. Establishing such relationships of mutual support and nurturance is the ultimate goal of customer orientation.

    That customers would support such a relationship for a long time in the future is the *final customer judgment* that all companies should strive for. Figure 20.6 presents an instrument to assess this final judgment by asking customers to rate a set of statements. The total of each customer's ratings is his or her judgment, conveniently scored as an index anchored at zero and 100, with 100 being the perfect score. Companies falling below this score should strive to bridge the gap.

Summary

In this chapter we presented various strategies and tools that businesses can employ to offer each of the six values to customers. For the universal, performance value, companies need to focus on programs of quality improvement, R&D to create innovations in products and services, mass customization, and warranties and guarantees. To differentiate themselves on service value, firms need to become more responsive in their dealings with customers. They need to offer better service during pre-purchase as well as post-purchase phases. Superior service value depends on employee competence, knowledge-ability, courtesy, and responsiveness. These employee traits can be managed by careful selection and training and retraining. Service value also requires an infrastructure capable of handling product repair or maintenance service without much downtime. Finally, price value can be offered by lower-margin or higher-productivity strategies. Firms can improve productivity by automation and process reengineering.

The three personal values, too, require certain strategies and tools. For social and emotional values, a marketer needs to manage its marketing communications. All its communications need to be strategically directed to create a focused social image and associations. Quality, price, and distribution exclusivity can be harnessed to give a product a social image of prestige. Situations and settings (i.e., ambiance) can be used to create mood and emotional association. The convenience value can be enhanced by increasing the "points of access" (e.g., by strategic location of product delivery and by 24-hour easy access by customers to a firm's employees). Another avenue of offering convenience value is by automating the recording of the transaction. Finally, firms can differentiate themselves on financing value by offering easy payment terms, low financing rates, and leasing arrangements.

Firms should attempt to differentiate themselves by exceeding on more than one type of customer value. Of course, what exactly will constitute value to a specific customer in a specific product/market situation needs to be constantly researched. Customer-driven companies are constantly listening to the voice of the customer and are continually striving to offer better value to their customers.

Key Terms

Value Delivery 772
Effectiveness 772
Efficiency 772
Mass Customization 778
Emotional
    Communications 780

Social Cause Marketing
    781
Lower Margin Approach
    782
Increased-Productivity
    Approach 782

Reengineering 784
Cycle Time 784
Form Utility 786

Review Questions

1. What is meant by effectiveness and efficiency in terms of creating value for customers? Are they the same thing? Why might both be important to marketers trying to deliver superior customer value?

2. What are the lower-margin and increased-productivity avenues, respectively? How are these part of an attempt by marketers to create value for customers?

3. What is mass customization? How does it differ from reengineering? How do these two business practices deliver value to customers? What specific values do they deliver, and how?

4. How might financing value be applied in business-to-business markets? Is it equally applicable for both products and services? Give examples of both consumer products and services and business products and services that benefit from financing values.

5. Identify the actions recommended in the chapter for creating value to the buyer role. Explain each briefly with examples.

6. Is it possible to measure the usefulness of a company's various actions in delivering value to customers? What approaches are there for this purpose? Briefly explain each approach.

Applications

1. Consider your own role as a customer of the following companies: (a) your supermarket, (b) your post office, (c) your physician and health-care facility, and (d) the mail catalog company you occasionally buy clothing from. For each of the company's products/services, reflect on your own needs, wants, and preferences for doing business. Identify what each company could do to offer you better marketing values, illustrating your answer for each specific market value you might desire.

2. Assume that you are the marketing director for a large chain of hotels. How will you ensure that you are delivering superior market values to your customers? Write your company president a memo outlining your plan of action to substantially enhance the market values your hotel chain is currently delivering to its customers.

   Now do the same exercise assuming that you are a health insurance agency. Consider all three roles of the customer.

3. Review Figure 20.5, Sample Questions for Measuring Customer Perceptions of Value Delivery Processes. The measures in the questionnaire are generic, and they may need adaptation (and wording change) for specific companies or product/service categories. Adapt these measures and design a questionnaire for use by (a) a bank, (b) a supermarket, and (c) a company selling office furniture and supplies to small home offices.

   Note: To make sure that the questionnaire makes sense, answer it yourself as a customer of these companies.

Practical Experiences

1. Contact three companies that are known for delivering superior customer value either in person or on the Internet. Identify which values they are most concerned with delivering. Are these companies attempting to increase the number of values they deliver? Should they deliver more values or should they focus on the excellent delivery of just one or two critical values? Why?

2. Survey three of your classmates or friends about the different social/emotional values they look for from each of the following products: (a) the brand of cologne/perfume they use, (b) the health club they belong to, (c) their favorite restaurant, and (d) the car they drive. Ask them how they came to associate the social/emotional values they seek and/or receive from these products. In what way are these products a source of social/emotional values? Then compare your answer to the sources described in the chapter. Based on your interviews, comment whether the value-creation actions described in the chapter for this market value really create that value.

3. Review Figure 20.5 to refresh your memory on customer values. Take the questions you designed in Applications Question 3 and add them to the 10 statements presented in Figure 20.6, Assessment of the Customer's Final Judgment.

   Now administer this questionnaire to five customers, for each of the three products/services: bank, supermarket, and office furniture and supplies company.
   Review their responses and identify similarities and differences across the three products/services.

4. Administer the same survey to about 50 consumers as a student group project. Enter the data in the computer, and for each product/service, identify the relationship between the Customer's Final Judgment scores on the one hand and the item scores from questions derived from Table 20.3.

Interpret your findings in terms of differences across the three products/services. Note: To identify the relationships, you may proceed as follows:

a. Compute an average score for the "customer's final judgment items."

b. Compute an average score for each of the value processes of Figure 20.5.

c. Compute correlations between the average score computed in (a) with the average scores computed in (b).

d. Run a regression analysis, where the average score computed in (a) is the dependent variable, and the average scores on value processes computed in (b) are the predictor variables.

Notes

[1] For theoretical essays on customer value, see Robert B. Woodruff, "Customer Value: The Next Source of Competitive Advantage," *Journal of the Academy of Marketing Science* 25, no. 2 (Spring 1997), pp. 139–53; A. Parasuraman, "Reflections on Gaining Competitive Advantage through Customer Value," *Journal of the Academy of Marketing Science* no. 2 (Spring 1997), 25 154–61; Stanley F. Slater, "Developing a Customer Value-Based Theory of the Firm," *Journal of the Academy of Marketing Science* 25, no. 2 (Spring 1997), pp. 162–67, for a practitioner's essay on the topic, see Bradley T. Gale, *Managing Customer Value* (New York, NY: The Free Press, 1994).

[2] For further reading, see Robert Jacobson and David A. Aaker, "The Strategic Role of Product Quality,"*Journal of Marketing* 51 (October 1987), pp. 31–44.

[3] Michael Schrage, "Few Try to Imitate 3M's Successes," *Boston Globe*, October 11, 1992, p. B2; also see, "Competing on Science: The Agenda for Senior Management," *Harvard Business Review*, November–December 1989.

[4] B. Joseph Pine II, Bart Victor, and Andrew C. Boynton, "Making Mass Customization Work." *Harvest Business Review* September/October 1993.

[5] Tom Richman, "Getting the Bugs Out," *Inc.* (June 1984), pp. 61–64; also see, Christopher W.L. Hart, "The Power of Unconditional Service Guarantees," *Harvard Business Review* (July–August 1988), pp. 54–62.

[6] George S. Day and David B. Montgomery, "Diagnosing the Experience Curve," *Journal of Marketing* (Spring 1983), pp. 44–83.

[7] "Productivity to the Rescue," *Business Week*, October 5, 1995, pp. 134–36.

[8] Robert D. Buzzell and Robert T. Gale, *The PIMS Principle—Linking Strategy to Performance* (New York: The Free Press, 1987); R.G. Wakerly, "PIMS: A Tool for Developing Strategy,"*Long-Range Planning*, June 1984, pp. 92–97.

[9] Christopher H. Lovelock and Charles B. Weinberg, "Columbia Plastics Division of Fraser Industries, Inc.," in *Marketing Challenges: Cases and Exercises* (McGraw Hill, 1993).

[10] Nick Adams, "New Warehouse Automation Improves Customer Service at Kinney Drugs,"*Industrial Engineering*, October 1993, pp. 21–23.

[11] William Wrennall, "Productivity: Reengineering for Competitiveness," *Industrial Engineering* 26, no. 12 (December 1994) p. 12 (3).

[12] John McCloud, "McDonnell Douglas Saves Over $1 million per Plane with Reengineering Effort," *Industrial Engineering* 25, no. 10 (October 1993), pp. 27–30.

[13] "Equipment Leasing Is a Wise Investment," *The Office* 118 no. 2 (August 1993) p.18 (3).

[14] Philip Kotler, *Marketing Management: Analysis, Planning, Implementation, and Control* (New York: Prentice-Hall, 1991), p. 701. 7th edition.

[15] General Electric 1990 *Annual Report*.

[16] For a research report on the conceptual distinction between customer satisfaction and customer delight, see Richard L. Oliver, Roland T. Rust, and Sajeev Varki, "Customer Delight: Foundations, Findings, and Managerial Insight," *Journal of Retailing* 73, no. 3, (1997), pp. 311–36.

CHAPTERS

	1	2	3	4	5	6	7	8	9	10	11	12	13	14	15	16	17	18	19	20	MAIN ISSUE TOPICS & CHAPTER NUMBER	SPECIAL FEATURES
Prepaid Wireless		●	❖									❖						●			Payer vs user roles (2); values each role seeks (3); segments the service will appeal to (12); is long-term contract necessary for loyalty? (18)	Service/Youth
Nike	❖					●	❖			❖											Cross-cultural influence on customer response to marketer communications (6, 10); need to mold corporate culture and personality (1, 7)	Product/International/ Europe
Islamic Banks			❖		❖	●				❖											Influence of religion (as a reference group (6); role of government (5); customer values of religious banks (3, 10)	Service/International Business/(Middle East, Asian)
NFL							●				❖	❖									Men-women differences (7); targeting women as a segment (12); channeling behavior (11)	Product/Service/ Sports Marketing
QWERTY Keyboard									●		❖										Habit and learning (9); resistance to innovation (9); incentive for attitude and behavior change (11); role of involvement (11)	Unique story
Insurance Fraud										●	●	❖	❖								Beliefs underlying attitudes (11); psychographic segmentation (10, 12); illustrative research (13)	Service; interpreting survey data
Rubbermaid	❖		❖					❖					●				❖			●	Researching customer behavior (13); researching trends (8); offering value to resellers and end-users (3, 17, 20); adopting a customer orientation culture (1, 20)	Market-oriented innovations
Four Customer Decisions														●							Individual decision-making, problem recognition, decision models, low/high involvement decisions (14)	Students' journals
Duquesne Light																●					Business customers' buying policies and procedures (16)	Sample "welcome booklet" for vendors
Design Plus				❖												●					Public institution buying, buying center (16); customer values for different decision makers (3)	Architectural design service/school board as customer
Customer Loyalty Index													❖					●			Analyzing customers' store loyalty (18); identifying data needs for understanding customer store choice (13)	Proprietary research report
Digital			❖											❖		❖			●		Loss of business customer due to misreading of values the customer was seeking (3, 16, 19); role of market values in decision models (3, 14)	Business customer; major purchase
National Motors								❖											●		Business customers seeking suppliers as partners (19); trends in business buying (8)	Business customer/ relationship-based buying
Oura Oil																		❖		●	In the face of fierce competition, a Japanese gasoline retailer explores avenues of delivering customer values to win customer loyalty (18, 20)	International (Japan) gasoline retailer

Key: ● Strong; ❖ Considerable & applicable

PREPAID WIRELESS: PROTECTING THE PAYER FROM THE USER!

Of the 452 messages your roommate will take for you this year, how many of them will you actually get?

Suppose you were a college student and you were to hear a pitch in a TV ad for a company selling its wireless phone service. Would you find this pitch appealing? You might if you have a lot of friends calling you while you are away from your room and if you are paranoid about not missing a message some caller may have left for you. The above message was actually used recently by Bell Atlantic Corp.'s wireless phone service division, called Mobile, in the Washington, D.C. area.

Early users of wireless service included affluent consumers and businessmen. But after a decade of promoting to these groups, the wireless companies are now casting their net wider. Wireless service is now being promoted to ordinary men and women as an emergency aid (e.g., stranded on the highway with a flat tire, or stuck in traffic on the way to an important social appointment). The current group that companies are trying to court is students. Historically, students have been the least attractive target, because their financial means are limited. But now companies are realizing that the wireless phone naturally appeals to the youth. This was humorously epitomized in the movie *Clueless,* where two high-school teenage girls constantly talked with each other on their wireless phones until they would actually bump into each other, still connected by wireless!

But the *Clueless* girls were rich; most students are not. Enter wireless services with a twist: prepaid wireless. "Worriless Wireless" is how a TV ad by Omnipoint Corp.—another provider of wireless phone service—promotes its prepaid wireless service. It goes on to say, "You control what you spend on your wireless calls—because you pay for them in advance."

According to a *Yankee* group report, in 1997 there were about 580,000 subscribers to prepaid wireless services in the United States, which is a small fraction of the 54 million wireless subscribers; by the year 2000, their number is supposed to grow to 1.9 million and by 2002 to 2.7 million. Correspondingly, prepaid wireless revenues are expected to grow from $400 million in 1997 to $1.5 billion in 2000 and $2.2 billion by 2002.

The market share leaders in prepaid service are not recent upstarts, but established phone companies. Omnipoint Corp. and PrimeCo Personal Communications LP. are two pioneers in promoting prepaid service; for each, as many as 50 percent of the total subscribers are prepaid customers.

Who buys prepaid? Initially, these were people who could not pass a credit check, accounting for some 30 to 40 percent of all wireless subscribers. Now, prepaid wireless is being offered as an insurance against getting bills one would find hard to pay. It is a check on overspending.

Prepaid doesn't come cheap. Vendors get lower sales commissions, and subscribers don't get subsidized phones. No one is certain about the longevity of customers of prepaid service. Is this a trend likely to grow? How long can one keep customers who are not tied down by a long-term contract? Will these customers stay brand loyal? These are the questions that wireless companies face. Correctly gauging customer interest in both wireless service and in prepaid cards would be crucial to companies as they pursue new markets for prepaid wireless.

Discussion Questions

1. The case is subtitled, "Protecting the Payer from the User." Is that subtitle apt? Briefly explain.

2. Why are students and youth a natural target for wireless? Why does wireless appeal to them?

3. What other customer groups might find the prepaid wireless useful?

4. Some companies fear that due to a lack of a long-term contract, prepaid customers would not be loyal to the company. Discuss this statement. Is this fear real? What can companies do to increase customer loyalty?

Based on Elizabeth Jensen, "Wireless Carriers Try New Hook to Win Customers," *The Wall Street Journal,* March 4, 1998, p. B4.

CASE TWO

NIKE: A REBEL LEARNING TO SCHMOOZE!

Europe, Asia, and Latin America: Barricade your stadiums. Hide your trophies. Invest in some deodorant. . . . As Asia and Latin America have been crushed, so shall Europe . . . The world has been warned.

A sales pitch from some deodorant salesman? A battle cry from some despot? No, none of these. It is, instead, a Nike ad in *Soccer America* magazine's Spring 1996 issue, targeting the European consumers and soccer fans. Nike, which after acquiring control of the Brazilian national soccer federation, wants to rock the European soccer world with its in-your-face advertising.

Nike's iconoclastic brand of advertising, happily embraced by its millions of American fans, has brought it trouble from its international audiences. In the Summer 1996 Olympics in Atlanta, for example, Nike used the slogan, "You don't win silver. You lose gold." At its headquarters in Switzerland, the International Olympic Committee (IOC) was not amused; the slogan "denigrated the Olympic spirit of competition and belittled all those athletes who came to the Games without a chance of winning gold," said an incensed IOC official. So intense was their disapproval that several IOC member nations considered banning all manufacturers' Nike logos from the game.

Not that Nike hasn't tried to incorporate local color in its foreign advertising. In one ad in Japan, for example, Charles Barkley was shown fighting Godzilla. In a European ad, Barkley wore a wig and a flowing robe as a character in an opera, called, "The Barkley of Seville." These adaptations work fine for promoting its shoes for basketball, a game seen as authentically American. Soccer, however, is a different story. Nike has no home base in it, and it is a foreigner to this Asian and European sport's tradition-respecting governing body—the International Federation of Football Association (FIFA).

Take a Nike ad on British TV featuring Eric Cantona (a French soccer player) who describes how his spitting at a fan and insulting a coach had won him a Nike endorsement contract. To Nike's millions of American sports fans, this image is all too familiar in the person of tennis star and Nike endorser John McEnroe. To the European officials of the Fédération Internationale de Football Association (FIFA), this was vantage irreverence. This was advertising that "glorifies violence and bad taste," wrote an angry FIFA official.

Another commercial depicts Satan and his demons teaming up against a team made up of various Nike endorsers—Air Jordan, Charles Barkley, and French soccer player Eric Cantona, among them. The commercial ends by showing Cantona kicking a winning goal through Satan. Mr.

Cantona flips up his collar, in the style of James Dean (a 1960s American movie screen idol), and says "Au revoir" as he kicks the final ball. In focus groups with European teens, the ad was a hit. As they left the room after viewing the test ad, they all flipped up their collars and said "au revoir." To the officials of FIFA, which controls access to consumers by granting licenses to merchandisers, this was too scary and offensive to show in prime time when kids would be watching!

At home, Nike would be unfettered by such controversy and outrage. Indeed, it would feed on it. But abroad, it had to think twice. American icon James Dean's rebel image comes across to the European establishment as the "irreverent ugly American." When dealing with tradition-bound Asian and European cultures, "we now have to add a sort of United Nations side," admits Philip Knight, Nike's own "rebel with a cause" CEO. That United Nations side shows up in its recent change in the slogan it uses on its basketballs: instead of "Sanctioned by players, not the powers that be," it now reads "The partners we need"! Nike has realized that if it is to expand globally, its "just do it" attitude has to give way to a "just schmooze it" mind-set.

Discussion Questions

1. "Culture is a significant, all-pervasive determinant of customer behavior." Discuss this statement, illustrating with Nike's experience.

2. Does Nike's corporate culture differ from the culture of its customers in Europe and Asia? In what way?

3. What specific cultural values were reflected in each of the Nike's communications described above, and in what way could these have been incompatible with the cultural values prevailing in Europe and Asia?

4. In order to succeed in Europe, how should Nike mold its attitude? What would a "just schmooze it" mind-set comprise of? Would Nike have to give up its characteristic personality altogether? What image should it try to portray?

Adapted from Roger Thurow, "In Global Drive, Nike Finds Its Brash Ways Don't Always Pay Off," *The Wall Street Journal*, May 5, 1997, pp. A1, A10.

CASE THREE

ISLAMIC BANKS: RESPECTING THE PROPHET'S WORDS

Bank Islam, a bank in Malaysia, operates by the principles of Islam. Its customers deposit money with the bank, but they do not receive any interest on it. The reason is that Islam prohibits any interest as usury. So instead of being paid an interest on their money, customers receive a share of the bank's profits.

The bank was founded in Egypt about three decades ago simply to give pious Muslims a way to keep their money safe. Today, Islamic banks are common in the Middle East, and they are spreading in the Phillippines, Europe, and the U.S. In these countries, many customers like the availability of a bank that follows the Islamic principles. Islamic banks pool deposits and in turn invest them in construction, commodities, and other businesses that do not pay any interest on these investments. Instead, these commercial borrowers pay the bank a share of their own profits. In turn, the banks share the profits with their individual depositors. The combined assets of all the Islamic banks now total over $70 billion. The leader of the pack in Malaysia is Bank Islam, with total deposits of 3 billion ringgit, or $1.2 billion.

Islamic banks have devised new ways of lending and investing money. A consumer who wants a car loan, for example, agrees to make a series of payments totaling more than the sticker price of the car, which remains the bank's property until all the payments have been made. In business markets, importers and exporters employ a technique they call *murabaha*. A bank buys goods and sells them to a customer who then pays the bank at a future date a total sum more than what the customer would have had to pay if the goods were bought with cash. This technique was approved by New York Fed.

In Malaysia, where the banks are expanding financial services most aggressively, Arab-Malaysian Bank has issued the first Islamic credit card—an interest-free Visa card. The bank charges no interest, but customers pay an annual fee that is a percentage of their purchases. The credit limit is equal to the amount in their deposit accounts in the bank.

The Malaysian government is pushing for the country's financial services to go global and attract foreign capital. A number of Malaysian Islamic investment funds hold shares worth $780 million, most of them in foreign companies. However, these companies are carefully screened to ensure that the stocks are not linked to liquor, gambling, or other activities regarded as sinful by Islamic teachings.

Conservative Muslims criticize the government for allowing banks to conduct both Islamic-oriented and interest-paying services under the same roof. According to these critics, some Islamic stockbrokers are handling companies that make some of their profits from interest received.

Some argue that it is impossible for Islamic financial institutions to become major players in the global financial industry because the interest-paying services are an inevitable part of modern day financial business. "That concern is true," says Nik Ramlah, an official of the Malaysian Securities Commission, "but it just underlines the need to introduce the necessary Islamic financial products to meet the needs of modern day investors."

Discussion Questions

1. What role does religion play in customer behavior? Illustrate with the behavior of customers who follow the Islamic religion.

2. Which of the market values do Islamic banks offer to Muslim customers, specific to each of the three customer role? Would Islamic bank products, such as the practice of *murabaha,* be of value to non-Muslim customers also? Under what circumstances?

3. Can modern economies and their financial institutions co-exist with traditional cultural norms? Do governments play a role in promoting such co-existence?

Adapted from Joe McDonald, "Malaysia's Islamic Banks Grow in Assets, Popularity," *The Detroit News,* January 3, 1997; Also, see **http://data.detnews.com/1997/03/01030062.htm** and Kirk Albrecht, "Turning the Prophet's Words into Profits," *Business Week,* March 16, 1998.

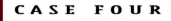

CASE FOUR

NOW THE NFL TURNS ITS SIGHTS ON WOMEN

During Superbowl 1998, the National Football League (NFL) had a contest with a twist; it was directed at women.

According to recent data, more than 40 million women in the U.S. watch professional football on an average weekend. In 1990, women made up 33 percent of the NFL's fan base; in 1998, this proportion is 43 percent. Of course, the level of interest in watching the game varies for both males and females: some watch it without getting too involved, while others are avid and knowledgeable watchers.

One of the league's findings was that men and women watch the game differently. Most women watch the game with their families, and, unlike men, they won't plan and spend the whole day around the game. Also, more than men, women like special segments like "a day in the life of a player."

The NFL is running a four-tiered women's initiative: participation, education, merchandising, and advertising. Under the education tier, NFL teams offer a course called Football 101, designed by the Women's Institute for Football Education (WIFE) and lasting about 2 1/2 hours, including a tour of the stadium and locker rooms and appearances from the team's players. The fee ranges from $25 to $35. The course is generally oversubscribed; in Jacksonville, Florida, for example, the course had to be run twice to accommodate 400 women who signed up.

Research also revealed that 70 percent of NFL-licensed merchandise is bought by women. To tap into the women's market, the NFL recently commissioned a licensed women's line of merchandise. Many of the items are made only for women, such as leggings, overalls, and scarves; but unisex items such as sweatshirts are also cut especially to suit women's tastes in style. The merchandise is being sold through mass merchandisers such as Kmart and Wal-Mart and sports shops.

In September 1997, the league also published the *NFL Family Cookbook,* which features recipes from well-known players. Finally, the NFL has launched media advertising, in magazines and TV shows skewed toward women: *TV Guide, Entertainment Weekly, Self, Cosmopolitan,* and *People* magazines, and *Friends, Melrose Place* and other TV shows.

For women who want to increase their appreciation of the game, now there is an easy guide called, *The Women's Armchair Guide to Pro Football.*

Discussion Questions

1. Why do women watch football? Could their reasons and motivations be different from those of men? Why is the proportion of women watchers on the rise?

2. Why does the NFL run the course, "Football 101"? Why is the course designed exclusively for women, rather than for both men and women?

3. It is stated that women watchers' viewing patterns vary from men's. In what way? Are there variations among women also? What implications do these variations have for marketers?

Adapted from Margaret Littman, "Women Fans Have Gridiron Pros Grinning," *Marketing News* 32, no. 3 (February 2, 1998), pp.1, 14.

CASE FIVE

THE QWERTY KEYBOARD: ARE CONSUMERS CREATURES OF HABIT?

QWERTY—the sequence of the first six letters on the second row of a standard keyboard. Every day, millions of people use it. Occasionally, some pause to wonder, why are the letters arranged in that sequence?

Clue: Look at the sequence of other letters on the keyboard: ZXCVBN, ASDFGH, YUIOP, and so on. Get the picture? These letters make no words! Yes, the keyboard was designed so that your fingers would have to travel all over to type almost any word in the English language. And it is not to give your fingers a workout; it is to slow you down. The story goes that early typewriters often jammed as typists hammered on the keys in quick succession. To avoid the jams, the typist had to deliberately slow down which was hard to do. So QWERTY was the answer!

Then, during the 1930s, inventor August Dvorak came up with a better keyboard, the one that arranged the most frequently used letters consecutively. A U.S. Navy study showed the Dvorak keyboard to be easier and quicker to use. And, of course, newer typewriters and modern-day computer keyboards would not jam at any speed. So it would be logical to switch over to the new keyboard, right? Not really. The Dvorak keyboard was never adopted because by then millions of people had gotten used to the QWERTY.

This quaint history made news recently. The neoclassical economic theory holds that markets always choose the right technology. Two economists, Paul David and W. Brian Arthur of Stanford University, challenged that theory in a 1985 essay. They argued that the inferior technology of the QWERTY keyboard should have been abandoned in favor of the more efficient Dvorak invention. But it was not, because people get locked into habit. Naming this idea "path dependence theory," Professor David suggests that it is human nature that "once you start down a certain path, it is hard to get off." And markets behave the same way, argues Professor David.

Professors David and Arthur's views have been challenged by other economists. Among them are Stan Liebowitz and Stephen Margolis, who argue that the Navy study was flawed, and that were the Dvorak keyboard indeed more efficient, businesses with large typing pools would have grasped the superior product to save huge sums on labor costs, even if the change-over meant retraining and short-term productivity loss. Echoing the same sentiment, economist Paul Krugman of MIT says, "Really large mistakes offer profit opportunities. If there is a really crummy technology out there that we have locked into, then it will be worth it for someone to pay the cost involved in getting people to switch."

Professors David and Arthur argue that their point was not to defend one keyboard over another. Rather it was to show that "historical events have a large and unacknowledged role in shaping economic choices"—that "path dependence" theory can explain a considerable portion of everyday human behavior. While economists have yet to discover indisputable evidence for the path dependence theory, Professor Krugman concedes that "QWERTY is a great metaphor."

Discussion Questions

1. What is the QWERTY metaphor? Do you believe that it summarizes customer behavior? Explain your answer.

2. Do customers behave according to "path dependence" theory? How would you synthesize the arguments of economists who argue for and against it, using customer behavior as the context?

3. What other examples can you think of that show the role of habit in customer behavior?

4. Does the model of "resistance to innovation adoption" (discussed in Chapter 9) apply to customer behavior that path dependence theory attempts to explain? How?

Adapted from Lee Gomes, "QWERTY Spells a Saga Of Market Economics," *The Wall Street Journal*, February 25, 1998, pp. B1, B6.

CASE SIX

CONSUMER ATTITUDES TOWARD INSURANCE FRAUD

What do consumers think about committing insurance fraud—like padding claims or ripping off the system in some way? A 1995 study by the U.S. Insurance Research Council found a sharp increase in public tolerance of "soft" fraud.

To understand the underlying reasons and motivations, in 1997 the Washington-based Coalition Against Insurance Fraud surveyed 600 American households. The principal finding of the study was that consumers are concerned about the rising incidence of fraud and deem the practice to be morally wrong, but they can understand why people do it and in some cases even sympathize with people who defraud because they are economically disadvantaged.

Based on consumers' levels of tolerance and their perceptions of why people commit insurance fraud, the researchers grouped consumers into four groups: moralists, realists, conformists, and critics.

Moralists (31 percent).	Moralists have the least tolerance for insurance fraud, and are the most in favor of strong punishment.
Realists (22 percent).	Realists have a low tolerance for insurance fraud but realize it occurs. They may feel some behaviors are justified, depending on the circumstances; they don't advocate strong punishment.
Conformists (26 percent).	Conformists are fairly tolerant of insurance fraud, largely because they believe many people do it, making it more acceptable. Accordingly, they believe in moderate punishment.

Critics (21 percent). Critics have the highest tolerance for fraud and tend to blame the insurance industry and its unfair business practices. Accordingly, they support little or no punishment.

Demographically, the four subgroups varied only slightly, with the exception that moralists included a higher percentage of females.

Respondents were asked to describe their attitudes towards the insurance industry in general, as well as their own insurer and agent, on a five-point scale—from very positive to very negative. The responses are summarized in the following table.

- People are only looking for a fair return on premiums paid (60%).
- People wouldn't lie to insurance companies if they were treated with more respect (39%).
- People are forced into this behavior to get insurance (33%).
- Nobody tells the truth on an application (27%).

Consumer opinion varied by subgroups: The critics were more likely to justify fraud by saying insurers make too much money and cause people to lie to them. But even the moralists join them in being more likely to justify fraud as a way to get a fair return on premiums paid, although they don't nec-

ATTITUDES TOWARD THE INSURANCE INDUSTRY

COMPONENT	TOTAL	REALISTS	CONFORMISTS	MORALISTS	CRITICS
INDUSTRY IN GENERAL					
Positive	53%	45%	60%	60%	47%
Neutral	20%	23%	20%	20%	20%
Negative	26%	32%	20%	20%	33%
INSURANCE COMPANY					
Positive	72%	65%	78%	78%	63%
Neutral	15%	25%	13%	12%	25%
Negative	10%	10%	9%	10%	12%
INSURANCE AGENT					
Positive	74%	71%	75%	79%	69%
Neutral	13%	21%	19%	17%	26%
Negative	6%	8%	6%	4%	5%
INSURANCE PREMIUMS					
Very/Fairly Reasonable	63%	53%	70%	68%	55%
Fairly/Very Unreasonable	31%	41%	23%	26%	40%

In exploring claims experience, about 40 percent of the survey's respondents reported that they had filed an insurance claim within the last two years. The claim categories were: 52 percent health insurance, 39 percent auto, 16 percent homeowners or renters, 3 percent disability, 1 percent life insurance, and 1 percent workers' compensation. Attitudes toward the industry were significantly more positive from people who filed claims on life and homeowners insurance, but much less so for other lines of insurance.

Respondents were asked whether they agreed or disagreed with a number of reasons that people might commit insurance fraud. The list of reasons and the percent of respondents agreeing follow:

- Fraud is justified because insurance premiums increase regardless of claims history and that insurers make undue profits (67%).

essarily condone the practice. Conformists tend to justify fraud by claiming everyone does it, while realists are more likely to believe that premiums will continue to rise regardless of claims history, perhaps suggesting there's no incentive not to commit fraud.

Respondents also were asked why they think people don't commit insurance fraud. A total of 63 percent felt that a person's moral character was the prime deterrent to committing fraud. Other reasons given included fear of being caught (15 percent), fear of prosecution (7 percent), lack of opportunity to commit fraud (3 percent) and a person's religious beliefs (2 percent). Seven percent answered "other" and 20 percent "don't know."

Consumers overwhelmingly believe insurers should take a number of actions to curtail insurance fraud. About 9 in 10 respondents believe insurers should verify applications more carefully, inform people how fraud increases costs, reduce premiums for people with few or no claims, investigate claims more thoroughly, and seek prosecution of suspected fraud more often. At the same time, respondents were less receptive to requiring more documentation to make it more difficult to falsify records (72 percent) or offering rewards to people who provide information about fraud (66 percent).

Critics are the least likely to believe any methods should be used to deter fraud, particularly asking consumers to provide more documentation. Moralists are most likely to believe insurers should verify applications more carefully and do more to inform the public about the costs of fraud.

Respondents were also asked to rate a series of possible consequences and punishments. The findings are summarized in the following table.

ernment to consider as a first step toward reducing consumer fraud.

Discussion Questions

1. How do consumer attitudes influence their behavior? In the present study, is there an association between consumer attitudes toward the insurance companies and their tolerance for consumer fraud, their underlying beliefs about insurance companies, and their support for various acts of punishment?

2. How does experience affect consumer attitudes? Why does that effect occur?

3. What approaches would you suggest for changing people's tolerant attitudes toward insurance fraud? What legislation would you recommend, if any?

PERCEPTIONS OF POSSIBLE PUNISHMENTS FOR FRAUD

METHOD	TOTAL	REALISTS	CONFORMISTS	MORALISTS	CRITICS
Prosecute for lying and falsifying information	57%	63%	63%	70%	29%
Deny unjustified portion of claims; pay remainder	53%	70%	52%	49%	48%
Deny insurance to customer who has submitted false claims	45%	48%	53%	58%	15%
Deny all claims in cases of applications fraud	42%	41%	54%	49%	20%
Customer pays investigative costs if claim is unjustified	40%	40%	54%	46%	17%
Process claims, no questions asked	10%	5%	8%	2%	30%

The Coalition believes that uncovering the public's attitude toward insurance fraud will make it easier to develop specific anti-fraud messages and programs to help change those attitudes. However, it remains to be seen which segments would be most amenable to any attitude change programs and what these programs could possibly be. Based on the study, the Coalition is drafting specific recommendations for insurers and for the gov-

4. What attitude models discussed in Chapter 11, if any, are reflected in the findings of the study?

Adapted from Dennis Jay, "Public Attitude Has Big Impact on Fight Against Insurance Fraud," *National Underwriter—Property & Casualty,* September 15, 1997, Special Report: Insurance Fraud Review Section, p. 23

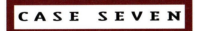

CASE SEVEN

RUBBERMAID: CAPTURING THE CUSTOMER'S VOICE

Rubbermaid, Inc., the maker of plastic household products, has regularly been included in *Fortune's* list of 10 most admired companies. In fact, in 1994, it stood at the top of that prestigious list. Today, Rubbermaid is a household name in the United States, and its array of products is dazzling. For a number of years now, one of the company's goals has been that one-third of its revenues come from products that did not exist five years ago. It floods its retailers with about 300 new products every year, and more than 90 percent of them turn out to be a success. Major retailers have set up inside their store a store-within-the-store, called "destination shops," dedicated entirely to Rubbermaid products.

Where does the company get ideas for this blizzard of new products? The answer is delightfully simple: from customers. By asking them, by observing them, by listening to them, around the year, across the organization, and on a large scale. On any given day, quite a few managers and engineers, marketing researchers and product development specialists—company personnel from all ranks—are scouring the kitchens, bedrooms, and bathrooms of America to discover what customers need or want. They engage in probing conversations with customers, sometimes to identify unmet needs customers themselves might be unaware of.

An often-told story at Rubbermaid is about Stanley Gault, its legendary former chairman. A few years ago, Gault was walking in Manhattan, the story goes, when he overheard a doorman muttering and swearing while sweeping the dirt into a Rubbermaid dustpan. Gault stopped to query the doorman and would not give up until he understood the cause of his griper's unhappiness. The lip of the dustpan was so thick that it was impossible to get all the dirt into the pan. Back in the office, Gault ordered engineers to redesign the product.

The company conducts regular focus groups to explore product improvements and tests new products with user groups with in-home trials where consumers are asked to write diaries on their experience with the product. In addition to reading these test results and focus group reports, managers are encouraged to read customer letters, visit stores, and chat with customers wherever they encounter them.

The company also analyzes social trends. For example, it came up with the idea for "litterless lunch kits" for school children after observing three related social trends: rising concern for the environment, consumer interest in healthier eating, and preference for home-prepared food. These lunch kits are colorful containers (to please children) with airtight modules that can be washed and reused. This eliminates food packaging, something that appeals to ecology-minded parents. They also are designed to fit compactly and attractively on store shelves.

This last point is noteworthy. The company spends an enormous amount of effort on identifying and responding to the retailers' needs and wants as well. Retail managers from across the country arrive in the marketing demo room at the company's headquarters in Wooster, Ohio, at the rate of three per week. In meetings with these retail managers, Rubbermaid's product team describes ideas taking shape and solicits retailers' feedback. They discuss consumer trends, product strengths and weaknesses from the retailers' point of view, pricing, packaging, store layouts, or whatever else might concern the retailer. A major outcome of these discussions is that the product design is influenced by retailer concerns: products must be acceptable to the household customer as well as to the retailer!

Rubbermaid aims to offer value both to end users and to retailers. For retailers, the value comes in the form of service and speed. The company offers higher trade margins and generous promotional allowances. And it does everything fast: it gets the inventory to the store just-in-time. If a customer needs help with promotion, it responds fast with a new ad or promotion concept. CEO Wolfgang Schmitt says that with retailers, "we simply do what we agreed to do," and the company constantly raises the bar on what it agrees to do.

In regard to the household customer, the company does not pretend to sell at the lowest price. Instead, it offers value by improving the product quality. For example, the company uses more and better resins and a thicker gauge. "No one surpasses our quality," was a constant claim by Gault, the famed former chairman. That unsurpassable quality is captured in its advertising slogan: "Don't you wish everything was made . . . like Rubbermaid."

Discussion Questions

1. Compare various methods the company employs to research its customers. What are the relative merit and limitations of each method for generating new product ideas?

2. Why does Rubbermaid expend effort at dealing with retailers? To what extent is that effort in the nature of research versus managing retailer relationships? What role do retailers play in the company's success?

3. Identify specific values the company offers its household and reseller customers, relating them to the market values framework described in Chapter 3.

4. Would you consider Rubbermaid a customer-oriented company? Why or why not? Is customer orientation paying off?

5. Based on your reading about Rubbermaid, Inc., identify the key ingredients needed to implement a customer oriented culture in a company.

Adapted from Jean-Philippe and Nayak P. Ranganath, "Fomenting a Customer Obsession: Rubbermaid's Product Development Strategy," *National Productivity Review* 14, no.4 (September 22, 1995), pp. 89—105.

CASE EIGHT

FOUR CUSTOMER DECISIONS

Marketing Professor Dan Wardlow of San Francisco State University asked his students to describe some personal instances of individual customer decision making. Excerpted below are four student submissions:

I went into the bookstore the other day to buy oil painting materials. Since I was about to paint for the first time, I knew nothing about what or what not to buy . . . [So] I started asking someone that worked at the store to advise on the type of paper I needed for oil painting. This person did not know so I went on and asked a woman in the aisle who was also going to buy similar products. Because she had been painting for many years, she knew exactly what to get and she told me. Since my urge to paint had become so urgent and I didn't want to take any more time in making a careful and studied purchase, I decided to follow a stranger's advice based on her own past experiences. So far, I am quite happy with this purchase.

(Submitted by Nadege Bossut)

Recently, my favorite Nike sweatshirt, which I've worn for at least 8 years, started to form holes. I desperately needed a new one because the sweatshirt was one of my staple pieces of clothing. Before I made the purchase, I had to decide whether to buy a Nike sweatshirt that costs about $40 or an Old Navy sweatshirt for about $15. As I went about my information search, I compared the value between the two and clearly the Old Navy sweatshirt was much cheaper; however, Nike was much better in quality and fit. My parents have always taught me to go for lower prices, but only to a certain extent. That is, I shouldn't purchase an item just for the price and end up unsatisfied. I hate to admit it, but I have purchased many items in the past which unfortunately are now sitting in the corner of my closet as junk. I live in a middle class household and spending $40 just for a sweatshirt is a bit extreme. And as an American born citizen, I've been constantly exposed to the Nike fad, which in this case doesn't influence me much if the price difference is $25. However, from my past experiences, quality does impact my decision. If I buy a sweatshirt that's warm, has a good fit, and is durable, I definitely think it's worth it for an extra $25. In conclusion, I'm now the proud owner of a new Nike sweatshirt.

(Submitted by Rene Tam)

I've bought a Playstation system recently. In fact, when I wanted to buy a TV game system, I did ask my friends about the games among Nintendo, Sega, and Playstation. Before asking my friends, I knew that Playstation offers more new games than Nintendo and Sega. When I was in Hong Kong, my friends there and I usually played either Sega or Nintendo because they offered more exciting games, for example, car racing, street fighting, and so on. However, most of my friends here said Playstation was better than the other two in the United States in terms of the number of games, and the number of other people who had the Playstation games. So, eventually I bought a Playstation system with several games. However, I don't think I am really happy with my decision because the games are not as exciting as the other two companies' games! I finally told my friends that because of them I had made a wrong decision.

(Submitted by Polly Tam)

Just the other day I noticed that I ran out of mousse. So I put it on the shopping list for our shopping trip on Saturday when my wife and I went shopping. I prefer Salon Selective Styling Mousse; the reason: there's one that smells like apples that my wife introduced to me. She uses that type of mousse and its smells real good. When I first tried it, I loved it. It left my hair feeling soft and smelling fresh, unlike other types of mousse I had tried before that used to leave my hair feeling hard and looking like stale curly fries, not to mention leaving my hair smelling like alcohol. Salon Selective Mousse is not as expensive as other name brands. They also put it on sale often enough to buy one and get the second at half price off. If and when the store runs out of this product at the time I go to purchase it, I wait and go back when they restock the item.

(Submitted by Guadelupe Villalpondo)

Discussion Questions

1. For each journal narrative, identify the type of problem recognition that occurred. Explain your answer.

2. For each journal narrative, identify whether it was a low- or a high-involvement decision and also whether the decision was made in an information processing mode (IPM) or affective choice mode (ACM).

3. For each student as the customer, what decision model was used? Illustrate your answer.

Reproduced with permission from Professor Dan Wardlow and his students identified above. Adapted from the Web site: **http://www.sfsu.edu/~mktgwww**

CASE NINE

WELCOME TO DUQUESNE LIGHT COMPANY

"Welcome to Duquesne Light Company." This is the heading of a brochure from the Pittsburgh, Pennsylvania based company mailed to all prospective vendors and suppliers. Excerpts from the booklet follow:

Duquesne Light is engaged in the production, transmission and distribution of electric energy to 580,000 commercial, industrial and residential customers in Allegheny and Beaver counties. Our purchasing staff is committed to fulfilling a role within our organization which provides superior service to our intenal clients and ultimately to our customers.

The Corporate Purchasing and Contract Administration Unit is responsible for the procurement of materials and services for all strategic business units within the Company.

Purchasing Objectives

To obtain materials and services at a competitive price, on schedule and in accordance with the quality, technical and commercial requirements of the procurement.

To develop reliable sources of supply for current and future needs and maintain sound and mutually beneficial relationships with vendors, based on their ability and desire to be a quality supplier.

To recommend and promote the standardization of materials whenever practical and in the best interest of the Company.

To examine new or alternative materials and services consistent with established quality standards at competitive prices.

To be knowledgeable of leading edge technology that supports our Company in being a low cost producer and profitable supplier of electric services, recognized for its excellence and quality.

Ethics Policy

Duquesne Light Company provides standards for ethical business conduct to its employees to be used as guidelines as they manage their responsibilities to the Company's customers, fellow employees, suppliers, shareholders and the general public. Employees and representatives of the Company shall avoid any conflict of interest, which might interfere with or adversely influence their obligations to the Company. The cooperation of all suppliers is requested in observance of this policy.

Evaluation and Selection of Vendors

Vendor representatives are encouraged to provide buyers with current product brochures and information regarding the companies they represent. Vendors may be asked to complete a Duquesne Light Company vendor questionnaire to provide additional information to Purchasing for evaluation.

A uniform approach is used in qualifying vendors to furnish materials and provide services to the Company. The Company's qualification process is a joint effort between Purchasing and other areas within the Company who may be involved in the evaluation; i.e. Operations, Finance, Risk Management and Legal. A vendor's qualifications and capabilities shall be measured both commercially and technically.

We expect all suppliers and contractors to be knowledgeable of, and comply with, all local, state and federal laws, codes, rules and regulations, including safety and environmental. Upon request, vendors may be asked to submit any required certifications to the Company.

The Company reserves the right to select vendors to receive Requests for Quotation (RFQ) and reject any and all bids, for any reason, at its sole discretion.

On a periodic basis, Purchasing will evaluate suppliers to review performance, quality, price and customer service.

Duquesne Light's procurement policy emphasizes competitive bidding. All quotations are to be solicited by, and directed to, the responsible buyer. Vendors are not to address or send copies of their quotations to nonpurchasing personnel.

All vendor contact during the Request for Quotation (RFQ) process shall be with the assigned buyer. Inquiries from vendors to users regarding an RFQ shall be first referred to the buyer. During this period, vendors may not contact users directly regarding the RFQ without the buyer's prior consent. Failure to comply with this requirement may disqualify the bid.

It is the responsibility of all Duquesne Light buyers to obtain the best value for the Company. To accomplish this objective, price analysis shall be utilized to arrive at the lowest total evaluated cost. We realize the importance of our supplier's contributions to our cost reduction efforts and welcome any suggestions or information that will help maintain our high quality standards and present an economic benefit to Duquesne Light Company.

Conclusion

We hope this booklet provides the information, guidelines and assistance necessary to begin or continue a long-term working relationship. The Duquesne Light Company Purchasing staff welcomes the opportunity to develop and maintain a mutually beneficial business environment with qualified suppliers.

Discussion Questions

1. What is the purpose of "welcome booklets" such as the one published by Duquesne Light Company?

2. What is the significance of procurement function in a customer company's overall business performance? Does its more or less significance have any implications with how the organization will act as a customer?

3. Identify the concepts discussed in Chapter 16 which are evidently in use at this company.

4. Does the welcome booklet show whether or not the Duquesne Light Company is practicing relationship-based buying?

Supplier welcome booklet obtained courtesy of Jody Kelsey, general manager, Corporate Purchasing and Contract Administration Unit, Duquesne Light Company.

CASE TEN

DESIGN PLUS: DEALING WITH SCHOOL BOARDS AS CUSTOMERS

The architectural firm of Design Plus is a medium-sized privately held company, located in Cincinnati, Ohio. Its partners, architects Cora Moore and David Tessler, started the firm some 10 years ago, soon after graduating from the school of design at the University of Cincinnati. To date, they have worked exclusively on the design of commercial buildings in the booming suburban business districts of Blue Ash and Riverfront. Recently, they learned of a school district in the city of Mariemont having received funding and approval for the construction of a school building.

Cora and David had long wanted to get into designing school buildings. Whenever they visited their fourth grade children's schools, as architects, they could not help noticing how very antiquated and dysfunctional the old school buildings typically were. They would often talk about how, if they ever had the opportunity, they would redesign the school building. The news of the Mariemont school district project was therefore very exciting for them.

While in college, Cora and David had also majored in marketing. They knew that in all likelihood, the school board was a different customer, and their experience of dealing with corporate customers may be of little help in dealing with a school board. Therefore, they began to research how the school district goes about buying the products and services it needs. They were able to piece together the following description of how the school board acted as a customer.

The key role in the buying process is played by Sarah Rolfes, the school district superintendent. But other individuals also play a role. These include a couple of school board members and one or two community members (prominent among them is Chris Solomon, a wealthy stockbroker), Peggy Monroe, the principal of the school for which the new building is being built, and a number of teachers who are on the buying team. For elementary schools, PTA members are also involved.

Very few of these participants have a "global" view of the purchase. The superintendent is the person with the most global view and is also the primary contact for the architect.

Usually, the school district puts out an RFP to invite architects to hear a request. The list of architects comes from referrals, past experience, word of mouth, and from calls by the architects themselves seeking new business. The district outlines what it wants. The RFP must address these needs as well as provide information on who will be handling the project, architects' resumes, and the firm's past experience with similar projects. In addition, the price must be included. The RFP is generally required to be limited to 10 pages.

From the initial proposal, the district creates a short list of architects and invites them for an interview. Generally, three or four architects are invited for an interview and sales presentation. The buying team provides an outline for the interview which lasts about an hour. It includes a brief history of the company, an introduction to the assigned project team members, an explanation of the firm's approach to the design task, and a presentation of the firm's strength. Slides of past projects are shown, and fees are discussed, followed by a question and answer session.

The entire buying process takes about six to eight weeks—about 2 to 3 weeks for RFP and another 3 to 4 weeks for the final decision from the short list.

Insiders would confide that price is generally not a big factor in the final decision. The decision makers understand that "you get what you pay for." Also, the purchase decision is often made based on chemistry between the buying team and the architectural team. In fact the process is sometimes very political in the sense that the interviewing process is a formality to demonstrate that the school board is following the procedure.

Based on this research, Cora and David are now wondering what their approach should be to obtain this business. They know that in addition to some politicking, they will have to "educate" the buying team into their philosophy of architectural design.

Discussion Questions

1. How is buying by public institutions different from business buying? Illustrate with the above case.

2. Identify the various members of the buying center team, along with their sphere of influence. How should Cora and David "sell" their service to each one?

3. Being marketing majors, Cora and David are well aware of the three customer roles and six market values framework. How should they use that framework in planning their selling strategy?

Excerpted and adapted from "Johansen and Lundgren Architects," in Robert W. Haas, *Business Marketing: A Managerial Approach* (Cincinnati, OH: South-Western College Publishing, 1995), pp. 688–695.

CASE ELEVEN

CUSTOMER LOYALTY INDEX (TM) OF DRUCKER'S MARKET

Drucker's Market is a supermarket in Bakersville, Oregon. Its customers came from the city of Bakersville as well as surrounding rural areas, comprising a population of 31,819. The area is served by three other supermarkets: John's Big Deal, Low-Buy Foods, and Hometown Foods. To find out how loyal its customers were and what motivated them to shop at the store, Drucker's recently commissioned the market research firm of National Market Research, Inc., Beaverton, Oregon, to conduct a study. The research firm conducted telephone interviews with a random sample of 400 primary supermarket shoppers in the households selected from the telephone listing of the area.

Using the survey data, the research firm calculated the market shares of the four stores to be as follows: Drucker's 23 percent, Hometown 29 percent, John's 26 percent, and Low-Buy 22 percent. It also calculated a loyalty index based on market share patterns among the store's primary customers and the total market. The table below shows the loyalty index for Drucker's Market as well as its competitors, for the store as a whole as well as for individual departments.

LOYALTY FOR:	DRUCKER'S	JOHN'S	LOW-BUY	HOME-TOWN
Total Store	70	108	68	153
Produce	86	98	106	110
Meat	79	58	138	125
Bakery	106	190	N/A	104
Delicatessen	100	143	53	124

The research firm prepared the following profile of supermarket shoppers in the Bakersville area.

Drive Times. The primary customers of Low-Buy Foods travel an average of 13 minutes from home to the store. The driving time for Drucker's customers is 9 minutes, for Hometown's customers it is 8 minutes, and for John's customers it is 5 minutes.

Food Expenditures. The average customer in the trading area spends $36.82 at supermarkets in a week. The average customer of Drucker's spends $40.18; that of John's, $33.09; of Low-Buy, $37.54; and of Hometown, $36.47.

Customer Motivations. Seeking low price is the overall motivation for customers in the trading area. Fifty-three percent of all respondents indicated price as their most important consideration in selecting the supermarket. Eight percent chose a store based on selection, 26 percent on quality, and 14 percent on service. The motivations for selecting a supermarket varied among the primary customers of individual stores, as shown in the table below:

	DRUCKER'S	JOHN'S	LOW-BUY	HOME-TOWN	TOTAL
Price	25%	86%	73%	28%	53%
Selection	4%	3%	14%	9%	8%
Quality	47%	10%	10%	36%	26%
Service	24%	1%	3%	27%	14%

Demographics. Finally, the National Market Research, Inc. put together the following profile of primary shoppers of each store.

	DRUCKER'S	JOHN'S	LOW-BUY	HOMETOWN	AVERAGE
Age (years)	37	26	29	33	31
Income (per capita)	$32,550	$19,990	$23,538	$29,809	$26,472
Highest education	Grade 14	Grade 11	Grade 12	Grade 13	Grade 13
% female	86%	77%	81%	74%	80%
Persons/household	2.2	3.1	2.9	2.4	2.7

Henry D'Aveni, the general manager of Drucker's has the research report submitted by National Market Research, Inc., in front of him. He has studied the report and finds it fascinating. He now needs to interpret what those results mean for his store and identify what actions, if any, he needs to undertake to improve his store's position in the trading area. "Let me mull over it for a couple of days," he says to himself, and turns his attention to the more pressing task of reviewing the accounts payables.

Discussion Questions

1. Is there a relationship between a loyalty index and market share? What would the relationship imply? Should a store seek more loyal customers or go for the large market share?

2. Are the research data consistent with the model of store loyalty presented in Chapter 18? Does the model apply differently to different stores? How?

3. Given the data that the research firm collected, would you as a store manager ask for further data analysis, and what would you ask for?

4. If you had the option of collecting further information from survey respondents in future surveys, what information would you collect?

Adapted from *The Loyalty Index Report,* National Market Research, Beaverton, Oregon, downloaded from the Internet site: **http://www.nmresearch.com/loyalty.htm**

(E-mail: Johnl@nmresearch.com).

CASE TWELVE

BUT THIS TIME DIGITAL WAS LOOKING TO THE LONG-TERM

By 1980, business videos—private television programs—were a booming business. One company, VideoStar Connections, Inc., was specifically founded to take advantage of this market trend. VideoStar would set up temporary satellite networks for one time delivery of private television programs for corporations—programs such as product announcements, training programs, or sales meetings. From this one-time event broadcast on temporary networks, businesses began to move to permanent private television networks. VideoStar could easily extend its "special video event" expertise to installation of permanent satellite networks. And this is exactly what it did in 1983 for its first customer—Hewlett-Packard, already a customer of its temporary satellite network.

Then in 1984, Digital Equipment Corporation (DEC), also a client of VideoStar for its temporary networks, issued a "request for proposal" (RFP) for a permanent satellite-based private video network worth more than a million dollars. After several months of hard work by VideoStar, however, Digital awarded the contract to Private Satellite Network (PSN), a recent upstart in this new line of business.

What went wrong? Its price was surely competitive, as it later learned from Digital. It was perceived to be techni-

cally competent. And Digital was very satisfied with VideoStar's past performance. Indeed, Digital assured the company that it would continue to get its temporary network business. What went wrong was that Digital thought that VideoStar was right for temporary networks but not for the permanent system. "Digital thought," says David Green, vice president of sales and marketing for VideoStar, "we were great for one-night stands, but not right for a long-term relationship."

Discussion Questions

1. Does this case illustrate the pitfalls of being product oriented instead of being customer oriented? How?

2. Which decision model best captures Digital's decision making? Explain how.

3. Is Digital practicing a "relationship-based buying" customer behavior? Explain your answer.

Based on David Green, "Learning from Losing a Customer," *Harvard Business Review,* May–June 1989, pp. 54–58.

CASE THIRTEEN

NATIONAL MOTORS, INC.—GETTING A TASTE OF RELATIONSHIP-BASED BUYING

Veronique Dussart has just returned from a meeting with Abdul Kalam, the purchasing director of Alpha Appliance Co. Veronique is the marketing director of National Motors, Inc., a manufacturer of electric motors and controls. Alpha, a manufacturer of household appliances, had been buying electric motors from National for the last 10 years. Veronique believed that the relationship between the two companies had been on solid ground, notwithstanding some recent quality and delivery problems. Abdul Kalam gave Veronique an earful about these problems and then proceeded to explain the company's change of direction in procurement policies. In the face of these changes, National was unlikely to retain Alpha's patronage, despite its lower prices over its major competitors, unless National too changed its way of doing business.

As Veronique tried to recover from the shocking news, she pieced together the key details of her meeting with Abdul Kalam as follows.

Abdul Kalam explained that his company had launched a program to become a leader in the industry with a three-prong attack on quality, cost, and delivery. His company had initiated a total-quality program committing all organizational units. Cross-functional teams had been set up to develop an integrated customer-oriented product development/delivery system. Two key elements of this program were just-in-time (JIT) and early supplier involvement (ESI). Kalam explained each as follows.

Just-in-time (JIT) program. JIT focuses on waste elimination by ensuring that perfect quality products are made available to customers in exact quantities at the precise time needed by the customer and at total minimum cost. Alpha considers both external and internal customers. Its procurement department therefore has the responsibility to ensure that all user departments inside the company get their supply of materials from suppliers on a JIT basis and without any need for inspection by them.

Early supplier involvement (ESI). The ESI approach at Alpha would be a companion to JIT. Its goal would be to bring key suppliers into the product/service planning stage very early during the product concept development phase. By doing so, Alpha expects to benefit from its supplier's expertise in product design, material selection, and processing techniques. In effect, the supplier becomes a part of the customer company, and often partnerships are formed. The ensuing close relationships allow them to work together to find optimum solutions to the final customer needs.

The JIT and ESI programs have caused Alpha to become very selective about their suppliers. The company would want to drastically reduce the number of suppliers it does business with and select suppliers based on their long-term capability to meet rigorous quality and delivery requirements. For example, the company was exploring the possibility of suppliers delivering the materials in exact sequence in which they are required on the assembly line.

At the conclusion of the meeting, Abdul Kalam had told Veronique that in light of the recent delivery and quality problems, National would have to make a detailed presentation outlining how it would prepare itself to be a supplier to Alpha as Alpha extends its total quality program to its procurement of electric motors. "We will need to hear from you within a month," Kalam had told Veronique. It was now Veronique's job to prepare a plan of action.

Discussion Questions

1. Relationship-based buying is a new practice being increasingly embraced by industry. Why is this practice in vogue?

2. What should a supplier do to prepare itself for a customer who wants to engage in supplier partnering?

3. What would be Veronique's role in the new strategy? Would other managers of National also be involved, and why?

4. Is Alpha's strategy change an isolated phenomenon? Can National simply ignore Alpha's new demands and turn its energies to the rest of the market?

Adapted from Charles O'Neal, "Electrotech, Inc," in Robert W. Haas, *Business Marketing: A Managerial Approach* (Cincinnati, OH: South-Western, 1995), pp.717–722.

CASE FOURTEEN

OURA OIL: DELIVERING CUSTOMER VALUE

You arrive at a gas station and are quickly greeted by a couple of attendants dressed in gleaming white uniforms. They sprint around your car, pump the gas, clean all the windows, check tire pressure, promptly process payment, and courteously guide you out of the station, with a flourish of bows.

What gas station is it? It is Oura Oil, located in the Osaka region in Japan. Its customer pampering pays off: it commands a 35 percent of the share of the market. However, its comfortable lead is now being threatened with the advent of hypermarkets in Japan. These stores offer rock-bottom prices and one-stop shopping for a huge variety of consumer products; and they have an outsized gasoline station. Another development is a new law enacted in 1997, permitting self-service stations.

These new types of stores will surely force Oura to cut its margins. Yoshio Oura, managing director of Oura Oil, estimates that about 30 percent of his customers would willingly give up superior service for lower prices. But Oura believes that he must not cut the service levels. "Even if I charge the same price as the hypermarkets," he explains, "I'll still need a point of differentiation from my competitors, and service is one of those points."

So Oura has instead responded to increasing competition by starting a loyalty program, called the "Five-Up Club." Customers who sign up receive a card that earns points with every purchase. These points can be redeemed for gift certificates, merchandise, or cash purchases. The awards are determined through a simple Recency, Frequency, Monetary Value (RFM) formula; the more recent the last purchase, the more frequently the customer makes the purchase, and the more money the customer spends, the more points he or she earns. One popular reward is a birthday gift, sent to qualifying club members.

Customers who purchase over 5,000 gallons a year receive a special card. The card entitles customers to extra-special service by attendants, who deliver such extras as vacuuming the car and refilling the windshield-washer free of charge.

To pay for the program, Oura is dropping more expensive promotions such as free gift boxes of facial tissue or detergent, common in the industry. It has also signed up with some Marketing partners such as Kentucky Fried Chicken, SOGO Department Store, and the Japan Travel Bureau. These partners help pay for the program by purchasing points from Oura and then awarding them to Five-Up cardholders.

The company also promotes activities based on shared interests among customers. For example, recently the company sponsored an outing to an orchard, where customers picked their own fruit. The company also has plans for special-interest clubs and an Internet chat site for customers. To promote a two-way dialogue with its customers, the company uses a club newsletter that also contains a questionnaire for respondents to give the company feedback. From these surveys, the company learns customer preferences as to the kinds of rewards customers would value. Recently, the newsletter has been used to extend value-added privileges to members by offering mail-order merchandise. "Japanese women love to buy brand-name imports," notes Oura, so he has recruited a merchandising partner who imports key items such as handbags and accessories. Special offerings to Club members extend right down to the staple of the Japanese diet, rice. "Now that the rice market is opened and Japanese can buy rice from anywhere they want, we sell rice by mail directly from the place of production," Oura explains.

This small but growing mail-order business, begun as a loyalty-building device, could well become a profit center in its own right. "In 1997, we plan to put together a complete mail-order catalog for our club members," says Oura. "They can use the points they earn from buying gasoline to pay for merchandise. But they can also earn more points by buying merchandise."

The program has proven immensely popular. As of January 1997, a total of 170,000 people had joined. Within a year of the program's launch, about 80 percent of all cash sales were recorded using the card. And its gasoline sales in the closing months of 1996 were up 5 percent, while overall gasoline sales in the Osaka region were down 3 percent. There are other payoff from the database—Oura knows who his customers are by name and address. He can segment them according to their current and potential value. And he knows that with the right mix of communications and rewards, he can increase their value. Now Oura is using the database and a mapping software to identify trading areas for each station. Based on these maps, he will be able to target promotions more effectively.

Oura is also eagerly cooking up new ways to encourage increased business from existing customers and collecting the data that will ultimately form the basis for every marketing decision. He knows there is plenty of room for improvement: even his best customers buy only about half of their gasoline at his stations. Oura figures that if he can increase his share of customers with these heavy users to 60 or 70 percent, he can more than make up for any business he may lose to hypermarkets and self-service stations.

Discussion Questions

1. Why does Mr. Oura feel that he cannot cut down on personal service levels? How does he manage to thwart the dual competitive threat from hypermarkets and self-service stations?

2. In what way is Oura's loyalty program different from other loyalty or frequent buyer programs you might be aware of? Is its program likely to produce true customer commitment? Why or why not?

3. Identify market values Oura Oil delivers, specifying the customer roles to which those values are directed.

Adapted from Richard Cross, "High-Octane Loyalty," April 1997, Marketing Tools, *American Demographics*.

GLOSSARY

Acculturation The process of learning a new culture.

Acquisition centrality The tendency to place material possessions and their acquisitions at the center of one's life.

Activity-based costing (ABC) Trade discounts and fees based on specific services the reseller asks of the supplier.

Actual self A person's self-image of who he or she is.

Addressability A feature of a database wherein each customer's address is known in order to enable a marketer to address marketing communications individually on a one-on-one basis.

Advocate sources Communication sources that have a vested point of view to advocate or promote.

Affect The feelings a person has toward an object or the emotions that object evokes for the person.

Affective choice mode (ACM) A decision mode wherein affect or liking for the brand ensues a choice based not on attribute information, but based on holistic judgments.

Affinity A person's identification with and conformity to the norms and standards of a particular reference group.

Affinity marketing A strategy used by vendors of goods and services to offer special incentives to association members in return for their endorsement.

Affordability The possession of adequate economic resources needed to buy and use a product or service.

Aftermarketing The process of providing continued satisfaction and reinforcement to individuals or organizations that are past or current customers.

Aggression To become aggressive and display or inflict pain on someone out of frustration and without justification.

Aggressive personality A person who values personal accomplishment over friendship and seeks power and admiration from others.

Annual purchasing agreements Agreements made by government agencies with specific suppliers, which allow the governmental entity to purchase small items routinely.

Approach/avoidance motivation The human desire to attain a goal-object and desire to avoid an object of negative outcomes.

Arousal-seeking Humans' innate need for stimulation.

Arousal seeking motive The drive to maintain the organism's stimulation at an optimal level.

Assimilation and contrast Information within the acceptance range is assimilated and accepted; information outside of this range is contrasted and rejected.

Asymmetrical power One party has more power over the other.

Atmospherics The physical setting of the store that influences customer behavior.

Atomistic family unit A person living alone.

Attitude Learned predisposition to respond to an object or class of objects in a consistently favorable or unfavorable way.

Attitude hierarchy The sequence in which the three components of attitude—cognition, affect, conation—occur.

Attitude molding Forming a new attitude or changing a preexisting attitude.

Attitude strength The degree of commitment one feels toward a cognition, feeling, or action.

Attitudinal brand loyalty A customer's consistent repurchase of a brand due to his or her preference for it.

Attraction of alternatives How attractive a customer finds alternative brands to be.

Attribution motivation Humans' innate need to assign causes to events and behaviors.

Attributions	Inferences that people draw about the causes of events and behaviors.
Authoritarian parents	Parents who exercise strict authority over children; children learn to obey their elders in all matters.
Autonomous decisions	Decisions that are made independently by the decision maker.
Awareness set	Brands a customer is aware of.
Baby boomers	Persons in the U.S. born between 1946 and 1964.
Bargaining	A method of conflict resolution, based on distributive justice for all, wherein the dissenting members negotiate a give and take.
Behavioral brand loyalty	A customer's consistent repurchase of a brand.
Behavioral compatibility	The degree to which an innovation requires no change in existing behavior.
Behaviorally anchored scales	Measurement scales that utilize descriptions of specific behaviors to which the respondents express their reactions.
Behaviorism	The theory that a person develops a pattern of behavioral responses because of the rewards and punishments offered by his or her environment.
Beliefs	Expectations that connect an object to an attribute or quality.
Benefit segmentation	Grouping of individual customers according to the benefits they seek from a product or service.
Biogenics	The study of biological characteristics of people.
Biological determinism	The belief that human behavior is determined by biological factors such as genetics and DNA.
Birth order	The sequence among all siblings born of the same mother.
Brand belief	A thought about a specific property or quality associated with a brand.
Brand equity	The enhancement in the perceived utility and desirability that a brand name confers on a product.
Brand parity	The concept of how similar and mutually substitutable the brands are.
Brand valuation	The financial worth of a brand name.
Business	A licensed entity engaged in the business of making, buying or selling products and services for profit or nonprofit objectives.
Business climate	The condition of the national or international economy.
Business cycle	A cycle of boom and recession experienced by the business world and caused by fluctuations in the economic environment.
Business process reengineering	The redesign of business processes to make them more efficient.
Buyclass	Type of purchase need in terms of its newness.
Buyer	A person who participates in the procurement of the product.
Buyers' remorse	The regret customers feel after buying a product or service because they are unsure if buying it was wise.
Buying center	All the members of a customer firm who play some role in the purchase decision.
Category management	The merchandising decisions that would maximize the reseller profits on an entire product category.
Central processing route	Message *content* is attended to and scrutinized actively and thoughtfully.
Change agent	A person or organization that brings about a planned social change.
Change targets	People whose behavior is sought to be altered by change agents.
Channel partnership	Relationship between a reseller and a supplier in which they agree on objectives, policies, and procedures designed to further each other's business.
Circadian rhythm	The 24-hour cycle of activities that most humans repeat day after day in their lives.

Classical conditioning	The process in which a person learns an association between two stimuli due to their constant appearance as a pair.
Climate	A component of the geophysical market environment, consisting of temperature, wind, humidity, and rainfall in an area that affects consumers' needs for food, clothing, and shelter.
Cocooning	The habit of staying at home rather than going out.
Cognition	A thought about an object.
Cognitive consistency	The principle that a person desires consistency among all his or her beliefs or thoughts.
Cognitive dissonance	A tension between two opposite thoughts, typically manifested after a customer has bought something but is uncertain whether a correct choice was made.
Cognitive learning	The acquisition of new information from written or oral communication.
Commitment	An enduring desire to continue the relationship and to work to ensure its continuance.
Communicability	The extent to which an innovation is socially visible or easy to communicate about in social groups.
Competitive promotional activity	Special price deals available on competing brands.
Complexity	Extensiveness of effort it takes to comprehend and manage the product during its acquisition.
Complexity of an innovation	The difficulty in comprehending an innovation.
Compliance	Steering customer behavior by government regulation.
Compulsive buying	A chronic tendency to purchase products far in excess of one's needs and resources.
Compulsive consumption	An uncontrolled and obsessive consumption of a product or service, likely to ultimately cause harm to the consumer or others.
Conation	The action a person wants to take toward an object.
Concept-oriented families	Families that are concerned with the growth of independent thinking and individuality in children.
Concurrent protocols	A record of respondent thoughts at the time of decision making.
Conditioned stimulus (CS)	A stimulus to which a new response needs to be conditioned.
Conjunctive model	A decision-making procedure wherein the customer examines all alternatives on a set of attributes or evaluative criteria in order to identify an alternative that would meet minimum cut-off levels on each attribute.
Consideration set	All the brands in a product category that a customer will consider assessing for purchase.
Consignment buying	An arrangement wherein the reseller receives the title and pays for the merchandise only after it is in turn sold to the end user.
Consumer behavior odyssey	A qualitative research project undertaken in the late 1980s in the U.S. that involved personal visits by an interdisciplinary team of academic consumer researchers to a variety of consumer sites.
Consumer socialization	The acquisition of knowledge, preferences, and skills to function in the marketplace.
Convenience value	Saving in time and effort needed to acquire the product.
Corporate image	The public perception of a corporation as a whole.
Corrective advertising	Advertising whose message includes a correction of a previous deception.
Country-of-origin effects	Bias in customer perceptions of products and services due to the country in which they are made.
Credit value	Freedom from having to exchange cash at the time of purchase or from becoming liable for immediate payment.
Cultural context	The culture to which a customer belongs.

Culture	Everything a person learns and shares with members of a society, including ideas, norms, morals, values, knowledge, skills, technology, tools, material objects, and behavior.
Customer	A person or an organizational unit that plays a role in the consummation of a transaction with an organization.
Customer behavior	Mental and physical activities undertaken by customers that result in decisions and actions to pay for, buy, and use products and services.
Customer culture	A culture that incorporates customer satisfaction as an integral part of corporate mission and plans.
Customer decisions	Decisions customers make in the marketplace as buyers, payers, and users.
Customer equity	Customer support for a supplier's well-being.
Customer expectations	Customers' economic outlook about the near future that shapes their spending.
Customer loyalty	A customer's commitment to a brand or a store or a supplier, based on a strong favorable attitude, and manifested in consistent repatronage.
Customer militancy	The behavior of frustrated and dissatisfied customers entailing the taking of the law into their own hands.
Customer orientation	Gaining a thorough understanding of customers' needs and wants, and utilizing them as the basis for all of the firm's plans and actions in order to create satisfied customers.
Customer problem	Any state of deprivation or discomfort or wanting (whether physical or psychological) felt by a person.
Customer satisfaction	A positive feeling ensuing from a successful outcome of a market transaction.
Customer visits	A research program wherein a marketing firm's managers visit customer firms to interview buyers as well as users of their product and to observe their product in-use.
Customization	Receiving the product or service in a manner tailor-made to an individual customer's circumstances.
Customized data	Data that are collected at the behest of a small group of pre-identified customers, and made available only to sponsoring companies.
Cycle time	The total time it takes for the entire production and/or delivery task to be completed.
Deceptive advertising	Advertising that has the capacity to deceive a considerable segment of the public.
Deep involvement	A customer's extreme interest in a product or service on an ongoing basis.
Defense Acquisition Regulations (DARs)	Procurement regulations that apply to the Department of Defense.
Defense mechanisms	Psychological processes that stem from a person's need to protect his or her ego.
Democratic justice	A family norm in which each family member is given a voice in family decisions.
Democratic parents	Parents who give every family member an equal voice and encourage self-expression, autonomy, and mature behavior among children.
Demographic segmentation	Segmenting the market based on demographic characteristics of customers.
Demographics	Easily verified, objective characteristics of a group of customers.
Desert	A climate consisting of dry heat.
Detached personality	A person who is independent minded, entertains no obligations, and admits little social influence on personal choices.
Differentiation	The way marketers present their offerings differently from their competition.
Diffusion Process	The spreading of an innovation's acceptance and use through a population.
Direct purchase method	A method usually adopted by the U.S. government for orders costing up to $25,000, which entails directly contacting a few suppliers and placing an order with one of them, usually on the lowest quote basis.
Discretionary expenditures	The purchase of goods and services to make life physically or psychologically more comfortable beyond sustenance.

Disguised-nonstructured technique	A questionnaire design wherein the research purpose is not apparent to the consumer nor are the response categories provided.
Disguised-structured technique	A questionnaire design wherein the real intent of the question is disguised, but the response categories are provided.
Disintermediation	A practice in which the customer is enabled to transact directly with a firm without any intermediaries.
Disjunctive model	A decision-making procedure that entails trade-offs between aspects of choice alternatives.
Distribution intensity	The number of outlets at which a product is available in any market.
DNA	An acronym for deoxyribonucleic acid, which refers to the cell nuclei that form the molecular basis of heredity in organisms.
Door-in-the-face	A strategy of eliciting a behavior by first making a large request whose refusal is followed by a small request.
Drive	An internal state of tension that produces actions purported to reduce that tension.
Ecological design	A strategy of influencing behavior by the design elements of the physical facility surrounding the customer.
Ecology	Natural resources and the balance and interdependence among vegetation, animals, and humans.
Economic context	The economy in which the customer lives.
Economy	The state of a nation with respect to levels of employment, wages, inflation, interest rates, currency exchange rates, and aggregate household savings and disposable income.
Effectiveness	How well a product or service meets the customer's needs and wants.
Efficiency	How little it costs the customer in money, time, and physical effort to receive the value he or she seeks.
Efficient consumer response (ECR)	Practiced by the food industry, suppliers and resellers work together to "bring better value to the grocery consumer."
Ego	The conscious mediator between the Id and the superego.
Elaboration likelihood model	(ELM) The proposal that a message is elaborated upon by the consumer to examine and interpret it.
Electronic data interchange	(EDI) A computer-based link between a supplier and its business customer that transmits customer inventory data to the supplier and automates reordering and shipping of the depleted product.
Elimination by aspects (EBA)	A decision-making procedure wherein the customer examines all alternatives one attribute at a time in the ranked-order sequence with minimum cut-off attribute values.
Emotional communications	Communications that evoke some emotional experience in the viewer or reader.
Emotional hierarchy of attitude	A sequence of attitude components in which a person first feels an emotion toward an object, then acts on it, and then becomes knowledgeable about it.
Emotional value	The enjoyment and emotional satisfaction users obtain from products and services.
Emotions	The consciousness of the occurrence of some physiological arousal followed by a behavioral response along with the appraised meaning of both.
Enculturation	The process of learning one's own culture.
Enduring involvement	A customer's ongoing interest in the product or service.
Enduring involvement	The degree of interest a customer feels in a product or service on an ongoing basis.
Engel's law	Economist Ernst Engel's theory that the lower the per capita income of a nation, the more its people tend to spend on basic necessities such as food and clothing.
Environmental marketing	Marketing of products and services in a manner that attempts to minimize the damage to the environment.
Environmentally conscious consumer	A customer who actively seeks out products with minimal impact on the environment.

Equatorial	A climate consisting of high humidity and high temperature.
Ethnic diversity	The rising proportion of persons who do not belong to the major ethnic origin of the place.
Ethnic identity	The ethnic heritage in which a person is born.
Ethnographic research	A research method in which the researcher takes on the cultural perspective of the population being studied.
Evaluated new unplanned purchases	Purchases for which the need had not been recognized prior to the purchase occasion.
Evaluative consistency	A process wherein the missing attribute is assumed in order to conform to the overall evaluation of the brand.
Evoked set	Brands in a product or service category that the customer remembers at the time of decision making.
Exclusive distribution	The product being sold only by one reseller in a given market.
Experiential consumption	The use of a product or service in which the process of use itself offers value.
Experiment	A research method in which respondents are placed in a controlled situation, and then their response is observed or recorded.
Expertise	Possessing knowledge about the innovation that is not yet common knowledge.
Exploratory shopping	Just browsing around after collecting the planned items.
Extended problem solving (EPS)	A product or service selection strategy wherein the customer engages in an extensive information search and prolonged deliberation in order to minimize the risk of a wrong choice.
External attributions	Assigning the cause to situational demands or environmental constraints that were beyond the control of the individual.
External stimuli	Marketplace information that causes problem recognition.
Family	A group of persons related by blood and/or marriage.
Family life cycle	The different stages a family goes through—starting from the time a person is young and single to the time when he or she becomes a single solitary survivor.
Family relationship	The degree of mutual respect and trust between parents and adult offsprings, and the harmony of relations and communication among them.
Federal Acquisition Regulations (FARs)	Procurement regulations that all agencies of the government have to follow.
Financial well-being	Financial products and services such as financial planning, wills and trusts, mutual funds and stocks, and so on acquire new significance in aging customers' lives.
Financing value	Offering the terms of payment more affordable by distributing the liability over an extended period of time.
Firmographics	Easily verified, objective characteristics of a business firm.
Fiscal policy	Government decisions on trade practices, procurement, spending, and taxation.
Fishbein model	Psychologist Martin Fishbein's formulation that attitude toward an object is the sum of the consequences of that object weighted by the evaluation of those consequences.
Fishbein's extended model of behavioral intention	Psychologist Martin Fishbein's formulation that a person's intent to engage in a behavior is the weighted sum of his or her own attitude toward that behavior and others' expectations about his or her performing that behavior.
Focus groups	A research method wherein a small group of customers participate in a group discussion steered by a moderator on specified issues.
Foot-in-the-door	A strategy of eliciting a behavior by first asking for a small favor whose acceptance is followed by a larger request.
Forward buying	A practice wherein customers buy an item for future consumption.
G.I. generation	Persons born in the United States during the period 1901–1924.

Gender orientation	The degree to which specific behaviors and norms are linked to a person's gender rather than being shared across genders.
Generation 'X'	Persons born in the United States between 1965 and 1975.
Generic differentiation	A global (or overall) differentiation on a nontargeted basis, wherein a firm presents an improved offering to the entire market.
Genetics	The biochemical basis of heredity of an organism consisting of specific sequences of nitrogenous bases in DNA.
Geodemographics	Identifying customer segments based on geographical location.
Geographic redistribution	Refers to the shift in population density from one region of a nation or world to another.
Gerontographics	A segmentation approach based on the premise that the factors that make older consumers more or less receptive to marketing offerings are directly related to their needs and lifestyles, which are in turn influenced by changing life conditions.
Global warming	Earth's climate becoming warmer due to an increase in hydrocarbons in the atmosphere resulting from increased industrialization.
Goal-object	Something in the external world whose acquisition will reduce the tension experienced by an organism.
Government	Legal entities empowered to organize and govern a city, state, or nation.
Government policy	A market context factor comprising monetary/fiscal policy and public policy.
Green consumer	A customer concerned about the deteriorating environment and willing to modify his or her customer behavior to save the environment.
Group traits	Common biogenic categories such as race, gender, and age.
Groups	Two or more persons sharing a common purpose.
Habit	A learned sequence of responses to a previously encountered stimulus.
Habitual purchasing	Simply repeating previous purchases.
Hedonic consumption	The use of products/services for the sake of intrinsic enjoyment rather than to solve some problem in the physical environment.
Heider's balance theory	The principle that a person will modify some of his beliefs to make them balanced or congruent with the rest of his or her beliefs.
Heuristics	Quick rules of thumb and shortcuts used to make decisions.
Household	A consumption unit of one or more persons identified by a common location with an address.
Id	A division of the human psyche that refers to the basic source of inner energy directed at avoiding pain and obtaining pleasure; it represents the unconscious drives and urges.
Ideal self	A person's self-image of who he or she would like to be.
Identifiability	A desirable segmentation criterion stating that every segment must be identifiable to provide the marketer the opportunity to know who the customer is.
Ignorance paradox	The tendency of less knowledgeable customers to seek less information rather than more.
Imitative behavior	Adopting the behavior of those whom a person admires or considers successful.
Imitators	Those who adopt an innovation after observing others who have it.
Importance of purchase	How important a purchase is in the customer's life.
Impulse purchase	The implementation of previously unplanned purchases, with purchase decisions made on the spur of the moment.
Increased productivity approach	An approach in which a firm strives for a lower cost of production by raising productivity.
Index of consumer sentiment	A nationally tracked measure of economic pessimism/optimism felt by customers in the United States.

Individual context	The background that is specific to customers as individuals.
Individual traits	Unique biogenic and psychogenic aspects of the individual customer.
Inference making	Reaching a judgment about an object based on incomplete information.
Information board	A table of information in which the cells contain the information about the extent to which the brand specified in the corresponding row contains the attribute specified in the corresponding column.
Information overload	Customers are exposed to so much information that they are unable to process it to make a decision.
Information processing mode (IPM)	A decision mode wherein the customer acquires, evaluates, and integrates information about brand attributes to arrive at an overall brand evaluation.
Information processing research	A class of research whose focus is on studying the information customers process for reaching a decision.
Innovation adoption	A person's acceptance of an innovation for continued use.
Innovation	A product, service, or an idea that a customer perceives as new.
Innovators	Customers who are the first ones to adopt an innovation.
Instant gratification	The desire for an immediate satisfaction of a need or want.
Instant marketing	Being ready to offer without delay a product or service when the customer wants it.
Institutional context	The organizations and institutions to which a customer belongs by birth or by choice.
Institutions	Relatively permanent groups with a pervasive and universal presence in a society, such as schools, religions, and the family.
Instrumental conditioning	The learning of a response because it is instrumental to obtaining some reward.
Instrumentality	A relationship in which something is a means to a given goal.
Intensive distribution	The product being sold through as many resellers as possible to make the product conveniently available.
Interattribute inference	A process wherein the customer infers the value of one attribute based on another attribute.
Intergenerational influence (IGI)	Influence of family members and the transmission of values, attitudes, and behaviors from one generation to the other.
Internal attributions	Ascribing the cause of someone's behavior to personal dispositions, traits, abilities, or motivations and feelings.
Internal stimuli	Perceived states of physical or psychological discomfort that cause problem recognition.
Interpretation	A step in the perception process in which meaning is attached to the stimulus.
Interpretative research	A method of research in which a researcher observes a group of consumers in their natural setting and interprets their behavior based on an extensive understanding of the social and cultural characteristics of that setting.
Inventory turnover	The number of times the inventory is completely restocked during a given year.
Invitation for bid (IFB)	A method of government procurement wherein the government specifies the item being sought exactly and invites sealed bids.
Involvement	The degree of personal relevance of an object or product or service to a customer.
Joint decisions	Decisions wherein more than one decision maker participates.
Just noticeable difference (j.n.d.)	The magnitude of change necessary for the change to be noticed.
Laddering	A research technique to identify means-end linkages.
Lead users	Innovative users of a product who use it in ways that suggest how the product should be modified for better utility.
Learning	Any change in the content of long-term memory.
Learning hierarchy	A sequence of attitude components wherein a person thinks first, feels next, and acts last.

Lemon law	A law, adopted by many U.S. states, that protects a car buyer from being sold a substandard car.
Level of adaptation	A person developing adequate familiarity with a stimulus so that the stimulation is perceived as normal or average.
Lexicographic model	A decision model wherein the available alternatives are compared in sequence by the rank-ordered attributes.
Life status change	Major events in a customer's life that change his or her status or personal context.
Lifestyles	The way a person lives.
Lifetime revenues	The cumulative revenues a firm can obtain from a customer over his or her lifetime.
Limited problem solving (LPS)	A product or service selection strategy wherein the customer invests some limited amount of time and energy in searching and evaluating alternative solutions.
Low-involvement attitude hierarchy	A sequence of attitude components in a person's acquisition of attitude toward objects that are of low salience or importance.
Lower margin approach	Selling at a low-profit margin in order to attract customers.
Loyalty	A customer's consistent patronage of the same brand of a product or service.
Maintenance/labor agreements	Agreements made by a business firm or government for obtaining a maintenance service throughout the year on an as needed basis.
Market characteristics	The physical characteristics of the surroundings in which customers buy, use, and pay for products and services.
Market conditions	Unpredicted events causing a shortage or surplus of supply or changes in access to markets.
Market context	Refers to the man-made (not nature-made) market forces that impact on customer needs and wants.
Market mavens	Individuals who possess information about markets and disseminate it to other customers.
Market segmentation	The process of identifying subgroups of customers within a market whose needs, wants, and/or resources are different in a way that makes them respond differently to a given marketing mix.
Market values	The benefits (tangible or intangible) a customer receives from a product or service.
Marketer sources	Communication sources that act on behalf of the marketer of the product or service itself.
Marketing concept	A firm focuses on making what the customer wants.
Marketing myopia	A narrow vision wherein a firm views itself in limited, product- or service-centered ways—as makers and sellers of products and services they produce and sell.
Maslow's hierarchy of needs	Psychologist Abraham Maslow's theory that human needs and wants exist in a hierarchy so that higher level needs are dormant until lower level needs are satisfied.
Mass customization	Tailoring the product to the customer's specific needs, without sacrificing the speed or cost efficiencies of conventional mass production methods.
Materialism	The importance a consumer attaches to material possessions.
Maturation	A self-perceived obsolescence of prior preferences.
Means-end chains	Linkages between the product's physical features and customers' fundamental needs and values.
Membership clubs	Buying organizations that buy in large quantities and then act as resellers to their members.
Membership groups	Groups in which an individual claiming to be a member is recognized as such by the leader and/or the key members of the group.
Mental activities	Processing information about a product or service alternative, making inferences about it, and appraising it for purchase and use.
Mental budgeting	The idea that customers mentally set aside budgets for product categories.

Model stock quantity	The number of units needed to cover the expected demand at a prespecified percent of the time between the order placement and receipt of merchandise.
Modeling	The learning of a response by observing others.
Modified rebuy	A purchase item that is similar to the previously purchased item, but entails some changes either in design/performance specifications or in the supply environment.
Monetary policy	Government decisions on interest rate changes, money supply, government borrowing, and regulating financial institutions.
Moods	Short-lived and less intensely felt emotions.
Motivation	The state of drive or arousal that impels behavior toward a goal-object.
Motivation research (MR)	A research method directed at discovering the conscious or subconscious reasons that motivate a person's behavior.
Multiattribute models of attitude	A rule that suggests that overall attitude is formed on the basis of component beliefs about the object weighted by the evaluation of those beliefs.
Mutual goals	Those goals that require each exchange partner's cooperation and by whose achievement each partner profits.
National culture	The culture prevalent in a nation.
Necessary expenditures	The purchase of products and services needed for minimal sustenance.
Need	An unsatisfactory physical condition of the customer that leads him or her to an action that will remedy that condition.
Need for cognition	Humans' need for information and for understanding the world around us.
Negative Cue	An inference-making strategy wherein the customer simply treats the missing information as a negative cue, which then affects the overall judgment negatively.
Neglectful parents	Parents who remain distant from their children and neglect them.
Negligent consumer behavior	Customer behavior that puts oneself or others at risk, or that would, in the long run, impose heavy costs on society.
Neo rich	Persons who have recently become affluent.
Net worth	Financial resources available to a customer—comprising income, inheritance, and borrowing power.
Networks	A group of firms that deal with each other on a preferential basis.
New task	A purchase item new to the buying organization.
Nondisguised-nonstructured technique	A technique in which the purpose of the study is *not* disguised; however, the consumer response categories are not predetermined.
Nondisguised-structured technique	A technique that makes the research purpose obvious and seeks responses along prespecified response categories.
Nonfamily household	A household that does not contain a family.
Nonmarketer sources	Communication sources that are independent of marketer influence.
Norm of reciprocity	An expectation that an act of favor or concession toward someone must be returned by a comparable act of favor.
Nuclear family unit	A family comprising a married couple with children.
Odd pricing	The setting of prices just below the next round number.
One-stop shopping (OSS)	The practice of acquiring all related products from one supplier.
Opinion leadership	The giving of information and advice, with acceptance of the advocated position by the opinion recipient.
Optimal level of stimulation	A level at which balance is reached so that the person is neither bored nor overwhelmed by new experience.

Organization	A process of stimulus categorization in which the sensed stimulus is matched with similar object categories in one's memory.
Other-brand averaging	A process wherein the missing attribute value is assumed to be an average of its values across all other brands.
Outsourcing	Procuring products and services that were once produced by the customer him/herself.
Partner-specific investments	Investments that one party makes on processes dedicated to the other party.
Passive consumers	Persons who are not consuming the product themselves but who, as bystanders, are being negatively affected by the consumption of others.
Payer	A person who pays or finances the purchase.
Perceived justice	Customers' perception that they were treated fairly during the conflict resolution process and that the decision outcome itself was fair.
Perceived risk	The degree of loss (i.e., amount at stake) in the event that a wrong choice is made.
Perceived risk of an innovation	The uncertainty that the innovation might cause an unanticipitated harm.
Perception	The process by which an individual selects, organizes, and interprets the information received from the environment.
Perceptual and preference mapping	An analytical technique of obtaining a visual map in a multi-dimensional space that shows consumer perceptions of similarity among and preference for various product or service alternatives.
Perceptual distortion	In interpreting a stimulus, a person's prior beliefs interfere and distort the meaning to conform to those beliefs.
Perceptual threshold	The minimum level or magnitude at which a stimulus begins to be sensed.
Performance risk	The probability that the product may not perform as expected or desired, or that there may be physical side effects or unwanted consequences.
Performance value	The quality of physical outcome of using a product or service.
Peripheral processing mode	A message is interpreted cursorily by attending to its form rather than its content.
Permissive families	Families wherein children are given relative independence in conducting their own affairs, especially in their adolescent years.
Personal characteristics	The individual customer's biogenic makeup, comprising one's biological and physiological features.
Personal context	The characteristics of the socioeconocultural environment of the customer.
Personal safety	The safety of one's own person from crime or harmful consumption.
Personal values	Product or service benefits that satisfy the *wants* of the customer.
Personality	A person's consistent ways of responding to the environment in which he or she lives.
Personality trait	A consistent, characteristic way of behaving.
Persuasion	A rational method of conflict resolution wherein some members persuade others by demonstrating how the other person's position will lead to a suboptimal outcome.
Phased decision strategy	A two-stage decision procedure wherein the alternatives are first eliminated, and then the remaining alternatives are compared for a final choice.
Physical activities	Bodily actions undertaken by a customer toward buying a product or service.
Pioneer brands	Brands that are the first to enter the market and that have significant advantage over existing substitute products.
Planned purchases	The purchases that a customer had planned to buy before entering the store.
Planned social change	Active intervention by an agency with a conscious policy objective to bring about a change in some social or consumption behavior among the members of a population.
Polar zone	The areas of earth that are always cold and quite dry.

Politicking	A conflict resolution method wherein members form partisan coalitions and then "manage" the decision with behind-the-scenes maneuvering.
Popular culture	The culture of the masses in a nation, with norms, rituals, and values that have a mass appeal.
Poverty	Income levels insufficient to provide an adequate, nutritious diet for sustenance.
Power	The ability of one party to influence the decisions of the other in a reseller and supplier pair.
Power bases	The specific resources one party has over the other as the basis of exercising relative power.
Power dependence	The relative dependence of one party on the other because of the resources the other party possesses.
Price as a quality cue	Customers' use of price as a basis for judging the quality of a product or service.
Price points	Price ranges for alternatives within the same product category.
Price value	A fair price and other financial costs incurred in acquiring the product.
Pricing proposal	A proposal made by a supplier to government, using a specific government form, certifying current cost and pricing data for each line item.
Primary data	Data that does not already exist and which a researcher must collect anew.
Primary demand	Demand for the product or service category itself.
Primary emotions	Basic human emotions that humans have acquired based on the evolutionary process.
Primary groups	Groups with whom a person interacts frequently and whose norms are considered important.
Primary research	Collection and use of primary data to answer specific questions of interest to the marketer.
Problem recognition	A realization by the customer that he or she needs to purchase something to get back to the normal state of comfort—physically and psychologically.
Problem routinization	Defining a decision problem so that no *new* decisions need to be made.
Problem-solving	A rational approach to conflict resolution wherein participants search for more information, and deliberate on the new information.
Processing by attributes (PBA)	The process of assessing brands wherein all the available brands are compared simultaneously on one attribute at a time.
Processing by brands (PBB)	The process of assessing one brand entirely before moving on to the second brand.
Projection	Blaming others for one's own shortcomings, or projecting one's own feelings on to others.
Projection technique	A research technique wherein a fairly vague stimulus is presented to respondents who then interpret it by necessarily "projecting" themselves into the stimulus.
Proprietary data	Data collected by private business firms that are in the business of collecting and marketing information of interest to a class of clients.
Protocols	Customers' verbatim responses to certain information-processing tasks, often elicited by asking the respondent to speak out his or her task-related thoughts aloud.
Psychogenics	A customer's needs based on psychological tensions and influenced by differences in personality and social relationships.
Psychographics	Characteristics of individuals that describe them in terms of their psychological and behavioral makeup.
Psychology of complication	The customer desire to redefine a problem so that decisions have to be made anew.
Psychology of simplification	The customer strategy of simplifying the task.
Public policy	Government rules and regulations that affect customer choices and behaviors.
Pull marketing	A strategy in which the marketer directly appeals to end users, inducing them to ask the purchaser to buy the marketer's product or service.
Purchase-decision involvement	The degree of concern and caring that customers feel in a purchase decision.
Purposive behavior	When a person expends energy to attain some goal-object.

Push marketing	A strategy in which the marketer appeals to the buyer to induce him or her to buy the product and then promote it to the end user.
Qualitative research	A method of gathering data wherein the respondent states the answer in his or her own words rather than being limited to preassigned response categories.
Quality of life	Living condition measured by the absence of crime, traffic congestion, and pollution, and the opportunity for education, recreation, and general well-being.
Quantitative research	A research method wherein a person's answers are obtained on a numerical scale.
Quick response	Suppliers offering fast product replenishment to resellers.
Race	The genetic heritage group in which a person is born.
Rationalization	To explain some action by a motive more acceptable, suppressing the actual motive from consciousness.
Reachability	A desirable segmentation criteria stating that every segment must be reachable without wasting resources on everybody.
Reciprocity	The customer practice of buying from a supplier because he or she (the supplier) in turn buys something else from the customer.
Recreational needs	A person's need for entertainment and recreation.
Reference groups	Persons, groups, and institutions that we look up to for guidance for our own behavior and values.
Reference price	The price customers expect to pay.
Regional economic integration	The realignment of nations into region-based economic blocs, such as the European Free Trade Association (EFTA).
Regional marketing	The practice of adapting the marketing program according to customer diversity from one region to another.
Regression	A defense mechanism in which a person reverts back to childhood behaviors.
Relationship-based buying	The customer practice of limiting his or her choice to a single supplier.
Relative advantage	The superiority of an innovation compared to the current product it will substitute.
Relative expertise	The acknowledgement by offsprings that parents possess expertise about a product.
Repression	A defense mechanism in which the ego devotes a great deal of its energy to keeping a particular thought or feeling at the unconscious level.
Request for proposal (RFP)	A method of government procurement adopted for products or services that are new, complex, or entail large sums of money, and where negotiations are deemed necessary.
Reseller	A licensed business entity that buys someone else's products and services, adds some value for the customer, and sells it to other customers who may themselves be resellers or end users.
Restocking unplanned purchases	Purchase of items that the shopper had not thought about buying at the time but had been using regularly.
Retrospective protocols	Respondents' reports of their thought processes about a decision made in the past.
Reverse marketing	The practice of developing, maintaining, and motivating suppliers, current or prospective ones, to get set up to become long-term suppliers.
Role formalness	The degree to which interactions between the supplier and customer are limited to the formal roles of the parties.
Roommate families	Families whose members structure their time, location, and activities independently of one anotherand with minimal sharing.
Rosenberg model	Psychologist Milton Rosenberg's formulation that attitude toward an object is a function of the extent to which the object is instrumental in obtaining various values, weighted by the relative importance of those values.
Rote memorization	The rehearsal of information until it gets firmly lodged in the long-term memory.

Routine problem solving (RPS)	A product or service selection strategy wherein the customer considers no new information, and instead simply repeats previously made choices.
Satisficing	Customer (or decision maker's) acceptance of an alternative that he or she finds satisfying, rather than an arduous search for the most optimal alternative.
Schachter's two-factor theory	Psychologist Stanley Schachter's theory that the experience of emotion depends on two factors: autonomic arousal and its cognitive interpretation.
Search strategy	The pattern of information acquisition by customers to solve their decision problems.
Secondary data	Data already existing and collected by someone else.
Secondary demand	Demand for a specific brand of product or service.
Secondary groups	Groups with whom a person interacts infrequently and whose norms are considered weakly binding.
Secondary research	An examination of secondary data to answer the questions of interest to the marketer.
Segment-of-one marketing	Customizing the market offering to each individual customer.
Segmented differentiation	Identifying different homogeneous segments of the market by some characteristics of its customers and then offering each segment a different marketing mix.
Selective demand	Demand for a specific brand of product or service.
Selective distribution	The product being sold by more than one reseller but by a limited number of resellers.
Self-concept	A person's image of oneself—who he or she is.
Self-perception theory	The idea that people often infer their attitude by observing their own behavior—thus making attitude an inference from behavior rather than a cause of it.
Self-selection	The idea that customers self-select themselves to be the customers of the firm that offers the advantage they seek.
Selling concept	The firm focuses on persuading the customer to buy what it makes and offers.
Sensation	A step in the perception process in which the person attends to an object or an event in the environment with one or more of the five senses.
Service value	The assistance customers seek in buying a product or service.
Shopping motives	The reasons customers have for visiting stores.
Silent majority	The U.S. generation of people born between 1924 and 1946.
Simulation	A research method wherein real-world conditions are created in a laboratory to study the behavior of customers.
Single source data	Organization of both purchase incidence and consumer characteristics data collection in a single integrated record.
Situational involvement	The degree of a person's interest in a specific situation or on a specific occasion.
Smart products	Products that can communicate their "functioning status" to an outside agent or receive communication from an outside agent to adapt their function within predefined limits.
Social-cause marketing	Marketing programs that promote social causes.
Social class	The relative standing of members of a society reflecting a status hierarchy.
Social marketing	The application of the principles and tools of marketing for planned social change.
Social-orientation families	Families that are more concerned with maintaining discipline among children than promoting independent thinking.
Social risk	The probability that significant others may not approve of the innovation adoption.
Social value	The benefit of a product or service directed at satisfying a person's want for gaining social approval or admiration.
Stimulus	Any object or event in the environment that a person perceives.
Store image	The sum total of perceptions customers have about a store.

Store loyalty	A customer's predominant patronage of a store, based on a favorable attitude.
Store visiting	The practice of visiting various stores and shopping centers without necessarily having any plans to buy anything.
Straight rebuy	A purchase item that has been processed and procured before.
Subculture	The culture of a group within the larger society.
Subjective norms	A person's perception about what others expect from him or her.
Substantiality	A desirable segmentation criterion stating that every segment that is targeted must be big enough to be profitable to the company.
Superego	The moral side of the psyche, which reflects societal ideals.
Supplier-customer partnering	Establishing a partnership-like relationship with one's supplier or with one's customer.
Switching costs	Costs a customer would have to incur if he or she switched suppliers.
Symbolic groups	Groups with which a person identifies himself or herself without a formal membership, voluntarily adopting its norms and values.
Syncratic decisions	Decisions in which all family members play an equal role.
Syndicated data	Data that are of interest to a potentially large number of users, regularly collected by standardized procedures and made commercially available to all interested marketers.
Synergy in value	The concept that one value enhances the utility of another value.
Systematic search	A comprehensive search and evaluation of alternatives.
Targeted differentiation	Identifying a specific market segment and then designing a marketing program to target and appeal to this particular segment.
Technical proposal	A proposal required by the government as part of the bid document submitted by commercial firms.
Technology	Use of machines and devices to facilitate a practical task.
Technophiles	Customers who are deeply interested in technology.
Technophobes	Customers who fear new technology.
Temperate zone	Located well north and well south of the equator, its temperature varies greatly by season, with significant rain or snow for the most of the year.
Test marketing	A research method of testing a marketing mix on a limited market as a precursor to deciding whether to implement that mix in the entire market.
Thematic apperception test	A series of ambiguous pictures shown to respondents who are then asked to describe the story of which the picture is a part.
Time shift	A period when nonwork related activities may be pursued.
Time shortage	The lack of free time.
Tolerance for ambiguity	The degree to which a person remains free from anxiety in the face of uncertainty and lack of complete information.
Topography	The terrain, altitude, and soil conditions of a location on Earth where customers buy and use the product or service.
Trait theory of personality	The view of a person as a composite of several personality traits.
Transaction-specific investments (TSIs)	Any special equipment or technology or human resources that need to be dedicated for meeting the needs of a particular customer/supplier partner.
Trialability	The extent to which it is possible to try out the innovation on a smaller scale.
Trust	A willingness to rely on the ability, integrity, and motivation of the other party to act in the best interests of the trusting party.
Trustworthiness	The perceived benevolence and dependability of the opinion giver.

Unconditioned stimulus (UCS)	A stimulus toward which a person already has a pre-existing specific response.
Universal values	Product or service benefits that satisfy the *needs* of the customer.
Unplanned purchases	Purchases that a customer did not intend to buy before entering the store.
Usage segmentation	Segmenting the market based on the brand, product, and quantity customers use.
User	A person who actually consumes or uses the product or receives the benefits of the service.
Valence	The favorable and unfavorable direction of attitude.
Value compatibility	The degree to which an innovation is free from contradicting a person's deeply held values.
Value delivery	A firm fulfills a customer's need or want.
Values	The end states of life; the goals one lives for.
Values and lifestyles (VALS)	A well-known psychographic segmentation scheme, widely in use, based on customer responses to a set of questions on their values and lifestyles.
Verbatim	The recording of respondent answers exactly in their own words.
Verifiable benefit	An advertising claim that can be verified by independent scientific tests.
Virtual reality	An interactive, computer-generated 3D immersive visual and sound display of stimuli and situations representative of their real (physical) versions.
Visual image profile	A research technique to elicit the nonverbal response of customers by presenting them with visual images of human emotions to identify their own emotional experiences.
Voluntary simplicity	A tendency to simplify life and adopt economic behaviors of low consumption and ecological responsibility.
Want	An unsatisfactory psychological/social condition of the customer that leads him or her to an action that will remedy that condition.
Weber's Law	Named after the German Scientist Earnst Weber, the law states that the larger the base quantity, the larger the magnitude of change needed for being noticed.
Withdrawal	A defense mechanism in which people simply withdraw from those situations in which they are unsuccessful.
Word association	A research technique wherein the respondent is asked to state whatever association the presentation of each word in a set evokes.
Zaltman metaphor elicitation technique (ZMET)	Consumer researcher Gerald Zaltman's patented research technique to help respondents identify and report the rich imagery they hold as a result of their experience in the consumption of a product or service.

Company Index

Name Index

Subject Index

Photo Credits

Literary Credits

Pages 6–7 Eye on Customers: Putting Theory into Practice: List of questions adapted from Professor Jawaroski and Kohli's research.

Page 23 Courtesy of McDonald's Corporation.

Page 50 Courtesy of Auto-by-Tel.

Page 68 Courtesy of the Honda Motor Company of America.

Page 80 "Values Customers Seek in Various service Purchases" from "The Role of Personalization in Service Encounters," by B. Mittal and W. Lasser, *Journal of Retailing*, 72(1), 1996, pp. 95–109. Reprinted with permission.

Page 87 Table 3.1: Measuring Customer Value: An Extended Example, from *Consumption Value and Market Choices: Theory and Adaptations* by J. Sheth, B. Newman & B. Gross. Cincinnati, OH: South-Western, 1991, pp. 90–91. Reprinted by permission.

Page 105 Map Showing Geographical Differences in Customer Behavior: "Ride 'em Cowboy: Map of Bicycling to Work in U.S." reprinted from *American Demographics* magazine with permission. Copyright © 1985, American Demographics, Inc., Ithaca, New York.

Page 115 Map Showing Camcorder Consumers from "Camcorder Consumers" reprinted *from American Demographics* magazine with permission. Copyright © 1994, American Demographics, Inc., Ithaca, New York.

Page 121 "Economic Downturns and the Customers' Buying Mood" from *Economic Change and Consumer Shopping Behavior*, by Ben A. Oumlil, 1983. New York: Praeger Publishers.

Pages 122–123 Consumer Sentiment List from "Indicators of Consumer Behavior" from "The University of Michigan Surveys of Consumers," *Public Opinion Quarterly*, 46, 1982, pp. 340–352. Copyright © 1982 University of Chicago Press.

Page 135 Southwest Airlines Home Page. Courtesy of Southwest Airlines.

Page 144 Indian man in traditional Indian dress (a "kurta" shirt) from *Femina* magazine, January 15, 1997. Photographer: Madhur Shroff.

Page 160 The Consumer Revolt Against the Saints of Commerce" from "Hypereality and Globlization: Culture in the Age of Ronald McDonald," by Russel W. Belk, *Journal of International Consumer Marketing*, 8(3/4), pp. 23–37.

Page 164 Private-Public, Luxury-Necessity, Product-Brand Influences from "Reference Group Influence on Product and Brand Purchase Decisions," by William O. Bearden & Michael J. Etzel, *Journal of Consumer Research*, (1982) 9: pp. 183–94. Copyright © 1982 Journal of Consumer Research, Inc.

Page 170 Engel's Law: Lower Income Customers Spend Large Proportion of Income on Necessities from *Economics*, 14th edition, by Paul A. Samuelson and William D. Nordhaus, 1992, Figure 25–2, page 436. Copyright © 1992, McGraw-Hill, Inc., New York.

Page 175 Table 6.4: Consumption Patterns among U.S. Social Classes adapted and modified by the authors, based on Paul Fussell, *Class*, Summit Books, 1983, pp. 190–192. Copyright © 1983 by Paul Fussell.

Page 206 Tall City Homepage, Geocities. Courtesy of Tall City.

Page 216 Window on Practice: Why Do Hispanics Prefer Vended Water? from "Quenching Hispanic Thirst," reprinted from *American Demographics* magazine with permission. Copyright © 1989, American Demographics, Inc., Ithaca, New York.

Page 238 "Sixteen Factors or Personality Traits Identified by Cattell" by R.B. Cattell, H.W. Ever, and M.M. Tatsucka, from *Handbook for the Sixteen Personality Factors Questionnaire*. Champaign, IL: Institute for Personality and Ability Testing, 1970, pp. 16–17.

Page 239 Table 7.2: "A Summary of Personality Traits Measured by the Edwards Personal Preference Schedule" from the *Edwards Personal Preference Schedule*. Copyright © 1953, 1954, 1959 by The Psychological Corporation. Reproduced by permission. All rights reserved.

Page 241 "Classification of Personality into Social Styles" adapted from *Personal Styles and Effective Performance: Make Your Style Work for You* by David W. Merrill and Roger H. Reid. Radnor, PA: Chilton Book Company, 1981.

Page 242 "Identifying Social Styles: Verbal and Nonverbal Cues" from *Personal Styles and Effective Performance: Make Your Style Work for You* by David W. Merrill and Roger H. Reid. Radnor, PA: Chilton Book Company, 1981.

Page 275 "Technology: The Hotel of the Future" originally appeared in the March/April issue of *The Futurist*. Used with permission from the World Future Society, 7910 Woodmont Ave., Suite 450, Bethesda, Maryland 20814. 301/656–8274.

Page 296 Photo of aseptic boxes for milk from *Marketing News*, May 20, 1996, p. 19. Used by permission of the American Marketing Association, Chicago, IL.

Page 302 Excerpt from "National Affairs" on Dole/Clinton debate showing poll taken from a *Newsweek*/NBC News Focus Group of 36 registered voters conducted by pollster Frank Luntz of Luntz Research Companies, from *Newsweek*, October 14, 1996, pp. 30–31. Copyright © 1996 Newsweek, Inc.

Page 320 Line diagram of Adopter Categories from *Adopter Categories: Diffusion of Innovations*, Fourth Edition by Everett M. Rogers. Reprinted by permission of The Free Press, a division of Simon & Schuster. Copyright © 1995 by Everett M. Rogers. Copyright © 1962, 1971, 1983 by The Free Press, NY.

Page 325 Window on Practice: "Making Modern Technology Customer-Friendly for South African Rural Customers" adapted from "ITs New ATMs in Place, A Bank Reaches Out to South Africa's Poor," by Ken Well, *The Wall Street Journal*, June 13, 1996, pp. A1, A10. Copyright © 1996 Dow Jones, Inc.

Page 327 Table 9.2: Illustrative Measures of Opinion Leadership and Innovativeness from "Measuring Consumer Innovativeness," by Ronald E. Goldsmith and Charles F. Hofacker, *Journal of the Academy of Marketing Science*, 19 1991, pp. 209–221. Reprinted with permission.

Page 328 Table 9.3: "Characteristics of Business That Are Innovative in Adopting New Technology" adapted from "Corporate Culture, Enviromental Adaption, and Innovation Adaption: A Qualitative/Quantitative Approach," by Susan Kitchell, *Journal of the Academy of Marketing Science*, 23, no.3, (Summer, 1995) pp. 195–205. Reprinted with permission.

Page 346 Window on Practice: "Germ Busters Feed on Consumer Germ Phobia" adapted from "Fear of Disease Has Consumers Resorting to Germ Warfare," by Tara Parker-Pope, *The Wall Street Journal*, February 7, 1997, pp. A1, A4. Copyright © 1997 Dow Jones, Inc.

Page 349 Table 10.1: "Murray's List of Needs: Examples of Psychogenic Needs" adapted from *Explorations in Personality* by H. A. Murray. (1983) Copyright © 1983 Oxford University Press. Used by permission of Oxford University Press, Inc.

Page 355 "Conditions for Internal & External Attributions" from *Psychology: Themes and Variations*, by Wayne Weiten, 1989, Brooks Cole Publishing Company, a Division of Wadsworth, Inc., Belmont California 94002. Copyright © 1989 Wadsworths, Inc.

Page 358 "Emotion Typology: Plutchik's Circle" from *Psychology: Themes and Variations*, by Wayne Weiten, 1989, Brooks Cole Publishing Company, a Division of Wadsworth, Inc., Belmont California 94002. Copyright © 1989 Wadsworths, Inc.

Page 363 Table 10.5: "The Rokeach Value Survey Instrument" adapted from *Rokeach Value Survey* by Milton Research. Modified and reproduced by special permission of the Publisher, Consulting Psychologists Press, Inc., Palo Alto, CA 94303 from *Understanding Human Values* by Herman A Witkin. Copyright © 1979 by Consulting Psychologists Press, Inc. All rights reserved. Further reproduction is prohibited without the Publisher's written consent.

Page 365 A Means-End Chain for a Hypothetical Customer: "Hypothetical Hierarchical Value of Map of Wine Cooler Category" from "Laddering Theory, Method, Analysis, and Interpretation" by Thomas J. Reynolds and Jonathan Guttman, *Journal of Advertising Research*, 28, February/March, 1988, p. 19.

Page 370 AIO Statements, adapted from "Activities, Interests, and Opinions," by William D. Wells and Douglas J. Tigert, *Journal of Advertising Research*, 11 (August 1971): p. 35. Reprinted courtesy of the Advertising Research Foundation.